Raymond Aron

Volume 1

1905–1955

Raymond Aron

Volume 1

The Philosopher in History
1905–1955

Robert Colquhoun

SAGE Publications Ltd
28 Banner Street
London EC1Y 8QE

 SAGE Publications Inc
275 South Beverly Drive
Beverly Hills, California 90212 and
2111 West Hillcrest Drive
Newbury Park, California 91320

SAGE Publications India Pvt Ltd
C-236 Defence Colony
New Delhi 110 024

British Library Cataloguing in Publication Data

Colquhoun, Robert, *1938-*
  Raymond Aron.
  1. Aron, Raymond
  I. Title
  194   B2430.A/
ISBN 0-8039-9739-6

Library of Congress catalog card number   86-060448

Printed in Great Britain by
J. W. Arrowsmith Ltd, Bristol

Contents

For Eliane

La plupart des grands hommes expriment leur destin avant même de l'avoir vécu;
phénomène étrange que toutes les biographies nous permettent de vérifier.
The majority of great men foreshadow their destinies before having lived through
them – a strange phenomenon which all biographies confirm.
André Malraux, in Claude Mauriac, *Un autre de Gaulle* (1970)

Je ne suis plus ni de droite ni de gauche, ni communiste ni nationaliste, pas plus
radical que socialiste. J'ignore si je trouverai mes compagnons...
I am no longer on the Right or the Left, a communist or a nationalist, no more a
Radical than a Socialist. I have no idea if my companions will join me...
Raymond Aron, "Lettre ouverte d'un jeune Français à l'Allemagne",
Esprit, February 1933.

Résumer une philosophie, c'est toujours la trahir.
To summarize someone's philosophy is always to betray it.
Raymond Aron, "La Philosophie de Léon Brunschvicg",
La France libre, June 1944.

List of Abbreviations

AAAPSS	Annals of the American Academy of Political and Social Science
AJS	American Journal of Sociology
AS	Annales sociologiques
ASR	American Sociological Review
BAS	Bulletin of the Atomic Scientists
BJS	British Journal of Sociology
BSFP	Bulletin de la Société française de philosophie
Fig.	Le Figaro
Fig. Lit.	Le Figaro littéraire
FL	La France libre
IA	International Affairs (London)
LE	Liberté de l'esprit
LP	Libres Propos
NC	La Nouvelle Critique
NRF	Nouvelle Revue française
PE	Politique étrangère
RFS	Revue française de sociologie
RFSP	Revue française de science politique
RMM	Revue de métaphysique et de morale
RP	Recherches philosophiques
RTASMP	Revue des travaux de l'Académie des Sciences morales et politiques
TLS	The Times Literary Supplement
TM	Les Temps modernes
TR	La Table ronde
ZS	Zeitschrift für Sozialforschung

Preface

Raymond Aron, the French social and political writer who died in October 1983, is an incomparable guide to anyone seeking to understand our turbulent century, for his life and work have involved him with some of the most momentous events (the rise of fascism, the Second World War, the Cold War), striking personalities (Sartre, Malraux, de Gaulle) and influential ideas (Marxism, existentialism, structuralism) of our time. The aim of this intellectual biography of Aron's first fifty years is to trace the development of his thought, place it in its historical context and show the unity which underlies the apparent diversity of his interests: sociology and philosophy, history and economics, strategy and international relations, and political analysis and journalism. The companion volume, *Raymond Aron. Volume 2: The Sociologist in Society, 1955–1983*, completes the study of a thinker who is arguably the greatest political sociologist since Weber.

An important part of my research was carried out during a sabbatical year spent as a French Government Scholar at the Ecole des Hautes Etudes en Sciences Sociales in Paris, 1979–80. I should like to acknowledge the help given by that award and to thank my colleagues at Goldsmiths' College, University of London, who shouldered my teaching and administrative responsibilities during my absence. I am particularly grateful to the following, who all figured in Raymond Aron's life at various times and who kindly agreed to let me interview them in the course of my research: Georges Canguilhem, Jacques Hepp, Robert Marjolin, the late Lord Robbins, and the late Manès Sperber. Professor Donald MacRae of the London School of Economics and Political Science, who supervised my earlier thesis on Aron, was a constant source of advice and encouragement. I have also benefited from discussions with Dr John Hall of the University of Southampton, whose informed comments have been of great value. I should also like to thank my half-brother, David Leney, for reading the text with a non-specialist's eye.

My greatest debt is to Raymond Aron himself. Not only did I have two lengthy interviews with him in 1977 and 1979, but we met on a number of other occasions and corresponded frequently. In all our contacts he was unfailingly courteous, helpful and understanding. At the same time, true to his liberalism, he always left me free to pursue my research in whatever way I wished and wherever it led me. In 1981, four years after I had begun my own work, Aron published a book of autobiographical interviews, *Le Spectateur engagé* (*The Committed Observer*). Even more importantly, in 1979 he began writing his own memoirs; these were published in September 1983, only a few weeks before he died. And in 1985 the review *Commentaire* published a valuable collection of writings commemorating its founder. I have therefore been able to make use of all these sources in writing this intellectual biography and, since Raymond Aron's death, I have been particularly grateful for the cooperation and goodwill shown me by his wife, Madame Suzanne Aron, and his daughter, Dominique Schnapper.

Finally, I owe very special thanks to my wife. Not only has she typed several drafts of the manuscript, but she has borne the years of her Aronian widowhood with understanding, fortitude and humour. The moral and material support which she has so unstintingly given has been inestimable. Without her, the work would quite simply never have been completed.

* * *

I have normally used the first edition of Aron's writings, except – as indicated – where a subsequent edition is more readily available. I have invariably given references both to the French text and, where available, to the English translation. Whenever possible, I have used existing translations, but where these have proved inadequate, I have retranslated them, with the indication "(R.C.)". Reference to the French text alone means that any English translation is my own.

References to Aron's publications up to and including 1955 – e.g., "1931a" – will be found in Section A of the Bibliography: Aron's Publications in French, 1905–1955. Publications in French from 1956 onwards are listed in the Bibliography of Volume 2.

English translations up to and including 1955 – as in "tr. 1945a" –

will be found in Section B of the Bibliography: English Translations and Writings in English, 1905–1955. English translations from 1956 onwards are likewise listed in the Bibliography of Volume 2.

A surname followed by a date – e.g., "Abel, 1958" – indicates that the full reference to the author will be found in Section C of the Bibliography: Writings on Aron Mentioned in Volume 1.

Attention is also drawn to the Chronological Table (1905–1955) of personal, national and international events in Aron's life. An equivalent Chronological Table for 1956–1983 will be found at the end of Volume 2.

Finally, readers may like to know that since Aron's death a specialist library and research centre has been established at the Institut Raymond Aron, 10 rue Jean Calvin, 75005 Paris, France.

Introduction

During his lifetime Raymond Aron was described as "probably the most brilliant sociologist alive"[1] and "the greatest 'sociologist of the middle range' of our time".[2] Both these judgements are correct, and yet one can go further. As Ralf Dahrendorf declared when Aron was presented with the Goethe Prize in 1979:

Raymond Aron is the only social scientist of recent decades who, in view of his wide sphere of interest, his combination of analysis and action, commitment and power of understanding, his blend of critical revolt and critical reserve, may be compared in terms of significance with Max Weber.[3]

He is, on this view, the greatest social thinker since Weber, who died more than half a century ago and whom Aron himself considered to be "*the* sociologist".[4]

Despite his renown, Aron has not been the subject of a full-length study which seeks to take a comprehensive view of his life and work. A number of books have, it is true, been devoted to him in his native France, but they concentrate on particular – if central – aspects of his achievement. One, written by a jurist, Alain Piquemal, focuses on his theory of international relations,[5] while another, the posthumous publication of a lifelong Jesuit friend, Gaston Fessard, is a very personal interpretation of Aron's philosophy of history.[6] A more orthodox analysis is to be found in Sylvie Mesure's penetrating monograph on his critique of historical reason.[7] Aron has also been the subject of several theses in French which have yielded valuable discussions of his social and political philosophy.[8] Since his death, too, his friends and students have compiled a fitting commemorative volume of tributes and more extended analyses, including a number of excellent essays on his thought – among them those by Pierre Manent (possibly the best introduction to Aron's achievement in any language), Franciszek Draus, Allan Bloom and Pierre Hassner.[9]

In the Anglo-Saxon world, where he has long had a considerable reputation, Aron figures, if somewhat marginally, in *The Obstructed Path*, H. Stuart Hughes' account of the development of French social thought between 1930 and 1960.[10] More importantly, he was accorded a prominent place as one of the thinkers discussed by Roy Pierce in his analysis of *Contemporary French Political Thought*.[11] Both studies were published in the 1960s, but since then he has also been the subject of sympathetic and perceptive essays by Tracy Strong, Miriam Conant and, above all, Ghita Ionescu.[12] All these writers, however, concentrate on Aron's political thought. The only commentator to go further is John Hall in his recent discussion of six contemporary thinkers who provide *Diagnoses of Our Time*.[13] Hall offers an analysis which rightly seeks to link the work on international relations, the philosophy of history and the sociology of industrial society, but the space that he is able to devote to Aron is inevitably limited by the nature of his project.

There are several reasons why a study of Aron's life and work as a whole has not so far been undertaken either in France or, to my knowledge, elsewhere. The most obvious is the sheer quantity of his writings. In the fifty years since his first publication appeared, Aron completed nearly forty books and contributed more than six hundred articles to periodicals and reviews; in addition, as a journalist since the Second World War, he wrote some four thousand newspaper and magazine editorials – and these form an integral part of his work which none of his commentators have so far sought to incorporate into their analyses. It did not seem possible to do justice to such an output in a single volume and this is why the first part of this intellectual biography ends in 1955. In that year Aron reached his fiftieth birthday, completed his famous book, *The Opium of the Intellectuals*, and embarked on a new career as Professor of Sociology at the Sorbonne.

A second problem is that Aron's thought covers a range of disciplines

2

and interests which is perhaps unique among contemporary social scientists. First and foremost he is a sociologist, but he is also a philosopher, economist, contemporary historian, political analyst and student of international relations. For analytical purposes, therefore, his *oeuvre* can be divided into a number of different categories: for example, the philosophy of history, the sociology of industrial society, the history of sociological thought, studies in political theory, international relations, the critique of ideologies, and the analysis of French politics. At its root, however, lies the essentially pre-war work, culminating in the *Introduction to the Philosophy of History* published when Aron was thirty-three, which established the theoretical and methodological foundations for all his subsequent writings. For, as he once put it, "If there is a philosophical problem which is mine, it is: how is one to reflect upon history-in-the-making?"[14]

At the same time, as a direct consequence of his philosophical concerns, Aron was fascinated by the problem of the relationship between thought and action – in particular, the relationship between social theory and political practice. As we shall see, questions such as these soon led him into what proved to be a lifelong dialogue with Marx. Aron rejects all forms of historicism and determinism, but he does not fall into the opposite trap of idealism. For him, man is an active being, but the margin of freedom within which he may make choices and take decisions is constrained by social, economic and political conditions and circumstances. From the beginning, therefore, a main impetus of Aron's sociological work has been to explore the nature and scope of such limitations on men's freedom of action, in an attempt to locate what he once called "the points of application of the human will".[15] Thus the central theme which runs through all his books is, in his own words, "a reflection on the twentieth century, in the light of Marxism, and an attempt to illuminate every sector of modern society: the economy, social relations, class relations, political regimes, the relations between states, and ideological debates".[16]

Aron is more than anything else a *political* sociologist who stresses the primacy of the political in social life. As such he locates himself in what he describes as "the French school of political sociology", whose central figures are Montesquieu and Tocqueville – "a school of sociologists who are not very dogmatic, who are above all interested in politics, who do not disregard the social infrastructure but recognise the autonomy of the political order, and who are liberals".[17] Aron's liberalism, which derives from Kant, Weber and his own philosophy of history, made him the unwavering enemy of totalitarianism of the Right and the Left; but this also served to isolate him in Parisian intellectual circles, where it appeared only too easy to dismiss him as a man of the "Right" in a city in which so many of the intelligentsia have automatically placed themselves on the Marxist, revolutionary and Stalinist "Left".

Furthermore, Aron is not a "literary" writer – the author of novels and plays – and in Paris this, too, is a considerable handicap for anyone who wishes his political judgements to be taken seriously. The French seem to like their political oracles to be creative writers – in Aron's time, such figures as Mauriac, Malraux, Camus and, above all, Sartre.[18] On the contrary, Aron is, as he admits, "wary of the imagination, whether in philosophy or politics".[19] As a social thinker, therefore, he is essentially an analyst who keeps his eyes firmly on the real world and refuses to engage in flights of abstract theorizing (Maurois once said of him that "He would be our Montesquieu if only he were willing to take off from historical reality").[20] In addition, although Aron has what he calls "a global representation of the world", he is like Weber and unlike Marx, or indeed Durkheim, in that he has no "system" and certainly no key either to sociological understanding or to "the good society". Thus he has often been accused of embodying a sceptical "pessimism", whereas in fact throughout his life he was careful to argue against the two extremes of deterministic fatalism, on the one hand, and naive optimism, on the other; in their stead, his social and political stance was invariably one of cautious hope tempered by reason and realism.

What is true, however, is that, both because of his philosophy of history and because of the times in which he lived, Aron was an inveterate opponent of all forms of "prophetism", especially revolutionary millenarianism and what he calls "romantic utopianism". As a consequence, he felt it necessary to curb his natural instincts:

> I am strongly opposed to utopianism and romanticism, above all because such attitudes have cost our century too dearly. If we lived in a bourgeois, conservative century, I would probably allow freer expression to my spontaneous romanticism. But as our century has seen Stalin, Hitler and appalling massacres, I have reacted against these catastrophes by developing the more rational half of my soul. I am not reasonable and cold by nature; I am reasonable and cold by design.[21]

Aron was, of course, conscious of the fact that such an attitude was likely to limit his appeal, but he accepted this as virtually inevitable: "I am aware, obviously, that my message – if there is one – is less exalting for the imagination than the grand historical syntheses of a Toynbee, Spengler or Marx. I know that people prefer their dreams to reality because, as Renan said, 'The truth is sad'".[22]

4

Not surprisingly, therefore, Aron was never a glamorous figure in the French cultural landscape – and this, too, may explain why, compared with some of his contemporaries, relatively little (apart from book reviews) was written about him during his lifetime. In the first place, he had a reputation for being cold, even icy, somewhat aloof, an inhuman intellectual machine. He was none of these things; the evidence of many who knew him, and my own experience, bears witness to his warm humanity. He was in fact a passionate man who, on his own admission, "strove constantly to conceal his passions by the use of reason and the appeal to reflection".[23] One of the keys to understanding Aron's personality lies, I am convinced, in an injunction of Malraux's: "Réduire en soi la part de comédie" – "One must reduce the element of play-acting in oneself". Aron once used this phrase to refer to the liberal historian, Elie Halévy,[24] but it could serve equally well to highlight a trait in Aron's own character which Ralf Dahrendorf has caught perfectly:

Aron belongs to those who do not have to prove the radical nature of their thinking through their outward appearance or life-style. He values the virtues of an age which did not treat the integrity of human beings so cavalierly as ours does. For him politeness, respect, and *amitié* (in the untranslatable French sense) are values which both bind people together and protect them in their individuality.[25]

Thus he eschews all posturing, moralism and demagogy ("I don't like pretending to be some kind of universal conscience: it strikes me as indecent")[26] and this explains why, in contrast to the heady flamboyance of a Sartre, Camus, or even Malraux himself, Aron may come across as a dry, distant, perhaps colourless, figure.

Any such impression is the consequence of what he saw as a necessary "intellectual asceticism" in an age rife with "secular religions". For similar reasons – and despite evidence of his growing influence in his own country at the time of his death – he was never one to encourage "disciples" or the formation of an Aronian "sect". There are only individuals, in France and elsewhere, who have come to value the wisdom, morality and courage of the sanest of travellers through what Nietzsche foresaw would be a twentieth century of great wars fought in the name of ideologies.

Notes

1. Gellner, 1966, p. 255.
2. Hall, 1981, p. 195. The terminology is Robert Merton's.

5

3. Dahrendorf, 1980, p. 30.
4. Tr. 1970b, p. 250.
5. Piquemal, 1978.
6. Fessard, 1980. See also Jeanne Hersch's introduction (Hersch, 1980).
7. Mesure, 1984.
8. For example, Eric Werner, *La Pensée politique et morale de Raymond Aron* (no date), and Franciszek Draus, *La Philosophie sociale de Raymond Aron* (thèse pour le doctorat de 3ᵉ cycle. Ecole des Hautes Etudes en Sciences Sociales, Paris, 1981). Both theses are available at the Institut Raymond Aron. See also Werner, 1973; and Draus, 1983, 1984.
9. Manent, 1985; Draus, 1985; Bloom, 1985; Hassner, 1985.
10. Hughes, 1966.
11. Pierce, 1966. His other subjects are Mounier, Simone Weil, Camus, Sartre and de Jouvenel.
12. Strong, 1972; Conant, 1978; Ionescu, 1975.
13. Hall, 1981. Hall's other thinkers are Marcuse, Habermas, Daniel Bell, Dahrendorf and Gellner.
14. "Comment penser l'histoire qui se fait?" (1967i).
15. 1943g; reprinted in 1944a, p. 327.
16. 1981a, pp. 299–300: tr. 1983b, p. 254 (R.C.).
17. 1967a, p. 295: tr. 1968b, p. 258 (R.C.).
18. Compare Pierce, 1966, p. 122: "France...is unusual in the historical regularity with which literary figures have appeared prominently in political contexts and in the public attention which is given to their political pronouncements. Voltaire, Chateaubriand, Hugo, Zola, Malraux, Mauriac, Sartre, and Camus all share a common tradition which is without counterpart elsewhere".
19. 1967j, p. 90.
20. "Il serait notre Montesquieu s'il consentait à décoller de la réalité historique", ibid.
21. 1977g; reprinted 1978b, pp. 631–2.
22. 1967j, p. 79.
23. Ibid.
24. 1971d.
25. Dahrendorf, 1980, p. 35.
26. 1981a, p. 100: tr. p. 86 (R.C.).

Part One

Youth: 1905–1930

1

Schooldays

———

On 14 March 1905, at her home in the Rue Notre-Dame-des-Champs not far from the Luxembourg Gardens, Suzanne Aron, the wife of a Parisian law professor, gave birth to her third son, Raymond Claude Ferdinand. A first son had died at birth; two others, Adrien and Robert, had been born in 1902 and 1903. She had desperately wanted a daughter, and the earliest photographs of the infant Raymond show him dressed as a girl with long curls reaching down to his shoulders.[1]

Raymond Aron's family was of Jewish origin. On his father's side, it had been established in Lorraine since the eighteenth century. Under the Ancien Régime, the Jews in France endured an isolated and wretched existence in which, restricted as to where they might live and excluded from all but a few trades and occupations, they were neither citizens nor foreigners.[2] There were, however, exceptions. Thus one of Aron's ancestors, a doctor by the name of Cerf, who lived at Metz, had earned a number of privileges for his family. In 1744 Louis XV had fallen ill in the town; the royal physicians having given up all hope for him, the local Jewish doctor was summoned as a last resort and he succeeded in curing the King.[3]

But it was the French Revolution which changed the legal position of the Jews in France; it gave them civil rights and abolished the occupational and residential restrictions to which they had been subject. The effects of the reforms of 1791 may have been exaggerated and further liberalizing measures were taken under the Restoration;[4] nevertheless, it was not long before the Jewish pedlars, ragmen and money-lenders of Eastern France were starting to emerge as tradesmen, industrialists and businessmen – a process which continued throughout the years of the July Monarchy and the Second Empire. The generation born with the Third Republic, however, did not always follow their successful fathers into business; many of them studied instead to enter such professions as medicine, journalism, the law and the civil service, or to become teachers in the lycées – the state secondary schools – and the universities.[5]

Aron's family background fitted this pattern closely, for in the mid-nineteenth century his paternal grandfather, Ferdinand (1843–1905), together with a younger brother, Paul, had founded a textile firm at Rambervillers, a small town about fifty kilometres south-east of Nancy, a city to which Aron Frères moved as the business prospered. Aron's father, Gustave, however, who was born in 1870, did not wish to go into the family firm but decided on an academic career in law instead. His studies began brilliantly. After being top of his class at Lyon, he won the prize for best student at the end of his first year at the Faculty of Law in Paris and completed his doctorate by the time he was twenty-five. But he was unable to obtain the intensely competitive *agrégation de droit*, which would have entitled him to be a *professeur* in a university faculty of law; he tried at the turn of the century and was placed second, but at that time only one *agrégation de droit* was awarded every two years and he abandoned the attempt. After being a lecturer (*chargé de cours*) at the University of Caen and then at the Sorbonne, he had to be content with a professorship outside the University at the Ecole Supérieure d'Enseigne-ment Commercial and the Ecole Normale Supérieure d'Enseignement Technique; but, once he was married, he ceased "working" in a creative sense and, as he used to put it, devoted himself to his children.

Aron's mother, Suzanne *née* Lévy (b. 1877), was the daughter of a textile manufacturer from the north of France. She herself had not had any higher education, but was married early and lived for her family. She had a brother, Julien, who began to study philosophy at school and might have embarked on an academic career, but he died young.[6] She also had two sisters to whom she was very close. The younger of these married the historian, Robert Anchel, author of two standard works, *Napoléon et les Juifs* and *Les Juifs de France*.[7]

Not long after Aron's birth his parents moved to a new apartment in the Boulevard Montparnasse, where they remained for several years. His grandparents on both sides were well-off (his mother brought a dowry with her when she married) and he could remember the large chauffeur-driven car that belonged to his paternal grandmother in the years before her death in 1914. It was in the previous year that his parents decided to leave Paris for Versailles, where they lived in rented accommodation until their own architect-designed house was completed in 1915.

Of the three Aron sons, Adrien, the eldest, was the first to break away from the family. A playboy and ladies' man, for years his parents' indulgence enabled him to live in comfort without having to work. He was "remarkably intelligent" and excelled at those pastimes which interested him – tennis, bridge and stamp-collecting; indeed, Aron's remark in his memoirs – "He was endowed with exceptional intelligence and he put it at the service of bridge and stamps"[8] – might serve as an epitaph for Adrien. Ranked ninth in France at tennis during a decade in which the first four places were taken by Borotra and "the three musketeers", he was also an international bridge champion. After the Second World War, which he spent first at Cannes and then in Switzerland, he turned his hand to stamp-dealing – living, until his death from cancer in 1969, in the small, neglected flat which had been his since the early 1930s: "Until his last day", wrote Aron in 1983, "he remained on the margins of a society whose hypocrisy he scorned, gradually succumbing to cynicism". Yet Aron, who for whole periods of his life had seen almost nothing of an elder brother from whom he was utterly different, was with Adrien in his last days, as if held to him by some bond: "He was the perfect incarnation of the man of pleasure, the kind of man whom my philosophical self (mon moi philosophique) despised but whom another part of me, barely conscious and humiliated by his overriding lack of seriousness, both admired and envied".[9]

Aron's other brother, Robert (to be distinguished from the historian of the same name), seems to have left less of a mark on him. From the start Robert was somewhat overshadowed by his older and younger brother – the sporting prowess of the one and the academic brilliance of the other. Nevertheless, he was no intellectual sluggard. He simultaneously obtained two degrees (licences), one in philosophy and the other in law, and then went on to take a higher diploma in philosophy, the subject of his dissertation being a comparative study of Descartes and Pascal. He even published an article based on this work in the prestigious Revue de métaphysique et de morale.[10] But Robert decided against an academic life, went into banking and eventually became Director of Studies at the Banque de Paris et des Pays-Bas. Despite such apparent success, he seems to have been disappointed in his professional career, feeling that his capacities were not given adequate recognition. Like Adrien he never married and lived increasingly embittered and alone, trying his hand at detective stories and a history of the Normandy landings which would put right the official versions, until he was gradually overcome by the paralysis which in 1978 eventually killed him.[11]

The philosopher, Léon Brunschvicg, used to enjoy joking, "In the Aron family there are two good philosophers and two good tennis-players and yet there are only three of them. A *polytechnicien* of my acquaintance never managed to solve the problem".[12] The family had their own tennis-court in the garden at Versailles and Aron himself was an excellent player. As a boy, tennis was (with cycling) his "greatest passion", and he took part in many tournaments, ending as a "ranked player" – even if, compared with Adrien, he was always known as "le mauvais Aron".[13] His parents disapproved of scholastic "work" after dinner; instead, every evening, beginning when Aron was about ten, the three sons played bridge with their father – until, that is, Adrien began seeking his distractions elsewhere. Marcel Ruff, a veteran of the First World War who first met the family in 1920 when he was a student of literature at the Ecole Normale Supérieure, remembered a warm, lively and talkative household. "In our house we always argue the point", the Aron boys told him, and it was true: whether it was a question of tennis, bridge or politics, the words flew freely between parents and children. They were also keen mountaineers, and sixty years later Ruff could still recall the impressive array of climbing-boots that lined one of the passage-ways of the house in Versailles.[14]

Although his father was cheerful and outgoing in character – and thus very different, Aron told me, from himself[15] – as a boy Aron took his father's abortive academic career very much to heart. At the same time, Gustave Aron placed all his own frustrated hopes and ambitions in his youngest son, who as a consequence was determined to succeed in his studies: "Gradually", Aron recalled at the end of his life, "as I grew older and was able to understand him – no longer as the all-powerful father but as one who had been humiliated – I felt myself to be the bearer of his youthful hopes, whose mission was to bring him a kind of revenge; I would wipe out his disappointments with my own successes".[16] In addition, however, Gustave speculated on the Stock Exchange and the family was financially ruined in the Great Crash of 1929. As a result, Aron wrote, he could not remember his father's last years without "a feeling of guilt and an immense sadness". Nor was he ever to forget the "debt" which he felt he owed his father or the latter's "legacy" to his son:

In some vague way, every time I was conscious or afraid of making a mess of my life, I thought of my father as though life was inflicting a new defeat upon him; the son whose task was to remedy injustice, the son to whom he had confided his message, he too, though with fewer excuses, was choosing the easy way out, or failure, through the same faults of character – with fewer excuses, because my father had long been happy despite failure, whilst I could not be happy if I failed.[17]

Gustave Aron eventually died of a second heart-attack in 1935, a few weeks after the birth of his first grandchild, Aron's eldest daughter. It was "his last joy", though to the young Aron, weeping tearlessly before the laid-out corpse, he had died of misery.[18] His whole life had been, in Aron's phrase to me, "a kind of bourgeois tragedy". Aron's mother, as we shall see, survived her husband for another five years to die, alone, in the midst of the débâcle of June 1940.[19]

* * *

In 1913, when he was eight, Aron went to the Lycée Hoche in Versailles. Until then he was given private lessons by an *institutrice* (Mademoiselle Lalande was still alive fifty years later when she wrote to him on his election to the Institut de France in 1963). He was "the typical good pupil"; he "liked learning and enjoyed working". Somewhat behind his contemporaries when he began at school, he soon caught up and from the age of ten aspired after – and usually achieved – first place in class. "In short", Aron told me, and repeated in his memoirs, "I was afflicted by an *amour-propre* that I cannot now recall without shame".[20]

As a boy he read widely, if not precociously, outside his formal studies – Dumas and Tolstoy, Corneille and Racine. Significantly, perhaps, in view of the lack of illusion that characterized Aron's later writings, Prince André, gazing at the heavens in *War and Peace*, filled him with an intense emotion that he was never able to recapture at subsequent readings: "I expected too much from this passage and, as a consequence, it lost its charm". Similarly, the words of Corneille's tragedy *Horace*, which he spoke aloud to himself, "transported me into a sublime world", but when, in high expectation, he went to see the play at the Comédie Française, "the miracle did not take place":

Several years later I read Proust and understood the simple reason for my disappointment; one cannot experience perfect moments to order. Proust gave me a number of such moments, but I am reluctant to reread particular passages of *A la Recherche du Temps perdu*, out of a fear of not reliving those perfect moments or even of spoiling their memory.[21]

13

Aron was not yet ten when he discovered and eagerly devoured his father's collection of documents on the Dreyfus Affair. Not that there is any evidence to suggest that he was particularly marked by its effects – "The Dreyfus Affair", he stated in his memoirs, "did not trouble my feelings as a young Frenchman". Like many other "assimilated" French Jews, the Arons were completely secularized. The three sons had once been given some token religious instruction, but Aron had hardly even been in a synagogue and, like most French children of his middle-class background (Catholics were the most common exception), he attended the local lycée. Notwithstanding the occasional taunt of "Sale juif!" ("Dirty Jew!") or "Youpin!" ("Yid!"), as a boy he felt – as he wanted to be – totally integrated and wholly French.[22] At the beginning of one school year, for example, when the rest of the pupils were being taken to a church service, he simply followed them in.[23] Certainly, the "Affair" was a subject of discussion at the lycée, and the young Aron, who was of a disputatious frame of mind, was not afraid to join in the debate (friends of his parents nicknamed him "l'avocat" – "the barrister" or, perhaps more to the point, "the barrack-room lawyer"). Thus his classmate, Jacques Hepp, remembered a particular history lesson in which the young Aron listened to the teacher "with rapt attention":

At the end of an exposition whose ambiguous conclusions left a doubt hanging over Dreyfus' role, he raised his hand to speak. The teacher gave him permission and we heard him begin an amazing speech for the defence, buttressed with quotations, dates and irrefutable arguments. At the age of fifteen he had read, assimilated and remembered everything (newspaper articles, manifestos and accounts of the trial). We listened spellbound and the teacher, aware of the unsettled atmosphere in the class, did not interrupt, wisely deciding not to confront a pupil already endowed with an exceptional gift for argument.[24]

Aron himself recalled the incident in his *Memoirs*:

A history teacher of right-wing opinions, who sympathized with the Action Française, was discussing the Third Republic...He told us that it was impossible to say, even with the passage of time, whether Dreyfus was guilty or innocent, that the question did not matter very much in any case, and that the Affair had been the occasion, or the excuse, for the unleashing of partisan passions – those of the enemies of the Army or of the Church. I argued with the teacher (who had, furthermore, been wounded in the war) as best I could and brought in the lot...The teacher replied with the classic phrase: "It's more complex than you say". He also used false arguments ...But in the discussion with the teacher, neither of us, as far as I can remember, mentioned – or at any rate underlined – the fact that Dreyfus was a Jew and so was I...[25]

14

Later, at the Ecole Normale Supérieure, Aron's Jewish origin was a matter of complete indifference to his fellow students:[26]

My Jewishness was in a way projected onto me, from outside, by the milieu surrounding me. Without that milieu I would not have made any distinction, inwardly, between other French people and myself. Thus, every time I come to consider the question, I experience a feeling of unease: I insist on affirming that I am Jewish because that is the wish of the world around me, but in a part of my being I do not feel it.

It was not until he encountered the full force of anti-Semitism in Germany in 1933 that he resolved to "assume the responsibility" of his Jewishness. "Since Judaism was becoming an object of horror and contempt, it was out of the question to run away from it. But I have always accepted it with a certain uneasiness".[27]

Aron's best friends at the Lycée Hoche were in fact two Protestants – Jacques Hepp,[28] who was to become one of the foremost surgeons of his generation, and Léonard Rist,[29] son of the economist, Charles Rist. Aron was, Hepp recalls, an outstanding pupil: "He clearly had no liking for disorder, rowdyism in class ('le chahut') or anything that was trivial, bawdy or vulgar" – but he was not a prig and was quick to enjoy himself with his friends.[30] Conscientious and well-behaved, he was "always first in class", apparently without the slightest effort; he was "exceptionally gifted" ("surdoué") and "seemed to know everything". It was, however, in the philosophy class, when he was sixteen, that Aron's "extraordinary maturity" was particularly evident: "la classe de philo" became "a dialogue between Aron and the teacher", Georges Aillet, while Hepp and Rist left them to it and read Laforgue and Nerval under the desk.[31] Up till then Aron had had "no intellectual passions",[32] but he was as if "transfigured" by this new experience. Although his other subjects – French, Latin and Greek, mathematics, history and geography – interested him ("more or less"), after three months he decided to devote his life to philosophy, and his "intoxication" with the subject never left him.[33]

"I have long since reconstructed my intellectual biography", Aron wrote at the end of his life. "Before the philosophy class, darkness; after the philosophy class, light":

Historically, the academic year 1921–1922, which I regard as decisive for my existence, was marked by the last convulsions of the great crisis of war and revolution. I learnt nothing about politics or economics, Bolshevism or Karl Marx, but I glimpsed, for the first time, the enchanted world of speculation or, quite simply, thought...Aillet philosophized before us; armed with no system, he sought, hesitatingly and out loud, the truth...For the first time, the teacher did not already know, he was searching; he did not have a truth to transmit but a way of thinking to put before us.[34]

But there was another, and even more important, lesson to be learned, which marked Aron out from his contemporaries:

The philosophy class taught me that we can reflect upon our life instead of submitting to it, that we can enrich it through thought and carry on a dialogue with great minds. A year's familiarity with the work of Kant cured me, once and for all, of vanity...That class opened up for me the world of thought but, despite Descartes, it did not give me any lessons of method...To think, yes, but also – first – to learn and study. Only philosophers, Bachelard once wrote, think first and study afterwards. For ten years I was to put forward political opinions, whereas in fact I simply preferred some men to others; my sympathy went to the meek and the oppressed and I abominated the powerful, with their arrogant belief in their rights. But between philosophy and my emotions a chasm formed – the ignorance of society as it is and as it can and cannot be. Most of the friends of my generation have not filled, or even tried to fill, that gap.[35]

Aron's schooldays were, of course, overshadowed by the 1914–1918 war. Nine years old when it began and thirteen when it ended, he was filled with all the naive patriotism of the unthinking schoolboy: he dreamed of military glory and, set to write a composition in class about what he hoped to be when he grew up, he sang the exploits of *le petit capitaine*. When he entered the philosophy class, however, and started to question things he had hitherto taken for granted, his whole attitude began to change; he realized that he had at no point suffered as a result of the war or felt any compassion for the miseries of the participants. He was sickened by his childish self-centredness and his loathing of the war now became as strong as his boyish patriotism had once been.[36]

It is easy to see, therefore, why the philosophy class also brought with it Aron's "conversion to the Left". The post-war elections of 1919 had resulted in a landslide victory for the Right, the Bloc National, and the creation of the "Chambre bleu horizon" (named after the sky-blue of the victorious soldiers' uniforms); but by 1921–22, the "patriotic exaltation" of the war years was beginning to wane and the Left to rediscover its strength and ideas. Aron's father, for example, a Dreyfusard in his youth and a fervent patriot in the Great War, was returning to his former moderate socialism. Aron, too, was affected by this "resurgence of the bourgeois, academic Left, which till then had been smothered by national feeling". But there was also a more general reason for his leftward shift. This was the fact that

16

philosophy itself gives a lesson in universalism. Men think and they are all capable of thinking. They must therefore be educated and won over. War denies man's humanity, since the victor has demonstrated nothing except his superior force or cunning. The climate of the philosophy class, whatever the opinions of the teacher, normally encourages a left-wing emotional stance.[37]

Aron passed his school-leaving examination, the *baccalauréat*, with the top classification of *très bien* at the age of seventeen and (a fact that he did not record in his *Memoirs*) was also chosen by his lycée to enter for the 1922 *concours général* in philosophy, a competition just revived after a twenty-year gap and open to the best pupils in Paris and the provinces. He came fourth in the contest for the Paris lycées and, amid much pomp, received his prize from the President of the Republic, Alexandre Millerand, himself.[38]

That same year he moved to the Lycée Condorcet to prepare for the entrance examination to the most prestigious of France's institutions of higher education, the Ecole Normale Supérieure. The two best-known lycées for this purpose were the much larger Louis-le-Grand and Henri-IV, but Condorcet, being close to the Gare Saint-Lazare, was convenient from Versailles (neither his parents nor Aron fancied his becoming a boarder) and less of an academic forcing-house than its two more famous counterparts. The usual practice was to spend two years preparing for the entrance examination to the Ecole Normale, but at Condorcet the two preparatory classes only comprised about twenty-five pupils and were taught together. His friends now included Daniel Lagache, the future psychiatrist, who entered the Ecole Normale Supérieure in the same year as himself, the philosophers Jacques Heurgon and Olivier Lacombe, the geographer Jacques Weulersse, and the industrialist Edmond Lanier.[39] According to another of their number, Jean Maugüé, "three pupils dominated the class" – Heurgon (who was a year senior), Aron and Lagache:

Others had their chance, and did indeed pass into the Ecole Normale, but none enjoyed the same respect from our teachers. Born, all three, into the world of business, and dressed as if they were already men of the world, they recognized each others' worth, knowing as they did that. . .they were destined for brilliant careers. And our teachers assumed as much. . .Nevertheless, the figure who most impressed me was Raymond Aron. . .With that sad, disdainful, inner beauty of his, he was already the one who understands everything – in other words, that men must be taken as they are and that they are, moreover, incurable. He was, furthermore, the only one of the three not to doubt my chances of success. . .[40]

17

Of his years at school, the two spent at Condorcet were the ones Aron remembered "not as the happiest but as the most enriching", although "we learned next to nothing about the world in which we lived".[41] His philosophy teacher was André Cresson (1869–1950), a man of great charm and sensitivity. Cresson was a close friend of Léon Brunschvicg and Célestin Bouglé, with whom he had been a student at the Ecole Normale Supérieure and who were to play an important part in Aron's life in the years before the Second World War.[42] However, Aron felt most drawn to his Latin teacher, Charles Salomon (1859–1925), who was a friend of the Socialist leader, Jean Jaurès, and a master at Condorcet for thirty-six years. According to the writer and philosopher, Paul Desjardins, Salomon was

an authentic humanist, or teacher of *humanity* (not *humanities*). He belongs, moreover, to a fine lineage, one which is wholly French and descends from Montaigne to Stendhal and to Proust – subtle analysts all, and passionate lovers of human spontaneity... There is about them no trace of moral dogmatism, and yet they have great wisdom... "It is through our nature," he used to say, "when we succeed in fully realizing its essence, that we act on our life. That is why I so insist on our being ourselves. It is our only real source of strength".[43]

Aron's French teacher was the astringent Hippolyte Parigot, who wrote for the newspaper, *Le Temps*, and made Aron aware of the importance of literary style.[44] He was taught Greek for a year by Georges Dalmeyda (1866–1932), who left to become Professor at the Sorbonne in 1923; and Aron's history teacher was Léon Cahen, a specialist on the French Revolution[45] and the author of a standard political history of nineteenth-century England.[46]

The first year at Condorcet, where half the class were a year his senior, was evidently a salutary experience for Aron. On his arrival he felt himself to be lagging behind the others in general cultural awareness as well as in Latin and Greek, although in philosophy he at once found that he was "at an honourable level".[47] He failed to come first at the end of the year – which he later saw as very good for him. Nevertheless, his marks were sufficiently high for his teachers to advise him to take the entrance examination for the Ecole Normale a year early. He did so and, much to his mortification, failed, although he came to believe it was just as well: it was unusual to pass after only one year and at Louis-le-Grand and Henri-IV pupils did not even make the attempt.[48] At the end of his second year, however, Aron did succeed in coming first in all his subjects: philosophy (with eighteen marks out of twenty), French (though for Parigot's taste he was "not literary enough"), Greek, Latin, history and German. Cresson considered him to be "An excellent pupil; wide knowledge, maturity, and a personality in full development", and the headmaster (proviseur) described him as possessing "Intellectual worth. Clear, strong mind. Has the knowledge and maturity of the best. Excellent in every way".[49] This time, too, he passed the examination for the Ecole Normale Supérieure. After the initial selection, there still remained 180 candidates in the arts section, of whom twenty-nine were accepted. Aron was placed fourteenth, and a student from Louis-le-Grand, by the name of Jean-Paul Sartre, seventh. According to *normalien* legend, a poor ancient history oral on Pergamum cost Aron a number of places.[50]

Notes

1. The source of much of my information on his family was an interview I had with Raymond Aron in 1979. See also his *Memoirs* (1983a), Chapter 1. I am grateful to his daughter, Dominique Schnapper, for letting me see the family photographs.
2. Robert Anchel, *Les Juifs de France* (Paris, 1946), pp. 17–18.
3. André Harris and Alain de Sédouy, *Juifs et Français* (Paris, 1979), p. 38.
4. Philippe Bourdrel, *Histoire des Juifs de France* (Paris, 1974).
5. "A hundred years after their legal emancipation, the Jews of France took part in practically all of the nation's activities, sometimes attaining the highest levels of intellectual fame: it is enough to mention Bergson and Durkheim. Soon, it would be Marcel Proust...". Bourdrel, op. cit., p. 194. Compare Pierre Aubery, *Milieux juifs de la France contemporaine à travers leurs écrivains* (Paris, 1957), p. 53.
6. Aron told me that while at school Julien was taught philosophy by Léon Brunschvicg, who was later to become an important influence on Aron at the Ecole Normale Supérieure. Before reaching the Sorbonne, Brunschvicg, as was the normal practice, taught philosophy in a number of provincial lycées, including the Lycée Corneille at Rouen (1895–1900). It was presumably here that he taught Aron's uncle.
7. Published in 1928 and 1946 respectively. The latter is referred to in note 2, above.
8. 1983a, p. 11. Adrien was also author of books on bridge and stamp-collecting – e.g., Adrien Aron and Jean Fayard, *L'Art du bridge* (Paris, 1937); Adrien Aron, *Les Secrets de la philatélie* (Paris, 1959).
9. 1983a, pp. 10, 11.
10. Robert Aron, "Note sur le pari de Pascal", *RMM*, 23, 1926, pp. 85–91.
11. 1983a, pp. 24–6.
12. Ibid., p. 232.
13. 1978b, p. 621. Tennis is listed as Aron's recreation in *Who's Who*. He also loved watching rugby; although he never played the game, he remained "an obstinate admirer" of what was for him "a marvellous spectacle". Aron recounted this in a television programme, *On n'a pas tous les jours vingt ans: 1925* – in a series produced

by Anne Sinclair and broadcast by Antenne 2 on 5 August 1981. In addition, he remained a keen follower of football. See "Confession d'un fan", *L'Express* (1605), 16 April 1982: tr. 1982e.

14. Ruff, 1985.
15. His father was, Aron once said to me, "bien dans sa peau".
16. 1983a, p. 14.
17. Ibid., p. 16.
18. Ibid., pp. 25–6. Aron states in his *Memoirs* (p. 26) that his father died in January 1934, but this is a slip.
19. See Chapter 9, below. Paul Aron, the younger brother of Aron's grandfather, Ferdinand, had a son, Max, who like his first cousin, Aron's father, also embarked on an academic career, but in medicine. Max Aron became Professor of Biology at the University of Strasbourg and in his turn had three sons, all of whom subsequently became well-known in their varying fields. The eldest son, Robert Aron-Brunetière (b. 1915) became a noted dermatologist; the second son, Claude, like his father before him, was to become Professor of Biology at Strasbourg; while the youngest, Jean-Paul, has written a number of books including a novel, essays on biological epistemology, studies of French food-habits in the nineteenth century and, probably his best-known work (with Robert Kempf), *Le Pénis et la démoralisation de l'Occident* (Paris, 1978).
20. 1983a, p. 17.
21. Ibid.
22. Ibid., pp. 18, 19.
23. 1981a, p. 32: tr. 1983b, p. 29.
24. Hepp, 1985, p. 10.
25. 1983a, pp. 18–19.
26. 1978b, p. 622.
27. 1955j.
28. Jacques Hepp, who won the Croix-de-Guerre in the Second World War, later became Professor at the Collège de Médecine des Hôpitaux, and a member of the Académie Nationale de Médecine and the Académie de Chirurgie. Many years later, Professor Hepp happened to be one of the surgeons who operated on Simone de Beauvoir's mother, when she was dying of cancer. In her account of her mother's death, de Beauvoir singled out Hepp ("Docteur P.") for warm comment: "I liked Dr P. He did not assume consequential airs; he talked to Maman as though she were a human being and he answered my questions willingly". Simone de Beauvoir, *Une Mort très douce* (Paris, 1964), pp. 78–9: tr. (by Patrick O'Brian) *A Very Easy Death* (Harmondsworth, 1969), pp. 45–6.
29. Léonard Rist later worked for the World Bank in Washington.
30. Hepp, 1985, p. 10.
31. Jacques Hepp, interview with the author, 1980. Aillet had been a student at the Ecole Normale Supérieure in 1896 and died in 1943.
32. R. A., interview with the author, 1977.
33. Aron recounted this in a television programme devoted to him in the series *L'Homme en question*, broadcast by the French television channel FR3 on 30 October 1977. I am grateful to FR3, and especially the Atelier Michèle Vallon, for enabling me to see a videotape of the programme in December 1979. Cf. 1981a, p. 26.

34. 1983a, pp. 19, 20, 21.
35. Ibid., p. 22.
36. 1981a, p. 26: tr. p. 24.
37. 1983a, p. 22.
38. *Revue universitaire*, 1928(2), pp. 231–2. The distinction of beating Aron in philosophy went to two pupils from the Lycée Janson-de-Sailly by the names of Pierre Debauvais and Gilbert Boris, and one from Henri-IV, Max Bercot.
39. 1983a, pp. 28–9.
40. Jean Maugüé, *Les Dents agacées* (Paris, 1982), pp. 40–1. Maugüé subsequently entered the Ecole Normale Supérieure where he studied philosophy. He taught in Brazil in the 1930s, joined the Free French during the Second World War, and then served in the diplomatic corps for ten years before returning to France to teach in the Lycée Carnot.
41. 1983a, pp. 29, 30.
42. On Brunschvicg and Bouglé, see Chapter 2, below. Cresson wrote over forty books, from his doctoral thesis, *La Morale de Kant: Etude critique* (Paris, 1897) to the "philosophical testament" of the end of his life, *Les Lambeaux de la vérité* (*Fragments of Truth*). Two of his "guiding ideas" were that "our knowledge is always on a human scale and we can only ever affirm what is most probable". See François Canac, "Cresson (André)", *Association amicale de secours des anciens élèves de l'Ecole normale supérieure*, 1951, pp. 24–6.
43. Paul Desjardins, "Salomon (Charles)", ibid., 1927, pp. 39–46.
44. Parigot entered the Ecole Normale Supérieure in 1881 and died in 1948.
45. Cahen's doctoral thesis had been on *Condorcet et la Révolution française* (Paris, 1904; new edn, Geneva, 1970).
46. Léon Cahen, *L'Angleterre au XIXᵉ siècle: son évolution politique* (Paris, 1924; 5th edn, 1957).
47. 1983a, p. 27.
48. R. A., interview with the author, 1977.
49. Sirinelli, 1984, pp. 19–20. This article is especially concerned with the youthful Aron's relationship to Alain and his disciples – see Chapter 2, below.
50. Sirinelli, 1982. This article compares the political attitudes of Sartre and Aron in their student days.

2

The Ecole Normale Supérieure

_____

The Rue d'Ulm

Founded – and quickly disbanded – during the Revolution, the Ecole Normale Supérieure was originally designed, under the organization of the French higher education system in 1808, to provide arts and science teachers for the lycées. Together with its great scientific counterpart, the Ecole Polytechnique, it soon became the most famous of the _grandes écoles_, the major institutions of higher education outside the University which had been created at the beginning of the nineteenth century. The difficulty of its highly competitive entrance examination – in Aron's day the Ecole still took fewer than sixty arts and science students a year – contributed to the prestige of the School; so, too, did the subsequent fame of many of its students, not only in teaching and research, but also in literature, politics and the diplomatic service. Thus the students of the Ecole Normale Supérieure, which was residential, were widely considered to form an academic elite and developed a unique esprit de corps.

Such an institution was almost bound to attract enemies, and hostility to the School reached a peak at the turn of the century. It was criticized for taking the most able students away from the university faculties –

students who then went on to take the most sought-after jobs in the lycées and, to an increasing extent, in the universities – and, largely on account of the influence of its legendary librarian, Lucien Herr, it was accused of being a centre for the indoctrination of the country's young intellectual elite into socialism. As a result, in 1903 it was made part of the University of Paris; though retaining its financial independence, its budget was severely cut. Its unique professorial system, by which in the nineteenth century gifted *maîtres de conférences* had been specially appointed to the Ecole, was largely discontinued and henceforth its students had to attend lectures in the ordinary way at the Sorbonne, with the result that the Ecole was in danger of becoming little more than a hostel for exceptional students. By 1914 its prestige had suffered a decline, particularly in science, and the proportion of applicants to places, though still in a ratio of five to one, had been halved by comparison with twenty-five years earlier. Significantly, its Director during this period (1904–1919), the historian Ernest Lavisse, did not even live in his official residence at the Ecole and allowed considerable relaxation – some said deterioration – of discipline. Indeed, there was even talk of the School closing, but the heroism of its students in the First World War helped to save it – half of them died in battle and the School as a whole was awarded the Croix de Guerre.[1]

By the time Aron became a student at the Ecole in 1924, Lavisse had been succeeded as Director by the literary historian, Gustave Lanson. Cold and authoritarian, though a conscientious administrator, Lanson had been appointed in 1919 to preside over an institution filled with veterans of the war and he sought to "restore order" to the Ecole – an aim in which he appears to have been singularly unsuccessful, at the cost of considerable personal unpopularity among the students.[2] Lanson was succeeded in 1927 by the School's first scientific Director, the mathematician Ernest Vessiot, who began a building programme which led the Ecole to be described in the inter-war years as "an anarchist monastery sprouting laboratories".[3] Indeed the Ecole, which in 1847 had moved to the site on the Rue d'Ulm where it still stands, looked like a cross between a monastery and a barracks. The state of the building, already filthy and dilapidated in the nineteenth century, had been made even worse by its use as a hospital during the war: the roof leaked, conditions in the dormitories and studies were primitive and uncomfortable, there was no central heating or running water (these were introduced ten years later by Vessiot's successor, the genial sociologist Célestin Bouglé), and the students frequently complained about the food. Nevertheless, the intellectual atmosphere at the Ecole was remarkable.

When Aron arrived in 1924, the final-year students included Alfred Kastler, winner of the Nobel Prize for Physics in 1966. The philosopher, Vladimir Jankélévitch, was in his third year, as was Pierre Brossolette, who during the Occupation died a hero's death at the hands of the Gestapo. Second-year students included the philosopher and mathematician, Jean Cavaillès, who became a close friend of Aron's and was to be shot by the Germans as a Resistance leader in 1944;[4] the sociologist, Georges Friedmann; and the writer and literary critic, Pierre-Henri Simon.

Aron's year – the "*promotion*" of 1924 – was a particularly brilliant one. It consisted of fifty-two students, of whom twenty-nine were in the arts section (*lettres*) and twenty-three were studying science. The arts students read either Greek, Latin and French (literature or philology), or philosophy, or history and geography, or modern languages (English or German). The scientists took either mathematics, or physics and chemistry, or natural sciences (biology and geology). The course normally lasted four years, students taking the four *certificats* in their chosen discipline which comprised the *licence d'enseignement*, followed by a dissertation, the *diplôme d'études supérieures*. At the end of their final year they took the *agrégation*, the competitive examination which entitled them to teach in the lycées.

Among the arts students in Aron's year there were five studying philosophy, all of whom were to become well-known: Sartre; Paul Nizan, Communist writer, journalist and militant in the 1930s; the psychiatrist Daniel Lagache, who became Professor of Pathological Psychology at the Sorbonne; the philosopher Georges Canguilhem, who was subsequently Professor of the History and Philosophy of Science at the Sorbonne; and Aron himself.[5] The other arts students included the diplomats, Jean Baillou and Armand Bérard; Albert Bédé, Professor of French at Columbia University; the Socialist deputy, Jean Le Bail; the historian, Georges Lefranc; the Latinist, Jacques Perret; and the Hellenist, Louis Robert.[6] The science section of the 1924 promotion included the 1970 Nobel Prizewinner for Physics, Louis Néel, and the mathematicians, Jean Dieudonné and Charles Ehresmann.

Aron's generation at the Rue d'Ulm in subsequent years included, in the 1925 promotion, the philosopher Jean Hypollite, who later became Director of the Ecole, the historian Henri Marrou, and René Maheu, the future Director-General of Unesco ("André Herbaud" in Simone de Beauvoir's memoirs); in the 1926 promotion, the philosopher and mathematician Albert Lautman, who was to be shot as a member of the Resistance in 1944,[7] and the philosopher Maurice Merleau-Ponty; and in 1927 – the first year in which women were fully accepted as students at the Rue d'Ulm – Simone Pétrement, philosopher, Conservateur of the Bibliothèque Nationale, and biographer of Simone Weil, who herself entered the Ecole Normale Supérieure in 1928.[8]

Aron's first impression on arriving at the Rue d'Ulm was a sense of wonder: he had never encountered so many intelligent people in so small a space.[9] The five philosophers in the 1924 promotion – Sartre, Nizan, Lagache, Canguilhem and Aron – formed a close-knit group and in their first year were "almost always together at the Ecole and outside".[10] They used to go together to Georges Dumas' lectures on pathological psychology at the Hôpital Saint-Anne[11] and even planned to write a scenario together for a film of Jules Renard's novel, *Poil de carotte*.[12] Aron told me that he "lacked self-confidence" and was therefore "very flattered" to be admitted into the company of Sartre and Nizan, who had known each other while preparing for the Ecole Normale at the Lycée Louis-le-Grand. Thus the "petits camarades" became close friends.

Nizan was in some ways the most precocious member of the group.[13] At the Ecole Normale he and Sartre were "indistinguishable" – they were even known as "Nitre et Sarzan". Nizan, wrote Sartre,

had a cast in one eye, like me, but in the opposite direction, so that it was agreeable. My divergent squint gave my face the appearance of an unploughed field. His eyes converged, giving him a mischievous air of abstraction even when he was listening. He followed fashion closely, insolently. At seventeen he had his trousers cut so tight around the ankles that he had trouble pulling them on. A little later they flared out into Oxford bags (pattes d'éléphant) that hid his shoes. Then, all of a sudden, they changed into plus-fours (culottes de golf) that came up to his knees and stood out like skirts. He carried a Malacca walking stick and wore a monocle, little round collars, and wing collars. He traded in his steel-rimmed glasses for enormous tortoise-shell spectacles which, with a touch of the English snobbery that afflicted all the young people of the time, he called his "goggles". . . At the Ecole Normale nobody paid any attention to dress except for a few provincials who proudly wore spats and tucked silk handkerchiefs into their jacket pockets. But I don't remember that anyone disapproved of Nizan's outfits – we were proud to have a dandy in our midst.[14]

It was the element of mystery in his personality which, Aron recalled at the end of his life, attracted Nizan's fellow students – a mystery which went beyond his natural elegance, wit and "exceptional speed of mind". But it was also apparent, despite the intermittent gaiety with which he concealed it, that he was full of an anguish that he was determined to overcome by serious thought or action. During his second year at the Ecole, he was offered the post of tutor to the son of a leading businessman in Aden, Antoine Besse (subsequently the founder of St Antony's College, Oxford). Aron was one of those present at Nizan's "deliberation": should he, or should he not, interrupt his studies and spend a year in Arabia? There was, Aron believed, an element of play-acting in such scenes, for Nizan had already made up his mind to go.[15] He left in October 1926, returning the following May in order to resume his studies at the Ecole, joined the Communist Party (having flirted with Georges Valois' right-wing *chemises bleues*) and became engaged.

Aron was drafted in to help break the ice between the families of the engaged couple: the Nizans were a provincial, petit-bougeois family from Quiberon in Brittany (Paul's father was a railway official), while his fiancée, Rirette Alphen, came from a very different background – upper-class, Jewish, Parisian society ("la grande bourgeoisie juive parisienne"). Whatever Aron's part in the affair (he spent several weeks at Quiberon in the summer of 1927 where, he claims, his presence was redundant), there were no major incidents, despite the reservations of *curé* cousins on the Nizan side, suspected of slight anti-Semitism. The wedding itself took place on Christmas Eve 1927 at the Mairie du Panthéon, with Sartre and Aron as witnesses. The couple had had their clothes specially made ("d'un chic très britannique") by Aberdeen, an English tailor in the Boulevard Malesherbes. Unfortunately, the day before the wedding, Nizan was smitten by an attack of acute appendicitis. The surgeon agreed to postpone the operation for twenty-four hours on condition that the groom, whose pallor contrasted strikingly with the red carnation in his button-hole, went straight home after the ceremony and lay down with an ice-pack on his stomach.[16]

At the time, Aron wrote in 1983, he had no doubt that Nizan would become a writer: Aron considered him Sartre's inferior in intellectual force and philosophical power, but he believed that Nizan had the greater literary talent.[17] Four years after the Arabian interlude, in 1931, Nizan was to publish a short book, *Aden-Arabie*,[18] which contained a searing attack on the Ecole Normale and "that official exercise which is still called philosophy", both of which, in spite of his initial high hopes, "soon inspired in me all the disgust of which I was capable".[19] The only exception to Nizan's indictment was the famous librarian at the Ecole, Lucien Herr:[20]

In 1924 there was still one man at the Ecole: Lucien Herr. When you saw that giant bent over a mountain of books, his clear eyes peering from beneath a bulging forehead, from beneath a steep cliff of thoughts, when you heard his voice that never lied pronounce judgements with the sole object of rendering to each his due, you knew that you were safe in that filthy abode. But he died. The Ecole Normale remained, a ridiculous and, more often, odious thing, presided over by a patriotic, hypocritical, powerful little old man who respected the military.[21]

Nizan followed *Aden-Arabie*, which Aron "liked and admired", with *Les Chiens de garde* (1932), an attack on the idealist philosophy prevailing at the Sorbonne and in particular its chief exponent, Léon Brunschvicg. Aron thought this "a terrible book" ("un livre épouvantable"), [22] which both displeased and shocked him (he was not sure that he ever finished reading it): "Our teachers did not deserve such insults for the sole crime of not being revolutionaries. Why should they have been?"[23]

Although his friendship with Nizan was "very lively and intimate, it was a student friendship",[24] and they saw little of each other in the 1930s. During this time Nizan wrote regularly for the Communist Party's daily paper, *L'Humanité*, and then for its evening paper, *Ce Soir*. He also spent a year in the Soviet Union (1934–5) and during the Civil War visited Spain as a journalist, but he resigned from the Communist Party after the signing of the Stalin-Hitler non-aggression pact in August 1939. He was killed near Dunkirk in May 1940 while serving as liaison officer with a British regiment. After his death Communist-inspired rumours circulated that while a Party member Nizan had been a police-informer, and in 1947 a group of writers, which included Aron and Sartre, published an open letter in the press challenging the Communist Party to provide proof of the allegation.[25] This met with an evasive reply;[26] the failure to produce evidence was noted in a further open letter,[27] and no more was heard of the rumours against him. Nizan's writings subsequently remained relatively forgotten until the 1960s when *Aden-Arabie* was republished with a dazzling introduction by Sartre.[28] New editions of his other works followed and, as a result, Nizan became one of the *maîtres à penser* of the student generation of 1968.

If Aron's friendship with Nizan was strongest in their third year at the Ecole, his relationship with Sartre was closest in their fourth year, when he shared a *thurne* or study with Sartre and the "charming" Pierre Guille ("Pierre Pagniez" in Simone de Beauvoir's memoirs and later Secretary to the French Parliament).[29] "Was I convinced", Aron asked at the end of his life, "that Sartre would become what he did – philosopher, novelist, playwright, prophet of existentialism, Nobel prizewinner for literature?"

If the question is put in this form, I should unhesitatingly say "no". Even if I had been asked if he would be a great philosopher or writer, my reply would have varied and never been unqualified. On the one hand, I admired (and still do) his extraordinary fertility of mind and expression. We used to pull his leg about the ease with which he wrote (I myself, at the time, wrote with difficulty, haunted by the blank page and the pen that refused to move). "No more than three hundred and fifty pages of manuscript in three weeks? What's going on?", we used to say to our *petit camarade*. As well as his facility as a writer, his wealth of imagination and creativity in the world of ideas dazzled me then (as it does now). Not that doubts never crossed my mind. Sometimes he would develop an idea at length, aloud or on paper, simply through a failure to seize it in its entirety and give it pertinent expression. He constructed theories whose faults could easily be shown.[30]

One of the subjects of conversation between Sartre and Aron concerned how to come to terms with their mutual ugliness. Sartre, says Aron, often talked about his looks – and Aron about his – but Sartre's ugliness disappeared the moment he opened his mouth to speak; it was as if his intelligence wiped away the spots and swellings that disfigured his face. "Moreover, being small, thick-set and sturdy, he could climb a rope, keeping his legs horizontal, with a speed and agility which amazed us all".[31]

* * *

In his first two years at the Ecole Normale, Aron took his *licence* in philosophy. This consisted of four "certificates": psychology, general history of philosophy, general philosophy and logic, and morals and sociology. He received the mark of *bien* for each certificate, with the ironical exception of the last – (Durkheimian) sociology and morals (*assez bien* only).[32] At that time neo-Kantianism dominated French academic philosophy, particularly under the influence of Léon Brunschvicg, who had been teaching at the Sorbonne since 1909 and became Professor of the History of Modern Philosophy in 1927. The philosophy syllabus included the study of Plato, Aristotle, Descartes and their successors, but there was little on the post-Kantians, no Hegel and almost nothing on Marx. A prominent place was given to epistemology, particularly in relation to science and mathematics, but there were no lectures on political philosophy (while he was at the Ecole Normale, Aron never heard mention of Tocqueville).[33]

The philosophy licence was "very easy" after the relative difficulty of the entrance examination and Aron consequently had plenty of free time. He played tennis (in his first year at the Ecole he won the singles and, with the future sociologist, Georges Friedmann, the doubles competition).[34] He frequently visited the Louvre[35] and, like many French intellectuals, he was a keen cinema-goer. Above all, he read novels and poetry – both that of great writers such as Proust (his favourite author), Claudel and Valéry, and the fashionable literature of the day (Paul Morand, Giraudoux, Valery Larbaud, and Breton and the Surrealists).[36] In addition, he followed, for a time, Edouard Le Roy's philosophy lectures at the Collège de France, embarked upon large volumes of civil law and began books on mathematics.[37]

Apart from a teaching practice (*stage pédagogique*) at the Lycée Louis-le-Grand in January 1927 where he was described as being "a young master full of talent",[38] Aron's third year was spent on the dissertation which he had to write for his *diplôme d'études supérieures*. For his subject he chose Kant's concept of "the intemporal", because it was to Kant that he felt most drawn. This involved him in studying all of Kant's work from the writings that preceded the *Critique of Pure Reason* to the *Religion within the Limits of Pure Reason* of the last years, and he now spent eight or ten hours a day reading Kant, though with what results he could not be sure. For years the dissertation was lost – he lent his copy to Nizan and Sartre (Aron believed that some of its themes can be detected in *Being and Nothingness* as well as in Sartre's theatre)[39] – although he told me in 1977, and repeated in his *Memoirs*, that he would be curious to see it again. It so happens that at the very end of his life the widow of Albert Lautman found a copy among her papers. Its full title was *La Notion de l'Intemporel dans la Philosophie de Kant: Moi intelligible et liberté* (*The Notion of the Intemporal in Kant's Philosophy: Intelligible Self and Freedom*). Despite its densely technical nature, the 40,000-word text clearly shows Aron's early preoccupation with the problem of liberty, as the quotation from Kant on the title page reveals: "Die Freiheit läszt sich nicht theilen. Der Mensch ist entweder gantz oder gar nicht frei" ("Freedom is not divisible. Man is either completely free or not at all").[40] The ninety pages of poor-quality typescript which follow are divided into six chapters together with an introduction and a conclusion: The Formation of the Problem of Freedom; Freedom in the *Critique of Pure Reason*; Intemporal and Eternal; Autonomy and Intelligible Self; Original Freedom and Actual Freedom; The Intemporal in Religious Thought.[41] The dissertation was supervised by Brunschvicg, who gave it seventeen marks out of twenty.[42] Aron never, he confessed, succeeded in reading the newly rediscovered text, but he retained, nonetheless, "a memory of austere exaltation from my year spent in the company of a philosopher":

There is no substitute – even for those who are not destined for a life of philosophical toil – for the unravelling of a philosophical text. For many years after my year with Kant, all other books seemed easy to me. I evaluated their level by the mental tension that each one required.[43]

The final year (1927–8) was spent preparing for the *agrégation* and this involved the study of Aristotle, Rousseau and Comte, together with the writing of three dissertations. By now Aron had given clear evidence of his gifts as a philosopher. By temperament he preferred high-level abstraction and metaphysics. During his first year he had read a paper on the ontological argument in Saint Anselm and Kant to Brunschvicg, who was so impressed that he went to tell the Director, Lanson, that here was a student with a real talent for philosophy. During his final year Aron read a paper on Aristotle's physics to Léon Robin, the specialist in Greek philosophy, and an American philosopher who was present told Robin that Aron was a born metaphysician and ought to work in this field.[44] However, he also had an intellectual reputation among the students: Simone de Beauvoir recounts how, in the oral examination for the agrégation (candidates were given one day in which to prepare a lecture-topic), "there was a crowd to hear the lesson presented by Raymond Aron, for whom every one foretold a brilliant future as a philosopher".[45] He had to comment on a passage of Aristotle and Spinoza and, despite an error of interpretation in the latter for which he was subsequently docked a point,[46] he received the top mark of sixteen out of twenty. The subjects of the written papers were "Reason and Society", "Language as a Means of Communication between Individual Consciousnesses", and "Plato's Theory of Ideas".[47] Overall Aron was placed a comfortable first, with Emmanuel Mounier, who later founded the review *Esprit*, second, and Daniel Lagache third (Georges Canguilhem had taken the examination the previous year and Nizan was now a year behind). Aron was pleased at his success, but in his mature view only one of his three dissertations – that on Aristotle and Comte – contained anything original.[48]

Sartre failed the agrégation that year. Pierre Bertaux, who entered the Ecole Normale in 1926 and struck up an early friendship with Aron, recalls the latter's reaction when the results were posted up: "I can still see Raymond Aron read the list through, utter a cry of rage, hurl his hat to the ground...and trample it saying: 'Ah, the fools, the fools! They've failed Sartre'".[49] According to Aron's interpretation, Sartre had deliberately courted failure that year by presenting his own philosophy instead of sticking to the rules of the academic game, but he too came first in the agrégation (with higher marks than Aron) when he took it again in 1929 – Simone de Beauvoir was second.

* * *

Already, as a student, Aron's chief interest, apart from philosophy, was politics. The Cartel des Gauches, consisting of Radicals and Socialists, had won the general election of 1924 and formed a government under Edouard Herriot. Aron, who was "completely left-wing", was "beside himself with joy" at their victory. He became a member of the Socialist Party – "to do something for the people". Having been introduced by his cousin, Durkheim's nephew, the anthropologist Marcel Mauss, he joined the branch of the fifth *arrondissement*, in the heart of the Latin Quarter, but he remained a member – "with difficulty" – for only a few months. What made him decide to leave was an incident one evening when an impeccably dressed bourgeois student declared in emphatic tones, "Above all, we must not forget that we are a revolutionary party!" As Aron later recalled, he found this remark, coming from such a source, "so ridiculous", since the Party was obviously not revolutionary, that he decided he had had enough; the bad faith evident in the contradiction between words and action stuck in his throat and he left the Socialists. However, he did not feel the need to join any other party; although extremely interested in politics, he devoted little time to them.[50] Nevertheless, he was present at a dramatic session of the National Assembly in July 1926 when, in the midst of a financial crisis, Herriot presented a second government which was immediately rejected by the Chamber of Deputies.[51]

In contrast to his "vague socialism", however, Aron's strongest political feeling – one shared by many of his generation – was of revolt against the Great War. This made him into a fervent pacifist. In 1925 or 1926, for example, through a League of Nations association of which he was a member, he spent a fortnight in Geneva during the annual meeting of the General Assembly. Here he heard a speeech in favour of "indivisible peace" by the eloquent Socialist deputy, Joseph Paul-Boncour, whom Aron much admired. It was in Geneva, too, that he first met Bertrand de Jouvenel; only two years older than Aron (they had not known each other at the Lycée Hoche, where de Jouvenel had also been a pupil), he was already a journalist of repute.[52]

Again, when in March 1927 a military law was introduced envisaging "an orientation of the country's intellectual resources in the direction of national defence", Aron was one of fifty-four *normaliens* who signed a petition stating that for the first time in war the law abrogated "all intellectual autonomy and freedom of opinion". Text and signatures were reproduced in the pacifist monthlies, *Europe* and *Libres Propos*.[53] Similarly, a year later Aron signed a declaration in support of a historian, Georges Demartial, who was about to be deprived of his Legion of Honour for five years for writing an article in which he challenged the view that Germany alone was responsible for the First World War.[54] This declaration of support was followed by a petition to the Minister on Demartial's behalf.[55] Above all, Aron dreamed of reconciliation between France and Germany, and this was one of the reasons which led him to go to that country in 1930.

A number of politicians and writers visited the Ecole Normale in his time – for example, Blum, Herriot and Alfred Fabre-Luce – and it was one such visit which led to the publication of Aron's first article. The occasion was a discussion between Julien Benda, whose controversial *La Trahison des clercs* (*The Betrayal of the Intellectuals*) had recently appeared, and a group of students at the Ecole. Aron's three-page "note" of the meeting was published in the April 1928 number of *Libres Propos*.[56] Even in this first short piece, published when he was barely twenty-three, one passage is particularly striking because it alludes to a theme which was to remain central to Aron's work – the relation between thought and action. Thus, having criticized Benda for his philosophical idealism, Aron added: "Hence. . .a certain contempt for the intellectual who seeks to reflect upon our world (penser notre monde) and gradually bring intelligible relationships to bear upon it – in other words, to bring heaven down to earth". Surely, he asked, it was possible to "conceive, without betraying it, an attitude of mind that is attached to truth and inspired by generosity, though nonetheless engaged in action?" The tone, too, was sharp as Aron took Benda to task for his "radical pessimism": "We expected a man. All we had before us was a man of letters".[57]

Alain and Brunschvicg

At the time when Aron was a student at the Ecole Normale Supérieure there were three names to conjure with as far as French philosophy was concerned: Bergson, Alain and Brunschvicg. Bergson was, as Aron put it after the former's death during the Second World War, "the greatest French philosopher of our time";[58] yet by the time Aron entered the Ecole in 1924 Bergson's influence, which had been at its height in the first two decades of the century, was already on the wane. Overcome by paralysis, he had gradually gone into retirement after the First World War and, although he won the Nobel Prize for Literature in 1927, he wrote little in the last twenty years of his life. "So far as I can recall", wrote Aron in 1975,

we read him even then as if he belonged to the classics and the dead. As Professor of Philosophy at the Collège de France he attracted his own crowds; as Nobel laureate in 1927 he reached during his lifetime the height of his renown. After World War I he retained disciples and admirers but no longer influenced philosophical instruction in lycées or universities.[59]

Alain's case was different, however. His real name was Emile Chartier, and he was the author of the famous series of *Propos* as well as chief philosophical spokesman of Radicalism. Seeing himself as champion of the underdog, and refusing all honours including the Sorbonne, he taught at the Lycée Henri-IV in Paris, where his ideas had a considerable influence upon pupils entering for the Ecole Normale Supérieure. In the 1920s his prestige "inspired a fanatical minority" on the fringe of the Sorbonne[60] and at the Ecole Normale itself there was a group, which included Canguilhem, calling itself "les élèves d'Alain". Aron, who had not of course been a pupil at Henri-IV, did not belong to this group and "did not see in him the Master". Nevertheless, through friends and by reading his books, he did come under Alain's influence[61] and occasionally accompanied the great teacher on his celebrated walks from the Lycée Henri-IV to his home in the Rue de Rennes.[62]

This influence was the subject of the second article Aron wrote, published in *La Psychologie et la vie* in 1929:

There is at the Ecole Normale a group of young men furiously active in body and soul. Strong and healthy, they are keen to apply – on the sports field and in the Popular Universities, through hard toil and political petitions – the counsels of the Master. They are known as "the disciples of Alain", a term applied by the authorities and some students out of fear and by others out of friendship – sometimes even respect. Differing markedly in taste and temperament, they are united in a common admiration for the Master, and at the same time in a shared contempt for whatever is base and feeble, a contempt for those who, while still at the Ecole, are preparing careers for themselves as self-seeking yes-men, and a general contempt for much of humanity and its affairs: slaves, profiteers, those who give themselves airs, trouble-makers, militarists and nationalists...

It is these hatreds which unite them, for they have no desire for a common theory. Alain teaches them that everyone must think freely for himself. He is neither a builder nor a refuter of systems. He does not argue. For him it is enough to think and put ideas in place. He does so in front of his pupils with unadorned sincerity and an ever-renewed desire for truth...Is it this absence of affectation and dialectic, this ceaseless contact with truth, that his former pupils, turning their backs on the professorial lectures of the Sorbonne, return to find – sometimes for several hours a week – at the Lycée Henri-IV? Is this the secret of the extraordinary sway he holds over the generations of pupils who adopt his ideas, imitate his style even, share his enthusiasms, and read and reread Descartes, Stendhal and Balzac...?

Perhaps, but it must first be said that this real thinker is a great one. Then, at the risk of arousing his annoyance, one must add the example set by his life. Previously, thinkers were partly judged by their conduct during the Dreyfus Affair. Since then the "clerks" have been put to a harsher test. By doing more than his duty as a citizen and all his duty as a philosopher, Alain – free mind and admirable soldier – returned from the War an even greater man. Finally, the friend of his pupils, it is he who by his kindness and cordiality gives them strength and joie de vivre. His look and his smile are a source of joy for others. And I have never understood the truth of Spinoza's words better than when I saw him: "Joy is the passage from a lesser perfection to a greater one"...

His pupils may not always derive a philosophy, a politics and a morality from this teaching. But even if they were no longer to subscribe to the Master's thought, they would, I believe, be happy to write, with Maurois: "To Alain, teacher of philosophy, I owe everything". However limited it may be, this influence is enough to spread, a little mysteriously, the name of the philosophy teacher of the Montagne-Sainte-Geneviève. How many only know Alain through the passion of one of his disciples, or at any rate first came to know him through one of them. For my part, I owe a great deal to the friendship of a number of his pupils, as well as to his books. Or rather it was the life and the man, sensed through the admiration of his disciples, which added to the power of his writings. Thus one respects, admires and likes him, even before meeting him. One can therefore understand the fanaticism of his pupils, which some find slightly ridiculous. But they would say in reply, as Alain did of Lagneau: "He is the only Great Man I have met". And to this Great Man, who has succeeded in remaining a man and a friend as well as a Master, disciples "in spirit and truth" are happy to pay homage.[63]

As he wrote after Alain's death in 1951, what most impressed Aron and his fellow students were the "great man's" personality and conduct:

A pacifist, he had joined up on the first day of hostilities. He had served as a common soldier, but took no pleasure in fighting. He rejected high office and refused to avoid the obligation that the community imposes on its humblest members. At the time we were still in revolt against the great massacre and, even more so perhaps, against eye-wash of any kind (le bourrage de crâne). We judged our elders in terms of their deeds and words between 1914 and 1918. To us, Alain's seemed to have the mark of greatness.[64]

Yet, even in the 1920s, Aron was "reluctant to subscribe to Alain's political principles". He was not sure that Alain's quietism was preferable to Jaurès' socialism:

At the time, like most non-Catholics at the Ecole Normale, I inclined towards the Left and declared myself a Socialist. It goes without saying that I had almost no idea how a socialist economy differed from a market-economy and that I was quite incapable of pointing to the probable advantages and drawbacks of each. As an "intellectual of good will", I sided with the people against the privileged classes, and with progress against tradition. Society must be rebuilt on a rational basis and traditional institutions destroyed. I was more affected by the symbols of Republicanism or Revolution than those of Conservatism. Not that such preferences committed me to anything very much, any more than their opposite would have done.[65]

It was only when he went to Germany, witnessed Hitler's rise to power and began the study of economics, sociology and history, that Aron broke with opinions which were "the product of convention rather than thought". As a result, his admiration for Alain gave way to a revolt against an influence which, in the years leading up to the Second World War, appeared to him "pernicious" ("néfaste").[66]

Of his teachers at the Ecole Normale Supérieure it was Léon Brunschvicg who impressed Aron the most; Brunschvicg had a high opinion of Aron and professor and student became friends. Although Aron was by no means uncritical of Brunschvicg, throughout his life he continued to hold him in "the greatest respect"[67] and referred to him in later years as "mon maître".[68] Few people today read Brunschvicg, but in the 1920s and 1930s he was an important and extremely influential figure in French philosophy – "the mandarin of mandarins", as Aron called him in his memoirs.[69] To Aron, writing in 1975, Brunschvicg with his "critical idealism" was "the last representative of one style of philosophy or one moment of French thought, a style and a moment whose origins go back to the last quarter of the nineteenth century, to the era when the Third Republic tried to re-establish the universities, which had been eclipsed since the French Revolution".[70]

Born in 1869, Brunschvicg had been educated, like Aron after him, at the Lycée Condorcet in Paris, where his fellow pupils included Xavier Léon the philosopher, Elie Halévy the historian, and Célestin Bouglé the sociologist, all of whom were to remain lifelong friends and colleagues.[71] From 1888 to 1891 he was a student at the Ecole Normale Supérieure, where Léon, Halévy and Bouglé were again his contemporaries. Shortly afterwards, in 1893, Léon and Halévy founded the *Revue de métaphysique et de morale*, the philosophical journal with which Brunschvicg was associated throughout his life and to which he was a frequent contributor. The three of them were later instrumental in founding the Société Française de Philosophie, of which Brunschvicg became President on Léon's death in 1936. In 1909, having taught in

36

various lycées in the provinces as well as at the Lycée Condorcet and the Lycée Henri-IV in Paris, he was appointed *maître de conférences* at the Sorbonne, where he remained for over thirty years, becoming Professor of the History of Modern Philosophy in 1927 and presiding over numerous juries for the agrégation and the doctorate including, as we shall see, Aron's defence of his doctoral thesis in 1938. In 1919 Brunschvicg was elected to the Académie des Sciences Morales et Politiques, of which he became President in 1932.[72] Aron saw him for the last time at the beginning of 1940;[73] with the defeat of France in the following June, Brunschvicg, who was Jewish, left for the Unoccupied Zone – his house and library in Paris were subsequently ransacked by the Germans – and when the Unoccupied Zone was invaded in November 1942 he was compelled, now in ill-health and using an assumed name, to move again, until he eventually reached Aix-les-Bains. It was there that he died in January 1944.[74]

Aron was to discuss Brunschvicg's "critical idealism" on several occasions during the early part of his life. The first was a respectful enough review, published in 1932, of the master's *De la Connaissance de soi* (*On Self-Knowledge*),[75] even if Aron used the occasion to go beyond Brunschvicg and develop some of his own ideas – in particular, the need for "a doctrine of political and social action". This involved "choosing, in accordance with a system of values, between the possibilities offered by every historical situation":

To pick out from history the directions which man's development is taking, to gauge the degree of certainty of our knowledge and its significance for the past and the present, and to deduce from this the real freedom of action that is available to us, is a problem of thought before it is a problem of practice.[76]

The second occasion on which Aron discussed Brunschvicg's work was a lengthy, hundred-page article which he wrote in order to try to rid himself, once and for all, of his teacher's influence. At the time (still the early 1930s) he was strongly – if temporarily – attracted by Mannheim's sociology of knowledge and, in his eagerness to explain the thought in terms of the social conditions of the thinker, he alluded to Brunschvicg's Jewishness, the French context and the bourgeois social milieu. Aron sent the article to Brunschvicg who approved of the exposition of his philosophy, but thought the critique offensive and left to Aron the decision whether or not to publish the piece. Aron decided against, and the text was lost during the war.[77]

The third occasion was a commemorative lecture which he gave at the French Institute in London during the war, shortly after Brunschvicg's death.[78] "Like all philosophers worthy of the name", said Aron, "Léon Brunschvicg was above all a moralist".[79] To Brunschvicg the positive sciences, in particular mathematics and physics, were central to humanity's spiritual development, and it was for this reason that his writings, though essentially concerned with morals, took the form of a critical history of science. Thus his "three major works" – *Les Etapes de la philosophie mathématique* (1912), *L'Expérience humaine et la causalité physique* (1922) and *Le Progrès de la conscience dans la philosophie occidentale* (1927) – traced "the progressive creation of the universes of mathematics and physics and the process by which the mind becomes conscious of the conditions and significance of its achievements".[80] In this sense Brunschvicg's was "a philosophy of human destination": man was "a being destined to discover the truth" and science "the essentially human activity".[81]

Brunschvicg's ideas might, Aron acknowledged, appear to be simple, but

all philosophies, in a sense, come down to simple truths. Philosophy is always the formulation not of common sense, but of good sense. Furthermore, because it rejects all dogmatism and any kind of system, and because it teaches no *credo*, this philosophy has nothing "dialectical" about it. It puts considerable emphasis on criticism – the critique of false science and false wisdom, of superstition and myth. It puts considerable emphasis on history, the setting for the surprising adventure through which man becomes human. In the final analysis, this philosophy is not an affirmation, but an appeal: an appeal to each and everyone to bring about in himself the conversion from childhood to maturity, from natural egoism to hardwon spirituality, from illusion to truth.[82]

Nevertheless, Aron had a number of reservations about Brunschvicg's thought, even if, as we have seen, he never subscribed to the kind of intemperate attack on neo-Kantian idealism made from a Marxist point of view by Nizan. Although Brunschvicg's philosophy was, said Aron, "profoundly historical", it was also "somehow not of our time" – in the sense that it "undemonstratively invites us to live every moment as if it were our last and in a way that will make it endure for ever". Secondly, it was a philosophy in which "anguish has no part" and " the consciousness of spiritual unity" was emphasized at the expense of "the revolts of the irrational". Thirdly, Brunschvicg used to advocate that one should teach what one understood and ignore what one did not know, but this, said Aron looking back at Brunschvicg's philosophy in 1944, was "a strange sort of wisdom at a time when secular religions are rampant. Brunschvicg is our contemporary, but he is the contemporary of Einstein, not of Hitler".[83] Finally, even though Brunschvicg recognized the discrepancy between humanity's spiritual destination and the tragic destiny of men today, was it enough for a philosophy simply to point to the goal?

If the ideal is too elevated, if man's lot is too wretched, will the philosopher not lose the capacity to engage with reality? The problems which attracted the attention of my generation seemed to us so removed from the precepts of that lofty wisdom that we were tempted to throw overboard what should have served to guide us.[84]

Notes

1. On the Ecole Normale Supérieure, see Theodore Zeldin, *France, 1848–1945, Vol. Two. Intellect, Taste and Anxiety* (Oxford, 1977), Ch. 7; Pierre Jeannin, *Ecole Normale Supérieure, Livre d'Or* (Paris, 1963); Alain Peyrefitte, *Rue d'Ulm. Chronique de la vie normalienne* (Paris, new edn, 1963).
2. Jeannin, op. cit., Ch. VI.
3. "Un couvent anarchiste où poussent des laboratoires" (ibid.).
4. See Chapter 9, below.
5. There was one other philosophy student in Aron's year, but he died in 1928.
6. Four of the twenty-nine arts students in Aron's year were to be killed during the Second World War.
7. See Chapter 9, below.
8. Simone Pétrement, *La Vie de Simone Weil, Vol. I. 1909–1934* (Paris, 1973). A separate Ecole Normale Supérieure de Jeunes Filles had been in existence at Sèvres since 1881.
9. 1983a, p. 31.
10. Daniel Lagache, interview with Claude Bonnefoy, *Arts*, 11 January 1961. Cf. Aron, 1978b, p. 622.
11. Georges Canguilhem has told me (interview, 1980) that it is untrue that Aron, Sartre and Nizan entered for the first-year examination in medicine – physics, chemistry and natural science ("PCN") – as stated in Didier Anzieu, "Daniel Lagache", *Association amicale de secours des anciens élèves de l'Ecole normale supérieure*, 1974, p. 108.
12. Lagache, op. cit.
13. Of the seemingly endless succession of books on Nizan, the one that deals most directly with Aron (he gave an interview to its author) is Annie Cohen-Solal, *Paul Nizan, communiste impossible* (Paris, 1980).
14. Jean-Paul Sartre, "Avant-propos", Paul Nizan, *Aden-Arabie* (Paris, 1960), p. 20: tr. (by Joan Pinkham) *Aden-Arabie* (New York, 1968), pp. 18–19 (R.C.).
15. 1983a, pp. 32–4.
16. Cohen-Solal, op. cit., p. 64; 1983a, p. 33.
17. 1983a, p. 33.

18. Paul Nizan, *Aden-Arabie* (Paris, 1931; new edn, 1960). References are to the 1960 edition.

19. Ibid., p. 66: tr. p. 60.

20. Lucien Herr was in charge of the library at the Ecole Normale Supérieure from 1888 till his death in 1926. He used the position to exert considerable influence on the students who passed through the School and it was in large measure through him that such figures as Jean Jaurès and Léon Blum were converted to socialism. See Charles Andler, *La Vie de Lucien Herr* (Paris, 1932); and Daniel Lindenberg and Pierre-André Meyer, *Lucien Herr: Le Socialisme et son destin* (Paris, 1977).

21. Nizan, op. cit., p. 68: tr. p. 61. This last reference was to Gustave Lanson who, as we saw, was Director from 1919 to 1927.

22. 1981a, pp. 46–7: tr. 1983b, p. 41.

23. 1983a, pp. 33–4.

24. Cohen-Solal, op. cit., p. 38.

25. *Fig. Lit.*, 29 March 1947; *Combat*, 4 April 1947.

26. *L'Humanité*, 4 April 1947.

27. *Fig. Lit.*, 28 June 1947.

28. See n. 14, above.

29. On Guille, see 1983a, p. 45.

30. 1983a, pp. 34–5.

31. Ibid., p. 35.

32. Sirinelli, 1984, p. 21.

33. 1981a, p. 27: tr. p. 25.

34. *Bulletin de la Société des amis de l'Ecole normale supérieure*, 1925.

35. Aron's taste in painting was "eclectic", although he did not like modern art. The painters he admired included Le Nain, the Dutch primitives and the Rhenish school (R.A., interview with the author, 1980). Dominique Moïsi, who was Aron's student in the 1970s and accompanied him as secretary to a congress at Venice in April 1971, reports that "His relationship to art was distant. He had the artistic taste and culture of 'the honest man' ('l'honnête homme'). He was able to appreciate the beauty of Venice, but he was not stirred by artistic creation in the way that he could be by ideas or people" (Moïsi, 1985, p. 108).

36. Aron, in the television programme, *On n'a pas tous le jours vingt ans: 1925*, broadcast by A2, 5 August 1981 (see Chapter 1, n. 13, above).

37. 1983a, p. 37.

38. Document supplied to the author by Dominique Schnapper.

39. 1983a, p. 36.

40. *Kant's gesammelte Schriften*. Herausgegeben von der Preukischen Akademie der Wissenschaften. Band XVII (Berlin and Leipzig, 1926), No. 4229, p. 467.

41. I am very grateful to Madame Aron and to Dominique Schnapper for arranging for me to see the manuscript in March 1984.

42. Sirinelli, 1984, p. 21.

43. 1983a, p. 38.

44. R. A., interview with the author, 1977.

45. Simone de Beauvoir, *Mémoires d'une jeune fille rangée* (Paris, 1958), p. 272: tr. (by

James Kirkup) *Memoirs of a Dutiful Daughter* (Harmondsworth, 1959), p. 276. Compare the economist, Gaston Leduc, who as a student was living at the Fondation Thiers at the time: "I used to hear my friends from the Rue d'Ulm singing the praises of a star pupil ('un crack') who would certainly get himself talked about one day" ("Discours de M. Gaston Leduc, Président pour 1977", *RTASMP*, 1er semestre, 1975, p. 390).

46. 1983a, p. 37.
47. *Revue universitaire*, 1928 (2), pp. 291–9.
48. 1983a, p. 37.
49. Bertaux, 1985, p. 14.
50. See n. 35, above. Aron's left-wing contemporary at the Ecole, Georges Lefranc, who knew about such things, told Aron that he only joined the Etudiants Socialistes and not the Socialist Party itself. But since Aron could recall the presence of elderly people, he concluded in his memoirs that he went to Party meetings without being a card-carrying member (1983a, p. 48, n.i). See also Sirinelli, 1984, pp. 22–3, who discusses this question.
51. 1983a, p. 46.
52. Ibid., p. 45.
53. *Europe*, April 1927; *LP*, April 1927.
54. *LP*, February 1928.
55. *LP*, July 1928. See also "L'Affaire Demartial", *Europe*, June 1928, pp. 249–80. A year later, after he had left the Ecole, Aron helped organize a petition defending the right of normaliens to oppose compulsory military service (*LP*, July 1929 and *Europe*, August 1929). Two years after that, he signed a letter to the Minister for the Colonies, asking for a reprieve for those found guilty of rioting in Indo-China (*Europe*, April 1931).
56. 1928.
57. Ibid.
58. 1942j, p. 81.
59. Tr. 1975a, p.x. Compare the Marxist sociologist Henri Lefebvre, who was a student at the Sorbonne in the 1920s: "If there was one thinker for whom, at that time, we...unhesitatingly expressed the most complete scorn, it was Bergson. We had an almost physical horror of that flabby, shapeless thought of his...We read Bergson's books as a diversion, in the same way as we would have gone to an exhibition of furniture or photographs of 'la belle epoque'. We argued about Brunschvicg; we weighed up his strengths and weaknesses; we attacked him, and someone could always be found to plead in his defence. And that was true even when a little later Paul Nizan was planning to write *Les Chiens de garde*. But the condemnation of Bergson was in our view irrefutable, definitive and absolute. There was no need to prolong the argument...His thought seemed quite simply alien to us, our problems and our preoccupations". Henri Lefebvre, *La Somme et le reste* (Paris, 1959), pp. 383–4.
60. Tr. 1975a, pp. x–xi.
61. 1952b; reprinted 1972a, pp. 75–6.
62. 1981a, p. 25: tr. p. 23. For a discussion of Alain's influence on Aron at this time, see Sirinelli, 1984.

63. 1929. Jules Lagneau (1851–1894) was an idealist philosopher who had a strong personal influence on Alain. See the latter's *Souvenirs concernant Lagneau* (Paris, 1925).
64. 1972a, p. 76.
65. Ibid.
66. Ibid., pp. 76–7. See Chapter 11, below, and, for Aron's final thoughts on Alain, 1983a, pp. 41–5. The other influential political thinker in France in the inter-war years was Charles Maurras, leader of the right-wing Action Française. Aron read him "with complete indifference", however. "Maurras represented a positivist theory of monarchy, with an ideology of French order. I did not read him much; he bored me. I found him 'hexagonal' to an exaggerated degree. Even at the time when I still knew nothing of the wider world, I found his political philosophy strictly French and provincial" (1981a, pp. 36–7: tr. pp. 32–3 (R.C.)).
67. Tr. 1975a, p. ix.
68. 1945s.
69. 1983a, p. 38.
70. Tr. 1975a, pp. ix–x.
71. Another close friend of Brunschvicg's from his schooldays was Marcel Proust.
72. Brunschvicg also lectured abroad a great deal – for example, at Cambridge in 1923, the year in which he was invited to the annual meeting of the British Institute of Philosophy and received an honorary degree from the University of Durham.
73. 1945s, p. 128.
74. On Brunschvicg, see: Marcel Deschoux, *La Philosophie de Léon Brunschvicg* (Paris, 1949); Marcel Deschoux, *Léon Brunschvicg ou l'idéalisme à hauteur d'homme* (Paris, 1969); René Boivel, *Brunschvicg: sa vie, son oeuvre avec un exposé de sa philosophie* (Paris, 1964); and the Special Numbers devoted to Brunschvicg by two journals: *RMM*, 50, 1945, and *Les Etudes philosophiques*, 20, 1945.
75. 1932a.
76. Ibid., pp. 206–7.
77. 1983a, p. 72. Cf. 1981a, p. 39: tr. p. 35.
78. 1944l, reprinted 1945s. Aron also paid tribute to Brunschvicg in *France*, the French-language daily paper published in London during the war (1944z[4]).
79. 1945s, p. 128.
80. Ibid., p. 129. Compare tr. 1975a, p. ix: "To summarize in a single phrase the titles of his three great books, the progress of consciousness may not be isolated from innovations in mathematical thought or experimental physics".
81. 1945s, pp. 129–30.
82. Ibid., p. 134. Brunschvicg's view of science was at times strikingly close to the much better-known account subsequently put forward by Karl Popper in his *The Logic of Scientific Discovery* (1959), first published in German as *Logik der Forschung* in Vienna in 1934. Aron himself has noted that another point of similarity between Brunschvicg and Popper was the former's anticipation of Popper's criterion of falsifiability in science: Brunschvicg "had already taught us the formula that, from the pen of Sir Karl Popper, presently enjoys universal recognition: a proposition must be falsifiable in order to be scientific" (tr. 1975a, p.x).
83. 1945s, p. 138.

84. Ibid., p. 139. Compare Henri Lefebvre: "We were completely unfair to Brunschvicg... It was only after the rise of fascism and the Second World War that I came to appreciate the high quality of an intellectualism that was born of the Dreyfus Affair and involved a somewhat abstract but strong love of freedom, justice and truth, based on individual judgement (moral as much as intellectual) in the face of the forces of passion, including political passion." Lefebvre, op. cit., p. 376.

Part Two

The 1930s

___

3

Germany, 1930–1933

A Life Project

On leaving the Ecole Normale Supérieure, Aron did his eighteen-months'
military service (from October 1928 to March 1930). Alain's teachings
had done their work and he failed, in part through lack of conviction,
the officers' selection examination which allowed normaliens to do only
a year's military service; his inadequacies as a map-reader and platoon-
commander "did the rest" (at least the examination must have the distinction of being the only one Aron ever failed). As a result, after a few
weeks with an engineers' regiment at Metz and a brief interlude as a
telephonist in Paris, he became an instructor in meteorology at Saint-
Cyr, and it was on his advice that Sartre joined him there at the end
of 1929.[1]

Simone de Beauvoir, who saw Aron quite frequently at this time, was
somewhat in awe of his intellect.[2] She and Sartre were, she claims,
scornful of Aron's decision to join the Socialist Party; although they
themselves had no political affiliation, they believed that it had become
a bourgeois party and they disapproved of its gradualism. Nevertheless,
Sartre and Simone de Beauvoir rarely talked politics with Aron.
Philosophical questions, however, were a different matter. On these

Sartre and Aron "argued sharply", while Simone de Beauvoir kept silent; she felt that she did not think quickly enough, but if anything she would, she says, have sided with Aron, because she too inclined towards the idealism which, in her view, he had inherited from Brunschvicg. In contrast to Sartre, who had a tendency to try to construct all-embracing philosophical systems on the model of the Stoics or Spinoza, Aron

enjoyed critical analysis, and set himself to tear Sartre's rash syntheses to bits. He had the knack of getting his opponent in the fork of a dilemma and then crushing him with one sharp hammer stroke. "There are two alternatives, *mon petit camarade*", he would say. "Take your choice". And a faint smile would flicker in those vivid blue eyes, which always had so intelligent and cynically disillusioned a look about them. Sartre struggled hard, to avoid being cornered, but as there was more imagination than logic in his mental processes, he had his work cut out.[3]

However, in these contests Simone de Beauvoir cannot remember either Sartre ever convincing Aron or Aron ever shaking Sartre's beliefs.

On completing his military service Aron hesitated about the intellectual direction he should take. It may seem surprising in view of the brilliant manner in which he had passed the agrégation, but as soon as he left the Ecole Normale he had experienced "a kind of inner crisis".[4] He felt depressed that he had not put his four years there to full use in order to accomplish all that he should have done; instead, he had only done what came easily to him.[5] Of course, he had acquired some knowledge of the great philosophers, but he wanted to free himself from the "narrowly national" education he had received.[6] After all, up to that time he had seen little but teachers, students and books; French society and thought seemed to him to be suffering from a kind of sclerosis and he knew nothing of modern science or social reality. In short, he wanted to discover a world that was different.[7]

Furthermore, although by "temperament and natural ambition" he was "inclined towards metaphysical speculation", Aron experienced radical doubts about the very possibility of doing philosophy in the twentieth century and in particular about constructing a philosophical system. Metaphysics seemed impossible in an age when the natural sciences were "demonstrating in action their correspondence with reality" and "overturning our civilization" – a view in which he was encouraged by Brunschvicg.[8] He had no wish to devote himself, like contemporaries such as Vladimir Jankélévitch, to the history of philosophy – "the ultimate

48

refuge of professors who no longer believed that, in our era, philosophy retained a function".[9] Philosophical analysis on a particular subject-matter such as physics or mathematics alone seemed possible, but Aron had studied relatively little of either of these and he calculated that it would take him years to acquire an adequate education in one or other of them.

Finally, Aron had to earn a living. During his childhood and youth he and his parents had enjoyed a comfortable middle-class existence, but his father, as we have seen, had been ruined in the financial crisis of 1929. Aron was anxious to get away from the gloomy family atmosphere that prevailed. In order to earn a living he had to teach, and it seemed to him almost impossible both to do this and devote himself to the study of mathematics and physics in a serious way. Thus began a little-known episode in Aron's career. He decided to study the science which he believed he would have least difficulty in mastering – biology – and, at Brunschvicg's suggestion, to begin a doctoral thesis on the notion of the individual in the realm of living matter. He would do this, however, while teaching not in France, but in Germany.[10] Not only was this the country to which young French philosophers seeking to complete their education traditionally went (Durkheim and Bouglé, for example, had both gone to Germany at the end of the nineteenth century); Aron was also attracted there by a feeling of revolt against the Great War and against a French foreign policy which seemed to him "totally devoid of any generosity". His dream was of Franco-German reconciliation.[11]

Accordingly, in March 1930, Aron arrived at the University of Cologne as *Lektor* to Leo Spitzer (who was perpetually surrounded by a "garland of young girls in flower") in the Department of Romance Languages.[12] Aron lectured to German students on a variety of historical and cultural topics, such as the "Counter-Revolutionaries", de Bonald and de Maistre, and his favourite writers – Proust, Claudel and Mauriac.[13] In his spare time he read German philosophy and French and German books on genetics, for which he had developed a passion, especially the work of Mendel and Morgan (at a time when the Professor of Biology at the Sorbonne, Etienne Rabaud, would have nothing to do with the subject). Thus two months after his arrival at Cologne he wrote to Pierre Bertaux:

I have started reading Scheler. I am thinking of tackling Husserl next week. I don't yet dare to talk of my progress. I don't dare to talk of myself. I take pleasure in my solitude, my freedom, and the monotony of this existence of work. I refuse to look at myself or ask myself questions, for I don't want to fall a prey again to doubts that are foolish (because they have the annoying habit of always looking back to the past), pointless (because I nevertheless remain strong enough not to let them have the last word), and debilitating (because, after all, regret and anxiety do not "give joy" to the present). What's more, I find life austere and beautiful (even today, when I am very tired, so if you want to get an idea of my real "state", put everything up a notch), and I feel more than ever that the solution is always simple, the moment one is prepared to stop looking at oneself living or to treat oneself as the object, the end or the norm of one's thoughts, desires, ambitions and hesitations (the list could be made longer). If I add that I have encountered a few human beings and have confirmed that a little sport and outside pleasure remain necessary for my complete equilibrium, then you have my first experiences abroad in a nutshell...[14]

By now he had decided on the subjects of the two theses which had to be completed for the doctorate. The secondary thesis would be on *Le Mendélisme: essai d'epistémologie et de critique* (*Mendelism: An Epistemological and Critical Essay*) and the principal thesis an *Essai d'une philosophie du socialisme* (*Essay on a Philosophy of Socialism*). The latter, he wrote to Bertaux in November 1930,

is not only still alive – in embryonic form – but has filled me with light. In it the different problems which preoccupied me have all come together: philosophy becoming conscious of itself, philosophy chasing the ghost of the historical, socialism becoming a spiritual reality through the rediscovery of the will embodied in values, etc., etc., everything seemed to me connected – one Sunday morning, while walking on the banks of the Rhine.
...Since then, this clarity has disappeared somewhat, though something remains. But I should add that I shall probably go on changing until the unlikely day when I finish my thesis or the more likely day when I resign myself to the fundamental incompatibility between my philosophical anxieties and the discipline of academic life.[15]

Aron was referring here to an incident which had occurred to him a short time before and revealed to him what he later called his life's project ("mon projet d'existence").[16] One day, as he described it to me in 1977, he was walking by the river at Cologne when he was suddenly "overcome by an intense emotion" ("saisi par une passion"). The realization came to him that man can only live his life in accordance with his nature and in the situation in which he finds himself; but, at the same time, if he wishes to be a philosopher he must detach himself from the way in which his situation determines his interpretation of his time. Aron had become aware of the problem which was to underlie not only his pre-war writings and in particular the *Introduction to the Philosophy of History*,[17] but his whole life's work. He had become aware, that is, of the "dialectical relationship" between the almost inevitable relativity of man's perception of the world in which he lives and the duty of the

50

philosopher and man of action to doubt his own perception: in other words, the duty to be both detached and committed at one and the same time. Aron subsequently sought therefore to live his life in such a way that, on a philosophical level, he always remained conscious of the relativity of man's perception of history and of the social world, while also taking as far as possible the understanding of those relative perceptions; and, secondly, he aimed to be both an observer of history and an actor in history. He succeeded in being the former through his academic work, of course; and he was an actor, although in a way he could not foresee, through his journalism, in which he attempted to analyse and influence events as a political columnist and commentator. Thus all of his writings, as Aron put it in 1978, "illustrate and carry out my initial and permanent plan conceived forty-five years ago and of which the *Introduction to the Philosophy of History* revealed only a part: I wanted simultaneously to be a spectator of history in the making and an actor, through words written and spoken, in politics".[18]

One consequence of the way his ideas were changing at this time was an eventual decision to abandon the thesis on Mendelism. After working on it for a year he came to the conclusion that he would either have to become a biologist himself or "leave to the biologists the task of criticising their science".[19] It seemed to him that any intelligent biologist with a minimum of philosophical training had as much to say about biology and genetics as he did. He was "easily convinced that reflections upon science by those who were not committed to it were generally inferior to those of the scientists themselves".[20] The subject of the thesis did not sufficiently excite him. It seemed a poor way of using his abilities and, above all, he had the feeling that a gulf existed between his philosophical studies of biology and his personal life:

Brunschvicg's neo-Kantianism, which had turned me away from metaphysics, still left me dissatisfied. Ethics, drawn from the history of science or epistemology, seemed to me both partial and every bit as arbitrary as any other philosophy. The attitude of the scientist in his quest for truth, the detachment from self by which one sees a situation and oneself through the eyes of another – I admire the grandeur and accept the necessity of all this. But the total, flesh-and-blood man that I am – that we all are – does not live each moment like a scientist over his test tubes or microscope; he loves, hates, acts, believes; he is a citizen, soldier, teacher, militant, bourgeois, rich or poor, French or German, in the midst of others and of events. Because science and science alone brings true knowledge since its findings can be verified, philosophy no longer possesses a field of its own in which it can attain verifiable knowledge; however, this does not mean that philosophical thought, for lack of system, relinquishes all ambition and leaves it up to the novelists to ponder the human condition. A society cannot do without a certain overall vision of itself and the world. A philosopher still has the choice between the two

51

paths: the analysis of the natural sciences or reflections of a moral and historical nature. It may well be that these two paths meet somewhere. [21]

Aron's "life project", therefore, as he formulated it in 1930–1, "at a time when I was finding life hard to cope with and severely judging the narrowness of the philosophical training I had received", involved him in subjecting his political opinions to a critique. In so doing, he wrote in 1978,

I hoped to overcome a duality that was perhaps inevitable but one that made me suffer. On the one hand, I read Kant's *Critique of Pure Reason*; on the other, I observed Weimar Germany, where I had been living since 1931. Kantian philosophy fascinated the student and scholar in me but not the social and historical man who was painfully witnessing the rise of German National Socialism and the conditions that spawned a second European and world war. In asking myself several questions (Why did I join the Socialist Party? Why did I leave it after a few months, tired of the idle revolutionary talk of the young bourgeoisie of the Latin Quarter?), I discovered, almost in spite of myself, another critique: to question my political opinions was also to question the limits of socio-historical knowledge. On the way I discovered Marxism, which already, in the Germany of 1931, obstructed the future. Thus I travelled from a critique of biology to a critique of the human or social sciences, and in so doing I re-established a unity between myself and my life – a unity, both dangerous and exhilarating, of thought and action, of teaching and journalism, of history and politics. [22]

In the autumn of 1931, after eighteen months at the University of Cologne, Aron moved to the Maison Académique of the Institut de France in Berlin. Here he read voraciously, tackling books which, he says, were "quite impossible"; and it was now that he had his first real contact with the social sciences – sociology and economics. The stimulus for this was his first encounter with Marx's writings, because his recently conceived "life project" had quickly led him into a dialogue with Marx: [23]

When I set out on my intellectual journey, having made up my mind to be both an observer and an actor in history, I began by studying Marx and *Capital* in particular. My wish was to discover a true philosophy of history which would have the incomparable advantage of teaching us not only what is but also what must be. Marxism, vulgarly understood, is a global interpretation of history, with a conclusion: one must side with the proletariat and eventually arrive at the socialism which is the end of prehistory. But, after studying Marxism for almost a whole year, I concluded, with regret, that such a conception was false. It was not possible, from the analysis of history, to deduce which policy to follow or foresee the ultimate end of a society in which the contradictions between men would be eliminated. It is in this sense that, initially, I defined my ideas in relation to Marxism. [24]

Aron had begun studying *Capital* while he was at Cologne in 1931. The following year, however, Marx's early writings, such as the *Economic and Philosophical Manuscripts* and *The German Ideology*, were first published in Germany. Aron was, therefore, favourably placed to read these, too. Thus he became one of the first Frenchmen to be able to form a view of Marx's work in something like its entirety, from its Hegelian beginnings through to the final volumes of *Capital* – an awareness which is transparent in the masterly article he published on Marx a few years later in 1937.[25]

In addition to Marx, Aron also discovered contemporary German philosophy and with it a whole new philosophical language:

When I first arrived in Germany, I was completely dazzled. The German language is an exceptionally supple instrument for philosophy, and we always tend to think German philosophers are more profound than they really are. There are two languages for philosophy – German and Greek. When one immerses oneself in the German language, one feels enriched almost to the point of drowning. To begin with, I considered all the German philosophers to be great. That did not last long, but I discovered some who taught me a great deal.[26]

Aron read the German phenomenologists and in particular the two thinkers who most impressed him, Husserl and Heidegger. Neither of them was well known at the time, but their influence was to be implicit in his first major work, the *Introduction to the Philosophy of History*. However, the importance of this encounter with the phenomenologists lay not only in the impact these writers were to have on Aron, but also in the effect they were to have, through Aron, on Sartre. Although the two do not appear to have corresponded while Aron was in Germany, Aron kept in touch on his visits to Paris. Thus Sartre wrote to Simone de Beauvoir in October 1931 recounting how a mutual friend with whom he was staying

woke me at nine o'clock, ushering Aron into the room. He was suitably accompanied by a flood of electric light. There he sat, like an old eagle, expounding the thesis of the French *lecteur* at Cologne whilst I, fascinated, lay quietly panting in my moist sheets. Then Guille, who was due to go out with him, arrived. The two of them served me breakfast in bed; Aron poured the coffee while Guille buttered the bread, accompanied by such remarks as, "Ah! you naughty little widower, how happy you are! You'll never catch Le Castor [Simone de Beauvoir] bringing you breakfast in bed".[27]

And it was Aron who, while on a visit to Paris which Simone de Beauvoir locates in 1932–3, brought the existence of the new German philosophy to the attention of Sartre and, as she recalls, convinced him that he should go to Germany to study phenomenology:

53

We spent an evening together at the Bec de Gaz in the Rue Montparnasse. We ordered the speciality of the house, apricot cocktails. Aron said, pointing to his glass: "You see, *mon petit camarade*, if you are a phenomenologist, you can talk about this cocktail and make philosophy out of it!" Sartre turned almost pale with emotion at this. Here was just the thing he had been longing to achieve for years – to describe objects just as he saw and touched them, and extract philosophy from the process. Aron convinced him that phenomenology exactly fitted in with his preoccupations... Sartre decided to make a serious study of it and, on Aron's instigation, he took the necessary steps to succeed his *petit camarade* at the French Institute in Berlin for the coming year.[28]

It was also during this period that, as part of the critique to which he was subjecting his political opinions, Aron began to read Max Weber and the other German sociologists whom he was to discuss in his first book, *La Sociologie allemande contemporaine* (*German Sociology*).[29] He also read the German philosophers of history who were later to form the subject of his preliminary doctoral thesis – Dilthey, Rickert and Simmel, as well as Weber.[30] Not that his interest in the philosophers of history stemmed from any particular concern for professional historians and their work; because of the neo-Kantianism he had "absorbed" at the university, he was "fascinated" by the notion, derived from Dilthey, of a critique of historical reason: thus Aron's interest in philosophical reflection on history arose out of his intellectual project as he had begun to formulate it in 1931 and in particular his concern with the problems of relativism and objectivity in the perception of history. At the same time he was also fascinated by Marx's notion of a critique of the economy. Indeed, when his principal thesis, the *Introduction to the Philosophy of History*, "inspired by the critiques of Dilthey and Weber", was published in 1938, Aron "conceived the idea of writing a critique of political economy, or rather an introduction to the social sciences, along the lines of Marx's critique of the economy". After the war, however, he "largely lost interest in writing introductions to the social sciences or to political economy; concrete problems won out over formal or epistemological problems".[31]

It is important to note here, as the historian Henri Marrou has pointed out, the impact which Aron's stay in Germany was to have on the development of French culture. "Europe had not yet been created and the French intelligentsia grew up in a confined atmosphere which, with hindsight, appears to us to have been cramped and, as it were, highly provincial".[32] Aron, as we have seen, felt these restrictions not merely retrospectively but at the time, and this was the main reason for his leaving for Germany. He certainly succeeded in his aim of discovering a new intellectual world; and it was he who brought back to other French intellectuals of his generation the knowledge and understanding of the German phenomenologists, sociologists and philosophers of history which he had derived from his stay in Cologne and Berlin.

It was, above all, the work of Max Weber which had impressed Aron the most among the writers he read at this time and which was to be the greatest single influence on his intellectual development:

It was in Max Weber that I discovered what I was looking for: in him was to be found a combination of historical experience, political understanding, a striving for truth, and, ultimately, decision and action. The determination both to grasp truth and reality and at the same time to act in the world seem to me to be the two imperatives which I have tried to follow throughout my life – and I found these two imperatives in Max Weber.[33]

On reading Weber, Aron appears to have felt immediately an "elective affinity" with a thinker whose concerns seemed to correspond closely with his own. Thus nearly forty years later, in his Inaugural Lecture at the Collège de France, he was to say in recalling his stay in Germany in the early 1930s:

Thanks to Max Weber I believed in the possibility of combining, without confusing them, scientific curiosity and political concern, detached thought and resolute action . . .Between the sociology of Max Weber – a sociology of the war between classes, parties and gods – and the lived experience of an *agrégé de philosophie*, a Frenchman and a Jew, living in Berlin during the first months of the Third Reich, there existed, it seemed to me, a sort of pre-established harmony or, to put it more modestly, a shared sensitivity . . .Lacking any all-embracing vision, in the midst of the tumult of events, incapable of adhering to any faction, I wanted to live in all lucidity the historical condition of man, of which the personal and philosophical experience of Max Weber gave me both an example and a theory. Dialectic of incomplete knowledge, contradictory values, adventurous decisions: the Europe of the thirties filled these abstract formulae with an already tragic resonance.[34]

The Rise of National Socialism

Aron, who was in Germany from March 1930 to August 1933, lived through the final, turbulent years of the coming to power of nazism and, from January 1933, experienced the first months of the Third Reich. In the elections held in 1928 the National Socialists had won only twelve seats in the Reichstag, polling 810,000 votes; but six months after Aron's arrival in Germany, in the elections held in September 1930, the National Socialists won 107 seats, with six and a half million votes, thus becoming the second largest party in the Reichstag.

Aron's first impression on arriving in Germany was an intuitive feeling that, as he later expressed it in a phrase of Toynbee's, "History is again on the move". What "struck, shocked and shattered" him was the "nationalistic violence" of the German people. From that moment onwards he lived in a psychological state that was completely different from that of the Ecole Normale. "The problem was no longer the follies of the previous war. The problem – the obsession – became: how to avoid the next war?"

The moment I came into contact with Germany, I had the feeling that the German people refused to accept the fate that had been imposed upon it; there was a kind of deep-seated, fundamental revolt, aggravated by the economic crisis. As a result I hesitated between my former pacifism and the decisive question in politics: what is to be done? The articles I wrote while in Germany are all awful (détestables). They are awful because, in the first place, I did not yet know how to observe political reality; furthermore I did not yet know how to distinguish clearly between the desirable and the possible. I was not yet capable of analysing the situation without revealing my emotions, and these were split between my education in what might be called "university idealism" and a growing awareness of politics in all its pitiless brutality. The fact is, when matched against Hitler, my teachers, whether Alain or Brunschvicg, were (it has to be said) woefully inadequate. At any rate, they were living in a different world from that in which I found myself when I saw Hitler and listened to his speeches at public meetings.[35]

The other shock experienced by Aron was the "violent anti-Semitism" of the Nazis. This, in his view, undoubtedly played a part in his growing awareness of the significance of national socialism. "When I arrived in Germany, I was conscious of being a Jew but, if I may so put it, only faintly so". His consciousness of his Jewishness was, as we have seen, "extraordinarily feeble":

But in Germany the shock was not only German national socialism, but anti-Semitism. It would be an exaggeration to say that this was the only question. The fact is, however, that national socialism, in addition to the nationalism that was shared by other political parties, was distinguished by its rabid anti-Semitism, so much so that from 1930 onwards I always presented myself as first and foremost a Jew.[36]

What were the articles, written in Germany, of which Aron later spoke so disparagingly? Although, as we have seen, he read enormously during this period, he had great difficulty in putting pen to paper at this time; he had "a dread of the blank page" and was afraid that he would never be able to write.[37] Nevertheless, between 1930 and 1933 he published some fifteen pieces in the pacifist *Libres Propos* (*Le Journal d'Alain*, as it was subtitled), to which Georges Canguilhem and Simone Weil were also regular contributors; the monthly was edited from Nîmes by two of Alain's most fervent disciples, Jeanne and Michel Alexandre.[38] In addition, he wrote half a dozen articles for the left-wing political and literary review, *Europe*: similarly pacifist in outlook, it had been founded in 1923 by Romain Rolland and was currently edited by Jean Guéhenno.

Subsequently, in his memoirs, Aron qualified – with good reason – his earlier blanket condemnation of the "awful" German articles, which he had reread "without pleasure but without humiliation". In writing for Alain's *Libres Propos* he tended, as he explained, to conform to the views that were expected of him by its editors, and "moral judgements are constantly intermingled with the analyses".[39] Furthermore, his ignorance of economics was apparent: "In order to become a commentator on history-in-the-making (l'histoire-se-faisant), I still had a lot to learn".[40] In particular, he should, he believed in retrospect, have analysed the Weimar Constitution; he failed to understand the "aberration" of Brüning's economic policy – deflation and a balanced budget; and, like most others, he underestimated Hitler.[41] Nevertheless, as he increasingly came to grapple with political and social realities, his commentaries from Germany, whatever their faults, give a clear indication of the journalistic talent that was to emerge, apparently so unexpectedly, a decade and a half later, after the war.

The first of Aron's articles was a "letter from Germany" ("from a young teacher on a study trip"), signed "R.A.", which appeared in *Libres Propos* at the end of 1930.[42] In it he commented that the September election had been a "vote of despair" on the part of the German people; the situation nevertheless "remained tragic" with "mutual incomprehension" growing on both sides of the Rhine; it was the duty of French pacifists to call for a revision of the Treaty of Versailles in the name of justice.

Further "letters from Germany" followed. At the end of February 1931 Aron wrote with prescience that national socialism was moving "towards illegality along the path of legality".[43] To a communistic propaganda was being added one of racialism, nationalism and imperialism, although it had to be admitted that there was among the majority of the militants a "moral desire for regeneration, devotion and sacrifice". There was no doubt that the Nazi leaders were followers of fascism: the problem as they saw it was not that of a precise and reasonable programme, but of how to gain control of the state. If they came to power, would the Nazis take measures against the Jews? It was impossible to say. It was, however, certain that, although things had not gone well for the Nazis in recent weeks as the democratic forces in Parliament had taken steps

57

to reinforce themselves, there was no cause for "complacent optimism": "In national socialism millions of beings have seen a last resort against their lot. The liquidation of such a revolt by peaceful means is a mere hope, perhaps a utopia".[44] Nevertheless, "balanced disarmament" and Franco-German reconciliation based on equality of rights were still possible; it was being unduly pessimistic to believe in a sudden attack by Germany – even a National-Socialist Germany – without provocation or warning signs and in spite of the treaties of guarantee, although it was true that only a different kind of social regime would ensure peace. The solution, Aron concluded, lay in a "revolutionary pacifism".[45]

These themes also appeared in his first article for *Europe*, published early in 1931.[46] It was impossible, he declared, to exaggerate the seriousness of the situation in Germany: unemployment, financial instability, social crisis and "the wave of national socialism...rising...with the inflexible power of a natural force".[47] The article also contained some strong criticism of French policy towards Germany, a call for the revision of the Treaty of Versailles, the urging of Franco-German reconciliation within a united Europe, and an eloquent plea for an "uncompromising pacifism". But this, said Aron, was to be sharply distinguished from communism: ·

Communism is above all a doctrine of fanaticism: under the eye of the prophet, all means become the same. The final goal is humane, but the ways which lead there are violent. It is not enough to say that during this process peace becomes subordinate to other values: communists often assert that catastrophe is necessary for rebirth. Through faith in an inevitable dialectic, they consider world war unavoidable and productive. An uncompromising pacifism, open to individual criticism, has nothing in common with such a doctrine. It rejects any closed system and refuses to deduce everyday action from an external determinism. It is an act of faith in man and his will.[48]

"If", Aron observed in his memoirs, "the 1931 articles still bore the mark of my inner uncertainties and of the oscillation between my ideals and the analysis of the political situation, I can read without embarrassment the articles I wrote in 1932, during the last year of the Weimar regime. On several important points my analysis was correct and my articles shed light on the present and the immediate future".[49]

This judgement is borne out by the second of his articles for *Europe*, published in February 1932, in which he began by asking how seriously Hitler should be taken.[50] In spite of recent electoral gains it was unlikely that the National Socialists would obtain a majority of votes and thus form a government, but they could still make any other legal government impossible and they might find allies. What were Hitler's intentions? One thing was certain: he had not forgotten the failure of his putsch in 1923 and would not attempt one again without the support of the army. For the time being at any rate, Aron correctly predicted, Hitler would respect his promise of legality. What sort of man was he? There was no doubt about his ability as a political orator and organizer, but whether he was a statesman was less certain. In any case, he was a sufficiently good tactician not to sacrifice the unity of his party in return for an immediate share in power. If he entered the government, it would not be in order to give up his freedom of action, in other words his right to intolerance and brutality.[51]

Although it was pointless to try to make predictions in the volatile context of German politics, it was possible to analyse the forces working for the Right. To begin with, the place was half theirs already: for example, the legal system had for years been peopled with reactionaries. Then there was the nationalistic atmosphere which was everywhere apparent in Germany, together with the view of France as the hereditary enemy. Finally, it was necessary to take into account the feeling of resignation and passivity among the German people – a passivity in the face of destiny and in the expectation of a miracle. For, Aron asked, in strongly Nietzschian and Weberian accents:

Where is the individual to learn independence, virile choice, and a rational mastery over fate? Neither in his career, nor in the industrial process, does he see freedom operating. All that the future appears to hold for him is a long march through an unwieldy bureaucracy, in which second-class qualities emerge more easily and achieve more success than does original worth. He has the feeling that the "system" tyrannizes those who serve it. The triumph of the masses or of the machine is everywhere. Everywhere man is the slave of a social or economic determinism which he rarely understands and never controls. It is no wonder that by far the most striking, even if superficial, characteristic of the political psychology of the Germans is their acceptance of a fate which is always hidden and always inevitable. It is no wonder that stupor, dejection and revolt mingle strangely in the soul of the fanatical masses.

To this might be added a mixture of indifference to politics, together with obsession, revolutionary will and the desire to obey. Many, particularly among the pre-war generations, consider affairs of state (although they deny it) as something distant and foreign, which is of interest to specialists, technicians and politicians, but not to private individuals. Furthermore, the younger generations are obsessed by the problem of revolution because revolution seems to them the only hope. Every German has learnt to what extent his fate is bound up with that of the nation as a whole; they have all discovered the reality of the nation even if they have not learnt respect for the state. In short, their fanatical love of order, which is perhaps the Germans' strongest political passion, their acceptance of deep-seated forces and all-powerful leaders, and the desire among many of them to be given orders and to be relieved of their anxieties, all this paves the way for the acceptance of dictatorship.[52]

Yet, said Aron, in spite of all the indications, there was nothing inevitable about such an outcome. The problem was, he stressed, both an economic and a moral one. Because of the complexity of the situation all that could be foreseen with any certainty was the decay of liberty, the increasing integration of the individual into the group and the triumph of nationalism. However, despite all the difficulties, a repair-job was still possible which would allow the organization of industry to readapt progressively to the forces of production, "without a revolution and without a dictatorship that would endanger the whole of Europe".[53]

France had a role to play in helping Germany to solve its problems. "The Germans believe that their horizon is blocked on all sides by walls erected by France".[54] France had to give back to the Germans a sense of freedom and hope. In particular, the French should renounce reparations and seek a balance of forces through disarmament. The time for recrimination and blame was over. Germany was largely responsible for the seriousness of its economic situation, but France by its continuing "clumsy lack of understanding" and "apparent aggressiveness" bore "a crushing responsibility" for the violence of the hatred directed towards itself.[55] The answer lay in a unification of the two countries. In this way Germany would satisfy its claims and France achieve security; it would then be "genuinely possible to talk once again of the society of nations, a European federation, and a super-state".[56] It was for this reason that Aron welcomed the talks on a Franco-German customs union that were currently taking place, for "this growing economic solidarity of France and Germany is our best cause for hope". To communists who protested about a capitalist alliance against Russia, Aron's reply was that

the "capitalism" of communist invective only exists in propaganda speeches. There are *different* nations and *different* capitalists, more preoccupied with their rivalries than with their common enemy – for the moment at any rate (I am not a prophet)...

I am quite aware that such capitalist pacifism will hardly arouse enthusiasm. But do you really believe that it is intellectuals who will prevent war? Or conscientious objectors? Or social democrats? Or Herriot's Radicals?

Today the narrow path of reformism lies in the understanding between the capitalist economies.

Otherwise, go and make the revolution.[57]

Much had happened in Germany by the time Aron wrote his next article for *Europe* in June 1932. In March of that year presidential elections had taken place in which Hitler stood against Hindenburg – the first of five major elections in Germany within the space of nine months. The National Socialist vote had risen from the six and a half million polled in the parliamentary elections of September 1930 to eleven and a half million – an increase of 86 per cent – giving Hitler a third of the total votes. Hindenburg, on the other hand, had received eighteen and a half million votes. Nevertheless, this fell just short of the absolute majority required and a second election had therefore to be held. This took place in April. On this occasion Hitler won thirteen and a half million votes (36 per cent); Hindenburg received nineteen and a quarter million (53 per cent), thus obtaining the majority necessary for his re-election.

A few days later the Chancellor, Brüning, whom Aron had earlier described as "attempting, with a heroism which no one appreciates, to resist with patience and prudence" the advance of nazism,[58] had issued a decree dissolving the SA (the Storm Troopers), the SS and their affiliated organizations, on the grounds that such private armies constituted an unacceptable state within the state. In May, however, General von Schleicher, who was anxious to come to an arrangement with the Nazis, let Hitler know that he did not approve of the ban on the SA. First, with the help of the Nazis in the Reichstag, he forced the resignation of General Groener, the Minister of the Interior. Then, with the agreement of the Junkers, he offered Hitler the resignation of Brüning and his replacement by Papen, the lifting of the ban on the SA and the SS, and new elections for the Reichstag, all in return for the Nazis' tacit support. On 30 May Brüning was forced to resign, to be succeeded as Chancellor by Papen, who duly lifted the ban on the SA and dissolved the Reichstag, "thus ensuring", as Aron wrote in *Libres Propos* two days later, "almost certain success for the Nazis".[59] Aron was indignant;[60] France would have to be very careful in negotiating with Hitler, "but, that having been said, let us not meddle with the internal politics of Germany. After all, a parliamentary regime is not the only one possible".[61]

On Brüning it was, Aron reasoned, difficult to form a judgement:

...the injustice of his disgrace and the aggressive mediocrity of his successor have added to his stature and, if one will excuse the expression, "republicanized" him. Yet his courage does not wipe away his faults. Having come to power with the aim of governing on the Right, he was pushed to the Left by the violence of the nationalists. But he neither would nor could choose between his attackers and his supporters. He never succeeded in undoing the damage of his initial mistake (the dissolution of the Reichstag in September 1930) and, faced with an increasingly acute crisis, he only put forward partial measures, with no clear plan. Thus he failed, just as anybody else would have failed. The cure for Germany's present troubles lies either in fundamental reforms or a foreign policy that learns to adopt a different tone and a new form of patience. The significance of the

61

Brüning experiment will depend on the future: has it been the period of maturation before decisive changes take place, or the vain resistance of bourgeois men of reason yielding finally to blind passion? Has it prepared the way for a new Germany, or been the prelude to a reaction, the like of which has not been seen before? Or does it herald chaos and revolution?[62]

Writing in *Europe*, Aron asked why it was that Hindenburg, who had been elected by the Centre and the moderate Left, had turned to the Right.[63] Aron's answer was that Germany had become virtually impossible to govern democratically: "Too many interests clash – too many parties, groups, states and communes – and every day an excess of metaphysics and a surfeit of poverty dig a deep pit of anarchy beneath the apparent order. One way or another, if chaos can be avoided, an authoritarian regime (which could well preserve the form of a republic) will be set up".[64]

On the question of disarmament Aron's position had now changed in view of the events in Germany. France should still reduce its armaments, but without renouncing a superiority in arms which had now become a necessary guarantee of peace.[65] The proposal for a general cancellation of all war-debts should be supported, but France could not go further than that in the face of Germany's new masters: "For the future we can have no confidence in either Schleicher, or Papen, or Hitler. With none of them do we have, or do we wish to have, anything in common. We shall sacrifice neither 'liberalism' nor 'formal democracy' to 'the order desired by God' which today's Chancellor claims to be re-establishing". Nevertheless, France must continue to think in terms of collaboration with Germany rather than conflict, for "whether we like it or not, the destiny of Germany is also the destiny of Europe".[66]

The elections which followed Papen's dissolution of the Reichstag were held in July, and the National Socialists won 230 seats.[67] They had more than doubled their support since the last elections for the Reichstag in September 1930. With over thirteen and a half million votes, they were now far the largest party: the Social Democrats had obtained nearly eight million votes, the Communists five and a quarter million and the Centre four and a quarter million. Hitler had gained nearly thirteen million votes in the four years since 1928. Yet, at 37 per cent, the Nazi vote still fell short of a majority and, moreover, seemed to have reached a peak, for in the last five elections its proportion of votes had been: September 1930 (Reichstag) 18.3 per cent; March 1932 (first presidential election) 30 per cent; April 1932 (second presidential election) 36.7 per cent; April 1932 (Prussian Diet) 36.3 per cent; and July 1932 (Reichstag) 37.3 per cent.

In August 1932 the SA, ready to seize power, was concentrated round Berlin. Hitler demanded complete power from Hindenburg, but the aged President outmanoeuvred him, offering him only the Vice-Chancellorship and a place for the Nazi Party in a coalition. On 12 September, after it had been sitting for less than a day, Papen again dissolved the Reichstag, amid farcical scenes under its President, Goering. Elections – the fifth in eighteen months – took place on 6 November. Writing a few days later, Aron commented: "Last Sunday the German people gave evidence, not by a wiser vote, but by a more sceptical attitude, that in the last two years it has learnt a great deal and that its 'political education' is in progress".[68] Although the press had made much of the apathy of the electorate and the unimportance of the November elections, they in fact marked "a decisive turning-point in the history of national socialism". The Nazis had lost thirty-five seats in the Reichstag and their total of votes had fallen by over two million, their proportion dropping from 37 per cent to 33 per cent. The signs were that "Nazi ideology has lost its power of attraction" and that the movement "is very close to being doomed. In particular it is beginning to be short of money".[69]

In Aron's view only the KPD (the Communist Party) now stood for "clear and violent protest against the capitalist regime", and they benefited from the "cowardly patience" of the Socialists. For although the Socialist Party (the SPD) had plenty of leaders and rank-and-file members, fine newspapers and journals, "the best Marxist theorists in Europe" and good trade-union organization, the Party itself had become bureaucratized. Led by old men, lacking any youthful drive or vigour, it had become a party of "cautious opportunism". A Popular Front could only come from below and "the first condition would be a truly revolutionary situation".[70] Nevertheless, in spite of the November election results, Hitler and Papen would continue to dominate Germany. As for a dialogue with Germany, nationalist though it was, this was still possible, provided France had "the courage to consider other interests than her own".[71]

On 17 November, after Aron had completed his article, Papen resigned the Chancellorship, apparently leaving the way clear for President Hindenburg to invite Hitler to become Chancellor in a coalition, provided that Hitler could form a majority in the Reichstag. Ostensibly this was a reasonable offer, but in fact the conditions were bound not to be met. Hitler could not obtain a majority and, even more importantly, Hindenburg refused to grant Hitler what he really wanted. Hitler had no wish to be a parliamentary Chancellor bound by a coalition, but a presidential Chancellor with the same full powers as Hindenburg had granted to

Papen. In a note on the ministerial crisis appended to his article, Aron foresaw that Papen would "probably go" and commented justly: "It has never seriously been a question of a Hitler cabinet. The old Marshal who, with age, is giving evidence of a political intelligence that we never knew he had, assured himself of Hitler's refusal by setting him impossible conditions...But national socialism on the decline could well either become more revolutionary or disintegrate".[72]

The answer came all too quickly. On 2 December Schleicher, who had earlier sounded out the possibility of a coalition with the Nazis under his own Chancellorship but been refused by Hitler, himself became Chancellor. In early January 1933, however, Papen, perhaps from motives of revenge, began to intrigue with Hitler against Schleicher. By 28 January Schleicher had resigned and two days afterwards Hitler agreed to become Chancellor in a Nazi-Nationalist coalition with Papen as his deputy.

For the past two years, Aron wrote six months later,

Loud-mouthed demagogues have been stirring up crowds of unemployed and desperate men. Idle officers, playing at being politicians, have been busying themselves in obscure intrigues around a tired old man...The decisive event emerged when the orator of the Sportpalast was called to the Wilhelmstrasse. On 31 January, the Hitlerites, beside themselves with joy, paraded before their leader and before a motionless ghost, who had come, as the representative of the old Germany, to ensure that the way was open to the Germany of tomorrow.[73]

Since the fall of Brüning in May 1932, German nationalism had, Aron continued, followed an inevitable course. The question to be answered had been: who – Hitlerites or German Nationalists – would take control and gain advantage from it? Till January the outcome had been uncertain. The details of the intrigues and the struggle might be of only historical interest, but they served to explode the myth of the official version of events that "Hitler, fortified by the will of the people, seized power." Thus,

Papen has been able to direct the course of German history in a decisive way. For – in spite of all the forecasts *post eventum* in which the lovers of necessity take such pleasure – nothing was less inevitable, in view of the general circumstances, than the Nazi dictatorship...It is impossible to gauge at this point how much efficacy history will grant to Papen, as living proof of the commonplace idea that historical action is the privilege of neither superior minds nor great leaders, but of individuals placed in favourable positions who intervene at the right moment. Thus it only needs a push from a half-wit or an adventurer to give a new direction to a people's future.[74]

The Reichstag fire on 27 February, which was immediately followed by a decree suppressing individual liberties and by the arrest of political opponents of nazism, was the signal for the "National Revolution". In the elections called for by Hitler earlier in February and held on 5 March, the National Socialists, their campaign financed by leading industrialists and now with the use of the state radio and press, increased their vote by five and a half million to over seventeen million, their proportion rising from 33 per cent in the last elections in November 1932 to nearly 44 per cent. Yet it was only with the support of the Nationalists that they were able to form a majority in the Reichstag. On 23 March, in a building filled with stormtroopers, opposed only by the Social Democrats (the Communists had been virtually proscribed), Hitler was voted full powers for four years. He was now independent both of the Reichstag and of the President, and the work of the "National Revolution" could be carried out in earnest.

"What struck me the most, during the first weeks of the regime", Aron wrote in his memoirs, "is the almost invisible character of the great events of history. Millions of Berliners saw nothing new. There was only one sign or symbol: within three days the streets of the capital were swarming with brown uniforms". The other thing that struck him was "the spread of fear" – without large numbers of suspects or opponents of the regime actually being thrown into prison or concentration camps. Nevertheless, the feeling of mortal danger and the threat of arrest made their presence felt everywhere: "We were no longer breathing the same air. In the spring of 1933, my friends, Jews or liberals, used to say, as the sun shone on the terraces of the cafés in the Kurfürstendamm: 'Den Frühling werden Sie uns nicht nehmen' ('they won't take the spring away from us')".[75] But Aron was himself present, with his friend Golo Mann, the historian and youngest son of Thomas Mann, at the burning of the books on 10 May 1933 – the notorious *auto-da-fé* which he described fifty years later:

The scene itself, as I witnessed it, not in the midst of the SA but from a few metres away, near the university, was devoid of all grandeur. There was no crowd, no enthusiasm –perhaps a hundred Nazis in uniform, and Goebbels' speech. . . Neither Golo Mann nor I said a word, joined in silence by our solitary thoughts. In a civilized country, a country of high culture, the old ruling class had entrusted to these thugs the mission of restoring to Germany her independence and power. The books were consumed *Unter den Linden* as those of the Library had once burned in Alexandria; the flames were the symbol of barbarism in power.[76]

Aron analysed what he saw as the main features of the "National Revolution" in the last of his articles for *Europe*, written later that summer at the end of his stay in Germany. These features were: the purging of the civil service and the substitution of Hitler's nominees; the completion of the political unification of Germany through the abolition of federalism; the achievement of moral unity by means of demonstrations in which "Germany offered herself the spectacle of a deep harmony which appeared to be a prelude to greatness"; the necessity of Party membership for office-holders (as in Communist Russia and Fascist Italy); the suppression of opposition parties; the ending of the political role of the Catholic Church and the domination of Protestantism by the nationalist and racialist Deutsche Christen; the loss of university autonomy and the removal of socialists, liberals and Jews from their posts "without a gesture of protest"; in short, the spread of the "Gleichschaltung" (totalitarianism) throughout all areas of life – political, administrative, artistic and sporting.[77]

It was difficult, Aron observed, to confirm the reported acts of violence. Atrocities should of course be condemned, but it was important also to guard against "being enticed into a 'moral' (and patriotic) crusade against German barbarity. The immense majority of Hitlerites, in all sincerity, do not believe in these 'Greuelmärchen' ('horror-stories')".[78] As for the concentration camps, about which dreadful reports were emerging, Aron stated that he had no knowledge of what went on there and preferred to say nothing until he had reasons for believing their truth.

Next he turned to the question of anti-Semitism. The immediate cause lay in the need to find a target for hatred and in the conspicuous position of the Jews. However, there was a further and deeper cause: the importance which the Germans, unlike the French, attached to the racial composition of the nation. The Jews were seen as the "poisoners of the German soul"; the German and Jewish races were said to be "inassimilable". A number of measures had been taken against the Jews. They had been "purged" from the civil service; Jewish entry to higher education had been limited to 5 per cent; there had been sacking of Jewish employees; and Jews were socially ostracized. It was impossible to say where it would stop. The methods were said to be "civilized", but did they not constitute "a cruelty as cold and as revolting as the pogroms? The attempt to be objective must give way to a wholly justifiable indignation".[79]

Why did the Germans not protest more strongly? Partly through prudence, but also because of indifference:

After all, it is a question of displacing unemployment. Is this unjust? Of course, but are not the millions of men who do not work, the millions of young people who have never worked, also the victims of injustice? Are they responsible for their misery? Having grown accustomed to social disaster, many Germans have lost the sense of moral protest and are incapable of distinguishing between the movements of crowds and the stoppages of fate.[80]

Was any general judgement finally possible? In the first place, although Hitler had not brought the Germans work or food, he should be given credit for solving the political problem, in that he had taught the Germans obedience once again. Secondly, the German revolution was a petit-bourgeois revolution and not the proletarian revolution of Marxist theory. Lastly, it was also a revolution of the younger generation against the old. The young, who had only known "the bitterness of defeat, despair and misery . . . sincerely thought of themselves as inaugurating a new era":

The metaphysics of the irrational and of the "gemut" ("the feelings") are often a justification for mediocrity. But this protest of healthy vitality against over-refinement and scepticism deserves neither contempt nor irony. Collective faiths are always crude and it is easy to show their absurdity, but history does not always judge rational intelligence to be right.[81]

Meanwhile, in spite of their noisily proclaimed pacifism of recent months, the Nazi leaders had not abandoned their imperialist ambitions. The task was clear: "Whatever our personal opinions, it is absolutely necessary to help (and compel) national socialism (and fascism) to opt for a peaceful solution".[82]

This article, Aron wrote in his memoirs, left him with "a kind of unease"; in particular he was disturbed by his "excessive objectivity", especially in the discussion of anti-Semitism where his Germanophilia, together with his sense of French rather than Jewish identity, had not been entirely effaced by his detestation of nazism. Indeed, the article in question was attacked for its "feeble defence" of the Jews by Serge Quadruppani in a book published shortly before Aron's death,[83] although Aron was able to defend himself against such charges – convincingly, in my view – in his memoirs.[84]

* * *

Two years later, in 1935, Aron returned to the question of Nazi Germany in a lecture he gave at the Ecole Normale Supérieure's Centre de Documentation Sociale as part of a series organized by Elie Halévy on "The Social Crisis and National Ideologies". Aron's lecture was entitled "An Anti-Proletarian Revolution: Ideology and Reality of National Socialism" and it was published with the other lectures in the series in the following year.[85] He began by pointing out that it was difficult for him to be impartial, because Hitlerism had always been anti-Semitic and it was now increasing the danger of war; and although he would try to understand rather than pass judgement, he warned his audience that he was a strong critic of national socialism.[86] Furthermore, since his subject was a vast one, he would limit himself to two problems. How was a popular anti-proletarian revolution possible, since the German revolution was a mass movement against Marxism, if not against the proletariat? And how far had the ideology been put into practice once national socialism had attained power?

In order to understand the idea of a popular revolution of the Right, it was necessary to begin by distinguishing the terms "proletariat" and "people". "People" was the more general word; if "proletariat" referred to factory workers, then the "proletariat" constituted a minority of the people. That minority was certainly more active, more homogeneous and better organized than the rest of the population; nevertheless, in so far as it was "isolated in the struggle, it would not have the right to speak in the name of the people (unless one accepts Marxist ideology, according to which the proletariat today represents the masses because it has a historic mission to fulfil)".[87]

Even if this distinction were accepted, there was another problem. In France all those on one side of the barricades were thought of, however mistakenly, as being on the Left, that is, against those in power and on the side of the proletariat. Such a judgement was even more false in the case of Germany, where the ideology of what the French called the "Right" was as spontaneous and deep-seated as the ideology of the Left was in many French circles. Modern Germany had become self-aware during the wars of liberation. In Germany one had to be a nationalist.[88]

From which social groups had national socialism recruited its support? First of all from the young. German youth was "nationalistic", "in its way socialist", and "above all in revolt". There was a conflict of generations that was "both moral and, one could say, utilitarian":

The young were born into a world which was too narrow; they had no hope of success; even when they had the good fortune to find work, they were crushed by a monstrous and inhuman administrative machinery; and they who combined the impatience of all youth with the indignation of those who are in revolt had no other prospect than a slow advancement.[89]

Furthermore, between the generation which grew up before the war and those who were in their twenties in the decade between 1920 and 1930, "too often communication was no longer possible: they did not speak the same language, and they did not have the same conception of existence".

Nor were relations much easier between the generation which had fought in the war and the post-war generation, "even though today, thanks to Hitlerism, reconciliation seems to have been brought about". One phrase which could frequently be heard in the years between 1930 and 1933 perhaps best expressed what underlay the general feeling at the time: "es muss etwas geschehen", "something has to be done". However,

In a Germany which had been humiliated and beaten, one had to see this renewal, not as pointing towards a socialist international, which in the eyes of the young was too abstract and utopian, but in the context, which was real, close-at-hand and living, of the German nation.[90]

In addition to the young, two other groups provided Hitlerism with some of its most militant elements: the "white-collar proletariat", allegedly cut-off from the means of production, and the "intellectual proletariat" with their pockets full of useless diplomas. Yet why had they failed on the whole to join the proletarian camp? Partly because of differences of life-style, but also of class-consciousness: most white-collar workers and unemployed intellectuals refused to see themselves as members of the proletariat and loathed a Marxist ideology which saw them as having interests in common with the manual workers. Similar views were held by the lower middle-classes – small shopkeepers, commercial travellers and artisans; unlike the proletariat, they were critical not of capitalism itself, but of particular forms of capitalism such as the large stores, high finance, the influence of the Jews, monopoly capitalism and excessive rationalization.

Furthermore, the peasantry had not joined the proletariat, either. This was partly because of the subtlety and power of Nazi propaganda compared with that of the Socialists and Communists, but in particular because, unlike the other two parties, the Nazis could promise the abolition of the burdensome interest on debts incurred by the peasantry, without this involving social upheaval. Thus,

between the capitalist bourgeoisie and the proletariat, there are ranged a number of broad strata of the population. They constitute neither a class, nor even middle classes, but remain there, floating, as long as no party has mobilized them. And if they stand up against certain forms of capitalism, they stand up equally against a predetermined proletarianization, against certain Marxist ideologies, and against the necessity of revolution.[91]

The proletariat was also weakened by divisions on the Left ("The Communists kept their strongest blows for the Socialists"). At the same time, by creating a new class of unemployed, the economic crisis increased the disunity of the workers, because the unemployed, demoralized by inactivity, failed to develop the necessary class-consciousness and were lost to the proletariat. The two Marxist parties in fact had their own ideology working against them, for people wanted neither international socialism, nor materialism, nor revolution, but "the resurrection of Germany".[92]

How did national socialism succeed in mobilizing and unifying the masses who were in revolt? And if the social situation created the possibility of a right-wing revolution, how did that possibility become a reality? It was Aron's view that "resentment, hope and a particular ideology have passionately united millions and millions of people who wanted a new world". The sources of resentment were "France, the Jews and certain capitalists"; hope, kindled by "a collective faith of a religious kind", lay in the better future promised to all Germans, workers and capitalists alike; and the ideology rested on a critique of equality, rationalism, liberalism, democracy, internationalism and, above all, Marxist materialism.[93]

These were, Aron emphasized, only the main constituents of the ideology. A thorough analysis would need to examine the part played by totalitarian thought in the social sciences, the role of irrationalism in philosophy, and the influence of political ideas in literature and law. It would also be necessary to consider whether or not the Nazi revolution had created, as it claimed, a new "anthropology" – an original conception of man. But such had not been Aron's aim.[94] He had, he pointed out, merely tried to show how the ideology of national socialism coincided with "the historical situation and the aspirations of social groups". The ideology suited those who sought to transform their lot without over-throwing the economic structure. It promised a world in which men would be different and the unity of the nation re-established, without the need to destroy either capitalism or the class system.[95]

If such was the ideology, how far had it been put into effect in the two years since national socialism had come to power? The political programme had been largely completed: the unity of German society had been achieved, and national socialism had replaced parliamentary democracy with "an authoritarian constitution in conformity with its principles". Had the moral unity which Hitler had promised the nation been attained? One "moral satisfaction" achieved had been the putting of anti-Semitic ideology into practice. Another lay in the field of foreign policy. Hitler had given the country what he had promised: "a fight for equality in dignity".[96]

70

How far had the hopes of the different social groups been realized? Many of the young had found work in the administration of the Party or other organizations. The lower middle-classes – artisans, small traders and white-collar workers – had stayed faithful to the regime because their situation had improved materially and also morally in the sense that they "can obey a paternalistic leader with whom they are united by an oath of loyalty. They have the impression that everything is in order because the workers are well insulated from power".[97] As for the peasantry, they had gained in that the rate of interest on loans had been reduced. All these measures helped to explain why the Germans had not revolted – a question frequently asked by Marxists in France.

With regard to economic policy, the regime had launched a programme of major public works in order to reduce unemployment but also, unlike the United States or Italy, for military purposes. It had also sent the unemployed, especially the young, to labour camps. The economy had revived and there had been a 50 per cent reduction in unemployment. This was an undoubted improvement, even if rearmament was the central factor. Another element in the ideology had been national self-sufficiency and here, too, the Germans had experienced at least partial success. However, the regime was by no means socialist:

If by "socialist" is meant a regime in which class differences are abolished or at least reduced, then no regime is less socialist than national socialism. Not only do they proclaim the necessity of giving free play to individual initiative, and not only do they uphold and re-enforce the authority of the employer, who is thus made into a "führer", but the distribution of profits is also left untouched.[98]

Furthermore, workers' salaries had, if anything, decreased since 1933. Perhaps, then, as the ideology claimed, the regime promoted "fraternity", rather than equality or liberty. In reality, however, the social problem had not been solved: there had been over four million votes against national socialism in the last plebiscite and underground Communist Party propaganda continued in spite of persecutions and "pitiless repression". Nevertheless, it would be wrong to think that the workers had been "terrorised into submission to a regime they detested. They have not much to regret, they are not all conscious of the loss of their liberty and, today as before the war, they have become aware of the nation as a reality". The regime had settled down and become a part of people's everyday lives.[99]

In conclusion, Aron stated,

Hitler did not seize power: it was handed to him, by a *junker*, a soldier and a landowner from Eastern Prussia. Without seeking to diminish the part played by accident in the Papen-Hitler alliance against Schleicher, it is legitimate to comment upon it. It was in the shadow of the bankers that the ambitious mediocrity and the demagogue sealed the agreement between the old Germany and the Third Reich.[100]

A final question, one which governed the destinies of Germany and Europe, remained: would there be peace or war? Doubtless Germany did not consciously desire war, yet it was impossible not to be aware of the "intensive, systematic" preparations that were taking place, and it was difficult not to wonder where the mood of "nationalistic elation", the concentration of military might, and present economic policy were all leading:

French specialists on German affairs were wont to declare in 1933 that national socialism was contributing to a German revival and that this was a happy event for our inter-dependent Europe. In my view, national socialism is a catastrophe for Europe, because it has revived an almost religious hostility between peoples and because it has thrown Germany back upon its ancient dream and its besetting sin: under colour of defining itself arrogantly in its singularity, Germany is destroying itself in myths – a myth itself and a myth about the hostile world.

National socialism, as has been said, is very specifically Germanic: it remains to be seen if it is not, above all else, the caricature of eternal Germany. Of course we must seek understanding and agreement between neighbours. But understanding requires a common language; it also requires mutual confidence. Can we in honesty find that language and extend such confidence to one another? If we cannot, all that remains is a fragile peace based on force and fear.[101]

Notes

1. 1983a, p. 50. Simone de Beauvoir relates how Sartre and another *normalien*, "Pierre Pagniez" (Pierre Guille), used to fire paper darts at Aron while he was trying to instruct them in meteorology. Simone de Beauvoir, *La Force de l'âge* (Paris 1960), p. 37: tr. (by Peter Green), *The Prime of Life* (Harmondsworth, 1963) p. 32.
2. "One day, feeling very nervous, I drove out with him alone to Trappes to find a meteorological balloon that had gone adrift. He had a little car of his own, and sometimes took us in to Versailles from Saint-Cyr for dinner". Beauvoir, op. cit., p. 34: tr. pp. 29–30.
3. Ibid., p. 35: tr. p. 30. Referring many years later to this famous passage, Aron remarked to François George (like Pierre Guille, Secrétaire des Débats in the Chamber of Deputies): "Look at my eyes more closely. You'll see that they're not so cynically disillusioned. What's more, each of them has a different expression" (George, 1985, p. 113).

4. 1981a, p. 27: tr. 1983b, p. 25. Compare 1983a, p. 50.

5. Aron told me (interview, 1977) that, paradoxically for one with a reputation as a hard worker, there was a lazy streak in his character: he carried out the easy tasks, but sometimes avoided work which, though possibly more important, was more difficult. Thus he believed that on a number of occasions in his life he had failed to write books which would have been better than those he did write, simply through weakness – for example, through signing a contract with a publisher.

6. Tr. 1975a, p. xi.

7. R. A., interview with the author, 1977. Compare 1981a, p. 27: tr. p. 25.

8. Tr. 1978a, p. xviii.

9. Tr. 1975a, p. xi.

10. R. A., interview with the author, 1977.

11. 1981a, p. 28: tr. p. 25.

12. 1983a, p. 53. On Spitzer (1887–1960), see Jean Starobinski, "La Stylistique et ses méthodes: Leo Spitzer", *Critique*, 20, 1964, pp. 579–97. The Italian *Lektor*, Enrico de Negri, with whom Aron was to remain on friendly terms, used to get up early every morning in order to translate Hegel's *Phenomenology*.

13. Thus he lectured on Claudel's play, *L'Annonce faite à Marie* and Mauriac's novel, *Le Désert de l'amour* (1981a, p. 30: tr. p. 27). Later, in Berlin, he took part in the French play, acting the part of the doctor himself in Jules Romains' *Knock*. It was the only time in his life he ever acted and he thoroughly enjoyed himself – "The theatre belongs among the dreams I never took seriously" (1983a, p. 74).

14. 1985a, p. 281.

15. Ibid., pp. 281–2.

16. R. A., interview with the author, 1977.

17. See Chapter 6, below.

18. Tr. 1978a, p. xx.

19. Ibid., p. xviii.

20. Tr. 1975a, p. xi.

21. Tr. 1978a, p. xviii.

22. Ibid., pp. xviii–xix (R. C.).

23. R. A., interview with the author, 1977.

24. 1981a, p. 51: tr. p. 45 (R. C.).

25. 1937a. See Chapter 7, below.

26. 1981a, p. 38: tr. p. 34 (R. C.).

27. Jean-Paul Sartre, *Lettres au Castor et à quelques autres. I. 1926–1939*, édition établie, présentée et annotée par Simone de Beauvoir (Paris, 1983), p. 48.

28. Beauvoir, op. cit., p. 112: tr. pp. 141–42 (R. C.). Evidently Sartre had not attended the lectures on the German phenomenologists given at the Sorbonne between 1928 and 1930 by Georges Gurvitch and published as *Les Tendances actuelles de la philosophie allemande: E. Husserl, M. Scheler, E. Lask, N. Hartmann, M. Heidegger* (Paris, 1930). Aron, who was doing his military service at the time, did not go to these lectures, either (R. A., interview with the author, 1979).

29. 1935a: tr. 1957a. See Chapter 5, below.

30. 1938a. See Chapter 6, below.

31. Tr. 1978a, p. xx.

32. Marrou, 1971, p. 37.
33. 1981a, p. 38: tr. p. 34 (R. C.).
34. 1971a, pp. 23–5: tr. 1978a, pp. 65–6 (R. C.).
35. 1981a, pp. 28–9: tr. p. 26 (R. C.).
36. Ibid., p. 32: tr. p. 29 (R. C.). The first occasion on which Aron publicly underlined that he was Jewish and, as such, might be suspected of a lack of objectivity was a lecture on national socialism which he gave at the Ecole Normale Supérieure in 1935 (1936a) – see below, p. 67. Although Aron states (1981a, p. 32: tr. p. 29) that the date of this lecture was 1934, it is clear from internal evidence that it took place a year later.
37. R. A., interview with the author, 1977.
38. Jeanne Alexandre was the sister of the sociologist, Maurice Halbwachs. On *Libres Propos*, see Jeanne Alexandre and Léon Emery, "Alain: sa position sociale", *Le Contrat social*, 12 (2–3), 1968, pp. 111–15.
39. 1983a, p. 55. In his memoirs, for example (ibid., pp. 55–6), Aron was severely critical of the wishful generalities contained in his early "Simple Propositions of Pacifism", which dates from February 1931 (1931b).
40. 1983a, p. 55.
41. Ibid., pp. 61–2.
42. 1930.
43. 1931c, p. 138.
44. Ibid., pp. 138–9.
45. Ibid., p. 140.
46. 1931g. Cf. 1931b.
47. 1931g, p. 281. .
48. Ibid., p. 286.
49. 1983a, p. 59.
50. 1932m.
51. Ibid., pp. 297–8.
52. Ibid., pp. 301–2.
53. Ibid., p. 304.
54. Ibid.
55. Ibid., p. 305. Compare 1932e, in which Aron drew up figures showing how much Germany had paid in reparations and concluded that the "only solution" lay in "general suppression of all war debts".
56. 1932m, p. 305.
57. 1932d, pp. 152–3.
58. 1931g, p. 281.
59. 1932h, p. 314.
60. "A clique of obsolete nobles, their property threatened by the acquisition of land in the national interest, a band of generals believing themselves called to play Napoleon, have used their influence to suppress the last barrier temporarily halting the National Socialist advance" (ibid.).
61. Ibid., p. 315.
62. Ibid., p. 316. To which Aron added in a postscript a few days later: ". . .it must not be forgotten that on the day the National Socialist leaders, once in power, clearly

ally themselves with the capitalists and go back on their promises. . ., on that day the proletarians. . ., who now take part en masse in Hitler's movement, will end up by rebelling. But such a regrouping of popular forces on the Left cannot be envisaged so soon; the 'national system' must be experienced first; at the moment everyone blindly obeys the 'Führer' and will continue to do so. For fanaticized crowds have a wonderful capacity for not seeing reality. And in German politics, God is as important as bread. . ." (ibid., pp. 316–17).

63. 1932n.
64. Ibid., p. 497.
65. Compare 1932j, p. 423: "If we disarm, who will guarantee that Schleicher's Germany, if not Mussolini's Italy, will not try by risking war to satisfy ambitions that are too well advertised? Let us be frank: no democrat or Frenchman can today treat such disturbing questions lightly. What is more, I strongly object when a left-wing publicist like Kayser justifies his thesis with such simplistic arguments as: 'If we disarm, we have a chance of avoiding war; if we do not disarm, we are *certain* of war'. No, no and no! If we do not disarm, even if Germany partially rearms, all will not yet be lost. There will still be opportunities to negotiate with the Germans and to settle problems by peaceful means".
66. 1932n, pp. 497–8.
67. Cf. 1932i.
68. 1932o, p. 625. Compare 1932l.
69. 1932o, p. 625.
70. Ibid., p. 626.
71. Ibid., p. 630.
72. Ibid.
73. 1933c, p. 125.
74. Ibid., p. 127.
75. 1983a, pp. 74–5.
76. Ibid., p. 63. See also "A Berlin en janvier 1983", *L'Express* (1647), 4 February 1983 (an interview with Aron by Missika and Wolton on the fiftieth anniversary of Hitler's coming to power). In a tribute to Aron after his death, Golo Mann himself described the scene as follows: "It was on that evening that I first met Aron. We stood next to each other, close to the fire, and listened to the speeches. I cannot recall how we came to be there – it must have been by chance. He noticed that I felt sick when books by my relatives were consigned to the flames and curses, and he showed himself extremely sympathetic and helpful to me. (This was the man whom his interviewers were so fond of describing as an 'icy intelligence'.) At one point he whispered to me, 'When you think of *our* little old politics!', referring to the political life of his own country, so civilized and footling compared with the irrational fury and triumphal hatred being whipped up in Berlin" (Mann, 1984, p. 75).
77. 1933c, pp. 128–9.
78. Ibid., p. 130.
79. Ibid., pp. 132–3.
80. Ibid., p. 133.
81. Ibid., pp. 136–7.
82. Ibid., p. 138.

83. Serge Quadruppani, *Les Infortunes de la vérité* (Paris, 1981), pp. 50-5.
84. 1983a, pp. 63-7.
85. 1936a. Other contributors to the series included Elie Halévy (on England), Georges Friedmann (USSR), Robert Marjolin (USA), and Célestin Bouglé (France).
86. See n. 33, above.
87. 1936a, p. 26.
88. Ibid. Aron was presumably thinking of the war of 1813-14, for example.
89. Ibid., pp. 27-8.
90. Ibid., pp. 28-9.
91. Ibid., pp. 29-32.
92. Ibid., pp. 32-4.
93. Ibid., pp. 34-40.
94. Aron can be said to have undertaken such a programme in the articles written for *La France libre* during the war and collected in *L'Homme contre les tyrans* (1944a) – see Chapter 10, below.
95. 1936a, p. 41.
96. Ibid., pp. 42, 45.
97. Ibid., p. 46.
98. Ibid., p. 51.
99. Ibid., pp. 51-3.
100. Ibid., pp. 53-4.
101. Ibid., p. 55. Aron's contribution to the volume was singled out by several reviewers, notably R. Schroder in the *Zeitschrift für Sozialforschung* (5, 1936, pp. 427-8) and the anonymous critic of the *Revue de métaphysique et de morale* (44, Supplement to October 1937, p. 12). In particular, Gaétan Pirou (1886-1946), one of France's leading economists and editor of the *Revue d'économie politique*, commented: "Of all the chapters on foreign countries, that by R. Aron seems to me the most instructive. In it he presents the reasons for the success of Hitlerism with great clarity and penetration. The perfect objectivity of his analysis is all the more praiseworthy that, for all sorts of ethnic and doctrinal reasons, he must naturally be opposed to national socialism" (*Revue d'économie politique*, 50, 1936, p. 1443).

4

France, 1933–1939

Aron had left for Germany "an innocent"; he returned to France "an adult". He had passed an important milestone in what was to be the endless journey of his political education, for from now on, instead of asking himself which was the "right" attitude or ideology to adopt, his question would always be: what is to be done?[1]

I had understood and accepted politics as such and not as something reducible to morals; I would no longer strive, by making speeches or signing petitions, to give proof of my good intentions. To reflect upon politics is to reflect upon political actors, and thus to analyse their decisions, their goals, their means and their mental universe. National socialism had taught me the power of irrational forces and Max Weber the responsibility of every individual, not so much for his intentions as for the consequences of his choices.[2]

At the time, early in 1933, in the only article he ever wrote for the left-wing, Catholic periodical *Esprit* – an "open letter from a young Frenchman" in a special number on Germany – Aron expressed himself as follows, conscious no doubt that his words would be unlikely to find favour with that journal's moralistic readers:

If one wishes to think or act in the political sphere, one must above all take the world as it is and not, by means of ready-made ideologies, foreclose the possibility of concrete – and perhaps effective – thought. To observe things and people, statistics, unemployment figures or the line of a frontier – that is how I envisage the study of the Franco-German problem... I consider pseudo-philosophical formulae on the nature of the abstract and the concrete in modern societies to be pointless. And I am wary of moral revolutions if in them one seeks refuge from the servitudes of our historical situation.[3]

This new perspective on the world had been brought home to Aron in an incident in 1932 which he never forgot. Through friends of his brother Adrien, Aron was invited to share his concern about events in Germany with the Under-Secretary in Herriot's Foreign Ministry, a certain Joseph Paganon. After listening to what was doubtless a brilliant exposition of the problem, the Under-Secretary thanked the young normalien on behalf of his Foreign Minister and suddenly put to Aron the following question: "But tell me, since you have spoken so eloquently of Germany and the perils which loom on the horizon, what would you do if you were in his place?" The embarrassed Aron was unable to recall his reply – assuming that there was one.[4] But the Minister's lesson, as Aron put it, "bore fruit". Thus fifteen years later, when he had begun writing as a journalist for *Combat*, he replied to his fellow editorialist, Albert Ollivier, who had just written an article criticizing government policy: "What do you propose to put in its place?".[5] It was not enough just to criticize; it was also necessary, Aron believed, to suggest to those who governed what they should and could do.

The way in which Aron's thought was developing at this time is also illustrated by the change that was taking place in his attitude to pacifism as his early moralism gradually gave way to an attempt to think politically. Thus his first article on pacifism, published in *Libres Propos* in February 1931, was full of vague and wishful generalities about the revision of the Treaty of Versailles.[6] By early 1933, however, when his next article on the subject appeared[7] – a reply to a pamphlet by Félicien Challaye entitled *La Paix sans aucune réserve* (which had the support of Georges Canguilhem, among others)[8] – Aron had ceased being a pacifist in Alain's sense: that is, he no longer rejected war at any cost.[9] A further discussion – a more developed version of the former – was published a year later in the renowned philosophical journal edited by Xavier Léon with the assistance of Elie Halévy, the *Revue de métaphysique et de morale*.[10] Aron himself considered this final version important enough to bear reprinting in a collection of his political essays published nearly forty years later.[11]

The article in question, "De l'Objection de conscience", was occasioned by a motion in support of conscientious objection which had recently been passed by the elementary schoolteachers' union at their annual conference.[12] The main concern of Aron's argument, which he presented in schematic fashion in the form of a number of propositions and questions, was to make a distinction between a moral imperative, on the one hand, and a political judgement, on the other, through an analysis of what had been called the "epidemic" of conscientious objection. It was Aron's view that conscientious objection could only be justified in terms of an absolute religious imperative, as in the Christian command-ment, "Thou shalt not kill", or by a categorical imperative of the individual conscience, as in Kant's moral law. Such an imperative must, however, be unconditional and unselective; it must be directed against all wars and not just some. Otherwise, "If between moral imperative and action we interpose a consideration of reality and of our probable judgements, then the command of our conscience becomes a political opinion".[13]

By the same argument, the conscientious objector could not also be a revolutionary socialist or a communist. Not only would this be self-contradictory, but such a political *opinion*, while possibly being based on reasons of a moral kind, could not be reduced to a moral *imperative*:

Indeed, the person who desires the liberation of the individual, or justice, does not automatically become a socialist, or a communist, or a revolutionary: he must also, through the observation of reality, succeed in convincing himself that the most humane perspectives take shape on the side of revolution. In other words, every political decision always results either in a confrontation of values (fatherland or humanity, justice or order based on force), or an analysis of the facts, or judgement about the future. (Which class today has a historic mission or, again, which party gives most hope to those who desire justice?) I do not claim that all men examine reality before they adopt a particular attitude. A great many move directly from a moral claim to the party which finds a place for that claim in its doctrine, without examining the concrete situation. But, logically, all political decisions imply two judgements – of value and of fact.[14]

People sought to make an absolute distinction between national wars and revolutionary civil war, claiming that the former helped to main-tain existing institutions and injustices and the latter to destroy them. There were differences between the two, Aron admitted, but they were differences of degree and not of kind:

Revolution destroys institutions and its aim is justice, but it creates other institutions: in order to make a choice...it is necessary to compare the institutions which the revolution will create and those already in existence. Nationalists and revolutionaries,

79

then, fight equally for institutions, those of today or those of tomorrow...Doubtless justice seems a superior ideal, but what right have we to compare values which have been realized with an ideal that men will never attain? The defence of national greatness can be for certain individuals a supreme value, as justice may be for others...

Between these forms of war I do not see a difference which justifies *a priori* the moral acceptance of the one and the rejection of the other. The question is one of political choice, and not of an imperative derived from one's conscience...A political doctrine is and must be a philosophy of the real and not just a question of morality.[15]

Thus, he concluded characteristically, it was important to recognize that political choices could be no more than "probable opinions", for "certainty and total conviction" were, in such matters, "unattainable".[16]

During his years in Germany Aron's attitude of revolt against the past had slowly been replaced by a feeling of foreboding about the future. He had, as he put it, moved out of the post-war period to enter the pre-war years. His values had remained fundamentally unchanged but, over and above the Left and anti-fascism, "it was a question now of France and her security". By the time he returned home in the summer of 1933, his "reconversion", as he wrote in an important passage in his memoirs, was almost complete:

The patriotism of my childhood, of my family and of all my ancestors was getting the better of the ill-defined pacifism and socialism to which philosophy and the post-war climate inclined me. I still chose to be "on the Left" and I was afraid of compromising with the Right, so as not to be exploited by the opposition. This timidity still stemmed from a refusal, whose origins were social rather than intellectual, to accept the logic of politics. Later, much later, I often replied to those who reproached me for my dubious companions: "One chooses one's enemies, not one's allies". Furthermore, I rid myself fairly quickly of the myth that Sartre defended till his dying day, "La droite, ce sont les salauds", or – to put it in more academic language – the myth that political parties differ in the moral or human quality of their members and leaders. The parties of the Left do perhaps have a greater attraction for idealists (in the ordinary sense of the term). But when revolutionaries cross over to the other side of the barricades, do they preserve their moral superiority for long? There are virtuous people in every camp: are they so numerous in any?[17]

* * *

Aron left Berlin in August 1933 and on his return to France married Suzanne Gauchon, a graduate in literature whom he had met the previous year. The Gauchons were not Jewish: Suzanne's paternal grandfather was of peasant origin and had owned a café-restaurant at Les Roches-de-Condrieu, a village on the Rhone about forty kilometres south of

Lyon. Her father had attended the local lycée and, after completing technical studies at Lyon, joined the navy as an engineering officer. After the First World War, in which he was decorated several times, he became Commercial Director of a firm of oxy-acetylene welders. He retired to Toulon where he died in his nineties, remaining to the last "un peu paysan".[18] On Suzanne Gauchon's mother's side, her grandfather, whose surname was Faure, came from Lyon, where he had a small business selling artificial flowers for cemeteries. His daughter, Suzanne's mother, was, Aron told me, "very sensitive and intelligent", though not a cultured person. Suzanne, on the other hand, had "an intellectual vocation" and went to the Lycée Victor-Duruy in Paris, where she was an outstanding pupil and made a number of close friends. These included Christiane Martin du Gard (her father, the writer Roger Martin du Gard, was a witness at Aron's wedding); Edwige ("Edi") Copeau, the daughter of the theatrical director, Jacques Copeau (she later became Mother-Superior General to the Benedictine order of missionaries); and Simone Weil.[19] She then studied at the Sorbonne where she obtained her licence in literature in 1930.

Aron met his future wife two years later at one of the famous *entretiens* held every summer at the Abbey of Pontigny in Champagne. These international gatherings or *décades*, usually consisting of three ten-day sessions each year, had been founded in 1910 by Paul Desjardins and were designed to bring together teachers and writers, philosophers and novelists, to discuss moral, philosophical and political questions. The most well-known French participants included André Gide, Roger Martin du Gard, Charles Du Bos, Jacques Rivière and André Maurois. The first *décade de Pontigny* which Aron attended was on the theme of "L'Homme et le temps" ("Man and Time"), in August 1928, at which he gave a paper on Proust.[20] The décade of August-September 1932, at which Aron met Suzanne Gauchon, was entitled "De la Transmission des valeurs" ("On the Transmission of Values") and André Malraux, whom Aron had met briefly at Cologne in 1931, was also present.[21] Malraux, who was four years older than Aron, was already well-known as the author of *Les Conquérants* (1928) and *La Voie royale* (1930). The two immediately became friends and Aron was extremely flattered.[22] He admired Malraux's work and the following year published an enthusiastic review of *La Condition humaine* in *Libres Propos*, a few weeks before it was awarded the Prix Goncourt for 1933.[23]. Aron himself directed the 1937 décade, when the subject was the future of the League of Nations.[24] He was, he has said, "indebted for life" to those meetings – meetings which were "unique, inimitable, indefensible and indispensable". They complemented those of the Société Française de Philosophie and the literary gatherings of the *Nouvelle Revue française*: "Philosophers were not allowed to seek refuge in jargon and writers accepted the need to justify their views. They were the conversations of honest men, mid-way between the drawing-room and the lecture-theatre". Above all, Pontigny called for "liberalism in its true sense – acceptance of the other".[25]

Marcel Ruff, who was on holiday near Toulon, remembers how Aron came to introduce his fiancée: "He was radiant with love and happiness, as is usual in such circumstances, but with a sincerity, a spontaneity and a kind of enthusiasm which were his hallmark – in sharp contrast to his unjustly deserved reputation for icy dryness".[26] The Arons were married on 5 September 1933 and the eldest of their three daughters, Dominique, was born the following year.[27] According to Ruff, towards the end of his stay in Berlin Aron had applied for the post of lecteur at the French Institute in London but it went to another normalien of Aron's year, "M" – much to Ruff's indignation because Aron had earlier helped M to obtain a post in a German university (Aron, on the other hand, told a surprised Ruff that M had as much right as he to seek a post in London and that Aron had not the slightest reason to feel aggrieved).[28]

In the event, immediately after his marriage Aron went to Le Havre to take Sartre's place as philosophy teacher at the Lycée there. Sartre had in fact been teaching in Le Havre ("Bouville" in his novel, *La Nausée*) for two years and, having been successful in the application which Aron had suggested he should make to replace him in Berlin, was due to leave for Germany. Aron spent a year in Le Havre, at the end of which Sartre returned there from Berlin for a further year, while Aron went to Paris. One of his pupils at the Lycée du Havre was the writer, Albert Palle, who remembers Aron as "a marvellous teacher";[29] two others were Sartre's future friend, Jacques-Laurent Bost, and the anthropologist, Jean Pouillon. Palle felt himself to be torn between his two philosophy teachers, or rather between "the scepticism of Aron" and "the moral tyranny of Sartre", and wrote complaining about his plight to Aron. The latter replied in a letter dated November 1934 (by which time he had left Le Havre for Paris):

...Don't worry...Don't feel that you are betraying me if you discover that I have said something which is wrong to you. Don't hesitate to adopt opinions that are the opposite of mine. Let us even imagine the impossible – that Sartre, as an old friend, should make some joke or criticism at my expense. Don't feel embarrassed, don't think of him as a traitor, and don't believe him too much all the same. And when we give contradictory advice, listen and make your own choice...[30]

According to Aron, he never worked harder than during his year in Le Havre. Not only did he have to give eight or ten hours of philosophy lessons a week; he had now begun to write seriously, although he was "tortured" by the idea of not being able to put pen to paper,[31] thus inaugurating the only period of his life – that between 1933 and the outbreak of the Second World War – in which he lived "the life of a real 'scholar'".[32] He did a considerable amount of reviewing, especially of German social-science texts;[33] and, while at Le Havre, he worked on his first book, *La Sociologie allemande contemporaine* (*German Sociology*)[34] and began his preliminary doctoral thesis on the critical philosophy of history.[35]

In October 1934 Aron moved to Paris to become Secretary of the Centre de Documentation Sociale at the Ecole Normale Supérieure, a position which he was to hold until the outbreak of the war. The Centre's Director was Célestin Bouglé. Now relatively forgotten, he was one of France's leading sociologists and university figures in the inter-war years.[36] Bouglé was a robust Breton, born with the Third Republic in 1870. As a student at the Ecole Normale, he had been one of the group of lifelong friends which included Brunschvicg, Elie Halévy and Xavier Léon. A disciple of Durkheim, though not an uncritical one,[37] Bouglé was appointed *chargé de cours* at the Sorbonne in 1909 and in 1919 became Professor of the History of Social Economy. The following year he founded the Centre de Documentation Sociale at the Ecole Normale. In 1928 he became Assistant Director of the School itself and was a popular Director from 1935 until his death in 1940 – gravely ill with cancer, he took his own life when the Germans entered Paris.[38].

Bouglé was the epitome of the Third Republican academic with a social conscience. Affable, optimistic and apparently untroubled in character and outlook, he was "exceptionally eclectic"[39] and seems to have subscribed happily to beliefs which in others might have coexisted less easily. Vigorous Dreyfusard in his youth, member of the Central Committee of the Ligue des Droits de l'Homme, friend and correspondent of Alain, Bouglé was a liberal, an individualist and a social reformer.[40] He admired Saint-Simon, Proudhon (whose collected works he edited) and Jaurès, although he remained a member of the Radical rather than the Socialist Party (he twice stood unsuccessfully as a Radical deputy in the early part of his life); he was also an active and eloquent supporter of solidarism, syndicalism and the Popular University Movement. He was a pacifist, a patriot who detested nationalism, a strong defender of the Treaty of Versailles, an advocate of German reparations, and a supporter of the League of Nations. Above all, he was a brilliant lecturer and lucid writer. Even in his lifetime, however, there was something *démodé* about Bouglé: a great popularizer, he was both a generalist and a synthesist at a time when specialization was increasingly the vogue, and his style remained literary and rhetorical when it was the fashion to attempt to be "scientific".[41]

Nevertheless, Bouglé's creation of the Centre de Documentation Sociale was a major achievement. Financed through the generosity of its benefactor, Albert Kahn, the "*Docu*", with its specialist library and lecture programmes, established itself as probably the most important centre for social research in France during the inter-war years. The position of Secretary was usually filled by an *agrégé* in philosophy or history.[42] Bouglé clearly had a high opinion of Aron and was anxious to have him as his colleague at the Centre, even though the two men were by temperament very different: Bouglé's jovial belief in "progress" contrasted sharply with Aron's disabused realism – a realism moulded by the study of economics and by the three and a half years he had just spent in Germany. Indeed, Bouglé appears to have found the young Aron rather overpowering ("assez terrible") and once remarked that Aron was often right, but the trouble was that he knew it.[43] Among those who frequented the Centre was the future socialist economist, Pierre Uri (b. 1911): "We went there to while away the time", he recalled after Aron's death, "to borrow books, browse through the periodicals, and above all to chat with an elder in whom everyone recognized an outstanding intelligence, a curiosity that knew no bounds, and a willingness to engage in dialogue with his young *camarades*".[44]

At the time Aron was its Secretary, the Centre de Documentation Sociale shared its office at the Ecole Normale Supérieure with the Frankfurt Institut für Sozialforschung, whose Director was Max Horkheimer. As an "avowedly Marxist organization, staffed almost exclusively by men of Jewish descent",[45] the Frankfurt Institut had been closed down in March 1933, soon after the Nazis came to power, and had moved its administrative centre to Geneva. Its new board included Bouglé and another prominent French sociologist, Maurice Halbwachs (although the International Institute for Social Research, as it came to be called, moved to New York in 1934). As a Radical, Bouglé was unsympathetic to the Institut's Marxism, but was "willing to forget politics in considering the Institut's plight";[46] and it was at his suggestion, with the support of Halbwachs and Bergson, that in 1933 a branch of the

Institut had opened at the Centre de Documentation Sociale. Further-more, when in the same year it proved no longer possible for the Institut's journal, the *Zeitschrift für Sozialforschung*, to be published in Leipzig, Bouglé proposed that it be published in Paris by the Librairie Félix Alcan, an arrangement which continued until the outbreak of the war. All this, it should be noted, occurred at a time when German émigrés tended to meet with a "cold reception" from French intellectuals and it "took courage" to work openly on their behalf: "Bouglé, Halbwachs, and their colleagues" were among the exceptions who "had that courage".[47] Aron met Horkheimer, T. W. Adorno and Friedrich Pollock at this time.[48] He himself wrote two major articles for the *Zeitschrift für Sozialforschung* – one on Pareto[49] and the other on Descartes;[50] but he was also given paid responsibility for French book reviews, his activity reaching a peak in 1936 and 1937 when he wrote some twenty-five notices of more than forty titles for the journal.

In the 1930s Aron also reviewed for the *Annales sociologiques*. This had been founded in 1934 as a successor to Durkheim's famous *Année socio-logique*, which, having ceased publication in 1912, had been briefly revived in the mid-1920s.[51] Beginning at Le Havre in 1934, he continued to write for the journal throughout the decade, his last reviews appearing in Paris during the war before the *Annales sociologiques* closed down in 1941, while Aron was already in London.[52] In addition, he wrote a number of reviews,[53] as well as an important article on ideology,[54] for *Recherches philosophiques*, a recently founded journal whose editors included Gaston Bachelard, Alexandre Koyré and Jean Wahl.

During the 1937–8 academic year, after he had finished writing his doctoral theses, Aron was appointed as a temporary lecturer at the University of Bordeaux, where he replaced Max Bonnafous (later Minister of Food in the Vichy Government). Earlier, in 1935, thanks to Bouglé, he had begun teaching philosophy part time to trainee *instituteurs* at the Ecole Normale Supérieure d'Enseignement Primaire at Saint-Cloud. It so happens that, a year or so before Aron's death, one of his former students at Saint-Cloud sent Aron the pages of some unpublished memoirs in which he recalled his philosophy teachers of pre-war days. It is impossible to say with how much hindsight or knowledge of Aron's later works the anonymous author was writing, but Aron thought it worth quoting certain passages in his own memoirs:

We used to go to the lectures of the two teachers jointly responsible for philosophy at the Ecole; both of them were Jewish but they could not have been more unalike. The conscientious Dreyfus-Lefoyer was always there, but his lectures – comprehensive and even exhaustive, though predictable and unquestioning – left us indifferent. Those of the nimble Raymond Aron, in which, completely ignoring the syllabus, he offered us his thoughts on the philosophers of history, from Machiavelli via Hobbes to Sorel and Pareto, were provocative and impressive...He had just spent several years in Germany in the course of which he had been able to observe the rise of nazism – something which he visibly abominated but which fascinated him. He had been a socialist but he had acquired a profound knowledge of Marxism. He appreciated Marx's rigorous critique of the economy, but he rejected Marx's manichean prophetism...In the name of lucidity and realism, he was a shatterer of illusions. I was unwilling to abandon my faith, but I recognized the significance of his views. We were still anxious to carry on living in the nineteenth century...but he rigorously dissipated such myths and we found ourselves naked and defenceless on the edge of the abyss. We were tempted to feel angry with him, as if it were he who had led us there. And it is a fact that, as one who denounced a Nazi danger that brought with it the threat of war, he was a frightening figure; yet, at the same time, he was a disbander of troops whose revolutionary creed he had drained of all hope.

"It was not I who was frightening", Aron commented, "so much as the world both as I saw it between 1935 and 1939 and as, we now know, it was".[55]

* * *

Aron has been reproached for his "silence" in face of the dramatic political events in France in the 1930s.[56] But how justified is such criticism? At the time of the right-wing riots in Paris on 6 February 1934, for example, he was teaching at Le Havre; and it is true that he did not join such bodies as the Comité de Vigilance des Intellectuels Antifascistes which were set up in their wake. He was, of course, totally opposed to fascism, but he did not believe that there was a danger of its coming to power in France. Right-wing deputies were elected to Parliament, but they were moderates, not extremists. Of the right-wing Leagues, the Croix de Feu, which was by far the biggest, was an ex-servicemen's organization; its members were not authentic fascists and their head, Colonel de la Rocque, was not a charismatic chief capable of becoming a fascist leader. There were, on the other hand, a number of fascist intellectuals and sects, but a major fascist party did not exist. France did not experience anything resembling the German elections of the early 1930s in which huge numbers of National Socialist deputies were returned to Parliament, and it was for this reason that Aron used to argue that fascism did not constitute a danger in France in the way that national socialism had done in Germany.[57]

Aron also believed that the overriding imperative was to maintain

French unity in the face of the threat from Germany; in his judgement, all partisan movements, including those directed against fascism, weakened the country, heightened the risk of civil war – a hatred of civil war has always been one of Aron's strongest political passions – and consequently increased the danger from the Third Reich.[58] For the same reason, though a supporter of the Republican cause, he approved Blum's decision not to intervene in the Spanish Civil War: the French people were deeply divided on the issue and it would not have been easy to risk a diplomatic crisis with half the country opposed to the government.[59]

In addition, the Comité des Intellectuels Antifascistes was made up of a combination of Communists and disciples of Alain. The latter were pacifists at almost any price, while the former were fervent supporters of the alliance with the Soviet Union. Thus there was a fundamental contradiction between them. Accordingly Aron, who even at that time "had a certain taste for clarity and truth", concluded that the Committee of Anti-Fascist Intellectuals was internally divided and its work ineffective.[60].

Aron did, however, write one article specifically devoted to French politics during this period: a critique of the economic policy of the Popular Front.[61] Like most of his friends, Aron had voted for the Popular Front, though without excessive enthusiasm. "Will you join us?", called out Pierre Uri, catching sight of Aron watching from the pavement as Uri and his companions marched along the legendary route from the Bastille to the Place de la Nation. "I was a socialist before you", Aron called back, without moving.[62] He and a small group of economists strongly objected to the Popular Front's economic programme and especially the law introducing a forty-hour week. One member of the group was the economist and demographer, Alfred Sauvy;[63] another was Aron's close friend, Robert Marjolin.[64] Marjolin, who was born in 1911, had left school at the age of fourteen. After working in various jobs (as apprentice orthopaedist, office worker and on the Paris Stock Exchange), and with no *baccalauréat*, he began studying philosophy at the Sorbonne in 1931. With the help and encouragement of Bouglé, he went to Yale University on a Rockefeller Scholarship in 1932–3 to study American sociology. He returned from the United States convinced that only economic liberalism could solve the problems of the Depression, and, having completed his licence in philosophy, he turned to the study of economics, in which he took his licence, doctorate and, after the war, agrégation. Between 1934 and the outbreak of the war he worked under Charles Rist at the Institut Scientifique de Recherches Economiques et

87

Sociales. Meanwhile, he had caught the attention of Léon Blum and at Blum's suggestion he took over the economics page of the Socialist paper, *Le Populaire*, writing under the nom de plume of Marc Joubert. When the Popular Front came to power, Marjolin became assistant to Jules Moch, the Secretary-General to Blum's Cabinet, but he eventually resigned over the introduction of the forty-hour week; his repeated warnings had been to no avail. Aron, who had taught himself economics and with Marjolin had pioneered a series of lectures on political economy at the Centre de Documentation Sociale, had also written to Blum, though the Prime Minister never replied to his unknown correspondent.[65]

Surprisingly, Aron's "Reflections on the Economic Problems of France" were published in the philosophical journal, the *Revue de métaphysique et de morale*. Realizing that the article would probably be refused by left-wing periodicals, and not wishing for it to be politically exploited by an organ of the Right, Aron had sent it to the *Revue de métaphysique et de morale*, where Elie Halévy, by now its Editor, had agreed to publish it.[66] In the current political climate, Aron declared, intellectuals had too often become mere party-propagandists and had abandoned the attempt to be impartial observers. The "Blum experiment" had failed, because it had not aimed at a revival of the industrial activity on which everything else depended: social reforms, stability at home, a strong France and peace abroad. Obviously, Aron pointed out, he was not addressing professional economists, who would learn nothing new from his analysis, but "honest people" who might thus come to realize that "economic phenomena, far from being mysterious, are comprehensible to those willing to study them and accept the lessons of fact".[67]

The only serious attempt at deflation in recent years, Aron wrote, had been Laval's in 1935, but he had failed to devalue the franc: both policies – devaluation and deflation – must be applied together. Instead, once in power the Popular Front government had not only increased wages, as was "bound to happen once the factories were occupied", but also, "faithful to the programme which it had drawn up with an incredible lack of seriousness", within six months it had introduced a forty-hour week throughout the economy. This had been done "with a complete lack of common sense", involving as it did "an increase in industrial costs without an increase in the income of the working class".[68] A reduction in hours of work was "obviously desirable", because that was the whole purpose of technological development, but it was essential that this should be compensated by increased production, which was not in fact the case. Coming as it did at a time when devaluation had stimulated industrial activity, the forty-hour week brought with it "the most dire consequences. It made goods more scarce, rendered certain firms incapable of meeting orders, and contributed to the rise in prices at the very moment when the watchword should have been to produce more and reduce costs". Realism of this sort, Aron admitted, might offend certain readers. Yet before trying to improve the situation of those already in work, jobs should be created for those who had none. The forty-hour week should have been postponed, because at present it was incompatible with a high standard of living. It was wrong to lead people to think that they could enjoy a better life and do less work, at one and the same time.[69]

Thus Aron welcomed as "a victory for common sense" the "pause" in the Popular Front's reforms announced by Blum in March 1937, even though it had been "greeted by everyone on the Left as a defeat for democracy" and as "submission to the orders of capitalism".[70] In fact, he argued, the unions themselves had been more concerned to obtain wage increases and paid holidays than a forty-hour week. Furthermore,

If ministers had been less ignorant they would have found the strength, which they found in other circumstances, to make particular groups understand where their real advantage lay. Perhaps, moreover, it was not so much understanding and courage that were lacking as the subordination of the so-called demands of idealism to the arguments of realism and national greatness. Bad policies as well as bad literature are made with good intentions.[71]

It was true that the "Blum experiment" had coincided with what had been rightly called a trade-union revolution, but it was this which, in Aron's view, lay at the root of the failure. The unions had not realized that, with the Popular Front in power, they were now on the other side of the barricades and should no longer be pursuing their traditional policy of opposition. Up till then, in France as in all capitalist countries, the unions had carried out a defensive role, supporting the demands of the workers but without asking themselves whether or not those demands were either justifiable or realistic. Such a tactic was legitimate as long as the power of the capitalists was far superior to that of the workers, but to continue this tactic throughout the previous year was, it seemed to Aron, an "absurd mistake", even if it were an understandable one.[72] Finally, France would inevitably suffer from being the only nation with a five-day week. "For years our country, weakened in her capacity to compete internationally, will have to put up with what people call her progressive step". No doubt, after many a crisis, the French economy would eventually adapt to the forty-hour week; for the time being, however, the new law left the Popular Front's successors with "a heavy task".[73]

Aron's article "made something of an impact" because he had "explained why the experiment had failed".[74] He continued to think that the economic programme of the Popular Front was "perfectly absurd" – its folly being due largely to the "extraordinary ignorance" in economic matters of France's rulers at the time – and this judgement is now generally shared by historians.[75] Nevertheless, once again he found himself isolated in a small group caught between two blocks – "those who were passionately opposed to the Popular Front and those who thought that it was the dawn of a new society".[76]

Aron has also been criticized for his "failure" to alert public opinion to the danger from Hitler's Germany.[77] In the first place, however, the fact that he was Jewish seemed to him to be a possible source of mis-understanding and misinterpretation of his motives. As we have seen, he was conscious that, as a Jew, he could be accused of lacking objec-tivity. When Hitler came to power, French Jews were suspected of being anti-German and anti-Hitler not simply because they were French, but because they were Jews. Much of the propaganda aimed against "the war-mongers" ("les bellicistes") derived from the fact that, for obvious reasons, French Jews had strong feelings about nazism not only as Frenchmen but also as Jews. Since, deep-down, Aron did not primarily think of himself as Jewish, his reaction to national socialism and the threat from Germany was essentially that of a Frenchman. But it was precisely this "French reaction" which to a large extent "paralysed" him: he felt that, outside a circle of friends, it was difficult for him to express his views about nazism without being suspected of being carried away by his feelings as a Jew.[78]

Furthermore, except to a small group of academics and students, Aron was totally unknown at the time. He had not yet become a journalist, of course; he was an obscure, if particularly brilliant, young agrégé in philosophy working for his doctorate. Where, then, should he write? And, more importantly, what could he say? The main question was Germany and the crucial moment the German reoccupation of the Rhineland in March 1936. Aron believed that a military response was necessary and that this was the last chance to stop Hitler without a war. However, the decision had to be taken within forty-eight hours. Once the decision not to intervene had been taken, in Aron's view there was nothing which, politically, he could do, especially as it was impossible for him to *prove* his belief that Hitler was now intent on war.[79] From then onwards, it seemed to Aron that the only way to stop Hitler was through a war which the French understandably did not want. In March 1936, however, the course of history could have been changed, for Hitler had given orders that if the French army advanced, his troops would withdraw. This moment of decision illustrates Aron's philosophy of history: it required "lucidity and a little courage" to change the course of history. Unfortunately, however, Hitler was right: there was no likelihood of a French government taking such a decision.[80]

And Munich? With his habitual honesty, Aron has said that emotionally he was opposed to the agreement, but intellectually he was less sure. He certainly did not think the agreement "very honourable", but he was unconvinced by the argument that resistance was the best way of avoiding war: there seemed to him no means of telling.[81] Militarily, in September 1938 France and Britain were unprepared for war and, diplomatically, the German claim to the Sudeten areas of Czechoslovakia was not, in Aron's opinion, wholly unjustified: the Sudeten Germans were, after all, Germans. At this time Aron was on friendly terms with Hermann Rauschning, the former Mayor of Danzig and author of a number of critical analyses of national socialism,[82] who had remained in contact with military and conservative elements hostile to Hitler. He spoke several times to Aron about the generals' conspiracy, saying that the military leaders would have rebelled had Hitler given orders to attack Czechoslovakia. After Munich, Aron took Rauschning to see Gaston Palewski, Paul Reynaud's Chef de Cabinet, but Palewski listened to Rauschning "with evident scepticism".[83]

Whether or not the generals would have disobeyed Hitler and sought to depose him, at the end of his life Aron was strongly opposed to any attempt to pass moral judgements on people in accordance with their attitudes to Munich. Sartre and Simone de Beauvoir, for example, were in favour of the agreement on pacifist grounds – no one, they said, had the right to dispose of other people's lives. After the war, however, in his trilogy of novels, Les Chemins de la liberté, Sartre presented those who were pro-Munich as "des salauds", which to Aron ironically proved that "as far as Munich is concerned, it is possible to form contradictory judgements without being condemned to everlasting praise or damnation".[84]

To Aron, in retrospect, the most extraordinary diplomatic decision in the pre-war years was the British and French guarantee to Poland in April 1939. It was "extraordinary" because the French had refused to risk war over the Rhineland and Czechoslovakia but, following Britain, decided to risk war over Poland at a time when nothing could be done for the country. To guarantee Poland's security was to accept its destruction within a few weeks at most; it also meant a full-scale war in order to defeat Germany. The French could still have failed to honour the agreement to which they were committed by treaty, but by now Britain had altered its policy and had also undergone a psychological change. France was allied to Britain and thus the French embarked on a war which they had declared without fighting, and which they were unwilling to fight.[85]

Finally, Aron's overriding feeling, in recollection, of the 1930s was of his country's decadence:

I lived through the 1930s in despair at the decadence of France, in the feeling that France was sinking into the void. The disaster of the war should have been foreseen. Basically, France had ceased to exist. She only existed in and through the hatred the French felt for one another...

I felt that decadence deeply, with immense sadness and one obsessive idea: to avoid civil war. I should have liked to explain to the people on the Left that if there was a war to be fought, it was not against other Frenchmen but together against the real enemy, at that time Nazi Germany. I should have liked to explain the same thing to those on the Right who failed to understand the situation. As so often in my life, I found myself between two blocks, without much hope of being able to say what I thought or of being heard.[86]

Yet, as he movingly recalls, there was another side to Aron's life in the France of the 1930s, besides the sorrow and despair he felt in the years before the war:

I was young then and happy in my private life. It is possible to be happy with one's family, happy with one's friends, and happy in one's work, and at the same time to be overcome with despair at the nation's decline. When I try to evoke the 1930s, it is both these emotions together that I encounter, with exceptional intensity on either side. My companions and friends were people of outstanding intelligence: Eric Weil,[87] Alexandre Kojève,[88] Alexandre Koyré,[89] Robert Marjolin, Malraux, Sartre – in a word, all those who have made themselves a name and have achieved something. We used to discuss the history of the world with Kojève, and economic reconstruction with Marjolin. Alexandre Koyré and Eric Weil were philosophers of the highest rank. They too saw, with the same despair, the decadence of France and the approach of war. What more can I say? I have never lived in a milieu as outstanding in intelligence and warm in friendship as I did in the thirties, and yet I have never experienced such despair at the direction history was taking.[90]

Notes

1. 1981a, p. 43: tr. 1983b, p. 38.
2. 1983a, pp. 79–80.

3. 1933e, p. 743. *"Esprit"*, Aron wrote in 1983 (he had known its founder, Emmanuel Mounier), "irritated me not so much by its values as by its manner. I found in it the kind of literature that struck me as typically ideological: it failed to approach political problems in such a way that the reader could see the solutions or choices it recommended. Its main ideas, the variations on the theme of community, reminded me of a form of German literature sometimes exploited by the national socialists. When the testing-time came and events required decisons to be taken, the *Esprit* group was divided in 1938 (which was understandable) and even in July 1940 – which gives one more cause to think" (1983a, p. 102).

4. Ibid., p. 59.

5. "Comment sortir du tripartisme?", *Combat*, 27 June 1946.

6. 1931b. Aron dissected the article, in order to make this point, fifty years later in his memoirs (1983a, pp. 55–6).

7. 1933a. Cf. 1983a, pp. 56–8.

8. *Documents des "Libres Propos"*, No. 1, 1932.

9. 1981a, p. 67: p. 58.

10. 1934a. For an editorial letter on the subject, see Halévy, 1985.

11. 1972a.

12. The text of the motion passed at the Congrès du Syndicat National des Instituteurs is reprinted in *Libres Propos*, 1933, pp. 470–1 ("L'Hérésie des instituteurs").

13. 1972a, p. 347.

14. Ibid., pp. 347–8.

15. Ibid., pp. 350–1.

16. Ibid., p. 353. Compare the sociologist, Julien Freund, who rightly observed of "De l'Objection de conscience" when he first encountered it many years afterwards: "I was immediately struck not only by the continuity of Aron's thought, but also by its style. For the style with which we are familiar today was already formed in those days. Aron is the man of open firmness (*la fermeté ouverte*): he takes a position, but eschews dogmatism" (Freund, 1972, p. 217).

17. 1983a, p. 81.

18. R. A., interview with the author, 1979.

19. Ten years later during the war, Suzanne Aron, who had arrived in England just a few weeks before (see Chapter 9, below), was one of those present when Simone Weil, who had died in London, was buried in the New Cemetery at Ashford, Kent, on 30 August 1943. Simone Pétrement, *La Vie de Simone Weil, Vol. II. 1934–1943* (Paris, 1973), p. 519.

20. R. A., personal communication, December 1979.

21. R. A., interview with the author, 1979. Malraux's biographer, Jean Lacouture, is mistaken, therefore, when he states that Malraux and Aron first met at Elie and Florence Halévy's in 1927. Jean Lacouture, *Malraux, Une Vie dans le siècle, 1901–1976* (Paris, new edn, 1976), p. 331.

22. R. A., interview with the author, 1979.

23. 1933b. Aron wrote that with *Les Conquérants* ("un très beau livre") Malraux had become for the younger generation what Barrès had been for the generation of 1890, Gide for that of 1900, and "what Nietzsche must remain for all those who do not conceive of existence without an initial revolt". *La Voie royale* had "confirmed dazzling

gifts, but was a disappointment": although the ending of the book was a fine one, the beginning was "weak and slow, and encumbered with obscure dialogue". *La Condition humaine*, on the other hand, was "a great book", even if (fortunately) it did not wholly fulfil the promise of the title: "There is a slight lack of serenity in the consent it gives to our condition. The sense of a life that is simple without being base is missing. And an exaggerated taste for the tragic still prevents those who are united by love or satisfied by action from experiencing joy. But already a book such as this is quite enough to enable one to class an *oeuvre* and judge a man". For the author's reaction, see Malraux, 1985.

24. "Reconstruction de la Société des Nations: comment mettre ensemble la justice et la force". Aron was fairly certain that this was the *décade* in question (personal communication, December 1979).

25. 1949c, pp. 76–7. See also Anne Heurgon-Desjardins (ed.), *Paul Desjardins et les décades de Pontigny* (Paris, 1964). Aron also attended the meetings of the Union pour la Vérité, a society for the promotion of secular morality, which Desjardins had founded in 1906 and whose premises were in the rue Visconti, a narrow street lying between Saint-Germain-des Prés and the Seine. Thus Maurice Schumann, spokesman for the Free French in war-time London and later Foreign Secretary, recalls one such meeting in 1938 at which the speaker referred to Péguy's remark that "Mystics always degenerate into politicians" ("Les mystiques se dégradent toujours en politiques"). "Too much of a liberal to show his impatience, Raymond Aron turned to me and murmured: 'Nowadays it's the politicians who degenerate into mystics, and that's still more serious'" (Schumann, 1955).

26. Ruff, 1985, p. 12.

27. Dominique Aron, who married the art historian, Antoine Schnapper, Professor of the History of Modern Art at the Sorbonne, has become a sociologist in her own right. Director of Studies at the Ecole des Hautes Etudes en Sciences Sociales, her publications include: *L'Italie rouge et noir* (Paris, 1971); *Sociologie de l'Italie* (Paris, 1974); (with A. Darbel) *Morphologie de la haute administration française* (Paris, 1969 and 1973); *Traditions culturelles et société industrielle* (doctoral thesis, 1979); *Juifs et Israëlites* (Paris, 1980); and *L'Epreuve du chomage* (Paris, 1981).

28. Ruff, 1985, p. 13.

29. "Un professeur formidable" ("Albert Palle n'est pas l'homme des confessions", *Fig. Lit.*, 14 November 1959, p. 3).

30. Palle, 1985, p. 17. Aron was, for Palle, "a man of friendship", in the Aristotelian sense of *philia* – faithful, egalitarian and fraternal – and, as we shall see, he and Palle were to remain in touch over the years.

31. 1981a, p. 43: tr. p. 39.

32. R. A., interview with the author, 1977.

33. See. e.g., 1934b–f.

34. Particularly the second half, on Max Weber (R. A., interview with the author, 1977).

35. 1938a. See Chapter 6, below.

36. On this era of French sociology, see Terry N. Clark, *Prophets and Patrons: The French University and the Emergence of the Social Sciences* (Cambridge, Mass., 1973) and Philippe Besnard (ed.), *The Sociological Domain: The Durkheimians and the Founding of French Sociology* (Cambridge and Paris, 1983). On Bouglé, see: *Bouglé 1870–1940* (Paris,

1940); Maurice Halbwachs, "Célestin Bouglé, sociologue", *RMM*, 43, 1941, pp. 21–47; Georges Davy, "Célestin Bouglé, 1870–1940", *RFS*, 8, 1967, pp. 3–13; W. Paul Vogt, "Un Durkheimien ambivalent: Célestin Bouglé, 1870–1940", *RFS*, 20, 1979, pp. 123–39; William Logue, "Sociologie et politique: le libéralisme de Célestin Bouglé", ibid., pp. 141–61.

37. See Halbwachs, op. cit. Bouglé has been called "an ambivalent Durkheimian" (Vogt, op. cit.).

38. Clark, op. cit., p. 234.

39. Vogt, op. cit.

40. On Bouglé's brand of liberalism, see Logue, op. cit.

41. Vogt, op. cit.

42. Aron's predecessors in the post included one of Bouglé's favourite students, Marcel Déat (in 1921 they even published a *Guide de l'étudiant en sociologie* together), who moved from socialism to national socialism and finally to active collaboration with the Germans as Minister of Labour during the war. This led Aron, in 1941, to observe: "In his youth, he did not appear in any obvious way different from his *camarades normaliens*; his socialism was tinged with moral idealism and Durkheimian sociology, without any particular knowledge of economic realities" (1941j, reprinted 1945r, p. 40). Cf. 1973j: tr. 1973d, p. 82, where Aron remarked that "Déat's brilliant mind led him to faultless reasoning, but the final conclusions were all wrong. On the day he joined the German camp in July 1940 I said to myself: 'We've won'".

43. "Aron a souvent raison, mais il est toujours sûr d'avoir raison" (R. A., interview with the author, 1979).

44. Uri, 1985, pp. 116–17.

45. Martin Jay, *The Dialectical Imagination: A History of the Frankfurt School and the Institute of Social Research 1923–1950* (Paris, 1973), p. 29.

46. Ibid., p. 30.

47. Ibid., p. 38. The Paris office of the Institut, in its turn, was closed by the Germans in 1940. After the war, in June 1949, Aron was one of the signatories to a petition which successfully urged the reopening of the Institut in Frankfurt (ibid., p. 285). The other signatories included G. D. H. Cole, Morris Ginsberg, Paul Lazarsfeld, Robert Lynd, Talcott Parsons and Robert MacIver.

48. 1983a, p. 85.

49. 1937l. See Chapter 7, below.

50. 1937m.

51. The Editorial Committee of the *Annales sociologiques* at this time included Bouglé, Paul Fauconnet, Marcel Mauss, François Simiand, and Halbwachs.

52. 1941a–h.

53. 1934–5a, 1934–5b, 1935–6.

54. 1937d. See Chapter 7, below.

55. 1983a, p. 745.

56. 1981a, pp. 44ff.: tr. pp. 39ff. Cf. 1983a, Chapter VI.

57. Ibid., p. 74: tr. p. 64.

58. Ibid., p. 46: tr. p. 41.

59. Ibid., pp. 58–9: tr. pp. 51–2.

60. Ibid., p. 46: tr. p. 41.

61. 1937c.
62. Uri, 1985, p. 117.
63. Alfred Sauvy (b. 1898) later became a Professor at the Collège de France and is the author of a standard *Histoire économique de la France entre les deux guerres* (Paris, 1965).
64. See Marjolin, 1985 and the interview with Marjolin in *L'Expansion*, May 1979, pp. 207–19. Marjolin was "dazzled" by Aron's analytical capacity and his "greatest ambition at the time was to resemble Aron as much as possible" (Marjolin, 1985, p. 19).
65. 1981a, pp. 47–50: tr. pp. 42–4. He also broadcast on the subject (see 1979g).
66. 1937c, p. 793. As Aron wryly remarked, he subsequently lost such scruples (1981a, p. 48: tr. p. 43).
67. 1937c, p. 795.
68. Ibid., p. 802.
69. Ibid., p. 804.
70. Ibid., pp. 808–9.
71. Ibid., p. 813.
72. Ibid.
73. Ibid., p. 805. Aron later said of Blum: "Morally and intellectually, he was by far the best man among France's leaders...But it is absurd to try to make Léon Blum into the one who is always right. He was always courageous and worthy of respect, but he had no understanding of economics. He did not understand the Popular Front programme. He was often mistaken, like everyone else. But compared to many others, he had an intellectual and moral style that set him apart" (1981a, pp. 60–1: tr. p. 53 (R.C.)).
74. 1981a, p. 48: tr. p. 43 (R. C.). "It was a little bombshell" (Georges Canguilhem, interview with the author, 1980).
75. For a recent discussion, see Henri Dubief, *Nouvelle histoire de la France contemporaine. 13. Le Déclin de la Troisième République, 1929–1938* (Paris, 1976), pp. 183–93. In fact, at the end of 1938, after Munich, the length of the working week was increased by Paul Reynaud, an opponent of the Popular Front and now Finance Minister in Daladier's government. In the mid-1930s Reynaud's had been one of the few voices to be heard arguing in favour of devaluation. For Aron's high opinion of Reynaud, whom he came to know after the war, see 1981a, p. 61: tr. p. 53, where he also discusses Daladier. According to Jean-Claude Casanova, the only two men of the Third Republic Aron really admired were Reynaud and André Tardieu (Casanova, 1985, p. 255).
76. 1981a, p. 49: tr. pp. 43–4 (R. C.). Cf. ibid., pp. 69–73: tr. pp. 61–3, where Aron analyses the French Left's propensity to "celebrate its defeats".
77. Ibid., pp. 44ff.: tr. pp. 39ff.
78. Ibid., p. 33: tr. pp. 29–30.
79. Ibid., pp. 44–5: tr. pp. 39–40.
80. Ibid., p. 62: tr. p. 54 (R. C.).
81. Ibid., p. 35: tr. p. 31.
82. Hermann Rauschning, *Die Revolution des Nihilismus* (3rd edn, Zurich, 1938): tr. *Germany's Revolution of Destruction* (London, 1938); *Gespräche mit Hitler* (New York, 1940): tr. *Hitler Speaks* (London, 1939).

83. 1983a, pp. 147–8. Oversimplifying as was his wont, Sartre claimed that Aron's analysis of national socialism was largely based on Rauschning's. Writing to Simone de Beauvoir in December 1939 he remarked: "I have started reading Rauschning. It's very interesting, and then I had to laugh because you remember how Aron presented us with the trilogy, 'Charismatic power, Machiavellian élite, mass', as something he had discovered in nazism as a result of his own thinking. Well, it's the *major* theme in Rauschning's 400 pages. I despair of ever finding an original idea in Aron". Jean-Paul Sartre, *Lettres au Castor et à quelques autres. Volume I. 1926–1939*, édition établie, présentée et annotée par Simone de Beauvoir (Paris, 1983), p. 511.

84. 1981a, pp. 63–4: tr. p. 55 (R. C.).

85. Ibid., pp. 35–6: tr. pp. 31–2.

86. Ibid., pp. 74–5: tr. pp. 64–5 (R. C.). But see the letter from André Fermigier, quoted by Aron in his memoirs, which questions the "decadence" of the 1930s (1983a, p. 673).

87. It was to Eric Weil (1904–77) that Aron dedicated his principal doctoral thesis, the *Introduction to the Philosophy of History* (the other dedicatee was Malraux). Born in Hamburg and a student of Ernst Cassirer, Weil had written a doctoral thesis on the sixteenth-century Italian philosopher, Pietro Pomponazzi. Having left Germany in 1933 when the Nazis came to power, Weil moved to Paris where he became a French national. He served in the French army, was captured and spent five years as a prisoner of war in the land of his birth. After the war he returned to France, where he taught at the Universities of Lille and Nice. He obtained a second (French) doctorate on *Hegel et l'Etat* (Paris, 1950) and *Logique de la philosophie: Réflexions sur les concepts fondamentaux des grands systèmes philosophiques* (Paris, 1950; 2nd edn, 1967). His other works include: *Philosophie politique* (Paris, 1956); *Philosophie morale* (Paris, 1961); *Problèmes kantiens* (Paris, 1963; 2nd edn, 1970); *Essais et conférences: 1. Philosophie* (Paris, 1970), *2. Politique* (Paris, 1971). For an appreciation of Weil, see the essays in *Archives de philosophie*, 33, 1970. Cf. 1983a, pp. 99–100.

88. Aron has described Alexandre Kojève as "the most intelligent man I have ever met" (1981a, p. 68) – he "gave me the impression of genius" (1973j: tr. 1973d, p. 82). In the 1930s Kojève gave a famous and influential lecture-series on the phenomenology of mind at the Ecole Pratique des Hautes Etudes (see Chapter 7, below), but he remained unknown to the public at large. "In later life Kojève spent twenty-five years as a civil servant in the Ministry of Economic Affairs, where he was the *éminence grise* of French negotiations. The solutions he proposed were invariably interesting, sometimes brilliant, but they were not always those adopted" (ibid.). He died suddenly, while making a speech in Brussels, at the height of the crisis of May 1968 (1981a, pp. 253–4). See also 1983a, pp. 94–9.

89. The philosopher and historian of science, Alexandre Koyré (1882–1964), was born in Russia. In the 1930s he was a Director of Studies at the Ecole Pratique des Hautes Etudes in Paris. During the war he taught at the New School for Social Research, New York, and became a member of the Institute for Advanced Study at Princeton in 1956. In 1958 he established a centre for research into the history of science and technology at the Ecole Pratique des Hautes Etudes. See also 1983a, p. 100.

90. 1981a, p. 75: tr. p. 65 (R. C.).

5

Max Weber and
German Sociology

―――――

Aron's first book, *La Sociologie allemande contemporaine* (*German Sociology*), was completed in 1934, when he was not yet thirty, and published the following year.[1] Aron, who was teaching at Le Havre, was hoping to be made Secretary of the Centre de Documentation Sociale under Bouglé, and it was from him that the idea for the work came. The famous academic publishing house, the Librairie Félix Alcan, was launching a new series, the "Nouvelle Encyclopédie philosophique", for which Bouglé was going to write a survey of contemporary French sociology.[2] He suggested that Aron should contribute a similar volume on modern German sociology. But there was another reason for undertaking the work: it was something of a tradition that young French sociologists who had been to Germany should, on their return, write about what they had encountered there. Thus Durkheim, who had gone to Germany in 1885–6, wrote two articles about German philosophy and social science.[3] Similarly, in 1896 Bouglé himself had published a book written after a visit to that country.[4] For these reasons, Bouglé urged Aron to write a book about contemporary German sociology which would be published by Alcan in their new series.[5]

His years in Germany of course made him uniquely fitted for the task.

As one reviewer of the English translation of *La Sociologie allemande contemporaine* observed over twenty years later:

When Raymond Aron...went in 1930 to lecture at the University of Cologne, he found sociology thriving in Germany. Lectures in sociology were offered in all the German universities, a professional society was active, and three periodicals devoted to sociology were being published. The field of sociology had attracted scholars of outstanding ability. In abstract analysis of social phenomena and in the construction of comprehensive social systems, German sociologists were, as a group, unmatched elsewhere in the world.

The success of the Nazi movement brought to an abrupt end the growth of sociology in Germany. In 1933, the periodicals were discontinued, the sociological society became inactive, sociology was dropped as a course of study in the universities, and German sociologists were forced either to emigrate or to keep quiet.[6]

Consequently, Aron's account "affords a vivid sketch by a contemporary witness of a rare high moment in the history of sociology".[7]

Even more importantly, however, *La Sociologie allemande contemporaine*, published in 1935, was the book which introduced the work of Max Weber to a French audience. Weber, who had died fifteen years earlier, was virtually unknown in France at the time.[8] None of his writings had been translated into French. Maurice Halbwachs had published a short article on Weber's life and work in 1929 in the first number of the *Annales*, the subsequently famous historical journal founded by Marc Bloch and Lucien Febvre,[9] and a full-length study by Marcel Weinreich was to appear in 1938.[10] But it was Aron who, by devoting well over a third of his text to Weber, first provided the French with a substantial account of his ideas and achievement.[11]

* * *

Aron began *La Sociologie allemande contemporaine* by drawing a distinction, within twentieth-century German sociology especially as it had developed since the 1914–18 war, between "systematic" and "historical" sociology. Systematic sociology was concerned with "fundamental social relations, types of social group, the static structure of society", while historical sociology focused on "the laws, or at least the theory, of the development of 'bourgeois society'".[12] However, there were no insurmountable differences between the two schools, as was shown by Max Weber, who

100

fell within neither school but "dominates all by his genius".[13] His work on interpretative sociology and his analysis of social action belonged to systematic sociology, but his study of the relations between economics and religion brought him close to the historical and Marxist tradition. Furthermore, his sociologies of law, economics and religion were both systematic and historical. In his work there was "not a simple juxtaposition but a genuine synthesis". For example, "His sociology of religion explains doctrines by social conditions, analyses the groups in which religions express and organize themselves, and investigates the influence of religious belief on human conduct".[14] Thus the three main themes of Aron's analysis of contemporary German sociology were to be systematic sociology, historical sociology and the work of Max Weber. The book did not claim, however, to be exhaustive: for reasons of space, Aron pointed out, it contained no discussion of Marx, or anthropology, or other sociologists such as Scheler, who was already well-known in France.

Within systematic sociology Aron distinguished formal sociology (as illustrated by Simmel and von Wiese), the sociology of society and community (Tönnies), phenomenological sociology (Vierkandt), and universalistic sociology (Spann). The founder of formal sociology was, for Aron, Georg Simmel. Although strictly speaking he did not fall within the period under discussion, it was Aron's view that the "development of sociology as an autonomous discipline can...scarcely be explained without taking his work into account".[15] However, it was ironical that his book, *Soziologie,*

is by no means systematic; it is a collection of brilliant essays, the connection between which cannot always be seen and which themselves lack unity and organization. The reader becomes lost in an interminable succession, not so much of historical examples, as of theoretical cases and possible combinations. These dazzling exercises often seem like an elaborate game. The book has thus brought its author many admirers but few disciples.[16]

Aron also picked out as an exponent of formal sociology Simmel's "true successor", Leopold von Wiese, even though he employed different terminology and "entirely rejects the equivocal distinction between form and content".[17] The theoretical programmes of the two men were similar, but there were "very great differences" in their work, in particular "a contrast of scientific temperament". Von Wiese had tried to construct "a complete, harmonious and incontestable system", the whole of which could be analysed by a single method. "He has therefore rejected the brilliant, improvised, supple analyses in which Simmel delighted and has sacrificed everything to considerations of scientific exactitude and a sort of 'conceptual quantification'".[18] Furthermore, von Wiese

leans towards behaviourism, not in the narrow sense of a materialist psychology which is not interested in phenomena of consciousness (in his sociological analysis von Wiese retains the act and its motive, behaviour and states of mind) but in the wider sense of social behaviourism – of how men behave in society. Von Wiese's method is more positive and less psychological than that of Simmel.[19]

It seemed to Aron that some of the fundamental concepts of von Wiese's "sociology of relations" – for instance, his concept of distance – were unclear. There were also problems with his definition of the subject-matter of sociology, which he saw as both physical and moral. For von Wiese, the social fact of a handshake, for example, was neither the physical fact nor the motive of the action, but the two at once. For him, therefore, sociology occupied an intermediate position between psychology and natural science. However, to most German sociologists "trying to provide a philosophical basis for sociology, this compromise seems tainted either by naturalism or by individualism or with abstract theorising". On the other hand, it should be said in von Wiese's favour that his theory was "based primarily on a definite philosophy of the social, on a reduction of the essence of society to interpersonal relations". In view of its obscurities, however, his sociology could only be judged by its results. It seemed to be "more descriptive than explanatory. It describes, groups and classifies various social processes, but in order to explain them it would be necessary to go beneath the social to biological facts, or beyond social phenomena to the psychological or spiritual sphere. Undoubtedly. . .he makes use of the laws of biology and psychology". How useful was it, then, to construct such a system as von Wiese's? It was Aron's belief that the kind of conceptual quantification developed by von Wiese was of little use in "a world of pure qualities".[20]

The second element within systematic sociology discussed by Aron was the sociology of society and community as represented by Ferdinand Tönnies' famous book *Gemeinschaft und Gesellschaft*. Although it had appeared in 1887, "it deserves mention in a study of sociology".[21] Yet "in spite of, or perhaps because of, its wealth of material, the book remained almost unknown for many years" – until, that is, the publication of its second edition in 1912. The reasons for this "success after so long a silence" were, Aron argued, both scientific and political. At a time when sociology was developing as an independent discipline in

Germany, Tönnies' book was "pure sociology", employing concepts similar to Max Weber's ideal type; Tönnies' theory also appealed to phenomenologists, for they could find concepts of essence in it; his attempt to explain collectivities in terms of the will of their members formed the basis for a possible theory of groups; and his concepts of "community" and "society" had "both a historical and a supra-historical meaning", since "they referred to the basic structure of societies and also to different periods of social development".[22]

However, this was not enough to explain the importance in German sociology of the concepts of society and community, for the opposition between them also fed German political ideologies:

The reaction against mechanistic civilization and against an abstract social order has taken the return to "community" as its watchword. It must be recognized that this word, which is rarely used in political discourse in France, has to German ears the same sound as our "justice and equality". All the revolutionary movements against contemporary society in Germany aim at the same ideal of solidarity of feeling, of real unity in harmony with nature. They attack the same enemies – the individualism of economic man, the rivalry of various interests, brutal competition, and the inhuman organization created by law, by convention or by economic processes. All these vague aspirations crystallize around two antitheses: those of culture and civilization..., and those of community. Both the youth movement and National Socialism invoke the idea of an authentic community. Animated by a horror of discipline, formalism and artificiality, the movement has transformed the lives and minds of many young people. National Socialism, in spite of the enthusiasm and faith of its adherents has, by a tragic paradox, contributed to the creation of an order more tyrannical than that which it wished to destroy.[23]

Not that, in Aron's view, Tönnies – despite his preference for "community" – would have recognized his doctrine either in national socialism or even in cultural romanticism. Nevertheless, his work contained ambiguities both of value and of meaning. Intentionally or otherwise, Tönnies, like many other German sociologists, implied that "community" was of superior value; while, on the level of meaning, Aron doubted that the two types, "society" and "community", exhausted all the analytical possibilities.

Aron took Alfred Vierkandt as the representative of systematic sociology in its third guise, phenomenological sociology. Vierkandt could be seen as a disciple of both Simmel and Tönnies, in that he tried to combine Simmel's formal sociology, which studied the relations between individuals, and Tönnies' sociology, which analysed the types of social groups and social beings. In addition, he sought to combine Simmel's formalism with Durkheim's collective consciousness through a method of phenomenological reductionism. However, although it was an "undeniable merit" of Vierkandt's work that it tended towards pure description, his "essential types", "ultimate facts" and "directly intuited wholes" seemed to Aron to present many problems. Why, for example, was "submission" an "ultimate fact"? Why was it essential that the ideal type of a society be based on "inner bonds"? Vierkandt also oscillated uneasily between individualistic and holistic explanations of social reality. Finally, the predominance of the concept of community in Vierkandt's theory seemed to be based on nothing more than an emotional preference.[24]

Within systematic sociology the fourth and last tendency discussed by Aron was universalistic sociology – the doctrine that the sociologist must start with the whole and not study any particular aspect in isolation. Such a doctrine was illustrated by the work of Othmar Spann, although for a number of reasons Aron found it "difficult to give him his due":

He has already published an impressive amount of scholarly work. He is the leader of a school, followed by enthusiastic disciples and attacked by violent critics. It may be said that he himself incites a somewhat brutal criticism by his imperious demand that one should take sides and by the way in which he introduces emotional passions into scientific questions by the insertion of political and value judgements. Thus anyone (like myself), who finds the atmosphere of universalism uncongenial, is tempted to see, in his lengthy books, only words, literary talent and religious feeling, rather than philosophical rigour or contributions to knowledge.[25]

Although the emphasis within universalism on the study of the whole rather than isolated parts was "valid up to a point", Aron also stressed that there was a "spiritualist" and "romantic" side to universalism. Furthermore, it seemed to Aron that to try to relate universalism to Durkheim's sociology, as H. G. Wagner had recently attempted to do,[26] was "entirely to distort its meaning". However, Aron's main criticism of Spann's work was that "it rests wholly upon value judgements". He "refuses to separate science and ethics, sociology and political philosophy", with the result that his "treatise of sociology is at the same time an exposition of political philosophy". His method was "strictly conceptual and ideological, without any appeal to observation or experience (except to confirm or illustrate the theoretical propositions)".[27]

Aron's conclusion to his discussion of systematic sociology was that it would be inappropriate to talk in terms of any "Galilean discoveries", for that would be to mistake the significance of sociological activity. "Sociology . . . does not help us to foresee or calculate, but only to understand". On the other hand, from systematic sociology we could learn

to give up such simple concepts as "constraint" or "imitation", and to understand more fully the infinitely diverse relations between individuals, the conflicting types of social relation, the continual exchanges between individuals and between the individual and social formations, the existence of individual influences even in the most elaborate social constructions, and conversely the existence of collective influences in the most fugitive individual contacts. Systematic sociology adds to our conceptual resources and refines our sense of reality in the attempt to grasp this life which is at once so intimate and so mysterious.[28]

* * *

Aron turned next to "historical sociology". In his view, of the sociologists considered so far, only Tönnies was concerned with both systematic and historical sociology, because "community" and "society" were both ideal types and terms of historical evolution. Those whom he now went on to discuss were, it seemed to him, mainly concerned with historical problems. Of these, Franz Oppenheimer, who tried to present the general features of the history of mankind, seemed to Aron to be "the most Western-minded" of the German sociologists. He was a "vigorous critic" of racist interpretations of history, and his social ideal was "a genuinely liberal society". However, his work was difficult to assess in a short space: "The amplitude of his undertaking commands admiration, while his reforming zeal, which sometimes becomes an obsession, calls forth alternately respect and irritation".[29]

At first sight, Alfred Weber's sociology of culture also had "undeniable merits": it stressed the uniqueness of different cultures without neglecting their similarities, and it maintained the independence of the different cultural "spheres" without obscuring their interconnections. However, his list of "spheres" or "factors" was incomplete, omitting, as it did, race and physical environment, for example. Categories such as these were helpful for the kind of historical panorama that Alfred Weber sought to present, but the basis on which he distinguished the various "factors" and "spheres" was unclear and the real value of his view doubtful.[30]

The third doctrine of "historical sociology" considered by Aron was the sociology of knowledge, in particular as propounded by Karl Mannheim.[31] If up to this point in his survey Aron had been reticent in his criticisms of the German sociologists he had discussed, he now unleashed a biting attack on Mannheim's "historical relativism". Aron began with the problem of ideology, which he took to refer to "ideas which are determined by reality". Here Marxism seemed to him to raise three sets of questions. Was ideology a general phenomenon and, if so, how could the Marxist escape from the vicious circle in which he found himself and justify his standpoint and judgements? Was ideology universal, in the sense that all intellectual systems, ideas and categories were inseparable from their social situation? Finally, did ideology imply a negative value-judgement, in that the explanation of ideas in terms of their social situation was also a condemnation of them? More generally, was the genesis of a set of ideas relevant to their truth or moral value?[32]

Although as a sociology of knowledge Marxism was "perhaps naively dogmatic" in its condemnation of "bourgeois ideology" and in its justification of "proletarian ideas", it was not self-contradictory: "Marxism does not demolish the notion of truth, but simply decrees in more or less arbitrary fashion that the truth is accessible only to a particular class".[33] Instead, it had been left to a "bourgeois Marxism", as Mannheim's doctrine had been called, to move beyond Marxism and in the process fall into "a thorough-going historical relativism", of which the sociology of knowledge was "only the self-styled scientific expression".[34] According to Mannheim, and this seemed to Aron to be the central tenet of the sociology of knowledge, because each group occupied a particular historical situation, it had its own way of perceiving the world, and as a result there were as many perspectives as there were points of view and as many partial views as there were classes. To try, therefore, to escape the "naive dogmatism"[35] of the Marxist assertion that proletarian ideas are true while bourgeois ideas are false, Mannheim argued that neither proletarian nor bourgeois ideologies were either true or false, but both were "perspectives".

Mannheim's attempt to resolve the problem of truth and ideology by positing an impartial group of unattached intellectuals "may be judged as it deserves".[36] Indeed, he seemed later to have abandoned the idea in favour of the possibility of moving from one perspective to another in philosophical, historical and social theories:

But here the absurdity of the undertaking is revealed. It is not possible to "move" from one interpretation of the world to another. The Marxist and the liberal interpretations of an economic fact are not reconcilable. No equivalence can be established between them since it is a matter of two contradictory interpretations which cannot both be accepted. An empirical judgement is either true or false, in terms of known facts and of logical form. And if a number of rival theories coexist this must be attributed to the impossibility of verifying them in a strict fashion, not to the existence of several truths or "perspectives" which are equally valid...Finally, if the sociology of knowledge

106

claims to dispose of the notion of universal truth itself, . . . and to introduce in the form of "relationism" an intermediate form between absolutism and scepticism, then not only does it fall far short of justifying this revolution but it is demolished by the ancient argument against scepticism, for "relationism" itself cannot be objectively true.[37]

As a theory of knowledge, then, the sociology of knowledge seemed to Aron to contribute nothing, for "there is no sociological theory of knowledge. . . The theory of knowledge is not history but logic; it analyses the congruence of thought with reality. . .".[38] On the other hand, what the sociology of knowledge could and did do was to

remind us once again of the difficulties we all experience in thinking impartially in historical, political and social matters. But far from constituting a new theory of knowledge it teaches us nothing about the most important problems of the human sciences: the theory of understanding, historical causality, and methods of verification in fields where an appeal to experience is impossible.[39]

* * *

These were, of course, Max Weber's problems. Up to this point Aron had been sparing in any praise of the writers he had discussed. Not so, however, with the subject of the third and major section of his book, Max Weber, for whom he expressed an almost unqualified admiration. "Max Weber is, without any doubt, the greatest of German sociologists . . . His work, by its erudition, the variety of questions raised, its rigorous method, and the profundity of the philosophy upon which it is based, has established itself as the paradigm of a sociology which is both historical and systematic". His *Economy and Society*, for example, was "the most imposing construction which has yet been attempted in the social sciences".[40]

For Aron, Weber's "originality and greatness" lay in the fact that he was "a politician and a thinker at the same time", in that he "both separated and united politics and science". He separated them, in the sense that he argued that science had to be independent of preferences and value judgements, and he united them, since he conceived of science in such a way that it was indispensable for action. Thus Weber advocated "a science for the politician, and political action based upon science". Furthermore,

Beyond the politician. . . it is man as a whole who appears in Weber's work; man in a divided world where he is obliged to choose between different gods, man in conflict with the destiny against which his faith is shattered. These then are the ultimate themes of the human enterprise which history recounts: competing gods, and the conflict between ideals and necessity.[41]

Aron began by considering the logic of the social sciences in Max Weber, and in particular his theories of ideal types and of understanding and causality. His conclusion was that, despite their incompleteness, the theories involved "a continuous collaboration between history and sociology". What Weber offered was "a history which does not ignore irregularities and a sociology which does not eliminate either accidents, or ideas, or human strivings". As a result, "the historical world, as a whole, with its dramatic character" could "find a place" in Weber's sociological categories.[42]

Aron turned next to the relationship between political theory and political action in Weber. It seemed to Aron that, in making the logical distinction between fact and value, Weber was criticizing the Durkheimian view that a new morality could be established on the basis of sociology and also the Kantian belief that moral consciousness and moral imperatives could be raised to the level of universal truth. Weber believed such views to be dangerous for scientific truth, moral honesty and the dignity of the human person, and his rejection of them accorded with his "deepest personal strivings".[43] At the same time, it was

difficult to grasp the magnitude of Weber's political activity. He was never really engaged in political action, and he had no political doctrine in the ordinary sense of the word... Weber's political thought did not involve a system. He did not have any abstract knowledge of the "best form of government"... There is no politics except in the world, and no action except in the present... His politics were not those of a *littérateur* or moralist, but those of a historian and man of action. They were not a system, or a collection of mere opinions, but judgements. To act is to make a decision, to deal with events, and to aim at an end, in a unique situation which one has not willed. Political philosophy, therefore, can be nothing but a more profound understanding of temporal action, a reflection upon the conditions within which our desires are expressed and an analysis of political choices in their relation both to reality and to our ideal.

Weber, faithful to his theory, exemplified throughout his life this kind of reflection, applied to historical development, in order to grasp the moments when human will is able to intervene effectively. On every occasion he judged what, in terms of the facts and *his* values, should be attempted... Thus Weber... chose a morality of responsibility...[44]

Although Weber was a nationalist – a fact which Aron had no wish to minimize – his nationalism was lucid and neither bigoted nor based on "the triumph of force", but on the expansion of Western civilization

108

"within the framework of great states".[45] He also had a consciously idealized and "very elevated" view of "the leader", conceived in terms of the kind of leader he would have wanted to be. Herein lay the source of one of the several contradictions in Weber, for:

He had a conception of heroism which did not always accord very well with the actual conditions of human existence. He had a thirst for truth which was sometimes incompatible with the needs of democratic politics...Weber refused to employ the means necessary to obtain power. He was prepared, in the abstract, to calculate human reactions and to act in accordance with his calculations, but as a human being he refused to employ the means which he knew to be essential...That is why he remained a scholar.[46]

However, it was Aron's view that the contradictions in Weber's political thought were "not lacking in grandeur":

The nationalist had a strong feeling for the individual, supported working-class demands, and was ready to help all those who were victims of collective institutions. He accepted the struggle between gods, between nations and between men, but he had a horror of a "world in which everyone engages in deception". Let each man choose his ideal and fight for it under its true colours. This notion of rivalry between heroes or between enlightened and lucid nations is Weber's political Utopia. His desire to distinguish clearly between what is known and what is believed, between what is desired and what is the fact, represents the scruples of an intellectual. Without these scruples he could not have lived; with them he was unable to act.[47]

Weber's historical writings could in a sense be seen as "an expanded version of the Marxist problem". There was, however, an important difference between Weber and Marx: whereas Marx's categories were supposed to be universally applicable to all historical periods, Weber stressed the historical uniqueness and originality of contemporary society. In, for example, *The Protestant Ethic and the Spirit of Capitalism*, on which Aron concentrated his discussion, Weber had not sought to "refute Marxism by opposing to it an idealist theory of history", because to Weber that would have been "just as schematic and indefensible as historical materialism itself". Historical materialism was, in Weber's view, a necessary and legitimate method of research, provided the sociologist was aware of the simplification involved in studying "unilaterally the economic causes of historical events". What Weber was opposed to was "the dogmatic claim to provide a total explanation of history in terms of economic phenomena", although Aron added that this was not the "real meaning" of Marxism but rather the dogmatic Marxism attacked by Weber.

In such expressions as "real causes", applied to economic phenomena, he saw only a naive justification of metaphysical political assumptions, without any scientific value. The economic system, far from providing the basis for an explanation of all historical phenomena, is itself not susceptible of an immanent explanation; the development of the forces and modes of production is unintelligible if other factors are not taken into account. On the other hand, Weber did not believe that "ideas rule the world"; he presented the case of Protestantism as a favourable example which enabled one to understand the way in which ideas act in history...Protestantism is not *the* cause, but *one* of the causes of capitalism, or rather, it is *one* of the causes of certain aspects of capitalism.[48]

Finally, Aron turned to Weber's "general sociology" with an exposition of his types of action, his sociologies of religion and law, and his analyses of authority, power and rationalization. In Aron's opinion, *Economy and Society* remained "without question Weber's and sociology's master-piece";[49] and he concluded with a personal comment, not contained in later editions or the English translation of the book, in which he made his admiration for Weber quite explicit:

We have not sought here to say what kind of man he was. But we have tried to show the scientist he was, conscious of the limitations of a work that was essentially provisional, and the politician he wanted to be, conscious of the servitude that all action entails. In this way we have tried to justify an admiration, the expression of which I should like to repeat. As a scientist, he showed the paths that sociology should take. As a philosopher, he remains a master for all those who place the highest value on lucidity, that is, a true knowledge both of the world in which we have to live and of ourselves.[50]

* * *

Of the senior members of the University, Brunschvicg was "very compli-mentary" about *La Sociologie allemande contemporaine*, whereas Halbwachs, at any rate in private, said that he found the book "unreadable".[51] When he came to review it for *Annales*, however, he expressed approval of Aron's "very substantial and truly suggestive book"; readers in France had, for the first time, been presented with "a penetrating and objective analysis of the main currents of German general sociological thought" by a philosopher who had spent several years in Germany.[52] Indeed, the reviews were almost uniformly favourable, recognizing as they did that the work satisfied a long-felt need, for it was the first book devoted to German sociology to appear in French since Bouglé's forty years before. To Michel Schwartz in the *Zeitschrift für Sozialforschung*, for example, the book was "objective and useful",[53] while the anonymous reviewer in the *Revue de métaphysique et de morale* observed that the critical comments with which Aron accompanied his exposition made the analysis "more penetrating and sure". The chapter on the sociology of knowledge was "particularly remarkable" in this respect, Aron pursuing Marx and Mannheim with an "almost pitiless logic" and even "a certain malice".[54] The author's admiration for Weber, at the time when French sociology was dominated by the influence of Durkheim and his followers, was also generally remarked upon.[55]

In the United States, *La Sociologie allemande contemporaine* was reviewed with a number of reservations by V. J. McGill in *The Journal of Philosophy*:

A French review of German sociology appearing amid the present European tensions has a special interest. Unfortunately, the author does not deal with the newer sociologists of National Socialism who hold the German state, race, and Fuhrer to be the subject-matter and criterion of sociology. His attention is confined to such well-known figures as Von Wiese, Tönnies, Vierkandt, Spann, Oppenheimer, Mannheim, etc., of whom he gives a very brief but lucid account. Half the book, however, is devoted to Max Weber, whose abundant and resourceful mind, combining philosophy, sociology and politics, political realism and idealism, Marxism and liberal ideas of all descriptions, the author never ceases to admire, even when there appears to be no reason for it. Is Weber "the German Machiavelli" or "the idealist of Heidelberg"? he asks, and replies that "the contradictions in the political attitude of Weber are also a mark of greatness". And though he rightly criticizes Mannheim for attempting to combine a liberal interpretation of economic facts with a Marxist interpretation plainly incompatible with it, Weber is spoken free of the same offence. Marxist sociologists, as the author says, are not considered in this book, but quasi-Marxists, such as Tönnies, Sombart, Mannheim, Weber, etc., who combine Marxism with incompatible ideas, appear as the central figures. So the enemies of Marxism, as Lenin once said, are obliged to wear the garb of Marxism. Certainly the reasons the author gives why the complete "dogmatic" Marxism was, and must be, rejected seem to be inadequate and to rest on misunderstanding. For example: economic causes are the only determining factors in history is presented as a Marxist dogma.

The book concludes with a most interesting comparison of German and French sociology. The one is metaphysical, the other positivist; the one is devoted to culture and community, the other to freedom or justice. Several ingenious reasons, but probably not very satisfactory ones, are brought forth to explain this difference.[56]

La Sociologie allemande contemporaine does not appear to have attracted attention in Britain before the war, but it was generally well received when a clear and readable English translation, *German Sociology*, was published over twenty years later.[57] The *Times Literary Supplement*'s anonymous reviewer called *German Sociology* "the standard work on this topic in any language". Aron's exposition was "remarkable for its fidelity to the tortuous thoughts of the German sociologists, for its appreciation of the distinctive context in which they wrote, and for the lucidity with

111

which he presents his findings to a public unfamiliar with the German intellectual scene". His account of Weber ("whom he rightly holds to be the greatest of German sociologists") was "definitive".[58] Norman Birnbaum, in the *British Journal of Sociology*, echoed this judgement: Aron had written "the definitive work on German sociology" and the discussion of Weber's methodology, in particular, was "a brilliant exposition of a difficult and obscure topic".[59] Similarly, Theodore Abel, whose pioneering *Systematic Sociology in Germany* had appeared in the United States almost thirty years earlier,[60] drew attention to Aron's "lucid and valuable" account of Weber. For Abel, "the most interesting part of the book" was the chapter which compared sociology in Germany and France. In general, *German Sociology* was "a worthwhile addition to the history of social thought".[61] "Nothing that Professor Aron writes is without distinction", remarked Geoffrey Gorer in *The Observer*, "and everything shows his clarity, elegance of mind, and encyclopaedic knowledge":

There is probably no better short appreciation of the work of Max Weber, almost certainly the dominant figure in sociology of the earlier part of this century, than the forty pages devoted to him in this book, and no better depreciation of Karl Mannheim than the annihilating ten pages devoted to the man whose influence in England was momentarily so great.[62]

On the other hand, to Charles Wilson in *The Spectator*, Aron's book, although containing "some valuable ideas, some shrewd observation and intuition", was "too allusive, too discursive, occasionally, one is bound to add, too tolerant – as it is of some of Weber's sociology of religion, which is frequently inaccurate and unhistorical". Wilson wrote that he was "left with the feeling that German sociology is much more of a special case, that it contains much less of transferable value than is sometimes implied here".[63]

Peter Winch, whose controversial *The Idea of a Social Science* had recently been published, was also ambivalent. The first chapter, on "Systematic Sociology", he wrote, "illustrates well the virtues and vices of Aron's treatment":

On the one hand he has a great gift of succinct, sympathetic, impressionistic exposition. For instance, although Spann's work is obviously and admittedly uncongenial to Aron, he succeeds in giving such a sympathetic account of it that it appeared, at least to this reviewer, to contain a good deal more of the truth than the writings of those authors nearer to Aron's own way of thinking. But the impressionistic style is less satisfactory when it comes to criticisms: these are often acute, but there is such an air of being anxious to hurry on to the next writer on the list that one is frequently left with an air of superficiality. This is of course partly the fault of the epitomizing *genre* to which the book belongs. But one has the impression that Aron would be well worth hearing if he could allow himself to pursue his own lines of thought more extensively, and that possibly it was a waste of his very considerable talents to expend them on this compromise between panorama and criticism which occasionally falls rather heavily between the stools.[64]

The best part of the chapter on "Historical Sociology", Winch thought, was the criticism of the sociology of knowledge. "Here the heat of the chase has happily induced Aron to give freer rein to his own polemical powers".

If the treatment of Mannheim shows Aron's powers of criticism at their best, the full-length chapter on Max Weber does the same for his talent of exposition. The merits of this chapter derive partly from the fact that Weber's ideas are so much more worth expounding than those of most of the others in the book and partly from the related fact that here Aron has more space in which to develop an argument. What is particularly striking is the lucid way in which Weber's methodological insights are shown in relation to his historical researches and his general sociological theories...

In general the book can be recommended for its discussion of Max Weber; and apart from that for its stimulating and suggestive qualities rather than as a general guide-book to German sociology. Philosophers should find particularly interesting the light which is throughout shed on the intimacy of the relations between sociology and philosophy.[65]

Finally, one or two reviewers of the translation seemed unaware that the book had first appeared more than twenty years earlier. Thus, although Howard Becker – who had published an enthusiastic notice of Aron's complementary thesis in 1939[66] – considered Aron's treatment of German sociology to be "clear, succinct, and very well balanced", the work was "now rather badly outdated; for all practical purposes it could have been written before World War II". It was, he complained, "quite impossible to get any idea of what *current* German sociology was like from this book".[67]

Criticisms such as these were, however, the exception. Placed on the "Otto List" of banned books and reduced to pulp during the German occupation,[68] *La Sociologie allemande contemporaine* was republished in France in 1950 and has been reprinted at regular intervals since then, even though the "contemporary German sociology" of its French title is now half a century old.[69] It has also been translated into German, Japanese, Spanish, Italian, Greek and Portuguese, as well as English. It would not be an exaggeration to say that *German Sociology* has become a minor sociological classic – no small achievement for a first book which at the end of his life Aron saw as "a rather *ad hoc* work",[70] very much written by a student. Only someone very young, he told me, would have had the audacity to attempt it.[71] Nevertheless, this early book made an impact on such sociologists as Robert Merton, Arvid Brodersen, Edward Shils and Slatislav Andreski, and Aron never regretted finishing his "German pilgrimage" by publishing it.[72]

Notes

1. 1935: tr. 1957a.
2. Célestin Bouglé, *Bilan de la sociologie française contemporaine* (Paris, 1935). Bouglé's volume appeared a few months before Aron's.
3. See Steven Lukes, *Emile Durkheim: His Life and Work*, Ch. 4 (London, 1973).
4. Célestin Bouglé, *Les Sciences sociales en Allemagne* (Paris, 1896).
5. R. A., interview with the author, 1977.
6. Chambliss, 1958.
7. Ibid.
8. The 1933 edition of the *Larousse du XX⁰ siècle*, for example, made no mention of Weber.
9. Maurice Halbwachs, "Max Weber: un homme, une oeuvre", *Annales*, 1, 1929, pp. 81–8.
10. Marcel Weinreich, *Max Weber* (Paris, 1938).
11. Aron was to return to Weber almost immediately in his complementary thesis, *Essai sur la théorie de l'histoire dans l'Allemagne contemporaine*, and to a lesser extent in his principal thesis, the *Introduction to the Philosophy of History*, both of which were published in 1938 (see Chapter 6, below). Weinreich's painstaking study (also a thesis) appeared in the same year (Weinreich, op. cit.). In spite of this pre-war interest in Weber, however, no work of his was to be translated into French until 1959, when Aron introduced a translation by Julien Freund of *Wissenschaft als Beruf* (*Science as a Vocation*) and *Politik als Beruf* (*Politics as a Vocation*) under the general title, *Le Savant et le politique* (1959c).

   The first work by Weber to appear in English was a translation of the *General Economic History* (London, 1927). In the United States, Theodore Abel had discussed four of Aron's authors, including Weber, in a doctoral dissertation published six years before *La Sociologie allemande contemporaine*: Theodore Abel, *Systematic Sociology in Germany* (New York, 1929). Subtitled "A Critical Analysis of Some Attempts to Establish Sociology as an Independent Science", it examined the "formal sociology" of Simmel, the "phenomenological sociology" of Vierkandt, the "behaviouristic sociology" of von Wiese, and the "*Verstehende Soziologie*" of Weber. Two years after *La Sociologie allemande contemporaine* appeared in France, Weber was of course to receive extended treatment from Talcott Parsons in *The Structure of Social Action* (New York, 1937).

   In England, Parsons' translation of *The Protestant Ethic and the Spirit of Capitalism*, with a Foreword by R. H. Tawney, had appeared in 1930; and Werner Brock's *An Introduction to Contemporary German Philosophy* (Cambridge, 1935) was published in the same year as *La Sociologie Allemande Contemporaine*. Brock's work contained lucid discussions of Husserl, Dilthey, Weber, Nieztsche, Kierkegaard, Jaspers and Heidegger.

12. 1935, p. 2: tr. 1957a, p. 2.
13. Ibid., p. 3: tr. p. 2. Compare 1934b, p. 108.
14. Ibid., pp. 3–4: tr. p. 3.
15. Ibid., p. 6, n.i.: tr. p. 5, n.i.
16. Ibid., pp. 7–8: tr. p. 6. David Frisby has criticized Aron's "influential study" for classifying Simmel's sociology as "formal" (thus contradicting Simmel's own intentions and ignoring his work outside *Soziologie*) and for treating him as a mere precursor of Max Weber. David Frisby, *Sociological Impressionism: A Reassessment of Georg Simmel's Social Theory* (London, 1981), p. 3.
17. 1935, p. 10: tr. p. 8 (R. C.).
18. Ibid., pp. 12–13: tr. p. 9.
19. Ibid., p. 14: tr. p. 10.
20. Ibid., pp. 18–19: tr. pp. 13 14.
21. Ibid., p. 20: tr. p. 14.
22. Ibid., p. 23: tr. p. 16.
23. Ibid., pp. 24–5: tr. pp. 16–17 (R. C.). Compare 1934c.
24. Ibid., pp. 38–40: tr. pp. 26–8. Thirty years later an American specialist on Vierkandt, Paul Hochstim, could write: "Unquestionably the most detailed and exact, if somewhat brief, summary of the *Gesellschaftslehre* (*Study of Society*) is offered by Aron, who also launches a highly cogent critique of Vierkandt's use of the phenomenological method" – even if Aron, like others, failed to discuss Vierkandt's anthropology. Paul Hochstim, *Alfred Vierkandt: A Sociological Critique* (New York, 1966), p. 26.
25. 1935, p. 41: tr. p. 28 (R. C.).
26. H. G. Wagner, *Essai sur l'universalisme économique* (Paris, 1931).
27. 1935, pp. 44, 46, 48: tr. pp. 31, 32, 33.
28. Ibid., p. 52: tr. p. 36.
29. Ibid., p. 62: tr. p. 43.
30. Ibid., p. 70: tr. p. 48. Alfred Weber, who was Max Weber's brother, has described *La Sociologie allemande contemporaine* as the best introduction to the subject (1981a, p. 302: tr. 1983b, pp. 256–7).
31. While in Germany, Aron had met Mannheim, who was teaching at the University of Frankfurt, and at one time he was very much under Mannheim's influence ("For six months or a year I was a Mannheimian"). Aron even wrote an article about him which he sent to Mannheim, who lost it – "fortunately", in Aron's view, "because it was certainly very bad" (1981a, p. 39: tr. p. 35). Aron also met Norbert Elias at this time (1983a, p. 108).
32. 1935, p. 76: tr. p. 52. Compare 1934d.
33. Ibid., p. 80: tr. p. 55.
34. Ibid., pp. 80–1: tr. p. 55.
35. Ibid., p. 81: tr. p. 55.
36. Ibid., p. 88: tr. p. 61.
37. Ibid., pp. 89–90: tr. pp. 61–2.

38. Ibid., p. 90: tr. p. 62.

39. Ibid., p. 91: tr. p. 62. Aron met Mannheim again in Paris in 1935, after the latter had been forced to leave Nazi Germany. "He spoke with generosity to me about my book", Aron wrote many years later, "without extending his compliments to the chapter in which I treated him severely" (1981b, p. xiv). Aron subsequently saw Mannheim – " a decent man" – in London during the war (1983a, p. 108).

40. 1935, p. 97: tr. p. 67.

41. Ibid., p. 98: tr. p. 68.

42. Ibid., p. 118: tr. p. 81.

43. Ibid., p. 123: tr. p. 85.

44. Ibid., pp. 123–7: tr. pp. 85–7.

45. Ibid., p. 128: tr. p. 88.

46. Ibid., p. 132–3: tr. p. 91.

47. Ibid., p. 133: tr. p. 92 (R. C.). Compare 1934b, p. 109.

48. 1935, pp. 137–8: tr. pp. 94–5.

49. Ibid., p. 144: tr. p. 100. This was his view in 1935; in subsequent post-war editions of the book he wrote only that it was "Weber's masterpiece", removing the reference to sociology.

50. Ibid., p. 154. On Aron and Weber, see Raynaud, 1985.

51. R. A., interview with the author, 1977.

52. Halbwachs, 1937.

53. Schwartz, 1936.

54. Anon., 1936.

55. Pirou, 1936; Vignaux, 1936; Janelle, 1939. The only hostile review I have discovered was that by Tazerout, 1936.

56. McGill, 1936. This is the only pre-war American notice of *La Sociologie allemande contemporaine* that I have come across.

57. Tr. 1957a.

58. Anon., 1957a.

59. Birnbaum, 1958.

60. See n. 11, above.

61. Abel, 1958.

62. Gorer, 1957.

63. Wilson, 1957.

64. Winch, 1959.

65. Ibid.

66. Becker, 1939. See Chapter 6, below.

67. Becker, 1959. Cf. Stark, 1965.

68. 1981b, p. vii. There were several "Otto Lists" (named after the German ambassador to Paris, Otto Abetz) published during the war. Needless to say, Aron was in excellent company, for the List included such names as Benda, Blum, Malraux, Thomas Mann, Freud, Koestler, Aragon, Nizan, Zweig and Gide. See Herbert R. Lottman, *La Rive gauche: Du Front populaire à la guerre froide* (Paris, 1981), pp. 213–15.

69. 1950a, 1966b, 1981b. Cf. Arnaud, 1966: *La Sociologie allemande contemporaine* "has become a classic introduction to the methodology of the social sciences at university

level. . . Aron's account has not aged in the slightest, and if today Max Weber, for example, no longer remains to be discovered as he was thirty years ago, it is still through the precise and vigorous analyses contained in this short work that apprentice sociologists can best be initiated into his decisive contribution to the destiny of social science".

70. Tr. 1978a, pp. xx–xxi.
71. R. A., interview with the author, 1977.
72. 1983a, p. 107.

6

The Philosophy of History

_____

The Critical Philosophy of History

On his return from Germany Aron had begun working for his doctorate in philosophy. Candidates for the *doctorat ès lettres* had to submit two theses, a *thèse principale* and a *thèse complémentaire*, each of which was publicly defended in front of a different jury of three senior members of the University. Aron's original plan had been to write his principal thesis on the "critical philosophy of history" of the four German thinkers, Dilthey, Rickert, Simmel and Max Weber, and to follow this with a complementary thesis on the "philosophy of historical relativism" of Troeltsch, Scheler, Mannheim and possibly Spengler.[1] Indeed, he wrote the first volume, which he entitled *Essai sur la théorie de l'histoire dans l'Allemagne contemporaine: la philosophie critique de l'histoire* (*Essay on the Theory of History in Contemporary Germany: The Critical Philosophy of History*),[2] in 1934 and 1935, while he was still at Le Havre and after he had moved to Paris to become Secretary of the Centre de Documentation Sociale.[3] However, when he showed it to his supervisor, Léon Brunschvicg, it "met with severe criticism" – a judgement which led Aron, writing some forty years later, to comment:

This severity was probably excessive and today I understand its motivation; in any case it served me well. Since he, who had my interests at heart, predicted inevitable failure if I offered this historical essay (on German philosophers hardly known at the time to the French) as my principal thesis, I had to express my own ideas directly and not present them through thinkers of secondary rank.[4]

Aron was strongly affected by Brunschvicg's verdict and went back to work on the subject in the summer of 1935. Not long afterwards, however, *La Sociologie allemande contemporaine* (*German Sociology*) was published and, as we have seen, this was a book of which Brunschvicg thought highly. He therefore wrote to Aron saying that he had perhaps been too hasty and unjust in his judgement of the *Essai sur la théorie de l'histoire dans l'Allemagne contemporaine*. Aron then "somewhat ridiculously" showed the manuscript to Malraux and their mutual friend, the writer Jean Duval, and discussed it with them. As a result he resolved to abandon his original plan for the complementary thesis, although the sections on Mannheim and Troeltsch were well advanced;[5] instead, he decided to submit the *Essai sur la théorie de l'histoire dans l'Allemagne contemporaine* as his complementary thesis and to begin work on what was to become his principal thesis, the *Introduction à la philosophie de l'histoire* (*Introduction to the Philosophy of History*).[6] Written between autumn 1935 and Easter 1937, he was forced to complete it more hurriedly than he would otherwise have wished. War was coming and it seemed to him that, even if he survived, he "would not have the heart, at the close of hostilities, to resume an unfinished work".[7] In the end, he dedicated the complementary thesis, on the critical philosophy of history, to his academic seniors, Bouglé and Brunschvicg, and his principal thesis, the *Introduction to the Philosophy of History*, to André Malraux and another friend, the philosopher Eric Weil.[8]

The two works are, to say the least, daunting and difficult to read; their content is highly abstract and the style heavily Germanic. Nevertheless, as we shall see, they were both well received when they appeared in France in 1938, and the French originals even attracted favourable attention in the United States and Britain before the war. Not surprisingly, however, the complementary thesis, the *Essai sur la théorie de l'histoire dans l'Allemagne contemporaine*, is one of the few books by Aron never to have been translated into any language; yet it contains full and careful analyses of the ideas of the four thinkers whom Aron chose to study, and is an essential preliminary to the major work, the *Introduction to the Philosophy of History*.

Aron's aim in the *Essai sur la théorie de l'histoire dans l'Allemagne contemporaine* was, he explained, a limited one. He was not trying to encompass "the theory of history in contemporary Germany" in its vast entirety. Everyone was aware of the part played by the philosophy of history, in its various forms, in German thought. The logic of historical knowledge, as well as the visions – "panoramic, grandiose and uncertain" – of a Spengler, had exercised a profound influence on the consciousness which the Germans had developed of their time and culture. It was true that, since the beginning of the nineteenth century, the moral sciences in Germany had been imbued with a sense of history, and in particular one that derived from classical idealism; but since the end of the last century, philosophical interest in history had expressed itself directly in "theories of history".[9]

Aron's intention was to focus on one aspect of the historical problem and one period of German philosophy – that which was concerned with "the critical philosophy of history", as represented by Dilthey, Rickert, Simmel and Weber. He also stressed that his approach was philosophical rather than sociological. By this he meant that he was not interested in explaining the ideas of these thinkers in terms of their origins and milieu; his concern was to "treat these philosophers as philosophers" – in other words, to provide a rigorous examination of their ideas, not simply because they were little known in France, but in order "if possible, to approach nearer to truth".[10] Thus he was not aiming to provide a sociological, historical or biographical account of these writers, but an "internal understanding" of their philosophical ideas.[11]

Nevertheless, it was important, Aron believed, to situate the "critical" period in the history of philosophy, in order to specify the aim of his inquiry:

In the domain of speculative thought, the breakdown of Hegelian philosophy marked a crucial moment in nineteenth-century Germany. The philosophy of Hegel was continued by, on the one hand, Marxism and, on the other, the historians, economists, jurists and philologists who constructed what Dilthey called the sciences of the mind. In the middle of the last century, philosophy seemed dead in Germany and the moral and political sciences were in process of developing.[12]

It was in this situation that Dilthey set about trying to establish a new methodology for the moral sciences, together with a concrete doctrine of man in human history.

The other source for the critical philosophy of history, Aron explained, lay in the neo-Kantian movement which, after the break in speculative philosophy, sought its inspiration in the "return to Kant". Rickert's thought was linked to this movement, the "South-West German school", proposing to complete Kant's work by developing a critical theory of history.[13]

These two aims met in the idea of a critique of historical reason. But was it possible, Aron asked, to be precise about such a term, in view of the wide divergences of interest between the different thinkers? Thus Dilthey had wanted first of all to produce an encyclopaedia of the historical sciences, then a psychology which would be a kind of mathematics of the moral world, and was finally content to try to analyse the fundamental concepts of the sciences of the mind. Rickert sought to elaborate the logical principles of a science of the individual. Simmel was concerned to investigate the nature of the gap between the historical account and lived experience. Lastly, Weber attempted to define the limits of those historical judgements which are capable of universal truth.[14]

Nevertheless, in spite of this diversity, Aron believed that the four thinkers did have:

a common objective, which was to clarify the nature of the historical sciences, and a common philosophical principle: hostile to traditional philosophy of history, they see themselves as renewing the problem by substituting positive reflection for metaphysics. This is why we have placed the idea of a critique of historical reason in the forefront of our study, and have directed the whole of our discussion towards the fundamental question: is it possible to transpose the Kantian method in a way that makes the philosophy of history redundant and provides a logical foundation for the historical sciences?[15]

Aron began his discussion with an outline and evaluation of Dilthey's "critique of historical reason". Dilthey's thought was "critical" in the sense that the metaphysics of Aristotle, Descartes and the German idealists such as Hegel, was, Dilthey believed, a thing of the past. Man would never succeed in providing an all-embracing explanation of human existence. Such extravagant claims must be replaced by a more rigorous scientific inquiry. Dilthey's Kantianism was evident in his assertion that, in order to attain truth, philosophy must rely on the only immediate certainty, inner experience. However, for Dilthey a legitimate philosophy did still exist: the attempt to understand man through his past. In this way the philosophy of history merged, he thought, with the science of history as a means for the individual to situate himself historically and thus engage in an act of self-discovery. For this reason, Aron declared, Dilthey had "an exceptional place" in his investigation:

He is its starting-point, but also its resting-place. He has travelled along the whole of the dialectical road that we intend to take. From the rejection of the philosophy of history, passing through the critique of historical reason, he arrives at a philosophy of man...There is..., in his writings, at least the outline of all the philosophies that we will have to encounter: critique of historical knowledge, relativism of this knowledge, historical character of all values, absolute nature of historical development (absolu du devenir), relativism of truth, and finally, at the outset and at the end, philosophy of man in as much as historical being.[16]

There were, however, three main problems in connection with Dilthey's thought. First of all, his "philosophy of life" corresponded to the irrational-ism prevalent in post-war Germany, even though it was less relativistic and more rigorously grounded than, for example, Mannheim's sociology of knowledge. Secondly, Dilthey had failed to solve the logical or critical problem he had set himself – that of "founding" the moral sciences on first principles. It seemed to Aron that the fundamental concepts on which Dilthey had begun to work towards the end of his life (the circular nature of historical knowledge, the specificity of concepts, the interdependence of the narrative of events and of the historical sciences, and the privilege of retrospective thought), while providing a valuable starting-point, were insufficiently developed. Thirdly, Dilthey's philosophy appeared to end in relativism, since in spite of his achievement he had failed to show how man could choose between irreconcilable values and ends, and thus, in a universally valid way, take the decisions which involved his commitment.[17]

Aron turned next to Rickert's "logic of history and philosophy of values". Although Rickert's thought was now dead in Germany in a way which Dilthey's and Simmel's was not, Aron believed that historically it had been of considerable importance. In particular, it had been valuable in combating a narrow positivism, according to which history should become a "real" science, taking physics as its model. Nevertheless, Rickert had not succeeded in resolving the central problem, which was to establish the basis for an objective science of history. In Rickert's view, objectivity resulted from selection, because he thought that the same facts must be of interest to all, even though historians might have a special interest in politics, for example, or the history of ideas, or the economy. However, Rickert's theory offered no grounds for making a choice between these possible value-judgements. Aron's conclusion was that "in the last analysis there is little that is worth retaining from Rickert's immense efforts", for "there still remains the problem posed by the critique of historical reason: within what limits, and under what conditions, does an objective historical science exist?" Rickert had offered an answer to this question, but it was "so abstract and so far removed from real science as to be empty".[18]

Aron now considered Simmel's "philosophy of life and logic of history". Simmel had, in Aron's view, failed to solve a crucial problem, that of historical "understanding", since he argued, falsely, that in "understanding" we suddenly grasp the soul of another person. Furthermore, his concrete analyses, "though suggestive, are incomplete, because, on the one hand, Simmel avoids the difficulties by resorting to art, and, on the other, he sanctifies his antinomies by giving them a metaphysical significance". For example, "the opposition between understanding and explanation, between objective interpretation and causal explanation, is valid, but it constitutes a point of departure rather than a point of arrival for logical thinking".[19] At the same time Simmel's problems were, in Aron's opinion, "the major problems of a logic of historical knowledge: understanding and causality, plurality of significant relations, the necessity of organizing phenomena into wholes and the arbitrariness (because partial) of all wholes – these are indeed the themes of a logic which would seek to define the limits of historical objectivity". However, Aron believed that it was possible to "take critical analysis further before resorting to metaphysics", whereas Simmel had "encountered these problems from within the perspective of a particular philosophy which prevented any further investigation". It was impossible to discuss that philosophy because Simmel presented it as though it were "a personal vision". As a consequence, the problems posed by the critique of historical reason remained unresolved. Finally, like Dilthey, Bergson, Nietzsche and Schopenhauer, Simmel gave the philosophy of history an "irrationalist orientation: the principle of historical movement, the metaphysical substance, the carrier of history, is neither spirit nor man, but life, a life beyond the opposition between being and consciousness, feelings and reason".[20]

As in *German Sociology*, it was not until he turned to a discussion of Weber ("The Limits of Historical Objectivity and the Philosophy of Choice") that Aron felt able to give full rein to an almost unreserved admiration, for in Aron's view it was Weber alone who had come near to clarifying the problems posed by the critical philosophy of history. The originality of Weber's contribution was that instead of searching for a general theory of historical knowledge, as Dilthey, Rickert and Simmel had done, he had tried to define the *limits* of historical objectivity. For him their question, "Under what conditions is the science of the past universally valid?" was replaced by another: "Which elements of this science are independent of the perspective and the will of the historian, in a way which has universal validity?" Furthermore, as a politician as well as a scholar, Weber had, Aron believed, succeeded in "elucidating in a definitive way the characteristics of historical knowledge demanded by action".[21] Weber refused to allow scientists to make value-judgements and "with the same intransigence, in politics he fought against ideologists and moralists". In fact, Aron pointed out, Weber sought objectivity in history and in the social sciences "*because of, and not*, as one might be led to think, *in spite of* politics". In Weber, therefore, science and politics were united because "he asks of the cultural sciences the knowledge required by the man of action: the historian questions the past and, in the same way, the politician reflects on reality and considers his course of action". Thus any account of Weber should, in Aron's view, start with an analysis of "the conditions of action".[22]

Aron began, therefore, with the problem of selection in Weber and in particular the degree to which historical judgement can attain universal validity. As a neo-Kantian, Weber did not believe in the possibility of combining science and metaphysics. He thought that world-views were expressions of feeling or assertions of the will and, therefore, essentially unverifiable. For him, then, historical knowledge and understanding must be free of all metaphysics. At the same time, however, the historian had to choose between facts and he could only decide which facts were of interest or importance on the basis of some metaphysical viewpoint. As a result, Aron argued, "Weber's philosophical scepticism entails the subjective character of historical science". This led to what was for Aron "the central idea of Weber's methodology" – his belief that "only the relations between facts freely chosen are capable of universal truth". In this way, Weber "finds a place for subjectivity and objectivity, for the will of the historian and the force of circumstances. And his polemic against those who deny either is impassioned". It was, therefore, easy to understand why he fought with such bitterness against opponents of the Right and the Left, and against metaphysicians as well as artists, for they "limit the scientist's freedom and distort the significance of his findings". For Weber, as Aron expressed it,

Selection must be arbitrary, because world-views are contradictory and our concepts are inadequate for the richness of reality. Relations of causality must be objective, because, otherwise, the reconstitution of the past would disintegrate into a multiplicity of irreconcilable points of view, since the world is unthinkable without determinate relations.[23]

Thus the "guiding principles" of the logic of Weber's sociology were "the rejection of metaphysics and the assertion of causality, and the subjectivity of selection and the objectivity of relationships".[24] Sociology, like history, involved "understanding", and the "conditions" of understandable action were "the facts of nature, physiological or biological phenomena (heredity), and incomprehensible human reactions". The sociologist had to be aware of these external influences on behaviour as "given" (données), but he should, "as a result of a free decision", concentrate on the sphere of intelligible actions. Because of his concern with "understanding", the sociologist should consider the realities which were the objects of his study as being in principle reducible to the events of individual consciousness, since we only understand consciousness and the only consciousness is individual. Again, like the historian, the sociologist had need of ideal types, which were concepts peculiar to the understanding of human action. The sociologist also had to relate understanding and causality: regular relationships in sociology were both intelligible, because they clarified men's motives, and in accord with the norms of causality, because they must always be verified by the facts and if possible statistically. Furthermore, the sociologist must normally be able to show that the particular men he claimed to understand were indeed acting in accordance with the ideal type.[25]

There were, of course, a number of problems in Weber's account which required clarification. For example, what exactly were the "law-like regularities" of sociology? What was the relationship between chance and probability? How could one reconcile the reduction of all social phenomena to individual or inter-individual events and the necessity to consider social wholes and collective realities? What were the types of behaviour on the basis of which one could construct ideal types? There were also ambiguities in Weber's attempt to distinguish "rational" and "emotional" understanding as well as in his four "types of action". Nevertheless, Aron was conscious of having presented an account of Weber's logic of the social sciences which was "almost entirely positive".[26]

Unlike Rickert and Simmel, however, Weber's logic was not based on some personal system or individual attitude. His critique was solidly grounded in what was both a political philosophy and a philosophy of life:

The impossibility of proving value-judgements is central to Weber's thought. The union of science and action rests on this fundamental assertion, which allows their co-operation because it justifies the distinction between them.

Weber's polemic against the intrusion of value-judgements in scientific research has a double origin in both theory and practice. He sought impartial understanding and a politics of the will. Science itself makes free decision necessary in the sphere of action, on condition that it does not go beyond the limits of objectivity. And science *must* respect these limits, in order to avoid the arbitrariness of metaphysics or of emotional preferences.[27]

126

Aron had sought to show, therefore, through his discussion of Weber, why science, thus defined, could never tell us how to act:

Science is partial. There is no formula which predetermines the movements of the whole. There is no predestined evolution. Even laws express the regularities of likely consequences (between different orders of social fact, and between a particular human attitude and its consequence), not necessary connections. The tendencies of evolution, which we flatter ourselves that we perceive, are at most only typical patterns that leave room for other possibilities in the world of things and for other wills in the world of men. Thus determinism invites freedom, and only fatalism necessitates resignation.

Above all we should remember that social determinism, even that of the economy, does not transcend human action; it is not comparable to the Hegelian dialectic, whose law escapes individual consciousness. Marxist dialectic, although it can become conscious, is, in origin and essence, supra-individual. Weber's sociology, on the other hand, in principle only knows those wholes which are reducible to the sum of individual events. This places it at once at the level of problems of action as they present themselves to the individual person. Certainly, there are, at any moment in history, basic facts (des données de fait) against which the individual can do nothing. Science teaches us to define the limits of the possible. But since Weber always asks, "What must *I* do?", even collective interests and massively stable realities are once again submitted to the judgements of our conscience . . .

At the same time the science of culture is indispensable for action. It teaches us the consequences which human decisions have had in the past, and the regular relation between specific attitudes and events. . . Science enables us to discover what we can do, not what we ought to do. It also reveals to us what we wish to do. It can make us form a precise idea of the end that we are pursuing and of the reasons for our preferences. Instead of vague formulations and sentimental desires, it obliges us to express in articulated judgements – judgements of fact and judgements of value – an attitude which perhaps tradition or instinct, rather than reflection, has suggested to us. How many political programmes would resist this double test of lucid formulation and confrontation with reality?

Such a politics could, it seems to me, be justly called a "politics of understanding", or alternatively a "politics of determinism and freedom". Into the tissue of causal relations the individual inserts his action which is, in its turn, a determining factor. If the determinism is human, if it is made up of partially interwoven necessities, the individual sees the field of action open to his initiative as limited, but not entirely removed. He uses the determinism instead of being its slave.[28]

Just as science could not tell us what goals we ought to seek, so no philosophy could establish for us a universally valid hierarchy of values. Each person had to take his own moral decisions, "with no other witness than his conscience". In fact, men were beset on all sides by fundamental contradictions and each man could only overcome them by following what Weber called his "god". In the political sphere, for example, did justice consist in the distribution of goods according to merit or in attempting to compensate for natural inequalities? Should one favour the development of an elite or give preference to social equality? "All the highest concepts – liberty, equality, justice – are the object of oppositions as irreducible as the rivalries between groups and the struggles between individuals".[29] Indeed, for Weber there was a "pitiless contest" between rival gods and it was out of this that arose the necessity of choice. "To be a human being is freely to give oneself a god. Life is a 'chain of ultimate choices through which man chooses his destiny'".[30]

As far as the philosophy of history was concerned, the implication of Weber's view was that any synthesis was impossible. Clearly, Aron pointed out, such a philosophy ran the risk of irrationalism, and it was only saved by a faith in science. For Aron, it avoided despair only by "a kind of ascetic heroism", with the result that man was "reconciled neither with his milieu, nor with himself" – a theme which Weber shared with Marx. Thus, Weber's refutation of historical materialism had been an attempt to show that the social relationships which had now become a part of man's destiny had been created by men's will. Similarly, Weber's studies of religion had taken as their starting-point the question: how far had man willed the society in which he was condemned to live? Finally, Weber had taken the question a step further in his sociology and asked: how had the choices, which men must all ultimately make, been resolved historically? What was the relationship between the determinism of men's circumstances and the influence of their will?

However, the fact remained, Aron argued, that Weber's philosophy of choice was as particularistic and relativist as other world-views.

If all choices are arbitrary and rooted in history, one has no "reasonable reason" for preferring one choice to another. Certainly, Weber accepts such anarchy and does not assert the superior value of his personal choice. But he does not proclaim that the analysis of the conditions in which men choose is any less true. Is it possible to reintroduce this truth, which is of a philosophical order, into a doctrine that only seeks to recognize science and the will?

Weber's philosophy is the epitome of a philosophy of understanding and of the individual. Is it adequate? . . . Weber had no need to go beyond it because his political will was attached to a partial reality (German greatness) and his human will to an inexhaustible value, but one stripped of all content: freedom. Marx, because he wanted to reconstitute the totality of man, located himself in a historical dialectic, oriented towards and by a human truth. Weber, on the contrary, steeled himself in an attitude of despair, as if to test his endurance: "Wievel ich aushalten kann" ("To see how much I can stand"). But if man wishes to think of himself as something other than a creature of chance, devoted to perishable ends, he must be capable, after the event, of considering his choice as valid and of overcoming the relativity of his decision through his becoming conscious of it. But philosophy is precisely this act of becoming conscious. This does not remove the conflicts through which men make their history, but saves individuals from solitude, since relativity understood is already relativity overcome.[31]

Despite this limitation, "the only legitimate formulation" of the critique of historical reason was, in Aron's view, Weber's, since he had asked, not, "Under what conditions is the science of history universally valid?", but, "What elements of the science of history are universally valid?" In other words, Weber's question was the self-same question that Aron had put to himself in connection with his life's project in 1931: what conclusions are independent of the particular perspective of the historian, governed as he is by the epoch in which he lives and the philosophy he espouses? Weber's achievement was that, unlike the other "critical philosophers of history", he had seen that, in Aron's words, "the critique of historical reason determines the limits and not the bases of historical objectivity".[32] However, although Weber had correctly reformulated the central problem of the critical philosophy of history, his own answer was, in spite of the advances made, too relativistic. Thus, the position Aron had reached at the end of his complementary thesis was that the problem had been properly posed. The task now was to investigate further the question of the limits of historical objectivity and in so doing to move beyond Weber, away from relativism and nearer truth.

Introduction to the Philosophy of History

It was to this task that Aron turned in his principal thesis, the *Introduction to the Philosophy of History*.[33] All the charges that can be levelled against the complementary thesis – turgidity, abstruseness and aridity – can be made with equal justification against the second and more important work. Indeed, other criticisms can be added: Aron's meaning is often ambiguous and the writing contains too many high-flown passages which do little to advance the argument. Nevertheless, this forbidding and indigestible treatise is the theoretical fulfilment of Aron's life project as he had defined it at the beginning of the decade. Furthermore, as we shall see, the book quickly became a classic of its kind in France, although, when an English translation, poor in quality and containing no introduction, suddenly appeared in 1961, it met with incomprehension and even hostility from surprised British critics.

As its sub-title *An Essay on the Limits of Historical Objectivity* implied, Aron's purpose in the *Introduction to the Philosophy of History* was strictly epistemological.[34] Since the "critical philosophers of history" had failed to establish the fundamental principles of a universally valid science of history, Aron was now concerned to "replace the search for *fundamental principles* by the search for *limits*".[35] It was not his intention to see how far "historical knowledge measures up to some *a priori* criterion", or to try to "reduce it to a type of knowledge asserted in advance as the only truly scientific one". On the contrary, his aim was to use a "descriptive" or "phenomenological" method in an attempt to trace what he called the "natural movement" from knowledge of self to knowledge of collective development. Aron began, then, by making a distinction, which is now commonplace but was not widely accepted in France at the time, between the historical (human or social) sciences and the natural sciences. Thus he refused, he wrote, to separate knowledge and reality, because man's consciousness of the past was "an essential characteristic of history itself".[36] Unlike the natural world, human history was for man "not something external, but the essence of his being".[37] Consequently, it was crucial to distinguish between the *understanding* of human meaning and the *explanation* of the natural world ("We understand Kepler's laws, but we explain nature"), although Aron would, he stated, be primarily concerned with the distinction between understanding and causality – the "establishment of causal rules according to the regularity with which phenomena succeed one another".[38]

Aron therefore began his second study by attempting to go back to "the source of all understanding and meaning, namely lived experience and reflection".[39] This involved a discussion of what was meant by knowledge of self, knowledge of others, knowledge of a collective reality and, finally, historical knowledge. Knowledge of self implied that "at every moment we inevitably recreate the self by connecting the past to the present. In this way retrospective knowledge and choice, acceptance of the given and the effort to transcend it, are joined in an ever-renewed dialectic. One discovers oneself through action as well as through introspection".[40]

The discussion of knowledge of others which followed was clearly influenced by the writings of Alfred Schutz, whose *Der sinnhafte Aufbau der sozialen Welt* (*The Phenomenology of the Social World*) Aron had reviewed with apparent approval a few years earlier.[41] Between knowledge of self and knowledge of others there were, Aron wrote, both similarities and discrepancies:

In the first place...it is clear that each of us develops his own idea of himself through contact with others...But if my knowledge of myself is bound up with the knowledge that others have of me or that I have of others, there exists a real opposition between the perspective of the observer and that of the actor, between the construction of each one of us by and for himself and the construction of a person by and for an observer. One can come close to a person's effective identity by grasping their personal style, but the fact remains that one *lives* one's own experiences and that one knows the experiences of others *objectified*.[42]

130

Up to this point, Aron had, he continued, deliberately simplified his analysis by artificially isolating individuals from their "social or spiritual community". But to talk of a "society" implied the existence of "an explicit or tacit agreement, a common belief-system" between individuals, and human communication took place, of course, "within collectivities which penetrate and govern elementary relations".[43] Thus, "it is in and through individuals that common representations become clear, and in and through them that communities are realized which always precede and transcend individuals". However, this observation "justifies no metaphysic, either of *national souls* or of a *collective consciousness*, but it does confirm the existence of a reality both transcending men and within them – a reality which is social and spiritual, total and multiple".[44]

Lastly, Aron came to the question of historical knowledge. Historical knowledge lacked that sharing of consciousness which could exist between contemporaries. Communication with people in the past remained "strictly intellectual". The historian might reconstruct a person's ideas or values, but only rarely did he succeed in portraying feelings and emotions. This did not, however, imply that historical knowledge is always inadequate. Certainly, "the impression that only actual presence can give, the trivial yet significant details, the individual's personal style . . . all of this gradually sinks into oblivion". Yet this was not an irremediable loss, for "that which affects us most is not necessarily that which merits survival".[45]

What, then, by way of summary of this part of the argument, was the relationship between historical knowledge and knowledge of self, others and collective reality?

Historical knowledge is *part*, it is a *means*, of the knowledge of self. I discover the past of my collectivity partly in myself: when I interest myself in it, . . . I am trying to find out how my collectivity became what it is, how it made me what I am. Moreover, if I am, first and foremost, what my milieu and my environment have made me, if I do not spontaneously distinguish between the ideas I have received and *my* ideas, I am condemned to explore the world of mankind in order to show what perhaps makes me unique, and what, in any case, is mine, essentially because I have sanctioned it by my choice.[46]

The "fundamental idea" that emerged from Aron's discussion was that of the "dissolution of the object". "No such thing as a *historical reality* exists ready-made, so that science merely has to reproduce it faithfully. Historical reality, because it is human, is *ambiguous* and *inexhaustible*".[47] In other words, "theory precedes history".[48] The "plurality of interpretations" – the fact that many different interpretations of history are possible – was, therefore, "incontestable".[49] Nevertheless, he rejected

131

the argument that the study of history was invalidated by the impossibility of understanding other people's motives and intentions. On the contrary, to Aron, implicitly following Weber, it was not only possible, but indeed essential, for us to grasp other people's motives through rational understanding, by putting ourselves in their place and determining what they knew and intended.

Aron turned next to the question of causality in history and sociology. In his view, sociology attempted to "establish laws (or at least regularities or generalities)", whereas history was "limited to narrating events in their particular sequence".[50] History concentrated on "the antecedents of a particular fact", while sociology was concerned with "the causes of a fact which may be repeated".[51] Not that sociological and historical causality were mutually exclusive; on the contrary, they implied one another. Indeed, sociology could be defined as "the discipline which demonstrates general relationships between historical facts".[52]

This view led Aron to take issue with Durkheim, who in *The Rules of Sociological Method* had tried to draw a fundamental distinction between "society" and "history", and between "present" and "past". However, such distinctions seemed to Aron to be "vague and, frankly, not very intelligible", because "one cannot understand the present state of a collectivity without referring to its past, and without analysing that interdependence which always exists between different institutions".[53] Durkheim, Aron argued, was guilty of an "anti-historical sociological realism":

He seems to think of each society as an independent, self-contained whole. Furthermore, for him the sole object of scientific study is not society, as we see it in its concrete complexity, but the *social species* and its *constitutive characteristics*. He imagines that this enables him to ignore all the accidents that are evident in history. The real nature of collective life is caused by the *inner environment* and, in the last analysis, by social "density" (material and dynamic), which is then sanctified as the primary fact.

But how can such a claim be justified? How is it possible to define the idea of *primary fact*, or *factor determining the evolution of the collectivity*? Of course, Durkheim states these things in positive terms: a fact is primary when it is general enough to explain many others. But, on this account, the economic system, or technology, is also a primary fact. No one doubts the possibility of establishing any number of relationships in which "density" is the cause: such "density" might regularly entail some political, economic or moral phenomenon, but it, in its turn, requires explanation. Why, therefore, should it be primary? Why the only determining factor?[54]

In reality, such an assumption, Aron contended, served to hide "the prime necessity of selection, and the fragmentary character of sociological determinism", for there was in Durkheim an unwillingness to recognize that "sociological relations are, in so far as they are causal, scattered (dispersées), because they are not organized, like physical laws, into a deductive system". Nor, it seemed to Aron, could it be said that in *The Division of Labour* Durkheim had succeeded in demonstrating the thesis put forward in *The Rules of Sociological Method*, for *The Division of Labour* was guilty of the same errors:

In the first place, the demonstration relies on one of those striking dichotomies which Durkheim loved and used with exaggerated dialectical ingenuity. What are the causes of the division of labour?, he asks. Individual or social? Boredom, the desire for increased wealth – the hypothesis is inadequate. Only social causes are left, and in particular a cause internal to the structure of collective life, namely its volume and density. In reality, the very terms in which Durkheim poses the problem seem to us inexact. In fact, the division of labour, taken as a whole, does not represent a determinable and isolatable fact. Perhaps there is no point in looking for the causes of a global phenomenon which affects contemporary societies as a whole. In any case, it would be more appropriate to analyse the different manifestations of the phenomenon in order to discover its regular antecedent or antecedents. Now, Durkheim does not proceed to this systematic review (one can conceive of other hypotheses than the desire for happiness, or boredom, or social volume), and he poses another, specifically historical, question, namely: how was the transition made from primitive groups to the division of labour? It is as if he were sure in advance that all societies have gone through the same stages and obeyed the same laws, and that it is scientifically possible to reveal *the* cause of the historical process *as a whole*. Clearly, Durkheim is a prisoner of the old philosophies of history which he claims to be replacing with science; but he has not abandoned their premises, even though they are alien to scientific practice. The alternative of *individual or society* is as arbitrary as the alternative of *history or society*.[55]

Durkheim therefore seemed to be "the prisoner of an almost metaphysical realism",[56] because he thought that the development of history as a whole had to be explained by a single primary factor. For Aron, on the other hand, it was necessary to begin by analysing wholes into their elements and then try to establish the connections between them; and this was precisely what Weber, unlike Durkheim, had sought to do.

No one, Aron declared, had stressed the necessity of selection more strongly than Weber. Although his questions in *Economy and Society* were very general (for instance, what influence does the economy have on law, and what influence do religion and political constitutions have on the economy?), his answers – and this seemed to Aron crucial – were not general but specific. Even if it was impossible to say in any absolute sense how the political system influenced the economy, one could ask, for example, what effect charismatic power had on economic rationalization. However, the relationships were never those of necessity. Thus, for Weber, as Aron put it, "Protestantism *favours*, it *does not determine*, economic behaviour of a capitalist kind".[57] In other words, Aron argued, causal relations and "laws" in sociology are at most "partial and probable".[58]

It was not justifiable, therefore, to talk in terms of the *primacy* of any one cause. Claims such as "ideas rule the world" or "the relations of production constitute the determining factor in the evolution of history"[59] were, Aron maintained, "as banal as they were debated", but they had "rarely been subjected to criticism".[60] How valid, for instance, was the Marxist claim that the forces of production are the primary or exclusive or predominant factor in history? How could the proposition that the relations of production *determine* society as a whole be proved? One might try to show that a certain state of the "relations of production" regularly leads to a certain kind of "political regime" or "ideology", but this was not in fact the case: "equally developed capitalist regimes are combined with the most varying political constitutions, and the constitutions sometimes change in a country without these changes coinciding with or following economic transformations. Political evolution, for example, has a certain autonomy, although it does largely depend on economic evolution".[61] And if one attempted a historical proof, how would one know when one had arrived at the *true* or *final* cause, and what meaning could be given to the expression "in the last analysis"? It was, however, justifiable to "*describe* a society by starting with the relations of production, even though this legitimacy must be based on arguments external to causality, and the fruitfulness of the method varies, perhaps, with different societies".[62]

It might nevertheless be objected, Aron continued, that the search for a one-directional cause did violence to the idea of *dialectical* thought, according to which a cause could also be an effect and different historical forces acted upon one another. Aron was willing to accept this notion of reciprocal action, for it was certainly necessary to recognize the influence of the political and economic systems on one another.[63] However, it was inadequate simply to talk in general terms of a "reciprocal action"; instead, it was essential to engage in a detailed analysis and ask precisely how these influences were exerted. After all, no one doubted "the considerable influence of the economy in historical development". At the same time:

many ideological, religious or political phenomena do not appear to have an economic factor as their predominant cause. (What economic cause is sufficient to explain the transition from polytheism to monotheism? the evolution of modern physics? the Crusades or the Wars of Religion?) In the end, we keep coming back to the same argument: one has to weigh up the influence of different antecedents in each situation. How can we formulate in advance a single, unchanging conclusion to what are specific judgements?[64]

Not that he was claiming, Aron added, to have "refuted Marxism". Certainly, he had tried to refute the kind of causal analysis proffered by vulgar Marxism, but not the "anthropological" Marxism that was characterized by "a particular conception of man, rather than the efficacy of a particular cause".[65] Nevertheless – and this, he declared, might serve as the conclusion to his whole study – "*There is no prime mover of the total historical process*".[66]

However, the notion of cause was not incompatible with the study of mankind and history. It was sometimes said, for instance, that the accidents of history prevented one from inferring connections of cause and effect. Aron rejected this argument: there was "a constant bond" between cause and effect and an "intrinsic intelligibility" between motive and act. A more serious objection might be that it was impossible to state laws comparable to those of nature because of the "contingent, individual and free" character of historical events. But while granting that "accident plays a special part in history", Aron retorted that such an objection was "part and parcel of an already outmoded epistemology. Science no longer recognizes those absolute rules which force themselves on the world, as though decreed by a Creator".[67] Nor did the question of "free will" create insuperable difficulties, either:

As Max Weber pointed out, the typical act of free will is the reasonable act. This act is also the most understandable in terms of motives, and the one most likely to recur in so far as the situation to which it corresponds may be repeated. Metaphysical freedom, then, compromises neither prediction nor explanation – on the contrary.

There is no doubt that someone who believes in freedom will tend to attribute less importance to deterministic interpretations. He will question their validity since, as he sees it, things might have been otherwise. But usually, without being fully conscious of it, the philosopher is thinking of a historical freedom which has nothing to do with apparent metaphysical problems; he is thinking, that is, of the effect of chance encounters, or the power of men (and especially of individual wills). The necessity he denies...is one of institutions or collective movements. We admit that there may be some kind of affinity between metaphysical and historical necessity (or contingency): but that is all.[68]

Aron was nonetheless at pains to stress that his argument did not, as might be thought, imply moral relativism. It had become commonplace, for instance, to point to the obvious truth that moral rules vary with historical periods, societies and cultures. Historicism of this kind implied that it was impossible to arrive at any universally valid moral laws, or hold moral beliefs which were not the mere product of a social structure. But historicism, it seemed to Aron, substituted the myth of development for the myth of progress: "There is the same resignation to anonymous fate, but instead of the confident optimism that the future will be better than the present, there is a sort of pessimism or agnosticism. The process of history is indifferent to the desires of men, at least to their rational or moral wishes. The future will be different, neither better nor worse".[69]

In order to free oneself from such historicism, the first step was to "overcome fatalism":

The totality of history does not exist in itself, but for us. We compose it of the fragments collected and organized retrospectively by the unity of our interest or the unity we attribute to periods or cultures. Immediate observation shows us... the gaps in necessity. The discontinuity of the causal web leaves room for action, and the incompleteness and diversity of worlds leave room for personal decisions.

The power of history, it is true, is not entirely a myth. In social transformations, man stakes not merely his comfort or his freedom, but gambles with his very soul... Nevertheless, the dissolution of historical totality allows one to overcome resignation because it reveals the freedom and the duty of choice, and it allows one to triumph over nihilism through objective knowledge and philosophical reflection.[70]

Even if it were not possible to decide conclusively between different opinions, it was possible to reflect on them in order to "determine the conditions under which the individual, in practice and in theory, makes choices, commits himself and acts". This involved an analysis of "the historical nature of political thought and, above all, of the two decisive steps: *choice* and *action*".[71] However, one of the obstacles which prevented the recognition of the historical nature of politics was the positivist belief in a rationalist science of society or morality. The danger was that such a sociology would degenerate into sociologism; society would be set up as an absolute value and, as a result, "submission to the new divinity would be just as sacred as before". Furthermore, Aron rejected the claim that problems of political or moral theory and practice were primarily technical and could therefore be solved by technical means, on analogies drawn from industry or medicine, for it was a misconception to think of society as "coherent and unequivocal" and sociology as "total and systematic".[72] Moreover:

it is a strange illusion, all the more deep-rooted because it will not stand up to examination, to suppose that one will succeed in establishing, on rationalist principles, the image of a society obeying eternal rules and based on unselfishness, generosity and freedom.

Take, for example, current problems of the economy. To put it schematically, two systems of regulation are possible: one spontaneous, through the free action of prices in the market, the other deliberate, in accordance with a plan. In the first case, the capital needed for investment is supplied by personal savings, in the second by capital levies fixed by the administration of the plan. As well as implying profits, a self-regulated economy implies considerable inequality. A planned economy allows less inequality, but it requires strong power in order to determine, in accordance with collective needs (with a political conception of those needs), the share of the national income assigned each year to the various categories of citizens. The choice between these two systems is decisive: is a compromise, based on reason, conceivable? Not at all.

The choice can be made from various standpoints: the system which ensures greatest production is perhaps the most unjust or the one which allows the least personal independence. Fanatics try to conceal this plurality – their system would, they say, be the most effective, the most harmonious, the most just; it would do away with economic crises, poverty, and the exploitation of man. But such naive claims fail to grasp the basic facts. A just (or more just) society will, at the outset, have to sacrifice liberalism to equality and discipline. Even if it is stated that the contradictory claims of today will all be satisfied in the long run, risks must be taken. The order of the sacrifices to be made will depend on the nature of one's priorities.

The relations between men, whether economic or political, pose specific problems, which are not reducible to the abstract laws of ethics. Let us assume, with one philosophical tradition, that every individual is free because he has a certain capacity for judgement: how is one to specify those liberties to which he has a right, and those which he is prepared to give up momentarily in order to attain a particular goal? Concrete definitions are always taken from a historical reality and not from abstract necessity. In other words, . . . one either remains in the empyrean of empty principles, or else slips into making deductions from specific instances valid only for one time.

Let us add that one never has to choose between two ideal systems – self-regulated and planned – but between imperfect forms. At a certain moment in the evolution of capitalism, one must decide for or against the system, or for a specific reform. During periods of calm, when the established regime is not in question, a kind of politics of ideas, beloved of certain intellectuals, comes into its own; it formulates the ideal conceived by the existing society, or expresses a particular concrete claim. But during times of crisis, political choices reveal their true nature as historical choices. We take sides, join one class against another, or prefer the disadvantages of anarchy to those of tyranny. The illusion of the rationalist lies not so much in failing to recognize reality, as in clinging to the hope that he is, in spite of everything, choosing rationally. In truth, one chooses at and for a specific moment: it is not real liberalism one is rejecting, but decadent liberalism. One is not condemning parliament as such, so much as a corrupt parliamentarianism . . . [73]

The "science" of history, therefore, did not imply a deterministic fatalism but a concern with "observed regularities" – that is, "the relatively stable facts of a situation". These comprised: (i) elementary (or microscopic) regularities, connected with certain basic human impulses; (ii) historical and social regularities, characteristic of all collective organizations (e.g. class or group conflicts); and (iii) the causal relations analysed earlier. All these regularities, Aron emphasized, were partial and fragmentary, and their selection had an "inevitably political character". This raised once more the question of "the dialectic which has been at the centre of our work, . . . the dialectic of contemplation and action".[74] For it was not, Aron maintained, a question of *whether* politics had to draw on history, but of *how* it had to do so. This did not, however, imply that it was impossible to analyse the content of different doctrines, because although the historical nature of politics and of morality precluded any scientific pretensions, reflection was still possible.

Political choice, Aron argued, involved two distinct steps. The first – choice of a party – "requires me to recognize, within society as it is, those objectives which are attainable and desirable, or, again, the regime which could succeed the present one". The second step – joining a party – "assumes that I accept the members of a party or class as my fellows, and that I commit myself fully, rather than formulate a wish or express a preference. Not that one always proceeds from what one foresees or desires to an act of will".[75]

The content of political choice lay between conservatism, reform and revolution, although a conservative with any degree of intelligence was "to some extent always a reformer". The revolutionary, on the other hand, did not so much have a programme as "an *ideology*, that is, an image of another system, surpassing the existing one and probably unrealizable":

If . . . one were to restrict oneself to ideologies, one would automatically side with the revolutionaries, for they normally promise more than the others . . . Imagination, with all its resources, inevitably triumphs over reality, even when the latter is distorted and transfigured by lies. This explains the prejudice of intellectuals in favour of so-called progressive parties . . . Without the slightest doubt, all hitherto known societies have been unjust (in terms of present-day conceptions of justice). It remains to be seen what would constitute a just society, assuming such a thing were definable and realizable . . . Between partial predictions and future totality, there is still a vast margin – the margin of ignorance, and perhaps of freedom . . .

It would be too simple to say that one chooses the lesser of two evils, or that one chooses the unknown: let us say that a choice always implies sacrifices and that one chooses *against* something when one chooses revolution.[76]

Hence Aron's implicit preference for the modest and undogmatic "politics of understanding (entendement)", as exemplified by Weber, rather than the omniscient "politics of Reason" of the Marxists, "the confidants of Providence".[77] For, in an age of "blind allegiances", it was important for individuals not to think of the object of their political commitment as somehow "revealed" to them like a religious faith, but to see it as the result of a choice based on probability; and political commitments should not, like transcendental religions, divide the world into two opposing realms. It was the uncertain nature of our opinions that Aron wished to emphasize, rather than the absolute nature of our political commitments. As long as there was room for discussion, it was better to remember that no humanity was possible without tolerance, and the possession of the whole truth was granted to no one.[78]

After an epistemologically obscure and, it must be said, unconvincing passage in which he asserted that the individual, by exercising his capacity for reflection and choice, overcomes the relativity of history by the absolute of decision, Aron ended by reaffirming his faith in freedom, though a freedom tempered by realism:

Freedom, possible in theory, effective in and through practice, is never complete. The individual's past limits the margin in which personal initiative is effective, and his historical situation conditions the possibilities of political action...[79]

Aron then concluded with these words:

Human existence is dialectic, that is, dramatic, since it is active in an incoherent world, commits itself despite the transitoriness of time (la durée), and seeks an elusive truth, with no other guarantee than partial understanding and formal reflection.[80]

However, a philosophical inquiry such as this, Aron admitted in a final footnote, could not come to any conclusion in the strict sense. To try to go any further would require "a concrete interpretation of the existing situation of man and philosophy", but "that would be the object of another book".[81] Indeed, as Aron was to explain many years later, "The *Introduction to the Philosophy of History* represented, to my way of thinking, only one chapter, the most formal one, in the theory of historical knowledge. At the time, I was hoping to add to this introduction a theory of the social sciences, than a more concrete theory of historical interpretations – interpretations of epochs, civilizations, and the development of humanity". "Events", however, (i.e. the Second World War) distracted him from completing "this huge programme".[82] Nevertheless, the foundations for his life's work had been laid. Not only is Aron's philosophy of history implicit both in his wartime writings for *La France libre* and his post-war journalism; it is also, as we shall see, explicitly central to the

139

three major works he was to publish in the decade between the end of the war and his appointment to the Sorbonne in 1955 – *Le Grand Schisme* (*The Great Schism*), [83] *Les Guerres en chaîne* (*The Century of Total War*), [84] and *L'Opium des intellectuels* (*The Opium of the Intellectuals*).[85]

The Defence of the Theses

Aron defended his two theses in March 1938, and it is possible to reconstruct in considerable detail what he and his examiners said on that occasion, for two reasons. The first is that in 1938 the *Revue de métaphysique et de morale* decided to revive its former practice of publishing anonymous accounts of the defence of notable doctoral theses, and it began with Aron's.[86] Secondly, one of those present in the audience was his friend Gaston Fessard, a Jesuit, who made "several pages of notes" which, thirty years later, still survived.[87] Fessard used the summary in the *Revue de métaphysique et de morale*, which in his view was accurate, as the basis for his own account, but complemented it from his own record, arguing that, with the passage of time, his version could afford to be less reticent about the reactions of the venerable professors who comprised Aron's jury. The result was that, using both sources, Fessard was able to reconstruct a remarkably full account of the exchanges that took place during the examination of Aron's two theses and give a vivid impression of the tense atmosphere at the time.[88]

The actual date of this "historic joust", as Fessard called it, in which Aron was "the young *contestataire*, facing the members of a jury representing maturity and knowledge", was 26 March 1938 – that is, thirteen days after Hitler had proclaimed the *Anschluss* of Austria.[89] Because of Aron's three years in Germany, he was especially well-equipped to judge the likely consequences of Hitler's action, and Fessard points out that Aron introduced the first of his two theses, the *Essai sur la théorie de l'histoire dans l'Allemagne contemporaine*, "in a personal manner and with a personal emphasis that are barely visible in the account in the *Revue de métaphysique et de morale*". In this "charged and anguished atmosphere", Aron's "direct tone", and the fact that he was dealing with problems of German philosophy, helped create the unmistakable impression of a "confrontation", however courteous, and of a "clash between generations".[90]

Over thirty years later, in his Inaugural Lecture at the Collège de France, Aron himself recalled his feelings at the time:

I reproached the second generation of Durkheimians (Marcel Mauss, François Simiand and Maurice Halbwachs) not so much for their socialism, which was hardly subversive, as for the serenity of their choice, their unshakeable optimism, their indifference to Marx, and their tendency to neglect the sometimes inexpiable struggles between classes, parties and ideas...[91]

The rise of National Socialism in pre-Hitler Germany and the revelation of politics in its diabolical essence forced me to argue against myself, against my intimate preferences; it inspired in me a sort of revolt against the instruction I had received at the university, against the spirituality of philosophers, and against the tendency of certain sociologists to misconstrue the impact of regimes with the pretext of focusing on permanent and deep realities. How superficial were parliamentary developments when Hitler's coming to power foreshadowed a world war! How secondary were economic mechanisms when the Great Depression, with its millions of unemployed, was prolonged because of mistakes that today's students, even before graduating in political economy, could easily discern! ...The mood of my generation did not fit in with this attitude – one which was both resigned and confident, and still related to the positivism of Auguste Comte: an acceptance of a social determinism comparable to natural determinism, and an ineradicable optimism as to the eventual outcome...[92]

Just before the defence of my thesis, in 1938, Paul Fauconnet expressed surprise at the emotive tone of my *Introduction to the Philosophy of History* and questioned me about the reasons for my anguish. At the time, as I brooded on the near future, I was surprised at his surprise, or rather I felt indignant at the lack of historical awareness of professional sociologists...[93]

"...It is science and human industry that are superior, and not subject, to fate...it is this, without a shadow of a doubt, that will save humanity from the moral and material crisis in which it is struggling" (Marcel Mauss)...

Without a shadow of a doubt...Industry serves any end, including rationalizing the putting to death of defenceless men by men in arms.

It was against these values, or rather against the confidence, which seemed to me naive, in the inevitable realization of these values, that I rebelled, on leaving the University – a revolt against the professional sociologists who, before 1914, announced the withering away of the military functions of the state and, prior to 1939, had no presentiment of the age of contempt.[94]

The jury for Aron's complementary thesis, *Essai sur la théorie de l'histoire dans l'Allemagne contemporaine*, consisted of his supervisor, Célestin Bouglé, Paul Fauconnet, Professor of Sociology at the Sorbonne, and the Germanist, Edmond Vermeil. The scene was the Salle Liard at the Sorbonne and Aron began, as was the custom, by presenting a summary of his argument:

The starting-point for my work is a reflection on the Marxist philosophy of history, whose precursor was Hegel. But after the break-up of the Hegelian school into Right and Left Hegelianism and the collapse of absolute idealism, a whole movement of thought developed in Germany. This sought to replace the philosophy of history by an analysis of historical knowledge, in the way that Kant had sought to provide a critique of dogmatic metaphysics, and thus establish a new metaphysics. Dilthey, Rickert and Simmel are the representatives of this movement; it normally goes under the name of the "critique of historical reason", and the work of Max Weber in a sense marks its culmination.

Hence my first problem: what is the meaning and value of historical reason? Can it replace philosophy? The intention of the historical study I undertake in examining these four writers is philosophical. In my thesis, therefore, you will not find any attempt to explain their ideas in terms of their social context or circumstances, even though the kind of insight thus offered is not without value, as is shown for instance by Dilthey's use of biography and Max Weber's recourse to Protestant asceticism in order to account for the genesis of capitalism. I have been concerned above all to bring out the logical significance of these thinkers: is it, or is it not, possible to take historical reason as a basis for philosophy?

From this arose a second problem: since the four philosophers were concerned with the same question, it seemed to me that the best way to proceed was to present a rigorous reconstruction of their doctrines in their own terms, whilst considering each thinker and almost each language in its own right and at the same time showing the unity of the problem and the complementary nature of their solutions.

The essential result of this investigation serves as an introduction to my principal thesis. In fact, it shows above all, in particular thanks to Dilthey, the necessity of moving beyond positivism, engaging once again in speculation and then analysing its limits, since Rickert's failure signifies that there is a science of the particular and Simmel's that there is an unbridgeable gap between the fact itself and the account that is given of it. Finally, Weber leads us to the conclusion that the critique of historical reason does not succeed in specifying the conditions which make a historical science possible. Since the historian always engages his very being, as well as his philosophy, in his work, the search for the limits of historical objectivity must replace the search for its bases. In other words, the problem now is: to what extent can there be a valid science of the past?[95]

It was Bouglé who, after congratulating Aron on his personal qualities as well as the merits of his work, opened the attack. Aron was, he remarked, an adept at dismembering other people's work in order to suit his own purposes, and his style was highly compressed and at times even obscure. Furthermore, Aron had treated Simmel as a sceptic and failed to give an account of his important contribution to sociology. It was also necessary to clarify the distinction between "understanding" ("compréhension") and "explanation" ("explication"), as well as the relation between historicism and the critical philosophy of history.[96]

However, it was the orthodox Durkheimian, Paul Fauconnet, who seemed particularly disconcerted by Aron's theses. Aron's work was "honest and loyal", but Fauconnet could not see where it was leading. He could not decide whether Aron was possessed by the devil or had lost all hope ("un satanique ou un désespéré"). Aron criticized earlier sociologists, but muddled up all sorts of questions – historical, critical, political and metaphysical – perhaps because he was discomfited by Marxism. In addition, Weber's notion of "charisma" was, in Fauconnet's view, "grotesque and preposterous" ("baroque et saugrenue"). Nevertheless, Fauconnet ended with these words: "I conclude with an act of charity, in repeating to you my admiration and my friendship; an act of faith in the value of the theses you condemn; and an act of hope, the hope that future generations will not follow in your footsteps".[97]

Finally, the third member of the jury, the Germanist Edmond Vermeil, congratulated Aron on having thrown light on an important aspect of Germany's intellectual tragedy. He also admired the way in which Aron drew his conclusions together and the skill with which he paraphrased German philosophical terminology.[98]

There was now an interval before Aron defended his principal thesis, the *Introduction to the Philosophy of History*, of which the three examiners were his supervisor Léon Brunschvicg, the historian Emile Bréhier, and the sociologist Maurice Halbwachs. The audience had by now grown larger and even more attentive as Aron proceeded to outline his argument in what Fessard calls "the most direct manner possible":

Why am I a socialist? What does it mean to have a political position? These are the questions I put to myself while studying Marxism and political economy. It quickly became clear to me that, where such questions are concerned, desire and knowledge are mutually limiting and determining. But to state that judgements of value and judgements of reality are connected in this way raised a larger problem, one which was prior to the determination of political will: the problem of sociological and historical knowledge. The critique of historical thought and the logic of political thought condition one another. Hence my central thesis: the relativity of historical knowledge shows us the moment at which decision intervenes. In order to establish this thesis, I applied the phenomenological method to the subject who discovers history. Such a method shows that the subject of historical knowledge is not a pure subject, a transcendental I, but a living man, a historic I, who seeks to understand his past and his social circumstances. Such a profession of relativity is not anti-scientific, but it implies that causal relations are not the only ones in sociology. Both before and after they are posited, factors intervene which are not reducible to science, because science, by its very method, strives to eliminate them. Being fragmentary, causal relations require a synthesis of another kind: the *understanding* (compréhension) that entails elements which are objective but not purely scientific, because a plurality of perspectives is always possible and the past is constantly being renewed as it grows more distant. This is the basis of relativism. In other words, one always does history in terms of a philosophy, for otherwise one would be faced with an incoherent plurality of possible interpretations.

This implies that the general thrust of this thesis is, certainly, anti-scientist and anti-positivist. It does not, however, plunge us back into the arbitrariness or "anarchism" of individual preferences where practical decisions are involved, nor into an irremediable scepticism as far as philosophy is concerned. In life, decisions intervene that one can justify, but with other than scientific reasons. I have tried, therefore, to re-establish a sphere of validity for concrete man, by showing that, beyond science, philosophical reflection is possible; but this reflection is itself a function of history. In saying that there is no historical truth in history, I am neither driven to despair, because thinking is not everything – there is also the sphere of action; nor am I possessed by the devil simply because I have eliminated a certain number of ideologies that time seems to have condemned – for example, the idea of indefinite progress embracing the whole of society, or the belief that man's vocation consists of only two activities, objective research and pure contemplation. Though my book is a theory of historical knowledge, it is also an introduction to political science. It invites one to renounce the abstractions of moralism and ideology, in order to try to determine the true content of possible choices that are limited by reality itself. In conclusion, I have attempted to define the features of an attitude which ultimately attains the very essence of our activity as human beings. Since not all social science is content to establish causal relations, and since all historical knowledge presupposes a philosophy of history, we are all philosophers of history. We are not dealing with a specialism, then, but with the experience of human life. The philosophy of history is that part of the consciousness we have of ourselves, when we seek to live while reflecting on the influences that shape our lives.[99]

As supervisor of the principal thesis, Brunschvicg was the first to speak. Having expressed his admiration for Aron's talent, he did not hide his disappointment, both at the way in which Aron chopped up his problems and at the apparent gap between Aron's thought and his own. Aron, for example, contrasted ideology and dialectic. For Aron, the latter meant "a dramatic process lacking unity", whereas for Brunschvicg it was "a unity lacking drama". Brunschvicg was also anxious to hear Aron explain rather than justify himself, as was usual in the defence of a thesis.[100]

"I asked myself", Aron replied, "what it is to know oneself and others in history. And, beginning with the simplest forms of understanding, I arrived, not at a methodology of history, but a transcendental theory of knowledge...Having cleared the ground with a work which is above all critical, it becomes possible to pose the real question for the philosophy of history: what is the meaning for man of his own destiny? What is his destiny?"

"And what", asked Brunschvicg, "is your conclusion?"

"I have tried to follow through the implications of atheism and build from there, on the assumption that capitalism and progressive rationalization can disappear. Thus, I believe that I have shown the necessity of rediscovering a faith in man and seeking to understand our historical situation".[101]

On hearing this, Brunschvicg remarked that he preferred the philosophy of Voltaire in his *Essai sur les moeurs* and Condorcet's *Esquisse d'un tableau historique des progrès de l'esprit humain.*

144

The gap between the generations was again particularly evident when Aron was questioned by the historian, Emile Bréhier, with whom the dialogue at once took "an abrupt form". It seemed to him strange that Aron's essay on historical criticism should also claim to be an introduction to political science. Like Aron's other examiners, he objected to the way in which Aron had cut up his subject-matter into questions and sub-sections, thus, in Bréhier's view, losing any connecting thread. Furthermore whereas, say, the philosophy of mathematics concerned itself with mathematics, history seemed to be missing from Aron's philosophy of history. Aron, he continued, argued that the writing of history implied decision and choice, whereas to Bréhier the historian must be "*sine ira et studio*". He therefore put to Aron the direct question, "Ought the historian to be impartial?" To which Aron replied that it was possible to talk about impartiality in a psychological sense, in so far as each person "reconstructs the history of his truth", but from a logical viewpoint impartiality was "an illusion".[102]

Lastly, the sociologist, Maurice Halbwachs, focused on the relationship between history and sociology in Aron's account, sociology being, in Halbwachs' view, "superior" to history because it operated at a macroscopic level of analysis rather than the microscopic level of history. But Aron disputed this, arguing that one could say the very opposite – that sociology was the handmaid of history. The search for general relations in sociology implied an analysis of the particular and this involved the use of history. At the same time, historical analysis was only adequate if it went beyond disparate relations in order to recreate them as larger wholes, "thus enabling us to reconstitute the concrete development of humanity".[103]

Despite the hostility he had aroused in the eyes of some of his jury members, Aron was awarded his doctorate with *mention très honorable*. Even Fauconnet was generous enough to acknowledge that the *Introduction to the Philosophy of History* revealed "a verbal and intellectual virtuosity, and a steadfastness of purpose in the research, which placed its author in the very first rank". Fessard himself was left with the impression that Aron's examiners were like hens which have hatched a duckling and then watch in terror as it rushes towards the water, "to move with ease in an element unknown to them". Aron too, he believes, must have had something of the same feeling, because a few days later Aron wrote to him in reply to his letter of congratulation: "I didn't get the impression that my jury understood me and I am not sure that I explained myself clearly... But perhaps this is always the case in such matters".[104]

The Reception of the Philosophy of History

"The *Introduction* surprised the members of the jury", Aron wrote forty years later, "but the three leading judges at the University – Henri Bergson, Léon Brunschvicg, and Lucien Lévy-Bruhl – expressed, both publicly and privately, flattering or indulgent opinions. As a thesis, but also in the intellectual world at large, the book was a success".[105] Although it did not receive the prize for the best thesis of 1938 – that honour went to Henri Marrou, one of the earliest champions of Aron's philosophy of history, for his *Saint Augustin et la fin de la culture antique* – over a thousand copies of the *Introduction to the Philosophy of History* were sold within a year, which at that time was a remarkable number.[106]

Among the congratulations Aron received was a letter from Bergson, Nobel Prize winner in 1928, but now nearly eighty and gravely ill:

Mon cher collègue,

The state of my health has forced me to interrupt my correspondence for several weeks. This will explain to you why I did not thank you earlier for kindly sending me your *Introduction to the Philosophy of History*. I had, however, read it straight away, and with a keen interest. The book is full of ideas, and suggestive in the extreme. Indeed, if I had any criticisms to make, it would be that it launches the reader's mind in too many directions. *Felix culpa* (a good fault), without any doubt; but, as a result, I shall have to read it a second time in order to get an idea of the whole. I shall do this, if I possibly can, and to guide me on this occasion I shall take those ideas of yours which seem to fit best with my own thinking, in particular the discussion of the effects of *découpage* and *rétrospection*. But, in the meantime, I was anxious to send you my compliments on the book...[107]

Aron also received letters from the Polish sociologist, Florian Znaniecki, to whom the two theses represented "perhaps the most profound and significant contribution to the epistemology and general methodology of historical knowledge in recent literature", and from his friend, the philosopher, mathematician and future Resistance hero, Jean Cavaillès. Cavaillès wrote that he had read the *Introduction to the Philosophy of History* "with an ever-increasing admiration and interest". The book demonstrated "an analytical rigour and a masterly control over the whole, that one discovers throughout with the same intellectual joy". This was also true of Aron's "lucidity" in evaluating the different theories he had considered. The discussions of determinism and probability – and especially the distinction between understanding and causality, together with the critique of Weber – were "extremely important". As for Section II, and in particular the passages concerning knowledge of self and others,

146

they "go to the very heart of philosophy and are the finest things I have read in French for many years".

The reviews of the two theses were also favourable. In France's foremost literary journal, *La Nouvelle Revue française*, the philosopher, Bernard Groethuysen, praised the "sincerity" and "clarity" of Aron's two books. He also underlined the "passionate character" of his work, which reflected "the anguish of the citizen confronted by history", adding that Aron put his questions with "an unbending rigidity that refuses any wrong turnings (qui exclut tous les faux-fuyants)".[108]

Both works were discussed anonymously in the *Revue de métaphysique et de morale*. The reviewer of the *Essai sur la théorie de l'histoire dans l'Allemagne contemporaine* referred with irony to the "quality of high abstraction" which his subject imposed on Aron, so much so that his might be called "a philosophy of history to the power of two". Aron's reconstruction of Dilthey's philosophy afforded "such a remarkable example of 'the understanding of the other' that it seems at times as though his attempt at systematization adds to the work of the person whose thought he is studying". After a "merciless refutation" of Rickert and having "passed rapidly" over Simmel, Aron had at last come to Weber, with whom he could give "free rein to a sympathy of which till now he had shown himself so sparing". Finally, because the book was an "introduction to an *Introduction to the Philosophy of History*", the reviewer limited himself to saying "with the keenest sympathy" that it "not only presents the critical philosophy of history in an extremely remarkable way, but equally reveals Monsieur Aron himself".[109]

The *Revue de métaphysique et de morale* had discussed the *Introduction to the Philosophy of History* a few months earlier:

Information that is very broad-based, very reliable and almost always first-hand; subtle argument and a rich diversity of viewpoints; a precise sense of the complexity of the problems and a lively awareness of the uncertainties of the hour and of the intimate connection between theoretical and practical questions; the firmness of tone, and the tendency to formulate the conclusions of the discussion as though they are decisions of the will – all this gives the book a particularly modern accent and makes it a valuable example of the new philosophical generation's way of thinking. It also explains the expectation and the approval with which it has been greeted.

"Ultimately", the writer concluded, "this mighty epistemological effort (and this is not intended as a criticism) is entirely inspired by the temptation to ask of science more than it can offer – a practical orientation – and by the anguish of a personal choice to be made in the troubled political and social situation in which we find ourselves".[110]

Fessard himself reviewed both books in the Jesuit journal, *Etudes*. "The product of patient labour and deep personal reflection", he wrote, "these two theses have just been defended in the Sorbonne, in a brilliant manner, but not without causing something of a stir". Aron, "an atheist by up-bringing and a socialist by conviction", had succeeded in "determining very precisely the conditions that make history possible and, as a result, the conditions underlying rational political decision". He was, therefore, to be thanked for having "posed the problem of the meaning of history with both integrity and lucidity", for "at a time when the political decision of the Christian is no less important than that of the atheist, all minds capable of strong nourishment ought to read his book".[111]

Another Catholic periodical, *La Vie intellectuelle*, had been quick to note Aron's "remarkable" *Introduction to the Philosophy of History*.[112] The following year Henri Gouhier, who was to be Professor of Philosophy at the Sorbonne from 1941 to 1968, reviewed both volumes in the same journal. The analyses contained in the *Essai sur la théorie de l'histoire dans l'Allemagne contemporaine*, he wrote, constituted "a very useful contribution to the study of German thought in the last sixty years", while in the *Introduction to the Philosophy of History* Aron "takes each question to its furthest possible limit". It was Gouhier's hope that "this virtuoso of analysis" would com-municate with a larger audience by discussing his problem in a shorter and more accessible work, like *La Sociologie allemande contemporaine*. Aron's distinction between "understanding" and "explanation" enabled him to write some "very suggestive" chapters on knowledge of self and of the other, the different types of history and the sociological syntheses of Simiand and Durkheim. Aron had "a justifiably dramatic sense of recent events" and his "complex and thorough" work constantly raised questions for the reader, to whom his "pitilessly critical, steadfast and lucid mind" allowed no escape.[113]

By far the most sustained discussion of the *Introduction to the Philosophy of History*, however, was that by the historian, Henri Marrou, under the name of Henri Davenson, in *Esprit*.[114] Marrou, who had been a contemporary of Aron's at the Ecole Normale Supérieure, wittily wrote his article, "Tristesse de l'historien" ("The Historian's Melancholy"), in the form of a lecture by an "old professor" (vieux maître) to his young history students. Aron's was, he stated, "a great book", which "should henceforth serve as a basis for the training of all young French historians" in the fight against positivism. Yet,

No one will read it; and that is a pity. It is his fault, of course. I know Aron. He is an extraordinarily intelligent young man, but (does he realize, I wonder?) a bit haughty, *highbrow*; his book, like its author, is bound to discourage the well-intentioned. It is a difficult book. Aron deliberately writes as a logician. I don't criticize him for that, because a Logic of History, in the most technical sense of the term, was the very thing we needed; but a Logic is never a laughing-matter, and Aron really goes too far. He translates (that is the word he uses) every step in the historian's task into an abstract logical schema (we are lucky if he stops at the third degree of abstraction!). The result is an excessively arid exposition in which the reader is hard put to it to introduce a little living substance.[115]

Above all, the book was "too short"; "with evident coquetry", Aron had sought to emulate the "French philosopher style" ("le genre 'philosophe français'") – full of well-turned but highly condensed phrases and aphorisms. Aron would doubtless reply that he scorned "padding", but he ought to have paid greater attention to the fact that his book was "necessary and had a purpose to serve". This criticism, Marrou wryly confessed, sprang from the resentment of a reader who had spent three months on the book that summer, only to succeed in reading it twice; and it applied even more to Aron's complementary thesis, the *Essai sur la théorie de l'histoire en Allemagne contemporaine*, which was "too brief and too abstract, whereas a detailed, down-to-earth analysis of the theories of Dilthey, Rickert, Simmel and Max Weber, would have rendered the greatest of services to the French public".[116]

In Marrou's judgement, Aron's work contained:

the elements of an existential theory of history, a concrete doctrine, oriented towards life, and based on a philosophy of commitment and vocation, a philosophy of creative and conscious effort. In brief, if I may draw together his best aphorisms: anti-fatalism; and the acceptance of the history which makes us real, but also its transcendence, because it can be created.[117] Man only has an ephemeral and precarious existence; he demeans himself if he lacks the courage to devote himself to a purpose in history; he transcends historicism by the absolute of his decision. Man is in history, and man is a historical being, but man is *a* history, and this history is free, because it is not written in advance; it is also unforeseeable, as man is to himself...

Thus the proper role of historical experience is to educate courage and the will: to give man a sense of his responsibility, by preventing him from substituting a complacent nature or determinism for the real world offered to his energy...[118]

Nevertheless, in spite of the high praise he bestowed on the *Introduction to the Philosophy of History*, Marrou expressed a number of reservations about it. Aron's critique of historians was almost "too intelligent" and went "over the head of the real historian". He failed to analyse the material work involved in the elaboration of facts and only concerned himself with the logical structure of history. He thus idealized the historian. When

149

Aron defined history as "the intellectualization of the experience of time (la durée)", or as "the culmination of an attempt to theorize life by elucidating and reconstructing its immanent rationality", Marrou's reaction was one of amazement followed by anxiety. "'Understanding, explanation, placing in perspective, causal systematization'. . .Are we so intelligent? Alas, no. . ." In Marrou's view, historians were basically technicians. Yet even here, Aron was too generous. Like his German masters, he argued over the validity of the results obtained by a positivistic "science" of history; but no such thing existed, for the simple reason that such a science was technically unrealizable, because of the nature of documentary evidence. On a purely factual level, as well as at the logical level picked out by Aron, the historian could never attain "objective truth"; the best he could do was formulate probable hypotheses.[119]

Finally, Aron seemed to Marrou to be "too pragmatic and utilitarian". According to Aron, "In as much as he lives in history, the historian strives to act and searches for his past in his future", and "at a certain moment, an individual reflects on *his* adventure, a society on *its* past, and humanity on *its* evolution". But, on this argument, Marrou pointed out, the history of the Hittites would only be of value to a Turk. "Events are of interest to us", Aron wrote, "only in so far as they influence our existence". Yet, here, Aron's dislike of empty erudition, which Marrou fully shared, led him too far. For Marrou, "History can be contemplative without ceasing to be existential. History. . .is only one aspect, one part, and one means, of our knowledge of man". It was necessary, therefore, to "broaden the principles (schèmes)" of Aron's theory and "take them in their most formal sense: the less we try to find an immediate interest in history, the stronger is its influence on our existence".[120] However, these were relatively minor reservations and, as we shall see, Marrou was to remain an enthusiastic advocate of Aron's philosophy of history.[121]

The two theses were also noticed in the United States before the war. Howard Becker, for example, reviewing the *Essai sur la théorie de l'histoire dans l'Allemagne contemporaine* for the *American Sociological Review*, observed that Aron's treatise ran "strikingly parallel" with Maurice Mandelbaum's *The Problem of Historical Knowledge*, which had appeared in the same year, except that Aron gave Weber "the consideration he deserves". Indeed, Becker wrote, if he had to single out any part of a work which manifested "an almost uniformly high level of excellence", it would be the section on Weber. In general, "no single book" was "likely to be more enlightening either to the tyro or the seasoned specialist".[122] Similarly, to Horace Friess in *Social Research*, the journal of the phenomenologically inclined New School for Social Research, New York, the chapters on each of

150

the four German thinkers were "careful expositions" that could be "recommended both for their fidelity to the originals and for their skilful dissection of the implications for the central theme of the book". However, presumably unaware that this was only the first of two volumes, he added that "The brief final chapter scarcely gives enough indication of Dr Aron's own thought on the question of how historical science may be more adequately conceived than by the men he has treated".[123] Finally, in the *American Journal of Sociology* Floyd House remarked of the *Introduction to the Philosophy of History* that Aron had written "a searching and systematic critique" of the philosophies of history of Hegel, Marx and Spengler, and presented "carefully restrained" conclusions that were to some extent reminiscent of John Dewey's philosophy.[124]

In Britain, H. B. Acton discussed both books sympathetically a few months before the outbreak of the war and concluded his account of the *Introduction to the Philosophy of History*:

I tend to regard philosophical problems from a different angle, and to use a different philosophical vocabulary from that of Dr Aron, but I recognize the very great philosophical ability displayed in this book, and am interested in an attempt which few contemporary philosophers make – to bring rational reflection to bear, not upon the hypothetical duties of hypothetical and uncomplicated persons, but upon the duties of men in this unique and present juncture. It is to be hoped that Dr Aron will pursue and elaborate the view of morality which, in this book, is suggested and hinted at but still remains fragmentary.[125]

After the war, the second edition of the *Essai sur la théorie de l'histoire dans l'Allemagne contemporaine*, now titled *La Philosophie critique de l'histoire*, was reviewed for the new Scottish journal, *The Philosophical Quarterly*, by Jonathan Cohen. Aron's account was, he wrote, "lucid and interesting", although the historical picture had been drawn "even better" for English readers by H. A. Hodges in his *Wilhelm Dilthey: An Introduction* (1944). Cohen's main criticism was that Aron's treatment was insufficiently concrete and specific – in, for example, his discussion of the historian's "selection".[126]

Nearly a quarter of a century after the *Introduction à la philosophie de l'histoire* appeared in France, an English (or, rather, American) translation was published in 1961.[127] Its stilted literalness – Aron himself has admitted that it was an "imperfect" translation[128] – and the fact that it contained no attempt to set the book in any kind of context, compounded the vices of the original. Aron's Anglo-Saxon critics were understandably bewildered and the reviews generally hostile. Thus Ernest Gellner, who elsewhere places Aron in the very highest rank of contemporary sociologists,[129] frankly expressed his disappointment. The *Introduction to the Philosophy of History* was "an early work of a man who has since acquired, rightly, a quite outstanding reputation as a social thinker and an incisive writer"; but, in spite of the interest of its subject matter, it bore "too many unfortunate signs of its time and place of origin, of the youth of the author at the time he wrote it, and of a very hasty translation". The book was often obscure and contained "too many intellectual purple passages, much less acceptable in translation, at any rate in prose. . .". French philosophy had "suffered from German measles far too long" and the worst symptom was "loss of lucidity". Stimulating though much of the book was, it could have been much better if Aron had rewritten it recently – and translated it himself.[130] Geoffrey Barraclough argued, similarly, that, "Of course M. Aron has a great deal to say that is true and illuminating, particularly when he deals with such concrete subjects as the limits of historical objectivity; but too often he strays into abstruse Teutonic clouds, in which one reader at least finds it hard to follow him".[131]

In Colin Falck's view, the Wittgensteinian revolution in British philosophy had prepared a place for Aron's book, for according to Wittgenstein the study of concepts was the study of "forms of life" and these had a unity and changed historically. Aron's essay, therefore, had "a sharp contemporary relevance. Instead of treating history as a shoddy and recalcitrant kind of natural science, he follows Kant in deriving the various forms of human thought – including the natural scientific – from a philosophy of mind, and Hegel in setting this philosophy within the historical process itself." But in considering the problems of the philosopher's relation to action, Aron refused to take a firm position and ended up with "nowhere to put his feet". The best that he could offer was "a kind of lucid disillusion. . . This difficult and penetrating book may soon have a few philosophical pens falling lifeless from their owners' grasp. But if, like Wittgenstein, it makes us worry about questions where previously we sought answers, it, too, is conclusionless to the point of silence".[132]

Aron's most hostile critic, however, was Alasdair MacIntyre in the *New Statesman*. Rightly observing that the book seemed "singularly out of context", and justifiably complaining of its "turgidity and repetitiveness" compared with the clarity of *German Sociology*, MacIntyre correctly argued that in the *Introduction to the Philosophy of History* Aron had set himself the important task of moving beyond Max Weber. But the result, MacIntyre implied, was a failure. Aron exhibited "exactly what insular British scholarship has always supposed to be the characteristic vices of continental learning" – "glib paradox" and "fake profundity". The political conclusions were those of "a platitudinous liberalism". The book added nothing to the case against historicism, as presented by, for example, Karl Popper; but whereas one could disagree with Popper because he at least presented a clear case against which to argue, to try to disagree with Aron was "like trying to disagree with a fog".[133]

An altogether different view was taken by Bernard Semmel who, writing in the *Annals of the American Academy of Political and Social Science*, also made the comparison with Popper:

Aron is a thoroughly French phenomenon – it is difficult to imagine such versatility operating elsewhere – moving, in more than one way, within the tradition of *les philosophes*, the great publicists of eighteenth-century France . . .

Professor Aron's way of looking at history, like that of Karl Popper and Sir Isaiah Berlin, is that of the currently fashionable school of antihistoricism. The *Introduction* is possibly the most complete exposition of this point of view and serves the useful purpose of revealing to an age in search of faith the weaknesses which must be found in any historical system, such as that of Hegel or Marx, of Spengler or Toynbee.[134]

Toynbee himself was full of praise in *The Observer*: "The subject of the book is of abiding interest, and M. Aron's treatment of it does not date. Moreover, the book is a difficult one, even when one is reading it in one's own language". To him the work was more like a treatise of Aristotle than a dialogue of Plato, and he urged both philosophers and historians to read it:

One of M. Aron's characteristic intellectual virtues is that he takes a balanced view, as well as an all-round one. He rightly insists that there is a plurality of systems of historical interpretation. He does not admit that economics, politics, religion, or any other single one of man's various activities is the exclusive key to understanding. He is conscious of the limits of historical objectivity and therefore conscious of the relativity of historical knowledge, but he is also conscious of the limits of relativism in history.

This is a book that deserves to be read thoroughly. To master it requires time and labour. But the effort is rewarding.[135]

Such praise of the *Introduction to the Philosophy of History* was, however, very much the exception in the Anglo-Saxon world. Nevertheless, in spite of the intervention of the war, Aron's thesis soon became a classic of its type in France,[136] where it has frequently been reprinted.[137] As Henri Marrou, Aron's pre-war champion, expressed it many years later, "it was thanks to Aron that the historians of our generation . . . were able to tear themselves free from the tyrannical oppression of positivism . . .

153

Whether as a result of direct influence or by a kind of underground osmosis, the essentials of Aron's teaching have today passed into everyday consciousness".[138] Indeed, Marrou's own major work in the philosophy of history, *De la Connaissance historique*, was to a considerable extent inspired by Aron's "two resounding theses".[139] The same is true of a recent essay by a historian of a younger generation, Paul Veyne, Professor of Roman History at the Collège de France, for whom Aron's *Introduction to the Philosophy of History* remains "the fundamental book on the topic".[140] One Anglo-Saxon writer, at any rate, echoes this view: to the historian Gordon Leff, Aron's book "stands. . .in a class of its own among modern literature on the subject".[141]

Notes

1. R. A., interview with the author, 1977. Cf. 1983a, p. 112.
2. This was the title of the first edition of the book (1938a). However, when the second edition was published in 1950, the title was changed to *La Philosophie critique de l'histoire: essai sur une théorie allemande de l'histoire* (*The Critical Philosophy of History: Essay on a German Theory of History*) (1950b). Subsequent editions of the book have retained this title. My references are to the most recent edition (1970a).
3. 1970a, p. 13.
4. Tr. 1978a, p. xxi. Cf. 1983a, p. 111.
5. R. A., interview with the author, 1977. The manuscript was lost during the war.
6. 1938b: tr. 1961a.
7. Tr. 1978a, p. xxi.
8. On Eric Weil, see Chapter 4, n. 87, above.
9. 1970a, p. 9.
10. Ibid., pp. 9–10.
11. Ibid., pp. 10–11.
12. Ibid., p. 11.
13. Ibid., p. 12. For a recent discussion, see Thomas E. Willey, *Back to Kant: The Revival of Kantianism in German Social and Historical Thought, 1860–1914* (Detroit, 1978).
14. Ibid., pp. 12–13.
15. Ibid., p. 13.
16. Ibid., p. 25.
17. Ibid., pp. 99–109.
18. Ibid., p. 154.
19. Ibid., p.211.
20. Ibid., pp. 212–13.
21. Ibid., p. 19.
22. Ibid., pp. 217–18.
23. Ibid., p. 219.
24. Ibid.

25. Ibid., p. 251–2.
26. Ibid., p. 252–4.
27. Ibid., p. 258.
28. Ibid., pp. 258–60.
29. Ibid., p. 261.
30. Ibid., p. 262.
31. Ibid., pp. 267–8.
32. Ibid., p. 290.
33. 1938b: tr. 1961a. See also the discussions in Aron's memoirs (1983a, pp. 115ff.) and in Hall, 1981, pp. 174ff.
34. Cf. 1961a, p. 1.
35. 1938b, p. 10: tr. 1961a, p. 10 (R.C.).
36. Ibid., pp. 9–10: tr. p. 9 (R.C.).
37. Ibid., p. 11: tr. p. 11 (R.C.).
38. Ibid., p. 49: tr. p. 45 (R.C.).
39. Ibid., p. 51: tr. pp. 47–8 (R.C.).
40. Ibid., p. 62: tr. p. 59 (R.C.). See also the earlier discussion of Brunschvicg's *De la Connaisance de soi* (*On Self-Knowledge*) in 1932a.
41. 1934b. After the war Aron again referred to the "important" contribution to a theory of historical knowledge and reality contained in Schutz's early book. Although, Aron wrote, it was intentionally limited in scope (for example, it did not consider historical ensembles such as institutions and economic regimes), Schutz's theories of meaning and comprehension were "an essential part of every ontology of history" (1950c: tr. 1950b, p. 306).
42. 1938b, p. 71: tr. 1961a, p. 69 (R.C.).
43. Ibid., p. 73: tr. p. 70 (R.C.).
44. Ibid., p. 79: tr. p. 76 (R.C.).
45. Ibid., p. 81: tr. p. 78 (R.C.).
46. Ibid., p. 84: tr. p. 81 (R.C.).
47. Ibid., p. 120: tr. p. 118 (R.C.). In his memoirs Aron commented that the phrase "dissolution of the object" now seemed to him "gratuitously aggressive and para-doxical" (1983a, p. 122).
48. 1938b, p. 93: tr. p. 89.
49. Ibid., p. 95: tr. p. 91 (R.C.).
50. Ibid., p. 190: tr. p. 187 (R.C.).
51. Ibid., p. 229: tr. p. 226 (R.C.).
52. Ibid., p. 190: tr. p. 187 (R.C.).
53. Ibid., pp. 201–2: tr. p. 199 (R.C.).
54. Ibid., p. 202: tr. p. 199 (R.C.).
55. Ibid., pp. 202–3: tr. p. 200 (R.C.).
56. Ibid., p. 203: tr. p. 200 (R.C.).
57. Ibid., p. 204: tr. p. 201.
58. Ibid., p. 226: tr. p. 224.
59. Ibid., p. 246: tr. pp. 245–6 (R.C.). It is regrettable that the English translation repeatedly renders "les rapports de production" as "the profits of production" instead of "the relations of production".

60. Aron himself, however, had recently subjected such claims to critical examination in two articles published the previous year (1937a, 1937d). See Chapter 7, below.
61. 1938b, p. 247: tr. 1961a, p. 246 (R.C.).
62. Ibid., pp. 247-8: tr. p. 247 (R.C.).
63. See also 1937a and 1937d (Chapter 7, below).
64. 1938b, p. 249: tr. 1961a, p. 249 (R.C.).
65. Ibid., p. 250: tr. p. 249 (R.C.). See also 1937a (Chapter 7, below).
66. Ibid., p. 253: tr. p. 254 (R.C.). See also 1937b.
67. Ibid., pp. 255, 256: tr. pp. 255, 256 (R.C.).
68. Ibid., p. 256: tr. p. 257 (R.C.).
69. Ibid., p. 301: tr. p. 298.
70. Ibid., p. 301: tr. p. 298 (R.C.).
71. Ibid., p. 324: tr. p. 320 (R.C.).
72. Ibid., p. 325: tr. p. 321 (R.C.).
73. Ibid., pp. 325-6: tr. pp. 322-3 (R.C.).
74. Ibid., p. 328: tr. p. 324 (R.C.).
75. Ibid., p. 328: tr. p. 325 (R.C.).
76. Ibid., pp.329-30: tr. pp. 326-7 (R.C.).
77. Ibid., p. 331: tr. p. 328.
78. Ibid., p. 336: tr. p. 333.
79. Ibid., p. 349: tr. pp. 346-7 (R.C.).
80. Ibid., p. 350: tr. p. 346-7 (R.C.). Compare 1937d, p. 84: "In a world without God, man only overcomes his particularity through reflection. Without being either partisan or a historian, the individual transcends himself who thinks his action, confronts it with that of others, and, by standing back from himself, delineates the real conditions of human existence. But such reflection remains formal; to make this choice concrete, the individual must choose to commit himself in action and in history".
81. Ibid., p. 350: tr. p. 347.
82. 1961a, p. 1.
83. 1948a. See Chapter 16, below.
84. 1951a: tr. 1954a. See Chapter 17, below.
85. 1955b: tr. 1957b. See Chapter 20, below. In addition, Aron has continued to study – "as best he can" – the literature on historical knowledge, "in particular, the works of Anglo-American analysts" (tr. 1978a, p. xx); and since the war he has written a number of articles concerned with the philosophy of history, although they are less formal and abstract than his pre-war writings. See, for example, 1950c: tr. 1950b, and the studies collected in *Dimensions de la conscience historique* (1961a).
86. Anon, 1938b. Reprinted in Fessard, 1980, Appendix I.
87. On Fessard (1897-1978), see Marcel Régnier, s.J.., "Homélie prononcée aux obsèques du Révérend Père Gaston Fessard, s.J. le 22 juin 1978", *Commentaire*, 1, 1978, pp. 375-8; and Aron, "Chrétiens et Marxistes", *L'Express* (1453), 19 May 1979: tr. 1979d. On Aron and Fessard, see Baverez, 1985.
88. Fessard, 1971; reprinted in Fessard, 1980. Later in the same article Fessard went on to argue that there is "an unexpected parallel", in both form and content, between Aron's theory of historical knowledge in the *Introduction to the Philosophy of History*, and

Saint Ignatius of Loyola's "genesis of freedom" in his *Spiritual Exercises*. Fessard developed his highly personal interpretation of Aron's philosophy of history in a full-length work published shortly after Fessard's death (Fessard, 1980).

89. As Fessard makes clear, the account in the *Revue de métaphysique et de morale* (Anon., 1938b) wrongly gives the date as 18 March (Fessard, 1980, p. 36).
90. Fessard, 1980, pp. 36, 37.
91. 1971a, p. 19: tr. 1978a, p. 64 (R.C.).
92. Ibid., pp. 21–2: tr. p. 65 (R.C.).
93. Ibid., p. 25: tr. p. 66 (R.C.).
94. Ibid., p. 62: tr. pp. 80–1 (R.C.). The phrase, "the age of contempt", echoes the title of Malraux's novel published in 1935, *Le Temps du mépris*.
95. Fessard, 1980, pp. 37–8.
96. Ibid., pp. 38–40.
97. Ibid., pp. 40–1. Fauconnet died later that year.
98. Ibid., pp. 41–2.
99. Ibid., pp. 42–4.
100. Ibid., pp. 44–5.
101. Ibid., p. 45.
102. Ibid., pp. 46–8.
103. Ibid., p. 48. Halbwachs (1877–1945) was to die at Buchenwald.
104. Ibid., p. 49.
105. Tr. 1978a, p. xxi. Shortly after the outbreak of the Second World War, in a letter to Sartre dated 8 December 1939, Nizan wrote ironically that Aron and Armand Petitjean (now a forgotten Péguyesque figure whose review *Cahiers de Paris et de la Province* was *le dernier cri* before the Occupation) were "becoming rivals in the philosophical field. Between a neo-Péguy and a neo-Dilthey we won't have much to laugh about; but I suppose they'll regard us as incurably frivolous. . ." Simone de Beauvoir, *La Force de l'âge* (Paris, 1960), p. 440: tr. (by Peter Green), *The Prime of Life* (Harmondsworth, 1963), p. 340.
106. Marrou, 1971, p. 43. Marrou modestly adds that Aron's thesis "would undoubtedly have won the prize if the esprit de corps and professional jealousy of the historians had not claimed it for one of their own".
107. Unpublished letter, dated 30 June 1938. I am most grateful to Raymond Aron for letting me see this letter, and those from Florian Znaniecki and Jean Cavaillès referred to below, and allowing me to quote from them. The two concepts singled out by Bergson, *découpage* and *rétrospection*, are discussed on pp. 113–19 of the thesis (tr. pp. 111–18). Elsewhere, Aron has confirmed that these two notions are indeed "undeniably Bergsonian in inspiration" (1956c, p. 45).
108. Groethuysen, 1939.
109. Anon., 1939.
110. Anon., 1938a.
111. Fessard, 1938, pp. 410, 412.
112. *La Vie intellectuelle*, 56 (3), 10 May 1938, p. 348, n.i.
113. Gouhier, 1939, pp. 262, 264, 265–6.
114. Marrou, 1939.
115. Ibid., pp. 17–18.

116. Ibid., p. 18.

117. Marrou has since pointed elsewhere to the dangers of philosophical idealism in such a formulation: "...if one insists too much on the creative contribution of the historian, one ends up by describing the elaboration of history as a gratuitous game and as the free exercise of an inventive imagination" – a conception which undermines the validity of historical truth (Marrou, 1975, p. 51). At the same time – and Marrou has called this the "heart" of his own philosophy of history – history "appears as the fruit of an action, of an effort that is in a sense creative, which brings into play the living powers of the mind, as defined by its capacities, its mentality, its technical equipment and its culture. History is a spiritual adventure, in which the personality of the historian is completely committed; in a word, history is endowed, for him, with an existential value, and it is this which gives it its seriousness, its meaning and its price" (ibid., p. 197). Yet even this "existential value" of history should not be exaggerated (ibid., pp. 200ff.).

118. Marrou, 1939, pp. 41, 44. Cf. Marrou, 1975, p. 52: "History is a battle of the spirit, an adventure and, like all human enterprises, can only know victories that are partial, relative and out of all proportion to the initial expectation; and, as with every fight undertaken against the disturbing depths of his being, man returns with a sharpened sense of his limitations, his feebleness and his humility".

119. Marrou, 1939, pp. 27–34.

120. Ibid., pp. 44, 46.

121. The only hostile reference to Aron's theses which I have discovered in the pre-war French literature is a review by Henri Hauser. Surveying Aron's philosophy of history with an economist's eye, he saw little in it (Hauser, 1939). Aron had earlier savaged Hauser (1937o) – see 1983a, pp. 85–6.

122. Becker, 1939. Maurice Mandelbaum's *The Problem of Historical Knowledge: An Answer to Relativism* (New York, 1938) discussed "three historical relativists", Croce, Dilthey and Mannheim, and "four counter-relativists", Simmel, Rickert, Scheler and Troeltsch. Interestingly, Aron himself reviewed the book for the *Annales sociologiques* (1941e). He doubted that Croce, Dilthey and Mannheim could properly be called "historical relativists", since, as Mandelbaum himself pointed out, their philosophical intentions and metaphysical assumptions were very different. The placing together of the four "counter-relativists" seemed to Aron even more questionable. Thus Simmel had never sought to refute relativism. Scheler and Troeltsch's problem was that of the relativism of values rather than historical knowledge. As far as the latter was concerned, Scheler explicitly accepted perspectivism and Troeltsch combined a number of Rickert's ideas with arguments that were even more relativist. Nevertheless, even those who did not accept all of the arguments in Mandelbaum's attempt to provide "an answer to relativism" would benefit from his book and recognize the value of a number of his ideas, especially that of the unity of historical analysis and synthesis.

An Italian work, published at the beginning of the war – Carlo Antoni's *Dallo Storicismo alla Sociologia* (Florence, 1940), translated as *From History to Sociology: The Transition in German Historical Thinking* (London, 1962) – covered similar ground, analysing the thought of Dilthey, Troeltsch, Meinecke, Weber, Huizinga and Wölfflin. Antoni made no mention of Aron's philosophy of history but did refer to *La Sociologie allemande contemporaine* (Antoni, op.cit., Ch. IV, n. 65). In a recent edition of *La Philosophie critique de l'histoire* (1970a, pp. 13–14), Aron has drawn attention to another Italian study, Pietro Rossi's *Lo Storicismo tedesco contemporaneo* (Milan, 1956): like Aron's work, it considers Dilthey, Rickert, Simmel and Weber, but it also discusses Spengler and Meinecke.

123. Friess, 1940.
124. House, 1939.
125. Acton, 1939.
126. Cohen, 1951.
127. Tr. 1961a. The book has also been translated into Spanish (Buenos Aires, 1946), Japanese, Portuguese and even Serbo-Croat, but never into German.
128. Tr. 1978a, p. xxi.
129. Gellner, 1966.
130. Gellner, 1961.
131. Barraclough, 1961.
132. Falck, 1961.
133. MacIntyre, 1961.
134. Semmel, 1961. Compare George Catlin, who stated of the *Introduction to the Philosophy of History*: "Compared with some more trite and facile work that has appeared, here we have a solid and exhaustive study by an author of well-known brilliance" (Catlin, 1961).
135. Toynbee, 1961.
136. Cf. Delmas, 1951; André Rousseaux, "Les énigmes de l'histoire", *Fig.Lit.*, 17 May 1952; André Rousseaux, "Les incertitudes de Clio", *Fig.Lit.*, 29 January 1955; Arnaud, 1968: "Having quickly become a classic, Raymond Aron's thesis has, with the years, lost none of its striking and stimulating vigour, even if many of the paradoxes of yesteryear have become self-evident today. But that is the price of success...".
137. The *Introduction à la philosophie de l'histoire* was republished after the war (1948b) and, after regular reprintings, has now appeared in a student edition (1981c).
138. Marrou, 1971, pp. 38, 44.
139. Marrou, 1975, p. 20.
140. Paul Veyne, *"Comment on écrit l'histoire" suivi de "Foucault révolutionne l'histoire"* (Paris, new edn, 1978), p. 10. Aron himself has written a long article arising out of the book (1971c).
141. Gordon Leff, *History and Social Theory* (London, 1969), p. 24. See also the meticulous and illuminating analysis of his "critique of historical reason", published after Aron's death, by the young philosopher Sylvie Mesure (Mesure, 1984).

7

Marxism, Ideology and the Social Sciences

———

Marxism

Aron's earliest discussion of Marxism was an article published in 1931 on Henri de Man's *Au delà du Marxisme* (*Beyond Marxism*).[1] De Man (1886–1953), a Belgian, had been a member of the Second International in Germany until 1914. After the First World War, however, he abandoned his earlier revolutionary Marxism in favour of reformism and, as professor at the University of Frankfurt, became one of the most prominent theorists of social democracy in Weimar Germany.[2]

There was, Aron wrote in his review of *Au delà du Marxisme*, a danger of socialist theory becoming a "theology" (he was, for example, sceptical of talk about "destroying the foundations of the bourgeois state"), and de Man's "important" book was "the most vigorous effort yet" to rethink the growing problem of social reform or revolution.[3] True socialism must be democratic and non-violent. At the same time, as far as possible, "political democracy" used "peaceful means, such as universal suffrage, which allows different forces to appear in the state, not merely as the instrument of the ruling class, but as the moving expression of conflicting interests and wills". Aron also rejected the "dangerous" distinction, to be found in Marx, between ends and means, because

it forgets the psychological truth that the means employed arouse corresponding feelings in the human soul. The practice of violence arouses the instinct of violence, while to seek to move from violence to non-violence, from war to peace, and from armaments to security, is to ignore the immediate reactions of the human soul and is blind folly.[4]

De Man argued against a determinist Marxist materialism – rightly so, in Aron's view, for "mechanical-type causality cannot be applied to men's conduct". Utilitarianism was an equally false doctrine because it

turns the human being into a rationalistic calculator when in reality he is a passionate actor. The *"homo economicus"* of classical economy represents a type of ideal conduct which the real human being never attains. It is not enough, therefore, to say that other factors balance the economic factor: there is no economic factor in a "pure state". Indeed, the very notion of "factors" derives from a realist mode of thinking which imposes an arbitrarily simplified pattern onto a world that is in constant movement, made up as it is of numerous, inextricably interwoven relations...

Perhaps, therefore, by delineating a part of social reality, if not non-human in its origins at any rate uninfluenced by humanity, it would be possible to specify...in what sense and to what extent historical circumstances are the limiting, not determining, condition of our will. At the same time, we would once more become conscious of our freedom as a real cause, and perhaps the margin of indeterminacy contained within a given situation corresponds precisely with the power of our will. It is the belief in determinism which is the cause of our servitude. Faith in our will can be the basis of our autonomy. Such a faith is rational not mystical, because it depends on a critique of the determinist mode of thinking but also on an accurate appraisal of historical forces.[5]

Following Sorel, the latter would involve, Aron suggested, "a study of economic facts which is as free of bias as possible". In conclusion, de Man's ethical socialism was, in Aron's view, "more demanding as far as the present is concerned, because it puts less reliance on some future paradise".[6]

Despite this early discussion, it was, as we have seen, Aron's decision to subject his political opinions to a critique, which led him to study Marxism seriously while he was in Germany in 1931. He began by reading *Capital*, but his stay in Berlin happened to coincide with the publication there, in 1932, of Marx's youthful writings, and he became acquainted with them, therefore, before almost any other Frenchman.

162

Neither Marx nor Hegel were taught at the Sorbonne in the inter-war years and many French intellectuals in fact received their introduction to these thinkers at an extremely influential series of lectures on the phenomenology of mind given by Aron's friend, Alexandre Kojève, at the Ecole Pratique des Hautes Etudes between 1933 and 1939.[7] Aron himself attended these lectures, as did Alexandre Koyré, Raymond Queneau, Georges Bataille, Jacques Lacan, Robert Marjolin, Maurice Merleau-Ponty, Raymond Polin, Eric Weil, Gaston Fessard and (occasionally) André Breton.[8] Partly as a result of Kojève's lectures and in particular the influence they had on Merleau-Ponty and Lacan (Sartre did not go to them), Aron was later inclined to see what might be called a "new start" for French philosophy in the 1930s – "a return to Hegel" as opposed to the "return to Kant" of Brunschvicg's generation, with the consequence that "Marxism found its way into university studies in philosophy and became an integral part of the philosophical tradition that lycée teachers uphold and spread throughout France".[9]

It was against this background that Aron wrote his first major study of Marxism, a lecture on the relationship between politics and economics in Marxist theory, which was delivered at the Centre de Documentation Sociale and published in 1937.[10] It is an astonishingly "modern" analysis of what Aron called "philosophical" as opposed to "vulgar" Marxism, and it shows clearly how, from an early stage in his intellectual development, Aron refused to accept that politics was reducible to economics: on the contrary, he argued, though the two are interconnected, the political retains a certain autonomy from the economic.[11]

Aron began his analysis by defining the economy as "the ensemble – individual actions and collective institutions – in and through which men strive to overcome their original poverty, the disparity between needs or demands on the one hand, and resources on the other". Politics referred to "the ensemble which establishes stable relations of authority and dependence between individuals and groups animated by contradictory desires". "The instinct", he went on, "that the economy seeks to satisfy takes multiple forms, from hunger and thirst to greed and the desire for wealth. The instinct that politics aims to discipline is the will to power".[12]

Although analytically distinct, in reality the political and the economic were "always inseparable", and it was this conception of the relationship between the two which, Aron stated, was to be found in the writings of the young Marx, as opposed to his doctrinaire interpreters. The latter asserted "the *exclusive* or *predominant effect* of the economic factor", wheras "Marx, in his youth, does not seek to affirm the *primacy* of the economy over politics, nor the determination of the latter by the former". It was important to study Marx's youthful philosophical writings because they were "indispensable" for an understanding of *Capital* and undermined vulgar Marxism's "arrogant isolation" and "totalitarian pretensions". It was also essential for Marxists in particular to "ceaselessly confront theory with reality".[13]

What follows is a brilliant exposition of Marx's early writings from the standpoint of Aron's problem of the relationship between politics and economics in Marxism. He began with the "double critique" of democratic politics and liberal economics in the *Critique of Hegel's Philosophy of Right*, in which Marx argued that democratic revolutions were not enough to liberate man, since it was the economic system which engendered universal slavery; for Marx, "more than kings and their ministers, it is things which exercise tyranny".[14] The future revolution must, therefore, be economic. However, "before becoming an economist, Marx still had to discover, through philosophical reflection, . . . the conditions and the means of a humanity reconciled with itself".[15] He turned to this question in the *Economic and Philosophic Manuscripts* in which, by means of the concept of alienation, he analysed the inhuman nature of capitalism and presented his vision of man in a non-alienated society.

But, it will be said, is not this a pure utopia? How is it possible to unite the particular and the universal, the private and the public man? How is it possible to give to the individual all the riches of the species? . . .

Marx is not so naive as to believe that, under a different economic regime, the product will belong to the worker. But the collectivity will only have to impose its control and products correspond to real and legitimate needs, for alienation to disappear along with commodity-fetishism. The worker who labours for a plan established in the interest of all will be working for himself. Instead of being lost among the phantoms of the market, social relations will become intelligible to everyone. Specialization, reduced to a minimum, will not do violence to man's species being in as much as, reconciled with their destiny, men will communicate directly with each other and by their concord form a harmonious whole.

Once again, the ideal is a communal one; private life is inseparable from collective life because politics must merge with the very administration of the economy, because the individual fulfils himself in his labour which is a social activity, and because humanity, which has progressed as it has become alienated, must regain control over its alienations in order to achieve harmony with itself at last.

The inadequacy of political democracy showed us the primacy of the economic order and the necessity for the genuine revolution which will transform the condition of each and everyone. The humanist critique of contemporary society takes us back, in another sense, to this priority. Labour is the activity which defines man, and the relation of the worker to his product is the origin of all alienation. Thus, in our view, there has never been, in authentic Marxism, a primacy of the economy in any other sense. Neither in the causal nor the temporal spheres does the economy determine politics. The whole of history becomes the history of the relations of production because of the essential significance of labour. Contemporary society is dominated by the evolution of the economy because, left to itself, the capitalist system, in accordance with its dehumanized laws and contradictions, is heading for catastrophe. In other words, the primacy of the economy is either the expression of a philosophical anthropology, or a reflection of the structure characteristic of contemporary society.[16]

Aron turned next to *The German Ideology*, a work which contained "the outline of a philosophy of history" based on a particular anthropology. In *The German Ideology* man appeared as the being with the capacity to create his means of existence and each epoch was characterized primarily by its mode of production. "In this sense the forces of production are at the root of history". Again, however, this did not imply a single, causal "factor", but the interrelation of the forces of production, the social relations of production, and consciousness. "From the relations and, above all, the contradictions which develop between these three *moments*, historical movement is born":[17]

It is not, therefore, a question of asking how far the economy alone determines these other phenomena, for one does not move from the isolated causal action of one element (terme) on another to the action of this element on the whole. One starts from the historical totality, all of whose elements, related to one another by means of a ceaseless interaction, are organized...with labour as the premise and essential condition of existence.[18]

It was *The Communist Manifesto* which, in Aron's opinion, provided the central ideas of Marxism with "their most striking, systematic and perhaps eloquent form, but also the one most dangerously close to an oversimplified caricature". Aron did not accept the commonly held view that, having once settled accounts with his philosophical conscience, Marx then concentrated on his economic studies and became a naive materialist, uninfluenced by his youthful writings. It was easy to distort his thinking in this way; it was always tempting to adopt the language of "causes", because to do so was simple and seemed "scientific":

Hence the classic expressions: the economy conditions or determines political regimes, or the relations of production are the infrastructure on which the whole society depends. This is how one gets into insoluble difficulties which... reveal precisely *how the questions should not be posed*.[19]

It was easy enough to refute the claims of such a "vulgar distortion" of Marxist doctrine.[20] "Authentic" Marxism, however, was a self-confirming theory. It was not difficult to find economic causes behind political events, but the claim that causes are always economic resulted from the premises of the theory and did not depend upon empirical observation. What, for example, should one make of the orthodox Marxist claim that the state was now a "class state" or a "bourgeois state" – that is, the instrument of the ruling class? While of course recognizing the "undeniable influence" exercised by those who wielded economic power in democratic regimes, Aron cited Jaurès's view that, "There has never been a state which was purely and simply a class state, that is, one which was an all-purpose instrument in the hands of the ruling class, serving its every whim". Furthermore, argued Aron, "in as much as the proletariat becomes aware of its potential and . . . working-class parties win seats in parliament and local government, . . . the state ceases to be bourgeois".[21]

There was also in Marxist theory the question of the eventual withering away of the state in communist society, and the problem of the dictatorship of the proletariat as a feature of the transition from the reign of necessity to the reign of liberty. About both questions Aron was sceptical:

Marx took up the expression which summarizes the thought of Saint-Simon: the administration of things will replace the government of men. But as he always refrained from describing the regime of the future, everyone was free to imagine it as he wished: ancient millenarian hopes merged with and enriched scientific socialism . . . It is in fact doubtful that Soviet reality corresponds to this "liberty of each as the condition of the liberty of all". A society without classes and without privileges could perhaps do without the state, that is to say, without the police; but we are still a long way from this perhaps unattainable ideal.

Indeed, it is unlikely that Marx himself ever conceived the suppression of the state in so naive a way. The necessity for technical and administrative authority survives all revolutions; but the rulers of a collectivity who control the economy and distribute incomes justly would no longer be acting as individuals in the service of individual interests, but as representatives of all in the service of common interests.

More important than these arguments about the future have been the attempts to give content to the vague notion of the dictatorship of the proletariat. We know that the Paris Commune became, in the eyes of Marx and Engels, the model for the government to be established by the victorious proletariat . . . Today, the Soviets offer an example which is more concrete and near to hand. The danger is that the transitional regime increasingly becomes the definitive regime and that the classless society is combined with the dictatorship of one class, one party or even one man.[22]

As far, then, as the relations of politics and the economy were concerned, "no precise formula could possibly be valid for all societies".

The relationship between the two should not be asserted *a priori*, but had to be examined historically in terms of particular features of social organization. As for "the one and only victorious socialist revolution",

far from resolving the contradiction between the political order and the economic order by substituting the administration of things for the government of men, it is in danger rather of compromising the unity of the doctrine. Is control over the economy compatible with political and cultural liberalism? Is not the dictatorship of the proletariat, represented by a group of men who proclaim themselves its interpreters, . . . more dictatorial than proletarian? To unite the private and the public man, civil society and the state – is this the culmination of freedom or slavery?[23]

Only history, Aron concluded, would provide the answer.

The Problem of Ideology

One of the most striking passages in *German Sociology* was the fierce attack on the relativism of the sociology of knowledge and on Mannheim's failure to resolve the problem of ideology posed by Marxism. Aron returned to the topic briefly in a review article published the following year[24] and again in a substantial article which appeared in 1937.[25] Aron clearly, and rightly, felt the need to establish the grounds of his own epistemological position in order to provide the basis for that "critique of ideologies" which has formed an important part of his work.

Ideology, he began, had been defined as "my opponent's idea". This was not, he admitted, a bad definition, but was it possible to go beyond its implied relativism and "specify the conditions under which the critique of ideology can lay claim to objectivity"? In other words, was an objective study of ideologies possible? There was, Aron believed, a need for such an analysis because "the interpretation and disqualification of ideas through the revelation of interests and intentions represents a common practice today". For this reason, his analysis could, he suggested, be taken as "a contribution to the methodology of historical knowledge".[26] As such, his discussion of ideology was directly linked to his major concern at the time, the philosophy of history.

Aron first set about distinguishing "ideology" and "myth".[27] The term "myth" had been used by Sorel to refer to "vague ideas which become fixed in a striking form of words" – for example, such slogans as "The 200 Families", "The Plan", or "Jewish High Finance" – and thus become a social force. The term "myth", therefore, implied a judgement about the social consequences rather than the content or intrinsic value of a set of ideas – a judgement which, Aron remarked drily, was "unjust and inevitable". An "ideology", on the other hand, contained a judgement about the origins rather than the consequences of an idea, thanks in particular to a psychology which attempted to expose and thus disqualify the idea in question, especially through the use of psychoanalytic concepts such as dissimulation, sublimation and compensation. For example, Scheler had claimed that Marx's socialism was explicable in terms of "resentment". But such an "explanation" said nothing about the economic or political value of Marx's work:

An idea is true or false in respect of its object, it corresponds to the facts or it is contradicted by them, it is consistent with or opposed to our value judgements. We shall leave to the psychologist, therefore, those discoveries which perhaps make the man intelligible, but not the work...

Psychological criticism almost necessarily neglects the content of ideas (so much so that it completely dissolves them), because it considers predominantly, if not uniquely, their causes. Furthermore, the psychologist sees in society only individuals, or groups consisting of individuals, struggling against one another. He ignores the web of institutions which distinguish a society from an assemblage of individuals. Finally, he automatically places himself above history, indifferent as he is to the specific nature of the social problems which characterize each epoch, in the conviction that men always remain the same, since the motives of their conduct are unchanging.[28]

All these errors, Aron maintained, were avoided by those doctrines which situated themselves firmly in history, such as Marxism. The trouble was that Marxism raised another question in particularly sharp form: how could one avoid the accusation "proletarian ideology" when one began by accusing others of having a "bourgeois ideology"? As in his discussion of the relationship between the political and the economic in Marxist theory, Aron was careful to distinguish "vulgar" from "philosophical" Marxism. By "vulgar Marxism" he meant a

Marxism which sees itself as a science and not as a philosophy, and whose premise is that the infrastructure *determines* the superstructure. Ideas are explained in the last analysis by the forces or the relations of production; they must be related to historical and social situations, and in particular to social classes.[29]

However, it was important to distinguish a number of different meanings as far as so-called "materialist" interpretations were concerned. Explanation in economic terms could be direct or indirect; one could seek to establish relations of "determination" or "conditioning", either in terms of a single and sufficient cause, or one antecedent factor among others. More specifically, one could talk of "reflection" if one could somehow show that the categories of thought "reproduced" the techniques of production or the nature of social relations – if, for example, it could be shown that the medieval conception of the universe "reflected" the hierarchical structure of society. Lastly, it might be possible to trace modes of thought back to the interests or political attitudes of a particular group, although this would reintroduce the psychological interpretations examined above – as, for example, when it was claimed that fascism "expresses" the demands of the middle classes. It would be important, therefore, to make these distinctions if one wanted to use historical materialism scientifically, and to discover under what conditions such claims might be verified. Historical analysis became "indispensable" as soon as the claim was made that all ideas are determined by historical situations or are the expression of social classes. "But if one makes general use of the materialist method in this way, does one not become involved in insuperable difficulties?" [30] The result, Aron affirmed, was the destruction of any notion of truth, as he had tried to show in his discussion of Mannheim in *German Sociology*.

However, as Aron himself emphasized, so far he had only been considering a "vulgar Marxism" which stressed causality and resulted in

a scientific, pseudo-positivist distortion of Marx's original thinking. For, from the start, Marx does not conceive of a causal action of the infrastructure on the superstructure, nor of social class on ideas, for the good reason that he does not begin by perceiving a multiplicity of scattered elements. The grasping of the totality comes first: with the help of the concept of alienation Marx rediscovers the unity of history, because he sees in the struggle of man and his creations the immanent principle of evolution, and, in the transcendence of this struggle, the historic task of our epoch...

If one forgets the philosophy with whose help Marx criticized both society and theories, if one replaces dialectical understanding by causal explanation, one perhaps makes the doctrine more accessible and more active, but philosophically one makes it absurd.[31]

Nevertheless, there remained in Marxism "a residue of the Hegelian claim to grasp history from an absolute point of view". In reality, however, "Communist society is no more the accomplishment of human destiny" than was Hegel's Prussian monarchy.[32]

The conclusion to which Aron's discussion led him was that:

Any idea can be called an ideology, either because of its origins (psychological or sociological), or because of its consequences. In so far as the critique of ideologies confines itself to such judgements of fact, it is, in principle, objective. But objectivity disappears, or at least is compromised, as soon as, with the use of such terms as *logical*

169

or *illogical*, and *real* as opposed to *illusory*, one reintroduces an implicit appreciation of the content of the idea into psychological or social analysis.[33]

However, he was careful to point out that such a conclusion did not necessarily lead to relativism:

It does not follow that all ideologies are of equal worth, or that all choices are arbitrary. In the first place, certain ideologies fall beneath the hand of science, either because they contradict established facts, or because they hypostatize partial realities and distort their significance. Certain ideologies are self-contradictory (all those, for example, which combine revolutionary zeal and pacifist fervour). Beyond science and beyond logic, morality can, if not refute, at least appreciate ideologies. Generally speaking, value preferences, while not susceptible of proof, are nonetheless capable of reasonable, if not rational, justification.

In so far as this was not possible, then ideologies stood implacably opposed to one another, "irreconcilable, and capable only of being *experienced* and not *proved* (*éprouvées* et non pas *prouvées*)",[34] for man had to live and make choices, but without any certain knowledge.[35]

Objectivity and the Social Sciences

Aron took his analysis of the problem of ideology a good deal further in a paper on the related problem of objectivity in the social sciences. This paper was given to Léon Brillouin's seminar on theoretical physics and the philosophy of science at the Collège de France and published in the Swedish journal, *Theoria*.[36] It represents Aron's most specific pre-war discussion of the philosophy of the social sciences and is also one of the two articles which he wrote in the 1930s that discusses theoretical economics, the other being a review of Charles Rist's *Histoire des doctrines relatives au crédit et à la monnaie, depuis Law jusqu'à nos jours*.[37]

Aron had already argued, in an earlier article on sociology in France, that, if it were not to become over-speculative and abstract, sociology must cooperate with the other social sciences (psychology, economics, law and history).[38] His aim in the paper in *Theoria* was "to reveal, with the use of examples, both the possible objectivity (universal validity) and the temptation to *partiality*" of the social sciences, as well as "the inevitable connection between the object, scientifically constructed, and the subject who questions reality, works out the connections between phenomena, and organizes knowledge". As an example, he took "by far the most advanced" of the social sciences, economics, in its "most typical aspect"

– economic theory. Economic theory concerned itself with human actions which obeyed a logic of means to ends; in other words, it "reconstructs the behaviour of economic subjects by bestowing on them a strict rationality". This "rational reconstruction", as Aron called it, was a fundamental step in all social sciences, but the method contained "an obvious danger": too often economists confused the model and the ideal. They assumed that economic theory was both scientific and normative, simultaneously formulating scientific laws of economic reality and imperative laws of political economy. Furthermore, their theoretical model of free exchange held for an "ideal world that was very far from the world of reality".[39] In this way they slipped from theory to doctrine: their objectivity was compromised by a failure to distinguish their theoretical models from their normative preferences.

But such models presented other problems. By way of illustration, Aron examined three models used by economists in the study of unemployment. The first – the statistical approach which sought to establish correlations between such variables as proportion of unemployed and region, industry, type of job and age of worker – though "indispensable in economics as in all branches of science", lacked explanatory power.[40] Secondly, Keynes' "general theory" posed both logical and empirical problems. It was difficult, Aron maintained, to say whether or not his choice of variables was logically and empirically correct. Keynes' theory provided a model of dynamic equilibrium which was true in so far as it determined all the variables on which full employment depended and picked out certain mechanisms and correlations from among the variables, but it was still necessary to show that the actual situation was indeed as Keynes, without producing any proof, asserted it to be.[41] Lastly, the supposedly non-theoretical empirical analysis advocated by Simiand could be criticized on several counts. The idea that research could be totally separated from conceptual or ideological questions was quite false, since theoretical concepts inevitably came into the design of any study; and the statistics themselves always had to be interpreted – the interpretation of correlations or regularities was never somehow "inscribed" in the statistics.[42]

Thus none of these three modes of economic analysis "exhausted reality". In practice, different types of explanation had to be employed alongside one another. Not that such uncertainties should be cause for surprise or discouragement. They stemmed, not from the inadequacies of economists, but from the complexity of economic reality. The subjects of economics were men and their decisions were intelligible only if they were rational; but the fact was, Aron observed, that they were not

171

always rational.[43] This analysis pointed, therefore, to what Aron saw as the *historical* dimension of economics, properly conceived:

...economics is a historical as well as a theoretical science. It is historical, because it is concerned with facts that cannot be reduced to generalities. It is historical, because the generalities only apply in spatio-temporal frameworks marked out by the particularity of economic and social systems. It is historical, finally, because it arises out of a historical, i.e., human and changing, reality, which it consciously tries to grasp. It is with complex exchanges and with capitalism that economics comes into being and flourishes. Historical in its origins as in its purposes, it shares in the fortunes of the process it seeks to illuminate.[44]

From this "historicity" it was possible, Aron argued, to derive the two characteristics which "in the last analysis, define the originality of the social sciences":

The social sciences study human behaviour, which is intrinsically understandable in as much as it obeys a certain rationality. They are, therefore, *essentially conceptual* and contingently mathematical. They often resort to mathematical techniques to good effect, but they keep understanding (i.e., an interpretation of human consciousness) as their goal. Moreover, precisely because man figures at the centre of the reality they explore, the social sciences have more than one reference system at their disposal; they do not construct an edifice of laws, organized in such a way as to allow the deduction of particular relationships from general or elementary relationships. In so far as they form a composite of partial relations they arrive at a single whole. For example, it is the totality of an economic regime which provides the unifying principle: *horizontal unity and not deductive system*. Lastly, these two characteristics are just as applicable to the nature of the object as the curiosity of the subject; they derive from the ontology of historical reality, i.e., from their common nature and from the particular relations between subject and object.[45]

Compared with the other social sciences, economics was, Aron affirmed "in a privileged position", despite the problems he had already discussed in connection with it. This became clear, for example, if one compared economics and political science. There could not be "an abstract theory of politics" in the way that there was an abstract theoretical economics. An "eternal politics", as opposed to a "historical politics", would seek to reveal the universally valid rules by which power is obtained and preserved, whereas the nature of power, and the means to attain it, varied between societies. Furthermore, in order to understand human action it was necessary to try to reconstruct its motivation, and to do this it was necessary to reconstruct the particular political system in which the act in question takes place. Such partial reconstructions were, Aron maintained, possible: they corresponded to the construction of Weber's ideal types – in Weber's view, the most characteristic method in sociology. But in the absence of unequivocal ends and calculable means, and in the absence of a single model embracing successive acts, the understanding of political actions was subject to the ambiguity which characterized men's ordinary understanding.[46]

A science that aspired to objectivity, yet had to do with subjective meanings (meanings, that is, attached by human beings to their behaviour), was inevitably beset with subtle logical problems. In this connection, Aron considered two main difficulties. The first was the uncertainty that underlay the move from symptoms to consciousness, or from visible signs to conscious intentions; this assumed interpretative rules and could never be more than a question of probability. The second difficulty was that of ambiguity: even if one claimed to be uninterested in the "phenomena of consciousness" and to be concerned simply with "events", i.e., completed acts, these could only be grasped through the use of concepts. (Aron would not, he stated, discuss the pseudo-logical theories of the "Vienna School", which claimed to have introduced a radical empiricism into the social sciences; for any social scientist, he wrote, who sought to ignore the fact of consciousness and speak a behaviourist language would have nothing further to say or explain.) Uncertainty and ambiguity of this kind implied that a "plurality of interpretations" – the phrase Aron had used in the *Introduction to the Philosophy of History* – was inevitable, because, whether one was considering an act, an individual, or a global phenomenon, other interpretations were always possible. Just as an economic theory was the development of a question or the elucidation of a situation, the understanding of political events was the equivalent of the reconstruction of a set (un ensemble) of actions on the basis of a certain number of conditions (données). But there was nothing intrinsically subjective, partial or invalid about such interpretations; partiality entered in so far as these interpretations failed to grasp all the conditions or motives underlying decisions. They also became partial if, instead of the meaning which the behaviour had for the other, i.e., for the actor, they substituted the meaning which the act had for the observer. For in life, as in science, objectivity resulted from the attempt to put oneself in the place of the other; it required the social scientist to understand each object – be it an individual, an epoch, or a civilization – in itself. However, objectivity of this kind, Aron admitted, was an ideal: the social scientist was interested in men's lives and their creations, but these did not yield up their meaning without the reconstruction, and thus the margin of choice, which Aron had sought to establish in connection with economics. This margin of choice, however, was even wider in the case of political science: "In contrast", he wrote, "to the quantitative determinacy of economic reality, think of the indeterminacy of political reality. The latter only exists in actions and through intentions; it is refracted differently in every consciousness and only attains intelligibility in and through the consciousness of the social scientist".[47]

The principle of the plurality of interpretations did not imply, Aron argued, that all interpretations were arbitrary or that the impartiality of truth was destroyed. Nevertheless, he warned that the social scientist should not confuse his point of view, which was one legitimate point of view among others, with a philosophy which laid claim to absolute truth on the grounds that it alone was scientific. Positivist philosophies had not always avoided this danger of transforming a "point of view" into a dogmatic philosophy. The (Durkheimian) sociologist, for example, studied moral rules as social facts, but as soon as he took his research hypothesis to be a scientifically established proposition, he became partial, adopting a "philosophy of morality" which his research would never be able to confirm because all the findings were already implicit in the initial hypothesis. Arguments between social scientists were often of this kind, and stemmed from the fact that, in the social sciences, analytical method and conceptual system were dependent upon a particular philosophical view of the reality under study. In order to be objective, therefore, the social scientist had to make himself conscious of the particularity of his perspective; otherwise, he remained a philosopher.

There were, however, two other advantages enjoyed by economics compared with the other social sciences. Although of course difficult in practice, it was not theoretically impossible to enumerate all the variables on which the functioning of the economy depends; and the economy was *up to a point* separable from other social phenomena. Neither of these statements was true of the other social sciences. For example, it was impossible to enumerate all the variables of the political system; in any given situation, they could only be established in an approximate way, and, generally speaking, political variables were indefinite in number because "the collectivity as a whole expresses itself in its politics".[48]

These differences between economics and the other social sciences presented *difficulties*, i.e., they involved a greater margin of choice, in, for instance, the construction of interpretative models, the understanding of action and consciousness, the conceptual elaboration of lived experience, the determination of social wholes and the selection of variables. But such differences and difficulties did not, Aron emphasized, imply a *qualitative* distinction between economics and the other social sciences. Weber, for example, had succeeded in reconstructing political reality with the aid of rational models. His types of power corresponded, in Aron's view, to the models used in economic theory. They represented *types of social action*, which were clearly drawn from reality, but elaborated by understanding. Aron was, he stated, aware of the gap that existed between types of power and the models employed in theoretical economics: the latter enabled one to trace, and sometimes predict, actions as they unfolded, whereas the former merely isolated the motivations characteristic of different authority relations. Nevertheless, in both cases, he contended, reality was of the same order and the work of the social scientist was analogous.

Aron felt justified in concluding, therefore, that

the social-science disciplines all share the same purpose: to understand, in an objectively valid way, the "subjective meanings" of social actions. They all achieve this by the same method, that of "rationalizing reconstruction"; this ensures them a kind of *hypothetical objectivity*, an objectivity which is always of the same logical order, but which in practice varies considerably, depending on whether reality more or less imposes an interpretation, or the social scientist enjoys a greater or lesser degree of freedom. We have analysed the limits of this freedom in more detail elsewhere; suffice it to say that, theoretically speaking, it does not destroy the universal validity of findings that are partial, even though it connects the construction of reality to the mind of the social scientist. For historical reality never exists for men's consciousness alone: lived by the consciousness of some and understood by the consciousness of others, it changes with their consciousness, without ever being finally fixed.[49]

This analysis would, Aron admitted, doubtless surprise those who recalled to mind the traditional tenets of sociology, as defined by Durkheim: treat social facts as things; sociology, unlike the specialized social-science disciplines, should study society as a whole, through procedures analogous to those of the natural sciences; and it should search for the laws of social phenomena, seeking to determine the direction of human evolution, and its stages, through a comparative study of civilizations. In considering the vast ambitions of "general sociology" thus defined, Aron concentrated on the theories of causal primacy, beloved of "sociologists inspired by positivism". For J. S. Mill, for example, the prime factor was "the state of the speculative faculties of the human race"; for Marxism, it was the state of the forces of production, or of the relations of production; while for Durkheimian theory, though doubtless with qualifications, the prime factor was social morphology, the volume and density of population. The fact that they had all found the principal agent, though never the same one, was, Aron pointed out, in itself disturbing, but this left untouched the fundamental question: is it possible to discover a principal agency of history? From a logical point of view, Aron had tried to show in the *Introduction to the Philosophy of History* that the idea of a first cause was self-contradictory:

I am, of course, aware that Marxists accept the idea of reciprocal action and talk of first cause "in the last instance", and that Durkheimians, in their turn, talk of working hypotheses and disdainfully reject such philosophical niceties. But when all these dogmatists have woken from their slumbers, perhaps they will be kind enough to answer these elementary questions. The more one recognizes the plurality of causes, the more one softens and modifies the primacy of a cause, the more urgent becomes the question: by what criterion does one decide the first cause? Working hypothesis? If so, such a hypothesis must be capable of verification or refutation. It is always possible to arrange the facts as a function of a certain cause; consequently, the working hypothesis will never be either confirmed or disproved by the results. The supremacy of the cause will appear more or less complete; the primacy will remain. Causal analysis implies the construction of variables and the isolating of regularities, whereas in this case construction and analysis are carried on indefinitely in every direction, and the notion of primacy loses all meaning.[50]

From a sociological point of view, a "dogmatically true general sociology" was something to be feared rather than desired, because it would lay claim to the "total objectivity either of a system of natural laws or of a definitive metaphysic". The former implied a historical determinism and a dehumanized history; the latter could easily turn into a fanatical absolutism in which "a dominant factor becomes the demiurge and a future goal the absolute end of history". In Aron's view, "The only unity one can aim for should avoid such dehumanization and dogmatism: the unity of a true philosophy which respects both the contradictions of reality and human diversity". With regard to the problem of objectivity, therefore, although the particularity of viewpoints inevitably limited the validity of the social scientist's results, he could work to avoid partiality by becoming conscious of his own viewpoint. "Thus", Aron concluded, "the supreme virtue of the social scientist is the rejection of all dogmatism and the capacity for self-criticism. And philosophical reflection is an inseparable part of scientific research".[51]

Pareto's Sociology

In 1937 Aron published a long and critical article on Pareto in the *Zeitschrift für Sozialforschung*.[52] The Italian sociologist had died in 1923, but the late 1930s saw the spread of a veritable "Pareto fever" in certain intellectual circles. His most important work, the *Trattato di Sociologia Generale* (*Treatise on General Sociology*), had been published in 1916, to be followed almost at once by a French translation,[53] and Bousquet's standard French biography had appeared in 1928.[54] Nevertheless, the *Treatise* had been slow to make much impact on sociological thought in France or elsewhere; it had appeared during the First World War, French sociology was dominated by Durkheimianism, and Pareto was known to have flirted with Italian fascism in the year before his death. It was in America that, in the 1930s, interest in Pareto seriously began to develop, especially at Harvard, where a famous series of seminars on his thought was presided over by the physiologist L. J. Henderson, and attended by Talcott Parsons, Robert Merton and George Homans.[55] Books on Pareto by Homans[56] and Henderson[57] soon followed and an English translation of the *Treatise* appeared in America and Britain in 1935.[58] Its publication met with a flood of review articles (by Aldous Huxley and Morris Ginsberg, to take two notable examples);[59] a full-length critical study was published by Franz Borkenau, a former associate of the Institut für Sozialforschung who saw Pareto as "the precursor of Fascism";[60] and in 1937, the year in which Aron published his article, Parsons incorporated Pareto into his analysis of *The Structure of Social Action*.[61]

The importance of Aron's study is, as one authority on Pareto has put it, that "it shows very clearly what French sociologists reproached Pareto for: a kind of scientism which confused truth and reality and led straight to fascism".[62] *The Treatise on General Sociology*, Aron argued, held "a place apart in sociological literature":

By its size as much as by its pretentiousness, it offers features that might almost be called monstrous. Ideas that are basically simple are dressed up in language that is abstruse and bogusly rigorous. Pareto has abused the right to express himself at length, as though the multiplication of anecdotes made up for the uncertainty of the evidence and examples were the same thing as proof. No writer lays claim to science with such monotonous solemnity or reveals his preferences with so much frankness.

The posthumous destiny of the work is no less surprising. Ignored by many and scorned by others, it enjoyed a considerable reputation in scientific circles. Moreover, Pareto has been recognized by the Italian Fascists as one of their masters – Pareto the mathematician who constantly repeated that he sought to ignore the practical consequences of experimental methods. Finally, since the appearance of the English translation of the *Treatise*, it has found an enthusiastic public in the United States and has become fashionable: this passionate positivist responds to a real need of our time.[63]

Such paradoxes were, of course, apparent only and Aron's aim was, he wrote, to make it possible to understand them; for, in spite of his intentions, Pareto was "more interesting for the feelings he expresses than the truths he asserts".[64]

The theory of logico-experimental method, with which the *Treatise* began, was rooted in late nineteenth-century empiricism and, in Aron's view, lacked originality; nor was Pareto explicit enough about how his theory was to be applied to social reality.[65] The distinction between "residues" and "derivations" was also questionable. Residues were said to be the relatively constant part of human behaviour, whereas derivations represented its most superficial and changing aspect; yet, Aron argued, residues were unintelligible in isolation from derivations, and they could not be grasped without psychological analysis. There were problems, too, in the classification of both residues and derivations, but it was the discussion of the latter which was "probably the best part of the *Treatise*":

Aided by his passions, Pareto does not simply reveal errors, illusions and absurd beliefs; he analyses the methods used by demagogues, politicians and the press to spread derivations, strengthen residues, and maintain and reinforce authority, by making it self-evident, natural or sacred. On this point Pareto is an innovator; he is one of the first to have based a positive conception of propaganda on a psychology of the unconscious.[66]

But because, for Pareto, only logico-experimental thought was rational, he extended the sphere of derivations much too far and as a result any construction – religious, moral or philosophical – fell victim to his critical method. Non-experimental entities (and how, Aron asked, could notions like good or justice possibly be experimental entities?) implied an appeal to sentiment or authority and were thus disqualified by Pareto on logical grounds. At the same time he found a way of "giving vent to his pet hates", for contemporary religions such as humanitarianism, socialism, solidarism and democracy were, in his eyes, simply new expressions for eternal sentiments, neither more nor less reasonable than ancient religions.[67]

Aron turned next to the theory of the social system in Part Two of the *Treatise*, beginning with the concept of the utility of a society, viewed as an entity or a person. But what were the criteria of utility, and who

178

would decide them? Everyone had his preferences and ideals and, as soon as these were at issue, science was no longer competent. It was also difficult to distinguish clearly between actions based on interest and those based on sentiment.[68]

Finally, Aron considered the theory of social heterogeneity and the circulation of elites. Here, he argued, the "formalism" of Pareto's concepts failed to hide his personal feelings and considerably diminished the significance of his conclusions.[69] "The fact that every society has an elite and a government does not imply", Aron pointed out, "that all elites and all forms of authority are equivalent". The quality of Pareto's evidence was also dubious: "Pareto accepts the most varied and questionable testimony with the same confidence, as long as this evidence brings him fresh confirmation of his views or satisfies one of his hates".[70] Still more seriously, as Aron had stated at the beginning, he confused the enumeration of examples with experimental proof.

Aron's "main criticism" of the *Treatise*, however, was its "equivocal slide from logic to psychology and from psychology to sociology". The first part of the work depended on a logic and metaphysic of science, whereas the second suffered from the opposite error: instead of being sociological, it was dominated by an ambiguous psychology of the class struggle. Compared with Freudian psychoanalysis and the Marxist critique of ideologies, Pareto could show neither the historical significance nor the psychological roots of residues and derivations. His theory of the social system was mistaken because of his psychologism and his misunderstanding of the historical process. Formal, abstract concepts like social heterogeneity, elite, force and consent did not permit adequate analysis of the structure of a society or of the functions and bases of authority.[71]

Pareto was not just a polemical writer, but one who "thinks against", in the sense that his assertions only took on meaning in opposition to the doctrines they rejected.[72] In Aron's view, Pareto was correct up to a point in his polemic against a rationalist metaphysic, simplistic progressivism, democratic humanitarianism and economic liberalism. The problem was to decide how far and in what sense he was right: did he really go beyond the theses he refuted or was he the victim of the self-same prejudices? As far as his anti-rationalism was concerned, he fought against the absolutist religion of science, but fell into the identical error of ridiculing every effort of philosophical and moral reflection, because he considered positivism to be the only valid mode of thought. With regard to liberal economic theory, he failed to place economic life in its social context or analyse it historically, and in this sense he remained a disciple of the classical economists. Pareto was right to attack absolutist conceptions of pacifism, but his critique of humanitarianism resulted in the exaltation of violence and war. Similarly with his arguments against democracy: instead of refuting democratic ideas in the abstract, it would have been more relevant to compare them with social realities. Furthermore,

like other extremists, Pareto underestimates the meaning of formal democracy. Parliamentary regimes do not represent the fulfilment of human destiny and one can imagine sacrificing hard-won liberty to the necessities of another revolution. But the totalitarian regimes have shown the difference between dictatorship and democracy. The rights conferred by the latter are part of the rights one expects of a human society; interpreted concretely and in their full sense, they represent the ultimate requirement.[73]

Lastly, Pareto's anti-progressivism was based on a pessimistic conception of man. Of course, class distinctions could not disappear if by them were meant differences in intelligence, wealth and power; similarly, all societies required collective discipline and thus a government and some use or threat of force. What Aron refused to accept, however, was Pareto's assumption – never proven – that the class structure, the character of the elites and the functioning of authority were always basically the same. It was this assumption which led Pareto to ignore history and opt for violent elites and authoritarian regimes. Because he had no conception of human betterment, he shunned the present and fell back on unchanging experience and a theory of social equilibrium.[74]

How, then, did Pareto's thought relate to fascism, with which he had sympathized, though without ever becoming a party member? It seemed to Aron that Pareto's theories could in fact best be viewed as the system by which a fascist leader cynically and hypocritically justified and organized his behaviour through the irrational use of myth, propaganda and ideology, in a paradoxical combination of total relativism and naive dogmatism. Indeed, to use Pareto's own vocabulary, the whole *Treatise* was like "an immense derivation, whose residues are political hatred and an exclusive concern with relations between governors and governed".[75]

All "value-free" sociology, Aron concluded, treated value-judgements as objects of fact. Indeed, the various schools of sociology could be differentiated by the way in which they went about this objectification of values, and sociologists by the way in which they combined knowledge and decision. Thus the French school of sociologists had believed that the discovery of social laws would reveal the rules of action and that the very goals of action followed either from evolutionary tendencies or from "true" society ("la société authentique"). In reality, however, they had merely used science to confirm their own prior values. Weber, on the other hand, stressed that a partial science always leaves room for values and that the understanding of lived worlds does not entail a choice between them. Such a distinction was partially valid in theory, because he insisted on analytic knowledge and causal relations, but all his studies reflected the questions he posed both to the past and to the present.

Pareto's solution differed from that of both positivism and neo-Kantianism. It consisted in eliminating moral prejudices as non-factual, in seeing everything in terms of the problem of authority, and in suggesting the best means of maintaining social equilibrium without explicitly affirming any value. With idealism and morality thus removed and the basis common to all societies revealed, one remained theoretically free to prefer the impossible to the possible and the illusory to the real; in fact, however, one was condemned by Pareto as naive or hypocritical. The only alternative was scepticism or blindness. One either joined the abused masses or the exploiting elite; realism ended in cynicism. Scientism was not responsible for this cynicism, though it was the tool. It was scientism which allowed Pareto to confuse human facts with things and to ignore the crucial scientific procedures of selection, interpretation and organization. It was scientism which allowed him to treat general features as essential and to substitute an eternal social system for the evolution of human societies:

Social knowledge is not in fact separable from the concrete man. Formal generalities conceal those features of society which are essential (les données essentielles); if they draw closer to the concrete, they bear the mark of intention. Is this a failure of objectivity? Perhaps such an ideal is not so much unattainable by sociology as foreign to it.

The impartiality that is necessary in the establishment of facts and the criticism of sources and statistics does not mean that we do not have to choose between methods and concepts. But this choice, in its turn, is connected with a purpose (une volonté). Just as each person reveals the goal he sets himself by the idea he has of himself, so social knowledge is bound up with the dialectic through which man becomes conscious of himself in history and simultaneously discovers what he is and what he wants. Objective knowledge is one moment in this endlessly renewed dialectic, which passes from naive existence to lucid decision.[76]

Notes

1. 1931a. Originally published in Germany in 1926 under the title *Zur Psychologie des Sozialismus* and in a new edition in the following year, Aron's review was of the

second edition of the French translation (Paris, 1929). De Man's book was translated into English as *The Psychology of Socialism* (London, 1928). Aron's early article was reprinted in the journal, *Contrepoint*, in the 1970s (1975f).

2. On de Man, see "Sur l'Oeuvre d'Henri de Man", *Cahiers Vilfredo Pareto*, 12 (31), 1974.
3. 1931a, p. 43.
4. Ibid., p. 44.
5. Ibid., pp. 45, 46–7.
6. Ibid., p. 47. De Man, whom Aron came to know personally in the 1930s, enjoyed "exceptional prestige" at the time and was, as Aron put it more than forty years later, "the only theorist of democratic socialism in the inter-war years". Yet, although de Man had, as a member of the German Social Democratic Party, militated against national socialism until Hitler took power, after which he became a Belgian Cabinet Minister and introduced his own plan for the nation's economic recovery, he adopted a pro-German attitude after the defeat in 1940. In Aron's view, de Man was disillusioned with what he saw as the failures and weaknesses of economic and political liberalism and, though opposed to Bolshevism, national socialism and racism, "felt a vague attraction for the kind of community apparently created by authoritarian regimes". Nevertheless, de Man's "great merit" remained, it seemed to Aron, "the intellectual courage to submit received doctrines to constant examination", and the central question he raised was still relevant: could social-democratic parties combine the practice of reform with the ideology of revolution? (1975f, pp. 166–9).
7. Cf. 1983a, pp. 94ff. The lectures were published under Raymond Queneau's editorship after the Second World War: Alexandre Kojève, *Introduction à la lecture de Hegel, 1933 à 1939* (Paris, 1947).
8. Fessard, 1980, p. 51.
9. Tr. 1975a, p. xii.
10. "Les Rapports de la politique et de l'économie dans la doctrine marxiste" (1937a; reprinted – with slight alterations – 1972a). The 1972 text has been used here. The other contributors to the volume, whose general title was *L'Economique et le politique* (*The Economic and the Political*) and whose editor was Bouglé, included Raymond Polin (on Belgium), Georges Lefranc (syndicalism), and Marcel Déat ("Vers une Politique cartésienne").
11. Roy Pierce has argued that this article demonstrates "a mastery of Marxism unparalleled anywhere", as well as being "one of the clearest accounts of the distinction between 'vulgar' and 'philosophical' Marxism" (Pierce, 1966, pp. 27, 28). At the time, Aron's analysis was praised by R. Schroder in the *Zeitschrift für Sozialforschung* (6, 1937, pp. 457–8) and by the economist Gaetan Pirou (*Revue d'économie politique*, 51, 1937, p. 1493). Aron himself thought the article worth reprinting, virtually as it stands, thirty-five years later (in 1972a).
12. 1972a, p. 85.
13. Ibid., pp. 85, 86–7.
14. Ibid., p. 88.
15. Ibid., p. 90.
16. Ibid., pp. 91–2.
17. Ibid., p. 92.

18. Ibid., p. 93.

19. Ibid., p. 94.

20. See ibid., pp. 94–8.

21. Ibid., p. 99. The quotation is from Jean Jaurès, *Armée nouvelle* (Paris, 1911).

22. 1972a, p. 101.

23. Ibid., pp. 102–3.

24. 1936c.

25. 1937d (reprinted 1978m).

26. Ibid., pp. 65–6.

27. For a later discussion of this question, see Ben Halpern, "'Myth' and 'Ideology' in Modern Usage", *History and Theory*, 1, 1961, pp. 129–49.

28. 1937d, pp. 69, 74.

29. Ibid., p. 74.

30. Ibid., p. 75.

31. Ibid., pp. 77, 79.

32. Ibid., p. 81.

33. Ibid., p. 82.

34. Ibid., p. 83.

35. ". . .il faut d'abord vivre, et choisir sans savoir" (ibid., p. 84).

36. 1939c. Léon Brillouin (1889–1969) became Professor of Theoretical Physics at the Sorbonne in 1928 and at the Collège de France in 1932.

37. 1937–9.

38. 1937b. This "excellent study" was singled out for praise by Achille Ouy, "Les Sociologies et la sociologie", *Revue internationale de sociologie*, 47, 1939, pp. 471–3.

39. 1939c, pp. 164, 165, 166.

40. Ibid., p. 168.

41. Ibid., pp. 172–4.

42. Ibid., p. 175.

43. Ibid., pp. 177–9.

44. Ibid., p. 180.

45. Ibid.

46. Ibid., pp. 182–3.

47. Ibid., pp. 184–5.

48. Ibid., p. 186.

49. Ibid., pp. 186–7.

50. Ibid., pp. 190–1.

51. Ibid., pp. 193–4. Compare 1937b, p. 27, where, in connection with Durkheimianism, Aron argued that "far from becoming identified with a school, sociology should always remain critically self-conscious".

52. 1937l (reprinted 1978l). Aron had also discussed Pareto briefly in his article on ideology, published in the same year (1937d, pp. 72–4).

53. *Traité de sociologie générale* (Lausanne, 1917–19).

54. G. H. Bousquet, *Vilfredo Pareto: sa vie et son oeuvre* (Lausanne, 1928).

55. See Barbara Heyl, "The Harvard Pareto Circle", *Journal of the History of the Behavioural Sciences*, 4, 1968, pp. 316–34.

56. G. C. Homans and C. P. Curtis, *An Introduction to Pareto: His Sociology* (New York, 1934).

57. L. J. Henderson, *Pareto's General Sociology: A Physiologist's Interpretation* (Cambridge, Mass., 1935).
58. *The Mind and Society* (New York and London, 1935).
59. Aldous Huxley, "Notes on the Way", *Time and Tide*, 1 June 1935, pp. 811–15; Morris Ginsberg, "The Sociology of Pareto", *Sociological Review*, 28, 1936, pp. 221–45.
60. Franz Borkenau, *Pareto* (London and New York, 1936).
61. Talcott Parsons, *The Structure of Social Action* (New York, 1937).
62. Giovanni Busino, "Introduction à une histoire de la sociologie de Pareto", *Cahiers Vilfredo Pareto: Revue européenne des sciences sociales*, 12, 1967, p. 84.
63. 1937l, p. 489.
64. Ibid., p. 490.
65. Ibid., pp. 490–4.
66. Ibid., p. 497.
67. Ibid., pp. 497–8.
68. Ibid., pp. 498–500.
69. Nevertheless, two years later Aron was to make use of Pareto's theory of elites, in preference to Marxism, in the analysis of totalitarianism (1946d). See Chapter 8, below.
70. 1937l, p. 503.
71. Ibid., pp. 504–11.
72. Aron borrowed this expression *"penser contre"* from the Institut für Sozialforschung's *Studien über Autoritat und Familie* (Paris, 1936), p. 219. He also used it to characterize another thinker of whom he was highly critical at this time, Alain (1941v) – see Chapter 11, below.
73. 1937l, p. 514.
74. Ibid., pp. 514–16.
75. Ibid., p. 518.
76. Ibid., p. 521. Subsequently Aron was to return to Pareto on a number of occasions, beginning with his paper on totalitarianism to the Société Française de Philosophie in June 1939 (1946d) – see Chapter 8, below. He twice discussed Pareto during the war, once in a study of Machiavellianism in the first number of *La France libre* (1940b) and then in an analysis of "the romanticism of violence" a few months later (1941m) – see Chapter 11, below. Long after the war, however, in his Sorbonne lectures and elsewhere, he was to view Pareto in a more detached way. See Volume 2, Chapter 8.

8

Liberalism and Totalitarianism

The Age of Tyrannies

One of the pre-war professors for whom Aron was to develop a considerable respect was the liberal historian, Elie Halévy. Indeed, Aron came to place Halévy, with Montesquieu and Tocqueville, in that tradition of French liberal political sociology of which Aron thought of himself as a descendant.[1] Born in 1870 and elder brother of the writer, Daniel Halévy, of whom Aron had an altogether different opinion,[2] Elie Halévy was one of the group of subsequently influential academics – its other members were Brunschvicg, Bouglé and Xavier Léon – who had first met as pupils at the Lycée Condorcet and then been students together at the Ecole Normale Supérieure. Like them, he was also a close friend of Alain, with whom he was a lifelong correspondent.[3] He had founded the *Revue de métaphysique et de morale* with Léon and Brunschvicg in 1893 and in 1898 he was appointed as a lecturer, and subsequently to a Chair, at the Ecole Libre des Sciences Politiques. It was as a "pure" philosopher that Halévy began his career, with a book on Plato,[4] but he gradually turned to history with a study of Bentham and Utilitarianism,[5] before he embarked on his famous masterpiece, *A History of the English People*.[6]

Aron became a "disciple" of Halévy only after the latter's death.[7] Although Aron had met him once or twice at the Ecole Normale, he had neither gone to Halévy's lectures at the Ecole Libre des Sciences Politiques nor read his books. It was not until Aron's return from Germany that closer relations developed between them as a result of the articles on conscientious objection and the Popular Front which Aron wrote for the *Revue de métaphysique et de morale*.[8] During Halévy's lifetime Aron went only once to his house at Sucy-en-Brie, "La Maison blanche", but the visit left "a lasting impression" on him, because it was there that he met the two Rosselli brothers, Italian anti-fascist militants exiled in France, who only three days later were murdered on Mussolini's orders by members of the fascist group, the "Cagoule".[9]

At the time of his death in 1937, Halévy had been preparing his lectures on the history of European socialism for publication, and a group of friends and former students – Aron, J.-M. Jeanneney, Pierre Laroque, Etienne Mantoux and Robert Marjolin, under Bouglé's direction – decided to try to complete the work from Halévy's unfinished manuscripts and their own lecture-notes. This project was interrupted by the war and by Bouglé's death in 1940. After the war, however, the decision was taken to continue the work, and Halévy's *Histoire du socialisme européen* was published in 1948 with a Preface by Aron.[10] The book was dedicated to Bouglé and to one of the original members of the group, Etienne Mantoux, a former student, disciple and friend of Halévy of outstanding promise, who was killed in action ten days before the German surrender. Like Halévy, Etienne Mantoux had an exceptional knowledge and understanding of England and the English, which he had developed from a very young age: at the time of his birth in 1913 his father, Paul Mantoux, had just become Professor of Modern French History and Institutions at the University of London.[11] After graduating in law and studying under Halévy at the Ecole Libre des Sciences Politiques, Etienne Mantoux became a Research Scholar at the London School of Economics (1935–6), where he studied under Lionel Robbins and also attended Laski's and Hayek's lectures. A staunch, though non-party, liberal, he was a strong opponent of appeasement and keen advocate of Anglo-French cooperation and understanding during the 1930s. When war broke out he served in the French Air Force and after the Armistice tried unsuccessfully to sail to England with his two brothers. He then spent some months in Lyon working on his doctoral thesis on the monetary theory of forced saving, which he defended in May 1941. In July of that year he went to America to take up a Rockefeller Fellowship at the Institute for Advanced Study at Princeton. It was there that he wrote, in English, *The Carthaginian Peace*,[12] a powerfully argued reply to Keynes' influential attack on the Treaty of Versailles, *The Economic Consequences of the Peace*. On completing the book Mantoux returned to England early in 1943, joined the Free French Air Force, took a daring part in the liberation of Paris, and went on to be decorated several times for gallantry, before being killed in Germany at the end of April 1945.[13] *The Carthaginian Peace* was published posthumously in England after the war and translated into French with a Preface by Aron.[14]

In November 1936, shortly before his death in the following year, Elie Halévy had submitted a *"Communication"* to the Société Française de Philosophie, entitled "L'Ere des tyrannies".[15] This short paper, and the discussion which followed it, caused a considerable stir at the time – Aron, who was present and contributed briefly to the discussion,[16] has retained "a vivid memory" of the meeting[17] – and in 1938 the report of the session was reprinted in a posthumous collection of Halévy's writings, which took its title from the famous 1936 *Communication*.[18] The following year Aron reviewed the volume for the *Revue de métaphysique et de morale* and used the occasion to develop themes which Halévy had only presented in outline form. The result was a long article which clearly showed Aron's thinking about totalitarianism on the eve of the Second World War;[19] it was also the first occasion on which he discussed a problem that was to remain a lifelong interest – the relationship between war and society.

The studies "on socialism and war" contained in *The Era of Tyrannies* would, in Aron's view, hold "an honourable place" in Halévy's work. "Without attaining the level of the *History of the English People*, they demonstrate the same outstanding qualities of a historian-philosopher, a historian who rediscovered philosophy as he deepened a scrupulous understanding of the past". One chapter, "The Era of Tyrannies", seemed to Aron particularly striking, as it had to the members of the Société Française de Philosophie, and it was on this, therefore, that he concentrated.[20]

Halévy's central theses could, it seemed to Aron, be summarized as follows:

1. *Socialism is contradictory*...Within the doctrine, the idea of organization, hierarchy and authority is difficult to reconcile with the idea of liberation. Historically, bureaucratic socialism corresponds to the Bismarckian tradition, in contrast to England's liberal and parliamentary democracy. In theory and in practice, is a planned economy compatible with liberty?

2. *Socialism has resulted in failure everywhere*. Socialist parties have, through legal, parliamentary and municipal action, contributed to the improvement of the lot of the working-class. But they have not prevented war, which has shown nationalist feelings to be stronger than revolutionary feelings. Out of war and the action of armed groups tyrannies have arisen, in the face of powerless social-democracies.

3. In spite of their evident differences, fascist and communist regimes nonetheless have analogous origins and converging lines of evolution. The former move from an exacerbated nationalism to a kind of socialism; the latter, starting out from revolt and in the name of freedom, have resulted in a regime of authoritarian government and patriotic exaltation. The two forces...thus end in a paradoxical and perhaps odious reconciliation, thanks to "the almost limitless powers" which "the modern structure of the state places at the disposal of revolutionaries and men of action".[21]

Although its main outlines were clear, Halévy's account was, Aron suggested, only a "sketch". Aron's task, therefore, as he saw it, was, "not so much to refute as to analyse these propositions, confirm or amend them by studying the facts, and underline those conclusions which are firm and those points which are doubtful".[22]

Aron began with the "internal contradiction of socialism". In spite of the "dictatorship of the proletariat", which Halévy saw merely as an "extreme form of fiscal radicalism", Halévy was prepared to locate Marx "on the side of internationalism and freedom". However, Aron was "doubtful that freedom (in the sense in which liberals understand the term) ever constituted the highest goal for Marx". From his youthful writings onwards, Marx's was "a communal and not an individualist ideal". Man, according to Marx, had to realize his essence in "public" activity and not in pure consciousness or isolated individuality.[23] In addition, although Marx claimed to preserve – and even "transcend" – in "real" liberty "the formal freedoms of political democracy", it was, Aron maintained, "difficult to be precise about the exact nature of Marx's thought as far as the regime of the future was concerned, because his philosophy did not allow him to engage in prophecies and utopias and he hardly looked further ahead than the inevitable collapse of capitalism". As for the dictatorship of the proletariat, Marx certainly saw it as a provisional dictatorship to prepare for the society of the future, and not, as Halévy believed, simply as an "extreme form of fiscal radicalism". There was no evidence, either, that Marx believed that socialism would succeed capitalism without a revolutionary – i.e., authoritarian – period of transition. Furthermore, wrote Aron,

all socialists are, almost by definition, hostile to liberalism: whether they are supporters of hierarchy or equality, freedom or authority, nationalists or internationalists, they are critical of the independence that the capitalist economy and representative regime seek to preserve for individuals, in as large a measure as possible. In this independence, socialists denounce a form of egoism; in competition, a law of the jungle; in the separation of individuals, the dissolution of social groups. They revile capitalism because it ensures the triumph of the spirit of the market-place; because it only allows, as the young Marx put it, relations of interest to exist among men; and because it uses the profit-motive as the only motor of economic life. At the beginning of this century, Durkheim still gave as the essence of socialism the conscious organization by the collectivity of economic functions which today are widely dispersed and spontaneous. Moral propaganda against the reign of money, economic propaganda against freedom, and political propaganda against individualism, converge, then, on a common objective: the social system to which liberal doctrine seeks to give expression and justification.[24]

All socialists, therefore, whatever the differences between them, aimed at "the permanent liberation" of the human race, and this was held to depend on the suppression of private ownership of the means of production and of the free operation of the economy. But, Aron asked, what, in practical and concrete terms, would constitute an "organized" or "planned" economy, in which the means of production was in the hands of the state or the trade unions? What political and intellectual liberties would such an economy allow to individuals? The liberation aimed at by socialists, even Marxist ones, claimed to preserve "the rights of man", political rights and freedom of thought. But if these rights were not preserved, the result, Aron pointed out, would not be "the dialectical transcendence of formal liberty", but "the substitution of one form of slavery for another".[25]

Did socialism, then, which was born of a revolt against oppression, necessarily result in a new form of oppression? To answer this question, it was necessary to follow Halévy and move from the analysis of doctrines to the study of historical realities, and in particular "the two events in relation to which socialism defines itself today" – the 1914–18 war and the post-war tyrannies. The studies of war in Halévy's book loomed as large as those of socialism and this, Aron believed, was no accident. Historically, both war and socialism had, in Halévy's view, led to tyranny, since he contended that the tyrannical regimes, communist and fascist, all had a common origin, the European war. However, Aron argued, this, in its turn, originated, not in the economic rivalries or the contradictions of capitalism, but in a strictly political problem, the liquidation of Austria-Hungary. The analysis would not have to be taken very far, therefore, before there emerged a philosophy of history which, in contrast to Marxism, gave primacy of place to the political – that is, to "the fanatical and impartial passions" in individuals, and the quarrels of prestige, power and ideology between states.[26]

No one would deny that modern wars were "primarily economic", yet it required a Halévy to remind one that so trite an observation did not perhaps contain the whole truth. Most people, however, would probably agree on two points. The circumstances of the war were political: in spite of their rivalry, "capitalist circles did not for the most part consciously want war". Secondly, one of the main elements in the situation in Europe in which the conflict arose was "the competition between the great capitalist countries for the conquest of markets". Thus a Marxist was "always entitled to go back to the economic structure in order to explain political events, but this way of writing history could never be *scientifically* refuted". However, the same argument applied to a political interpretation of history, which in this case seemed to Aron to be "closer to the facts".[27]

Among the theses which Halévy had presented to the Société Française de Philosophie, "none aroused livelier protests than his implicit assimilation of the Soviet tyranny to the reactionary tyrannies". Yet, Aron maintained, Halévy's thesis was "in one sense, indisputable" – both kinds of regime were tyrannies:

The power of the state is absolute, with no legal or practical limitation. A single party represents the state throughout the country, even though it does not represent the people; a tyrant concentrates all power in himself; and an ideology is taught dogmatically as the official truth.[28]

There were, of course, other features common to both fascism and communism, but there were also a number of differences between the two kinds of tyranny. To begin with, they "derive from different classes: fascist regimes conserve the existing social structure, while communism destroys the former ruling classes and strives to prevent differences of income from crystallizing into class distinctions". Furthermore, although it was true that in the Soviet Union, as in both Fascist Italy and Nazi Germany, the trade unions were "entirely subordinate to the state apparatus and the single party", in the USSR "the party in power arose out of the working masses and communications are maintained between them and it". The two regimes differed also in ideology, that of fascism being "idealist, heroic, irrationalist and organic", while the ideology of communism was "materialist, internationalist and scientistic".[29] However, the major difference between fascism and communism – "as it appeared up to now" – lay in the contrast between the "imperialism" of the fascist regimes and the "pacific conservatism" of the USSR, although communism, too, was "capable of ideological imperialism".[30]

It might, of course, be objected that it was illegitimate to compare Soviet Russia, in its present state, to the fascist countries, on the grounds that the Soviet Union was still building socialism and that, in order for communism to be successfully achieved, there had to be world revolution. Yet, in Aron's opinion, Halévy was quite aware of the effect on the USSR of the threat from abroad and he recognized what Aron acknowledged as "the grandeur of the Russian endeavour"; it was simply that Halévy "refused to go beyond the 'immediate future' and try to imagine what lay beyond the existing tyranny". Halévy was acting with "a historian's prudence" – a prudence that Aron explicitly sought to emulate; but although it would be "unfair to dismiss the doctrine, strength of will and goal of communism", Aron was doubtful that nationalism would disappear with capitalism. Communism was "capable of the same realistic cynicism as fascist regimes", but did not pride itself on such cynicism to the same extent. Communism tried to teach everyone to read and people would not always be satisfied with *Capital*. Even the ideologies of the two kinds of tyranny, both of which claimed to be the one and only truth, had a different meaning: "Communism is the transposition and caricature of a religion of salvation, whereas the fascist regimes no longer recognise Humanity".[31]

Nevertheless, Halévy's basic assertion, that fascism and communism both suppress freedom, seemed to Aron to hold true:

> Political freedom: the plebiscites only represent the derisory symbol of the delegation by the people of its sovereignty to absolute masters. Personal freedom: against abuses of power, neither the German citizen, nor the Italian citizen, nor the Russian citizen, have any means of recourse; the bureaucrat and the member of the Communist Party, the local *führer* and the secretary of the *fascio*, are the slaves of their superiors, but objects of fear to private individuals. Intellectual freedom, freedom of the press, freedom of speech and scientific freedom – all the freedoms have disappeared. If, in English democratic practice, opposition is, as an admirable phrase has it, a public service, in the totalitarian states opposition is a crime.

Was a parliamentary regime compatible with total control over the economy? "Experience as much as reason" led Aron to doubt it, although as in all such matters one was dealing with probabilities, even if in this case the probability was a strong one. It was easy enough to "*conceive of* reformed democracies, capable of ordering the economy without constraining men", but historically the odds were against it. "Personal freedoms, and the citizen's right of recourse against the state, would be unlikely to survive the end of political liberty".[32]

There remained one further question: "is the intellectual tyranny of the single doctrine and the single party a provisional accident of history, or the fated destiny of a new era?" Halévy, wrote Aron, would have refused such a question, since he confined himself to observing the present. "Without claiming any more than Halévy did to give an answer", Aron pointed to "the violence of party quarrels", both in the last years of the Weimar Republic "and to a certain extent in our country today":

These divisions, in our age of political religions, ... spring from desires which deep-down are contradictory; they are upheld by metaphysical beliefs or, rather, rival dogmas. There is no room for talk of tolerance. Men demand that their deeds and sacrifices be justified by an absolute value. As long as the nation is torn apart in this way, it is condemned to impotence.[33]

To those who questioned him about the tyrannical regimes' chances of survival, Halévy used to reply: "It all depends on the alternative, peace or war". In order to resist the tyrannies, Aron believed, the democracies in their turn would have to submit to a war economy and censorship, and Halévy accepted such necessities:

A man of peace like all true liberals (only the free-trader, he said to me one day, has the right to call himself a man of peace), he was not a pacifist, either in the manner of Alain or that of the jurists. He did not put his trust in treaties or the individual's refusal to fight. He envisaged war as a historian-philosopher. Its permanent condition is that "man is not simply composed of common sense and self-interest; his nature is such that he does not judge life worthy of being lived, if there is not something for which he is prepared to lose it." It was also as a historian, and not as a moralist, that he used to answer questions about the prospects for the future. During a lecture at the beginning of 1935, he declared that there did not seem to him to be an immediate danger of war, but that, in six or seven years, the danger would be considerable. A year later, as I was reminding him of his prediction, he said to me quite simply: "I was being too optimistic". Since then events have justified his fears, but they have also revealed powerful forces for peace: the complicity between the bourgeoisie of all countries and the reactionary tyrannies; the decay – moral even more than material – of the democracies; and finally, a deep desire for peace on the part of all the peoples of Europe, terrified as they are at the approach of the catastrophe that will strike us all.[34]

Democratic and Totalitarian States

To Manès Sperber, the Austrian-born Adlerian psychologist, ex-Communist militant and – after the Second World War – writer and novelist, Aron was, with Malraux, "the most resolute and clear-sighted anti-Nazi" he knew in the years before and after Munich.[35] These qualities were strikingly evident in a paper entitled "Etats démocratiques et états totalitaires" which Aron gave to the Société Française de Philosophie on 17 June 1939.[36] The paper, and Aron's contribution to the discussion which followed, "caused a furore".[37] It was to be the last meeting of the Society before the outbreak of the Second World War and the last to be held under Brunschvicg's Presidency. The Munich agreement had been signed nine months before; on 15 March 1939 German troops had occupied Czechoslovakia; and two weeks later Britain and France had guaranteed the territorial integrity of Poland. On 23 May, less than a month before Aron gave his paper, Hitler had ordered the Wehrmacht to prepare to invade Poland.

Aron gave two reasons for his choice of subject. To begin with, he said, for the first time for several years Frenchmen were more or less in agreement about the foreign policy to be pursued, with the result that the problems could be raised without risk of unleashing partisan feelings. Secondly, poised as they were between peace and war, Frenchmen were experiencing a kind of respite or pause: everything was being called into question and perhaps one of the best ways of being rid of the obsession with war was to reflect on the problems which would continue to be posed, whatever the solution, "in the weeks, months or years to come".[38]

Aron's remarks could, he stated, be grouped around three themes. The first was that the nature of the totalitarian regimes depended essentially on the necessarily revolutionary character of their governing elite. The new elites could probably be understood best through Pareto's theory of revolutions which, in Germany's and Italy's case, seemed to Aron "more applicable than the Marxist model". Pareto had argued that the decisive factor in a revolution was not the economic institutions to which it gave rise, nor the class relationships from which it derived, but the coming to power of a new elite. In Pareto's view, there were basically two types of political man: the cunning politician, who preferred negotiation to violence, and the one who despised bourgeois humanitarianism and preferred the use of force. According to Pareto, the result was a fundamental opposition between elite and mass. Pareto argued that all regimes were built upon the masses, but also upon contempt for them: their rulers always more or less despised those who brought them to power. In

193

considering the totalitarian regimes, therefore, it was important to distinguish the ideologies aimed at the masses from the radical cynicism of the leaders, which implied another system of values. Finally, and in Aron's view this point was fundamental, the function of an elite was to ensure a country's greatness; but Pareto tended to confuse greatness with power, arguing that an elite justified its function and privileges by its capacity to resort to force in order to make a country greater. An elite incapable of violence was, Pareto thought, decadent and doomed. All of these propositions, it seemed to Aron,

apply closely enough to the totalitarian regimes and, to a large extent, determine the nature of those regimes, founded as they are on the masses and a contempt for those masses, and built by violent elites, which operate on the principle that the bourgeois democracies are so cowardly that one can try anything against them without the slightest risk.[39]

Aron's second theme concerned "the diplomatic problem": the dictatorships clearly put their main emphasis on foreign policy, and their imperialist ambitions were undeniable. However, those ambitions, Aron argued, were primarily political, rather than economic or ideological. They could not, for example, be satisfied by economic concessions. For these to be of any interest to Germany, it must first be convinced that it could not achieve its political and economic aims of territorial expansion: as long as this was not the case, it would reject all purely economic solutions. Nor were Germany's political ambitions strictly ideological: there were authoritarian states on both sides in the current diplomatic conflicts. The ideological aspect of those conflicts sprang from the fact that the totalitarian states took pleasure in the idea of attacking the democracies, because they despised them and thought of them as easy prey. Furthermore, countries which became totalitarian tended to become revolutionary in their foreign policy: because of the violent suppression of internal social conflicts, they tended to channel the country's energy into foreign adventures, as was now happening in Spain over Morocco. Finally, at first the demands of the totalitarian regimes had a nationalistic character and were supported by the majority of the country. When, for example, Germany regained its freedom to rearm and even when it annexed Austria, the German people as a whole were behind the Führer. Today, this was less certain, which was why, Aron believed, the democracies must distinguish between the people and the regime:

It is not that the people, up till now, have not been whole-heartedly following their masters, and it is not that I am claiming that we shall succeed in separating the people from the regime – I do not know: I am simply saying that it is the only tactic possible. The democracies must say to the ruling elites of the totalitarian states, who believe the democracies to be too cowardly to fight: "If you force us to it, we shall fight". But at the same time, since the democracies want peace, they must say: "We are ready to solve all problems by peaceful means". In this way they appeal over the head of governments to the people.[40]

Aron's third main theme concerned the relationship between the totalitarian and the democratic states. In the first place, the democracies must show themselves capable of the same virtues as the totalitarian states. By this Aron meant that, in the face of regimes which declared that might alone was right and they were heroic while the democracies were cowardly, it was "laughable" to be continually talking of pacifism, because this served to confirm the fascist leaders in their view that the democracies were in fact decadent. When speaking to people who professed to despise peace, one had to say that it was not out of cowardice that one loved peace. It was "ridiculous" to oppose regimes that were founded on work by regimes that were founded on leisure, and "grotesque" to believe that guns could be resisted by butter and effort by repose. When the totalitarian regimes threatened them, the democracies must reply that they were just as capable of heroism and hard work: that was what Aron meant when he said that they should be capable of the same virtues. The only difference, and it was an important one, was that, in the democracies, people must willingly consent to necessities which, elsewhere, were imposed.[41]

In what ways, asked Aron, did the democracies resemble the totalitarian regimes? How did the decomposition of the democracies manifest itself? Was there anything which the democracies might legitimately borrow from the totalitarian regimes? The "growing decomposition" of the democracies revealed itself, Aron maintained, not only on a material level, but also in the fact that the citizens of the democracies – "at any rate in France" – no longer believed in the value of the regime they lived under. "A large part of the opinion of this country wants another kind of regime".[42] Two "antithetical but mutually enforcing" phenomena dominated the democracies: the "limitless demagogy" of some and the "fascist sympathies" of others, the former serving to justify the latter, and vice versa. As a consequence, a number of the characteristics of the totalitarian regimes existed in France in embryonic form. For example, the "orthodox fanaticism", which "turns intellectuals into propaganda-delegates", was not to be found only in totalitarian countries, as shown by the "wholehearted cynicism" of the eminent author who had recently written: "The only justifiable war is one made by the very strong against the very weak; the very weak are gobbled up overnight and there is no more to be said". As Machiavellian advice this might be acceptable, Aron remarked, but "if elevated into a political maxim, it is difficult to see on what moral grounds it would be possible to base resistance to regimes which put such maxims into practice".[43]

Another example was the predilection of left-wing parties to employ methods of constraint, as opposed to normal economic methods, when confronted with a problem. For years left-wing parties in France had demanded exchange controls, first because capital was escaping – though the franc was, of course, overvalued – and then because they themselves had made a number of mistakes in the economic field. "This resort to procedures of constraint in order to get out of crises which one has oneself created or aggravated, seems to me typical, I am not saying of totalitarian regimes, but of the way in which one edges into them". The results which had been obtained in the last six months, in the most unfavourable circumstances, by measures that were "perfectly simple and reasonable", seemed to Aron to prove his point.[44]

Nevertheless, it was not necessary to think of the totalitarian regimes as incarnating absolute evil, nor to call it "fascism" every time someone proposed to restore some degree of authority or borrow certain methods from the regimes they were fighting. In the technical sphere, a number of measures taken by the totalitarian regimes were worth emulating, such as those to do with the birth rate as well as certain aspects of social policy. On the most delicate question, unemployment, Aron was not saying that there was nothing wrong with the methods used by the totalitarian regimes, but it would, he thought, be interesting to examine more closely which measures – for example, public works – might be borrowed by the democracies. He was not, he pointed out, advocating mere imitation, but the use of measures which would obtain equivalent results, such as the movement of workers: it was "ridiculous" that, in areas where old industries were dead, workers should be left to live on the dole, without being induced to move to parts of the country where work was available. Such acceptance of unemployment could be ruinous to the democracies.[45]

Obviously, Aron stressed, there were limits to state intervention and constraint. A regime of liberty implied certain social and economic conditions and if one sought to maintain a regime of political liberty, one also had to maintain a certain economic liberty. The totalitarian regimes of the twentieth century had shown that, if ever an idea was false, it was the idea that the administration of things replaces the government of persons. It had become abundantly clear that, when one sought to administer all things one was also forced to govern all persons. Secondly, in order for democratic regimes to survive, it was necessary to reconstitute a ruling elite which was "neither cynical nor cowardly, and possessed political courage, without falling into a pure and simple Machiavellianism". A ruling elite must, therefore, have "self-confidence and a sense of its own mission".[46]

Lastly, and this was most difficult, it was necessary to reconstitute "a minimum of faith or common will" in the democratic regimes. This brought Aron to his final question: how to put new life into the idea of democracy? It was necessary, first of all, to distinguish what was essential from what was of secondary importance. The idea of popular sovereignty was not, for example, essential because "it can lead as much to despotism as to liberty". It was, after all, the popular majorities which had, for the most part, abused their power. What was essential in the idea of a democratic regime was legality – "a regime in which there are laws and in which power is not arbitrary and without limits". A democratic regime was, in Aron's view, one which had "a minimum of respect for persons and does not consider individuals simply as means of production or objects of propaganda"; it was also a regime which "controls the authority of those who govern, through a system of representation".[47]

However, the task was not only to reconstitute a legitimate authority that was "neither magical, nor irrational"; those who held authority must also have the minimum competence necessary to administer a modern society. Such societies were "technically very complex" and in them "the masses, with the best will in the world, pray for measures which are the very opposite of their real interests. Democratic regimes are difficult regimes, and the weight of history is on the side of totalitarian regimes – in other words, of that particular mixture of demagogy, technology, irrational faith and police-methods which we see prevailing in other countries". When, therefore, Aron talked of "saving democracy", he did not, he explained, mean that this was the most probable outcome; he merely wished to state which measures seemed to him most desirable. "This is the form of conservatism which I would want to defend". But such a conservatism implied "not only the elementary virtues of discipline, consent to authority and technical competence, but also the intellectual courage to call everything in question and pick out the problems on which the very existence of France depends":

The present crisis will be a long and profound one. Whatever happens in the immediate future, we will not come out of it cheaply. The adventure in which France and the

197

countries of Europe are engaged involves no quick and miraculous way out. Therefore, I believe that we, as teachers, are capable of playing a small part in the effort to save the values to which we are attached. Instead of shouting party-slogans, we could strive to define, with as much good faith as possible, the problems that face us and the means to solve them.

In any case, it is essential that we should convince all those who are listening to us, and all Frenchmen, of this: the people of France have a heritage, but, in order to save it, we must be capable of conquering it anew.[48]

When Aron had finished speaking, the discussion was opened by the eminent economist, Charles Rist.[49] He confessed that it was difficult to add to an exposition "as full and concise as Monsieur Aron's", especially as he agreed with him on many points, and in particular his analysis of the totalitarian governments' economic measures. Similarly, the next speaker, the Catholic philosopher, Jacques Maritain, was "in entire agreement" with Aron, though he had a number of questions to raise.[50]

It was important, he argued, to qualify what Aron had said in urging the democracies to display the same virtues as the totalitarian states, because, in Maritain's view, if the democracies borrowed totalitarian methods and values, they themselves would become totalitarian in order to fight totalitarianism. Aron accepted the relevance of this objection, but the difficulty was that people thought they saw totalitarianism everywhere. The moment any proposal which smacked of the abhorred monster was put forward, the cry went up: "But, in order to resist, you are going to destroy your reasons for resisting!" Aron was, however, less pessimistic. Furthermore, when he spoke of "the same virtues" – a capacity for work, and heroism – the phrase was inaccurate because there were two differences: firstly, these virtues would be accepted voluntarily by the individuals themselves and, secondly, their goal would be quite different. After all, in history, in order to survive it was necessary to agree to effective means, and one only resisted arms through arms. He was reminded of a young man in the left-wing Catholic group, *Esprit*, who had said to him six months before: "If the English introduce compulsory military service, they will be acting in a totalitarian way!" This "really stupid" remark, it seemed to Aron, caricatured the idea that, the moment one was ready to resist, one destroyed the reasons for resisting, and it illustrated the kind of extremism one should be careful to avoid. Any nation wanting to survive had to have a will for power to some degree and had to accept a minimum of violence. When confronted by states which claimed to be carrying out a new division of land, and whose propagandists kept repeating that the democratic states were corrupt, the only way to resist was to show one was capable of the same virtues.

But, if one displayed those same virtues in pursuit of a different goal, then Aron did not believe that one was thereby destroying one's reasons for resisting. He did not, he emphasized, wish to underestimate the gravity of the question: assuming there was a war to defend the democracies, it was impossible to tell if the democracies would come out of it alive. He was not trying to present a prettified picture of reality. No one could say what would be the result of using methods which were essential to resistance:

At the present time, it is a question of pure necessity. This must be understood, together with the danger this necessity implies. One must prepare for it as best one can, but one must not invoke this danger in order to refuse those forms of discipline which are indispensable.[51]

Maritain's next point related to Aron's use of the word "heroism", because it was an idea which could be put at the service of moral values or nationalistic interests. Aron agreed: the notion of heroism was ambiguous and much used, often for ignoble purposes. In the authoritarian regimes, for example, "heroism" basically meant a willingness to march in rank and be a soldier! What was "terrible" was that the heroic virtues were used, successfully too, in totalitarian propaganda. The ideological propaganda which had seemed to Aron to have most effect on the young in Germany was that which promised them that a heroic life would soon be theirs. What they most detested about the democratic regimes was their comfortable, bourgeois character. That said, could one really claim that the destruction of seven million Czechs by a population of eighty million was a heroic act? Ever since history began and there were men to judge it, it had been considered cowardly for the strong to kill the weak. Aron had many reservations, therefore, about the use to which the totalitarians put the heroic virtues. Nevertheless, they spent their time repeating that they were ready to fight. It was quite simple: whatever one might say, as long as the democracies were not ready to do as much, they found themselves in a position of inferiority, even moral inferiority. That, Aron explained, was all he had wanted to defend.[52]

Maritain agreed, and asked a final question: should democracy try to retain its conservative character or should it attempt to become revolutionary? Aron replied as follows:

I believe that the democracies are fundamentally conservative, in the sense that they seek to conserve the traditional values on which our civilization is founded; in relation to those who would institute a totally new existence, a military existence based on permanent mobilization, in relation to them, we are conservatives.

In relation to those who seek complete control over the economy and . . . to use all men as propaganda objects, we are still conservatives, because we are liberals, who want to preserve something of personal dignity and autonomy. I think that even a revitalized democracy would be conservative in this sense. My fear is that a coefficient of value is given to the term "revolutionary" and a coefficient of contempt to the term "conservative". Historically, it is a question of deciding if one wants to conserve by transforming and improving. Revolution, on the other hand, is destruction.

I am not in favour of the radical destruction of our existing society.[53]

Up to this point, there had been a large measure of agreement between Aron and his questioners, but the emotional temperature of the discussion rose sharply with the intervention of the philosopher, Victor Basch, President of the League of the Rights of Man and a prominent anti-fascist and Popular Front militant.[54] He had, he declared, listened to Aron with the greatest interest, the more so because he did not agree with him on a single point. His first objection was that, in his view, the National Socialist revolution was to be explained not by Pareto's theory of elites but by a more deep-rooted German inferiority complex towards the "fertility, climate and beauty" of Italy and France. Secondly, he rejected Aron's contention that the totalitarian regimes were revolutionary and the democracies essentially conservative, for Aron was forgetting the democratic revolutions of 1789, 1830 and 1848. Thirdly, it was untrue to say that the anti-fascist movements had aggravated the political and moral faults of the democracies; on the contrary, Basch asserted, they had saved democracy. Fourthly, it was ironic that Aron, who talked of recreating a faith in democracy, should be so critical of democratic ideas, institutions and parties; to Basch, the democracies had always triumphed and would continue to do so, but in order for that to happen it was "necessary to nourish faith in democracy and not destroy it with arguments as strongly and eloquently developed as yours have been".[55]

In reply, Aron stated that he would "begin with a confession":

I, too, believe in the ultimate victory of the democracies, but on one condition – that they have the necessary will.

. . . I would like first of all, if possible, to rid my answer of any personal or emotive character. You have said that certain of my propositions were painful, and others saddening. I respect the emotions you felt, but I ask the right to express what I think in all sincerity, and I shall not hesitate to go on saying painful and saddening things to you, because I believe them to be true.[56]

In response to Basch's first objection, the criticism of Pareto, Aron pointed out that he was not trying to explain the origins of German totalitarianism, for this had frequently been done, but to use a method which might help one to understand how it had developed. On Basch's second point, whether the democracies were conservative or revolutionary, Aron agreed that the totalitarian regimes were quite different from the revolutions of the nineteenth century; but Aron was talking about the revolutions of the twentieth century, and for him a regime was revolutionary if it destroyed the existing world and its values, and replaced them with something else. However, with Basch's third point, the role of the anti-fascist movements, they came, Aron said, to the painful problems:

I am familiar with the part you have played in the anti-fascist movement and I know the view you take of that movement, just as you are probably aware of the attitude I have always had towards it. You said: "We saved France from fascism on the 6th February". But one must go back a little further than the 6th February 1934 and remember the disintegration of the parliamentary regime in 1932 and 1933, which to a certain extent explains the explosion of the 6th February. If it is said that the French anti-fascist movement saved democracy, one must also recognize the development of economic demagogy and the considerable and deep wrongs done to the French economy by measures that were insane: for I call "insane" an economic policy which consisted, in one and the same year, of diminishing the length of work by 20 per cent and increasing wages by 50 per cent – something which is not possible either in a capitalist or any other regime. I believe that many of the measures taken by the Popular Front government have, indeed, been harmful to the country, and that, in as much as people intensified still further the conflicts between French political parties, they made the normal functioning of parliamentary life impossible.

That said, I am certainly not claiming that the anti-fascist movement bears sole responsibility for the aggravation of social conflict.

I do not believe that a large section of opinion in this country is anxious for fascism. I think that the endless insults of "fascist" and "anti-fascist", which have been so generously exchanged for a number of years now, run the risk of driving France into a change of regime. For democracy, which implies opposition between parties, also requires that majorities do not abuse their power.

I am sure that you remain unconvinced, but allow me to say this. You said that you put an end to street movements. But you replaced them with other street movements.

I have no wish to condemn root-and-branch everything that this movement has done, and I should like to go back to the propositions contained in my summary: I think that, by making the functioning of the parliamentary regime more difficult, and the functioning of the present-day economy even more so, the Popular Front has indeed aggravated the faults of the democracies.

Basch: I wasn't defending the Popular Front government. What's more, you didn't mention it. You mentioned the anti-fascist movements; it was them I was defending. I never defend any government.

Aron: All the same, you can't say, "The anti-fascist movement is very good and the institutional realities provoked by that movement are very bad". A historical movement is judged by its concrete results.

Basch: It was a defensive movement against a danger which you minimize, against fascist ventures.
Aron: You then say to me, "You want to build a new faith, and yet, by your pessimism, you are destroying the very conditions of that faith".

Once again, our convictions and personalities are going to clash. I do not believe that we shall cause a new faith to arise by accepting responsibility for everything which the parliamentary regime and the parties of the Left have done since the war – to go back only that far.

Every time the parties of the Left have come to power, they have been incapable of governing for more than two years, as a result of mistakes that they themselves have made. If, as is often the case, left-wing ideas – the "great ideas" – are confused with certain concrete parliamentary realities, then I do not believe that we shall ever be able to restore faith, however small, to the young or to the French people as a whole. I do not believe that it is possible to arouse anybody's enthusiasm for the parliamentary regime, as it has functioned for the last twenty years.

My aim, therefore, was to distinguish the institutions, which do not seem to be irrevocably doomed but to be going through a temporary crisis, from the permanent values, which must be saved.

As for my phrase about the ideas of 1789...this is what I meant. If one takes the ideas of 1789 in their abstract sense of "liberty, equality and fraternity", these are only guiding principles; one still needs to know what institutions can translate them into practice. Above all, I want to save the fundamental ideas of respect for the person and the spirit. I spoke of calling abstract moralism and progressivism into question. Indeed, to think in terms of abstract justice, when faced with concrete economic and political problems, gets us nowhere. Between radical cynicism on the one hand, and abstract moralism on the other, I think that there is a third way: to pick out the institutional realities which, given the present situation, would best respect and express the values that we intend to safeguard.[57]

Relative calm seems to have returned to the gathering with the next speaker, the Socialist politician, Aimé Berthod.[58] He was, he stated, in almost complete agreement with "all the excellent things" that Aron had said, but Aron should, he thought, have paid more attention to two features of the totalitarian regimes which helped to explain their appeal: their egalitarianism and their claim to have destroyed capitalism. It was also important, he believed, to distinguish democratic and economic liberalism, for if that distinction were not made, the totalitarian regimes had a number of good arguments to use against the democracies. Aron replied that there was indeed a sense of equality, fraternity and community among the young in Germany, but wealthy classes still existed and capitalism had not been destroyed. As for the distinction between democratic and economic liberalism, he accepted it, but would want to add that, without a minimum of economic liberty, he did not see how one could preserve political liberties.[59]

202

Edmond Vermeil, the German specialist who had been one of the jury at Aron's defence of his complementary thesis the previous year, confessed that, although he had a high opinion of Aron, as Aron well knew, he preferred the attitude Aron had shown in the discussion to that in his exposition. Vermeil wanted to express what he called "the sadness I feel at the present time, a sadness which, I thought, weighed on us all a little as we listened to Aron's exposition: our democracies seem a little ashamed almost, in the face of the victories that have been won by the totalitarians".[60] Certainly, he believed, the democracies would have to revise their values and their pace of life, but not at the cost of sacrificing their principles. It was inadequate, however, to begin with Pareto and argue that the German revolution, like all revolutions, opposed elite and masses. "You said", he continued, turning to Aron, "that this implies contempt for the masses. I say: not in the democracies".

"Among the leaders of the democracies", Aron replied, "there is the same profound contempt for the masses that you find in *Mein Kampf*".[61]

The "really tragic problem of our time", Vermeil went on, was how to explain the surrenders, the lack of resistance, and lack of faith of the democracies in their own destiny and the values they represented. In his view, the tragedy could be explained in terms of two extremely dangerous forces. One, which came from the Right, imagined that Hitler, having saved German capitalism, would save French capitalism if he entered France; the other, on the Left, was a doctrinaire pacifism, which, said Vermeil, he could not understand.[62]

Aron confessed himself quite unable to understand the objection of his next questioner, the philosopher Dominique Parodi,[63] who had argued that it was not strictly possible to compare the democratic and the totalitarian states. The fact was, Aron pointed out, that they both existed. He had not sought to compare two doctrines, but two kinds of state which were there before their very eyes and in a short time might well be at war with one another. In reply, however, Parodi continued to maintain that they were not faced with two types of government "between which they had to choose". "But we are", insisted Aron.[64]

To the young economist, Etienne Mantoux,[65] Aron had "shown something quite rare in our time: that it is possible to admire democracy without ignoring its faults and to love liberty without being sentimental". He agreed with Aron that "in order to restore democratic values, we must be essentially conservative" and added:

Like you, I believe that it is the liberals who will succeed in safeguarding the values of which I speak – not those shamefaced liberals who dare not speak their name, but liberals ready to defend not only political but also economic liberty.

Finally, faced with these totalitarian regimes, I believe that, till now, we have given evidence of too great a confidence in the value of our own civilization.

Clearly, the future will be what we make it. There is no inexorable evolution in the direction of liberty, and democracy and liberty are threatened by a terrible crisis. If we do not defend them by reforming the methods with which we have defended them till now, they will surely perish.[66]

The Protestant theologian, Marc Boegner,[67] argued next that Aron had underestimated the importance for democracy of the idea of popular sovereignty, to which Aron replied that popular sovereignty, as conceived by Rousseau, implied the exclusion of political parties;[68] and to an objection from the Marxist philosopher, René Maublanc, that Aron had neglected the part played by economic factors in the rise of totalitarianism, Aron retorted that these had often been discussed already and, anyway, in Nazi Germany Hitler was master, not Krupp.[69] Finally, he added, Vermeil was mistaken if he thought that Aron sought a synthesis between the two kinds of regime:

I said that the democratic regimes had to examine their conscience; I believe that the best proof of this is their surrender in the face of the totalitarian regimes in the last few years. England and France were all-powerful when Hitlerism was in its early stages and they could have put a stop to the adventure before it was too late. The great capitalists played a part, that is unquestionable; but there was more to it than that. It is not only right-wing governments who were unwilling to resist the totalitarian regimes, and not only the great financiers who declared that it was stupid to defend the Czechs.

The crisis appears infinitely more profound to me. This is what I have tried to show, and I should like to end on this note. I have not sought to be pessimistic or to apportion blame; I have tried to show that it is too easy to appeal to immortal principles in the face of the totalitarian regimes. Principles are nothing when they are not animated by life and faith. It is a question, today, of giving them back their life.[70]

A description of Aron at this meeting has been left by the same "*Cloutard*" who had earlier[71] recalled his philosophy teacher at the Ecole de Saint-Cloud:

The scene is a stuccoed lecture-room in the Sorbonne where in the dim light a meeting of the Société Française de Philosophie is taking place under the presidency of Léon Brunschvicg – an Olympian figure with his huge forehead and a piercing look that seems to defy appearances. Raymond Aron – his body seemingly disjointed and his face with its projecting ears, hooked nose and bitter, ironic mouth assuming the exaggerated features of a mask – has just expounded, with cold detachment, views on the relativity of history,

204

the fragility of democracy and the uncertainty of humanity's future which arouse the anger of the massive Victor Basch. The latter, with trembling body and in a tribune's tones, declares his unshakeable conviction: liberty was born in Greece, it has never ceased to illuminate man's way and it is a light which will never be extinguished; it will triumph. In reply his interlocutor states with icy courtesy[72] that nothing is fixed in advance and nothing can be taken for granted; at best it is conceivable (but this is granted grudgingly and almost wearisomely) that in the very long term, perhaps, reason and morality will by their strength and power jointly triumph over violence and passion...It is evidently Aron who is right.[73]

* * *

On 21 August, two months after Aron gave his paper to the Société Française de Philosophie, the Nazi-Soviet Pact was signed – an eventuality which in June had seemed to him "fairly unlikely".[74] The Arons were on holiday near Bouglé's family house in Brittany when news of the Pact reached him. It "took his breath away". For five minutes he kept repeating, "It's impossible!" It was as if he refused to believe it, because he knew that it meant war, though on reflection he saw the logic of the "meeting of the two revolutions".[75]

Ten days afterwards, on 1 September, Hitler's troops invaded Poland and two days later Britain and France declared war on Germany. Aron had just been appointed *maître de conférences* (lecturer) at the University of Toulouse. He never took up the appointment.

Notes

1. 1967a, pp. 21, 295: tr. 1965a, p. 259. Cf. 1971d, p. 5. For appreciations of Elie Halévy, see Aron's own penetrating tribute in a lecture given to the Société Française de Philosophie to mark the hundredth anniversary of Halévy's birth (1971d); Michèle Bo Bramsen, *Portrait d'Elie Halévy* (Amsterdam, 1978) with a Preface by Aron (1978o); Myrna Chase, *Elie Halévy, An Intellectual Biography* (New York, 1980); and Anthony Hartley, "Elie Halévy and England Now: The Topicality of History", *Encounter*, January 1975, pp. 40–6.
2. In an article in *La France libre* written during the war, Aron called Daniel Halévy an "inveterate reactionary" (1943s, p. 431).
3. See Alain, E.C. *Correspondance avec Elie et Florence Halévy* (Paris, 1958). For Aron's view of the relations between Elie Halévy, Alain and Brunschvicg, see 1971d, pp. 22–4.
4. *La Théorie platonicienne des sciences* (Paris, 1896).
5. *La Formation du radicalisme philosophique* (Paris, 1901–4): tr. (by May Morris), *The Growth of Philosophical Radicalism* (London, 1928).
6. *Histoire du peuple anglais au XIXe siècle* (Paris, 1913–23). Aron reviewed a new edition of this work in 1973 (see 1973l). The nature of Halévy's shift from philosophy to history has been analysed by Aron in 1971d.

7. R. A., interview with the author, 1979. Cf. 1971d, p. 3.

8. 1934a, 1937c. See Chapter 4 above, and Halévy, 1985.

9. Halévy's wife, Florence, Aron recalls, "told us how shattered and overcome Elie was: pitiless and lucid in his diagnosis, he foresaw the time of the assassins and the coming of the barbarians" (1971d, p. 4).

10. 1948c.

11. Paul Mantoux, C.B. (1877–1956), was the author of a classic study of the English Industrial Revolution, *La Révolution industrielle au XVIIIe siècle* (Paris, 1906): tr. (by Marjorie Vernon) *The Industrial Revolution in the Eighteenth Century* (London, revised edn, 1948 and 1961). He subsequently became official Interpreter at the Peace Conference at Versailles, Director of the Political Section of the League of Nations Secretariat (1920–7), and Director of the influential Graduate Institute of International Studies at Geneva (1927–34).

12. Etienne Mantoux, *The Carthaginian Peace, or The Economic Consequences of Mr Keynes* (Oxford, 1946).

13. Paul Mantoux, "Foreword" to Etienne Mantoux, op.cit.

14. 1946g.

15. Elie Halévy, "L'Ere des tyrannies", *BSFP*, 36, 1936, pp. 181–253: tr. (by May Wallas) "The Age of Tyrannies", *Economica*, n.s. 8, 1941, pp. 77–93.

16. 1936r.

17. 1971d, p. 4.

18. Elie Halévy, *L'Ere des tyrannies: études sur le socialisme et la guerre* (Paris, 1938): tr. (by R. K. Webb) *The Era of Tyrannies: Essays on Socialism and War* (New York, 1965; London, 1967).

19. 1939b. Cf. 1983a, pp. 153–4.

20. Ibid., p. 283.

21. Ibid., pp. 283–4.

22. Ibid., p. 284.

23. Ibid., p. 285.

24. Ibid., p. 286.

25. Ibid., p. 287.

26. Ibid., p. 288. Aron was to develop this argument many years later in *Les Guerres en chaîne* (*The Century of Total War*) (1951a: tr. 1954a). See Chapter 17, below.

27. 1939b, pp. 290–1. Aron was less convinced by Halévy's claim that, although the war was political in its origins, it had decisive economic effects and the post-war tyrannies were a development not so much of Marxism as of the war economy (ibid., pp. 291–5). For Aron's later views on this question, see 1971d, pp. 18–19.

28. 1939b, p. 299.

29. Ibid., pp. 299, 300.

30. Ibid., pp. 302, 303.

31. Ibid., pp. 304–5.

32. Ibid., p. 305. For Aron's pre-war views on the USSR, as recalled forty years later, see 1981a, pp. 51–3: tr. 1983b, pp. 45–8 (R.C.): "I was both ignorant of the reality of the Soviet Union, somewhat neutral, interested nevertheless, but not attracted, because I dislike violence and, even at that time, I was by temperament a liberal. I did not believe in messianism or millenarianism. Thus, during the 1920s,

Bolshevism was not, for me, a privileged object of speculation. But, in the 1930s, we became increasingly obsessed by totalitarianism. And totalitarianism was Hitler, but also Stalin". It was the Nazi-Soviet Pact of August 1939 which, Aron states, "really freed" him in his view of the Soviet Union.

33. 1939b, p. 306.
34. Ibid., pp. 306–7.
35. Sperber, 1971, p. 548. The two men had in fact been introduced by Malraux (Manès Sperber, interview with the author, 1980). On Sperber, see Chapter 13, below.
36. The report of the session was published immediately after the war (1946d) and reprinted, with part of the discussion, at the end of Aron's life (1983f). See also the discussion in Aron's memoirs (1983a, pp. 154–7).
37. R.A., interview with the author, 1979.
38. 1946d, p. 43.
39. Ibid., pp. 43–4.
40. Ibid., p. 51.
41. Ibid., pp. 51–2.
42. Ibid., p. 52.
43. Ibid., p. 53.
44. Ibid. Aron was here referring to the economic measures taken by Paul Reynaud, Finance Minister in Daladier's Government. These included an increase in the length of the working week, reduction in the number of government employees, and new taxation plans, as a result of which a marked improvement had taken place in France's financial situation.
45. Ibid., pp. 53–4.
46. Ibid., p. 54.
47. Ibid., pp. 54–5. Compare the later discussion of this question in *La France libre* during the war (1942d). See Chapter 11, below.
48. 1946d, p. 55.
49. Charles Rist (1874–1955), the father of Aron's school-friend, Léonard Rist, was Professor of Economics at the Sorbonne. His most recent book was *Histoire des doctrines relatives au crédit et à la monnaie, depuis Law jusqu'à nos jours* (Paris, 1938) and a review of it by Aron was published in 1940 (see 1937–9).
50. Jacques Maritain (1882–1973) was Professor of Philosophy at the Institut Catholique. A strong opponent of totalitarianism, he spent the war in the United States, where he was to publish Aron's *L'Homme contre les tyrans* in a series which he edited for the Editions de la Maison Française in New York (1944a).
51. 1946d, pp. 62–3.
52. Ibid., p. 63.
53. Ibid., p. 64.
54. Victor Basch (1863–1944), who specialized in German philosophy, had been Professor of Aesthetics at the Sorbonne since 1918. He and his wife were to be murdered during the war by the pro-German French Militia, the *milice*.
55. Ibid., p. 67.
56. Ibid.
57. Ibid., pp. 68–70.
58. A Senator and former Minister, Berthod was subsequently arrested by the Germans and died as a result in 1944.

59. Ibid., pp. 70–5.
60. Ibid., p. 77.
61. Ibid., p. 78.
62. Ibid., pp. 79–80.
63. Dominique Parodi (1870–1955) had been Inspector General of Public Instruction since 1919. He had become Editor of the *Revue de métaphysique et de morale* in 1938.
64. Ibid., p. 83.
65. See above, p. 186–7.
66. Ibid., pp. 83–5. Compare the letter he wrote to Aron at this time: Etienne Mantoux, "Lettre à Raymond Aron: sur la maladie infantile du libéralisme", *Commentaire*, 6 (24), pp. 717–19.
67. Marc Boegner (1881–1970) was President of the Fédération Protestante de France and during the Second World War was to be a prominent opponent of measures aimed against Jews and political prisoners.
68. Ibid., p.91. See n. 47, above.
69. Ibid., p. 90. A *normalien*, pupil of Durkheim and a Communist, after the war Maublanc taught at the Lycée Henri-IV and became Editor of the Marxist journal, *La Pensée*. He died in 1960.
70. Ibid., p. 92.
71. See Chapter 4, above.
72. "Already (!)", Aron commented in his memoirs (1983a, p. 744, n.i.).
73. Ibid., p. 744. Aron submitted this portrait to another pre-war "*Cloutard*" for comment. The latter, although not present at this particular meeting, rejected the description of Aron's mouth as "bitter" and thought that the portrait omitted "the smile, kindness and good humour" of his former philosophy teacher (ibid., n.i.).
74. 1946d, p. 48.
75. 1981a, p. 54: tr. 1983b, p. 47. See also 1983a, p. 161.

Part Three

The War Years

———

9

La France libre

———

Aron was called up as soon as war broke out, though in a capacity
which involved little fighting because, as we saw, he had done his
military service in the Air Force as a meteorologist.[1] This was clearly
a source of irritation and regret to him; indeed, he wrote to Jean Cavaillès
at the Ministry of War in Paris to see if there was any chance of being
transferred to the tanks. But Cavaillès had already joined a combat unit
and Sergeant Aron spent the *drôle de guerre*, as the French called the
"phoney war", in charge of a dozen or so men at a meteorological station
on the Belgian frontier near Charleville. There was little to do apart
from launch weather-balloons, and he spent the time reading, editing
Elie Halévy's *Histoire du socialisme européen*,[2] and working on a book on
Machiavellianism in the twentieth century. Thus he wrote to his wife
on 28 November 1939:

I have corrected the part of the *Machiavellianism* you sent me. I am writing Essay II
which will be entitled "Machiavellianism and the Political Doctrines of the Twentieth
Century". Essay III will be called "Machiavellianism and Totalitarian Regimes". Essay
IV "1914 and 1939". Essay V will be "France in the Age of Demagogic Caesarism".
I have reached Essay II (the first being Machiavelli–Pareto). It will be a bit light, with
more ideas than facts and not enough specific study of texts. But the war allows one

to take liberties with scientific method. This work is quite distracting, at any rate on the days when some incident of military life doesn't detain me for hours because of some piece of stupidity.[3]

The German offensive, when it came, began on 10 May 1940, in just the sector where Aron happened to be. The disastrous weeks that followed were "morally unbearable". Aron had the feeling of being "totally useless"; he was overcome by "shame and humiliation".[4] Armed with their nineteenth-century rifles, the meteorologists saw action in Belgium and then gradually retreated with the routed army. Early June found him at Brie-Comte-Robert, a little to the south-east of Paris. It was at this time that he learned that his mother was dying at Vannes in southern Brittany. His commanding officer, having refused him leave to go to Vannes, entrusted him with a mission that enabled him to reach his mother before she died, although she was already in a coma. Aron's wife was also there, having made the difficult journey from Toulouse. "Never again shall I experience more desperate moments (des heures aussi désespérées)", he wrote to Albert Palle on 7 June, characteristically altering this at once to "closer to despair" ("proches du désespoir"). "Now I am armour-plated (blindé)", he declared, adding optimistically to his young friend (then heading for Dunkirk), "We mustn't forget that the first disasters are due largely to mistakes, strokes of misfortune and acts of betrayal which will not recur".[5] He rejoined his unit and, having crossed the Loire at Gien, he and his men reached a point just south of Bordeaux on about 20 June. There he was able to visit his former colleagues at the University, where he had lectured in 1937–8, including the Dean of the Faculty of Letters, the philosopher André Darbon, for whom he had a great respect. It was at Bordeaux that Aron heard Marshal Pétain's broadcast announcing that he was taking over as head of government and hoped to begin negotiations with the Germans for an end to hostilities. Aron did not, however, personally hear any of General de Gaulle's broadcasts from London.

Aron's reaction to the news, like that of most of the defeated army, was one of relief as much as anger; but he had no illusions about the intentions of the Pétain government and he refused to accept that any Armistice that might be concluded meant the end of the war. For Aron, the question in June 1940 was: would Britain hold out for the remainder of the summer? Either Britain would be quickly defeated, or the war would be a long one and France occupied for a number of years. Should he stay in France or carry on the fight in England? In a few days' time it would be too late to leave the country. Aron had, therefore, to reach a decision quickly, but first he wanted to discuss it with his wife who was with her parents 250 kilometres away at Toulouse. There was a motorcycle in his detachment and the driver – a mechanic from the North with whom Aron was on friendly terms (they met again after the war) – agreed to take him there on the pillion. At Toulouse he discussed the situation with his wife and friends, including Georges Canguilhem, who was later one of the founders of the Resistance movement "Libération". Aron thought that the war would go on and that he could be useful in England; there seemed to him little point in remaining in the south of France and he had no wish to go to the United States, even though he could have had a Chair in an American university, because there he would not have been able to take an active part in the war. Furthermore, he thought that it would not be long before laws were passed against the Jews and, should provision be made for exceptions, he would find it distasteful to take advantage of preferential laws if all other Jews were not treated as French citizens. In addition, he knew that, as a philosopher, a known democrat and an outspoken anti-Nazi, who had spent a number of years in Germany and attacked the mystique of nazism, he was certainly a marked man who risked being kept under surveillance and arrested. In any case, action on his part would be difficult, and he had no confidence in Pétain's government which, he thought, would gradually come to do everything that the Germans wanted of it.[6]

For all these reasons, he and his wife agreed that he should carry on the struggle in England. Thus he returned to his unit, said goodbye to his comrades and set off for Bayonne and Saint-Jean-de-Luz. All he had with him was a haversack containing his toilet things (and perhaps a book) and this gave him "a curious feeling of lightness":

What was the importance of things, furniture and even books? All that was disappearing into the distance. In the midst of the national disaster, only the essential remained – my wife, my daughter and my friends. Through these attachments, I remained myself. The catastrophe itself revealed the futility of everything else.[7]

At Bayonne he spent a night in a train which, to his amusement, contained all the shares of the Paris Stock Exchange. It struck him as "extraordinarily comical, and it even had its philosophical side: in the midst of the catastrophe the fleeting character of transferable securities was revealed".[8] From Bayonne he made his way to Saint-Jean-de-Luz, where a British liner, the *Ettrick*, was waiting to transport a Polish division to England. Someone suggested to Aron that he should put on a Polish military greatcoat, and he thus succeeded fairly easily in getting aboard dressed as a Polish soldier. The next day, 24 June, the ship set sail. Also on board were the internationally known jurist, René Cassin, who was to become one of de Gaulle's most valued associates, and some fifty French soldiers and airmen.[9] It was while he was on board the *Ettrick*, heading for England, that Aron learned that the Armistice with the Germans had been concluded.

He was to retain two memories of the crossing:

I was in the midst of clearing the table, wiping the cloth and perhaps doing the washing up when, for some reason or other, an elderly Englishman began talking to me and asked me what I did in civilian life. When I told him that I would have been teaching philosophy at the University of Toulouse had I not been called up, he burst into furious recriminations against the French and British governments – recriminations which he seemed to be addressing to his wife: "For years I've been telling you that this stupid policy would be the ruin of us all. Look where we are twenty years after victory!" For him the university teacher-turned-dishwasher had become the symbol of a topsy-turvy society and of the misfortune which the French and British had brought upon themselves.[10]

The other thing that left a lasting impression on Aron was the organization aboard ship:

Thousands of soldiers filed past with their mess-tins. There were no meal-tickets or identity-checks. Everyone was trusted. No steps were taken to guard against cheats or queue-bargers. On the *Ettrick* I first breathed *l'atmosphère britannique*. I at once felt at my ease, even though I did not understand a word of what the sailors, soldiers or, come to that, intellectuals said.[11]

The ship docked at Plymouth on the 26th, and the contrast between the distress and chaos in France, and an England as yet untouched by the war, was "extraordinary":[12]

I had just come from France, where the people were fleeing aimlessly along the roads, there were ruins almost everywhere, and there was an atmosphere of despair. I hardly spoke any English at the time. All the same, I did understand the words of encouragement of one good Englishman who said to me: "You'll get your country back by Christmas". The English were then in "their finest hour", but the mass of the population failed to understand the danger. The lawns were impeccable, as usual. The English, in their island, were undisturbed. But for me, coming from France to a threatened country where I had never been before, this impression of calm came as a shock.[13]

From Plymouth Aron was taken to an army camp at Birkenhead, where there were 20,000 Frenchmen, most of whom had been evacuated from Normandy during the German advance. A few days later the French were given a choice of three solutions: to return to France, to join the troops which had rallied to General de Gaulle, or to live as free citizens in Britain. Aron, who had left France in order to continue the war, decided to join de Gaulle's forces and at the end of June was sent with those who had made the same decision to the Empire Hall, Olympia, in West London. This huge, windowless building, normally an exhibition hall, had to house some two thousand Free French volunteers and, not surprisingly in the circumstances, soon became uncomfortable, dirty and malodorous. The men slept on mattresses – the infantry on one floor, the air force on another, and the artillery on the third. They had to do their own chores and Aron was to be seen, in forage cap and fatigues, taking his turn at cleaning out the latrines.[14] But no one complained: although the food was poor, there was enough of it and nobody stayed there for very long.

When he arrived in London, Aron, who of course spoke good German, knew virtually no English, although he could read it a little and had even reviewed a number of English books.[15] The only English people he knew were A. P. Herbert and his wife, whom he had met while on holiday at Varangeville, near Dieppe, in 1931 (he was reading Heidegger on the cliff tops; she was painting). However, through his friend Robert Marjolin, who was in London with the French Economic Mission under Jean Monnet, Aron soon met the liberal economists, Friedrich von Hayek and Lionel Robbins (later Lord Robbins). Early in July Aron paid his first visit to the Reform, the famous Liberal club in Pall Mall, where he subsequently dined nearly every Thursday throughout the war; here he had a long conversation with Robbins, who was then Director of the Economic Section of the Offices of the War Cabinet. Aron had just learnt of the British attack on the French fleet at Mers-el-Kebir on 3 July and was mortified by the news.[16]

The next day, Aron left Olympia and joined the Free French Forces in their camp at Aldershot. At the end of June there had been thousands of French soldiers, and at least ten thousand sailors, in England. During the course of July, however, the British authorities actively encouraged many of them to return to France, on the grounds that there was a shortage of arms but no shortage of troops. The attack on Mers-el-Kebir and the seizure of all French ships in English ports, together with the internment of their officers and crews, swelled the numbers returning to France. The great majority of French troops left and by the end of July the Free French Forces comprised no more than seven thousand men.[17]

On his first night in the camp at Aldershot, Aron shared a room with the twenty-year-old François Jacob, winner of the 1965 Nobel Prize for Medicine, who was serving as a medical orderly. There was also a young officer-cadet (*aspirant*) who had come to England from Morocco. That evening the three had a long conversation together. The next morning the officer-cadet asked Aron what the time was. "Twenty to seven", Aron replied. "Already!" he cried, and at exactly seven o'clock he put a bullet through his head. Aron and Jacob were the only witnesses at the inquest, the coroner's verdict being that the young Frenchman had taken his life "while the balance of the mind was disturbed".[18]

At Aldershot Aron asked to serve in the tanks, but he was told that, at thirty-five, he was too old, a decision which he thought "ridiculous". Nevertheless, though it was small consolation, he was put in charge of the tank company's accounts. He also had the satisfaction of being one of only 125 Frenchmen – twenty-five members of the Foreign Legion, a small armoured car section, thirty sailors and forty airmen – who took part in a procession through the streets of London on the fourteenth of July.[19] It was an emotional occasion, much acclaimed by the watching crowds, as General de Gaulle inspected the Free French troops in the presence of King George VI and laid a wreath at the statue of Marshall Foch near Victoria Station. In the afternoon they went to a special showing of the film, *Carnet de bal*, at the New Victoria Cinema and were served tea in the Central Hall, Westminster.[20]

One of those who came to know Aron in the camp was Daniel Cordier, then a young Maurrasian nationalist, later Secretary to the Resistance leader Jean Moulin, and after the war a successful (and left-wing) picture-dealer. He describes meeting the "vieux sergent" that July:

To us he was ageless – perhaps thirty or forty years old which, with the exception of the Colonel, made him the oldest man in the camp. He was called Raymond Aron – a name which was unknown to me or to my friends. Before the war he had been a teacher, which prejudiced me against him from the start. And yet he was approachable, straightforward and courteous. He was not very tall. His bare forehead, large ears and prominent nose gave his face an unusual appearance. He at once fastened his look upon me: it was attentive and searching, combining a fundamental melancholy with sudden flashes of malice. In the course of these meetings, I was astonished by the attention with which he listened to these young people. He would put questions to them and reply carefully to their arguments or questions with a moderation which, on occasions, did not exclude passion.

This wartime encounter with a twentieth-century Socrates was the beginning of Cordier's political education:

I spoke less and less, and listened more and more. And, although sometimes irritated by a democrat who was surely a former adversary, I began to appreciate his tolerance and his respectful demonstrations of reality.[21]

One of the main talking-points among the Free French in July 1940 concerned the attitude to be adopted towards Vichy, and it was here that Aron first began to put forward opinions which were considered heretical with regard to both Vichy and the orthodox Gaullists. Some, like René Pleven, who had been with the French Economic Mission in London and had at once rallied to La France Libre, argued that Vichy was an abomination and that any double game with the Vichyites was out of the question. Aron did not agree, and he annoyed those who wanted to continue the fight by arguing that Vichy's decision was probably justified, as long as England won the war. He agreed that the men of Vichy were reactionaries and, no doubt, foolish traditionalists, but he believed that they were basically patriotic: they at least seemed to be trying to spare the people of France the worst effects of a German occupation. It was therefore important, he argued, not to alienate them irrevocably but, on the contrary, to try to win them over to the right side. This is probably why Aron, who disapproved of the violent tone of the Free French broadcasts to France, was one of the very few who refused to broadcast for the BBC, except on such subjects as the death of Bergson.[22] In his view, it was necessary to manoeuvre in such a way that Vichy left North Africa and the fleet to the Allies, to whom both were indispensable. The danger in Vichy's policy, it seemed to Aron, was that England might be beaten in 1940 because she lacked the support of the French fleet. In his opinion, there was little to be gained from carrying on the war in North Africa. The Germans had no interest in opening up a front there and since it was clear that the Allies would eventually make a landing in North Africa, the neutralization of North Africa was, in the meantime, in the allied interest. For all these reasons, Aron thought that it was right that the Americans should play a double game with Pétain and useful that they should not recognize de Gaulle. Aron in fact had occasion to discuss these ideas with the General, but de Gaulle "had a horror of half-measures" and "wanted Vichy to carry its collaboration to its conclusion, because this is what he had predicted". As a consequence, between July 1940 and November 1942 Aron was often called a Vichyite by orthodox Gaullists, because he defended these ideas before the North African landings took place.[23]

Aron remained at Aldershot for about two months. At the end of August, however, he received a letter from a certain André Labarthe, who wanted to start a Free French monthly review and was looking for contributors. Knowing of Aron, whose *Introduction to the Philosophy of History* he professed to have read, Labarthe asked him to send an article; but Aron, whose time was completely taken up with military training, hesitated, not knowing what to write. It was at this point that chance played a part in his life. It was an open secret that a combined British and Free French attack was being planned on Dakar, the important naval base in French West Africa, held by forces which had remained loyal to Vichy. Aron was due to leave with this expeditionary force, but before doing so he went for the first time to General de Gaulle's headquarters at Carlton Gardens in London, where he had arranged to meet Labarthe. The latter proceeded to employ all his considerable powers of persuasion to get Aron to exchange his tank for a pen and join him in setting up the review. It was, Labarthe argued, folly for Aron to leave for Dakar, where his recently acquired military expertise was by no means indispensable, whereas an intellectual like him could be extremely useful in London.[24] Aron asked for a few days to think it over. He was torn between two arguments. On the one hand, he had come to England to fight; on the other, to start a review at that time did have a certain logic, since nothing of the kind existed outside France. Rightly or wrongly, therefore, and for motives which Aron himself could not wholly unravel, he decided to accept.[25] Thus, instead of leaving with the ill-fated task force which set off from Liverpool for Dakar on 31 August, Aron was posted to London, where he became Editorial Secretary (Secrétaire de la Rédaction) of *La France libre*, with Labarthe as Directeur.

Labarthe was a "curious mixture of journalist, politician and scientist", in whom, by all accounts, "imagination easily triumphed over the taste for truth".[26] Born in 1902, the son of a chambermaid and, it was whispered, a famous father (some said Maurice Maeterlinck), he had obtained a doctorate in physics at the Sorbonne. Before the war he had served with Pierre Cot, Air Minister in the Popular Front Government, and been on official scientific missions to the National Physical Laboratory at Cambridge, and to Germany. He had also visited the United States. In addition, he had been Director of the French National Establishment for Research and Technical Experiment, as well as Director of the Bellevue Group of Laboratories. However, he had also been active in left-wing politics and journalism. As early as 17 June 1940 he had left Bordeaux for London on board a ship carrying a cargo of copper, which he had requisitioned in his official capacity in the Armaments Ministry.

To Jean Oberlé, who became a famous broadcaster with the French

218

Service of the BBC as well as a regular contributor to *La France libre*, Labarthe was "one of the most brilliant personalities who rallied to General de Gaulle":

Physically, he reminded me of certain paintings of the Revolution, and I used to imagine him, with his thin face and blazing eyes, in the Committee of Public Safety, thundering against the impure and the factious. He liked to refer to himself as a man of the people, with his working-class accent, a voice that was sharp and sincere, and a style which was both concise and diffuse, but, on its day, excellent and quite overwhelming... His whole appearance – the black suit and hat, the lock of hair on his forehead, and the pipe – had something typically French about them. In four years, it never occurred to him to learn a single word of English. He was, moreover, an indefatigable talker and the English never tired of listening to him.[27]

De Gaulle was, apparently, very taken with Labarthe and decided to make him his Director of Armament and Scientific Research. However, Labarthe, who was politically ambitious and from the start seems to have felt that de Gaulle did not adequately appreciate and reward his talents, found a friend and ally in another politically frustrated member of the Free French in London, Vice-Admiral Emile Muselier. Like Labarthe, Muselier had a colourful personality and a leftist reputation. At the outbreak of the war he had been Admiral Commanding the Port of Marseilles, but he had been put on the retired list in October 1939 at the age of fifty-seven for, he implies in his memoirs, political reasons, although he had been able to continue to serve until the Armistice in the Air Ministry.[28] However, on 23 June he had escaped by ship from Marseilles to Gibraltar and arrived in England a week later, the only one of the fifty-five French admirals on active service at the beginning of the war to rally to London.[29] The next day General de Gaulle, who was his junior in rank as well as in years, appointed him Commander-in-Chief of the Free French Naval Forces.

Muselier was a brilliant officer and he organized the Free French Navy in a remarkable way, but politically he was unstable and inexperienced and he had a taste for intrigue.[30] In this, he was often urged on by Labarthe. Labarthe and Muselier were tireless conspirators and a constant thorn in the flesh of de Gaulle and his closest associates, and the result was a succession of petty incidents and quarrels among the Free French. The first of these occurred very quickly in the autumn of 1940. During General de Gaulle's absence on the Dakar expedition and elsewhere in Africa, "bitter personal conflicts and office tragi-comedies", as de Gaulle called them,[31] broke out at Carlton Gardens between Colonel Fontaine, whom de Gaulle had left in overall charge, and

Muselier. The latter, as the highest ranking officer among the Free French, resented this appointment. Labarthe, who was upset because de Gaulle had, without prior consultation, arranged for his Armament and Scientific Research Service to come under Fontaine's orders during the General's absence, "very quickly made a scene and left".[32]

"The atmosphere of emigration", as Aron himself was to put it, "creates conflicts which cannot be resolved in a vacuum".[33] The fact was that opposition to de Gaulle, for political and not just personal reasons, existed in London from the very beginning, stemming mainly from Socialist and Radical parliamentarians who believed that the General was neither a republican nor a democrat and was aiming at dictatorship.[34] De Gaulle's entourage in 1940 did indeed consist mainly of regular officers who, fired by traditional patriotism and hatred of Germany, were generally right-wing. Even in the camp Aron gained the impression that, while such people were not really anti-Semitic, "the Jewish question" existed nonetheless. Those on the Left who found themselves in London were very hostile to the "reactionary" officers surrounding de Gaulle; and the personality of the General himself – "authoritarian, curt and distant", as Aron later described it – was hardly sympathetic in the eyes of long-standing Socialist politicians, to whom this *"militaire"* was not far from being a "fascist". They were also wary of Colonel Passy, the head of Free French security, and resented seeing members of General de Gaulle's staff quietly earmarking post-war jobs for themselves.[35]

Labarthe had resigned as General de Gaulle's Director of Armament and Scientific Research in September and he now turned to the review which he was planning to set up. It was originally to have been called *La Relève (The Relief)*,[36] but its name was changed to *La France libre* (Labarthe subsequently claimed that General de Gaulle had taken the name of his movement from the title of the periodical).[37] Labarthe, as Directeur, was very much a figurehead; he was the review's *animateur* and public relations man. Although he wrote the editorials, he did not concern himself with details. The day-to-day editorial work was left mainly to Aron. "Though his title was editorial secretary, he was in reality editor-in-chief".[38] Aron wrote under the name of René Avord; officially he had been listed missing in June 1940, so that his wife might receive his pay from the French authorities, and he used this *nom de guerre* (after an air-force base near Bourges in central France) in order to protect this arrangement.

The review's administrator was a formidable lady, Martha Lecoutre. A Polish Jewess, Madame Lecoutre had come to England with Labarthe (her French husband lived somewhere in France), bringing with her

200,000 francs (£500) – the cost of one issue – and it was she who had taken the decision to found the review.[39] She, too, had a genius for public relations, read and corrected every article, and "managed the business office, where everything went as if by clockwork in the midst of what appeared to be wild disorder".[40] She was aided in this by the band of cosmopolitan society women who gravitated around the review, and in particular Baroness Budberg ("Moura"). A famous beauty in her time, this German aristocrat from Estonia still had her admirers. Indeed, she was the mistress of the ailing H. G. Wells, whom Aron met several times and who once memorably remarked of her: "Everybody likes her because she is so likeable".[41]

The other member of the editorial team was a Pole from the frontier region of Teschen. His real name was Stanislas Szymonzyk, though he was known to all as Staro. "An extraordinary person and a giant of a man",[42] he had served in the First World War as an artillery officer in the Austro-Hungarian army and then in the Polish army after 1918. For many years he had been a communist; he had lived in the USSR and been an activist in Weimar Germany, where he had known the famous propagandist, Willi Münzenberg. By now, however, he was cynically anti-communist: "Fascism", he used to say, "is the officers' regime; communism is the NCOs' fascism".[43] He had come to London with Labarthe and Madame Lecoutre, bringing his library with him.[44] Above all, he had an outstanding knowledge and understanding of military affairs, for which he had "a kind of genius" – he was "always quoting Clausewitz" and was to be an important influence in the development of Aron's love of that thinker.[45] As we shall see, it was Staro who, with Aron's assistance, wrote on military matters for the review.

La France libre's editorial offices were in the French Institute building in Queensberry Place, South Kensington, a short distance from the Maison de l'Institut de France in Queen's Gate, where Aron lived in 1940. The Maison de l'Institut, which in peacetime served as a lodging house for French scholars and graduate students visiting London, was presided over by its Director, Monsieur Cru, Tobin the butler, and a housekeeper fondly known to her French guests as "Mrs Custard" ("She was terrified of mice and of ghosts but was dauntless under the bombs"). Robert Mengin, former press attaché to the French Embassy and later a virulent leftist critic of de Gaulle, has described life there in the "still quiet" days at the end of July:

After dinner we played bridge. Raymond Aron was a crack player. But what we were really interested in was to get him to talk philosophy or political economy. Without

221

ever being pedantic, he seemed always to maintain the high level of his thought. His conversation had a charm we could not tire of. He handled ideas as he handled cards at bridge, and took every trick.[46]

But the house was struck by a bomb in the "baby blitz" of early 1944. Monsieur Cru, Mrs Custard and the butler were all killed. So, too, was a young war correspondent, Donald Monroe, an "exquisite being" of whom Aron wrote a movingly affectionate obituary in *La France libre*.[47] The review's editorial offices themselves were hit by a V1 in 1944 (they were subsequently moved a short distance to Thurloe Street) and even its presses were twice destoyed in air-raids. Throughout its eventful existence *La France libre* was published by Hamish Hamilton.

The first number of *La France libre* appeared on 15 November 1940 with, as its permanent sub-heading, the Republican call-to-arms of "Liberté, Egalité, Fraternité" – a formula held to be particularly daring in the current political climate among the Free French.[48] Beneath this there appeared a quotation from Ernest Renan, dated 15 September 1870, "La France humiliée, vous n'aurez plus d'esprit français" ("If France is humiliated, her spirit too will be no more"), followed by an appeal to the review's readers:

This French review is addressed to all Frenchmen. It is also addressed to all those who love France.

At the beginning of this summer of 1940, in every country where freedom still reigns, the humblest man coming home from work and hearing "the news" felt that something great was about to disappear. France had just been struck a blow.

Those who have had the good fortune to be born in those small villages of France, where every stone is heavy with memories and every path tells a story, have been robbed of what was for them, in their own small way, a source of greatness. The duty of all free Frenchmen is all the more imperative: to proclaim, the day after the disaster, their faith in the destiny of their native land.

Our country has given too much to the world for her fate to be a matter of indifference to those who respect spiritual values. France has too great a past for a military defeat to put an end to her mission to humanity.

The voice of France has fallen silent. When one listens to the words and reads the newspapers which come from our homeland, one no longer recognizes who is speaking. Held by the throat, France is forced to be silent or to deny herself.

On our desecrated soil, the Germans are already committing sacrilege. History books are being altered, paintings stolen from museums, books burned, people persecuted. Alas, Voltaire!

Against the crusade of force, against peoples who come too late in the history of humanity to make conquests, we intend to set the crusade of ideas. Battles are won through courage and force, but also through the force of ideas. This war which, behind the guns, sets doctrine against doctrine, must end with the victory of those who see in liberty and a discriminating respect for all beliefs the climate essential to the growth of culture. The victory of Germany entails the enslavement of the vanquished: it imposes every form of surrender, including that of the spirit.

The armies which Hitler has unleashed upon the world are supported by a technology which Germany has diverted from its true function. Germany has elevated the idea of war to the level of a principle which dominates the life of the whole nation. Her scientists, her engineers, one could even say some of her most eminent thinkers, have given the best of themselves to the development of a higher technology of war. Science is directed by Germany towards the art of battle. During the peace, which was for her only a time in which to gather her strength, the laboratory remained the faithful servant of the General Staff.

The drama which is unfolding at this time is putting a whole civilization at risk. Nothing is yet decided. The gigantic struggle which the British Empire is leading before the eyes of the world marks one of the turning-points of history. The cause of Great Britain is the cause of France; it is also the cause of all men who wish to think and work in peace and freedom. To each Frenchman it is a source of suffering not to be able to give anything more to those who refuse no sacrifice in order to spare humanity perhaps the most tragic step backwards it has ever taken.

It is because we keep our consciousness and hope alive in the face of today's events, that we wish to oppose the invader with the spirit of resistance until the liberation of our country. It is not defeat, but the moral acceptance of defeat, which makes a slave of the vanquished. It is because she has never surrendered in the past that our country has been a great one. France will not surrender.

We appeal to all Frenchmen throughout the world. We ask them to join with us in proclaiming their loyalty to the nation's soul, that is, to the values which were the honour and remain the glory of our country. For centuries the Frenchman has tried to uphold the flag of a humane liberty in Europe. He has borne it like a cross and his calvary is not at an end. It is in order that France may once again find her vocation that we shall struggle for the full restoration of her might.

> *Scientists, writers, engineers,*
> *send us your manuscripts.*
> *This review is yours.* [49]

The contents of the first number of *La France libre* demonstrate the unique range of topics – military, political, economic, literary and scientific – on which articles were published in the review. They also illustrate the varied nationalities of its contributors, who were by no means exclusively French or even British. Indeed, *La France libre* was almost a European periodical: during the war, as Aron was to put it forty years later, London was "for the first and last time, the capital of continental Europe" and Czechs, Poles, Belgians and Dutch were to be met everywhere. [50] Thus the first number contained an analysis of the military situation which was inspired by Staro, written by Aron and signed by Labarthe. [51] There were two articles by Aron himself: the first, unsigned, was on the defeat of France[52] and the second, signed René Avord, examined Machiavellianism as a totalitarian doctrine.[53] Other contributions included an eloquent memoir of the fall of France by the journalist, Alexander Werth ("Remember France"); a vivid description of London in the blitz by Eve Curie ("Cantine de Nuit"); and an essay on the nature of leadership in times of national trial by Denis Saurat, Director of the French Institute and Professor of French at King's College, London.[54] In addition there were articles by Sir Richard Gregory, President of the British Academy, on "The Universal Community of Science"; J. W. Beyen, the Dutch economist and statesman, on the material reconstruction of Europe after the war; and Camille Huysmans, Burgomeister of Anvers, on the linguistic problem in Belgium.

There was also a section, "Lettres Reçues", which reproduced a letter sent by a number of Englishmen eminent in the sciences and arts[55] to colleagues in America and England to ask for their support for *La France libre*:

France is now in German hands, and there is no longer any free expression of art, literature or science within her borders. Only a few have escaped of those who gave France so high a place in the world of learning. These are now possessed with the eager desire to express themselves, though they are exiles. They would strive to feed a flame which will recover its former brilliancy when France is herself again. They believe that their hope can best be accomplished through some concerted action among themselves. They would found a periodical publication, to contain a record of their thought and their work, so that their contribution to the advancement of learning will not be entirely interrupted, even in these troubled times. They propose to give to this periodical the name *La France libre*, and the very title draws the approval and sympathy of all their friends.

The periodical is not to contain propaganda.

The project if it is to justify itself must of course have such intrinsic value that scholars will welcome it for its own sake. There is no fear that it will fail in this respect: there will be many able contributors.

The collaboration of those who undertake this enterprise is well calculated to keep them in good heart and strength, by way of the encouragement and the opportunities for work which it affords. This will appeal to all the friends of French culture, who value every means of preserving the genius which they so much admire...[56]

There followed extracts from letters of support from, among others, Noel Streatfield, Somerset Maugham, Thomas Mann and G. M. Trevelyan who, in a message which must have gladdened Aron's heart, wrote: "It is with real joy that I hear of the venture of *La France libre* that you are about to make. I think at once of my friend Elie Halévy, so recently dead, who loved and understood both France and England, and wrote the finest piece of English history that this century has produced. He, if still alive, would have been for *La France libre*. . ."[57]

The review was an immediate success. The 8,000 copies of the first issue soon sold out and a reprint of 10,000 was produced. But the editorial team was small and copy was rare: often, half the manuscripts were still missing ten days before the date of publication and one of the staff had to fill the blank pages with his own prose, signing the articles with different signatures in order to give the impression that the review had an abundance of contributors. Its readers, however, were not taken in and enjoyed trying to recognize the authors by their tricks of style. René Avord apparently "had many such articles on his conscience".[58]

Aron was in fact by far the most frequent and regular contributor to *La France libre*. In only two of the fifty-nine monthly issues of the review which came out between November 1940 and September 1945 – the period in which Aron wrote for *La France libre* – did no article of his appear. He habitually wrote two, and occasionally three, pieces for each number, totalling well over a hundred articles, editorials and book reviews in just under five years.[59] However, there was an important addition even to this impressive output – his contribution to the remarkable series of articles by the review's anonymous military analyst, Stanislas Szymonzyk ("Staro"). As Szymonzyk spoke neither French nor English, he wrote his articles in German and Aron translated and adapted them into French by means of an operation which Robert Mengin has described as follows:

Aron was Socratic in his methods; in every issue the most interesting article was extracted by him, not from a little slave, but from an immense Slav called Staro. Staro was a genius at strategy, but he could not express himself in any language. He would be shut in a room with Aron, midwife *par excellence*, who after two or three hours of maieutics would bring forth the clearest, most intelligent, most prophetic analysis of military operations. At the War Office they looked forward impatiently to this monthly article; they would send over for the proofs.[60]

The resulting articles appeared month after month in *La France libre* until the end of the war and were indeed "treated as authoritative in the most serious military circles"[61] – at first they were even attributed to de Gaulle himself.[62] Thus, in addition to all his other work, Aron made a major contribution to some fifty further articles in *La France libre*. A number of these military analyses, going up to the end of the North African campaign in May 1943, were collected and published in a French edition in London during the war, with a Preface by "Strategicus", the military correspondent of the *Spectator*, who wrote that they "constitute a record which is perhaps unique of its kind". Their great merit, and the source of their success, lay in their method – "a logical and penetrating analysis which enables one to discover a significance and inner order" in an apparently confusing series of events. He went on to single out not only their "solid documentation" but also "their author's intellectual courage and the calm with which he considers unpleasant truths", their chief quality being that "he presents his readers with convincing arguments, which set courage and hope on a rational basis".[63] Szymonzyk and Aron also published a book together in 1944, an excellent military analysis of "the crucial year" from June 1940 to June 1941;[64] and the already outstanding quality of *La France libre*'s military writings was strengthened even further when the well-known French military commentator, Camille Rougeron, joined it as a regular contributor from April 1943.

In March 1941 one of Aron's friends from pre-war days, the economist Robert Marjolin, came to London and, under the *nom de guerre* of Robert Vacher (his mother's maiden name), worked for a time as the other Editorial Secretary of *La France libre*.[65] Marjolin had been in England once already, when Aron arrived at the end of June 1940. Having been sent originally to arrange supplies for the French army, throughout the weeks of the disaster he had been on a number of missions to France, carrying letters between Churchill and Reynaud as the French Government retreated from Paris first to Orleans, then Tours and, finally, Bordeaux. After the fall of France, he had left England to become assistant to Emmanuel Monick, the Secretary-General in Morocco,[66] but when their activities became suspect in Vichy eyes, Marjolin joined the Free French in London. As well as helping to edit *La France libre* in 1941 and 1942, he contributed regularly to the review on economic and political questions from June 1941 ("J'étais à Paris en janvier dernier") until July 1943. At first he had had doubts about de Gaulle – he had been Aide-de-Camp to Muselier in 1941 (Muselier's other ADC being the future Socialist politician, Alain Savary) – but he soon decided that the real leader of the Resistance was the General. He then worked for the Free French economic services under their Director, Hervé Alphand, until 1943, when, as a colleague of Jean Monnet, he went to the United States with the French Supply Mission, of which he became head in 1944.[67]

Another of the outstanding contributors to *La France libre* was E. M. Friedwald, who published his first article for the review in March 1941 and was the only one of the early contributors who continued to write for it until publication ceased in 1947. Friedwald wrote a succession of solidly impressive articles on a wide range of economic subjects as they related to the war in Europe and elsewhere: these included the oil question (a theme in which he was particularly interested and to which he returned on a number of occasions),[68] the economic strategies of Germany, Japan and Russia, the food problem in Europe, "the battle of the Ruhr", German-Italian relations, the war in the air, the myth of German invincibility, disarmament, economic problems of Eastern Europe, cartels and trusts, military strategy in Europe, and the future of China.[69]

Another regular, if more lightweight, contributor to *La France libre* was the artist Jean Oberlé (1900–1961), who between June 1941 and August 1944 wrote a series of colourful and amusing descriptions of wartime England entitled "Images anglaises", which he illustrated with his own drawings. Oberlé, who was already in London at the time of the fall of France, joined the French Service of the BBC and became a well-known broadcaster, taking part in such celebrated programmes as "Les Français parlent aux Français", which included the famous series, "Discussion des trois amis", between Jacques Duchesne (the *nom de guerre* of Michel Saint-Denis, the theatrical director), Pierre Bourdan and himself.[70]

Oberlé's friend Pierre Bourdan, under his real name of Pierre Maillaud, also wrote for *La France libre*, between September 1942 and April 1944. Bourdan, a journalist, had been working for the Havas Press Agency in London for a number of years when the war broke out. He then joined the French Service of the BBC and became one of its best-known broadcasters. He was, however, outspokenly anti-Gaullist.[71] In 1944 he went to France as a war correspondent with the Leclerc Division and was captured by the Germans but escaped. After the war he was elected to the Constituent Assembly in October 1945 as a Radical and in November 1946 became Deputy for a Paris constituency. In January 1947 Ramadier made him his Minister for Youth, the Arts and Information, but he was drowned in a sailing accident in the following year at the age of thirty-nine.[72]

Another anti-Gaullist contributor to *La France libre* was Louis Lévy, who had previously been a journalist on the socialist daily paper, *Le Populaire*. Lévy was a prominent member of the left-wing, pro-Republican "oppositional" group which centred on the daily paper, *France*; he was also the author of a book entitled *The Truth about France*, which was published by Penguin in both an English and a French edition in 1941 and given a complimentary review by Aron in *La France libre*.[73]

Other regular contributors were Matila Ghyka, Albert Cohen and Roger Caillois (who was also Director of the French Institute in Buenos Aires, where he edited the Free French publication, *Lettres françaises*). The review contained articles by René Cassin, de Gaulle's chief jurist; P. O. Lapie, the Socialist deputy and one of the only parliamentarians to join de Gaulle; Henri Focillon, the art historian and Professor at the Collège de France and later Yale University, where he died during the war; and Hervé Alphand, who became the French National Committee's Director of Economic Affairs. Writers whose work appeared in *La France libre* included Georges Bernanos, Jules Romains, Joseph Kessel, Jules Roy, Louis Martin-Chauffier and Romain Gary (Aron was, he believes, the first reader of Gary's first novel, *L'Education européenne*, which he admired greatly).[74] There were pieces by Jacques Maritain, the philosopher; Etiemble, the specialist in French language and literature; Edmond Vermeil, the Germanist who had been one of the jury at Aron's defence of his theses; and Jacques Duchesne, alias Michel Saint-Denis, the theatrical director and BBC broadcaster. Articles by Jean Guéhenno and Sartre were published after the Liberation.

There were verses by the *chansonnier*, Pierre Dac, and poems by Aragon, Eluard and Pierre Emmanuel. *La France libre* also contained accounts and diaries, often anonymous, of military actions and of life in occupied France; "Lettres de France" – listeners' letters broadcast by the BBC; "Où sont nos écrivains?" – an attempt to inform readers of the whereabouts of well-known French writers in June 1941; photocopies of the clandestine press; reproductions of satirical anti-German cartoons ("Etudes racistes"); obituaries and book reviews; and a remarkable series of photographs of the buildings, landscapes and people of France and the Empire which "filled Frenchmen in England, and Englishmen who loved France, with melancholy".[75]

La France libre also published many contributions, in French, by British writers: these included Charles Morgan, H. G. Wells, Victoria Sackville-West, Harold Nicolson, Rosamund Lehmann, Storm Jameson, Max Beerbohm, Raymond Mortimer, Desmond MacCarthy, Stephen Spender, J. B. Priestley, Herbert Read, Bernard Shaw, Elizabeth Bowen and Graham Greene. There were extracts from the books of the journalist, Alexander Werth; articles by the historians, D. W. Brogan and G. M. Trevelyan; Wickham Steed, former Editor of the *Times*; the diplomat, Sir Robert Vansittart; the art critics, Denys Sutton, John Russell, David Cooper, and Sir Kenneth Clark; Gilbert Murray, the classicist and President of the League of Nations Union; the political theorists, Harold Laski, Max Beloff and John Plamenatz; and the scientific writers, Julian Huxley and Ritchie Calder. In addition, towards the end of the war there appeared a four-part series entitled "What France Means to You", which was introduced by Raymond Mortimer and counted among its contributors Gilbert Murray, C. S. Lewis, Harold Nicolson, David Eccles, Victoria Sackville-West, David Garnett, T. S. Eliot, Harold Laski, Kathleen Raine, Violet Trefusis, Sir Kenneth Clark and Sir Edward Grigg (later Lord Altrincham).[76] Not that *La France libre* limited itself to contributions from French and English writers. As well as pieces by Americans (including John Dos Passos), there were contributions from members of many of the allied countries of occupied Europe: Belgians, Dutch, Poles, Czechs and Norwegians.

La France libre's early success was not shortlived and its first volume, containing the first six issues, had to be reprinted. Significantly, as circulation rose, the amount of advertising increased steadily.[77] The first anniversary issue (November 1941) included letters of congratulation and messages of goodwill from Churchill himself, General Sikorski, Head of the Polish Government-in-Exile, Dr Eduard Benès, his Czech counterpart, and E. N. van Kleffens, the Dutch statesman, as well as the text of a recent speech by de Gaulle to the Royal African Society. By November 1943 *La France libre* had a circulation of 40,000 (not counting an American edition then in preparation in New York).[78] Indeed, it came to have 76,000 subscribers[79] and the largest circulation of all the monthlies published in England – no small achievement for a periodical written entirely in French.[80] As a result, *La France libre* generally came to be seen as *the* organ of expression of the Free French movement[81] and "can claim to have been the main vehicle for the expression of French thought" from November 1940 to June 1944;[82] it "bore witness to the vitality of the French spirit in exile"[83] and was "the rallying point for all free minds exiled from the Continent",[84] constituting by its style and tone "a remarkable voice speaking on behalf of French culture".[85] "Nowhere", wrote J. G. Weightman, introducing a selection of articles from the review to English readers at the end of the war, "can we find a mass of French writing of a certain standard, representative of those four years, comparable to that published by *La France libre*".[86] Above all, *La France libre* rendered a considerable service to its country by bringing to the rest of the world, particularly South America, the essence of what there was to be read and known about France during the war years.[87] In addition, there was a clandestine edition of the review, in smaller format, which was parachuted into France every month by the RAF, and copies were also sent into other countries of occupied Europe, such as Greece, Belgium and Holland.[88]

There is no doubt that the "high literary and intellectual merit" of the periodical was "mostly attributable" to Aron.[89] Even Jacques Soustelle, who became a bitter critic of Labarthe and was later to reproach Aron for his "anti-Gaullism",[90] admitted that the review was "very well done, largely thanks to Raymond Aron".[91] Nevertheless, in Aron's own view, there was "nothing heroic" about his work with La France libre: indeed, the reputation which he gained as a result of his years in London with the review became "a kind of burden" ("une espèce de poids") for him. The only time when his conscience at having left France did not trouble him was during the blitz. The blitz did not worry him at all; on the contrary, it gave Aron the feeling that it was those who, like himself, had left France who were now experiencing the danger, and not the French themselves. Moreover, during the blitz Aron, normally a bad sleeper, slept soundly, undisturbed by the noise of anti-aircraft guns and, as his friend Denis Brogan used to put it, under the protection of the theory of probability.[92]

It was understandable, in view of its title, that people should identify La France libre with General de Gaulle and the Free French movement; yet the review was not sufficiently Gaullist for the General and his closest followers. This was undoubtedly due in large part to the political intrigues of Labarthe and his friend, Muselier. We have already seen how in September 1940, shortly before the first issue of the periodical appeared, both men were involved in ugly scenes at Carlton Gardens. Nevertheless, on his return from Africa in November, de Gaulle saw Labarthe and agreed to give financial support to the review.[93] De Gaulle himself says in his memoirs that he gave La France libre – "which owed its existence to the initiative of MM. Labarthe and Raymond Aron" – all the help he could.[94] Indeed, its fourth issue, dated February 1941, contained a letter from de Gaulle addressed to Labarthe ("mon cher ami"), in which he expressed the conviction that this "excellent review" would be "one of the important elements in the success of our cause".[95] Aron's own relations with de Gaulle were "excellent" and, although Aron kept his distance, they occasionally dined together.[96]

Labarthe and Muselier, however, continued with their intrigues and were at the centre of several "incidents" involving the Free French. The first of these has always remained something of a mystery. In January 1941 Muselier was placed under arrest by the British, having been accused of various acts of treason, including revealing to Vichy the plan for the attack on Dakar. De Gaulle, apparently convinced that the affair was part of a plot mounted by Vichy, protested strongly. A week later, having examined certain documents further and questioned two Free

French security agents, he wrote to the British government disproving the accusations and showing the documents to be forgeries. De Gaulle was allowed to visit Muselier in custody and a few hours later he was set free. Churchill apologized personally to de Gaulle, virtually admitting that the two security men in question were British agents. They were in fact arrested, found guilty and subsequently imprisoned. Muselier was even granted an audience of the King. Although at the time Muselier seems to have been grateful to de Gaulle for the way in which he had acted, he later suggested in his memoirs that the affair was part of a plot against him by the head of de Gaulle's Secret Service, Colonel Passy.[97]

A more serious crisis occurred in September 1941 in the days leading up to the formation of a French National Committee under de Gaulle's Presidency. De Gaulle had intended to make Muselier Commissioner for the Navy and Labarthe, as Editor of *La France libre*, Commissioner for Information. However, Muselier and Labarthe rejected these posts and put forward their own proposals: de Gaulle should remain President of the "Movement", but an "Executive Committee" should be set up, with Muselier as President, in which Muselier would have control over military affairs and Labarthe would be Political Director responsible for propaganda and action in France and the Empire. In addition, Muselier threatened to sever the Navy from the rest of the Free French Forces and carry on the war independently alongside the Royal Navy. However, when de Gaulle refused to accept this, Muselier seems to have climbed down quickly, and although he retained his responsibility for the Navy in the newly constituted Commission, there was no place for Labarthe.[98]

The fact is that Labarthe demanded much more than the General was prepared to give him. Labarthe wanted to be responsible for action and propaganda in France; in other words, he sought complete political control over the BCRA, the Bureau Central de Renseignement et d'Action, which was headed by Colonel Passy. Politically this was a key position, for if de Gaulle was to succeed he had to have the support of all the resistance movements in France. The Director controlled the money and arms distributed by the BCRA and the way he did so was of fundamental importance. All this was seen very clearly by Labarthe and it resulted in a quarrelsome rivalry between himself and Passy. Furthermore, he accused Passy of being a right-wing *cagoulard* (which was not, in Aron's view, the case) and distrusted him: Labarthe believed that he was being pursued by Passy's agents and by the security services responsible for Muselier's arrest, and he was, as we have seen, on bad terms with Colonel Fontaine, whom de Gaulle had put in charge of civilian affairs in London. In addition, on a personal level, Labarthe, a man of unbridled passion and ambition, aroused strong feelings of sympathy and hostility. A number of people believed him to be dangerous and would have liked to see him arrested. This was repeated to him and he held Passy responsible.[99]

However, the final break between Labarthe and de Gaulle came in March 1942 at the time of what came to be known as the "Muselier Affair". The previous December, Muselier had led a small naval force to the French islands of Saint-Pierre-et-Miquelon, off the coast of Newfoundland, and succeeded, much to the annoyance of the Americans, in winning them over to the Free French cause. Shortly after his return, Muselier, again with Labarthe's backing, enumerated a list of complaints against de Gaulle and handed in his resignation from the National Committee.[100] De Gaulle dismissed him from his command of the Free French Navy and, when Muselier once again threatened to secede with his forces to the Royal Navy, had him placed under thirty days' house-arrest. Muselier refused to comply but was finally prevailed upon by the British to leave London for a month. On his return, however, he rejected de Gaulle's offer to appoint him Inspector-General of the Free French Forces and "from that moment broke off all contact with the Free French, devoting himself with Labarthe to a virulent campaign of rumour and slander in British circles".[101] According to Soustelle, Labarthe even succeeded in penetrating Churchill's entourage and gaining the ear of the Prime Minister.[102]

After the American landing in North Africa in November 1942, the conflict between Labarthe and the Gaullists became "inexpiable"[103] and Labarthe pinned his hopes on General Giraud, to whom the Americans had decided to give their support. However, when the United States recognized Admiral Darlan, the former Chief Minister of Vichy who was now its Commander-in-Chief, as supreme authority in North Africa, support for Darlan apparently grew among the anti-Gaullist opposition in London, especially after he had given orders for the scuttling of the French fleet at Toulon to prevent its falling into German hands. The chief advocate of this thesis was Labarthe in an editorial entitled "Armée de la République", which appeared in *La France libre* in December 1942. "This article", says Soustelle, "marked the rallying of the so-called 'left-wing' anti-Gaullist opposition to the Vichy regime now being prolonged in Africa. An exchange of letters between Labarthe and myself made the break final". The National Commission for Information, of which Soustelle was Director, was in the habit of buying a large number of copies of *La France libre* every month for despatch to the overseas territories. Soustelle refused to purchase and distribute the December issue, as a result of which Labarthe accused him of "censorship".[104] It was presumably editorials such as this which led General de Gaulle in his memoirs to complain that by 1943 *La France libre* was one of the many Free French organs of expression which "openly declared themselves for Giraud".[105]

Then, on Christmas Eve 1942, Darlan was assassinated in Algiers[106] and Giraud was at once appointed Civil and Military Commander-in-Chief by the Imperial Council of Vichy Governor-Generals in North Africa. Not long afterwards, in February 1943, Labarthe, now leaving *La France libre* entirely in Aron's hands, went off to Algiers in order to drum up support for Giraud against de Gaulle. It was a forlorn hope: the order to fire on the allied troops, Pétain's refusal to go to Algiers and the scuttling of the fleet had made the eventual downfall of Vichy and the triumph of dc Gaulle virtually certain.[107] But by now Labarthe had developed an almost "metaphysical antagonism" towards the General,[108] accusing him of being a fascist and of seeking to become master of France by employing Nazi methods.[109] As a consequence, Labarthe "increasingly became the centre of anti-Gaullism",[110] and in May Giraud, who had by now been "completely taken in hand by Labarthe", made him his Minister of Information.[111] This appointment was interpreted as "a declaration of war on Gaullist propaganda",[112] as a result of which Labarthe "introduced a more rigorous censorship and the name of General de Gaulle was once again banished as in Darlan's day".[113] In May, too, Muselier, who had been flown in by the Americans and whose hostility towards de Gaulle apparently exceeded even that of Labarthe,[114] reached Algiers, and on 2 June, three days after de Gaulle's arrival, Giraud appointed him Prefect of Police in all but namc. An anti-Gaullist putsch seemed imminent but, says Soustelle, Muselier "gave way".[115] On the following day, the French Committee for National Liberation was formed, with de Gaulle and Giraud as co-Presidents, and by October Giraud and his supporters, including Labarthe and Muselier, had been outmanoeuvred and politically eliminated by the Gaullists.[116]

Aron himself took virtually no part in Labarthe's political intrigues.[117] Indeed, he very much regretted them and felt that they placed him in a false and difficult position. On Labarthe himself, however, he refused to make any judgement, saying, "I think too well of him to say anything ill, and I think too ill of him to say anything well".[118] Nevertheless, although he did not regret *La France libre*, this was a period of his life which Aron was to remember with little satisfaction. Inevitably, he was drawn – partly through inexperience, partly through weakness and partly through force of circumstances – into the conflicts between Gaullists and non-Gaullists, but he felt that his first duty was to the review and not Labarthe's political activity (not that Labarthe asked Aron for advice, in any case).

Nevertheless, Aron was certainly not an orthodox Gaullist. As we have seen, it was his view that the Gaullist movement should try to win over as many as possible of the supporters of Vichy to the allied cause, because it seemed fairly obvious to him that the Allies' first step would be to land in French North Africa. Aron believed, therefore, that it was important not to exasperate the Vichyites and treat them as traitors, because this would be likely to lead to civil war, and a detestation of civil war is one of his great political passions. Thus in 1941 and 1942 he judged that the Gaullists' anti-Vichy propaganda was excessive and was to all intents and purposes ushering in the civil war which resulted in the purges of 1944. As Aron was to write after the war: ". . . we did not have the right to refuse anyone the benefit of the doubt or of extenuating circumstances, or to equate with the traitors the many Frenchmen of good faith who, in 1940, for varying motives agreed to serve the Vichy regime".[119]

Furthermore, Aron's democratic convictions made him dislike the passionate, personal nature of the Gaullist movement particularly in the earliest days, as exemplified by the statement of allegiance to the General's person which people were made to sign.[120] Later, Aron wrote two powerful articles (which he came to regret[121]) in *La France libre* in which he warned against the authoritarian direction which Gaullism might take. The first of these was a signed editorial, "Vive la République!", written in June 1943,[122] shortly after de Gaulle's arrival in Algiers and the setting up of the French Committee of National Liberation with de Gaulle and Giraud as joint Presidents. Aron forcefully welcomed this development because it implied that a choice had been made for a liberal, democratic parliamentary republic and against a mystical, authoritarian "personal adventure". Two months afterwards, at the height of the period in which de Gaulle was succeeding in establishing his authority in Algiers and eliminating Giraud, Aron wrote a second article, "L'Ombre des Bonapartes", in which he analysed Louis-Napoleon's coming to power as "both the forerunner and the French version of fascism".[123] Although he did not mention de Gaulle at the time, Aron subsequently admitted that it was of course de Gaulle whom he had in mind in writing the article, while granting that his fears had been misplaced: "General de Gaulle, if he had not had his sense of mission, could have become the head of a moderate coalition, although his troops were those of the Popular Front, reinforced by patriots of every tendency".[124]

Later still, he came to see de Gaulle's ambition as "historic rather than personal". De Gaulle had to convince the French that they had resisted; they had to conceal the truth from themselves. "I did not", Aron admitted, "see this clearly, perhaps because de Gaulle's exclusivism got on my nerves, and above all because I was exasperated by the ferocity of the small Gaullist circle, which caused him to lose all sense of proportion".[125] At the time, however, orthodox Gaullists such as Soustelle were critical of Aron's reservations about the General. Thus Simone de Beauvoir recalls that, when in January 1945 she went to see Soustelle, who was then Minister of Information, to obtain an allocation of paper for the new review, *Les Temps modernes*, "Soustelle was very pleasant but the composition of the editorial committee made him shy away slightly. 'Aron? Why Aron?' He complained of his anti-Gaullist attitude".[126]

With the political eclipse of "Giraudism" in the autumn of 1943, Labarthe left Algiers and went to New York, where he edited an anti-Gaullist monthly, entitled *Tricolor*, until the end of the war. However, he continued to write some of the editorials for *La France libre* until September 1944 and occasional articles until August 1946.[127] Meanwhile Aron, who was now Directeur of *La France libre* in all but name, had remained at his post in London throughout the whole of this period. His wife and daughter, too, had managed to reach England. Having remained at Toulouse until 1941, they were able to move to Morocco, thanks to Marjolin. After the liberation of North Africa and with the help of Labarthe's American contacts, they sailed for England, arriving – with appropriate symbolism – on 14 July 1943. For a time the reunited family lived in a flat in Cromwell Gate, but when the Arons' second daughter, Emmanuelle, was born on 18 June 1944, mother and children moved to a cottage in the Hertfordshire countryside near Pinewood Studios, not far from the Free French airforce general, Edouard Corniglion-Molinier, who became Emmanuelle's godfather. Corniglion, a legendary figure and brilliant *raconteur* who hailed from the Midi, had been Malraux's pilot on the famous expedition in 1934 to the capital of the Queen of Saba in Arabia. One of the few Frenchmen to have been a fighter pilot in both world wars, he was later a Minister under the Fourth Republic and remained "an incomparable friend".[128]

Aron, meanwhile, lived in a small house in Queensberry Gate and it was here that he put up his old friend, now a Resistance leader,

Jean Cavaillès. Born in 1903, Cavaillès had entered the Ecole Normale Supérieure in 1923, the year before Aron. In 1928, like Aron, he had become Secretary of the Centre de Documentation Sociale under Bouglé; he, too, had been on a study visit to Germany in 1930–1, where he had become interested in the ideas of Husserl; and he had written his doctoral theses on the philosophy of mathematics under Brunschvicg, defending them in January 1938, only two months before Aron. We have already noted the letter he wrote to Aron in connection with the *Introduction to the Philosophy of History*. In the same year he and Aron had begun editing together a series entitled "Essais philosophiques" for the publisher Hermann, ending their introduction to the first volume with the Latin, "philosophia perennis sed in actione manifesta" ("a perennial philosophy but one revealed in action").[129] Taken prisoner in June 1940, Cavaillès succeeded in escaping. Later that year he returned to his post at the University of Strasbourg, now based at Clermont-Ferrand, where he became leader of the Resistance group "Libération Sud". In March 1941 he succeeded in being appointed to the Sorbonne so that he might continue his Resistance work from Paris. As leader of "Libération Nord" he was captured in September 1941, but again managed to escape. In February 1943 he was sent on a mission to London, where he spent two months, and while there he stayed with Aron. According to his sister's memoir, "Jean loved to recall their walks along the Thames, their visits to Cambridge and those long evenings in which the harmony that characterized their thoughts reinforced, even now, the bonds of a long-standing and constant affection".[130] When Cavaillès was about to return to France, Aron gave him "two antique ivory miniatures depicting harvest scenes", saying that they were supposed to bring good fortune: one was for Cavaillès and one for his sister – "'this sister about whom you have spoken to me so much', said Aron". They were later taken by the Germans during a raid. Cavaillès – "le plus brave, le plus pur", as Aron was to call him – was arrested in August 1943, imprisoned in Fresnes and shot at Arras in 1944.[131]

Aron himself returned to Paris in September 1944, but he continued to write articles, and indeed a number of editorials, for *La France libre* until September 1945. However, his role in the review was now over; he left it "with a heavy heart"[132] and from July 1945 his name no longer appeared as Secrétaire de la Rédaction. With the war at an end, a decision obviously had to be taken as to what the future, if any, of *La France libre* was to be, and in May 1945 a brave declaration of intent was published, "'*La France libre*' continue..." But although the review did continue to attract many distinguished French and British contributors,[133] there is no doubt that, deprived as it now was of its *raison d'être*, it gradually lost its sense of purpose and direction. In 1947, with a special number on the Low Countries, *La France libre* appeared for the seventy-fifth and last time. It died quietly, with no fanfares and no explanations, and with Labarthe's name still appearing as Directeur.

In conclusion, the most fitting tribute to *La France libre* was that paid by Jean-Paul Sartre in *Combat* at the end of the war, after Aron had given him a set of the review to read:

No hint comes through of the constant dangers which made of *La France libre* a perpetual risk of failure and a perpetual chance of success. It presents the most balanced, calm and level-headed of appearances. Written above all in the living heat of an ever-changing reality, whose very rhythm was unforeseeable, it always seems to be able to stand back from history. Where, then, did its contributors, constantly under pressure as they were, obtain the leisure to reflect on events which might at any moment overtake them by their speed? Cut off from their country, how did they succeed in retaining a sense of it, and in gathering abundant and precise information and always interpreting it correctly? Exiled in a foreign land, how did they acquire their understanding of Anglo-Saxon problems and points of view? Banished, reviled in France, and separated from their kin, how were they able, for four years, to maintain their dispassionate objectivity, while deep-down tormented by regrets, hope and hatred? Do you know many periodicals where "everything" has to be read? Are there many military chronicles that can be read with the same profound interest four years after the events? The most varied articles on Vichy, the state of France, Italian opinion and the German press, problems of international law, and accounts of war by officers and soldiers, were grouped around three regular chronicles, all three of them admirable in their intelligence: the chronicle by Raymond Aron (René Avord), which gives us a kind of spectral analysis of national socialism; that of the anonymous military critic, who was able to take a world-wide view in order to explain the battles and strategy of this universal war and show in each case how the military outcome and the economic struggle were closely related; and finally those of Robert Vacher (Marjolin), the economist, which examine the problems of the war and the post-war world. Politics, economics, strategy – the review, as a whole, offers us what, for four years, we so craved in the face of the lies of the Nazi press: an explanation of our time.[134]

Notes

1. This account of Aron's experiences in 1939–40 is based partly on an interview I had with him in 1977, and partly on unpublished evidence in the archives of the Bibliothèque du Comité d'Histoire de la Deuxième Guerre Mondiale (1948o). I am most grateful to Raymond Aron for allowing me to make use of this material. The interview with him reported in André Gillois, *Histoire secrète des Français de*

Londres de 1940 à 1944 (Paris, 1973) has also been useful, as has the account in *Le Spectateur engagé* (1981a, pp. 76ff: tr. 1983b, pp. 66ff.) and, of course, his memoirs (1983a, Chapter VII).

2. 1948c.

3. *Commentaire*, 8 (28–9), 1985, p. 233. Not surprisingly in the circumstances, the book on Machiavellianism was never completed; but Aron published an article on the subject in the first number of *La France libre* (1940b). See Chapter 11, below.

4. 1981a, pp. 76–7: tr. pp. 66–7 (R. C.).

5. Palle, 1985, pp. 17–18. This mud-stained, black-bordered letter was the last news Palle was to have of Aron for four years, when he wrote "on the off chance" to *La France libre*. A reply reached him out of the blue in Morocco in February 1944. "When I recognized your writing", wrote the "icy" Aron, "I felt like jumping for joy like a child". They met a few months later (Palle believes in Algiers) and Aron brought him a gold watch from London which he kept for twenty years (ibid.)

6. 1948o.

7. 1983a, p. 165.

8. 1981a, p. 80: tr. p. 69 (R. C.): "This is the only occasion on which I have had an intimate relationship with stocks and shares".

9. René Cassin (1887–1976) became Free France's outstanding jurist. He was later President of the European Court of Human Rights and won the Nobel Peace Prize in 1968.

10. 1983a, p. 166.

11. Ibid.

12. R. A., interview with the author, 1977.

13. 1981a, p. 79: tr. pp. 68–9 (R. C.).

14. Gillois, op. cit., p. 110.

15. 1941b, 1941e, 1941f.

16. Lord Robbins, interview with the author, 1979. Aron remembered Robbins saying to him in one air-raid during the blitz how much he regretted that Napoleon had lost the Battle of Leipzig (R. A., interview with the author, 1977).

17. Henri Michel, *Histoire de la France libre* (Paris, 3rd edn, 1972), pp. 9–11.

18. R. A., interview with the author, 1977. Cf. Gillois, op. cit., p. 103. Aron says that the camp contained some remarkable people, including a young man who had been hoping to enter the Ecole Polytechnique, the future Gaullist Minister, Robert Galley. Galley later fought in the Leclerc Division and married General Leclerc's daughter.

19. As Maurice Druon put it, "Three hundred Frenchmen marched past like the soldiers at the Battle of Thermopylae". Quoted in Gillois, op. cit., p. 246.

20. Ibid., pp. 245–6.

21. Cordier, 1985, pp. 22, 24.

22. Gillois, who worked for the BBC, says that the only two Frenchmen who, to his knowledge, refused to broadcast were Aron and General Koenig. The latter, when asked to broadcast to French prisoners in Germany, is said to have replied: "A true French soldier does not allow himself to be taken prisoner" (Gillois, op. cit., p. 312).

23. 1948o, pp. 6–7; Gillois, op. cit., pp. 101–2; R. A., interview with the author, 1977; 1981a, pp. 85ff: tr. pp. 73ff.

24. As Aron himself put it, "Labarthe m'a fait la scène de séduction" (R. A., interview with the author, 1977). Labarthe later recounted that de Gaulle himself had advised Aron to carry on his work as a writer instead of being a simple soldier; but, as with many of Labarthe's stories, "this was not wholly false, but not wholly true, either" (Gillois, op. cit., pp. 103–4).

25. 1981a, pp. 81–2; tr. pp. 70–1.

26. Jacques Soustelle, *Envers et contre tout, Vol. I. De Londres à Alger. Souvenir et documents sur la France libre, 1940–1942* (Paris, 1947), p. 47.

27. Jean Oberlé, *Jean Oberlé vous parle...Souvenirs de cinq années de Londres* (Paris, 1945), p. 102.

28. Vice-Admiral Muselier, *De Gaulle contre le Gaullisme* (Paris, 1946).

29. Laurent de Meauce, "Deux procès", *FL*, 9 (54), April 1945, p. 441.

30. 1948o, p. 10. Cf. Soustelle, to whom Muselier, with his "weather-beaten and sensitive face, which one could easily imagine swathed in a pirate's red handkerchief", was an "intelligent and lively person" who initially attracted sympathy but ultimately lost it because of the "feverish agitation and Florentine intrigues which flourished incessantly around him" (Soustelle, op. cit., pp. 41–2).

31. Charles de Gaulle, *Mémoires de guerre, Vol. I. L'Appel, 1940–42* (Paris, 1954), p. 124: tr. (by Jonathan Griffin) *War Memoirs, Vol. I. The Call to Honour, 1940–1942* (London, 1955), p. 150.

32. Soustelle, op. cit., p. 48. According to Muselier, op. cit., p. 95, Labarthe was dismissed by Fontaine.

33. Gillois, op. cit., p. 107.

34. One important centre of such opposition to the General was the group which formed round the daily paper, *France*, and had contacts in the Labour Party. *France* was edited by Pierre Comert, formerly head of the Information Service of the Quai d'Orsay, the French Foreign Office, and was subsidized by the British Ministry of Information. Other prominent members of this group were the journalists, Georges Gombault and Louis Lévy. Aron himself only wrote one article for the paper – a tribute to Brunschvicg, after the philosopher's death (1944z[4]).

35. 1948o, p. 5. The situation was to change, however, after 1941. Contact was established between London and France and numerous exchanges took place between the Resistance movements and the personnel in London. The "movements" were almost all democratic in character and de Gaulle realized – very intelligently, in Aron's view – that it was essential that the London Committee, too, should be seen to be democratic and republican, if he wanted to represent the whole of France (ibid., pp. 5–6).

36. Soustelle, op. cit., p. 48.

37. Robert Mengin, *No Laurels for De Gaulle* (London, 1967), p. 189.

38. Ibid., p. 188.

39. Gillois, op. cit., p. 103.

40. Mengin, op. cit., p. 189.

41. 1983a, p. 172.

42. Oberlé, op. cit., p. 103.

43. 1983a, p. 171.

44. Gillois, op. cit., p. 103.
45. 1981a, p. 82: tr. p. 71. See also 1976a, Vol. I., p. 10.
46. Robert Mengin, *De Gaulle à Londres vu par un Français libre* (Paris, 1965), p. 95: tr. *No Laurels for De Gaulle*, op. cit., p. 105 (R. C.).
47. 1944f.
48. 1948o, p. 5.
49. *FL*, 1 (1), November 1940, pp. 3–5.
50. 1981a, p. 94: tr. p. 81.
51. André Labarthe, "La Phase des guerres-éclairs est-elle terminée?", *FL*, 1 (1), November 1940. General de Gaulle read the typescript (which Aron kept) and wrote comments in the margin, like a schoolmaster marking an essay. Thus when the General came across a phrase of which he approved – for example, the statement that France had a superior road system but a static army – he would write "B" for "Bien" in the margin (1981a, p. 83: tr. pp. 71–2).
52. 1940a. See Chapter 10, below.
53. 1940b. See Chapter 11, below.
54. Saurat subsequently contributed a dozen times to the review.
55. William Bragg and A. V. Hill, respectively President and Secretary of the Royal Society; Frederic Kenyon, Secretary of the British Academy; the architect, Edwin Lutyens, President of the Royal Academy; J. B. Priestley; and Charles Scott Sherrington, former President of the Royal Society.
56. *FL*, 1 (1), November 1940, p. 92.
57. Ibid., p. 97. Trevelyan later contributed an appreciation of Halévy, "Elie Halévy, 1870-1937", *FL*, 5 (25), November 1942. The second number of *La France libre* (December 1940) contained a letter of support from Gilbert Murray, who also subsequently contributed an article (*FL*, 2 (8), June 1941).
58. Jean-Paul Sartre, "Une grande revue française de Londres", *Combat*, 7–8 January 1945.
59. Many of these were subsequently reprinted in three volumes, *De l'Armistice à l'insurrection nationale* (1945r), *L'Homme contre les tyrans* (1944a) and *L'Age des empires et l'avenir de la France* (1946b). See below, Chapters 11, 12 and 13 respectively. Aron also did a considerable amount of lecturing during the war. Thus in February 1941 we find him discussing "La Littérature politique au 18e siècle" at the French Institute (*France*, 12 February 1941) and giving a talk on Proust at the International Arts Centre, Bayswater, in December 1943 (*France*, 14 December 1943).
60. Mengin, op. cit., p. 187: tr. pp. 188–9 (R. C.).
61. Oberlé, op. cit., p. 103. Cf. 1981a, p. 82: tr. p. 71 (R. C.): "Staro's were the best military articles published in England. Specialists read them with great care".
62. 1948o, p. 7.
63. *La Guerre des cinq continents*, par le critique militaire de la revue *La France libre*, avec une préface de "Strategicus" du *Spectator* (London, 1943), pp. 5–7.
64. 1944z^2.
65. On Marjolin, see Chapter 4, above.
66. After the war Monick became Governor of the Banque de France.
67. Robert Marjolin, interview with the author, 1980. See also the interview with Marjolin in *L'Expansion*, May 1979, pp. 207–19; and Gillois, op. cit., pp. 46–7.

Marjolin was to have a brilliant career after the war. In 1945 he became Director of Foreign Economic Relations at the French Ministry of National Economy. From 1946 to 1948 he was joint Commissioner of the famous Monnet Plan for the regeneration of the French economy and from 1948 to 1955 Secretary-General of the OECE (Organisation Européenne de Coopération Economique), the forerunner of the Common Market. From 1955 to 1957 he was Professor of Political Economy at the University of Nancy and, after being Vice-President of the French delegation in the negotiations on the Common Market and Euratom, he became Vice-President of the European Commission from 1958–67. For two years (1967–9) he was Professor of Economics at the Sorbonne. He is also the author of several books and reports, including *L'Evolution du syndicalisme aux Etats-Unis: De Washington à Roosevelt*, (Paris, 1936); *Prix, monnaie et production: Essai sur les mouvements économiques de longue durée* (Paris, 1945); and *Europe and the United States in the World Economy* (London, 1953).

68. Friedwald published a book on the subject: *Oil and the War* (London, 1941).

69. Friedwald also wrote an analysis of the nature of the post-war world: *Man's Last Choice: Political Creeds and Scientific Realities* (London, 1948). Aron published the French translation, *L'Humanité doit choisir*, in the series he edited for Calmann-Lévy, "Liberté de l'esprit" (Paris, 1949).

70. See Oberlé, op. cit., and *Pages choisies de Pierre Bourdan*, présentées par Jean Oberlé (Paris, 1951), p. 18. Cf. Asa Briggs, *The History of Broadcasting in the United Kingdom, Volume III. The War of Words* (Oxford, 1970), pp. 246–9.

71. It is important to distinguish the French Service of the BBC from the Free French broadcasts. Although by mid-1943 the BBC broadcast five-and-a-half hours of French programmes per day, only ten minutes were allocated to the Free French, whose chief spokesman was Maurice Schumann, and these were subject to censorship by the Political Information Department (later the Political Warfare Executive) of the Foreign Office. The remaining air-time belonged to the French Service of the BBC whose members, being BBC employees, had to follow British instructions and at times – for example, after the American landing in North Africa in November 1942 – adopted an anti-Gaullist attitude. See Michel, op. cit., p. 32. Cf. Briggs, op. cit., pp. 239–57 and 441–60.

72. Pierre Bourdan's publications include his memoirs of the war years in London: *Carnet des jours d'attente, juin 1940–juin 1944* (Paris, 1945). For an account of Bourdan's life, see Oberlé's introduction to *Pages choisies de Pierre Bourdan*, op. cit.

73. 1941u. The French edition was entitled *Vérités sur la France*.

74. 1981a, p. 83: tr. p. 72.

75. Oberlé, op. cit., p. 103. An anonymous "officer of the Free French Naval Forces", in a lecture to the Oxford University French Club in November 1941, spoke of seeing the "astonishing photographs" published by *La France libre* displayed in houses in Africa. ("Nostalgie de la France", *FL*, 3 (14), December 1941, p. 124). Many of these photographs were later published in book form, with a French text by Alice Jahier, English translation by J. G. Weightman, and an Introduction by T. S. Eliot. See Alice Jahier, *Inoubliable France – France Remembered* (London, 1944).

76. These were subsequently reprinted with a Preface by Aron (1944z[3]). Aron seems to have met Arthur Koestler at this time. Thus Inez Holden (1904–74), novelist, journalist and friend of George Orwell, recorded in her diary for 11 September

1941: "Yesterday at the PEN world congress lunch I sat at a table with Koestler, Cyril Connolly, Stevie Smith, Guy Chapman, Koestler's girl friend Miss Hardy, ...René Avord, of *La France libre*, who has some other name, and a German refugee writer. Koestler was betting that Orwell would be the greatest bestseller in five years time and our bet was five bottles of burgundy". Bernard Crick, *George Orwell: A Life* (Harmondsworth, 1982), p. 395. The Congress was in fact held at the French Institute: see Storm Jameson, "Le 17e congrès international des PEN", *FL*, 2 (11), September 1941.

77. Thus from early 1941 onwards *La France libre*'s readers were reminded of the advantages of Nugget Shoe Polish, Jacob's Cream Crackers, 3% Defence Bonds, the war-time *cuisine* of La Cigale in Soho and La Coquille in Saint Martin's Lane, the delights of Dubonnet, Marmite and Pan Yan Pickle, and the benefits of reading *The Yorkshire Post*, as well as the fact that "Guinness vous fera du bien".

78. Gillois, op. cit., p. 103.

79. *The Listener*, 18 November 1943, p. 586.

80. Oberlé, op. cit., p. 104.

81. R. A., interview with the author, 1977; Soustelle, op. cit., p. 48.

82. J. G. Weightman (ed. and translator), *French Writing on English Soil* (London, 1945), p. 7.

83. Soustelle, op. cit., p. 48.

84. D. W. Brogan, "La France dans le monde", *FL*, 7 (38), December 1943, p. 89.

85. Oberlé, op. cit., p. 102. Cf. the recent testimony of Richard Cobb, the well-known British historian of the French Revolution, for whom *La France libre* was "la seule présence actuelle de la France". A faithful reader throughout the war years, he particularly appreciated the fact that it was not a propaganda organ (quoted by Aron in 1981a, p. 82: tr. p. 71).

86. Weightman, op. cit., p. 7. For press tributes to *La France libre*, see *"La France libre"*. *Numéro anthologique: novembre 1940 – septembre 1945* (Paris, n.d.), pp. 211–12.

87. 1948o, p. 8.

88. André Labarthe, "Après cinq ans", *"La France libre"*. *Numéro anthologique*, op. cit. The review also provided those who had spent the war in occupied France with a different perspective on events. Simone de Beauvoir, for example, has recalled how, thanks to the set of *La France libre* which Aron lent her when they met again in Paris at the end of 1944, she could "decipher the war not from the perspective of Paris but from the point of view of London, from the other side. I had been living in a prison; now the world was restored to me". Simone de Beauvoir, *La Force des choses* (Paris, 1963), p. 20: tr. (by Richard Howard), *The Force of Circumstance* (Harmondsworth, 1965), p. 10. Compare the young sociologist François Bourricaud, who came across some copies of the review in the autumn of 1944: "I was filled with amazement. Aron had shown that it was possible to speak of the events that had taken place since 1940, and to do so at the very moment they were happening, pertinently and soberly, while bearing witness – unreservedly, straightforwardly but without bombast – on behalf of a number of values to which one was unswervingly attached. This controlled and almost serene passion charmed me. It seemed the only fitting way of speaking of what had happened to France and the French since 1940, when one was not oneself a hero" (Bourricaud, 1985, p. 33).

89. Brian Crozier, *De Gaulle: The Warrior* (London, 1973), p. 135.
90. See below, p. 235.
91. Soustelle, op. cit., p. 48.
92. R. A., interview with the author, 1977. Cf. 1983a, p. 169. Simone de Beauvoir recalls an amusing story about the V1s in London which Aron told against himself when they met again after the war: "'When you heard one, you had to throw yourself flat on the pavement', Aron told us. 'Once as I was getting up, I saw a very old lady who had stayed on her feet. She was looking me up and down. I was so annoyed that I reprimanded her: 'Madam, in cases like this one should lie down!'" (Beauvoir, op. cit., p. 20: tr. p. 10).
93. Soustelle, op. cit., p. 48. The Free French were financed by British loans in accordance with the Churchill-de Gaulle agreement of 7 August 1940.
94. De Gaulle, op. cit., p. 131: tr. p. 158.
95. General de Gaulle, "Maintenir notre pays dans la guerre", *FL*, 1 (4), February 1941, pp. 309–10. De Gaulle apparently sought a rapprochement between himself and his adversaries. Thus, according to André Rabache, a journalist on *France*, on one occasion de Gaulle invited his opponents to lunch with Colonel Fontaine and himself at the Savoy: Comert and Gombault, of the newspaper, *France*; Labarthe and Aron, of *La France libre*; and Jacques Duchesne and Pierre Bourdan, of the BBC. Aron, however, had no recollection of such a meeting (Gillois, op. cit., p. 99).
96. Compare Gillois, ibid., p. 101, where Aron refers to the General's reaction to American anger at the Free French landing on Saint-Pierre-et-Miquelon on 22 December 1941: "I dined with him on the evening of the Saint-Pierre-et-Miquelon affair. He began to walk up and down, and exclaimed: 'Ah! They're marvellous, our allies!' It was both impressive and slightly ridiculous. His theatrical style seemed ill-suited to France's position".
97. There are many versions of the events surrounding Muselier's arrest. In addition to his own account (Muselier, op. cit.), see those in de Gaulle, op. cit., Soustelle, op. cit., and Jean Lacouture, *Charles de Gaulle. I. Le Rebelle, 1890–1944* (Paris, 1984), Chapter 25.
98. Michel, op. cit., pp. 31–2. Other versions of this incident, recounted from different viewpoints, are to be found in the memoirs of de Gaulle, Muselier and Soustelle, and in Lacouture, op. cit.
99. 1948o, p. 4.
100. Cf. Michel, op. cit., p. 82, and Lacouture, op. cit., as well as the accounts by de Gaulle, Muselier, and Soustelle. Aron also discusses the affair in his memoirs (1983a, pp. 182–4).
101. Soustelle, op. cit., p. 283.
102. Ibid., pp. 342–3.
103. 1948o, p. 7.
104. Jacques Soustelle, *Envers et contre tout. Vol. 2. D'Alger à Paris. Souvenirs et documents sur la France Libre 1942–44* (Paris, 1950), p. 65.
105. Charles de Gaulle, *Mémoires de guerre, Vol. 2, L'Unité, 1942–44* (Paris, 1956), p. 87: tr. (by Richard Howard) *War Memoirs, Vol. 2. Unity, 1942–1944* (London, 1959), p. 91.
106. Oberlé has left us this glimpse of Aron in London:
"On Christmas Eve, in London, there was a late-night party at Labarthe's. We were

among Frenchmen, drinking to Christmas Eve next year in Paris. The party went on very late. Towards three o'clock in the morning, the telephone rang in Labarthe's bedroom. When he came back he was quite pale. He said simply: 'Admiral Darlan was assassinated this afternoon, in Algiers'.

Labarthe, Raymond Aron and Duchesne remained silent. Héron de Villefosse said gravely: 'He did the navy a great deal of harm'.

Geneviève Brissot, who had experienced the German occupation in France, said: 'That's news which will please people in France'. I agreed with her and Villefosse". Oberlé, op. cit., p. 191. (Héron de Villefosse was a Captain in the Free French Navy and an associate of Muselier; Geneviève Brissot worked for the French Service of the BBC.)

107. 1948o, p. 7.
108. Ibid., p. 4.
109. See Soustelle, op. cit., Vol. 2, p. 204, and Paul-Louis Bret, *Au Feu des événements: Mémoires d'un journaliste: Londres-Alger, 1929–1944* (Paris, 1959), p. 388. Bret, formerly Chief of the Havas Press Agency in London, had worked for the Free French as a journalist and broadcaster before going to Algiers in 1942.
110. Soustelle, op. cit., Vol. 2, p. 230.
111. Ibid., p. 242.
112. Bret, op. cit., p. 400.
113. Soustelle, op. cit., Vol. 2, p. 216.
114. Bret, op. cit., p. 401.
115. Soustelle, op. cit., Vol. 2, p. 251.
116. Just how erroneous were Labarthe's (and Muselier's) judgements of both Gaullism and Giraudism may be seen from the analysis of the two movements in Henri Michel, *Les Courants de pensée de la Résistance* (Paris, 1962).
117. R. A., interview with the author, 1977. It is worth noting that throughout Muselier's detailed account of the events leading up to his break with de Gaulle in March 1942, Aron is never mentioned. See Muselier, op. cit.
118. Gillois, op. cit., p. 102.
119. 1946b, p. 7.
120. Soustelle denies the existence of any "oath" that had to be "sworn" to the General and asserts that this was a fiction entirely invented by Labarthe, or perhaps Muselier (Soustelle, op. cit., Vol. 2, p. 222). Henri Michel suggests that this so-called oath of loyalty to the General's person was no more than a military commitment limited to the duration of the war and that its significance was exaggerated by de Gaulle's enemies in order to show his political methods in a bad light (Michel, op. cit., pp. 32–3).
121. 1981a, p. 87: tr. p. 75.
122. 1943j.
123. 1943o, p. 83. Aron discusses the article, which "caused a scandal", in his memoirs (1983a, pp. 184–6).
124. 1946b, p. 17.
125. Gillois, op. cit., p. 101.
126. Beauvoir, op. cit., p. 25: tr. pp. 14–15.
127. When the war was over, Labarthe embarked on a career as a scientific journalist.

After a period as Foreign Scientific Correspondent of *France-Soir*, in 1948 he founded a monthly "revue d'information et d'éducation du grand public" called *Constellation*, of which he was Directeur till 1964. He also edited a monthly magazine entitled *Science et vie*. He died in 1967. After Giraud's elimination, Labarthe's friend Muselier wrote a number of articles for *La France libre* in 1944, though on military, and not political, matters. Muselier remained on active service till 1946, when he founded a political group, the Union pour la Défense de la République. He was made an Honorary KCB by the British, and died in 1965.

128. 1983a, pp. 191–2. Corniglion-Molinier's name was understandably a source of amused bewilderment to the British troops with whom he came into contact – see the witty pair of articles he wrote for *La France libre*, "Ces Français. . .", *FL*, 5 (27, 28), January and February 1943.

129. 1939e.

130. Gabrielle Ferrières, *Jean Cavaillès: philosophe et combattant (1903–1944)* (Paris, 1950), p. 195. A new edition, entitled *Jean Cavaillès, un philosophe dans la guerre, 1903–1944*, was published in 1982.

131. 1945y. Cf. 1962d, 1964j. A similar fate was suffered by Cavaillès' and Aron's mutual friend, the philosopher and mathematician, Albert Lautman, whose *Nouvelles Recherches sur la structure dialectique des mathématiques* had inaugurated the series "Essais philosophiques" (1939e). Born in 1908, he had been at the Ecole Normale Supérieure from 1926 to 1930. Also a student of Brunschvicg, he had been awarded the doctorate in 1937. He was captured in June 1940, but escaped from Germany to France at the second attempt in 1941. After working for various Resistance groups in the south of France, he was arrested on 15 May and shot on 1 August 1944. See the memoir by his widow, Suzanne Lautman, "Introduction", Albert Lautman, *Symétrie de dissymétrie en mathématiques et en physique: Le problème du temps* (Paris, 1946).

132. 1983a, p. 200.

133. After the war, *La France libre*'s regular contributors included (in addition to Labarthe and E. M. Friedwald) Roger Caillois, Raymond Picard, Roger Stéphane, Jean Dutourd, John Plamenatz and Stephen Spender.

134. Jean-Paul Sartre, "Une grande revue française de Londres", *Combat*, 7–8 January 1945.

10

Chronique de France

————

From November 1940 to April 1944 Aron wrote a series of regular monthly commentaries in *La France libre* under the general heading of "Chronique de France", many of which were republished in Paris after the war with the title, *De l'Armistice à l'insurrection nationale*.[1] These articles analysed the political, economic and cultural situation in Vichy and occupied France, their purpose being "to help readers, the majority of whom were foreigners, to understand events which the daily press reported in a more or less confused manner".[2]

Aron wrote his "chronicles" after studying the French, German and Swiss press:

I learnt that, even in a censored press like Vichy's, one can find practically everything. When one knows the country and reads the press (it is the only time in my life that, for three or four years, I really read the press), one can reconstruct a great deal of what is happening there. Today these articles are of only anecdotal or historical interest. There are now books by historians who have had access to archives which were not available to me. But my analyses were not that false, considering the information I had.[3]

Indeed, as a British reviewer commenting in 1948 put it, the articles provided "a monthly survey of the French situation which was unique at the time for its accuracy, fairness and balance and which even now remains impressively correct"; it was also significant that Aron "was able to reprint these studies as they stood for the educated public of liberated France, offering in this way the first coherent account of the internal developments in France under Vichy and the Germans".[4]

The articles contained in *De l'Armistice à l'insurrection nationale* are arranged in four sections. The first section, "Introduction", consists of the outstanding study in the collection, "La Capitulation", an analysis of the surrender of June 1940 which Aron wrote for the first number of *La France libre* the following November.[5] We have already seen the effect which the fall of France had on him. Thus, two years after the defeat he was to write, "On the whole of France, on every Frenchman, there weighs, as a kind of remorse, as a source of permanent humiliation, the memory of the tragic spring of 1940".[6] "La Capitulation" is a masterly analysis, intellectually powerful but suffused with a controlled passion (the *Times Literary Supplement*, welcoming the appearance of *La France libre*, singled out this "piercing and outspoken analysis of the causes of the French capitulation, unsigned...").[7] Furthermore, because of the desperate circumstances and the changed audience to whom Aron was now speaking, the writing is marked by a new directness and simplicity of style.[8]

In seeking an armistice, Aron declared, Pétain was forgetting that:

we were bound to Great Britain not only by solemn undertakings, but by the most certain and sacred interest, that of our very existence and "the spiritual liberties of our people". He was forgetting that, if the struggle was compromised in metropolitan France, the Empire, protected by an untouched fleet, still possessed immense resources.[9]

In trying to explain by what "aberration" the Armistice had come about, Aron turned first to the actors involved. He refused, he stated, to discuss the various intrigues surrounding the decision to seek an armistice, except to say that they only served to illustrate the "moral decay of the ruling classes" under the Third Republic and thus revealed "one of the profound causes of the surrender".[10] In his view, there were four groups of actors responsible:

generals seeking to save the remains of the army, reactionaries sincerely or hypocritically impatient to renovate the country, politicians anxious to obtain office in return for services rendered to new masters, and capitalists concerned for social order, if not for their country's greatness. All of them, sufficiently ignorant to hope for a reversal of alliances or a compromise with the victor, decided that France would submit before exhausting her means of resistance.[11]

248

How, he asked, could a decision of such historic importance have been taken or imposed by a few individuals, without Parliament being consulted and without the country being able to express its will? In the first place, a military defeat had been presented as if it were the downfall of a nation; secondly, for months censorship had been subjecting France to "a kind of despotism"; and, finally, "all the political organizations of the Third Republic were collapsing, and leaving the field open to myths and adventurers":

In the anaesthesia created by censorship during the eight months of war, the country's nerves had gradually been severed; the body as a whole seemed to be alive, but reduced to the reactions of a mere organism. The *élan* of Valmy, the Marne and Verdun could not be reborn. The country was taking no part in its destiny; its soul was no longer in it.[12]

As a result, "every military weakness was transformed into an irreparable misfortune". For example, because of the French army's inferior capacity of movement,

the columns advancing towards the front, or returning from it, found themselves crossing a vast region, peopled by fugitives and refugees, through which there blew a wind of panic. The morale of the troops, like their movements, suffered irreparable damage.

The pitiful procession of women, old men and children, encumbering the roads and machine-gunned by enemy aeroplanes as it searched vainly for shelter, illustrates France's tragic lack of preparation – material and moral – for the war, or rather the lack of preparation for modern war by a country that was a prisoner of an experience which, though still recent, had been overtaken by advances in military technique.[13]

At the same time, there was a complete breakdown of communication in the face of the German advance. "Public opinion no longer existed in France, because the material conditions for public opinion had disappeared. France was dumb because she no longer knew anything".[14] Nevertheless, a government determined to resist could have relied on the masses ("at any rate those who had not been affected by the new-found pacifism of the Communists"), since the people were fortified by that most ancient of traditions, resistance to the invader, and by a new passion, anti-fascism. "But in the middle of June 1940 there was no point in looking for representatives of the people. Beneath the shock of defeat, the Republic was collapsing of its own accord; it was dying without defending itself".[15]

How was it possible for a renunciation unparallelled in the history of France to be passively accepted by the French people? The answer,

Aron believed, could be summed up in two words: defeatism and misfortune. Defeatism, nourished by "the desire for a quiet life, the fear of war and the lack of confidence in our strength, . . . created the moral atmosphere in which the Armistice of June 1940 became possible". At the same time, this defeatism "stirred up passions on different sides":

Between pacifists and war-mongers . . . the hostility was as inexpiable as that between supporters and opponents of the Popular Front . . . People ended up by hating the enemy within more than the enemy without, and they exulted in the defeat because it confirmed the criticisms which for years they had been heaping upon the regime. Because they despaired of the Republic, they ended by doubting France.[16]

The acceptance of the Armistice had also been made possible by the misfortune of the French people. Thus, "When, on the roads, the news spread that Marshal Pétain was taking power and seeking an armistice, no one understood the meaning of the news. It was not interpreted in political but in human terms":

I remember a peasant woman from Lorraine who was pushing a pram and who was in her fourth evacuation in four weeks. This time, she said, her wandering journey was going to end: there would be no more planes to machine-gun and bomb her, and there would once again be a bed and milk for her baby. That is what the Armistice meant for her.[17]

Finally, there was one further "simple yet decisive" reason for the renunciation – the reputation of Pétain himself:

The man who recommended the Armistice was the victor of Verdun, the man described by the leader of the Socialist Party as "the most humane of our great generals". How could the French have suspected a political operation disguised as an attempt to save the nation? It needed the man who had said in 1916: "They shall not pass" to dare to say in 1940: "We must try to stop the fighting".

Alas! No one could be found to say to the French with authority: "We must try to continue the struggle".[18]

Aron rejected the view that it would have been both an act of cowardice to transfer the government to North Africa and impossible to carry on resistance from there. Certainly, there was no tradition of defending the country from without in this way, yet, "how great would have been the glory of France if, though completely occupied, she had refused to surrender!" And what of the 60,000 troops in Syria, the four divisions in Tunisia, the hundreds of aeroplanes in Morocco, and the untouched fleet with bases such as Bizerte and Oran? If, moreover, the French forces overseas were inadequate, whose fault was it but that of a defeatist High Command which had failed to persuade the government of the necessity of treating North Africa as "an integral part of the sphere of operations"? It was this which the military chiefs should have been doing, "instead of moving out of their spheres of competence to impose surrender . . . But the vocation of politics often comes to generals with defeat . . .".[19]

Aron also rejected the argument that the unity of the French nation and Empire would have been compromised still further if the government had moved to North Africa and France had been completely occupied by the Germans. On the contrary, France, with its different zones, was already a divided country; and, in the face of a total occupation and with its legal government in North Africa, the people, Aron maintained, would have united in a common resistance.

> In an ancient country like France, politically and ideologically divided, unity requires a unanimous will to national greatness. By surrendering, our country was condemning herself to tyranny. The capitulation not only obliges the French to do apparently of their own free will something which in reality they find it difficult to endure; it also accentuates their quarrels by depriving them of their ultimate collective faith, the love of a free country.
>
> Moral conditions determine the climate in which a temporary ordeal is endured. The momentary surrender of the territory of metropolitan France as a higher strategic necessity of modern war, and the continuation of the struggle in another form by falling back on the Empire, would have inspired the forces of resistance. People would not have lived in a hopeless and morbid atmosphere of renunciation . . .[20]

Finally, the Vichy generals, industrialists, bankers and politicians were deluding themselves if they thought they would obtain anything of significance by negotiating with Hitler. Once peace had been made with the Führer, there would be no French army and no general staff, even if a few individuals succeeded in advancing their careers. There would be no French capitalism, because the real capitalists – the masters – would be German; and there would be no French policy, because the rulers of France would be the servants of Germany. For had not Hitler himself said that "The countries conquered in the future war in Europe will be wiped off the map of the world"?

"French history", Aron emphasized in conclusion, "does not just date from the summer of 1940. The capitulation does not seal the destiny of our country. Meditation on the past must have no other end than to give more strength and lucidity to our action".[21]

* * *

Following this "Introduction", the first part of *De l'Armistice à l'insurrection nationale* concerned the period of the "wait-and-see" policy ("l'attentisme") of Pétain, Darlan and Laval, from December 1940 to October 1942. It also included analyses of the material and moral situation in France after the Armistice,[22] the various political regimes at Vichy,[23] German exploitation of the French economy and industry,[24] the food problem in France,[25] German and Vichy propaganda,[26] French cultural life under the Occupation,[27] and the trial at Riom in February 1942 of Blum, Daladier and other politicians of the Third Republic accused of responsibility for the collapse of France.[28] In addition, there was an impressively detailed analysis of the military problems surrounding the defeat of 1940, in the light of the evidence that emerged at the trial.[29]

In Part Two, which covered the period of the "collaboration" of Pétain, Laval and Darnand, the key article is that which analysed the "disintegration" of the Vichy regime in November 1942, as a result of the accession of Darlan to power in North Africa, the German invasion of the Unoccupied Zone and the scuttling of the French fleet at Toulon.[30] The problem, Aron wrote in January 1943, was to explain how, two and a half years after the Armistice, French Africa had not fallen into German hands. The *attentistes*, who provisionally favoured French neutrality, had triumphed over the *collaborateurs*, who wanted France to join the Axis. But the important question had been how the *attentistes* would react at the crucial moment, when the Allies landed in North Africa and a choice had to be made. In November 1942, it seemed to Aron, it was not the out-and-out *attentistes* like Maurras who had won, but those who had not been responsible for the Armistice and had been waiting to join in on the Allies' side. Such a victory in the face of German pressure would not have been possible, however, if most of the administration and the army had not been anti-German and acted in favour of the Resistance. "Thus nothing would be more absurd or unjust than to extend to all the men and institutions formally attached to Vichy the condemnation which rightly falls upon the collaborationist politicians".[31]

Furthermore, since the Armistice, the French Empire had given "striking proof of its solidarity and loyalty", as had the army and air force, but how would they react when the decisive moment – the allied invasion of North Africa – came? In the event, the agreement made with the existing authorities served to restore peace and order after three days, and the invasion of the Unoccupied Zone rallied the rest of the Empire to the allied cause. As a Swiss newspaper had written, Darlan's order to cease fire had rendered a considerable service to the Allies, while the "tragic events" of 27 November, when the fleet was scuttled at Toulon, prevented any French ship from falling into German hands.[32] These events had revealed to the world, and confirmed to the nation, that the fiction of a sovereign French state was dead. The struggle had been resumed in French Africa. All that remained was a band of traitors and a handful of fanatics, clinging to a sham collaboration or the myth of neutrality. "Through its resistance, its loyalty and its heroism", Aron concluded in January 1943, "the French people have finally brought the whole of France back into the war".[33]

Subsequently, however, in an important epilogue to *De l'Armistice à l'insurrection nationale*, written in Paris in February 1945, Aron returned to the events of June 1940 and November 1942 – "the dates at which the fatal decisions were taken" – in order to re-examine them "coolly, *sine studio et ira*".[34] Here he felt inclined to "soften the rigour" of the analysis presented in "La Capitulation" and "harden" what he now saw as his over-indulgent earlier judgement of the events of November 1942:

In June 1940, revolted by what appeared to us a breach of honour and an abandonment of the struggle and of the Ally before resources were exhausted, we were concerned only to pass a judgement of condemnation and to justify that condemnation by amassing reasons and by outlining in general terms what could have been. In November 1942, on the other hand, consoled by the speedy end to the fratricidal battle in North Africa, relieved of the dull agony which had been weighing on us for more than two years, and reassured that there would be no reversal of alliances, we did not stress sufficiently strongly that the men of Vichy, repentant though they might be, had finally disqualified themselves by sacrificing thousands of French and American lives to the myth of the defence of the Empire. In short, today we would be less severe towards the decisions of June 1940, *considered in terms of their effects*, and more severe towards those of November 1942, *as far as the responsibility of the actors is concerned*.[35]

The first proposition would doubtless "surprise and shock", but it was impossible to say how events would have turned out if France had continued the struggle from North Africa. For example, would Germany have attacked Russia in June 1941 if the Allies had been masters of the Mediterranean? The answer to such questions would never be known. Not, Aron stressed, that he was now implying that his judgement of the Armistice at the time had been mistaken. Militarily, the surrender had increased the chances of a lightning German victory, but France had been brought into moral disrepute as well: "If, today, the moral authority of France is not too diminished, we owe it to the other act of June 1940, that which kept France in the war and ensured the continuity of the Resistance and the maintenance of French honour". Furthermore, the Armistice worsened the divisions between Frenchmen, for if it had been wholly occupied, France would have been united against the occupant. As it was, "Half-occupied, and half-governed by a half-French government, she was doomed to the quarrels arising out of conflicting loyalties, to doubts, and to a war of religion all the more absurd because political unity existed on neither side of the barricades". In this sense, the Armistice damaged France more than it did the allied cause. Militarily, therefore, the two-year neutralization of North Africa was the least bad solution – it served the interests of both parties; however, the same could not be said of the Vichy government as far as its moral legacy was concerned.[36]

How did Aron now view the crucial events of November 1942? If, he wrote, the rulers at Vichy had possessed the foresight, the courage, or simply the good sense to make an unequivocal choice in favour of the Allies, their whole past would in retrospect have taken on another meaning. But the indispensable condition of any indulgence was that the story should have the right ending. At the first opportunity, Pétain should have gone to North Africa to win back to the cause of France the honourable French people whom he had, by his prestige, led astray. But the conclusion to this "lamentable adventure" was in fact quite different, for at a time when there was no longer any cause for hesitation the men of Vichy continued to prevaricate:

The majority of them were, at the bottom of their hearts, anti-German like all Frenchmen, but with so much uncertainty, Anglophobia, anti-democratic fervour and opportunism, that they were incapable of shaking off the chains of lies that they had themselves forged and of returning of their own accord to the straight path of a Frenchman's duty.

Thus, ironically (par une ruse de la raison), the Armistice did more wrong to the prestige of France than to the Allied cause, and was more harmful to French unity than to the unity of the anti-German coalition. As to the reversal of alliances of November 1942, it justified American diplomacy without justifying those who no longer knew who was the enemy. It was useful rather than meritorious.[37]

Finally, Aron examined the "moral crisis" of the *épuration* – the "purge" of the collaborators which followed the Liberation. The motives of those responsible for the Armistice had varied considerably: some hoped to deceive the enemy and save the Empire, others believed in the imminence of German victory, others wanted a national revolution arising out of the defeat, while others were simply willing to accept the new order. But in Aron's view it was important to distinguish those who were defeatists under the impact of the catastrophe from those who had actively conspired for it; it was wrong to attribute the worst motives to all.

However, until light had been thrown on the events surrounding the Armistice and its consequences, the purge itself would continue in an atmosphere of "unease and ambiguity". Once the High Court had given judgement on the leaders of the Vichy government, then it would be possible to deal logically with their subordinates and take account of differences in motives and circumstances. There was, for example, one motive which might have weighed heavily in people's minds – the genuinely patriotic desire to save French lives and thus preserve the country's future (possibly the Armistice and Vichy did indeed, for a time, soften the harshness of the Occupation).[38]

It seemed to Aron from his survey of the main events that took place between 1940 and 1944, that a number of "fundamental distinctions" could be made. Up until November 1942, the confusion was inevitable. Recognized by Russia until the spring of 1941 and by the United States until the liberation of North Africa, Vichy could be seen by most civil servants and officers as the legitimate government. Once the Armistice was signed, a major interest for France and its Allies was to save the fleet and the Empire. It was understandable, then, that some patriots at Vichy should try to maintain their position, in order to limit the degree of collaboration and work for France's re-entry into the war. There were grounds for sanction, in Aron's view, only against the originators of the policy of collaboration and against those of their subordinates who gave proof of exceptional zeal, as well as those who took personal initiatives (in Syria, for example) and were dedicated to repressing the Resistance. There was, by contrast, a presumption of guilt against those who followed Pétain to the very end. Clearly, Aron added, so crude a distinction did not cover the complexity of particular cases. Responsibility varied, depending on whether one was considering civil servants or ministers, and whether or not the executants went beyond what their functions implied.

It was even more difficult to apportion responsibility when it came to economic collaboration. Between the patriotic company directors who deliberately sabotaged themselves, at one extreme, and those who rushed to meet German orders, at the other, there existed every shade of response. Furthermore, every *attentiste*, however patriotic, was compelled to give pledges, in words at least, to collaboration, just as there were hardly any collaborators who did not try to take out a little counter-insurance. "Who", Aron asked, "could fathom the hearts and minds, and establish the merits and demerits, of the men who were engaged in this diabolical game?" Nevertheless, in order to satisfy public opinion, it would have been enough to deal sharply with the non-controversial cases.[39]

255

It would take years to overcome the economic effects of the catastrophe, but the moral traces would be even more difficult to remove. Would France manage to recreate its unity? In one sense, this unity had been progressively rebuilt during the war years: the "immense majority" of the French population now accepted the authority of General de Gaulle. But the attitudes associated with Pétainism and collaboration had not disappeared. It was rightly said that men of all backgrounds – believers and non-believers, Jews and Christians – met and recognized one another in the Resistance. But one must still have the courage to say that the unanimity in war did not necessarily extend into political action. Nevertheless, to talk of the "schism of Vichy" seemed to Aron to be an exaggeration and a distortion. The earliest resistants constituted a character-type rather than a spiritual family. They comprised not only officers who refused to compromise their sense of combat and honour, but also men of the Left and targets for racial persecution who could not accept an armistice with the Nazi evil. Both groups, obeying their patriotism and their conscience, refused to conform. They had, at that critical moment, the same reaction, not the same doctrine – and the same was true of the earliest Pétainists.[40]

After a few months, however, the lines of demarcation deepened. Pétain's clientele, in the Unoccupied Zone, was recruited primarily among former right-wing circles, the Parti Social Français and the Action Française. It remained anti-German for the most part, but because of its hatred of the Popular Front, the Jews and democracy, it believed in the Marshal as saviour and at times was even inclined to think that an arrangement was possible with the conqueror. Yet it was false to speak of the schism of Vichy, if this implied that a significant body of French people would have subscribed to the myth of the new order and taken the enemy's side: the die-hard collaborationists were always a small minority that had cut itself off from the rest of the nation. But it was true that the traditional schism of the French nation, which was again evident after 1934, took on a new form after the Armistice. The expression used by Maurras after his conviction – "the revenge of the Dreyfusards" – would have been inappropriate, if in its early days, when the traditionalists were in the ascendant, the Vichy regime had not indeed been to some extent the revenge of the anti-Dreyfusards.[41]

It was, then, not so much a question of establishing whether or not one could talk about a "schism of Vichy" as of specifying the effect of the Vichy regime on what was already a long-standing schism. Aron's "gloomy impression" was that things had changed less than might have been thought or hoped. On the one hand, certain conservatives had been infected by poisons of German origin and contaminated by doubt, so cleverly spread by Vichy, as to where their duty to the nation lay; on the other hand, in the course of the last few years they had been obliged to draw nearer to the mass of the French people taking part in the fight. But, Aron concluded,

I fear that, all things considered, the French bourgeoisie, business circles and all "right-thinking people" ("les bien pensants") have remained strangely true to themselves. In so far, then, as one wishes to spare the country a bloody revolution, one is calling for a renewal of the French bourgeoisie, one is asking it not to abandon or cling anxiously to its position, but to understand the new times, to have the clearsightedness to make reforms, and not to adopt a peevish attitude towards popular movements and aspirations; in a word, one is asking it to become a real elite again.

...In short, it is certainly necessary first of all to surmount these four tragic years, that is to say, remove the guilty and restore the weak, the conformists and those who have gone astray, to the French community; but it is above all necessary to overcome the traditional divisions of the nation.

The quarrels of yesterday weigh heavily upon us. If the purge had been better handled, and those chiefly responsible had been speedily and solemnly punished, it would have been easier to ignore the small fry and avoid one section of opinion protesting against the excesses and the other against the inadequacies of the purge. But let us leave regrets aside: the difficulties of the task incline the sincere critic to be indulgent. It is no longer a question of looking backwards. The French will not change to order and it is with the French as they are that we have to rebuild France. The hope is not to tear them suddenly from themselves, their prejudices and their passions, but to unite them in a common goal, and place before them a mighty task to be achieved together.

The national insurrection marked the triumphal completion of an effort carried on for four years in the dark. Today, it is a question of building in broad daylight, but without hope of dazzling days and without the prospect of triumph. The task is endless and it requires daily effort.[42]

Notes

1. 1945r.
2. Ibid., p. 7. Compare 1981a, pp. 95–6: tr. 1983b, pp. 82–3, where, implicitly criticized for his interest in what was happening in France under Vichy, Aron justifies his motives perfectly convincingly in similar terms.
3. 1981a, p. 96: tr. p. 83 (R.C.).
4. Stewart, 1948.
5. 1940a.
6. 1942l; 1945r, p. 177.
7. *TLS*, 30 November 1940, p. 597. The Free French daily, *France*, spoke of the "astonishing lucidity" of this article (11 December 1940).

8. Aron has been taken to task for writing about Vichy "without anger". His reply is: ". . . I simply do not like people who belch in front of blank paper. . . In general I prefer to understand and analyse my opponents, rather than abuse them. . . I believe that many of my readers at that time were grateful to me for preserving a certain decency of expression and for not being carried away by easy emotions – emotions which, I should add, I felt" (1981a, pp. 96–7, 99: tr. pp. 83–4, 85–6 (R.C.)).
9. 1945r, p. 11.
10. Ibid., p. 12.
11. Ibid., p. 14.
12. Ibid.
13. Ibid., pp. 14–15.
14. Ibid., pp. 15–16.
15. Ibid., p. 16.
16. Ibid., pp. 16–17.
17. Ibid., p. 17.
18. Ibid.
19. Ibid., p. 18.
20. Ibid., p. 19.
21. Ibid., p. 21.
22. 1940d.
23. 1941j, 1941l, 1941w, 1942i, 1942m.
24. 1941k, 1941t, 1941y, $1941z^3$, 1942p.
25. 1941n.
26. 1941p.
27. 1941r.
28. 1942f.
29. 1942l. *La France libre* contains no articles on Vichy's policy towards the Jews and Aron came to regret this. He suggests several reasons for this reticence. Firstly, the members of the Resistance in London thought of themselves primarily as French. As such, they were obviously opposed to Vichy's anti-Semitic measures, but there was "a kind of convention" to mention them as little as possible – an attitude which was probably accentuated in Aron's case by the fact that he was Jewish. Secondly, the measures taken by the French against the Jews affected Aron deeply precisely because he was, as it were, a Frenchman first and a Jew afterwards; for him it was "a kind of emotional precaution" to think as little as possible about what some of the French were doing to the Jews. Thirdly, because Nazi propaganda kept repeating that the Jews were the cause of the war, there was a convention of silence in the Allied press whereby it was stated that the war was being fought to liberate France and to combat totalitarianism – but not to free the Jews (1981a, p. 101: tr. pp. 87–8).
30. 1943b.
31. 1945r, p. 245.
32. Ibid., p. 249.
33. Ibid., p. 250.
34. Ibid., p. 355.
35. Ibid., p. 356.
36. Ibid., p. 358.

37. Ibid., p. 360.
38. Ibid., pp. 361–3.
39. Ibid., p. 366.
40. Ibid., pp. 366–7.
41. Ibid., pp. 367–8.
42. Ibid., pp. 368–9. Aron also analysed the events surrounding the Armistice in a review of Marc Bloch's *L'Etrange Défaite* (1947a), in which he compared the historian's posthumously published account of the collapse in 1940 with the analysis of the defeat of 1870 in Renan's *Réforme intellectuelle et morale de la France*. Renan's three key explanations, Aron argued, were close to those put forward by Bloch. To both writers, France's defeat was primarily intellectual – its military ideas were outmoded – rather than, as was commonly suggested, moral; the French army had been overtaken by a kind of sclerosis, because it had become socially isolated from the rest of the nation; and a politically and socially divided country was incapable of making war. Aron agreed with all three diagnoses, but felt that both writers had underestimated a fourth factor, the part played by numerical inferiority in both defeats.

11

Man against the Tyrants

The second collection of Aron's war writings, *L'Homme contre les tyrans*, was first published in New York in 1944, in a series edited by Jacques Maritain[1] and reprinted in Paris after the war.[2] Without ever losing sight of social realities, "these remarkable studies", as Maritain justly called them,[3] are on a higher philosophical plane than the articles in *De l'Armistice à l'insurrection nationale*. *L'Homme contre les tyrans* is the most significant and enduring of Aron's three volumes of *France libre* writings, because in it his liberalism is made explicit in a particularly lucid and powerful way. Despite its origin as a number of separate articles, the book which was never translated into English, is a neglected masterpiece of liberal political thought.

The twenty studies which comprise the collection were written between November 1940 and June 1943 and are arranged in five parts: "Tyrannie: Rationalisation et déraison" ("Tyranny: Rationalization and Unreason"); "Faiblesses des démocraties" ("Weaknesses of the Democracies"); "Séduction des tyrannies" ("Lure of the Tyrannies"); "Guerre impériale" ("Imperial War"); and, finally, "Perspectives".

Tyranny: Rationalization and Unreason

The first part of *L'Homme contre les tyrans* began with the analysis of Machiavellianism as a "doctrine of modern tyrannies" which Aron had written for the first number of *La France libre*.[4] "If", he argued, "Machiavellianism consists in ruling by terror and cunning, no epoch has been more Machiavellian than ours, . . . because the violent elites which have brought about the revolutions of the twentieth century automatically conceive of politics in the Machiavellian mode".[5] Like Machiavelli, Pareto, "who was one of the masters of fascism",[6] was led albeit using different arguments, "to exalt the virtues of the leader who makes decisions and gives orders, and of the masses who devotedly obey".[7] Machiavellianism, Aron believed, had three features which were common to all totalitarian philosophies: a pessimistic conception of human nature, out of which arose a philosophy of the development of history and of the techniques necessary for obtaining power; an experimental, rationalist method which, when applied to the political domain, led to an aggressive amoralism and an exclusive concern with power; and the glorification of action for its own sake.[8]

There were also a number of techniques typical of Machiavellianism, which served in the different stages of the march to power and the "imperial adventures" which followed: (i) The coup d'état, as practised by the Bolsheviks in 1917, and by the supporters of Hitler in Austria in 1934 and in Holland in 1940. (ii) The destruction of parliamentary democracy, as in Germany between 1930 and 1933, although "the revolutionary leaders admittedly receive the unconscious collaboration of many democrats in this work of destruction". (iii) The organization of the totalitarian party, as in the case of the Communist Party in the USSR, the Fascists in Italy, and the National Socialists in Germany. (iv) Revolution from above, as carried out by Hitler. (v) Economic tyranny, although on this point there were marked differences between tyrannies – in Hitler's case, for instance, state planning derived not from an economic theory but from political will, whereas with communism the order was reversed, the economic theory coming first and the authoritarian practice flowing from it. (vi) Propaganda techniques, and (vii) the extermination of conquered peoples, such as the Poles. The enemy was not, Aron concluded, invincible: but it was necessary to understand him in order to defeat him.[9]

Next, Aron attacked "the romanticism of violence",[10] singling out Georges Sorel as its most typical twentieth-century exponent. Sorel's *Réflexions sur la violence* had had most influence in Italy, especially on Pareto and Mussolini. Violence, thus conceived, was viewed not just as "a provisional necessity of the march towards power or empire", but as "a permanent necessity of the new order", as in Nazi Germany, with its "concentration camps, proscriptions and persecutions of minorities and opponents".[11] In the writings of Nietzsche and Sorel, the romantic view of violence had been inspired by noble ideals; but today's men of violence were "a tragic caricature" of those dreams, for such men did not seek to match themselves against equals, but to tyrannize the weak. Indeed, the sharpest corrective to romantic illusions about violence was "the inhuman reality of those who claimed to raise themselves above simple humanity".[12]

However, the unprecedented ordeal which the men of violence were imposing upon Europe forced everyone to remember what Aron called "the authentic facts of human existence". To go to one extreme and refuse force at all costs, or to go to the other extreme and exalt violence for its own sake, was to fail to recognize "the truth of civilization: the necessity to justify force by the goal at which it aims and the duty to commit oneself entirely to the service of the cause recognized as valid". This was why

only actions refute the doctrine of violence. When free peoples display as much discipline, courage and strength of purpose, in the defence of their freedom, as do the fanaticized masses in the service of their tyrants, then they dissipate romantic mythologies and revive the hope of all those who refuse to believe that peoples are forced to choose between civilization and power, between humanity and temporal greatness. Athens and Sparta, Carthage and Rome – these simplistic historical precedents do not foreshadow the fate of Western culture. There is room in the future for regenerated, militant and virile democracies which believe in themselves and their mission.[13]

In "Mythe révolutionnaire et impérialisme germanique",[14] Aron examined the term "revolution" as used by the Nazi regime. German pro-paganda, he wrote, portrayed national socialism as a "social revolution" and the invasion of France as the beginning of a "European revolution"; but it was important that "the word 'revolution', which has served to express the highest hopes of humanity, should not be used today to mask the most terrible degradation threatening European civilization".[15] There was, of course, a romantic revolutionary tradition, full of a heroic optimism, which put its faith in the forces of production and their organization, and announced the liberation of mankind and the pros-perity and happiness of all. This Promethean and millenarian myth of the kingdom of heaven on earth was, however, severely compromised by the actual revolutions which had taken place in the twentieth century, resulting as they had done in the one-party state, a state-directed economy and a politicized, authoritarian bureaucracy, from which "all trace of liberalism, even – or, rather, above all – intellectual liberalism, is removed".[16]

It was this latter point which revealed "the true character of the revolutionary task in our time. This is, certainly, to progress along the path of social justice and to remedy through organization the ills of a mechanistic civilization, but it is also to save the most precious values proclaimed by liberal civilization – respect for persons and for liberties".[17] In both theory and practice the German revolution contradicted such principles, for German propagandists deliberately confused socialism with Prussianism. This was true of, for example, Spengler in his *Preussentum und Sozialismus*, for whom the socialist state and the Prussian state (in reality, the bureaucrats' state) were one and the same – an almost military organization of hierarchical relations of command and subordination. This was a far cry from socialism, under which there were to be no separate classes, and whose aim was "the reconciliation of the proletariat, as of all the workers, with the national community".[18]

Not that all German socialists, even now, had abandoned this Western democratic revolutionary tradition. Nevertheless, it was true that the ideology of the "New Order" had its origins in Germany's political and intellectual past, for it was in Germany that the civil servants – the universal class, as Hegel called them – were collectively "honoured, respected, admired and metaphysically transfigured"; it was the German Socialist Party which had the strongest sense of organization in the International, and the least feeling for political liberties; and it was in Germany that the individual was "capable of respecting organization and hierarchy to the point of finding the highest satisfaction in the consciousness of being a cog in an immense machine".[19] Thus, national socialism had taken up the tradition of German socialism but had "vulgarized and degraded it and made the doctrine more brutal and aggressive".[20] Furthermore, because of its ambition and its conception of the relations between races, national socialism sought to impose the Prussian state on the rest of the world, and, as such, the socialism it professed was indistinguishable from imperialism. In a German socialism of this kind, what remained of "the dream which soothed men's misery and the ideal which stirred the wretched and the just to revolt"?[21] Capitalism continued to flourish under German socialism and Europe was being plundered at the expense of the Third Reich.

In "Bureaucratie et fanatisme",[22] Aron argued that although bureaucracy was becoming increasingly characteristic of Western society, it was no accident that only Nazi Germany, with its lack of political liberties, its love of order, and its military tradition, had experienced bureaucratic absolutism in its entirety. Thus, "To employ and adapt the expression used by the nineteenth-century Utopians, we should no longer say that the administration of things is replacing the government of persons, but that the government of societies is ending in the *administration of persons*".[23]

Already, Aron pointed out, there was concern that, in the factory, the organization specialist was pitilessly fragmenting manual work and reducing it to a small number of indefinitely repeated movements, in order to increase profit; and even if the psychologist intervened to introduce variety, arouse motivation and diminish fatigue, it was deplorable that rationalization took man himself as its object, at the risk of transforming him into a simple appendage of the machine. Under Hitler's regime, however, the state organized not only industry, but culture as well, and it monopolized the means of propaganda; it was therefore the whole person, and not merely a partial activity, which the state claimed to shape in its image. Thus even the freedom which the individual once preserved outside his work had been stolen from him. Operated by the bureaucrats, rational techniques pursued him into his very conscience and into the very act of intellectual creation.

And it was here, Aron contended, that "a kind of dialectical reversal" took place. These techniques were rational, in the sense that they were based on a theory, but their aim was not to make men reasonable. On the contrary, rationality in its ultimate form seemed to result in a total irrationality, not only because the bureaucratic-military machine, as a whole, obeyed a will to power which knew no limit, but also because national socialism had cultivated the most frenzied feelings among its followers, since the regime tended to produce men of passion and violence.[24]

However, Aron characteristically insisted, there was nothing *inevitable* about an authoritarian and totalitarian bureaucracy:

We are pointing to the existence of administrative rationalization and accepting it; man's task consists precisely in preventing the demands of public administration from making us forget the aspirations of individual persons and in refusing to allow military bureaucracy, dominated by a group of demagogues, to exercise an arbitrary authority. In other words, the more bureaucracy spreads, the more this bureaucracy needs authority, and the more the pluralism of parties and a certain form of representative regime become indispensable. Democracy is one of the counter-balances necessary to the growing weight of bureaucracy.

In the years to come, political democracy would have both to maintain an efficient bureaucracy and fix its limits, while interpreting the wishes of individuals and preserving the essential elements of what Aron was "still prepared to call the rights of man".[25]

The final study in the first part of *L'homme contre les tyrans*, "Tyrannie et mépris des hommes",[26] took its title from two pre-war books which seemed to Aron to "epitomize our epoch": Elie Halévy's *L'Ere des tyrannies*, about which, as we saw, Aron had written a major article shortly before the war,[27] and *Le Temps du mépris* (*The Age of Contempt*), Malraux's novel about an anti-fascist militant in a German concentration camp.[28] "Tyrannie et mépris des hommes" contained the first of several attacks which Aron has made on philosophies of pessimism and nihilism – in this case, Machiavelli's view that man is fundamentally evil, immoral and wicked. This theme had been taken up by Carl Schmitt – "an official theorist of national socialism", as Aron called him – and echoed by Spengler, for whom man is *naturally* evil. Such a view, Aron maintained, recalling the argument he had earlier developed in a discussion of ideology,[29] was akin to Nietzsche's nihilism – a demasking of the enemy's ideas in order to show the "instincts" behind them. This could take a sociological form which denied the possibility of universal truth and reduced all knowledge to the perspectives of interest groups, as in Marx's writings; or it could take a psychological or psychoanalytic form, as when the attempt was made to "explain" religious faith in terms of repressed or sublimated instincts. In either case, the claims made by opponents were not so much refuted as disqualified, and the use of this kind of argument could, Aron warned, result in scepticism or irrationality: "*all* ideas risk being shown in the same light, and, by the same token, being victims of the same disenchantment", with a consequent sapping of men's confidence in their ideals and capacity for rational will.[30]

Nietzsche may not have had the same racial views as Hitler ("he had an exceptionally high regard for Jews as well as the sons of Prussian officers"), but his critique of democratic and Christian values, his view of a morality based on power, and his advocacy of the reconstruction of European society, all seemed to converge in what was perhaps the basic idea in Hitlerite politics – "a biological politics, defined in terms of the culture of two human types, the superman and the man in the crowd".[31] Thus, in order to triumph over Hitler's evil, it was essential to "overcome biological nihilism and reaffirm the spiritual mission of humanity":

It is not a question of setting against Hitlerite pessimism an optimism which risks being just as simplistic. Today's events are enough to show that man is not simply bent on aspiring after good and that there are also tendencies to brutality and evil in him. But it is essential to set against the Hitlerite idea of man, and against the Hitlerite philosophy of the curbing of human variety, . . . the idea of the presence, in each individual, of a soul or spirit, a presence which is the foundation of dignity and the right to respect.[32]

Weaknesses of the Democracies

The second part of *L'Homme contre les tyrans* opened with an analysis of the philosophy of pacifism,[33] the problem which had so concerned Aron before the war.[34] Pacifism, in the sense of "peace at any price", was, he now wrote, not so much a coherent, systematic doctrine as "a state of mind, a state of the soul, a faith". Although it was "the most respectable of sentiments", pacifism in its extreme form – the unconditional rejection of all war, whatever its origin or reason, as in conscientious objection – ran the risk of generalizing about war. The problem was that "in the real world any willingness to defend a cause held to be just – territorial status, national independence – implies the risk of struggle and demands consent to the use of force against the enterprises of force. Peace supposes not the denial but the right use of power".[35] It required the triumphs of Hitlerism for the immense majority of pacifists to discover that "one evil, in any event, is worse than war: slavery".[36]

The drama of recent years, Aron argued, stemmed from the meeting of two types of men, whom he called the men of violence and the moralists. Both were born of the First World War: the moralists had never forgotten its horror, while for the men of violence it was the decisive experience of their lives. The former were among those avid for peace at any price, while the latter exulted in combat, swelling the ranks of the totalitarian parties:

Those whom the war had revolted were no less capable of courage and devotion, but they were lost in illusion and were guided by men even more blind than themselves. The honest men were incapable of understanding the gangsters: misfortune would have it that the gangsters understood the honest men only too well.[37]

One of the leading figures among the moralizing pacifists in the inter-war years had been the philosopher, Alain. Aron had, as we have seen, come under his influence in his student days,[38] and while in Germany he had written for "Alain's journal", *Libres Propos*, but his attitude towards the great man had changed during the course of the pre-war decade. Thus, having given a respectful welcome to a German study of Alain in 1932,[39] Aron had delivered a sharp attack upon him in a review of his "spiritual autobiography" in 1937.[40] He now developed his criticisms in a new essay, "Prestige et illusions du citoyen contre les pouvoirs", which was published in *La France libre* in 1941.[41]

Alain, "the disgruntled citizen" ("le citoyen grognard"), had, Aron wrote, "convinced part of French left-wing opinion that the moral opposition of the citizen to the powers constituted the best guarantee of liberties and of peace". He had "fashioned generations of young Frenchmen in a sterile hostility towards the state, and an almost wilful ignorance of the dangers threatening the nation and of the tasks incumbent on every member of the French community".[42] But events had shown Alain to have been wrong: it could no longer be argued that a state was assured of peace, if only it was restrained by the criticisms of its citizens, or that, for war to be avoided, all that was necessary was to refuse any risks or initiatives. "Never has that ancient truth, which was lost to sight in the years of peace, been more clearly revealed: a nation has no chance of preserving her independence unless she is ready to defend it with weapons in her hand".[43]

In essence, Alain's citizen was "the private individual who puts up with social life as if it were some base necessity; he asks the state to leave him quietly to cultivate his garden; and he refuses to take part morally in the destiny of the city or recognize that he, like everyone else, has to cooperate in the running of the state and is accountable, in his modest way, for the nation's greatness".[44] Nothing, it seemed to Aron, was more characteristic of the inter-war years than the desire to "think against" the social order, and Alain's historical importance was perhaps that he had formulated the philosophy underlying such a "thinking against".[45] Nothing was more anachronistic than this kind of anarchic refusal, for "if there is something noble about the rejection of honours, a peevish isolation is fruitless and absurd".[46] For democracies to survive, there had to be properly chosen leaders and a relation of confidence between them and the people. But, Aron concluded, the state of mind which Alain had fostered made this impossible:

> The true citizen wants to choose his leaders, not gag them with perpetual suspicion; he wants national greatness as well as personal security; and he wants powers which are legitimate but capable of acting.
>
> It is not in a struggle against the powers that the citizen fulfils himself, but in a free membership of the community.[47]

Aron concluded the "Weaknesses of the Democracies" with an analysis of "The Birth of Tyrannies".[48] Throughout history, he began, there recurred a type of power, which he proposed to call "popular despotism" or "demagogic Caesarism". It always featured "the same combination of personal, arbitrary power at the top and consent, even rapturous approval, on the part of the masses". This type of power was "the distinguishing characteristic of modern tyrannies".[49] There followed a comparison of the origins of tyrannies in ancient Greece – especially the conquest of Athens by Philip of Macedon, in spite of the warnings of Demosthenes – with the origins of national socialism in Germany. This was not, Aron explained, in order to argue for any political or historical determinism, but to show that the change from democracy to tyranny was not the result of chance or mere accident. A study of the similarities *and* differences in the origins of tyrannies could be instructive: it could point out the mistakes to avoid and the needs which required satisfaction if free democracies were to survive.

These needs were threefold. There must be a basic security for the ordinary man, especially security of work, if the masses were not to become a prey to demagogues. Political struggle must be within the framework of majority law; no group must seek absolute authority and all parties must be ready to compromise; and peaceful reform, in freedom, presupposed both foresight on the part of the ruling elite and moderation among the people. Finally, in genuine democracies opposition was a public service, but on condition that it did not see party rivalry as a struggle for absolute power, for no party should place itself beyond the law: "One does not owe tolerance to the person who professes intolerance. Just as one can and must respect the diversity of beliefs and particular associations, so one must defend oneself against the progressive infiltration of democracy by tyranny".[50] For the term "liberal" did not imply a readiness to accept everything, and too often "democracy" had been confused with a taste for the easy life.

Imperial War

The third part of *L'Homme contre les tyrans*, "Lure of the Tyrannies", consists of a "penetrating analysis", as a reviewer rightly called it,[51] of four French writers who were "in the enemy's service": Jacques Chardonne and Drieu La Rochelle,[52] Alfred Fabre-Luce,[53] and Henry de Monther-lant.[54] Aron then turned to an analysis of "imperial war" in Part Four.

The study with which this part opens, "La Stratégie totalitaire et l'avenir des démocraties", was first published in *La France libre* in May 1942[55] and was one of Aron's earliest excursions into a field which was to become a central concern – the relationship between war and society.[56] He began by pointing out that this question had not received the serious attention it deserved:

War is both a permanent feature and an essential factor in the life of collectivities. It was fashionable, a few decades ago, to reject with contempt the history of battles and to be concerned only with the history of civilizations, as if the development of civilizations could be understood without taking wars themselves into account. Today no historian would fail to acknowledge the complex interrelation between the art of fighting and other human activities. Civilizations have been saved or destroyed on the field of battle. And, generally speaking, social groups are as much characterized by the weapons they wield as the tools they use. Methods of war appear both as cause and effect of technology on the one hand, and of political and social organization on the other.[57]

Thus there was a clear parallel between the feudal regime and the technique of war which gave the predominant place to steel-cased knights requiring the help of numerous valets, while the large-scale appearance of firearms, by putting an end to the supremacy of heavy cavalry, was one of the causes of the disappearance of the feudal system. To take another example, but one in which the relationship worked in the other direction, the French Revolution transformed the way in which armies were organized; indeed, it changed the very nature of the conflicts from being dynastic to national.

Today, of course, the correspondence between the system of production and the military system was clear, but it was difficult to establish relations of causality between the different phenomena. The most that one could do was point to two sets of relations: certain features of the regimes which had come into being between the wars were the consequences of the First World War, and the current revolution in the art of war was a result of political revolutions which themselves had arisen out of the same war. However, this dual relationship presented problems for the politician as well as the sociologist:

For if preparation for war requires a certain organization of society and of the state, then peace and security depend on the political regimes established in different countries, as much as on the balance between powers. The traditional distinction between diplomacy and internal politics is no longer condemned, then, simply by the old lesson of experience, that despotisms normally end in imperialist adventures; it is also condemned by military technology itself.[58]

This argument implied that it was the moral and political duty of the democracies to guarantee the independence and security of the nations

270

which were today the victims of Hitler's Germany, through the enlargement of frontiers and the spread of democratic ideologies and political institutions. The need to increase the size of military, if not political, units was a direct result of changes in military technology. For example, without a large-scale arms industry small countries could not manufacture modern weapons of war and would only receive such weapons if they joined a much larger security organization. Similarly, because of changes in the military use of space, small nations, if strategically important, inevitably served as battlegrounds in any conflict. This did not, of course, imply that such nations no longer had the right to exist, but that neutrality was no longer a possibility, because this so-called independence allowed an aggressor to attack when he wished. Thus, "The characteristics of military technology mark the boundaries not of states but of military groupings". As for the major powers, if totalitarian despotisms concentrated their energies on material and ideological preparation for war, those neighbouring countries which wished to survive had no choice but to do likewise, in some form or other. Otherwise, the present tragedy might at any moment repeat itself. For all these reasons, Aron emphasized in conclusion that, "the installation of a totalitarian regime must in itself be considered an act of aggression and the expansion of democracy is clearly one of the conditions of collective security".[59]

Nevertheless, in a later article,[60] Aron defended the right of independent states, including small ones, to exist in post-war Europe, although their existence would depend on one condition: "the establishment of international bodies responsible for coordinating the development of diverse units and of regularizing relations between these units". What was doomed, in the economic as well as the political sphere, was "the temptation, to which too many nations had succumbed, to seek safety outside the common safety. The Hitlerite venture will have taught a double lesson: the vanity of conquest and the vanity of nationalist isolation".[61] It seemed to Aron, therefore, that "The Europe of tomorrow will be made up of independent nationalities. . . For Europe's only hope of progressively attaining an authentic unity is through the experience, in the freedom of each, of a life common to all".[62]

Perspectives

The final part of *L'Homme contre les tyrans* opened with a brilliant analysis of "historical pessimism"[63] – one of many such studies which Aron felt it necessary to write at different periods in his life. His starting point was a critique of the fatalism contained in James Burnham's *The Managerial Revolution*, which had appeared two years before. For Burnham, capitalism had been condemned to death by the Depression. In post-capitalist society there would be a totally planned economy and "the managerial society" would be typical of regimes whether of the Left or Right. However, such a society would not be socialist. It would contain distinct and even opposed social classes; the masses would be exploited by the privileged; parliamentary institutions would disappear; and totalitarianism and the one-party state would be normal, if not inevitable. To Aron, however, even if it were true that there was a movement towards planned economies, it was not possible to predict the political and moral institutions of the future. As he characteristically put it, "In arguing against these massive necessities, we will succeed perhaps, not in replacing totally pessimistic predictions by those which are equally optimistic, but in indicating the points of application of the human will".[64]

There was no need, Aron insisted, to assume that state control of the economy would inevitably be accompanied by the suppression of political parties and liberties. Even under a totally planned economic system built on a violent revolution, evolution towards certain forms of political democracy was "not inconceivable", in so far as the regime became more stable and groups such as trade unions were allowed to emerge. The "real question" was whether or not it was possible "to organize the economy progressively without resorting to authoritarian methods", although the difficulties, as experience showed, were obvious.[65]

Of course, it was easier to organize the economy as a whole if no opposition was allowed; on the other hand, the more the state assumed economic functions, the more desirable it was for the state to be limited and controlled. Thus "the primary task of our epoch" was "to safeguard the essential values of political democracy (that is, the right of opposition, the election and control of the governors by the governed, and intellectual freedoms), while at the same time adopting certain forms of economic planning". The experience of the democracies at war showed that such a goal, however difficult it might be, was not unattainable. Success would depend on many conditions: "the character of peoples, the quality of elites, the discipline of all groups, the consent of the parties to progressive methods, and the refusal to give in blindly to an absolute power". It was possible to gauge the likelihood of success in specific cases, but as soon as one tried to make general predictions in the abstract, one fell back into the error common to both historical optimism and pessimism.[66]

In the last century, the most popular philosophies of history, and even the consciousness of ordinary people, were dominated by the doctrine of progress, according to which a kind of parallelism or interdependence was said to exist between the accumulation of knowledge, increased mastery over nature, and the moral improvement of humanity. In other words, an indisputable fact – the development of knowledge and technology – was broadened into a naively confident vision of historical development as a whole. The catastrophes of the twentieth century have provoked a complete reversal of attitudes and brought into being a doctrine which is the exact opposite of the doctrine of progress. The same deterministic interpretation has been preserved, whereby the movement which is dragging capitalism to its death and the economy towards a planned regime is held to be irresistible. But instead of linking these transformations with the liberation of man, they are associated with tyranny, wars of conquest and fanaticism. What gave socialism its power of attraction was precisely the harmony which it asserted between the aspirations of man's consciousness and the spontaneous tendencies of history. What gives the current pessimism its debilitating poignancy is that it asserts an interdependence between ineluctable necessities and detestable phenomena. Thus both philosophies think in terms of totalities and assume that, by beginning with a particular economic regime or some characteristic of a particular social class, one can deduce every other feature of a society.[67]

Although it was wrong to be categorical in such matters, it was nevertheless "difficult to imagine a planned economy resulting in a rigorously egalitarian society, without a permanent political elite and without an economically privileged class". Just as it would be unusual for the same child to become both a great general and a great poet, so it would be unusual for humanity to preserve all the pleasures of freedom and all the benefits of organization. "But the end of myths", Aron declared, "must not be the end of hope. A totally rationalized and wholly tyrannical society is only a nightmare vision: a monster to be conjured up, not a destiny to be endured".[68]

The study which follows, "De la Liberté politique",[69] is a masterly exposition and a lucid comparison of the political theories of Montesquieu and Rousseau, focusing in particular on their implications for political liberty. Paradoxically, Aron argued, Rousseau's theory of popular sovereignty contained within it the seeds of totalitarianism. Montesquieu and Rousseau, he wrote,

share a hatred of tyrants – that is, of usurpers – and a hatred of despots – that is, of oppressive and arbitrary sovereigns. They are both imbued with the ideas to which the philosophers of the time subscribed: a demand for tolerance and legality, a critical approach to the examination of institutions, and an attempt to improve those institutions and make them more conducive to the well-being of nations. But in their social origins, the lives they led, their ways of thinking, and the ideals they propose, Montesquieu and Rousseau are as far apart from each other as it is possible to be. The citizen of

273

Geneva, full of a touchy pride rooted in the people, seems to be reviving a republican ideal, inspired by memories – or, rather, more or less imaginary myths – of the ancient *polis* and by his personal experience of a city-state; and, on the other hand, the President of the Parliament of Bordeaux, the admirer of the English constitution, appears anxious not about revolution or even brutal reform in his own country, but about the maintenance of intermediate bodies on which depend the moderation of powers and liberty itself. . .

Now, no idea better illustrates the contrast between the two thinkers than that of liberty. Liberty is an ambivalent notion that philosophers never weary of analysing and of which men tirelessly put forward contradictory definitions; it is also a decisive notion because so many strong feelings and aspirations crystallize around this word that there is not a tyrant who does not invoke it, even if he reserves for the nation as a whole the benefit of a good which is withdrawn from every individual. But this notion, charged as it is with uncertainty and passion, is also central to all political theories. . .[70]

Philosophers had always recognized a contradiction in the idea of liberty between, on the one hand, a definition of liberty as the capacity to do what one wants and, on the other, as "a certain quality of our conduct, the submission to the imperatives of reason, and an autonomy based on the absence of constraints and irrational drives". Montesquieu adopted the second, rejecting the commonly held view that the sovereignty of the people and the freedom of the people are one and the same. For him, a people which had the constitutional right to do whatever it wished would be no more free than a person who, in the name of liberty, gave full rein to his passions. For Montesquieu, political liberty was "the right to do whatever the laws permit", just as, for Kant, liberty was essentially the power to do one's duty. Thus the traditional distinction between monarchy, aristocracy and government, and even the distinction which Montesquieu made in *L'Esprit des lois* between republic, monarchy and despotism, was irrelevant to the question of liberty; or rather, if it were true that despotism by its very nature eliminated liberty, "neither republic nor monarchy in themselves guarantee its existence", since neither implied that the laws would necessarily be kept and the citizens "assured both of the full protection of the laws and of as much autonomy as is compatible with the laws themselves". In Aron's own words, "For peoples as for individuals, liberty is not recognizable by the more or less illusory consciousness which individuals have of it, but by respect for the laws, which also implies respect for persons".[71]

Hence the "exceptional importance", in Montesquieu's theory, of the division of powers, for this was, as Aron put it, "*par excellence* the bulwark of legality, and the barrier that the prudence of the legislators must erect against the arbitrary". Indeed, for Montesquieu the separation of powers seemed to be "a political necessity" and even "constitutive of liberty itself".[72] Of the three powers – legislative, executive and judicial – Montesquieu attached most importance to the independence of the judiciary because it was this which, combined with the limitation of the powers of the executive, gave the citizen what Aron called "the enjoyment of the most precious gift: security".[73] Security consisted of the citizen's conviction that he could not be imprisoned except in accordance with the law; the presumption of innocence and respect for the right of defence; and – the condition which, to Aron's mind, most clearly revealed Montesquieu's deepest aspirations and moral values – the existence of criminal laws in which the penalty derived not from the legislator's whim but from the nature of the crime itself. For Montesquieu, however, there was never any question of transferring the source or the exercise of absolute power to the people, but rather the people chose representatives "capable of discussing affairs", as he put it. Even here the representatives of the people would constitute only one of the assemblies invested with legislative power. Liberty, for him, was defined above all by "the mutual limitation of powers, as guarantee of legality", and only existed in limited governments.[74]

This, argued Aron, was in sharp contrast to Rousseau who, in spite of his liberalism, seemed to be in favour of "a new absolutism", because he "transfers to the people the absolute authority of the sovereign". Thus, the popular state implicit in Rousseau's theories suggested a strengthening of that centralization of the state which had already been taken very far by the French monarchy at the expense of the intermediate bodies.[75] Furthermore, in spite of a number of qualifications, Rousseau "does not hesitate to formulate a kind of religious and moral orthodoxy in the interest of the state", seeking to impose on the individual conscience a belief in the existence of an omnipotent and beneficent deity, a life after death and a last judgement, even though he wished to exclude what he called "theological intolerance". In Aron's view, therefore, "An unbroken chain leads from Plato who, in *The Laws*, recommended that those who do not believe in the gods should be put to death, to Rousseau, who declares that the sovereign can 'banish from the state' whomsoever does not believe in the articles of the profession of a purely civic faith".[76] Despite some reservations, for Rousseau,

the sovereign – that is, the people – is given the right to establish a creed which is binding on all citizens. Only public utility, and not the essential rights of persons, marks the limits of state intervention; and who knows how far, in the sovereign's eyes, the requirements of public utility can go? The political freedom accorded to the individual through participation in collective sovereignty does not necessarily entail the fundamental

275

liberties of thought, speech and action.
Democratic principles do not imply respect for liberal values.[77]

The opposition between Montesquieu and Rousseau was also evident in the constitutional debates after the French Revolution. Those Republicans who were influenced by Montesquieu favoured "an ingenious arrangement of institutions, a dual system of chambers, and the rigorous separation of powers". Those who took their inspiration from Rousseau advocated "a single chamber and, even if they preserve the independence of the judiciary, they grant the representatives of the people, invested with legislative power, supremacy over the executive power".[78] A similar opposition appeared over the question of deputies. Montesquieu, like Burke, wanted the people to choose its representatives but proposed that, once these had been chosen, they should be allowed to reach decisions in accordance wih their conscience. Rousseau, on the other hand, was against representation, believing as he did in direct assemblies of the people; but when these were physically impossible, he sought to reduce deputies to the role of delegates.

Whatever the source of authority, Montesquieu wants it to be shared and limited; Rousseau, placing the source of all authority in the people, does not accept that sovereignty can be either shared or limited.

All the time, Montesquieu's belief that the concentration of authority in a single hand results in tyranny, and that the omnipotence of the people is no less despotic than the omnipotence of a king, clashes with Rousseau's belief: the general will is subject to no law and it can be curbed by no rule, not even by those rules which it has itself proclaimed.[79]

In his conclusion, however, despite his evident preference for Montesquieu and his repeated strictures on Rousseau, Aron attempted to reconcile the beliefs of the two thinkers. Montesquieu had expressed "two ideas which remain ideals for democracy: security of the citizen and balance of powers, conceived as a bulwark against the arbitrary". Rousseau had shown, "with a matchless brilliance", that "legitimate powers presuppose the consent of the governed and that genuine communities are those in which the citizens themselves are conscious of having made their choice and of wishing to renew every day the order under which they live". Yet the thoughts of both men had their dangers, since Montesquieu's arguments might result in conservatism and Rousseau's in tyranny:

1. Aron's father, Gustave

2. Aron's mother, Suzanne *née* Levy

3. Adrien, Aron's eldest brother

4. The second brother, Robert

. Philosophy class, Lycée Hoche, Versailles, 1921–2. Aron is far right in the middle row,
Jacques Hepp is third from the left in the same row. Léonard Rist is seated far left on
he front row. Georges Aillet, their teacher, is in the middle of the front row (Aron family)

. The 1924 arts entry at the Ecole Normale Supérieure. Aron is seated far right, next to
Sartre, with Nizan seated second from the left. Georges Canguilhem is standing
n the middle row, far right, and Daniel Lagache in the top row, far right. (*L'Express*)

7. Alain (Dr Henriette Noufflard)

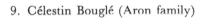

8. Léon Brunschvicg (Dr Henriette Noufflard)

9. Célestin Bouglé (Aron family)

10. Elie Halévy (Dr Henriette Noufflard)

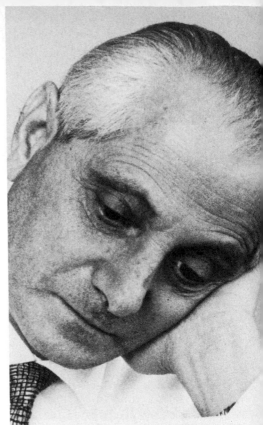

. André Malraux (Photo Harlinque-Viollet)

13. Robert Marjolin (Robert Marjolin)

12. Manès Sperber (Madame Manès Sper|

14. Jean Cavaillès – the photograph use|
false identity papers during the Occupa|
(Madame Gabrielle Ferrières)

15. Military service, 1928–30. Aron is seated fourth from the left (Aron family)

16. André Labarthe, Editor of *La France libre*, by Jean Oberlé (Roger-Viollet)

LA
FRANCE LIBRE

LIBERTE   EGALITE   FRATERNITE

Vol. 1, No. 1	15 novembre 1940	Prix 2/-

La France humiliée, vous n'aurez
plus d'esprit français
ERNEST RENAN (*15 Septembre, 1870*)

CETTE revue française s'adresse à tous les Français. Elle s'adresse aussi à tous ceux qui aiment la France.

Au début de cet été de 1940, dans tous les pays où règne encore la liberté, l'homme le plus humble revenant du travail et apprenant "la nouvelle" a senti que quelque chose de grand allait disparaître. La France venait d'être frappée.

Ceux qui ont eu le bonheur de naître dans ces petits villages de France, où chaque pierre est lourde de souvenirs, où chaque sentier raconte une histoire, ont tout perdu de ce qui faisait un peu leur grandeur. Le devoir de tous les Français libres n'en est que plus impérieux : au lendemain du désastre, ils proclament leur foi dans le destin de leur patrie.

Notre pays a trop donné au monde pour que son sort laisse indifférent ceux qui respectent les valeurs de l'esprit. La France a un trop grand passé pour qu'une défaite militaire mette un terme à sa mission humaine.

La voix de la France s'est tue. Quand on écoute des paroles, quand on lit des journaux qui viennent de chez nous, on ne reconnaît plus celui qui parle. Prise à la gorge, la France est contrainte de se taire ou de se renier.

3

18. The first editorial (Institut Raymond Aron)

LA
FRANCE LIBRE

LIBERTE   EGALITE   FRATERNITE

HAMISH HAMILTON LIMITED
90 GREAT RUSSELL STREET, W.C.1

17. The cover of the first number of *La France libre*, November 1940

19. The *Combat* editorialist, January 1947 (Collection Viollet)

20. With his daughter, Dominique, August 1954 (Aron family)

21. Summer 1954 (Aron family)

22. Aron's wife, Suzanne *née* Gauchon (Aron family)

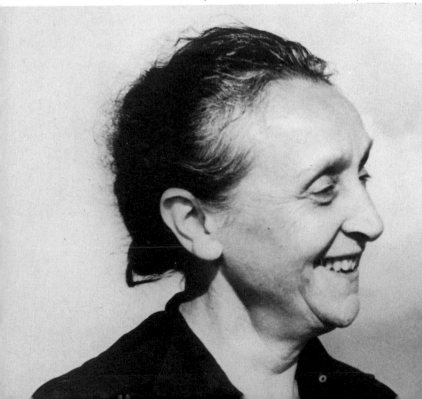

For Montesquieu, respect for legality, in the absence of a criterion enabling judgements to be made about the quality of legislation, runs the risk, even in the case of temperate regimes, of ending in resigned conservatism. And Rousseau's judicial fictions – social contract, popular sovereignty and general will – easily lend themselves to mythical transfiguration and, in their capacity as myths, run the risk of providing justification for new forms of tyranny. For example, if one assumes the infallibility of the general will, one hands over exorbitant powers to a majority or even a minority which, convinced that it incarnates the general will in an absolute form, uses the full power of the state in a violent way.[80]

Nevertheless, contemporary events had in a way "brought the supporters of Montesquieu and of Rousseau closer together", for "liberal values are denied by the totalitarian regimes in the same way as democratic values, and personal liberties are stifled at the same time as political liberties". To restore them both, it was necessary first to defeat the tyrannies:

The task will then remain to attempt a synthesis of autonomy, as defined by Rousseau, and liberty, as defined by Montesquieu. The synthesis of the moderation of powers and popular sovereignty is a task, always imperfect and always necessary, which all democratic constitutions, each in their own way, unendingly strive to achieve.[81]

Turning, lastly, to the problem of "Democracy and Enthusiasm",[82] Aron affirmed that countries only had a chance of preserving "the most precious of goods", independence and prosperity, if they remained ready at every moment to fight to defend them. This was why democracy, more than any regime, must "maintain patriotic feeling and keep intact those virtues – the capacity for sacrifice in the common cause, courage, and discipline in action – without which any collectivity is threatened with death". Democracies were peace-loving, but they could not be pacifist, if by that was meant the refusal to use force against force; for they would be a source of temptation to those who thought only of destroying them.[83]

To those who argued that democracies were incapable of arousing the kind of unanimity found in totalitarian states, the answer was that democracies would not even try to do so, since they considered "conflicts of ideas, interests and parties, to be normal, inevitable and fruitful". Democracies, "both by necessity and by vocation", were "condemned to uphold tolerance".[84] Furthermore, democracy not only supposed that those who governed were chosen in a certain way; it also implied that their authority remained limited and provisional. In other words, the right of opposition was as inseparable from democracy as was freedom of elections. The problem for democracies was "how to prevent party rivalry from degenerating into a battle for the conquest of the state". Too often, on the Continent, "the convictions of party members tended to crystallize into irreconcilable fanaticism . . . Thus, if democracies live by ideological and political conflicts, they die when conflicts take a fratricidally violent form".[85]

If, however, it were true that, between the wars, democratic ideas "seemed temporarily to have lost their power of attraction", the fault lay not with the discrediting of the ideas, but "the inadequacy of men and institutions". At the same time,

the democracies allowed themselves to be invaded by certain ideologies, such as anti-militarism and pacifism at any price, which have nothing to do with authentic democratic doctrine. And, which was even worse, they behaved as if they were resigned, on every front, not to defend themselves. Both internally and externally, they gave free rein to the activities of their enemies, either under pretext of liberty or under pretext of appeasement, as if one owed liberty to those who do not grant it to others, or one could appease ambition through sacrifice and renunciation . . .

"The enthusiasm of good sense" still exists. The eternal hope of humanity has lost none of its freshness. It is only a question of not dashing that hope and this is a matter, not for exaltation, but for lucidity and courage.[86]

Notes

1. 1944a.
2. 1946a.
3. 1944a, p. 11.
4. 1940b.
5. 1944a, pp. 15–17.
6. Ibid., p. 17.
7. Ibid., p. 19.
8. Ibid., pp. 21–2.
9. Ibid., pp. 22–9.
10. 1941m.
11. 1944a, p. 45.
12. Ibid., pp. 46–7.
13. Ibid., pp. 48–9.
14. 1941s.
15. 1944a, p. 52.
16. Ibid., p. 55.
17. Ibid., pp. 56–7.
18. Ibid., p. 61.
19. Ibid., pp. 60–1.
20. Ibid., p. 63.

21. Ibid., p. 64.
22. 1941z^1.
23. 1944a, p. 75.
24. Ibid., pp. 76–7.
25. Ibid., pp. 87–8.
26. 1942b.
27. 1939b. See Chapter 8, above.
28. Malraux's book had appeared in 1935.
29. 1937d. See Chapter 7, above.
30. 1944a, p. 97. After the war Aron was to be much more indulgent towards Schmitt, who died in 1985 at the age of ninety-seven. See Volume 2, Chapter 20.
31. 1944a, p. 100.
32. Ibid., p. 107.
33. 1941i.
34. 1933a, 1934a. See Chapter 4, above.
35. 1944a, p. 114.
36. Ibid., p. 118.
37. Ibid., p. 126.
38. See Chapter 2, above.
39. 1932k.
40. 1937f.
41. 1941v.
42. 1944a, pp. 129, 130.
43. Ibid., p. 141.
44. Ibid., p. 142.
45. Aron had earlier used the expression "penser contre" in his pre-war study of Pareto (1937l). See Chapter 7, above.
46. 1944a, p. 146.
47. Ibid., p. 147. Aron returned to Alain's political philosophy in two articles written after the latter's death in 1951 (1952a; 1952b, reprinted in 1972a). Although, Aron confessed, he did not feel much closer to Alain's political views in 1952 than he had done ten years earlier, nevertheless he held his "previous severity" to be "as excessive and unjust as the boundless admiration of those who rank the *Propos de politique* alongside Aristotle's *Politics* . . . The total adherence of so many men of good will to Stalinism forces one to recognize a truth . . . contained in Alain's teaching: the adoration of the powers or, even more, the claim of the powers to be adored, lies at the source of all tyrannies . . . It remains as true today as it did yesterday that power corrupts and that absolute power corrupts absolutely. Thus, criticism remains necessary whatever the epoch. Yet one must still be careful not to criticize in an exaggerated way the limited powers which need support if they are to endure – that is, if they are not to open the way to absolute powers" (1972a, pp. 77–8, 84).
48. 1941q.
49. 1944a, p. 148.
50. Ibid., p. 167.
51. Anon., 1947.
52. 1942r.

53. 1942s.
54. 1943c. Not surprisingly, Aron distanced himself from these articles in his memoirs (1983a, p. 205).
55. 1942h.
56. His first discussion of the problem was contained in his pre-war review of Elie Halévy's *L'Ere des tyrannies* (1939b). See Chapter 8, above.
57. 1944a, pp. 227–8. Compare the later discussion of this question in *Les Guerres en chaîne* (1951a: tr. 1954a). See Chapter 17, below.
58. 1944a, p. 229.
59. Ibid., pp. 243–4.
60. 1943e.
61. 1944a, pp. 318–19.
62. Ibid., pp. 320–1.
63. 1943g.
64. 1944a, p. 327.
65. Ibid., p. 339.
66. Ibid., p. 341.
67. Ibid., pp. 341–2.
68. Ibid., p. 342.
69. 1942d.
70. 1944a, pp. 343–5.
71. Ibid., p. 346.
72. Ibid., p. 347.
73. Ibid., p. 348.
74. Ibid., p. 352.
75. Ibid., p. 356.
76. Ibid., p. 357.
77. Ibid., p. 358.
78. Ibid., pp. 361–2.
79. Ibid., p. 362.
80. Ibid., p. 363.
81. Ibid., pp. 363–4.
82. 1942k.
83. 1944a, p. 372.
84. Ibid., p. 373. Compare 1940c, p. 133, where, in an article rejecting the view that France was on the brink of revolution in 1940, Aron argued that "In itself, competition between ideas and groups is not a pathological symptom; it is the normal sign of a living democracy".
85. 1944a, p. 374.
86. Ibid., pp. 381–2.

12

The Renovation of France

The third and last volume of Aron's war writings, *L'Age des empires et l'avenir de la France*[1], contains the major part of his contribution to the debate about post-war reconstruction. Aron had felt humiliated by his country's decadence in the 1930s and the defeat of 1940 and, as the allied victory seemed increasingly assured, he began to turn his attention in the pages of *La France libre* to the many questions surrounding France's future. *L'Age des empires et l'avenir de la France* consists of twenty such studies published in the review between August 1943 and September 1945. However, the key to the volume is its Introduction, completed in Paris in July 1945.

"For nearly a century", Aron wrote, "France has been afraid of thinking about her future (penser son avenir)". The French were reluctant to "throw themselves into their destiny in a virile way", because of their "absurd" rejection of any philosophy of history bound to a "project".[2] The crucial question today was: did France have a project? To Aron the answer was emphatically affirmative. France must become a great power again;[3] but to achieve this required "a twin effort of clear-sightedness and strength of will". The kind of "blind passion" seen in Nazi Germany would be no solution in "an ancient country with a tradition of reasonableness and scepticism". On the other hand, "the fondness for pitilessly denouncing our miseries and our faults runs the risk of perpetuating our disagreements and discouraging action on our part, unless self-criticism is guided by hard resolution". The goal of any such analysis must be "the expression of a strong will".[4]

On three occasions now France had found it necessary to question itself about its destiny: in 1815, 1871 and 1940. In 1815, France had begun, without realizing it, to "gnaw away at the twin pillars of power in the modern world" – population growth and industrial expansion. In 1871 there had occurred a fall which was "incomparably more profound". In analysing its causes, republicans sought to criticize the Empire and the exercise of personal power, while others, such as Prévost-Paradol, Tocqueville, Renan and Taine, went back to the French Revolution and what they saw as the evil consequences felt throughout the nineteenth century. Thus, "to the best minds the crisis appeared to be *essentially political*, allied to the vicissitudes of our history".[5] To Aron, however, such a proposition was "only approximately true", because although these writers showed admirable judgement and good sense in their analysis of France's position in the Europe of their day, they failed to examine "the economic system, the social structure and the style of French life". Since 1940, on the other hand, France had been made "suddenly and brutally" conscious of its situation and was no longer unaware, as in 1918, of "either its internal weaknesses,...or the decline of its human and industrial resources,...or the decadence of Europe itself, divided as it is into national states, while to the East and West there arise continental states and multi-national empires".[6]

France, Aron believed, was faced by a threefold crisis: first, "the prolongation of the moral and political crisis which dates from the Great Revolution and reveals itself in the violence of our internal quarrels and the instability of all our regimes";[7] second, "the fall in the birth-rate ...and the mediocre level of productivity in industry and even more in agriculture"; and, third, the crisis experienced by "all the nations of the old continent, dominated as they are by young states which apply technology developed by Western civilization to their unexploited and limitless spaces".[8]

It would have been tempting to follow the example of other writers and reiterate the counter-revolutionaries' polemic against democracy, or that of the republicans against the Empire. But such an analysis would today have been "irremediably superficial", for one of the basic theses of the book was, Aron stated, that the schism which continued to exist between the party espousing justice, liberty and equality, and the party advocating authority, order and hierarchy, "now only constitutes the primary substance of our quarrels":

282

If the war of political religions has resumed its virulence in the last fifteen years, the cause lies on the one hand in the stagnation of the French economy, and on the other in the influence of foreign ideologies (one might almost say the irruption into our country, as in all second-rank countries, of foreign parties). In other words, it is the sluggishness of the French economic body and the crushing of national states by empires, which have made the chronic disorders of the French nation so serious.[9]

Thus, if in the nineteenth century it was the political crisis which appeared decisive, today the political crisis was an expression of a profound demographic and economic crisis:

The point of application of the will has therefore changed. We shall try to act on the causes rather than the symptoms, on the lack of manpower and wealth, and on the lack of an inspiring idea, rather than on revolutionary and fascist convictions, which are more deep-rooted and immovable in our country than even the structure of our industry.[10]

It was often argued that the answer to France's problems lay in an authoritarian regime, but Aron rejected this: "Whether we like it or not, France is engaged in the adventure of liberty", and this implied democracy and pluralism. However, the irony here was that "the spiritual liberties which people revere appear to be inseparable from the competition between parties which they revile". Aron went on characteristically:

One always chooses, in history, between wholes: the worst form of utopian thought consists in a failure to recognize the relationships between those things which are good and those which are evil, or the incompatibilities between equally precious values. In so far as foresight is possible, a decision always involves some degree of resignation.[11]

To renounce political pluralism would be an act of self-mutilation on France's part, because it was ripe for neither a communist revolution nor a fascist reaction. Not that the future of democracy in France was assured, for "democracy functions in so far as the opposed groups consent to submit to the rules of the game and to agree on essentials". The powerful Communist Party in France turned non-Communists into anti-Communists ("a Party-Church exasperates all those who are not of the faith"), and although there was a danger of authoritarian reaction and a Franco-type regime, "fascism, in France, can only be a regime of decadence and an admission of failure". None of the material tasks which faced the country could justify the removal of its liberties; France must not be led to "hide democracy under a bushel", and it was against such an eventuality that Aron had written the earliest piece in the collection,

283

"L'Ombre des Bonapartes".[12] It was necessary, therefore, to accept, and try to influence, the movement of the Left. To choose democracy was to choose "a dangerous existence, but it is a danger from which we can only escape by surrendering in the face of our difficulties". There was no other way.[13]

There were, Aron emphasized, two tasks facing France in all sectors of national life: reconstruction and renovation, but not revolution.[14]

For a century and a half many French have loved the word "revolution". But they love the word more than the thing itself; of the great nations, France is the one which has offered itself the luxury of the largest number of revolutions and also the one which has stuck most obstinately to its traditional mode of existence.[15]

Furthermore, revolutionary phraseology had "too often served as an instrument for fascist activities not to inspire a salutary mistrust".[16] Instead, it was necessary to rebuild the ruins, put the factories back to work, find the capital to re-equip industry, establish priorities among public works, reorganize the civil service and draw up a constitution in order to "put an end to the arbitrary and return to a normal regime".[17]

It would be wrong, however, to be tempted to take the easy way out and simply go back to the pre-war state of affairs. It was necessary, rather, to be innovative ("faire du neuf"). But the French should be under no illusion: "No spectacular or grandiose task presents itself to us, because the grandiose tasks are those of conquest or revolution and neither appears to be an immediate possibility. There is much to be done from day to day and step by step: we have no creed to teach". With regard to the economy, for example, there was no "unique and glorious" or "transcendent and sensational" solution to offer, but a number of "reasonable measures to try", allied to "humble and steady effort".[18] Furthermore, there was a gap between the simplicity of the main economic ideas currently being put forward, such as nationalization, and the complexity of putting them into practice. Thus Aron was in favour of the nationalization of coal and possibly insurance, the chemical industry, transport and electricity. However, nationalization was "not a panacea". A change in the legal status of companies would not in itself alleviate the condition of the working class; it was the *quality* of state control that must be improved, since it was the state which "directly or indirectly controls economic life as a whole". There was also the problem of liberty, because individuals might be put at the mercy of the state. In order, therefore, to avoid tyranny, the introduction of nationalization must be gradual, especially

284

if "a pure and simple establishment of state control is rejected and the intention is to ensure the participation of workers' representatives in the running of affairs". For all these reasons, it would be wrong to expect any great miracles from nationalization.[19]

Finally, Aron turned to France's position in the world.[20] Here there seemed to be three possibilities for both France and Europe, with whom France's fate was inseparably linked. Europe might become the site for a struggle between non-European (i.e., Russian and American) empires, in which case there would be terrible civil war in France. Alternatively, Europe might be united under a conqueror, though here, writing in the middle of 1945, Aron was prepared to give the benefit of the doubt to the USSR: unlike nazism, "The Soviet Union, which provisionally resorts to means which we find repugnant, at least appeals to a universal ideal. Once it has overcome the problem of poverty, it will perhaps renounce those measures, involving constraint and violence, with which it has built up its economy". Nevertheless, the influence of the Anglo-Saxon world would still be felt in Europe in the next two decades. It was in this initial phase of reconstruction that the fate of Europe would be decided because, supposing that unification were brought about, its meaning would depend on whether it was "more or less freely desired by a restored and vigorous Western Europe, or shamefully endured by exhausted nations". The third possibility was that an independent Europe would come into being, cooperating with, but not dominated by, the Soviet Union and the Slavs, and able to find its own solution to the problem of reconciling the two key ideas of liberty and planning or plurality and organization.[21]

The present situation, however, contained "a fundamental ambiguity". One aim was to create larger economic and political units, without suppressing the nation state or destroying that love of country which was "the binding force of our historical collectivities". But the idea of a global unit of Western Europe which would comprise Germany and Italy, as well as France, Spain and England, was "pure utopia". Although it was idle to imagine a grouping which "would combine the economic and military advantages of Empire with respect for nationalities", nevertheless "for the time being the idea remains as seductive as it is vague". At one time Aron had thought that a Western federation would be the solution[22] and he still believed that it should be the long-term goal; but, in the immediate future, there were a number of obstacles in the way of such a proposal which "one must have the courage to state". For example, any union of France and Britain would be a union of unequals. Because of its empire, Britain would never be wholly linked to the Continent, and because of Britain's friendship with the United States, if France were to join with Britain, the result would be "not to bring a third Great Power into being, but to enter the Anglo-Saxon universe".[23] As for a "Latin Union" of France, Italy and Spain, this was no more an immediate objective than Western Union; the British, jealous of their position in the Mediterranean, would be suspicious, and the proposal was not one that aroused enthusiasm in France.

France had to find its own way. As early as 1835, in *Democracy in America*, Tocqueville had "with an unsurpassable lucidity" announced the age of empires – Russian and American;[24] but there was no need, Aron believed in 1945, for France to be aligned wholly with either. France should, however, maintain its own empire intact, at any rate in North and West Africa, whose economic importance was crucial. Not that this implied, he added, that the colonial system had to be preserved as it was. "On the contrary, reforms, liberal in inspiration, are probably the indispensable condition of the Empire's survival".[25]

Nevertheless, the fundamental task was the internal reform of France, for "one influences the world by what one is, not by the flattering self-images which propagandists strive to present to outsiders". Without internal reform there would be no salvation for France either in the Western bloc or through other alliances, because it would have lost the strength to exist as an independent political community. If, on the other hand, France rose to its feet again, it would be able to play a major part in restoring Europe's sense of unity, "without sacrificing Europe's heritage of a rich and fertile diversity".[26]

* * *

What domestic reforms did Aron advocate? To start with, France must renew its elites.[27] Too often, he wrote, politicians paid lip-service to democracy, but thought that it was *de bon ton* to smile at it in private. It was natural to call for a return to democracy and for its renewal – but on one condition: the legitimate search for fresh institutions must leave intact those principles – freedom of expression, plurality of parties and responsibility of the executive before Parliament – without which there was only despotism and adventure. Thus in all his studies of political reconstruction Aron would, he stated, keep three ideas in mind: the democratic will of the people; the need to resolve, or at least attenuate, the economic and social conflicts which had been the origin, occasion or excuse for totalitarian regimes; and the risk that the infernal cycle of wars engendering tyrannies, and tyrannies provoking new wars, would continue. The orderly life of societies presupposed the existence of elites that were capable not only of taking in hand the destiny of the community, but also of gaining the confidence of the masses. How could this be brought about?[28]

The answer to this question involved the kind of analysis of elites that foreshadowed Aron's later studies of comparative social stratification.[29] It was a fact, he argued, that in all places and at all times, power and wealth were unequally distributed, and in all societies, including communist society, some people exercised a disproportionate influence over their fellows. At the same time, contemporary civilization had a number of distinguishing characteristics. First, all the regimes of the twentieth century were "popular", in the sense that they invoked "the people", but none were egalitarian: differences in authority and prestige survived even when they were not obvious. It was clear that the complexity of social mechanisms, in an age when millions lived massed together and sophisticated technology was constantly developing, inevitably created a hierarchy of technical capacities and responsibilities.[30]

Secondly, in every European country which had known democracy, the masses aspired to take part in the life of the nation; not only did they want to receive their fair share of the common income, but also to exercise an influence on the community to which they made the contribution of their work and, in case of conflict, their blood. If, therefore, these popular aspirations were to express themselves in a positive and fruitful way, the masses must be guided by people in whom they had confidence. A modern society required leaders of the masses (meneurs de masses) in the same way that industry required engineers and the state had need of civil servants.[31]

Lastly, there were three kinds of elite in contemporary society: the administration – executives in business, industry and the professions (les cadres de l'activité professionnelle) as well as the civil service (la bureaucratie étatique); leaders of the masses – those who, in the parties or the unions, sought to guide popular movements; and the ruling classes of the state – politicians, generals and higher civil servants. Of course, these elites were not entirely separate. The distinction was simply designed to show the three functions of modern elites: the organization of the economy and public services, leadership of the popular masses, and defence of national interests. They should also have three corresponding virtues: technical competence, popular authority and a patriotic sense that went beyond particular and transitory interests. But all three functions, Aron stressed, were essential; thus the technocratic conception of government (le gouvernement des compétences) was a utopia, because it ignored the fundamental fact of the awakening of the masses to political consciousness. Authoritarian regimes, on the other hand, were concerned with *manipulation* of the masses, the leaders of the masses also being the rulers of the state.[32] As a consequence, authoritarian elites were characterized by a radical pessimism towards the masses and an aristocratic vision of history. Because the emphasis was always put on the few with responsibility, the masses were reduced to the passive role of serving as raw material for human achievements. Even under communism, it was the Party whose function it was to guide and eventually constrain the working masses.[33]

As a result of this analysis and an examination of the weaknesses of the Third Republic, Aron made a number of proposals for reform. Although the democracies must adapt speedily and vigorously to the modern age, it was equally important that they should preserve a respect for rights and persons and avoid the cult of violence. The only way to meet these twin requirements was through a pluralist method of recruitment to the elites. A "monistic" method, or single party, would fail to improve the quality of the elites and thus lead to totalitarianism. Aron therefore proposed reforms in three areas: professional training – the education system should be reorganized to include, for example, the creation of a faculty of social sciences;[34] recruitment – new life should be injected by going beyond the traditionally narrow social-class groups; and status – the pay of civil servants should be made comparable to that in the private sector.

At the same time, he put forward several suggestions for the selection of political leaders. This should be by a "baptism of fire" (on which Aron did not elaborate) in order to find men who were "firm and courageous". Recruitment to Parliament should be more broadly based, to put an end to the excessive predominance of lawyers and teachers. Unlike in the past, socialist leaders must be allowed to play their political part properly, without inspiring fear: professional associations, unions and parties must be allowed to carry out their function, which was to interpret and guide popular aspirations and be an organic part of democracy. Finally, the restoration of France's greatness should be the unifying idea of the nation, one capable of orienting people and parties towards the same task; for a powerful France was "the condition of the radiance of her culture".[35]

It was also essential, Aron believed, to strengthen the power of the executive.[36] In a democracy, the existence of a strong executive depended on three main factors: constitutional practice, the technical quality of the administration, and the support of public opinion. An essential reform for France was the creation of more stable government. Ministers must not feel that their position was under constant threat, but that they were the holders – "provisional but legitimate and sufficiently lasting" – of an authority that was real.[37]

How could this be guaranteed in the democracy of tomorrow? Various constitutional proposals had been put forward, of which Aron examined three. The first was a return to a Parliament of personalities or un-organized parties, as in the period up to 1914. But this would restrict the growth of intermediate bodies and was anti-democratic and totalitarian in its implications, for the existence of intermediate bodies, such as trade unions and employers' organizations, was to be found in all democracies. Their existence could not be half-heartedly accepted. Either they must be replaced by empty state organs, as under totalitarianism, or they must be recognized in good faith and integrated into the functioning of democracy.

A second proposal (advocated by Jacques Maritain, for example) was for a presidential system on the American model, which Aron was against on practical if not on theoretical grounds. Cooperation between President and Assembly was usually difficult. The 1848 Constitution, for instance, which was of this kind, had not been a success and conflict between the President and the Assembly would be likely to lead to some form of coup d'état. American circumstances were, in any case, different – an uninterrupted democratic tradition, autonomy of the states, limitation of the powers of central government, and absence of foreign danger.

Aron himself favoured a third solution – a combination of better organized parties and the normal practice of dissolution: in other words, a Parliament of parties organized along British lines. The two-party system could not be transferred lock, stock and barrel to French conditions, but it was possible to reduce the number of parties and re-establish a direct relation between the votes of the electors and the formation of governments. There might, Aron suggested, be four or five major parties (including a major party of social reform to the right of the Communist Party) and they would be obliged, under threat of dissolution, to maintain any electoral agreements throughout the parliamentary term. The party with most votes would normally provide the President of the Council or Prime Minister. In this way voters would no longer merely express their habitual preferences every four years, but would respond clearly to the questions posed by the parties' programmes. But such reforms, Aron added, would not be enough in themselves, for they failed to touch

289

the economic and social roots of the crisis and they also required corresponding changes in psychology and custom. The unions and parties of the Left must be prepared to take on the responsibilities of government and not simply make demands in opposition. "Tomorrow, democracy will flourish insofar as *all* republican parties feel determined to make it work".[38]

Administrative, technical and scientific changes were also necessary, but how, in a democracy, could they be brought about without falling into the twin snares of "technocratic despotism and the incompetence of ignorance"? Aron suggested a number of reforms. First, the application of the natural sciences to certain areas of human life, such as nutrition, though even here there were limits to how far such rationalization should go – the uncertainties of science and "the necessary safeguarding of freedom and imagination".[39] Second, a general system of social security, as in the Beveridge Plan. Third, measures to halt the decline in the birth-rate – technical measures to reduce disparities of income between large and small families, and moral measures to create a climate of confidence for having more children, although it was also "supremely important to avoid the despotism of 'the technicians of race' and to submit the proposals of the specialists to control".[40] Fourth, the setting up of an economic secretariat to the Presidency of the Council (like that of the British War Cabinet), which would study problems as a whole and advise governments of the likely consequences of their decisions. It was also important to create a new type of civil servant – "new men who are expected to have a feeling for action, a taste for responsibility and a desire for enterprise", and with a training whose culture was "less bookish and more international". Such suggestions might appear obvious, but "the key to all reforms is that there are men capable of giving them life".[41] Finally, there was a case for partial "plans" to cover particular branches of industry: "a country...which produces more slowly or more expensively than its rivals is doomed in the industrial battle...The strength of a nation is measured by its statistics of steel and not its statistics of novels or paintings". And who could say, today, that France was threatened by a surfeit of technology?[42]

Aron considered next the "guarantees of liberty",[43] beginning his argument with this stiking passage:

All regimes in our epoch, however authoritarian they are, pay lip-service to the sovereignty of the people, even though they use and abuse the inexhaustible resources of publicity and the police in order to manipulate the masses. On the other hand, it sometimes seems as if the most precious of gifts, freedom, is everywhere under threat:

freedom for the individual to say no or yes, with no other judge than his conscience; freedom not to enroll in any of the factions which dispute control of the state and its benefits; and freedom for minorities to oppose, within the framework of respect for the law, those who provisionally hold power. In order to denounce the heterodox, rival orthodoxies suddenly discover a mysterious affinity. In this sense, one can say that contemporary societies loathe liberalism even more than they loathe democracy, or at any rate that in democracy they hate the very guarantee of a certain liberalism.[44]

The threat of enslavement stemmed from causes that were deep-seated and universal for, as Montesquieu had suggested in his theory of the separation of powers, the chances of liberty diminished with the concentration of power. Today, economic power tended to become concentrated either in a small number of giant enterprises or in public bureaucracies. Thus,

men often feel themselves condemned to choose between a number of private tyrannies and a single, omnipresent tyranny. Even the political movements that have been brought into being by revolt against the oppressive weight of these institutions run the risk, by a paradox that is not rare in history, of stifling their own inspiration. Freedom only blossoms in an atmosphere of tolerance. But the doctrines of our time all teach a creed which, concerned though it is with the temporal order, nevertheless has an absolute character. It is not surprising, therefore, that the transfer to the political order of passions that were once reserved for transcendental faith should give our national and social struggles the character of wars of religion.[45]

If, then, the work of reconstruction required a strengthened (i.e., stable and effective) executive, the return to democracy no less urgently required certain guarantees of liberty. For democracy to function harmoniously it had to be rooted in the way of life of a people, as in Britain. But the Third Republic had, in spite of its faults and after a difficult beginning, "laid down deep roots in French soil". It would have been possible to reform it without destroying it, "without again handing France over to the hazards of revolution, and without claiming, in accordance with the eternal illusion of the simple-minded (les esprits légers), to be starting from a *tabula rasa*".[46] The principle without which no democracy was conceivable was respect for the law, and the guarantees of a return to democracy were threefold: the restoration of personal liberties, without which there was no security; the restoration of independence to the judiciary; and the placing of limitations on the present omnipotence of the executive by giving authority and prestige to the Consultative Assembly.

In addition, despite the evident problems in judging the attitudes

291

and actions of the press under Vichy, freedom of the press should be re-established. Thus Aron was against a recent proposal that government and party representatives should decide which journalists should be allowed to publish, for this was "so contrary to traditional conceptions of liberty".[47] "The number one enemy", he emphasized in an outstanding defence of the press in a free society, "is and remains the state monopoly of information, the press and radio".[48] To those who argued that a newspaper should not be a commercial enterprise but belong to an ideological or political group, it was important to recall "the almost inevitable characteristics of the press in democracies where there is private ownership of the means of production". If such ideas were put into practice, the result would be the disappearance of newspapers that aimed at a mass circulation, on a commercial basis, and required enormous capital:

I do not claim that the disappearance of all the *Paris-Soirs* of this world – and they exist in every country – would be a mortal blow to civilized values, but I can see the drawbacks rather than the advantages of their disappearance. Competition favours and stimulates the development of the press and helps to maintain that spirit of initiative and adventure without which every publication runs the risk of committing the worst sin of all – boredom. Why should France try to give every newspaper a provincial outlook and a doctrinaire tone?

To be independent, the press must be rich and varied...To reduce it to a single type (the party newspaper) would result in a deplorable impoverishment. In addition, the scope left to individuals would be diminished still further...Let us not lightly sacrifice freedom of enterprise, where publications are concerned: it is likely to favour the financial powers, certainly, but also to offer guarantees of liberty and, to non-conformists, a chance of action.

...In the final analysis, to choose a policy is to establish an order of preferences from among all the risks. We have the right to prefer, in spite of everything, the wager on liberty.[49]

Aron concluded with a magnificent passage on the "two types of men – opposed but at heart related to one another – who ravage the politics of our time":

One type believes in a man, a movement, a doctrine. For them, there is no salvation outside the Church. There is only one way of conceiving the good of the country or the future of humanity. Those who deny them are traitors or lost souls, who must be punished or brought back to the fold, or the slaves of private interests, to be unmasked or exterminated. The other type believes in nothing but power. The only reality is the struggle between factions for the control of the state. Ideologies are only masks or rationalizations. And yet, in the last analysis, having yielded to an ineluctable necessity,

292

those in power act in the same way, whatever the slogans they brandish. The first group provides the troops, and the second group the leaders, of authoritarian movements. . .

Nevertheless, if the politics of our time are to avoid the tragi-comedy of successive tyrannies, their slogans clashing as they ape each other's practice, and if the material organization for which the bureaucracies take responsibility is not to destroy the last traces of human dignity, what other recourse, what other hope have we but the autonomy of persons and the irreducible solitude of our consciences? [50]

Aron turned next to the problems involved in the reform of French education. [51] Educational systems ensured "the incessant reproduction" of the collectivity, and no social formation was, he wrote, more resistant to change. Two of the main talking-points in post-Liberation France were the problem of the birth-rate and that of education: France needed more men and women, and in the meantime needed men and women of better quality. In making his contribution to this debate, Aron suggested that there should be three objectives of reform: to give a logical structure to France's educational institutions (without being as diverse as the English system, historically the French educational system had developed in a more irrational way than was commonly believed); to remedy the vices revealed by the defeat of 1940 – particularly the failure of part of the country's elites; and to increase efficiency, by providing industry and public administration with men of competence. Thus the three main aims of educational reform were justice, efficiency and unity, and it was under each of these headings that Aron considered the problem. [52]

In order to bring about greater equality of educational opportunity – an aim recognized as just by the immense majority of opinion – a common school ("l'école unique") had been proposed: instead of being two parallel and separate systems, primary and secondary schooling would form a single, continuous system. All children would go to primary school and then into one of three branches of secondary education (classical, modern, and technical), according to aptitude. This would involve a number of changes: an end to elementary classes in the lycées; the transformation of senior elementary schools ("écoles primaires supérieures") into technical schools; free secondary schooling; and compulsory secondary education up to the age of fifteen in one of the three branches, with a common curriculum in the first two years ("premier cycle" or "années d'orientation") to facilitate transfer between branches. [53]

Such a plan seemed to Aron broadly acceptable, but it also contained a number of difficulties. The first was that of cost ("the most simple question and the one which it has become *de bon ton* not to raise"). Secondly, there was "the indisputable fact of the inequality of individuals"; there was "no point in imposing compulsory schooling up to the age of fifteen or sixteen on those who have no liking for study and look forward to going to work as a kind of liberation" (flexibility in applying the principle did not affect its validity).[54] Thirdly, what would be the method of selection for the different branches? Fourthly, there was unlikely to be any "pre-established harmony" between the numbers of pupils in the two humanities branches and the corresponding job opportunities in society: how would it be possible to avoid "the plethora of intellectuals or semi-intellectuals" likely to be created by the influx of pupils into the two humanities sections?[55] Finally, if future primary teachers went to the lycée rather than the école primaire supérieure, would they still be content to become *instituteurs*? Might not the quality of the instituteurs suffer as a result? Aron was not, he stressed, against these proposed reforms; his intention was simply to "confront abstract plans with social reality – a social reality which does not, at a word of command, submit to our ideal of logic and justice".[56]

In the interest of promoting greater social efficiency, Aron argued for a number of university reforms. It was necessary to "restore life to the provincial universities and relieve the overcrowding in the University of Paris", perhaps by encouraging the universities to specialize more.[57] He also advocated reform, but not abolition, of the *grandes écoles* and the university examination system. In addition, he recommended the creation of one or more faculties of economic and social science, with political economy as a central discipline instead of being a mere appendage to the degree in law: "France needs a school of good, if not great, economists and she needs to renew her political thought, which has suffered from sclerosis for the last half-century".[58] Such a reform would help in preparation for the higher civil service, since the new faculties of economic and social science "could provide the means of common access to all the competitive examinations, and even to a single examination for all state *fonctionnaires*, similar to that for civil servants in Britain, with specialization entering later".[59]

As to the problem of unity, i.e., the religious question, Aron's (very tentative) conclusion was that, since a sudden upsurge of understanding between Catholics and laymen was unlikely, it would be best to go back to the pre-war situation – "the one that is least divisive because we are used to it".[60] In this matter, moral reform was a necessary condition of institutional reform, but the former would not appear to order.

The "crisis of the University" (if one could use the expression) did not, Aron concluded, date from 1940 or 1944, but had been developing for years, as the contrast grew between "the stagnation of the University's practices and curricula, and the tumultuous *élan* of a society in search of a new order, and also as the University became increasingly isolated and lost contact with the latest and most lively intellectual movements":

The fact is that the faculties remain hostile or strangers to too many of the ideas that excite our contemporaries. When students fail to find any lectures on Hegel and Marx at the Sorbonne, they place a higher value on the books (however vulgarizing) and the lectures (however propagandist) that satisfy their curiosity. There is no need to introduce the clamour of the forum into the lecture-theatre, in order to breathe fresh life into places to which the young flock but from which too often the mind is absent. Even if a professor is not in the creative vanguard of his discipline, he should at least be capable of communicating the living science.

. . . By reducing the distance between the generation which teaches and the generation which learns, it will perhaps be possible to restore the unity between research in progress and teaching, and re-establish livelier contacts between the faculties and intellectual life in general. But, in the end, the question posed by the University is no different from that posed by the nation. They are both searching for the meaning of France in the twentieth century.[61]

* * *

L'Age des empires et l'avenir de la France also contains Aron's first sustained discussion of Marxism since before the war – an outstanding study of "L'Avenir des religions séculières" ("Secular Religions and their Future"), which was first published in *La France libre* in two parts in July and August 1944.[62] Aron coined the term "secular religions" (now a commonplace) to refer to doctrines, such as millenarian socialism and nazism, "which, in the souls of our contemporaries, take the place of a vanished faith and situate the salvation of humanity here on earth, in the shape of a social order to be created in the distant future".[63] The reign of socialism, as Marx described it in his youthful writings, was the reign of men who were free, equal and fraternal – an ideal which, Aron pointed out, was akin, in its deepest inspiration, to the Christian ideal. Indeed, the very idea, revived by socialism, of a liberation of man through history, stemmed from the philosophy of progress, itself a secularization of the Christian vision of a humanity marching towards the kingdom of the millennium. Where Condorcet had imagined a continuous movement towards more knowledge and civilization, Marxism saw a dialectic – in its own case, a series of social regimes succeeding one another in accordance with the law of oppositions, the passage from one regime to the next taking place as a result of a violent break, a revolution. It was by the negation of capitalism that man would transcend the particularity and servitude to which he was condemned by the system of private ownership.

The revolution, the decisive element in what could be called socialist eschatology, was not therefore simply a social upheaval, the substitution of one regime for another. It had a supra-political value, and marked the leap from necessity to liberty. Salvation lay beyond this apocalyptic catastrophe, this Promethean act by which humanity would break its chains and re-enter, so to speak, into possession of itself. Through its spontaneous evolution, capitalism was supposed to lead to this event, thus inaugurating a new era. Any interpretation, therefore, which cast doubt on the inevitability of capitalist development, struck at the very heart of the doctrine. This explained the passionate controversies aroused by Eduard Bernstein's reformism, which was finally condemned by a congress of the Social Democratic Party (prominent socialists themselves likened it to the synods at which Catholic dogmas were fixed). It was a heresy rather than a scientific opinion that was at issue; and socialism had continued to give rise to competing groups which, appealing to the same prophet and sacred book, excommunicated one another with great ferocity.

It might be objected that such analogies ignored the scientific character of Marxist socialism, and Aron was, he stated, willing to grant this aspect of many of its propositions. Historical materialism, for example, in the "brilliantly simplified" form given to it by *The Communist Manifesto*, was "a landmark in the development of sociological theories"; and even those who did not accept the economic ideas of *Capital* recognized in it "a monument of constructive analysis".[64] On the other hand, it was difficult to deny that the influence of *Capital* was largely independent of the truth or otherwise of the theories it contained. Its influence stemmed from the justification it appeared to give to the moral condemnation of capitalism and the intellectual support it seemed to offer socialist faith (an example of *fides quaerens intellectum* – faith seeking understanding).

The case of historical materialism was similar. The idea that societies "depend upon" the means and relations of production had become part of common consciousness and there was not a non-Marxist who had not learnt from it. On the other hand, however easy it might be to explain different phenomena in economic terms (and here it was unclear exactly what was meant by "economic factor" – the technical instruments or the social relations of production?), the explanation became increasingly

296

indirect, uncertain and even arbitrary, as one moved from material organization to the political regime and then to the intellectual sphere. "To bring everything down to the infrastructure, or to decree dogmatically that a particular cause is the final cause, is, from a scientific point of view, purely arbitrary". The moment one admitted an interaction between different causes, how could one decree that a certain cause was the final cause? The truth was that the choice of a final cause stemmed from the intention of the observer. The Marxist was interested above all in the economic system, determined as he was to change it. Since this change must, in his view, entail a total transformation of human existence, he saw in the economic system the final cause of the evolution of society. Indeed, the very purpose of the overstatements contained in the theory of historical materialism was precisely to arouse the indispensable conviction that an economic revolution would in itself bring about a total revolution.[65]

This conviction lay at the heart of Marxism, giving its power as propaganda and its confident *élan*; and it was this, too, which established the crucial identity between the historically necessary and the morally desirable. Marxism, in contrast to utopian socialism, claimed to be "scientific" and to reflect the "real" transformations in society. It was certainly a fruitful hypothesis to present a picture of capitalism sliding towards its death, the more it appeared to flourish; yet, Aron argued, the implication that the post-capitalist economy would give birth to a human, egalitarian order was "unscientific" in that it went beyond our knowledge and derived from an act of faith. The compatibility of political and intellectual liberalism with a planned economy (a theme that was central to current controversies) at least called for demonstration; and this was now possible, for the very idea that gave socialism its expansive force – the identification of the desirable with the necessary – instead of continuing to enjoy the benefit of the doubt, could now be put to the test of totalitarian experience.

Socialism's optimistic vision of a radiant future beyond capitalist exploitation originated in a boundless confidence in man and human reason: humanity, without God or master, armed with science and lord of nature, would inevitably be peaceful and satisfied. The First World War, however, dealt a rude blow to "the religion of hyper-rationalism", because, at the crucial moment, country won over party. Above all, the war and the Russian Revolution led to an increase in the number of secular religions, the division of the socialist Church into rival parties and the birth of violent anti-socialist religions, in which comparable means were employed for opposed ends. For the analogies between the secular religions were, Aron contended, as evident as their differences. Apart from the obvious external similarities between socialism and national socialism (vast meetings, huge portraits, enormous slogans, uniformed militia, "political" music, numerous flags), nazism also had its manichean world-vision and millenarian doctrine of salvation.[66]

But what of the future? Even if a less dogmatic political age was beginning, socialist ideologies were still popular, nationalism was still alive, and it could be said that this was the very situation which led to the birth of national socialisms. Yet, Aron argued, the future was not preordained and to think otherwise was always a form of defeatism. Was the age of secular religions to be succeeded by an era of relatively doctrine-less fanaticism? Or would people emerge from the war of nations and myths to reconstruct a human order? Because the secular religions had been discredited by their conflicts and affinities, would a cynical nihilism prevail, or, as Aron believed possible, a faith in man and "the sense of universal values"?[67]

People today aspired to security, national independence and the manifold freedoms to think, speak, write and trade, of which the enemy and his accomplices had deprived a continent. Theorists would doubtless argue that the formal liberties of bourgeois democracy – the right to vote, speak and associate – were nothing compared to the concrete liberty that only a collectivist society could ensure. But, Aron replied,

Whether formal or concrete, there are freedoms which, on emerging from slavery, the peoples will demand tomorrow, unconditionally and without reservation. They will tolerate neither Gestapo, under whatever guise, nor suppression of the elementary rights of the individual, whatever the justification. Or rather, they will submit to them perhaps, if some tyrannical group seizes power by surprise and keeps it through violent means, but they will not resign themselves to it. And the world will continue to live in fear.[68]

It was from sentiments such as these – the rights of individuals, patriotism, and the demand for liberty – that an effort must be made to reconstruct a doctrine. It was not, however, a question of a new dogmatism but of a search for institutions which would provide a chance of safeguarding the liberal, rationalist heritage of the nineteenth century, while responding to the necessities of today. But because the revolutions of the twentieth century had employed despotic methods, it did not follow that such methods had become inevitable. The only thing that followed was that the desire to remake society at a stroke, through authoritarian means and in accordance with the wishes of one group, inevitably led to a total state. Before embarking on the road to tyranny, therefore, it was important to show that the problems of our time could not be solved gradually. A comparison of the similarities between the secular religions suggested the beginnings of a solution. Today all regimes, whatever they were, must guarantee individuals a minimum of security (especially of employment) and this implied that the state accept responsibility for guiding, whether directly or indirectly, the economy as a whole. But in order to avoid totalitarianism and safeguard pluralism and liberty, regimes must both assume the responsibilities which the masses would not forgive them for refusing, and allow a degree of freedom to the spontaneous mechanisms of the market, as the method most likely to accord with the general interest within given limits.

No doubt, in the twentieth century, people no longer believed in parliamentary constitutions, economic liberalism or national sovereignty, as they had in the previous century. Because they had at least been partially realized, these ideas had lost the charm of novelty. But it would be absurd to ignore the reawakening of nationalism and of a humane liberalism on the devastated Continent. Certain parliamentary institutions and forms of free enterprise were, Aron maintained, capable of again finding justification, even in the eyes of the masses, as the best means of satisfying this ardent desire for personal autonomy. He was, he wrote, convinced that an intermediate regime, free from rival dogmatisms, was economically and socially viable. The gravest uncertainty concerned the political future, for, if the infinitely complex mechanisms of such a regime were to operate effectively, nothing less was required than cooperation between elites recognized as having prestige and masses that were well led. Such cooperation had every chance of developing in Britain, but the prospects were less favourable on the Continent.

Nothing great was achieved in history, Aron concluded, without the faith of ordinary citizens in ideas and people. The crucial question was: however lofty its inspiration, would such faith learn to respect "the virtues of simple humanity"?

At the end of June 1940, at the Olympia Hall in London, the first order of the day read out to the Free French volunteers ended with William the Silent's famous maxim: *Il n'est pas besoin d'espérer pour entreprendre ni de réussir pour persévérer.* In those words I saw then, and I still see, the motto of revolt, always vanquished and always triumphant – the revolt of conscience.[69]

* * *

The first volume of Aron's war writings to be published was the 1944 New York edition of *L'Homme contre les tyrans*. In the United States it was reviewed by his old friend, Alexandre Koyré, now Secretary-General of the Ecole Libre des Hautes Etudes at the New School for Social Research in New York. Writing in the Ecole's journal, *Renaissance*, Koyré commented:

Everybody knows *La France libre*. This volume therefore requires no introduction. All I need say is that this collection of articles forms *a book* and that this is the most important book to have appeared among French writers in exile.[70]

In Britain, the *Times Literary Supplement*'s anonymous reviewer called *L'Homme contre les tyrans* "a very remarkable polemic" against "a pessimistic resignation to an unknown but fully determined future or an optimistic resignation before the laws of progress... By an acute and remarkably objective analysis of the present situation and of its more recent origins, M. Aron hopes to dispel the pessimistic and the optimistic illusions". Singling out Aron's discussion of Alain, the writer continued:

If there be any among us so foolish in 1944 as not to realize that the tone of a culture has profound importance for the life of the nation concerned – and of its neighbours – the section of this book called "Guerre Impériale" is what the Americans call "required reading". But of even greater interest is the discussion of the treason of so many French clerks, of the ignominious contrast between the resistance of the French people and the acceptance of the German triumph of 1940 by so many of the intellectual elite... The analysis given here is most timely and, for English readers, novel.[71]

Aron's writings for *La France libre* were also well received when they were published in Paris after the war. The historian Lucien Febvre, for example, in *Annales*, the famous journal which he had founded and edited with Marc Bloch, described Aron's studies in *De l'Armistice à l'insurrection nationale* and *L'Homme contre les tyrans* as "very fine – limpid, subtle and showing rare penetration". The direct simplicity with which Aron posed the problems was matched by the clarity with which he resolved them. Economist, sociologist, politician – Aron was all of these "and with equal felicity".[72]

In its anonymous notice of *L'Homme contre les tyrans* the *Revue de métaphysique et de morale* called Aron a witness of "outstanding clarity of vision" and "admirable firmness of judgement". His *France libre* articles derived particular value from "the sureness of their analysis and the high level of their thought". If *De l'Armistice à l'insurrection nationale* was above all the work of a historian, *L'Homme contre les tyrans* was that of a moralist and philosopher. Without having to change the text or the order of his studies in any significant way, Aron had written "a real book" with a coherently developed argument; and the prudent "perspectives" with which he ended gave ample evidence of his "clearsightedness and strength of mind". Aron was "without any doubt, one of our most vigorous political thinkers".[73]

However, the most elaborate review of the war writings was that by Roland Caillois in the newly founded journal, *Critique*.[74] Caillois confessed himself not in the least surprised that Aron, who could doubtless have been a Professor of Sociology, had decided instead to become a journalist. In the first place, there was a Plato in every philosopher, someone who was not content merely to contemplate ideas, but who also wanted to live them and make them penetrate reality, trying if possible to convince a people or a tyrant of their truth. Secondly, Aron had always sought a knowledge of the facts, preferring social documentation to purely theoretical inquiry. It was, of course, true that his *Introduction to the Philosophy of History* was one of the most abstract books imaginable, but it represented "a detour in abstraction" in order to rediscover concrete reality, and a theoretical tool without which the interpretation of the world was doomed to a fruitless empiricism. In his thesis Aron had clearly shown that he placed great value on "the rights of action", though not at the expense of thought, since thought and action were as inseparable in history as everywhere else. Was it not siginificant that Aron had dedicated his "critique of historical reason" to both the man of action, André Malraux, and the philosopher, Eric Weil? "One must transform as wide a range of experience as possible into consciousness", said Malraux. Aron had taken up this formula, and the term "experience" had only one meaning for him – the historical experience which we live from day to day and which illuminates the past and informs the present. If, Caillois wrote, Aron was to be compared with any one thinker, it was Max Weber who came to mind. There was the same concern to "know reality in order to master it", the same belief in the rationality of the past but in the liberty of the future, the same determination to commit oneself in order to understand, but also the same reserve in the face of over-insistent orthodoxies. There was no doubt that "Aron is above all determined to be a man of his time and that is why he is bent on understanding it".[75]

His studies for *La France libre* gave proof of this. Varying as they did in their subject-matter, they gained from being brought together in book form. Indeed, their unity of tone was striking, their singleness of purpose giving to the whole a force not to be found in the studies on their own.

301

Thus, it was essential to understand nazism if the same mistakes were not to be repeated, and *L'Homme contre les tyrans* would help in this task. Aron excelled, for example, in demonstrating the reasons underlying Alain's popularity, the seductive hold of tyranny over intellectuals, and the characteristics of the "managerial" class; and the historical studies were no less valuable than the analyses of ideas. Furthermore, whatever the subject, the human quality of the argument was always preserved. Above all, Aron "never gives in to the temptation to provide a one-dimensional explanation, knowing as he does how to tackle a problem from a number of 'super-imposed' perspectives – economic crisis, political crisis, ideological crisis – without ever deciding *a priori* on the fundamental cause".[76]

Nevertheless, Caillois had two criticisms to make, the first of which – that Aron's explanations remained fragmentary – seems somewhat illogical in view of his previous remark. One never knew, Caillois wrote, by what criteria Aron gauged the importance of different causes; indeed, one often had the impression that in the last analysis everything was equally contingent, even though Aron asserted that it was important to locate "the points of application of the human will" and that "men make their history but do not know the history they make". These were, in Caillois' view, "excellent formulas". Perhaps Aron had a clear conception of the relationship between freedom ("the future is open") and the ineluctable weight of the past, but "he does not enable us to understand it in concrete terms". At times, Caillois went on harshly, one was even led to wonder if,

by thus reacting against the enormous weight of one-dimensional explanations, he does not end up in a kind of superficial chronicle which only rarely connects with the profound rationality of history, a rationality which, we freely admit, is not pre-ordained but arises out of historical reflection, since everything that man does – whether or not he has explicitly willed it – necessarily takes on a human meaning, understandable to him.[77]

Caillois' second criticism was that Aron's conception of democracy was "insufficiently grounded" because, in Caillois' view, the formal freedoms of liberal democracy are nothing but a disguise for class interests – an assertion which Caillois unfortunately failed to substantiate. But he concluded that:

Raymond Aron's books nonetheless constitute the best expression today of a certain kind of political thinking. With their evident good sense and seriousness, they are bent on rediscovering the innocence of liberal thought, at a time when opposing ideological systems are emerging, between which we will have to choose. Aron is surely aware of this, when he writes: "One always chooses, in history, between wholes" and these constitute "incompatibilities between equally precious values".[78]

302

Notes

1. 1946b.
2. Ibid., p. 7.
3. Compare 1944r.
4. 1946b, p. 8.
5. Ibid.,p. 9.
6. Ibid., p. 11.
7. Compare 1944e: tr. 1945b.
8. 1946b, p. 12.
9. Ibid., p. 13.
10. Ibid.
11. Ibid., p. 15.
12. 1943o.
13. 1946b, pp. 16–18. Compare 1944y, 1945d.
14. Compare 1945o, 1945p.
15. 1946b, p. 209.
16. Ibid., p. 88.
17. Ibid., p. 19.
18. Ibid., pp. 21–2.
19. Ibid., pp. 224, 225.
20. Compare 1944c; 1946c: tr. 1945c; 1945k.
21. 1946b, pp. 24–5.
22. See 1944c.
23. 1946b, p. 25.
24. Ibid., p. 368.
25. Ibid., p. 350.
26. Ibid., pp. 26, 27.
27. 1943u, 1943w.
28. 1946b, pp. 87–9.
29. For example, *La Lutte de classes* (1964a), Ch. IX. See Volume 2, Chapter 5.
30. 1946b, pp. 89–90.
31. Ibid., pp. 90–1.
32. Ibid., pp. 91–3.
33. Ibid., pp. 93–4.
34. See below, p. 294.
35. Ibid., pp. 115–18.
36. 1944g, 1944i.
37. 1946b, p. 123.
38. Ibid., p. 135. For another discussion of the future organization of political parties in post-war France, see 1944t.
39. 1946b., p. 142.
40. Ibid., p.144.
41. Ibid., pp. 148, 149.
42. Ibid., pp. 149–50.
43. 1944k.

44. 1946b, p. 151.
45. Ibid., p. 152.
46. Ibid., pp. 152–3.
47. Ibid., p. 160.
48. Ibid., p. 163.
49. Ibid., pp. 163–5.
50. Ibid., p. p. 165.
51. 1945h, 1945m.
52. 1946b, pp. 179–81.
53. Ibid., pp. 181–5.
54. Ibid., p. 185.
55. Ibid., p. 186.
56. Ibid., p. 189.
57. Ibid., pp. 189–90.
58. Ibid., p. 194.
59. Ibid., p. 196.
60. Ibid., p. 201.
61. Ibid., pp. 205–6.
62. 1944o, 1944p.
63. 1946b, p. 288.
64. Ibid., p. 291.
65. Ibid., p. 292.
66. Ibid., pp. 295–302.
67. Ibid., p. 314. Compare Aron's contribution to the so-called "end of ideology debate" in *The Opium of the Intellectuals*, published ten years later. See Chapter 20, below, and Volume 2, Chapter 10.
68. 1946b, pp. 314–15.
69. Ibid., p. 318. "There is no need to hope in order to begin an enterprise nor to succeed in order to persevere".
70. Koyré, 1944–5.
71. Anon., 1944.
72. Febvre, 1948.
73. Anon., 1947. Compare Pierre Prévost, reviewing *L'Age des empires et l'avenir de la France* in *La Nef*: "Raymond Aron, sociologist and philosopher of history, is also one of our most brilliant political writers" (Prévost, 1946). Raymond Millet in *Le Monde* called this volume "a captivating collection of essays" and was particularly impressed by Aron's discussion of elites (Millet, 1946).
74. Caillois, 1946. Roland Caillois is not to be confused with the anthropological writer, Roger Caillois.
75. Ibid., pp. 430–1.
76. Ibid., p. 435.
77. Ibid., pp. 435–6.
78. Ibid., p. 437.

Part Four

The Cold War

———

13

The Journalist

On 26 August 1944, General de Gaulle marched in triumph down the Champs-Elysées. The following month, "with beating heart", Aron set foot once again on French soil and returned to Paris, empty-handed and unknown to the public (his had not been among the familiar voices broadcasting from London). The war was not over yet and material conditions were extremely difficult. Furthermore, when he met members of the Resistance, Aron had "a feeling of inferiority". In retrospect, his decision to leave for England in 1940 now took on a quite different significance. In Aron's own eyes he had escaped the sufferings and dangers experienced by those who had remained in France – which had clearly not been his intention or the meaning of his decision in June 1940.[1]

Not having experienced the euphoria of the Liberation, Aron has contrasted the gloomy atmosphere of VE Day with the emotion which greeted the Armistice at the end of the First World War:

In November 1918, I was thirteen years old. I lived in Versailles. My parents took me to Paris, and I experienced the unique and unforgettable day when the people were united in joy. Without having been there, it is impossible to imagine what Paris was like on Armistice Day...People were embracing one another in the street. They all were – bourgeois, workers, employees, young and old alike. The people had gone mad, but mad with joy. There was no feeling of hatred, but rather of joy and relief. Everyone kept repeating the same thing: "We've beaten them!" ("On les a eus"). But it was above all joy they felt.

In May 1945, on the other hand, Paris was mortally sad – at any rate, as I experienced it. I remember a conversation with Jules Roy that day. He was struck, as I was, by this feeling of sadness, an absence of hope. It was the end of the war, but it was the Allies' victory rather than that of France. There was nothing like the delirious enthusiasm of November 1918. I only have one particular memory of 8 May. I went out into the streets, all the same, in order to share this moment with the people of Paris, and I saw – I forget where – General Giraud. He was alone. He had a sad look about him and seemed lost. I went towards him to greet him and show my feelings in some way, but then I saw him move off without a word. His was the sadness of a man who could have had an important role to play, but who had failed despite his courage. That day no one remembered him. Politics are like that.[2]

Nevertheless, in spite of this air of despondency, something did give Aron cause for hope. There was among his generation "a deep and resolute determination to rebuild the country".[3] Indeed, on his return to Paris, Aron at once threw himself into his writings on post-war reconstruction. That October he analysed "the conditions for France's greatness" in *Combat*, the renowned Resistance paper edited by Camus.[4] By the end of the year he had completed three articles for later publication in *La France libre*;[5] and he wrote a further three in 1945,[6] as well as a study of French foreign policy for *International Affairs*[7] and the important Introduction to *L'Age des empires et l'avenir de la France*.

It was at this point, however, that Aron made what he has himself called "the most foolish mistake of my life": having turned down a post at the London School of Economics, he was offered, but refused, the Chair of Sociology at the University of Bordeaux, where he had taught part-time for a year before the war. The decision was, he says, "absurd", and his reasons for refusing were "stupid". He wanted to live in Paris; he had been an exile for more than four years and all his friends were there. He had no wish to live in Bordeaux, nor did he think it was a good idea to commute from Paris (in any case, he had unpleasant memories of the pre-war train journey). More importantly, because of his experiences in London, he had become "corrupted" by his close contact with the world of politics – "poisoned by the virus of politics" – so much so that by the time he returned to Paris he no longer had any real desire to go back to university life. He felt that to teach sociology to a few students at Bordeaux was not the most effective way to help put France back on its feet and that he could make a more useful contribution to this end by engaging in "quasi-political" activity of some kind in Paris.

It was a decision which was to have two consequences: his university career was held up for a number of years – he would probably have been elected to the Sorbonne when a Chair became vacant in 1948, rather than in 1955 – and, if he had gone back to the University after the war, it is most unlikely that he would have become a journalist in the way that he did.[8]

Nevertheless, Aron did lecture at the newly founded Ecole Nationale d'Administration (ENA) and Institut d'Etudes Politiques ("Sciences Po") – at the ENA, for example, on "The Twentieth-Century Crisis" (1946), "One Hundred Years of the *Communist Manifesto*" (1948) and "Introduction to Political Philosophy" (1952), and at Sciences Po on "Comparative Political Sociology" (1951–2).[9] These lectures left their mark on the first post-war generation of French students. Thus the sociologist François Bourricaud who, with the economist and future Prime Minister Raymond Barre, followed his course on Marx and Pareto at Sciences Po in 1948, recalls the unique sense of "ease and rightness" that characterized Aron's teaching,[10] while another student, the diplomat Henri Froment-Meurice, dates the beginning of his lifelong confidence in Aron's judgement and power of persuasion from his 1948 ENA course on Marxism.[11]

Although Aron's entry into journalism is usually taken as dating from April 1946 when he made his spectacular debut with *Combat*, it is not generally known that he in fact started writing editorials over a year earlier – in the seemingly unlikely setting of a new illustrated weekly called *Point de vue*. Its Editor was Lucien Rachline ("Rachet" in the Resistance) and Aron was persuaded to join the magazine by his London friend, Corniglion-Molinier.[12] The three men comprised the Editorial Board and every week Aron wrote a leading article on international relations or French politics – some three dozen in all – from 23 March (the date of the first number) to 29 November 1945. Aron himself has remarked ironically of these articles that they were "neither better nor worse than those in *Combat* and *Le Figaro*, but nobody read them".[13] In style, length and quality they are in fact identical to the celebrated editorials he later wrote for these great newpapers. The other distinction to which the *Point de vue* articles can lay claim is that in them Aron twice used the expression "rideau de fer" ("iron curtain"), on 26 July[14] and again on 13 September[15] – at least six months, that is, before Churchill employed the phrase in his Fulton speech of March 1946.

Aron left *Point de vue* in November 1945 to embark on what turned out to be a brief spell in a government post. As a result of the referendum and elections held in October 1945, the Third Republic had been brought to an end and a Constituent Assembly elected for seven months. General de Gaulle, who had headed a provisional government since September 1944, was unanimously elected Head of Government in the new Assembly, in which the three major parties were the Communists, the new pro-Gaullist Catholic Party – the Mouvement Républicain Populaire (MRP) – and the Socialists. De Gaulle formed his government on 21 November, though he gave none of the key ministries – Foreign Affairs, Defence or the Interior – to the Communists, the largest group in the Assembly. The new Minister of Information was André Malraux and he asked Aron to be his Directeur de Cabinet. They had, as we have seen, been friends since the early 1930s[16] and Aron had dedicated his *Introduction to the Philosophy of History* to Malraux.[17] Their last meeting before they were separated by the war had been in October 1939, when Aron spent a whole evening trying to persuade Malraux to break with the Communists after the signing of the Nazi-Soviet Pact. But Malraux had refused, saying that he would have done so had Daladier not imprisoned them. By the time the two men met again, however, Malraux had become passionately anti-Communist.[18]

According to Malraux's biographer, Jean Lacouture, Aron was "one of the few men who could not say with Gide that 'when one is with Malraux, one does not feel very intelligent'".[19] Furthermore, the Ministry's Secretary-General was the young Resistance general and future Prime Minister and presidential candidate, Jacques Chaban-Delmas. With three such personalities, this ministry, as Lacouture put it, "ran no risk of sinking into somnolence",[20] especially as another member of the ministerial team was Malraux and Aron's mutual friend from pre-war days, Manès Sperber.[21]

Aron's work at the Ministry did not exactly fill him with enthusiasm. He had to spend most of the time seeing people in his office, particularly about which newspapers should be allowed to publish in view of their attitudes during the Occupation. By the time Aron entered the Ministry of Information at the end of 1945, most of the major decisions had been taken, although Malraux and he did authorize the *Figaro littéraire* to re-appear. Another problem with which he had to concern himself was the distribution of paper. The one thing Aron did try to do was to prevent the creation of a state printing corporation, consisting of those printing works which had been confiscated by the state at the end of the war. He was opposed to such a proposal because he was convinced that a state organization would prove incapable of administering the various printing works effectively; the presses should instead be transferred to the newspapers themselves and to those who were directly responsible.[22]

310

But there was no time for Aron to put these counter-proposals into effect. De Gaulle, in spite of his "extraordinary talent" as a parliamentarian, had no wish to head a parliamentary government. On 20 January 1946, therefore, he summoned his ministers and, apparently convinced that within six months he would be recalled to power, announced his resignation.[23] The "traversée du désert", as Malraux later called it, was to last twelve years, and Aron's only experience of political office had ended, after only two months. The experience had been "instructive" and "quite amusing", but he had the impression that "it is less tiring to work for eight or ten hours a day in a ministry office than to spend three hours reading Kant's *Critique of Pure Reason*. The work is irritating and annoying, but does not require intellectual effort".[24]

On leaving the Ministry of Information Aron, who had a wife and children to support, was faced with the problem of earning a living. Malraux was a close friend of Pascal Pia, the Director and *éminence grise* of *Combat*, the Resistance paper which, since the Liberation, had been published as a daily. At Malraux's suggestion, therefore, Aron went to see Pia[25] – *Combat's* Editor, Albert Camus, had withdrawn from the paper, exhausted by politics and in poor health, and was in the United States[26] – and as a result Aron wrote a series of seven articles on "the political scene" for *Combat* between 14 and 23 April 1946. They constitute a remarkable entry into journalism.[27] Much to his surprise – for he had no idea that he was capable of writing them – the articles "caused something of a stir in the journalistic world",[28] and at the end of April he joined Albert Ollivier as a columnist ("éditorialiste") on *Combat*, to which he now contributed two or three times a week on political, economic and international issues. Thus, at the age of forty-one, Aron embarked on a new career. He had never considered it before and he started in it at the top.[29]

Less well known is the fact that shortly after this, in June 1946, Aron joined the new illustrated magazine, *Réalités*, as an Associate Editor. This sumptuously produced monthly was to enjoy a huge national and international success – an English-language edition was published in Paris between 1950 and 1974. Aron wrote occasional articles on domestic and international affairs for *Réalités* from 1947 to 1964 (some twenty in all), though his formal relationship with the magazine came to an end in 1958 (for a brief period in the late 1960s, he was an "external contributor").

Looking back on his early years in journalism, Aron recalled:

It amused me at the time. And then, there is always that accursed *amour propre*. There I was, a philosophy teacher who had written some obscure books which hardly anyone

311

had read. I wanted to prove, therefore, that I too could do this job. But, once the demonstration had been given, after a few weeks or months my initial enthusiasm waned. A number of philosophers (who, I should add, wrote for *Combat*) used to say to me: "It's odd that you should prefer writing newspaper articles to the *Introduction to the Philosophy of History*". I thought they were right, but there was this intoxication with politics... and the idea, the illusion, the determination to take part in political life and in the restoration of France.[30]

Combat was "a marvellous enterprise, typically French and a trifle mad". It was a highly intellectual paper, whose pages contained "a density of grey matter to the square centimetre" that was "absolutely exceptional".[31] Aron particularly valued the debates that used to take place between the columnists of different newpapers – for example, Camus, Ollivier, Mauriac, Blum and himself; such debates no longer occurred today and he believed that the French press was the poorer for it. In the immediate post-war years there was argument and discussion – about the purge, General de Gaulle and the provisional government, everyday events and the future of France. "That is why", he says, "my memory of *Combat* is probably the happiest of all my memories of journalism".[32]

Aron joined *Combat* at the time of the first political battles after the war. The campaign for the referendum on the Constitution was at its height and in almost his first editorial Aron announced that he would vote against the all-powerful, single-Chamber assembly supported by the Communists and Socialists.[33] *Combat* was by tradition a Socialist paper and not surprisingly, therefore, the article caused a considerable upheaval among its staff and readership. A few days later, on 2 May, Simone de Beauvoir, who was now drawing apart from Aron politically and personally and may not therefore be a trustworthy witness, noted in her diary that her friend, Jacques-Laurent Bost, Sartre and Aron's former pupil at Le Havre and now a reporter on the paper, "told us a lot about *Combat*, about the passion Pascal Pia was bringing to the task of killing the newspaper and himself with it, about Ollivier, whom everyone loathes and who knows it, about Aron, who's also getting himself disliked by understanding *Combat* so intensely and insisting on saying so".[34] The next day, she wrote, Bost "told us that there was a great to-do at *Combat* because of the recent articles by Ollivier and Aron championing the *no*; many of the people on the paper were going to vote *yes*; and they wanted to start a campaign urging people to vote Socialist; otherwise *Combat* would become a right-wing paper. It appears that everyone stays on only because of Pia's personal charm, and he's so absorbed by his anti-communism that he forgets that he's supposed to be a leader of the Left".[35]

312

Although Camus looked in on *Combat* when he returned to Paris in the autumn, and even wrote a series of articles for the paper in November ("Ni Victimes ni bourreaux"), "he was only morally one of the editors and directors of the newspaper in 1946".[36] During his absence, as Simone de Beauvoir later expressed it,

Aron and Ollivier had used *Combat* to support the SFIO [the Socialist Party] which now drew most of its members from the lower middle-classes; Camus did not dissociate himself from them. Shortly after his return Bost was going to see him in his office and passed Aron on the way out as he was saying in a sarcastic tone: "Well, I must be off to write my reactionary editorial". Camus expressed astonishment; Bost made it clear to him what he thought about the paper's current policy. "If you don't like it, why don't you leave?" Camus asked. "I'm going to", said Bost. He broke with *Combat* and Camus was indignant: "There's gratitude!" However, if Camus stopped writing in *Combat* for a long while, it was because he resented, or so I was told, Aron's increasing influence there. But I think he was also disillusioned with politics in general. . .[37]

Indeed, as Camus' biographer, basing his account on an interview with Aron, put it, "it is true that on Camus' return his relations with Aron were not of the best. Aron mocked the presence of so many intellectuals on the staff, the uncertainty of its leadership; workers confided to him: 'If only we had a boss' – for Pia wasn't interested in being one. There was a faithful readership but a pitifully small one, growing smaller all the time. Aron would joke: 'We're read by everybody, of course, but everybody is 40,000 people'". In short, the paper was an intellectual, but not a commercial, success.[38]

By 1947 *Combat* was in serious financial difficulties, aggravated by a month-long newspaper strike in February and March. Its circulation had more than halved since its post-Liberation peak of 200,000 copies and various schemes were put forward to try to save the paper. Aron himself consulted bankers to see if they would support a paper under his direction; but each banker had his own political views and "Aron also knew that the staff would not have accepted his leadership, because he himself was politically committed" – to the newly-created Gaullist Rassemblement du Peuple Français.[39] Camus even returned to lend his prestige to the paper in an attempt to save it in February 1947, but to no avail: Aron wrote his last article for the paper on 27 May and on 3 June the political and administrative directorate announced that it was resigning. The Editorship was taken over by Claude Bourdet, who had helped found *Combat* during the war, while financial support was provided by Henry Smadja.[40]

Two papers now approached Aron in the hope that he would write for them – *Le Figaro*, whose Director was Pierre Brisson, and *Le Monde*, which had recently been founded by Hubert Beuve-Méry. Aron's motive for choosing *Le Figaro* was not, as was said in some quarters at the time, financial (the offers made by both papers were in fact similar); he decided to join *Le Figaro* for other reasons. Malraux thought that Aron would get on better with Brisson than with Beuve-Méry, and the events of the Cold War were to prove Malraux right: *Le Monde* soon adopted a neutralist stance with which Aron and Brisson both strongly disagreed.[41] Malraux also believed that Aron would have more freedom on *Le Figaro*: he knew that Aron was interested in international relations, economics and French politics, whereas Brisson, a literary man, considered himself an amateur in such matters and was ready to listen to others.[42] Finally, Aron wanted to be free in the mornings to do his "serious" academic work and this would not have been possible on *Le Monde*, which appeared in the afternoon.[43] It was at this time, therefore, that Aron established a work routine which, when he was in Paris, did not normally vary. On his own admission, he had "great self-discipline", but if he tried to do too much, he slept badly and was unable to continue the next day. Accordingly he used to work at home every morning, from 7.30 till lunch-time, weekends included, and this left him free to see people in the afternoons and to read after dinner. Thus to those who asked him how he managed to write so much, his reply was: "I don't work long hours, but I work every day".[44] Even on his daughter's wedding day he simply stopped working a little earlier than usual.[45]

Le Figaro had begun life as a satirical weekly in 1854 (reviving a title which had already been used under the Restoration and the July Monarchy) and had become a daily in 1866. Monarchist in the aftermath of the Franco-Prussian War, it had subsequently moved towards a moderate republicanism. Brisson, who was born in 1896, had been its Director since 1934, having previously been drama critic of *Le Temps* and Director of the *Annales politiques et littéraires*. After the fall of France in June 1940, *Le Figaro* withdrew to Lyon in the Unoccupied Zone where it continued to appear, but it ceased publication on 10 November 1942, immediately after German troops crossed the demarcation line. Because it had closed down before 25 November 1942, the date judged crucial by the Resistance, *Le Figaro* was allowed to reappear under its old name after the war, unlike its evening rival, *Le Temps*, which had continued publication until 30 November.[46] There was, however, some opposition to the proposal at the time, although Aron himself had had few doubts about the matter: the *Figaro* was, he wrote in *La France libre* in May 1944, "for two and a half years, the expression of a camouflaged but courageous form of the Resistance...There is hardly room for argument, now or in the future, about the patriotism of the *Figaro* staff, taken as a whole".[47] Thus *Le Figaro* reappeared in August 1944, whereas *Le Temps* was reborn as *Le Monde* the following December.

Aron joined *Le Figaro* in June 1947. It was the start of an association which was to last almost exactly thirty years. The paper was then entering "the most brilliant period it has ever known",[48] thanks partly to the quality of the writers, many of them members of the Académie Française, whom Brisson was able to attract: during the post-war years these included François Mauriac (who won the Nobel Prize for Literature in 1952), Jacques de Lacretelle, André Siegfried, Georges Duhamel, Pierre Gaxotte, Gérard Bauer, André Billy, Jean Schlumberger, Thierry Maulnier, André Rousseaux and Jean Guéhenno. Brisson allowed his contributors enormous freedom; at the same time his authority was unquestioned. Consequently, *Le Figaro* was, in a saying of the time, "an anarchy tempered by the absolute monarchy of Pierre Brisson". Aron, too, felt "wholly at ease" and was free to write what he liked.[49]

Not that there were never any difficulties between the two men. Brisson, like his newspaper, was a liberal conservative, moderate and republican in outlook; but he inherited a pre-1914 nationalism, which he never lost, and was, for example, deeply attached to the Empire. In Aron's view, Brisson's attitude to politics was primarily emotional. Political judgement was not his forte. He allowed himself to be carried away by his feelings; deeper analysis did not interest him. He only gave way when events proved him wrong; he then accepted the situation, even though he had resisted with all his might. Over French policy in North Africa, for example, Brisson had disagreements with both François Mauriac and Aron. Mauriac in fact abandoned *Le Figaro* for *L'Express* in 1955 because he supported Moroccan independence, although he continued to write for *Le Figaro littéraire*. Aron himself published a major series of articles, arguing for independence of the North African colonies, in *Le Figaro* as early as October 1955.[50] Brisson subsequently requested him not to discuss the Algerian question in the paper.[51] Aron instead brought out two separate books on the Algerian problem – *La Tragédie algérienne*[52] and *L'Algérie et la République*.[53] Ironically, it was *Le Monde* which, on its own initiative, decided to publish extracts from the latter.[54] Not that either Mauriac or *L'Express* gave Aron any credit for what he had done; on the contrary, as Aron himself put it, "It is always my misfortune to be wrong at the time" ("Mon infortune est toujours d'avoir tort sur le moment"). Nevertheless, Aron had the feeling that Brisson would have liked to be able to agree with him – indeed, that Aron's

315

arguments moved and even troubled him – but that Brisson's passionate temperament was too strong. Their disagreements remained shortlived, however, and never took a harsh turn.[55]

Aron normally wrote one or two articles per week for *Le Figaro*, either a front-page column on international affairs or a regular economics commentary. In addition, he often discussed the problems of the French educational system and took part in debates organized by the paper. However, doubtless because of his exasperation with the Fourth Republic and his commitment to the Rassemblement du Peuple Français,[56] he virtually ceased writing about France's internal politics in *Le Figaro* from the end of 1948 to the setting up of the Fifth Republic ten years later.

Aron also went abroad for the paper. Thus he made the first of many visits to the United States in November 1950, a combined academic-journalistic trip in which he spent a few days at the Institute for Advanced Study at Princeton followed by several weeks in Washington with James Burnham, author of *The Managerial Revolution*, and Léonard Rist, Aron's old schoolfriend who was then with the World Bank. In Washington he met the Secretary of State, Dean Acheson, as well as such journalists as Walter Lippmann and Joseph Alsop, and on his return wrote a series of eleven articles on "The Great Ordeal of the United States" in *Le Figaro*.[57] The following September he "covered" the San Francisco Conference on the Japanese Peace Treaty for the paper, his main problem being his inability to use a typewriter.[58] Furthermore, in the autumn of 1953 he went to the Far East, visiting Japan (where he had a long interview with the Prime Minister, Yoshida Shigeru), South Korea, Hong Kong, India (here he met Pandit Nehru) and Indo-China.[59] He also paid his first visit to Israel in June 1956, just six weeks before Nasser nationalized the Suez Canal.[60]

* * *

Aron discussed some of the principles on which his work as a columnist was based in a relaxed, witty and penetrating lecture which he gave in 1948 at the Institut d'Etudes Politiques as part of a series on the press.[61] He defined an "editorial" as "the expression of an opinion in a form that is direct and as persuasive as possible, in which the rigours of proof are sacrificed to the necessity of convincing and striking the reader".[62] Thus an editorial was to be distinguished from news (*"information"*), on the one hand, and a more developed study (*"étude"*), on the other.

316

The most common type was the polemical editorial, which sought to bolster the arguments of the party faithful, as in the articles of Maurice Schumann and Léon Blum. Its "rules", Aron ironically suggested, were never to reason justly, never to understand one's opponent, never to give credit to his good faith, and always to point out his weaknesses and never one's own.

The second type was the analytical editorial, as exemplified in *Combat*. About these Aron had, he confessed, no illusions. Their problem was that they appeared to be impeccably objective, when they could not be, since no political commentator could be uninvolved ("en dehors du coup"): his commitment might be more or less disguised, subtle or hypocritical, but he was engaged in action nonetheless. In analysing party attitudes, for instance, it was impossible not to imply where one's preferences lay, and one was therefore acting either for or against particular parties. Not that this was a criticism, for if, in politics, one had nothing to say, but merely explained the actions of others, it was better to say nothing at all.

The third kind of editorial was the one which took a stand ("la prise de position"). This was illustrated by the work of Camus, who for two and a half years had been not only the most talented columnist in France, but "probably the only one capable of expressing fundamental value-positions in the daily press, without being pompous. To find a style which prevents us from losing sight of our values in the midst of the daily political battle requires a great deal of talent, and it is very rare".[63]

Lastly, there was the "action editorial", which sought to cause a political upheaval and subsequently made history, as in the case of the famous *Times* editorials on Sudeten nationality during the Munich crisis of 1938 and on "spheres of influence" in 1943. Everyone, added Aron, wanted to write that type of editorial, "but one has very little chance of being the columnist who makes history...".[64]

What were the qualities required of a columnist? The first was knowledge, though in practice this was least demanded. "If we are concerned with real journalism – that is, with being capable, when faced with a political, diplomatic, economic or financial event, of commenting upon it, giving an explanation and offering a judgement – one must first acquire a knowledge of political economy, history and the political sciences".[65]

Another quality was journalistic talent, and this took two forms. The first was speed of intellectual reflex. For example, the main obstacle for the academic who entered journalism was that he was used to studying problems in depth and was reluctant to give a hasty opinion. "Being serious, when there isn't the time to be, is perhaps what constitutes the merit of the journalist".[66] The second aspect of journalistic talent was the capacity for clear, rapid and striking expression. When he began as a journalist, Aron said, he had only one rule of conduct, which had been passed on to him by an old teacher:[67] a newspaper article contained two essential elements – the first and the last sentence. The first sentence must make the reader want to go on to the end, and the last must stick in his memory. It was certainly important, Aron believed, that any article should have at least one key sentence, preferably the last; and this last sentence often took him as much time as the rest of the article. Furthermore, an editorial must be written quickly and must not contain too many ideas if it was to achieve its aim of being simple, direct and to the point.

However, the final quality of the columnist was a sense of responsibility, both towards the paper and towards the public:

People are always saying how it is the newspaper owners who limit journalistic freedom. But what counts much more is concern for the public: the journalist is much less anxious about his financial masters than about the reaction of the public. There are some things one cannot say without reaping a harvest of abusive letters which end up by making an impression on the paper's Director. The columnist we have all dreamed of some day being is one whose signature carries enough weight for his writing to have an influence, and who works for a paper which is sufficiently prosperous and liberal to let him say whatever he likes. This ideal columnist does not exist and the job of columnist, like many others, entails more servitude than grandeur – a little grandeur when he fulfils the task of fittingly, and almost always a great deal of servitude, when either he or the paper lacks the one and only condition of independence: success.[68]

* * *

"Success", in *Le Figaro*'s case, was the operative word. For many years the paper prospered. The problems were to begin, however, with Brisson's sudden death in 1964. Nevertheless, Aron was to remain with *Le Figaro* until 1977, when he joined the weekly news magazine, *L'Express*.[69] At the end of his life, thirty-seven years after he wrote his first article for *Combat*, Aron was still writing a regular column as a journalist. It is, of course, impossible to gauge with any precision the effect which his newspaper commentaries have had in the political world – the American diplomat McGeorge Bundy, for example, rates his journalism particularly highly;[70] but the unswervingly patient and realistic analyses contained in his regular articles on the economy were undoubtedly influential in financial circles and thus made an important contribution to France's post-war rise as an

318

industrial nation – the noted economist, Robert Marjolin, has singled out these articles for especial praise,[71] as has Guy Berger.[72] Aron himself was characteristically sceptical about the impact which his journalism has had in French political circles. His articles were, he admits, read by many politicians, but he had "no illusions": a commentator such as himself "has an influence less on the specific moment than in the long term". In his view – and he was surely correct in this – what distinguishes him from other columnists is that his specific judgements were always implicitly integrated in a particular global vision of the world.[73]

Who else, then, in this century has written commentaries of such weight and significance over so long a period? The figure with whom Aron has been most often compared is another journalist and writer on foreign affairs, the American, Walter Lippman,[74] although the Chicago philosopher, Allan Bloom, disagrees:

The comparison is in fact ridiculous, but it was a way of arousing respect for a type of man that is rare, essential to democracy but almost impossible to find in such a regime: someone who educates public opinion and who is at the same time truly wise and knowledgeable. Such was the ideal to which Aron approached. The difference between the two men is very instructive. Lippmann was almost always mistaken on the great questions, on Hitler and Stalin. His instinct was uncertain. He was a snob. His judgements on people were too often wide of the mark (he despised Truman). He was ashamed of being Jewish. His knowledge was superficial, and determined by the necessities of journalism and not by a real love of learning. He always considered power more important than knowledge. Aron had the qualities that were the obverse of these faults. Whilst Lippmann postured and preached, Aron really did the work. He was a companion on whom we could rely to help us judge the events of the modern world.[75]

Nevertheless, a comment which Aron made about Lippmann is perhaps even more applicable to his own work as a journalist and to the philosophy of history that underlies it:

The commentator, especially the one who writes about international politics, is able to point up the significance of current events, even the most fleeting, only by reporting the event in connection with the whole background. In its turn, such an interpretation implies a philosophy of history with a dual obligation: a concept of the relationship between sovereign states, and a view of the fundamental problems posed, in our time, by the nature of these states and the redivision of power. Philosopher of history by necessity, the commentator becomes inevitably a teacher. He is forced to explain to his compatriots the kind of world in which they will have to live, and what they will have to do in order to help their country survive, prosper and grow.[76]

Notes

1. 1981a, pp. 108–9: tr. 1983b, p. 93.
2. Ibid., p. 110: tr. pp. 94–5 (R.C.). Cf. 1983a, p. 195.
3. 1981a, p. 112: tr. p. 96 (R.C.).
4. 1944z^5.
5. 1944y; 1945h, 1945m; 1945o, 1945p.
6. 1945d, 1945e, 1945k.
7. 1946c: tr. 1945c.
8. R. A., interview with the author, 1977. Cf. 1981a, pp. 113–14: tr. p. 98; and 1983a, pp. 195–8.
9. These lectures are unpublished but available in typescript at the Institut Raymond Aron.
10. Bourricaud, 1985, p. 34.
11. Froment-Meurice, 1985, p. 42. For a Marxist view of the course, see Hartman, 1948, 1949.
12. On Corniglion-Molinier, see Chapter 9, above. Simone de Beauvoir recalls that soon after the Liberation, "Aron took us to lunch with Corniglion-Molinier who had been condemned to death by Vichy; his furniture had been confiscated, and he was camping out in a vast, luxurious but empty apartment on the Avenue Gabriel; attentive and charming, he was full of stories about the French in London". Simone de Beauvoir, *La Force des choses* (Paris, 1963), p. 20: tr. (by Richard Howard), *Force of Circumstance* (Harmondsworth, 1965), pp. 9–10.
13. R. A., letter to the author, 1982. Cf. 1983a, pp. 201–2, where he rightly emphasizes that as early as April 1945 he began trying to "free the French from their obsession with Germany".
14. "Le partage de l'Europe", *Point de vue*, 26 July 1945. Discussing the three-power Potsdam conference, Aron wrote: "Everyone hopes for something different from the unification of Germany. The Anglo-Saxons' hope would be that the iron curtain, which for more than two months has been lowered over the demarcation line, will be raised at last. But the Russians see in German unity the chance to extend their ideological influence and the activities of their representatives as far as the west of the Reich".
15. "Démocraties balkaniques", *Point de vue*, 13 September 1945. "The iron curtain", he stated, "has not yet been raised, but the silence has been broken". According to Brewer's Dictionary of Phrase and Fable, the expression was first used by Count Schwerin von Krosigk, the German statesman, in 1945.
16. See Chapter 4, above.
17. See Chapter 6, above.
18. 1981a, p. 108: tr. p. 93.
19. Jean Lacouture, *Malraux, une vie dans le siècle, 1901–1976* (Paris, 2nd edn, 1976), pp. 330–1: tr. (by Alan Sheridan), *André Malraux* (London, 1975), p. 359.
20. Ibid., p. 331: tr. p. 359.
21. See Chapter 8, above. Sperber had served in the French army in 1939–40 and gone into semi-hiding in the South of France before eventually escaping to Switzerland. After the war he settled in Paris and Malraux appointed him Chargé de Mission to advise on the organization of the press, radio and publishing in the French zones

of Germany and Austria. Sperber stayed in his post till 1948, long after Malraux's and Aron's departure from the Ministry. Subsequently he concentrated on writing and in particular published a trilogy of novels, *Et le Buisson devint cendre* (Paris, 1949), *Plus profond que l'abîme* (Paris, 1950), and *La Baie perdue* (Paris, 1953); a further novel, with a Preface by Malraux, *Qu'une Larme dans l'océan* (Paris, 1952); a collection of essays, *Le Talon d'Achille* (Paris, 1957); and an autobiography, *Ces Temps-là*, in three parts: *Porteurs d'eau* (Paris, 1976), *Le Pont inachevé* (Paris, 1977) and *Au-delà de l'Oubli* (Paris, 1979). The playwright, Eugène Ionesco, has called Sperber "one of the most lucid thinkers of our time" (Eugène Ionesco, "Sauver la culture", *Fig.*, 22 July 1976). For a "portrait" of Sperber on his reception of West Germany's *Friedenspries* (Peace Prize), see Fred Kupferman, "Une mémoire européenne", *L'Express* (1690), 2 December 1983. He died in February 1984. For a tribute, see M. J. Lasky/F. Bondy, "Manès Sperber", *Encounter*, June 1984, p. 46.

22. 1981a, pp. 112–13: tr. pp. 96–8.

23. Ibid., p. 119: tr. pp. 102–3.

24. Ibid., p. 113: tr. p. 98 (R.C.). Cf. 1983a, pp. 205–8.

25. 1978b, p. 625. Cf. 1983a, p. 208ff.

26. For the origins and subsequent history of *Combat*, see H. R. Lottman, *Albert Camus: A Biography* (London, 1979).

27. The articles in question are discussed in Chapter 14, below.

28. 1978b, p. 625. Cf. 1981a, p. 115: tr. p. 99 (R.C.): "I don't know why, but they were a real success in *le petit milieu parisien*".

29. The term *éditorialiste* has no exact equivalent in English. Aron was never an anonymous, editorial "leader writer". His articles were always signed and therefore "columnist" is a satisfactory translation, as long as the term is not taken to refer, as it sometimes does in the United States, to a writer who does not belong to the staff of a single newspaper and whose articles are syndicated. The English word Aron himself seemed to prefer is "commentator"(tr. 1959b).

30. 1981a, p. 115: tr. p. 99 (R.C.). Elsewhere Aron has remarked in lighter vein, "Prior to 1939 I composed my editorials aloud in conversation. Subsequently I wrote them down" (ibid., p. 123: tr. p. 106 (R.C.)).

31. Ibid., p. 115: tr. p. 99 (R.C.).

32. Ibid., pp. 115–16: tr. p. 100 (R.C.).

33. "Le moindre mal", *Combat*, 28 April 1946. See Chapter 14, below.

34. Beauvoir, op. cit., p. 86: tr. p. 73.

35. Ibid., p. 87: tr. pp. 73–74.

36. Lottman, op. cit., p. 403.

37. Beauvoir, op. cit., pp. 121–2: tr. p. 107.

38. Lottman, op. cit., pp. 402–3. Cf. 1981a, pp. 117–18; 1983a, pp. 215–18.

39. Lottman, op. cit., p. 415. On Aron's membership of the RPF, see Chapter 14, below.

40. Bourdet and Smadja fell out in 1950 and *Combat* continued publication, under Smadja's ownership, till 1974.

41. 1978b, p. 626. Nevertheless, when, thirty years later in 1977, Aron, who was still with the *Figaro*, suffered a heart-attack, Beuve-Méry wrote him "a very friendly letter", in which he wondered how different the evolution of the two papers would have been if Aron had joined *Le Monde* (1977h, p. 75). See also 1983a, p. 218.

321

42. 1977h, p. 75.
43. 1981a, p. 136: tr. p. 118. See also 1978b, p. 626.
44. 1978b, pp. 624–5. Compare the journalist, Roger Priouret: "One can ask anything of Raymond Aron, save a single hour of his mornings" (Priouret, 1959), and Wolton, 1985, p. 110: ". . . he worked non-stop every day – the morning for writing, the afternoon for meetings, and the evening for reading".
45. Dominique Schnapper, quoted in *Volcano on Ice*, BBC Radio 3, 14 January 1985.
46. An order dated September 30 1944 forbade the publication of all newspapers and periodicals which had continued to appear in what was formerly the Unoccupied Zone two weeks after 11 November 1942.
47. 1944k; reprinted 1946b, pp. 158–9. Compare 1981a, p. 109: tr. p. 94 (R.C.): "Despite a certain number of texts which I did not like, I had always located the *Figaro* on the right side of the barricades".
48. Jacques de Lacretelle, *Face à l'événement: "Le Figaro", 1826–1966* (Paris, 1966), p. 170.
49. Compare the *Figaro* journalist, Denis Perier Daville: " . . .we lived happily in an absolute monarchy tempered by a well-mannered anarchy, that is, with a feeling of complete freedom. To write freely for a newspaper that is successful, respected and has the wind in its sails – what more could a journalist who likes his job ask for?" Denis Perier Daville, *Main basse sur le Figaro* (Paris, 1976), p. 36. Similarly, François Mauriac observed in 1952: "The success of *Le Figaro* stems from the fact that . . . an air of freedom pervades it: not only the ideas but even the moods of each contributor blossom at their ease. No instruction or call-to-order ever restricts us . . .". François Mauriac, "La dégelée", *Fig.*, 28 April 1952.
50. "La France joue sa dernière chance en Afrique", *Fig.*, 12–15 October 1955. See Volume 2, Chapter 3.
51. 1981a, p. 196: tr. p. 168.
52. 1957b.
53. 1958b.
54. 1958j. On Aron and the Algerian War, see Volume 2, Chapter 3.
55. André Lang, *Pierre Brisson: Le journaliste, l'écrivain, l'homme (1896–1964)* (Paris, 1967), pp. 297–8. See also 1977h, p. 75. On his relations with Brisson, see Aron's memoirs (1983a, pp. 223–6).
56. See Chapter 14, below.
57. "La grande épreuve des Etats-Unis", *Fig.*, 8–20 December 1950.
58. 1983a, pp. 241–2. His *Figaro* articles on the Peace Conference, and the "Big Three" Washington Conference which immediately followed it, ran from 5 to 17 September 1951.
59. For Aron's impressions of this voyage, see 1983a, pp. 242–4.
60. "Visite en Israël", *Fig.*, 12, 14 June 1956. See also 1983a, pp. 245–6, and Volume 2, Chapter 2.
61. 1948e. One of those present was the future specialist in international relations, Stanley Hoffmann: ". . . Aron addressed himself in a very bantering way to this audience of young people, full of confidence in their future, on the subject of 'the way to become a journalist'. And he seemed to be saying: 'You'll see, it's not easy . . .'" (Stanley Hoffmann, "Un penseur adapté à nos catégories", *Le Matin*, 18 October 1983).
62. 1948e, p. 71.

63. Ibid., p. 81. Another *Combat* columnist who exhibited this rare talent was Aron himself: e.g., "L'illusion du progrès", *Combat*, 6 November 1946. See Chapter 14, below.

64. 1948e, p. 82. In Aron's own view, his "greatest journalistic success" (1981a, p. 264: tr. p. 224) was an article which he wrote during the 1973 parliamentary election campaign, attacking the "Common Programme" of the Socialists and Communists: "Le programme commun de la gauche ou le cercle carré," *Fig.*, 8 February 1973. See Volume 2, Chapter 17.

65. 1948e, p. 82.

66. Ibid. Aron himself often went some way towards overcoming this difficulty by writing his editorials as a series of articles.

67. Doubtless this was Hippolyte Parigot, Aron's French teacher at the Lycée Condorcet, who used to write for *Le Temps*. See Chapter 1, above.

68. 1948e, p. 83.

69. See Volume 2, Chapter 22.

70. Bundy, 1985, p. 127.

71. Robert Marjolin, interview with the author, 1980.

72. Berger, 1985.

73. 1981a, pp. 197–8: tr. p. 170.

74. E.g., Priouret, 1959, although in Priouret's view Lippmann lacked Aron's philosophical culture and awareness. Lippmann (1889–1974) was a columnist on the *New York Herald Tribune* from 1931 to 1966. See Ronald Steel, *Walter Lippmann and the American Century* (London, 1980).

75. Bloom, 1985, p. 174, n.i.

76. Tr. 1959b, pp. 114–15. Aron went on to describe Lippmann as just such a "political teacher, inspired by a certain philosophy of diplomatic history. It seems to me that the two essays written during the war, *US Foreign Policy* and *US War Aims*, offer a clear and synthesized exposition of this philosophy and make understandable in a larger context the diplomacy the author has recommended during the years since 1945" (ibid., p. 115).

14

The Rassemblement du Peuple Français

On 7 April 1947, in a speech at Strasbourg, General de Gaulle called for that *"rassemblement du peuple français*, which, within the framework of the law, will promote and cause to triumph, over and above differences of opinion, the mighty effort of common salvation and the far-reaching reform of the state". A week later the Rassemblement du Peuple Français (RPF) officially came into being and Aron, who had not been a member of any party since leaving the Socialists twenty years earlier, joined it. It was a decision for which he has often been criticized. Thus, to his steadfast friend and admirer, Manès Sperber, Aron's membership of the RPF was the only position he ever adopted which was "unconvincing and, in the last analysis, completely foreign to his nature", though Sperber is quick to add that it was an episode that was "shortlived and inconsequential".[1]

Why, then, did the wartime author of "La Menace des Césars"[2] and "L'Ombre des Bonapartes"[3] join a movement which has often been called Bonapartist and even fascist and totalitarian? Sperber explains Aron's decision partly, and perhaps fundamentally, in psychological terms: the man of forty was tired of the solitude of the outsider in a fanatical world.[4] Malraux used to say that Aron joined the RPF out of friendship for him. There is, Aron admits, some truth in this. Nevertheless, Malraux's influence should not be exaggerated, since their friendship would never have led Aron to adopt positions in which he did not believe. Aron himself says that no one has ever really understood his reasons for joining the RPF.[5] In order to do so, it is essential to understand his attitude to the problem which dominated French politics in the immediate post-war years – the nature of the regime and in particular the question of France's Constitution.

General de Gaulle, who had become Head of a Provisional Government in September 1944, had decided, in spite of opposition, to hold a referendum on whether to end the Third Republic. This took place in October 1945, at the same time as the election of an Assembly. An overwhelming majority (96 per cent) voted that the Assembly should be constituent and the Third Republic brought to an end; a smaller majority (two-thirds) voted that this Constituent Assembly should have limited powers and that within seven months it should produce constitutional proposals which would be submitted to the electorate in a further referendum.

Aron's initial contribution to the ensuing debate was a carefully argued analysis of the constitutional problem, which he completed that November.[6] France's Constitution would, in his view, be democratic in character, because the psychological and political structure of French society offered no other possibilities; and it would be defined in relation to the Constitution of the Third Republic of 1875, since the habits which had grown up over the past sixty-five years had survived and it was better, as the saying went, "to continue rather than start afresh". In practical terms, he believed, the arguments were over a small number of points: whether there should be one or two Chambers, the powers and composition of an eventual second Chamber, the right of dissolution, and the prerogatives of the President of the Republic.[7]

Aron began by making a powerful case for democratic pluralism – a multi-party system based on free elections – as opposed to the totalitarian monism of a one-party state, on the grounds that only the former was "pacific", "normal" and "natural".[8] However, in order to avoid the political instability which had paralysed the French state in the last twenty years of the Third Republic, governments should be formed directly as a result of elections and not through parliamentary combinations. The only way to ensure this, he argued, was through the threat of dissolution: in a crisis the President of the Republic must have, and if necessary exercise, the optional right to dissolve the Assembly.

But Aron was against a presidential Constitution of the American kind, because it seemed to him that a President who was elected by universal suffrage and was both Head of State and Head of Government would be too narrowly identified with a political party. The Prime Minister should be the man of the parliamentary majority, and the Head of State the man of the nation and not of a party. The Prime Minister should, he thought, be chosen by the President of the Republic rather than elected by the Assembly (though the two should normally coincide), since this allowed more flexibility in a crisis. On balance, Aron was in favour of a second Chamber. Above all, however, the government must be allowed to govern. The Chambers should no longer be free to make and break ministries, as under the Third Republic; but they should remain free to overturn them and provoke new elections. It was nevertheless important to remember, he emphasized in conclusion, that "the vitality of institutions is not determined by constitutional texts; in the end it is men who decide . . .". For in a party-based democracy, "institutions are less important than men, laws than parties, and principles than states of mind".[9]

* * *

Aron completed this essay on the Constitution on the day before General de Gaulle formed his second government – the one in which Aron became Malraux's Directeur de Cabinet and which came to an end when de Gaulle resigned the following January. Aron's attitude to the parties at this time, which is crucial to understanding his motives for joining the RPF, is revealed most clearly in the series of articles he wrote as his journalistic début in *Combat* in April 1946, during the referendum campaign on the Constitution. Until 1939, he argued, France had been a nation of the first rank in the context of European and even world diplomacy. It had chosen its path as circumstances permitted, but within a fairly broad margin of liberty. In the unified post-war world, however, in which events had repercussions throughout the globe and power was almost wholly concentrated in two state-continents, France had lost the greater part of its autonomy. Historically the most fundamental decision, which should dominate all internal preferences, was that of a diplomatic orientation. As far as this choice was concerned (one which was never mentioned, although people thought about it all the time), the line of separation passed somewhere between the Communist Party, which was pro-Moscow, and the Socialist Party, which, like most of the nation, was on the whole pro-Western.[10]

327

Whether one liked it or not, French politics were "magnetized" by the actions of the Communists. Privately, if not publicly, it was in relation to them that each person took up a position. Not that there was anything surprising in this, for the Communist Party was a revolutionary party and experience had shown that a communist revolution set up a totalitarian regime, with a single party, obligatory creed and omnipotent police. For the time being the Communist Party was playing the democratic and parliamentary game, but no one knew for how long. No one even knew if the Party itself knew, because in the end the decision was liable to be taken by others. The Communist Party presented itself as a national party. It had indeed played a considerable part in the Resistance. Millions of good French people supported it, without separating their patriotism from their revolutionary fervour. On the other hand, for years the Party had never questioned the foreign policy of Moscow, whatever was at stake, as the signing of the Germano-Soviet Pact in 1939 illustrated. Today, even supposing that since the dissolution of the Komintern the Party was free of all material attachment, it nevertheless remained, as Blum had put it, bound to the USSR by ties of love. By its aims and its view of foreign policy, the Communist Party was not, therefore, "a party like any other", although the political game entailed treating it as just that. What was the good, people asked, of saying out loud what everyone was whispering in private? Possibly one should resign oneself to silence, Aron replied, but there should be no mistake: this silence was poisoning the atmosphere, because it forced everyone into insincerity.[11]

The simple fact of raising such questions, which were normally reserved for editorial offices, would, Aron realized, earn him the charge of being anti-communist; but he rejected such an accusation, which was usually brought to prevent non-communists from justifying their position.

If anti-communism consists of failing to recognize the virtues of the militants, ignoring the attachment of a majority of the working class to the hope of communism, and forgetting the social reforms which party workers insist are essential, we are not anti-communist. But if, in order to avoid the charge of anti-communism, one has to approve all forms of action, resign oneself to a totalitarian regime, and believe that Stalin is always right and that Bevin's diplomacy is enough "to make a monkey blush", then we shall be willing to accept the accusation and we shall claim the rights of free thought.

No country, in the present world, chooses its destiny freely. A communist-type revolution in the narrow compass of a nation of forty million inhabitants makes no sense. Thus, in the position imposed on us by geography, how could attachment to a Union of Socialist Soviet Republics be brought about peacefully, as long as that Union does not extend to the whole planet?[12]

Turning to the Socialist Party, Aron argued that it was "the microcosm of France as a whole", reflecting as it did the nation's "hesitations, contradictory tendencies, good will, and also its weakness". *Dirigiste* and liberal, at one and the same time, it refused to choose, like the nation itself, and it, too, ended up in precarious compromises. As a workers' party, the Socialist Party would remain the younger sibling of the Communist Party, incapable of shaking off the inferiority complex which paralysed it. Every time it tried to outdo communism on the left or rival it in demagogy, it would fail; but if it presented itself publicly for what it was – a democratic party, committed to social reforms, but anxious to safeguard liberties and resolved to integrate France in the Western world – it would have every chance of success. The Socialist Party was both the party of synthesis and the party which could build bridges. As the party of synthesis, it was trying to construct an economic regime mid-way between capitalism and socialism. Such a regime was neither inconceivable nor unrealizable (the British Labour Party was in the process of demonstrating this). Unfortunately, for the moment, the French Socialists had not even mapped out the key features intellectually. They were rushing into nationalization, without having a clear idea either about how to run the nationalized industries, or how to orient the economy as a whole, or how the nationalized and the free sectors should co-exist.[13]

"France's situation", Aron stressed in his conclusion to the series, "far from justifying indifference, calls on everyone to take a position. Today more than ever, politics is our destiny: everything hangs upon them". On the problem of creating a parliamentary majority, there were three possibilities: a Communist-Socialist coalition; a tripartite majority of Communists, Socialists and the new pro-Gaullist Catholic party – the Mouvement Républicain Populaire (MRP); and the solution which Aron himself favoured, a coalition between the Socialists and the MRP. The latter represented "the majority about which no one breathes a word, but which from many points of view would be the most logical, one which would leave the Communists to one side and the extreme Right to the other, and group together all those who support a kind of Labourism" – in other words, "a union of all those who want liberal socialism and a Western orientation to our diplomacy".[14]

* * *

When, shortly after writing this, Aron joined *Combat* as a regular political commentator, the campaign for the referendum on the Constitution was in full swing. The left-wing majority of Communists and Socialists in the Constituent Assembly had voted for a powerful, single-chamber Assembly and was opposed by the MRP, which wanted to preserve the rights of the President of the Republic. As we have seen, at the end of April Aron published an editorial in which he argued for a *no* vote. "This time", he wrote, "I shall not obey the instructions of the Socialist Party, for which I have regularly voted. . .". In his view, a *no* vote meant three things. First and foremost, it meant that the proposed Constitution, which would institute a single all-powerful Assembly and consecrate the reign of the parties, was bad. Secondly, a *no* vote signified that a Constitution must be acceptable to a large majority of the nation. A Constitution sought to define the rules according to which the peaceful struggle of the parties would take place. It was doomed in advance if half the country rejected it. The weakness of the majority was of little importance where a programme of government was concerned; but when it was a matter of laws which were as fundamental and essential to the opposition as to the party in power, the division of the country into two almost equal blocks was itself proof that the legislators had failed. Finally, whether one liked it or not, a *no* to the referendum implied the rejection of a Socialist-Communist majority. The fate of coalitions between a democratic and a totalitarian party was too familiar: the Socialists – and they knew it – would be the victims. Were people willing to entrust the country's destiny to an opportunistic Communist Party which had never made a mystery of its ambitions? A *no* vote, Aron declared, was a vote for liberty.[15]

This article, as we saw earlier, caused an outcry among many of *Combat*'s staff. Nevertheless, a week later, on 5 May, the electorate voted, albeit narrowly (42 per cent to 37 per cent, with 20 per cent abstentions) against the proposed Constitution. Socialism, Aron argued, had probably been saved by this defeat. Since France had rejected any possibility of a totalitarian adventure, it was now necessary to combine social reforms with the safeguarding of formal liberties, and this implied the democratic socialism of Jaurès and Blum. The collaboration of the Communist Party in the reconstruction of France was, said Aron, to be welcomed, but only if that collaboration was not a step towards the complete seizure of power and it left freedom to manoeuvre in foreign policy.[16]

Fresh elections for a new Constituent Assembly were now called for the following month and on this occasion the Socialists lost votes to the Communists and the MRP, which became the largest party. The Left (Communists and Socialists) no longer had a majority in the Assembly. However, Aron still felt unable to give his support to the Socialist Party.

"Three kinds of men", he observed, "found themselves in the Resistance: Communists, humanists and Christians. The humanists, those who believe in neither God nor Stalin, are still looking for the party which will translate their message into daily action. Communists and Christians have each found a party which embodies their convictions and corresponds to their hopes".[17] On the day of the election, Aron argued in *Combat* for a second Chamber, a President of the Republic with strong powers, and the separation of powers.[18] Two weeks later, however, General de Gaulle, who had stayed silent since his withdrawal in January, re-entered the political scene. In a speech at Bayeux commemorating the Liberation, he pronounced himself in favour of a semi-presidential regime. "Was the occasion", Aron asked, "a ceremony of remembrance or the inauguration of a new movement?" The Constitution outlined by the General, "midway between the British parliamentary and the American presidential systems", was, Aron commented, "probably not viable in periods of calm", although one day the parties, however reluctantly, might be forced to try it.[19]

Nevertheless, Aron announced that this time he would vote for the Constitution, though with reluctance. In May, he explained, he had voted not only against a bad Constitution, but also against a likely Socialist-Communist majority in government. Furthermore, he had hoped that a revision would allow a real improvement to be made in the country's institutions. Such hopes had not been fulfilled. The two Constitutions were very similar, with an all-powerful Assembly, a second Chamber which had no veto, and a President whose powers were feeble (he had no right to choose the Prime Minister or dissolve the Chamber). No steps had been taken to ensure that a serious measure could be delayed for several months or sanctioned by new elections. No institution endowed with real powers had been raised above party interests, i.e., the will of party headquarters. It was true that politics was only marginally dependent on constitutions and that these, in their turn, depended as much on men as on texts. Yet the least one could say was that the opportunity had not been seized to try to improve a system whose faults were readily apparent. "For the citizen", Aron concluded, "abstention will probably be the only means of showing both his desire to put an end to the provisional and his repugnance for the proposed Constitution. Perhaps, even, a sufficiently large number of abstentions will make the revision of a supposedly definitive Constitution possible in the near future".[20]

It was difficult therefore, in his view, to disagree with the opinion of the constitutional proposals expressed by General de Gaulle: the

Assembly would be omnipotent and the President of the Republic and the Prime Minister would have no real authority.[21] However, he did not believe that the General was motivated by a desire for personal power. From the time of the Liberation till his resignation, he had shown "a sense of authority, feeling for the state and respect for legality. The impression he gave was of a legitimate sovereign, not a usurper or tyrant". On the other hand, Aron felt no sympathy for the recently formed Gaullist Union: "We have no relish for those unions which are above parties, but which, at the same time, consider putting up candidates". He was also concerned about "the political origins of certain neo-Gaullists": they had nothing in common with the Resistance.[22] In his Bayeux speech, de Gaulle had proposed that the President of the Republic should choose his Prime Minister, who would then choose his Cabinet and present it to the National Assembly, on the British model. This "classic mechanism of representative institutions" did not, Aron wrote, present a threat to democracy, as had been claimed. "Perhaps it is enough to go forward along this path for the Trojan War not to take place and to enable personal power to rally, without too much difficulty, to a parliamentary regime".[23]

Meanwhile, at the end of September, the MRP, the Communists and the Socialists all voted in favour of the new constitutional proposals. These would, Aron correctly predicted, probably be ratified by the country. "At the risk", he wrote ironically, "of satisfying nobody (as is *Combat*'s wont), I shall rejoice moderately in the agreement of the Big Three, and I shall only accord a resigned adherence to the Charter of the Fourth Republic". It was still a precarious Constitution.[24] When, therefore, ten days later, de Gaulle said a firm "no" to the proposals, Aron welcomed this as "a good piece of news, because it brings some light into an impossibly confused situation". De Gaulle had, he wrote, rejected the idea of presidential and personal power, declaring that he was only concerned with the separation and balance of powers. He had thus clarified his somewhat ambiguous earlier statements, which seemed to imply a presidential regime. But Aron would, he declared, still vote "yes": the Fourth Republic needed a Constitution.[25] The referendum itself was held a few days later, on 13 October, and resulted in the Constitution being accepted by nine million votes (53 per cent) to eight million (47 per cent) but with eight and a half million abstentions – the high figure for which Aron himself had hoped. It was, he commented, "unarguable and fortunate that the small majority obtained by the Constitution leaves open the eventual possibility of a revision".[26]

A National Assembly now had to be elected and Aron expressed himself hesitant about how to vote. There was, he reasoned in *Combat*, little prospect of the united and resolute government that France's reconstruction required. As long as the Socialist Party persisted in assuming its main enemy to be the Right and the trade unions continued to obey the instructions of the Communist Party, the only solution was the anxious search for the lesser of two evils.[27] A few days later, however, at the height of the election campaign, Aron produced an editorial of outstanding quality on "the illusion of progress"[28] – the kind of *prise de position* which, as he himself said of Camus, "reminds us of values in the midst of the daily political battle".[29] At the risk of shattering people's illusions, Aron wrote, it seemed to him that the Soviet myth was already in decline because in the long run the gulf between myth and reality would become clear to everyone. When the socialist system took the form of a compulsory creed, pitiless discipline (strikes and opposition were a crime), a ubiquitous police force and an inequality between manual and white-collar workers as great as that under capitalism, the least that could be said was that such "liberation" did not fulfil the dreams of the humanists. French communism fed on revolutionary romanticism, and the misapprehension would not remain hidden for ever. Such thoughts were, Aron granted, far removed from electoral arguments and political games. And yet, he asked, was not one of the profound causes of the mediocrity into which the party struggle had fallen the death of our gods? It was often said, and rightly, that only communism offered a total doctrine allowing total commitment. But this doctrine survived thanks to its ambiguities. A much greater threat than the blindness of those who clung to an illusion was the general scepticism. Fanaticism was the reverse of the nihilism announced by Nietzsche half a century before. It had to be recognized – and Aron did not, he said, mean this unkindly – that the republicans and the socialists had not so far aroused the kind of fervour which the secular religions stirred up. Myths could not be conjured up to order, especially when summoned by intellectuals. He would therefore refrain from dogmatism or prophecy, though he would risk one observation:

Man does not resign himself to the image which the manipulators of souls and the propaganda-specialists persist in imposing on him. In the age of the camps of slow death, at a time when the deportation of millions of human beings no longer even manages to move us, perhaps the simple rights of man, authentically stated, will take on a new freshness and an unexpected force. A living faith can grow from humble and eternal truths.[30]

As a result of the elections for the National Assembly, which were held on 10 November, the Communists became the leading party with 28 per cent of the votes, followed by the MRP (26 per cent) and the Socialists (18 per cent). The Socialist Party had, in Aron's view, missed its opportunity at the time of the Liberation when, as it renewed itself through contact with the Resistance, it could have become the head and inspiration of a vast Labourite formation. It should now, he urged, be less cautious and dissociate itself from the Communist Party,[31] for the dividing-line between liberalism and authoritarianism in economic matters lay not between the old Right and the old Left, but somewhere within the Socialist Party.[32] As for the election of the second Chamber, the senatorial Conseil de la République, through a complicated mixture of proportional representation and designation by the National Assembly, Aron argued that the electoral laws had accentuated the division of the country into two groups, one pro-communist and the other anti-communist. The so-called "Chambre de réflexion" would simply reflect the first Chamber.[33]

In December the veteran Socialist leader, Léon Blum, was chosen as Prime Minister in an all-Socialist caretaker government. "The success which from the bottom of our heart we wish him", wrote Aron, "is a tribute to his person, rather than to his ideas", although it seemed to Aron a pity that the Assembly could only find someone from the previous Republic.[34] In the following month the Socialist, Vincent Auriol, was elected President of the Republic, and another Third Republican Socialist, Ramadier, succeeded Blum as Prime Minister a few days later. Thus began a further period of "tripartism", a coalition of Socialists, MRP and Communists which was to last until the beginning of May. At the end of March, however, de Gaulle made the speech at Bruneval which foreshadowed the creation of the Rassemblement du Peuple Français. France's "tragic dilemma", Aron wrote in *Combat* two days later, was that it was faced with "either a coalition of opposites, vegetating in mediocrity and at every moment threatened by paralysis, or with scission, with the risk of civil war and recourse to authoritarian methods":

Perhaps there is no third possibility, as both the supporters and the opponents of General de Gaulle basically believe. I am not so sure, however. Potentially a majority of democrats does exist and, provided they overcome quarrels that are minor and outmoded, they could restore life to Parliament by re-establishing the distinction, essential in a democracy, between majority and opposition. In the absence of such a realignment, no regime will be viable – either today's or the one people will try to set up in the hour of distress.[35]

334

A week after Aron wrote these words General de Gaulle made his Strasbourg speech, in which he called for the Rassemblement du Peuple Français. He had, as Malraux put it, crossed the Rubicon.[36] "In truth", Aron commented the next day, "there is little doubt about the justice of the critique". The real question was a different one: how to overcome the problem. "No one", he continued, "is thinking of a *rassemblement* against Parliament. The aim is to replace fragmented coalitions with a majority that is capable of conceiving a programme and putting it into effect. A man's prestige can help in the formation of this majority, but in the last analysis what is essential is to rally round ideas with a view to action".[37]

* * *

Thus Aron joined the RPF because of his hostility to the Constitution and working of the Fourth Republic. But there was another reason, too. He had a guilty conscience at not having played a greater part in the Gaullist movement during the war. He now regretted the "one-sided and exaggerated" attitudes which he had adopted towards the General in London. After the Allied landings in North Africa he should, he believed, have thrown himself wholeheartedly behind de Gaulle, instead of standing aloof with his "reservations, criticisms, second thoughts and suspicions".[38]

Another issue on which Aron saw eye to eye with General de Gaulle and the RPF was communism. The RPF was strongly anti-communist. To de Gaulle they were "separatists" and "Public Enemy Number One"; France was in grave danger, externally from the USSR and internally from the Communist Party. As one of the most reliable analysts of Gaullism, Jean Touchard, reminds us,

In order to understand the origins and rise of the RPF, it is important to recall the climate and principal events of 1947: the world, divided into two blocs, was experiencing the beginnings of the Cold War. On 5 May 1947, the Communist Ministers were excluded from Ramadier's Government. The conference of Communist Parties in Poland, in September 1947, saw the creation of the Kominform; parallel to this, the French Communists were hardening their position in their own country, in the face of a government unable to overcome the difficulties of daily life; bread rationing...was introduced in August 1947; in October and November, huge strikes shook the country – a country that was a prey to fear of civil war and also to fear of a Russian invasion. No doubt such fear appears totally unfounded and improbable to us today, but it was very widespread in the France of 1947.[39]

335

It was the time of the Prague coup, the trials and purges in the "People's Democracies", the revelations of Soviet concentration camps and police-terror, and "the period when half the French intellectuals regarded as 'slimy rats' those who so much as doubted the democratic virtues and aesthetic genius of Stalin. It was a time worthy of the wars of religion".[40] De Gaulle, too, in his public speeches (though it is also clear that he sincerely believed what he said) helped create an atmosphere of impending disaster, to which Malraux added "his touch of personal pathos: the aesthetic of the Apocalypse".[41]

Malraux, "perhaps the most active and steadfast of the militants for the Restoration"[42] and the movement's most prestigious orator, was one of the two leading figures in the creation of the RPF. The other was Jacques Soustelle. Earlier they had formed a Working Party for the Return of General de Gaulle (Comité d'Etudes pour le Retour du Général de Gaulle), of which Aron was a member together with other "Gaullist intellectuals" like Georges Pompidou, Gaston Palewski and Michel Debré.[43] However, Malraux and Soustelle had differing conceptions of the RPF. Malraux had a poetic view of politics and history; during this period his "romantic catastrophism", as Aron put it, "triumphed over his sense of reality".[44] Soustelle, on the other hand, took a more "legalistic" view of the RPF, seeking to create a political organization.[45]

The movement was in fact structured along the lines which de Gaulle had proposed for the French Constitution in his speech at Bayeux: de Gaulle was its President and it had a cabinet, the Executive Committee, in which Malraux was responsible for "propaganda", together with a prime ministerial Secretary-General, Soustelle. There were also two consultative Assemblies – the parliamentary National Congress, and the senatorial National Council. The latter contained 140 members – 120 elected by the Congress and twenty *notables* who were nominated by the movement's Directorate (the President and the Executive Committee), though in practice by de Gaulle. Aron was one such nominated member of the National Council, together with Paul Claudel and Albert Ollivier.[46]

The task of the Council, which met for three days three times a year, was to work out the RPF's long-term philosophy and general policy-goals. In 1949, at the Lille Congress, Aron was chosen to act as *rapporteur* on one of its most important study groups, concerned with the "Association Capital-Travail". Its aim was to promote cooperation between workers and management in order to establish legally binding contracts over wages and salaries, stimulate production for the benefit of all and thus transcend Marxist notions of exploitation and class struggle. However, Aron himself was considered as "something of a sceptic" in RPF policy-forming circles – not, he acknowledges, without justification, since he attempted to translate "this vague and generous idea" (which foreshadowed later ideas of "worker participation") into a certain number of "practical and prosaic" measures.[47]

* * *

The initial success of the RPF was spectacular. At the beginning of May, only three weeks after General de Gaulle's Strasbourg speech, the RPF had received over 800,000 requests for membership. Support continued to grow throughout 1947 and in October the movement claimed one-and-a-half million members. But the first important test came with the local elections held that month. The result was a landslide victory for the RPF, which won about 40 per cent of the votes, capturing the largest cities in France, as well as over half the departmental capitals.

Commenting on the elections in *Le Figaro*,[48] Aron observed that General de Gaulle's resignation in January 1946, surprising as it might have appeared at the time, now seemed logical. After the election of the first Constituent Assembly in October 1945, the parties held the reality of power. De Gaulle, with no group or party supporting him, was gradually losing his authority. He was encountering increasing economic difficulties, without having either the taste to study them or an overall conception of how to overcome them. He was having to take on the increasingly illusory role of arbiter, in the name of a national unity whose fiction had not survived the war. As none of the existing parties reflected his own views, he was unable to join the party battle. He was not yet willing to abandon the Gaullism of unanimity in order to launch a political party. There had first to be an intermediate step: the unrestrained operation of the party system.

That experiment had now been carried out and the result was conclusive, if not in the eyes of the majority, at any rate in the eyes of a significant portion of the country. What was at issue, Aron stressed, was not the principle of the electoral system, nor even the division of power between the legislature and the executive, but the powerlessness of governments. This sprang, he argued, from the incoherence of the majorities and the massive and encroaching strength of the trade unions and especially the Confédération Générale de Travail (CGT), which had become a mere tool for Communist Party manoeuvres. As long as this structure, which was not so much constitutional as social and political, remained unchanged, the regime would be paralysed and the country condemned to stagnation and chaos.

On the other hand, if one reconstituted not a national union (for that only made sense in time of war) but a homogeneous majority, if one wrested the unions from the grip of the Communist Party, if one succeeded in restoring them to their legitimate function of defending occupational interests, then the parliamentary system, whose decline had been precipitated by the crystallization of social groups, would have another chance. It was legitimate to wonder if the RPF could fulfil this task; but there could be no doubt that the task was necessary. The RPF had a strength of purpose which was perhaps directed against the weight of history. At a time when everything conspired to reinforce mass parties and dictatorial unions, it attacked them both, in order to restore a margin of liberty to individuals and the state. "Strong powers and free citizens: the phrase has a Radical ring to it – as long as the first term does not crush the second".[49]

Thus Aron had no illusions about the wrong turning towards dictatorship which the RPF might take, and for this reason he urged that the RPF should combine with the Centre. "For the first time", he wrote a few days later, "one can see the possibility of a government supported by a homogeneous majority. But the anti-communist democrats must not be driven into the arms of the Stalinists by a fear of Caesarism". The choice made by the Centrists, who till now had been incapable of governing on their own, would be "laden with historical significance". Much depended on the way in which the losers reacted to their defeat, but also on the way in which the winners used their victory.[50]

The RPF's plan was either to win an absolute majority (which was out of the question) or to form a majority with the Communists. This could have compelled the parties of the Fourth Republic – "the third force" – to accept a revision of the Constitution.[51] But it was not to be. Between 1948 and 1950 the movement became a gigantic spectacle as General de Gaulle, "stage-managed" by Malraux, proceeded on a majestic Tour de France:

For three years Charles de Gaulle was a huge Gallic druid confronting the Tartars and Helots of the system, a tall silhouette and a mighty voice, with lighting and sound-effects by the director of L'Espoir. Music, lights, ornamental lakes, crowds in the shadows giving vent to their hopes and anger, platforms draped with the tricolour and balconies looking down over the shouting multitude, strong-arm attendants and short-sharp slogans – everything was done to give the great ceremonial a sacred, militant, sonorous character and to keep the crowds finely tuned and intensely responsive.[52]

338

None of this was likely to appeal to Aron; nor does it seem to have convinced the majority of French people, as the much heralded cataclysm failed to materialize and the Fourth Republic, unloved but tolerated, continued on its way. Although the RPF polled respectably in the elections for the Senate in November 1948[53] and in the cantonal elections of March 1949, it had in fact been in decline since the spectacular successes of October 1947. The real test, however, came with the General Election of June 1951, and this proved to be a setback for the movement. The RPF, with four million votes (21 per cent) was soundly beaten by the Communist Party, which polled a million more (27 per cent), although because of the new system of electoral alliances (apparentements), the RPF, with 117 seats, was the largest group in Parliament (even here, however, the number fell far short of the two hundred deputies it had hoped for). A year later General de Gaulle declared his indifference to the future of the RPF and Aron adopted the same attitude.[54] The final blow came in the municipal elections of April 1953. These were a disaster for the RPF, which lost half of its seats, and in the following month de Gaulle disbanded it as a parliamentary group.

* * *

The RPF published a weekly, *Le Rassemblement*, to which Aron contributed on five occasions between June 1948 and September 1949 (three of the articles being extracts from his book, *Le Grand Schisme*);[55] but although the publication was run by three talented ex-*Combat* journalists, Ollivier, Pia and Jean Chauveau, it was not a success.[56] Aron had in fact stopped writing about France's internal politics in *Le Figaro* at the end of 1948.[57] Nevertheless, there were some "difficult moments" when *Le Rassemblement* attacked *Le Figaro*, quoting a number of "disagreeable" texts that had appeared in the paper during the war. Aron offered to resign, but Brisson would not hear of it.[58]

Somewhat more successful was the RPF's monthly periodical, *Liberté de l'esprit*, to which Aron became a major contributor. The review had the same title as a series which Aron had been editing for the publisher, Calmann-Lévy, since 1947, the *Collection "Liberté de l'Esprit"*. This series, which he was to continue editing until the end of his life, has become one of the most famous and enduring in contemporary French publishing. In its early years it brought to the French public the work of such writers as James Burnham, Crane Brinton, Denis Brogan, Geoffrey Gorer, Basil Liddell Hart, Léon Poliakov, Bertram Wolfe, George Kennan, Salvador de Madariaga and Herbert Lüthy, as well as publishing the French edition of Koestler and others' *The God that Failed* with an Epilogue by Aron.[59]

The review, *Liberté de l'esprit*, first appeared in February 1949. Founded under Malraux's auspices, and edited by General de Gaulle's former Private Secretary, Claude Mauriac (son of François), it explicitly sought to be open to a variety of points of view, including those opposed to RPF doctrine. Its ambition was to rival the other great periodicals of the time such as *Les Temps modernes*, *Esprit* and *La Nouvelle Revue française*. It never achieved this goal, though it did publish pieces by Malraux, Thierry Maulnier, Roger Caillois, Pascal Pia, Jean Paulhan, Albert Ollivier and Jules Monnerot. During its brief life Aron contributed some twenty articles to *Liberté de l'esprit*, but with the demise of the RPF in 1953, it closed down.[60]

* * *

Aron's relations with General de Gaulle were "good" during the RPF period. Aron went to see him several times and they had some "interesting" political discussions together. They even had personal conversations because, at the end of 1950, Aron was struck by a private grief: his daughter, Emmanuelle, died of leukaemia at the age of six-and-a-half. Six months before that a Down's Syndrome child had been born to the Arons. De Gaulle, who himself had a mentally handicapped daughter, wrote Aron a "very moving" letter. Aron went to see him and de Gaulle spoke of his own misfortunes. For a few years, then, there were "genuine" relations between the two men, but the General was aware that Aron had not become "a trusty vassal".[61]

Their last meeting occurred in the summer of 1953, when Aron was on holiday not far from Colombey-les-Deux Eglises:

I rang at the gate to the General's property and, as he was away, I left my card and address. A few days later I received an invitation from him. My wife and I therefore had occasion to enter La Boisserie and know its rites: tea, then the General took me to his study and read me a passage from his *Memoirs*, the portrait of the Marshal. Afterwards, a walk in the garden. He referred to a lecture that I had delivered under his chairmanship; I cannot recall who organized it, but I do remember the words the General spoke after me. The lecture had been on France's economic situation and in the course of it I had put forward the idea – one which is commonplace enough – that the French occasionally carry out a revolution, but never any reforms. The General had rightly corrected me: "The French only carry out reforms in the midst of a revolution". And he recalled the reforms accomplished immediately after the Liberation.[62]

But Aron was never a Gaullist in the way that, say, Malraux was and de Gaulle recognized the fact. On one occasion, in 1961, after Aron had written an article – which he subsequently regretted – criticizing the General ("Adieu au gaullisme"),[63] de Gaulle remarked to Malraux, "Aron has never been a Gaullist". If to be a Gaullist was to be the General's faithful servant or to believe in him whatever one's own opinions, then Aron admits that he was never a Gaullist – either before the Liberation or after. Even during the RPF period, Aron continued to express opinions that diverged from those of the General on a number of issues. Yet, in a sense and at different times, Aron was, he says, a Gaullist. At the Liberation, for example, he thought that de Gaulle's government was "by far the best" and that he should give it his support. In 1958 he thought that de Gaulle's return to power, although the conditions were "unpleasant", was to be welcomed, because with him as Head of Government there was a chance that France would be capable of taking a decision over Algeria. But the manner of Aron's Gaullism "could not satisfy" the General. In order to be a "true" Gaullist, one had to have faith in de Gaulle and modify one's own convictions in accordance with his. Aron could not, he says, do that; but this did not prevent him either becoming Malraux's Directeur de Cabinet or joining the RPF.[64]

Aron's friendship with Malraux did not ("unfortunately") last until the end. Malraux became "very solitary and withdrawn". As one of General de Gaulle's ministers, he was frequently "irritated" by Aron's writings. Aron still saw him from time to time and retained the admiration and affection which he had felt for years, but "with age, distance and separation, a feeling of sadness weighed upon us". Aron does not believe it was the inadequacy of his Gaullism which was the basic cause of their gradual growing apart, but "something more personal", connected with the latter part of Malraux's life.[65]

* * *

A final judgement on the RPF is not easy and opinions differ sharply on the nature of the movement. "Le RPF", said Malraux, to whom most of the *bons mots* on the movement are attributable, "c'est le métro", by which he meant that support for it came mainly from lower middle-class and white-collar workers.[66] Alexander Werth has called the RPF "essentially totalitarian" and de Gaulle a "fascist demagogue" and "French Führer".[67] On the other hand, to Christian Purtschet, author of the most detailed study of the movement, the RPF, with its stress on the pre-eminent authority of the Head of State, the importance it gave to

341

the Sovereign People and its emphasis on social order, was certainly Bonapartist, but not fascist.[68] Jean Touchard, however, who has written an excellent study of Gaullist doctrine, is sceptical about attempts to locate the RPF in even a Bonapartist tradition. De Gaulle, he argues, never sought to attain power through a coup d'état but by parliamentary means; his criticism was aimed not at Parliament as an institution, but at the political parties, and he "never showed the slightest sympathy for Napoleon III, General Boulanger or the anti-parliamentary leagues of the 1930s".[69]

Aron himself, writing in *Le Grand Schisme* in 1948, admitted that the movement was in the Bonapartist tradition, but denied that it was fascist. Even its Bonapartism differed from its nineteenth-century forerunners in the personality of its leader: while in power de Gaulle had always shown a concern for legality and his aim now was a presidential democracy, not despotism. The Rassemblement itself had nothing in common with a totalitarian party either structurally or ideologically. It was undeniable that most of its votes came from the Right but its leadership, born of the Resistance, came partly from the Left. In any case, he asked, what did the words "Left" and "Right" mean now that the extreme Left sought to set up a totalitarian regime and despised liberty? Even if they had wanted to, the Gaullists would not have been able to install a fascist regime, because people were no longer susceptible to nationalistic fervour. Nevertheless, the question remained: in the face of communist subversion, could parliamentary democracy adapt to the requirements of a modern society? The RPF was a reaction to that crisis.[70]

Three years later, Aron did not see any necessity to modify his judgement. The Gaullism of the RPF, he wrote in *Les Guerres en chaîne*,

belongs to the Bonapartist tradition, which is specifically French. It combines the appeal to the soldier and the appeal to the people; it combines radical, republican, cockade-wearing followers, as well as conservatives, from the west, north and east of France. It does not rely on the rootless masses, revolutionary out of resentment, as German fascism did, but on heterogeneous masses, more conservative than revolutionary; some faithful to democratic slogans, but with a taste for authority, others traditionalists. But the Gaullist group has neither the strength nor the vices of the fascist parties. The brakes on authority in France are strangely powerful. For lack of an ideology, of popular fanaticism, of an organized party, a Gaullist government, should there ever be one, does not seem likely to break away from the traditions of a more or less clearly presidential republic.[71]

That prediction turned out, in 1958, to be correct.

Notes

1. Sperber, 1971, p. 548.
2. 1942q.
3. 1943o.
4. Sperber, op. cit., p. 548.
5. 1981a, p. 162: tr. 1983b, p. 138.
6. 1945u. *Le Monde*, in a brief notice (4 May 1946), called it "an important pamphlet". For a recent analysis, see Casanova, 1985.
7. 1945u, p. 84.
8. Ibid., p. 92.
9. Ibid., pp. 131, 133. In his memoirs Aron stated that he had reread this article with "agreeable surprise", although he believed it contained "a cardinal mistake" – a failure to make explicit, from the outset, the political content of the constitutional debate, i.e., the triangular battle which developed in France as a result of the war and the Occupation (1983a, p. 210).
10. "La scène politique", *Combat*, 14 April 1946.
11. "La scène politique: II. Le parti communiste français", *Combat*, 16 April 1946. Reprinted 1985b.
12. Ibid.
13. "La scène politique: IV. Le parti socialiste", *Combat*, 18 April 1946.
14. "La scène politique: VII. En quête d'une majorité", *Combat*, 23 April 1946.
15. "Le moindre mal", *Combat*, 28 April 1946.
16. "Le socialisme sauvé par sa défaite?", *Combat*, 10 May 1946.
17. "Le christianisme social au pouvoir", *Combat*, 5 June 1946.
18. "Du jeu électoral aux réalités politiques", *Combat*, 2 June 1946.
19. "L'Etat et les partis", *Combat*, 18 June 1946.
20. "Que faire?", *Combat*, 10 September 1946.
21. "De l'histoire à la politique", *Combat*, 20 September 1946.
22. "Pouvoir personnel?", *Combat*, 22 September 1946.
23. "Du pouvoir personnel au régime parlementaire", *Combat*, 25 September 1946.
24. "Une deuxième Constitution provisoire", *Combat*, 29 September 1946.
25. "Le 'Non' du Général de Gaulle", *Combat*, 10 October 1946.
26. "Le révisionnisme", *Combat*, 17 October 1946.
27. "L'unique problème", *Combat*, 3 November 1946.
28. "L'illusion du progrès", *Combat*, 6 November 1946.
29. 1948e, p. 81. See Chapter 13, above.
30. "L'illusion du progrès", *Combat*, 6 November 1946.
31. "Tactique socialiste", *Combat*, 15 November 1946.
32. "Union des gauches?", *Combat*, 1 December 1946.
33. "Réflexion ou reflet?", *Combat*, 26 November 1946. The Communists won 27 per cent of the seats in the Senate, the MRP 22 per cent and the Socialists 20 per cent.
34. "Autorité personnelle", *Combat*, 14 December 1946.
35. "Dilemme français", *Combat*, 1 April 1947.
36. It was Malraux who is reported to have later said of the RPF: "Le général de Gaulle nous a menés jusqu'au Rubicon, mais pour nous faire pêcher à la ligne" ("General

de Gaulle took us to the Rubicon, but then told us to get out our fishing-rods").

37. "En quête d'une majorité", *Combat*, 8 April 1947.

38. 1981a, p. 162: tr. p. 139 (R.C.).

39. Jean Touchard, *Le Gaullisme, 1940–1969* (Paris, 1978), pp. 99–100.

40. Jean Lacouture, *Malraux, une vie dans le siècle, 1901–1976* (Paris, 2nd edn, 1976), p. 347: tr. (by Alan Sheridan), *André Malraux* (London, 1975), p. 374. The epithet "*rats visqueux*" was Sartre's.

41. Ibid., p. 340: tr. p. 368.

42. Ibid., p. 335.

43. Ibid. Cf. 1981a, p. 165: tr. p. 141. Aron talks of Pompidou's "simplicity, good sense and impartiality" at such meetings (1983a, p. 230); but in his memoirs the former President chose (for whatever reasons) to refer to Aron as "describing the economic and monetary situation with great clarity and on that basis making confident predictions that were not confirmed by the facts" – particularly in connection with the problem of inflation in September 1948, after the formation of the Queuille Government. Georges Pompidou, *Pour rétablir une vérité* (Paris, 1982), pp. 51, 63–4.

44. 1981a, p. 122: tr. p. 105 (R.C.).

45. Touchard, op. cit., p. 97.

46. Christian Purtschet, *Le Rassemblement du Peuple Français, 1947–1953* (Paris, 1965), pp. 67ff.

47. 1981a, p. 165: tr. p. 141 (R.C.). Compare 1983a, p. 261. On the Association Capital-Travail, see Purtschet, op. cit., pp. 267–74.

48. "Du Gaullisme au RPF", *Fig.*, 23 October 1947.

49. Ibid.

50. "Portée d'une victoire électorale", *Fig.*, 26 October 1947.

51. 1981a, p. 166: tr. p. 142.

52. Lacouture, op. cit., pp. 342–3: tr. pp. 369–70 (R.C.).

53. "Nostalgie de la IIIe République", *Fig.*, 11 November 1948.

54. 1981a, p. 166: tr. p. 142.

55. "Il ne suffit pas de négocier pour s'entendre", *Le Rassemblement*, 5 June 1948 (on the proposed Washington-Moscow talks); three articles based on *Le Grand Schisme* (30 October, 6 November, 20 November 1948); and finally, "La Grande Bretagne et l'Europe", 24 September 1949.

56. Janine Mossuz, *André Malraux et le Gaullisme* (Paris, 1970), p. 77. See also Lacouture, op. cit., p. 342: tr. p. 369.

57. "Nostalgie de la IIIe République", *Fig.*, 11 November 1948.

58. 1981a, pp. 165–6: tr. p. 142.

59. 1950f. By the end of Aron's life, approximately a hundred titles had been published in the series, including works by Vance Packard, J. K. Galbraith, Hannah Arendt, Bertrand de Jouvenel, Richard Löwenthal, Arthur Koestler, Herman Khan, J. L. Talmon, Milovan Djilas, Zbigniew Brzezenski and George Lichtheim.

60. Other contributors to *Liberté de l'esprit* included Max-Pol Fouché, René Tavernier, Roger Nimier, Robert Poujade, Jean Lescure, Stanislas Fumet, Gaeton Picon, Jacques Lassaigne, Léon Werth, Pierre de Boisdeffre, Georges Cattaui, Jacques Soustelle, Henri Jeanson, Michel Debré, Branko Lazitch, André Stibio, Jean Chauveau, Claude Delmas, Jacques Robichon, Louis Sigean and Albert Palle.

Aron also spoke at some of the monthly "Conférences pour 'La Liberté de l'esprit'" organized by the RPF under the patronage of the review. Aimed at "la jeunesse intellectuelle", their object was to "treat the major aesthetic, ethical, economic and political problems of our time with an unswerving attitude of good faith, understanding and spiritual rigour".

61. 1981a, pp. 164–5: tr. p. 141 (R.C.).
62. 1983a, p. 235.
63. 1961m.
64. 1981a, p. 121: tr. pp. 104–5 (R.C.).
65. Ibid., pp. 122–3: tr. pp. 105–6 (R.C.).
66. Lacouture, op. cit., p. 341: tr. p. 368.
67. Alexander Werth, *De Gaulle: A Political Biography* (new edn, Harmondsworth, 1967), Ch. 6.
68. Purtschet, op. cit., pp. 128–39.
69. Touchard, op. cit., p. 125.
70. 1948a, pp. 225–6.
71. 1951a, pp., 327–8: tr. 1954a, p. 255.

15

The Break with Sartre

———

French thought, as Thibaudet[1] was fond of saying, develops through dialogues. We are not only thinking of what Barrès[2] used to call the diversity of France's spiritual families: in any one period, within a single family, French ideas find their most precise form of expression in the opposition between two men who present either the two most characteristic differences of emphasis within the same set of aspirations, or the two most extreme attitudes conceivable at that time, or indeed in any other era.

These words, written by Aron in 1942 about Montesquieu and Rousseau,[3] could equally well be applied to his own "dialogue" with Sartre, a dialogue which was to begin shortly after the war and to span a period of thirty-five years till the latter's death in 1980.

The intellectual atmosphere in Paris at the time of the Liberation has been evoked by Simone de Beauvoir, both in her novel, *Les Mandarins*,[4] and in her memoirs.[5] Among the "exiles" whose return she describes was Aron. "Although", she wrote, "he wasn't given to effusiveness, when he appeared one morning at the Café de Flore, we fell into each other's arms".[6] As early as September 1944, the month in which he returned, Aron joined Sartre and Simone de Beauvoir in setting up the editorial board of a new review, to be called *Les Temps modernes*. Relatively unknown before the war, Sartre had already achieved fame in intellectual and literary circles as the philosopher, novelist and playwright of "existentialism". Apolitical in the 1930s, he had now discovered the moral and political principle of *engagement* ("commitment") and had grown much closer to the Communists. He and Aron's other friend, Malraux, had in fact moved in opposite political directions and the two men did not like one another. Aron liked them both – "but never together, because there was practically no conversation between Malraux and Sartre".[7]

Not surprisingly, therefore, Malraux declined an invitation to join the editorial board of *Les Temps modernes*. Camus was too busy with *Combat*, but its other members were the Surrealist poet, writer and ethnographer Michel Leiris, the philosopher Maurice Merleau-Ponty, the journalist Albert Ollivier, and the former editor of *La Nouvelle Revue française*, Jean Paulhan. "In those days", as Simone de Beauvoir put it, "none of these names clashed".[8] Although before the war Sartre had been less "anti-Munich" than Aron, there had never been any serious political disagreements between them.[9] Sartre's wartime letters to Simone de Beauvoir and the notebooks he kept while in the army during the phoney war make several references to Aron. In his notebook for 1 February 1940, for example, he wrote of the year 1938: ". . . *History* was everywhere about me. Philosophically, first of all: Aron had just written his *Introduction to the Philosophy of History* and I was reading it".[10] On 9 May 1940, only a day or so before the German attack, he wrote to Simone de Beauvoir:

But there we are, it had struck me in Proust in connection with Albertine, one does not have the same age for everything: she is thirty for bridge, twenty for philosophy, thirteen for painting. There are partitions (cloisons). In Aron, too, there were partitions. He was a fifty-year-old for everything but that didn't make only one fifty-year-old, all his fifties had to be added together to arrive at his real age. I wonder if it isn't a fault to be found in Jewish intellectuals and in any case it explains his lack of authenticity, for authenticity is being the same throughout all situations, a single project.[11]

Despite these tart remarks, Aron was one of those he enquired after from his prison camp at the end of July 1940: "If you have any news of Nizan, Guille, Maheu, Aron, etc., let me know".[12]

After the war Sartre inscribed Aron's copy of *L'Etre et le néant* (*Being and Nothingness*) with the words: "To *mon petit camarade* Raymond Aron, to help him write 'against the fashion of existentialism', this ontological introduction to the *Introduction to the Philosophy of History* (written, like all introductions, after the event), with the friendship of Jean-Paul Sartre".[13] In an article written for *Combat* in January 1945 Sartre, as we have seen, paid a warm tribute to Aron's work with *La France libre*. That same month, however, Sartre went to the United States for *Combat* and, according to

Simone de Beauvoir, "began his career as a journalist with a *gaffe* that shook Aron to the core: he described the anti-Gaullism of the American leaders during the war with such satisfaction that he was almost sent straight back to France".[14] In April of that year Aron published a favourable review of Simone de Beauvoir's "rich and striking" existentialist essay, *Pyrrhus et Cinéas*, in *La France libre*.[15] But when, in September, her novel, *Le Sang des autres*, appeared to much acclaim, Simone de Beauvoir wrote:

Camus, though he disliked the book, did not conceal his surprise at this success; as for Aron, he told me straight out, with the frankness of true friendship: "The fact is, I find this success revolting!" What he disliked, I think, was the approval I was receiving from the middle-of-the-road orthodox intellectuals who had made my book a sort of fad. Writers, journalists, intellectuals, still united by the events of the recent past, we were all inclined to indulge in mutual admiration; and apart from this, my novel was the first to speak quite openly about the Resistance.[16]

The first number of *Les Temps modernes*, containing two articles by Aron, appeared in October 1945. The first of these – an analysis of France's political, economic and diplomatic situation in the year since the Liberation – can hardly have pleased Sartre.[17] Aron was quite clear that it was the internal restoration of France, and not any diplomatic successes, which would determine its future, and this necessitated America's friendship, because only the United States was capable of supplying French industry with raw materials and machinery. There was much talk of the American "invasion" threatening France's industry with slavery; but, he argued, French industry was also threatened with death and, there too, the restoration of prosperity was the primary condition for future independence.[18] Aron's other contribution to the first number of the review was on the trial of Pétain.[19] Of the four articles he wrote for *Les Temps modernes*, only this one, in his opinion, was "relatively acceptable"; it was "not at all conformist", but it was published in the review without difficulty.[20] In the following month he published an analysis of the Labour victory of 1945 and of the French Socialist Party's chances in the elections to be held in October.[21]

The review was an immediate success, although the increasing differences among the editorial committee were to be reflected in these comments by Simone de Beauvoir:

Paulhan, who had edited the *NRF* for many years, gave us the benefit of his experience; he usually made up most of the numbers, and he taught me the technique. Aron, who had acquired a lot of experience with *La France libre*, also gave us technical advice; he followed the progress of *Les Temps modernes* very closely, trusting, I think, that Sartre would not have the perseverance to find it interesting for long and that he would then take over. He was chiefly concerned with the political section and was very skilful at finding reasons for not publishing articles favourable to Communism. Excellent as an analyst, he was pathetic as a prophet: he announced a Socialist triumph on the eve of an election that was a landslide for the MRP and a defeat for the SFIO. Leiris was in charge of poetry, and our tastes rarely coincided. The committee met often and argued hotly.[22]

Aron and Simone de Beauvoir also quarrelled about Britain's policy in Palestine. According to de Beauvoir, Aron "thought England's higher interests justified the measures she was taking against immigration in Israel", whereas in her view, "the beauties of English democracy were so much hot air to these hopeless men jammed in the camps or on ships without harbour".[23] However, Aron, writing in 1968, had a different recollection of this conversation:

One day at the Café de Flore, Sartre and Simone de Beauvoir were loosing off their righteous wrath against the British. I pointed out that the latter had no easy task between the Jews and the Arabs, they had not created the Israeli-Arab conflict, they were trying to arbitrate in it. At that time, Simone de Beauvoir and Sartre were always looking for some simple dividing line between angels and devils, and could see nothing except the cruelty (or imperialism) of the British and the sacred cause of the martyrs. I could see – and who, mindful of the future, would not have seen it? – the struggle between Israel and the Arabs that would follow the departure of the British, who had been unable to impose peace or to reconcile perfectly legitimate but incompatible claims".[24]

By the time Aron's last article for *Les Temps modernes* was published, in the June 1946 issue,[25] the editorial committee had fallen apart and Sartre's name alone appeared as Director (Aron had in fact left when he joined Malraux's cabinet the previous November).[26] As de Beauvoir recounts it,

Ollivier was moving toward the Right; he sympathized with the Gaullist Union which had just come into being. Aron's anti-Communism was becoming more pronounced. At about that time, or a little later, we had lunch at the Golfe-Juan with Aron and Pia, who was also being attracted by Gaullism. Aron said that he had no great affection for either the USA or the USSR, but if there were a war he would be on the side of the West; Sartre replied that he himself had no relish for either Stalinism or America, but that if war broke out he would be found in the ranks of the Communists. "In short", concluded Aron, "we should make different choices between the two evils; but in any case we should both be making the choice over our dead bodies". We felt he went too far in thus minimizing an antagonism we regarded as fundamental.[27]

350

That November, another nail was placed in the coffin of their friendship at the opening of *Morts sans sépulture*, a play by Sartre about the Occupation which contained some much-criticized torture scenes. At the first night Aron's wife, having nearly fainted, left in the interval and Aron followed her.[28]

* * *

In February 1947, before the final break with Sartre occurred, Aron gave a lecture on the relationship between existentialism and Marxism at the Collège Philosophique.[29] As well as having introduced Sartre to phenomenology, Aron had also written about "existential philosophy" well before the war.[30] Furthermore, whereas Sartre had only begun reading Marx at the end of the war, Aron had been a student of Marx's writings since the early 1930s. He was, therefore, particularly well equipped to evaluate Sartre's post-war attempts to combine existentialism and Marxism in a single system, and his lecture at the Collège Philosophique is a devastating demonstration of the impossibility of fusing the two. It is also a fine example of Aron's willingness and ability to understand "the other" – in this case his twin adversaries, existentialism and Marxism.

He began by outlining Sartre's existentialist critique of Marxist materialism. Materialism, according to Sartre, could not explain consciousness and failed to recognize man's essential subjectivity; Marxist accounts of materialism confused positivism, rationalism and materialism; and there was a contradiction between the notions of materialism and dialectic. At the same time, in Sartre's view existentialism had a positive contribution to make to the philosophy of revolution. It offered man or thought "in situation" as the solution to the necessities of revolution; it demonstrated the "historicity" of values and thus helped towards their transcendence; and it preserved man's active freedom in the face of a total materialist determinism.[31]

Similarly, for Merleau-Ponty, rightly drawing on Marx's youthful *Economic and Philosophic Manuscripts*, existentialism, like Marxism, transcended idealism and materialism. Concrete man was the bearer of history and this obviated the problems of a vulgar Marxist determinism. No primary sector exclusively determined other sectors; each sector was intelligible in and through the totality. Both Marxism and existentialism sought to expose man's alienations – in existentialism's case, the ideological fictions of "bad faith". In other words, both Sartre and Merleau-Ponty had tried to define an existentialist anthropology which could serve as a basis for the revolutionary philosophy of Marxism.[32]

351

However, Aron pointed out, there were a number of ideological and psychological reasons why "official" Marxist theorists (such as Henri Lefebvre and Roger Garaudy) rejected existentialism. Existentialism weakened Marxist doctrine by questioning the notion of scientific truth. Existentialist (or philosophical) Marxism also undermined the simplicities of Marxist determinism in respect of the goal of socialism, movement towards that goal, and the relation between economic base and ideological superstructure. Finally, unlike Marxism, existentialism was not primarily concerned with revolution; *Being and Nothingness*, for example, exuded a "Pascalian atmosphere", in which the essential theme was the relation of the solitary individual to the absence of God.[33]

But there were also, Aron maintained, a number of strictly philosophical reasons why existentialism and Marxism were incompatible. In the first place, the Marxist idea of labour as the essence of man played no part in Sartre's existentialism. Secondly, there was in *Being and Nothingness* no suggestion of the Marxist belief that history is a creative process by which, through struggle with nature and among themselves, men arrive at liberty and consequently transcend contradictions. On the contrary, in *Being and Nothingness* the struggle of conscious individuals seemed to be eternal, and history did not appear to have a progressive and creative meaning. For the Marxist, unlike the existentialist, revolution provided the final solution to the problem of philosophy and this was the fundamental difference between them. The heir of Hegel-Marx could not also be the heir of Kierkegaard. It was understandable, therefore, that Marxists rejected existentialism: the two ontologies were different.[34]

Lastly, Aron argued that the existentialists had a doctrine of revolution that was romantic, abstract and rhetorical, and the reason lay in their unwillingness to examine realities:

Since 1848 and the youthful writings of Marx, history has advanced, new facts have appeared. Marxism as a revolutionary impulse, a movement to end alienation or go beyond present capitalist society, cannot be refuted by these facts. On the other hand, these facts make it necessary to refine the historical schema by which Marx explained the transition from capitalism to socialism. This schema involved aggravation of the capitalist contradictions, a progressive increase in the number of proletarians, and pauperization. A certain parallelism was assumed between the contradictions of capitalism, the development of the proletariat, and the chance of revolution.

The real evolution was quite different. The expansion of capitalism did not bring about a pauperization of the working class, but a rise in its standard of living. In the United States, the most capitalistic country today, the working class has the highest standard of living and the least desire for revolution. The only country where a revolution calling itself Marxist has succeeded is one where the objective conditions prescribed by Marxist doctrine were not given. This would suggest that revolution, even when it claims to be Marxist, is often a political phenomenon rather than the result of a gradual ripening of economic contradictions. Finally, the revolution having taken place in a single country, the post-capitalist regime has been associated with a historically singular society in which neither the state nor inequality has disappeared with revolution.[35]

In other words, both Marxists and existentialists had failed to analyse the present situation. Ironically, Aron declared, "I always have the impression that existentialism, while invoking commitment, seldom succeeds in committing itself; that it experiences extreme difficulty in adopting a concrete historical and political attitude". In conclusion, it seemed to him that "the discussion between existentialism and Marxism is richer in metaphysical controversy than it is in concrete study of the situation of France or the world, perhaps because neither group wants to see the original elements of this situation or to assume responsibility for it".[36]

* * *

Although Aron and Sartre were co-signatories of the open letter to the Communist Party in March 1947 challenging the rumours that were being circulated about the role played by their late friend, Paul Nizan,[37] the final break between the two men came in October of that year after the RPF's successes in the local elections held that month. The day after the elections Sartre and his friends, who included Merleau-Ponty and Simone de Beauvoir, used their radio programme, which was also called *Les Temps modernes*, to attack de Gaulle, comparing him – physically as well as politically – to Hitler. There was an outcry in the press at the monstrous injustice of the comparison. The next day Aron was invited to join Sartre and his opponents for a further radio discussion. According to Aron, when he arrived he found himself surrounded by "excited Gaullists" – General de Bénouville and Henri Torrès – who were heaping violent insults on Sartre and saying that it was impossible to have a discussion with someone who stooped to such base attacks. Sartre did not reply – "he never", says Aron, "liked direct confrontation". As for Aron, he too stayed silent, finding it impossible either to agree that Sartre was in the right or to join in the imprecations of Sartre's adversaries:

Certainly, I could have behaved differently and found a way of demonstrating my friendship without associating myself with his broadcast of the day before. I remember that short scene as an unbearable moment: on one side a group of Gaullists for whom I felt no sympathy and, on the other, Sartre, undaunted under the insults, and myself, silent. We each went off in different directions.[38]

353

A few weeks later, Aron learnt that Sartre refused to pardon Aron's "silence" while Sartre stood alone among enemies. When he heard that they had "fallen out", Aron went with Sperber to see Sartre: Aron tried to explain his attitude and above all to put the episode into its proper perspective. Sartre accepted Aron's explanations "with a minimum of good grace": "All right, we'll have lunch together one of these days", went the ritual conclusion of the conversation. But the lunch never took place.[39]

The difference between them was further symbolized by Aron's acceptance of the Legion of Honour in August 1947 – an award which Sartre had refused two years earlier – while a comparison of the two men at this time has been provided, albeit at a distance of thirty years, by the Anglo-French journalist and writer, Olivier Todd. Todd, who was not yet twenty years old, had recently become engaged to Nizan's daughter and in June 1948 he went with his fiancée to meet her two "spiritual uncles", Sartre and Aron. The latter was now living on the Quai de Passy on the Right Bank of the Seine. In contrast to the informality of their later meeting with Sartre,

The visit to Aron, in an apartment on the *quais* in the sixteenth *arrondissement*, was extremely stiff. Time was like a heavy piece of unleavened bread. With his enormous ears perpetually on the alert for false ideas, Aron was born to be caricatured by David Levine. His smile, which was very gentle, contrasted with his manner of hammering home certain words. His dress was bourgeois. A pair of braces kept his trousers well above the navel. He reminded me a little of Winnie the Pooh's donkey, Eeyore. If he had reached the conclusion that the world was in a sorry state, he freely admitted, as he does today, that things might have been even worse. Analytical, cold, almost icy, his thought could be stimulating, but never warming. To my mind, at that time, it lacked lyricism. I remember saying to myself, as I left, that here was a man who thought "like a dissertation". I preferred the looser form of the essay, English-style. Aron reminded me of some of the less fashionable professors at Cambridge – Broad and Ewing. I am afraid that, despite all his kindness, something of that first meeting has always remained, like a thin veil of mistrust on both sides, to cast a shadow over us. Aron, I believe, found it difficult to see the purpose of the visit. As for myself, what had I to say to him? Although I was not a communist, I was a progressive. For me, Aron symbolized the Right and reaction. In the first place, he was – horror of horrors! – political columnist of the *Figaro*. With his mocking blue eyes, he asked me a few non-committal, distant questions about my studies. He did not invite me to come and see him again. Because of my youthful but brutal aggressiveness (I remember calling him, in English, "wicked", almost perverse – "in the Bertrand Russell manner"), he could have shown me the door. Instead, he waited patiently till the cup was emptied and the last biscuit munched.

Looking back coolly today, I am convinced that I missed an extraordinary opportunity. If I had listened to Aron and read him more carefully, I, and so many others, would have been spared a great deal of time wasted on communism – all the more so because Aron was one of the few French thinkers to have been brought up first on philosophy (German,

354

in particular) and then economics (especially Anglo-Saxon). He could have helped me so much better than Sartre to reconcile contradictions that were pressing and ill-digested. Aron is a fairly pessimistic man of science. Sartre was always, above all else, a generally optimistic man of letters.

Another thing designed to separate me from Aron was the bourgeois, three-piece-suit, side to his character – an almost too perfect respectability which put me off. It seemed to me then, and for a long time afterwards, that his concern with general ideas prevented him from taking an interest in the lives of ordinary human beings and the specific, everyday misfortunes of the oppressed of every continent – perhaps because he rarely talked about such things. Aron *does* think about them, but he writes primarily for those who govern, not for the governed. Except on two occasions, I did not see him again until we met once more on *L'Express* in 1977.

In the 1950s and '60s, one could not be in the orbit of both Sartre and Aron. One had, so to speak, to make a choice.[40]

* * *

Sartre attacked Aron directly in the pages of *Les Temps modernes* towards the end of 1948. The occasion was a discussion with David Rousset and Gérard Rosenthal, with whom Sartre had recently founded the socialist, non-communist and neutralist Rassemblement Démocratique Révolutionnaire (RDR).[41] Aron, Sartre complained, had recently "made fun" of the founders of the RDR as "the inheritors of revolutionary romanticism"; Aron was also unjustified in declaring that if the RDR failed it would be through lack of support from the proletariat – Sartre found it difficult to believe that the proletariat supported the RPF. For Aron, the only social problem was that of the distribution of consumer goods in a society in which these were lacking. The task, therefore, was to combine authoritarian procedures and propaganda measures – or mystifications – in order to prevent the least favoured from causing disturbances which could only result in chaos. In other words, Aron's "realism" consisted in ensuring that existing society was not overturned, since the setting up of another type of society, which would not bring abundance either, could only lead to another kind of authoritarianism. Thus, for Aron, all societies were now similar, since they all had to be authoritarian in order to distribute insufficient goods.

This, Sartre maintained, led Aron to state that when the RPF came to power, its policy should be to freeze wages while letting prices move freely, because if purchasing power remained constant, prices would duly fall into line. But was it not utopian to believe that a party could remain in power, show its hostility to the working class by imprisoning its representatives, the leaders of the Communist Party, and introduce a wage-freeze which would lower the living standards of the working class? When asked how he thought that one third of the French nation would accept this without protest, Aron's reply was: "Bah! The working class is very tired!" Thus the utopianism and romanticism-in-reverse, not to mention unintelligent cynicism, lay with Aron.[42]

According to Sartre, this led Aron, like other leaders of the RPF, to side with one of the two world-powers likely to bring about war. To declare that war was inevitable was to hasten it, since the RPF begged America either to organize an international army which would include France, or help to rebuild the French army. "This theoretician, who claims that the misfortunes of society stem from the lack of consumer goods, believes that the right policy is to help bring about a war which, in any case, will lead to an even greater reduction in consumer goods and, in acordance with his own thesis, plunge the state into an authoritarian regime". Yet, at the same time as he prepared this apocalypse, Aron declared that those who sought to organize a peace-loving socialist democracy were being utopian. What, then, was the basic political hope of this "gloomy theorist, who sees no other solution than dictatorship and war"? Aron believed, said Sartre, that "we should keep things going, we and our descendants, long enough for scientific progress to bring abundance on earth".

At this point Rousset added that it was "utopian on Aron's part to believe that technical development necessarily brings social emancipation". Whereupon Sartre concluded that it was Aron who was the romantic myth-maker, because he had once told Sartre that "the emancipation and culture of a country are directly related to its industrial capacity".[43]

The article was a travesty of Aron's views, though he limited himself to the following letter to "Monsieur le Directeur", which was published in *Les Temps modernes* in November 1948:

I do not intend to reply in your columns to the attacks made by M. Jean-Paul Sartre. I would simply like to warn your readers against a misunderstanding. The opinions which M. Sartre attributes to me are not those that I have expressed in my articles or books, and the statements put in inverted commas were not made by me. M. Sartre probably considers them to be characteristic of my innermost thought, such as he believes he understood it from conversations that were once friendly. Unfortunately, as far as both the freezing of wages and the social consequences of technical progress are concerned, he grossly distorts what I think.

Your readers need only to refer to my latest book, *Le Grand Schisme*, to see that this is so. . .[44]

To which Sartre replied: "Raymond Aron made to me exactly the statements I report in 'Entretien sur la politique'. As I cannot doubt his good faith, I can only suppose that he must have simplified his thought in order to bring it down to my level, and that he has since forgotten about this provisional simplification. He reproaches me for having referred to a 'friendly' conversation. I would reply that our conversations have long ceased to be truly friendly, because his acts have ceased to be so".

When, however, Sartre published the interview in book-form the following year, leaving the text unaltered,[45] Aron felt obliged to reply in more detail in two articles in *Liberté de l'esprit*.[46] He began with Sartre's complaint that Aron sided with one of the two great world-powers likely to bring about war and that to say war was inevitable was to help hasten it. It was, Aron stated, true that he "sided with one of the two great world-powers", but he did so for many reasons that were quite clear. The Soviet Union was expansionist, like so many countries before it which were animated by a religion of universal salvation and which equated the enlargement of their empire with the triumph of their faith. Throughout the world, every nation threatened by Sovietism sought the support of the United States:

I consider it a duty of elementary honesty to declare that, opposed as I am to communist expansion, I stand in the camp of the only power capable of stopping it. If I, too, made use of private conversations, I would not be short of juicy quotations on this point. (This sentence does not apply to Sartre, who, unlike other "revolutionaries", is perfectly sincere and does not appear to believe that Western Europe in fact owes its freedom to American protection.)[47]

On the other hand, Aron had never said that a *hot* war was inevitable, nor that it was romantic to believe that peace was still possible. His thinking, on this point, was a little more subtle. He had written that the *cold* war was inevitable, but that a *hot* war was, for the time being, improbable. Thus Sartre made him say almost the opposite of what he believed. Aron had called the attitude implied by the double rejection – simultaneous opposition both to the Soviet Union and the United States – "moral rather than political", without refusing it a possible nobility. Sartre had borrowed from Alain the idea that one hastened war by declaring it inevitable. Leaving that particular argument aside for the moment, Aron pointed out that the accusation was true neither of himself nor, for that matter, of the RPF. To recognize the *reality* of ideological and diplomatic conflict was not at all the same as saying that war was *inevitable*, and to assert that all military preparation increased the risk of war, at a time when the Soviet Union possessed nearly 200 divisions, required, to say the least, some demonstration.[48]

He turned, secondly, to Sartre's contention that Aron was unjustified in declaring that if the RDR failed it would be through lack of support from the proletariat, since Sartre found it difficult to believe that the RPF could reply on the support of the workers. For once, said Aron, Sartre was referring to a text and not a conversation – an article in the *Figaro*, in which Aron examined the three possible paths for socialism: communism, an explicitly anti-communist, reformist social democracy, and Trotskyism.[49] The RDR, which adopted the slogans of revolutionary socialism, while remaining detached from both communism and existing society, seemed to be a variety of Trotskyism. The article had no intention of being aggressive; Aron was simply questioning the likely success of this new form of Leftism. The RDR claimed to address itself to the working class, but Aron doubted if it would manage to win over the troops of the Communist Party. It was a question of judgement. Events would show whether or not the RDR would succeed in winning over the working class, but why, Aron asked, was he disqualified from examining the reasons for the possible failure of the RDR? Everyone, including a member of the RPF, had the right to analyse a political situation and draw conclusions from it, with no other risk than that of being mistaken.[50]

To say that the RDR did not have the proletariat on its side was not to say that the proletariat was with the RPF. The number of workers ready to follow General de Gaulle was greater, it seemed to Aron, than the number faithful to Jean-Paul Sartre, but that was not the question at issue. The RPF did not claim to address itself specifically to the proletariat (whereas the RDR sought to be in the Marxist tradition). Above all, one did not refute an observer by reproaching him for his political affiliation. If, Aron added, he had appeared to go into tiresome detail, it was because he sought to make clear "the repugnance he felt for the dialogue":

A dialogue between a member of the RDR and a resolute anti-communist could be useful and fruitful. But a necessary condition is a mutual effort at understanding. Sartre certainly had no desire to understand my position. It was important to him, for reasons which I refuse to seek here, to discredit me or my political opinions, by presenting them as both cynical and unintelligent. One can, it is true, be unintelligent by being cynical, but there are many other ways, too.[51]

Thirdly, Sartre had "caricatured" Aron's views about wages and prices, making him say that two years would be needed for prices to adapt to wages – a proposition which, as Aron went on to show, was "strictly meaningless". Yet the controversy at least served to illustrate one of the obstacles which confronts the formation, in France, of a public opinion: the refusal, even (or above all) of intellectuals, to discuss serious problems seriously, and the propensity to prefer invective to discusssion and to replace arguments with moral accusations. Doubts are cast upon the motives of the economist, he is denounced as a starver of the people, and the merits of a benefactor of humanity are attributed to oneself, without even realizing that such procedures are strictly unworthy. That politicians, in the heat of battle, should resort to such measures is regrettable and doubtless inevitable. But why does Sartre hanker after politicians' laurels?[52]

Finally, Sartre presented a travesty of Aron's views about the social consequences of technical progress, attributing to him a remark that was "not even worthy of a first-year sociology student" – namely, "the emancipation and culture of a society are directly related to its industrial capacity". At the same time, "with comical gravity", Rousset had declared that "It is utopian on Aron's part to believe that technical development necessarily brings social emancipation". In the first place, Aron retorted, all one had to do was to look at *Le Grand Schisme*, where he had written, "Technical progress in itself resolves neither class conflicts nor conflicts of power", and, "Technical progress does not in itself imply moral or spiritual progress".[53] In other words, the two "revolutionaries" attributed to Aron the naivety he explicitly rejected.[54] Furthermore, the notion of "social emancipation" was ambiguous and required analysis on a number of different levels: the standard of living of the working class, the power and autonomy of its representative organizations (especially the trade unions), its share of political power, and the material and moral integration of the workers into society.[55]

Sartre, however, refused to recognize "the servitudes of action and the uncertainties of choice":

He ignores the nature of societies, just as he ignores that of men. When the novelist of *La Nausée*, the dramatist of *Huis Clos* and the philosopher of "la passion vaine", concerns himself with politics, he has all the sentimentality of an adolescent. Aided by his ignorance, he rejects, with contempt, the arguments of sociologists and economists, refusing to admit that the state of collective resources and the mechanisms of social relations place certain limits on the aspirations of the "humanists"...

The absurd or odious opinions he attributes to me are merely a way of disguising his own demagogy...Sartre refuses to follow either the path of reformist socialism or that of communism. By so doing, he amasses the most childishly contradictory pretensions. He wants to bring about a revolution – a brutal break with the established order, together with a complete change in the elite in power – while at the same time respecting formal liberties. He aspires after the collectivization of industry and the planning of the economy as a whole but, thanks to worker-control (the idea was a bold one a century ago), bureaucratic tyranny will be avoided and Europe united without the USSR, without the United States and even without Bevin. What a fine example of "intelligent realism"! And how useful it is, as a way of disguising the poverty of one's own ideas, to attribute a few derisory opinions to an "RPF man"!

The theory of technical progress has never been a total philosophy of history. Yet it still allows one to dispel the utopias indulged in by the young. After the seizure of power by whatever party, there will not be some mysterious and undiscovered source of riches for the collectivity to exploit. Tomorrow, as today, the same imperatives of work, organization, discipline and mobility will continue to impose themselves. As long as the progressive methods of reformist socialism are used, the inevitable disappointments do not degenerate into revolt and, by way of reaction, bring about the dictatorship of new masters. On the other hand, when power has been seized by violent means and legality has been broken, the impatience of the masses is sharper and the urge to re-establish order more pressing: in the middle of the twentieth century (we are not speaking for eternity), a brutal revolution which lays claim to socialism will inevitably involve a tyrannical phase lasting a few years or a few dozen years (even if it is not linked with Stalinism). All the revolutions of the twentieth century have been totalitarian ones.

Between reformist socialism and Stalinism, there is no third way for socialism in the present situation: there is only empty romanticism and a return to notions which were rich in hope a century ago but have been emptied by history of their emotional and intellectual value. A revolution by "democratic methods" is comparable to "the winged horse": a concept in itself contradictory, it allows the intellectual to run away from reality and dream about the reconciliation of his contradictory desires.

Revolution, said Simone Weil, rectifying Marx's famous phrase, is the opium of the people. At the level of the *Entretiens sur la politique*, it is now no more than the opuim of the intellectuals.[56]

For the first time, Aron had used the phrase which, six years later, was to become the title of one of his most famous (or infamous) books.[57] In it he was to return once again to the dialogue – "without hope and without issue"[58] – with "le petit camarade" of his youth.

Notes

1. Albert Thibaudet (1874–1936) was a literary critic and historian whose influence reached its height in the inter-war years. It was his book of that title, published in 1928, which led the Third Republic to be known as "La République des professeurs".
2. *Les Diverses Familles spirituelles de la France* by the nationalist writer, Maurice Barrès (1862–1923), was published in 1917.
3. 1942d. See Chapter 11, above.
4. Simone de Beauvoir, *Les Mandarins* (Paris, 1954): tr. (by L. M. Friedman) *The Mandarins* (London, 1960). Leopold Labedz says that de Beauvoir caricatured Aron in her novel (Labedz, 1977). He is presumably referring to the character of Scriassine, although Scriassine is obviously identifiable with Koestler – cf. Iain Hamilton, *Koestler: A Biography* (London, 1982), p. 379. The truth may be that the anti-communist Scriassine combines some of the traits of both men.

5. Simone de Beauvoir, *La Force des choses* (Paris, 1963); tr. (by Richard Howard), *Force of Circumstance* (Harmondsworth, 1965).
6. Ibid., p. 20: tr. p. 9.
7. 1981a, p. 108: tr. 1983b, p. 93 (R.C.).
8. Beauvoir, op. cit., p. 24: tr. p. 14.
9. Tr. 1975a, p. xiii.
10. Jean-Paul Sartre, *Les Carnets de la drôle de guerre: Novembre 1939 – Mars 1940* (Paris, 1983), p. 227. See also the entries for 18 February (p. 251) and 7 March 1940 (p. 357).
11. Jean-Paul Sartre, *Lettres au Castor et à quelques autres. Volume II. 1940–1963*, édition établie, présentée et annotée par Simone de Beauvoir (Paris, 1983), p. 215.
12. Ibid., p. 293.
13. *Commentaire*, 8 (28–9), 1985, p. 181. The November 1945 issue of *Les Temps modernes* announced a forthcoming article by Aron, "Contre la Mode de l'existentialisme", but it never appeared.
14. Beauvoir, op. cit., p. 29: tr. p. 18.
15. 1945j.
16. Beauvoir, op. cit., p. 49: tr. p. 36.
17. 1945v. Specifically, Aron discussed the formation in September 1944 of a provisional "Government of National Unanimity" under General de Gaulle, the "purge" of collaborators, the nationalization of certain branches of industry, the debate about the Constitution, France's "motor-less economy", the Franco-Soviet treaty of February 1945, France's exclusion from the three-power conference at Yalta, and the conflict with Britain over Syria.
18. Ibid., p. 99.
19. 1945w.
20. 1981a, p. 116: tr. p. 100 (R.C.). Aron had written: "Marshal Pétain could not but be sentenced to death, since a number of his subordinates had been so sentenced for obeying his orders. Because of his age, he could not be executed. The outcome was therefore both foreseeable and foreseen, in the same way that the convictions of his judges, chosen from among the members of the Resistance and the Consultative Assembly, were not open to any doubt. Hence the impression of a scenario written in advance, a kind of collective rite, in which the participants only half believed" (1945w, p. 153). See also the analysis of this article in Aron's memoirs (1983a, pp. 203–5).
21. 1945x. Cf. 1983a, p. 203.
22. Beauvoir, op. cit., pp. 59–60: tr. p. 47. She is presumably referring here to the election of a second Constituent Assembly in June 1946, though I have been unable to find any such "prophecy" by Aron.
23. Ibid., p. 81: tr. p. 68.
24. 1968a, p. 41: tr. 1969e, pp. 43–4.
25. 1946e.
26. 1981a, p. 116: tr. p. 100. He soon joined the Editorial Boards of several learned (and literary) journals. These included the *Revue de métaphysique et de morale* (1947–75), *Critique* (of which he remained a member from 1947), the *Revue d'histoire économique et sociale* (Conseil de Direction, 1947), *La Table ronde* (1948–50), the *Revue d'histoire de la deuxième guerre mondiale* (Comité de Parrainage, 1950) and the *Revue française de science politique* (1951).

27. Beauvoir, op. cit., p. 108: tr. pp. 93–4.

28. Ibid., p. 128: tr. p. 113.

29. 1948d, reprinted in 1970b: tr. 1969b, in tr. 1969a. The Collège Philosophique had been founded by Jean Wahl in January 1947 to provide lectures on philosophical topics not dealt with at the Sorbonne. Aron's lecture on existentialism and Marxism was given on 6 February 1947 (*Fig. Lit.*, 25 January 1947, p. 3) and not, as stated in 1948d, in 1946. The internal evidence of the text itself also confirms that the lecture dates from 1947.

30. 1937g, 1937p.

31. 1970b, pp. 30–8: tr. 1969a, pp. 21–6.

32. Ibid., pp. 38–41: tr. pp. 26–7.

33. Ibid., pp. 41–5: tr. pp. 27–30.

34. Ibid., pp. 45–56: tr. pp. 30–8. An American commentator, Mark Poster, has argued that in this article "Aron made Sartre into more of a Cartesian than he actually was" and that "existentialism insisted that reason was not ahistorical, that it was man *hic et nunc* who thought, not some transcendental ghost in a machine". Mark Poster, *Existential Marxism in Postwar France: From Sartre to Althusser* (Princeton, 1975), pp. 193–4. But this misses Aron's point. Aron was not arguing that existentialism was ahistorical (far from it, as I have shown), but that it lacked the specifically *Marxist* philosophy of history, according to which labour is the essence of man and the decisive relation is that of man to nature, by which he learns to master natural forces and at the same time creates his own living conditions.

35. 1970b, pp. 57–8: tr. 1969a, pp. 38–9.

36. Ibid., pp. 60, 61: tr. pp. 40, 41.

37. See Chapter 2, above.

38. 1983a, p. 317. For her version of this incident, see Beauvoir, op. cit., pp. 153–4: tr. pp. 137–8.

39. 1983a, p. 318.

40. Olivier Todd, *Un Fils rebelle* (Paris, 1981), pp. 98–100. Todd wrote these words before his dismissal from *L'Express* as a result of a disagreement with its owner, Sir James Goldsmith, in May 1981. Todd subsequently fell out with Aron over this incident. See Volume 2, Chapter 22.

41. David Rousset and Jean-Paul Sartre, "Entretien sur la politique", *TM*, 4, (36), September 1948, pp. 385–428. Rousset was soon to denounce the Soviet camps and, with Rosenthal, turn anti-communist, which resulted in a rift with Sartre.

42. Ibid., pp. 401, 402–3, 406–7.

43. Ibid., pp. 407–9.

44. 1948l.

45. Jean-Paul Sartre, David Rousset, Gérard Rosenthal, *Entretiens sur la politique* (Paris, 1949).

46. 1949f, 1949g.

47. 1949f, p. 101.

48. Ibid.

49. The article in question must be "Les incertitudes du socialisme", *Fig.*, 30 April 1948.

50. Aron was not, of course, mistaken about the RDR. Cf. David Caute, *Communism and the French Intellectuals, 1914–1960* (London, 1964), p. 175: The RDR "was to prove short-lived. The inevitability of choice between two dominant systems killed it".

51. 1949f, pp. 101–2.
52. Ibid., p. 103.
53. 1948a, pp. 312, 342.
54. 1949g, pp. 137–8.
55. Aron proceeded to this analysis, ibid., pp. 138–40.
56. Ibid., pp. 140–1.
57. 1955b: tr. 1957b. See Chapter 20, below.
58. 1970b, p. 8.

16

The Great Schism

———

Le Grand Schisme,[1] which was written between the Autumn of 1947 and April 1948, was Aron's first book for ten years (if one excludes the three collections of articles from *La France libre*). Two of its features were immediately apparent. The style was quite different from that of his pre-war work. The audience was no longer primarily an academic one; Aron was seeking to address a much wider French public, his message was urgent and important and, doubtless aided by his recently acquired experience in journalism, the expression was clearer. Secondly, the book's structure was strikingly symmetrical, consisting of four parts – "The Diplomatic Schism", "The Ideological Schism", "The French Schism", and "Reforms" – each of which contained four chapters and ended with a short untitled conclusion. The whole work was balanced by a Preface and a corresponding *Note finale*.

The kind of political analysis which he wrote for *Combat* and *Le Figaro*, Aron stated in his Preface, derived its value from a global interpretation of the historical situation; *Le Grand Schisme* was an attempt to provide such an interpretation. He was, of course, aware that he would be accused of being "obsessed by anti-communism", but his answer was that, faced with a sect which was both military and religious, and which rigorously applied the principle that he that is not for me is against me, the only honourable attitude was total assent or absolute refusal. There was "no half-measure". Yet he wanted to be clearly understood. His radical condemnation of communism did not apply to the feelings that inspired the doctrine and even less to its adherents:

The motives, which till recently turned young intellectuals towards the parties of the Left or the extreme Left, are the very ones which make us anti-communist. In spite of its words, Stalinism breaks with humanist, egalitarian tradition as brutally as Hitlerism. In practice, it rejects Christian, liberal values as radically as Hitlerism. Those who stay in the same camp but repudiate the generous impulse which led them there, have changed more than those who, though in another camp, continue to defend what they have always cherished.[2]

Nor, Aron added, did this political decision imply a judgement about the respective merits of the contending groups. The fact was that, on a human level, he sometimes felt closer to those who heaped insults upon him than those who took his side. It was only too true that anti-communism attracted the support of "fear, selfishness and privilege", but, in this sense, no cause was pure. Communism itself had largely gone beyond the heroic stage and attracted the support of "the will to power, cynicism and opportunism". In times of religious and civil wars – and the two always went together – neutrality was not possible. Nevertheless, this did not imply that one had to fight with insults at the ready and a heart full of hatred:

We detested the doctrine of racial pride and the master-race, but we shall never detest the ideal of a humanity reconciled with itself, or of the mastery of man over nature and society. We detest a mode of action and a social order which seems to us to betray its own ideal, and the cold cruelty of those who are the creators of mystification, the manipulators of naive masses. But that is as far as we have to go. Why stifle the last echoes of a dialogue which we shall have to begin again one day?[3]

Aron first analysed the "bellicose peace" ("la paix belliqueuse") of "the diplomatic schism". Hitler's shadow had ceased to haunt the imagination, but the shadow of a new Caesar was casting itself over the world. The rivalry between Russia and America, which had been latent during the war but was visible to all as soon as Germany surrendered, had not left the world any time to savour the joys of peace. Only the speed of events had taken people by surprise.[4] Europe, which yesterday had been the centre of civilization and today was a heap of ruins, now seemed a kind of "no man's land" disputed over by the two giants.[5]

The structure of diplomacy had undergone two important changes since the Second World War: the unification of the field of action, brought about by technological progress and the political and military solidarity of the continents; and the concentration of power in two giant states situated on the edges of Western civilization. To these two features, which were likely to be long-lasting, could be added two more, which were probably less permanent: the destruction of partial balances of power, both in Europe and Asia, and the expansion of the rivalry of empires into a total diplomacy. An inevitable consequence was that the countries lying between America and Russia took on the appearance of contested territories. Whether in the shape of a civil war, as in Greece or China, or an electoral and political battle, as in Germany or France, the struggle was taking place to decide which empire the nations – old or young, European or Asian – would join. Thus, whether in Berlin, Paris or Iran, the electoral campaigns became "spectacular episodes in the cold war" and took on international significance.

The traditional notion of peace implied the limitation of diplomacy in two senses: a limitation of what was at issue in the conflicts between states and of the means employed by diplomats when the guns fell silent. Today everything – economic regime, political system, spiritual convictions, survival or disappearance of a ruling class – was thrown into question. Thanks to the triumph of the Communist Party, a country risked defeat without a shot being fired. The party struggle inevitably took on the significance of a fight to the death. Peace was no longer possible. Before the age of what Hitler had called "the enlarged strategy", stable frontiers were the symbol of peace; now, the real frontiers were those which, in the very midst of peoples who were formerly united, separated the American party from the Russian party. The electoral map and the strategic map were one and the same. Peace was as precarious as the electoral map.[6]

In contrast to Soviet imperialism, however, the ruling class in the United States had not sought the leadership which fell to it when the industrial potential of the American Republic was transformed into military might. Public opinion in the United States, which counted in a democracy, thought of power as a burden rather than as a source of benefit. The Americans, with a touch of regret, called "commitment" what imperialists would call "conquest". Soviet diplomacy had aroused a counter-emphasis on "containment" – the determination to stop the rival's expansion – and not a desire for domination. American influence did not usually result in the radical removal of other influences. Opposition parties were not liquidated and the "American party" did not establish a police state or a monopoly of power. It was true that when the "Russian party" resorted to violence, the multi-party system and constitutional guarantees sometimes disappeared from countries "protected" by the United States, but this was a question of contingency measures, not the application of a doctrine. What nourished humanity's great fear was the fact that, in the Soviet sphere, the evolution was irreversible. Once the Soviet apparatus was in place, the machinery of lies and the political police came into operation. Nothing, short of war, would bring the peoples there to the light of liberty. The rivalry between Russia and America would have come into existence after the fall of Germany in any case, but the Kremlin's desire for communism – that is, for universal empire – made it inexpiable.[7]

Nevertheless, the absence of peace was not war. Total diplomacy, the disappearance of partial balances of power, the tendency to universal empire, even the "absurd division" of Germany and Europe, signified the end of peace in its traditional sense, but did not imply the immediate destruction of cities by atomic bombs. "Peace is impossible, but war is for the time being improbable". War of the kind now envisaged would not break out by mistake or as a result of an incident. The slide from a cold war to a bloody war implied that one side *resolutely* desired war, and for the moment that desire existed neither in Washington nor Moscow. The uncertainty created by the balance of military forces was "conducive to (bellicose) peace. One does not risk the destiny of humanity on the throw of a dice".[8]

However, as well as war by misunderstanding and war by resolute will, there remained another possibility: that one side should decide to achieve certain objectives and that the other should be no less determined to resist. Till now, the Soviet Union had carefully refrained from crossing the line of demarcation. The USSR had brought under control the countries which it had obtained the right to "liberate" and which it considered to be an integral part of the Soviet sphere of influence; but nowhere – neither in Trieste, nor Korea, nor Germany – had Russian troops crossed the frontier. On the other hand, the Communist Parties had spared neither invective, cunning nor violence within the Western countries. The United States, Aron believed, would not tolerate the conquest of one of the great Western nations by the Soviet fifth column. Even if, as was possible, the Communists did not seize power in Italy, France or West Germany, there was still a risk that internal conflict would degenerate into civil war. The two giants, at loggerheads through their intermediaries, could officially continue as spectators – but for how long?

Unlike Hitler, Stalin was neither a mystic nor a romantic. He was under no compulsion to draw up a timetable and hasten an evolution which in any case he considered inevitable. Stalin's imperialism was as unbounded as Hitler's, but it was less impatient. Still more importantly, the Soviet Union was growing stronger with time. It intended to organize the economy of the Soviet bloc, which comprised a hundred million people, and its five-year plans would enable it to increase its industrial potential. The only counter-argument was the temptation afforded by a vacuum. For a few months, or even years, Western Europe would be an easy prey. Would such a favourable opportunity occur again? What would the Kremlin do to prevent Western Europe from becoming not an aggressive threat but a force for resistance? Once again, the likely answer, it seemed to Aron, was "everything, except war".[9]

After an account of the origins and development of the Cold War,[10] Aron turned to the question of Europe. Europe's originality, in modern times, lay in its science, industry and social rationalization. None of these distinctive historical features was compromised by the coming of the giant empires. Far from it: science, technology and rationalization seemed destined for new triumphs, even if Europe slid towards a hopeless decadence. On the other hand, the atmosphere in which the conquest of nature by reasonable men took place would be profoundly changed. The problem was that Europe had never been conscious of itself as a political unity; there was perhaps a Europe *in itself*, but there was no Europe *for itself*. Nevertheless, it was possible to rise above nations without denying them. The nations of Europe belonged to a single culture but refused to acknowledge it. It was in their power to discover a common heritage, but they only took pleasure in evoking their hatreds and struggles. Their only future was a common one, but would they prefer slavery and death?[11]

Against the present division of Europe the strongest objection was the dangerous instability that resulted. The only possible solution was that of a Western Germany integrated into Europe, with a prestige and seductive power which East Germany would find hard to resist. The alternative was a trial of strength over the military and political evacuation of the Eastern zone by the Russians – a contest for which the Anglo-Saxons lacked resolution. At the moment, the countries of Western Europe required American aid, but, given time, Western Europe, together with its colonial territories, would represent an economic grouping capable of immense development. If Benelux, West Germany, Great Britain, France and Italy formed a unity, a new future would open up for the old nations of the Continent. Economically, Western Europe, even in isolation from the Soviet sphere, was still potentially one of the great industrial powers of the world. Politically, Western Europe could not but feel incomplete and mutilated. But one benefit could result from this misfortune. The European idea was inspired more by considerations of prudence than enthusiasm. The present threat could arouse the *élan* that was missing. The will, not to fight the Soviet Union but to resist it, could be the driving force behind the organization of the West. "It would not be the first time that unity was born from the consciousness of a common peril".[12]

Aron now considered the question of Western Europe's, and France's, foreign-policy orientation: should it be one of neutrality ("abstention") or commitment ("engagement")? He began by comparing so-called American "imperialism" with that of the Soviet Union, pointing out first of all that whereas a country which entered the Soviet sphere was "communized", one which entered the American sphere was not "Americanized" in the same way. The domination imposed by the continental power (the USSR) resulted in extreme forms of subjection; the influence exercised by the distant and discreet naval power (the USA) tolerated a strong measure of autonomy. Subjected to the Second or Third Reich, France would have felt itself a prisoner; but what would this entail in the case of submission to the Soviet Union?

Poor, the Soviet Union would export its poverty. The slave of its masters, it would teach other peoples to obey and acclaim their master-slaves. It would spread its primitive faith, its tentacular bureaucracy, its enthusiasm for technology and its scorn for the individual. Indeed, one would have to be a fanatical communist not to denounce in the Soviet triumph the equivalent of the calamity against which the whole world has just united.

The United States was too rich to dream of world conquest. If, today, it scattered naval bases, airfields and dollars throughout the five continents, this was to prevent its rival from conquering the planet. As a consequence, it was beyond dispute that to reject Soviet "liberation" was to accept the American presence. "In this sense, but in this sense only, there are only two alternatives between which a choice has to be made".[13]

The idea of a neutralization of Europe was, in Aron's view, "absurd". The industrial potential of Western Europe was too tempting a prize, and neutrality implied strength, which was what Europe currently lacked. As for an international "third force", there was only one thing wrong with it: it did not exist. It was obviously desirable that Europe should be capable of rising above its present condition, and be neither a pawn nor a satellite. But the intellectuals who refused to let people choose between one empire and the other, while reserving all their fervour for a

370

socialist United States of Europe, were giving proof "either of their ignorance or of their folly". The USSR would be extremely hostile to a prosperous and powerful socialist United States of Europe, because this would represent a barrier to Slavo-communist expansion. Ideo-logically, a socialist United States of Europe would be an unacceptable source of rivalry, for communists reserved their greatest hostility for non-communist socialists, making use of them when convenient, but ruthlessly eliminating them when they were of no further use or looked like becoming serious rivals. A Europe which belonged to the Europeans was in fact "the goal of American, but the nightmare of Soviet, diplomacy. Whether one likes it or not, only the United States offers Europe a chance to achieve its ancient dream of unity".[14]

On the German question, Aron rejected the argument, which he examined very carefully, that Western diplomacy, especially the Marshall Plan, ran the risk of resurrecting "the danger of eternal Germany".[15] As far as Germany was concerned, France must find

a language with which to address those who are and will remain our neighbours. It is not a question of wiping away the past, or of pretending to forget, as though the concentration camps had never existed. Nor is it a question of joining the chorus of those who, in the hope of winning over masses ripe for the taking, seek to flatter them in words, while maltreating them in deeds. The essential is quite simply to offer them a future and treat them as people destined to take their place one day, on an equal footing, in a European community. It goes without saying that the task is not just a question of issuing propaganda directives. A nation influences others by what it is and what it achieves, rather than by the slogans it spreads. The radiance of example carries further than the brilliance of words . . .

We are, in part, responsible for what Germany will be tomorrow . . . In order for economic understanding to blossom and bear fruit in the works of civilization, men must come together for a task that reconciles them. A defeated people only overcomes the past by envisaging a future which perpetuates neither its misery nor its guilt. Only the strength of the United States makes this future possible. Only the generosity of France will make it real.[16]

Finally, Aron argued against the "elimination" of Western Communist Parties, since this would bring "its own fatal consequences" – the curtail-ment of liberties and the reinforcement of powers. "Faced with communist totalitarianism, one will be driven to forms of despotism which may be less intrusive but in human terms are just as intolerable, since they will be inspired, not by faith, but by fear". Already, outside Europe, the Anglo-Americans had been induced, almost despite themselves, to support social groups anxious to maintain their privileges of power and wealth – in, for example, China, Korea and the Arab countries. The "law of polarization" operated everywhere. The logic of anti-communism was as undeniable as the logic of anti-Hitlerism. In order to fight Hitler, it had been necessary to collaborate with the communists: in order to fight the communists, it would be necessary to collaborate with the fascists. One would have to be blind not to recognize the danger, but the problem was one of *action*, of adaptation to circumstances, and there were no general principles in such a matter. "The anti-communist has to try to satisfy contradictory requirements: the safeguarding of liberties, the rejection of a reaction against the working class, social reforms, measures of repression against fifth columns, the affirmation of a political will, and restoration of the state". However, contradictions were not resolved through ideas, but through everyday practice.[17]

* * *

In Part Two of *Le Grand Schisme*, Aron turned to "the ideological schism" and in particular "the communist mystification". He began with an analysis of the "Protean doctrine" of Marxism – his first major discussion of Marxist ideology since the critique of "secular religions" four years earlier.[18] The elusive character of Marxism, he wrote, made it seem almost irrefutable. If one confined oneself to its popular versions, then one was accused by intellectuals of merely refuting vulgar Marxism; if one sought to avoid the over-simple formulae of the *Communist Manifesto* and went back to Marx's youthful writings, then one was accused by the orthodox of neglecting science at the expense of ideology.[19] But it was the duty of "historical criticism", as Aron put it, to "confront the Marxist schema with the course of events", the "Marxist schema" being "the simplified representation of evolution according to which the very movement of modern societies tends to accentuate the contradictions of capitalism and cause the final revolution to erupt". It was not difficult to show, however, that history had "ironically denied the predictions by means of which Marx asserted the parallel between rational necessity and socio-economic determinism". For a post-capitalist regime had been in existence for thirty years and it was, therefore, possible to confront the Marxist idea of the overcoming of alienation and the unity of the particular and the universal, with the reality of a regime of collective ownership and planning.[20] Accordingly, Aron examined two "myths": first, the myth of revolution and then the myth of the classless society.

The *intellectuel de gauche*, in France, is above all afraid of not being a revolutionary. He would sooner admit his ignorance of those questions about which he holds forth so confidently.

Damn it! One doesn't need to know anything about economics to condemn capitalism. To abandon the rank of revolutionary, on the other hand, is, it seems, the ultimate disgrace, for an intellectual.[21]

It would be impossible to underestimate the effect, in certain circles, of this "muddled and powerful" feeling. The communists played on it subtly, yet, when examined closely, the idea of revolution was unconvincing. Dissatisfaction was, certainly, normal in the contemporary world, but the wish to attenuate suffering or improve the condition of the masses did not necessarily lead to the romanticism of subversion. The latter was, on the contrary, "a kind of flight from reality, a vision, sometimes apocalyptic and sometimes seductive, of an event which would overturn existing societies. It seeks to overcome, at a stroke, the exhausting complexity of problems and to reduce creative effort to a simple act of force". In fact, Aron suggested, revolutionary romanticism lived off an almost verbal ambiguity. Revolution, in its broad, non-political sense, was viewed as prolonging the liberal, humanist tradition. But the implicit value-judgement assumed what had yet to be shown – namely, that political and social transformations, provoked by a specific historical revolution, marked a step forward on man's progress towards humanity.[22]

Marxist ideology serves to conceal, as though behind a smokescreen, the prosaic reality of communist revolution. Considered as historical materialism, Marxism sees the proletarian revolution, brought about by the contradictions of capitalism and the class struggle, as the inevitable outcome. As a dialectical philosophy of Hegelian inspiration, it announces that it does not know what the post-revolutionary regime will be like. Man is free and by his negativity creates his future. But, at the same time, it presents the proletarian revolution as an unprecedented Revolution, a passage from necessity to liberty, carried out by the immense majority in the interests of all and not by a few for a few. Beyond this Revolution, man will be reconciled with nature and with himself. Each individual will assume the totality of human nature. Clearly, the combination of these three themes gives Marxist ideology some outstanding advantages. An inevitable revolution, which introduces an unforeseeable social regime, but fulfils man's vocation, simultaneously satisfies those who have a sense of destiny, those who recognize the uncertainty of the future and those whose idealism turns them towards the people. Such an ideology has incomparable power as propaganda, but puts the critical mind to a severe test. How can one assert that a society, which cannot be known, will be the culmination of man's adventure? How can one decree that a revolution is inevitable from a deterministic point of view, when so many causes are intermingled and so many forces confront one another?[23]

In reality, Aron maintained, events had shown the Marxist conception to be false on "one decisive point" – the predicted growth and pauperization of the proletariat. Whether viewed in absolute or relative terms, the standard of living of the working class had risen more in the last century than in the previous ten.[24] Modern societies, where free competition prevailed, were not moving towards a simplified structure consisting of the vast mass of the exploited, on the one hand, and a small minority of exploiters, on the other; on the contrary, they were tending towards increasing differentiation.[25] Nor had there been the erosion of nationalism which Marx had anticipated.[26] The only "proletarian revolution" that had so far taken place had involved the seizure of power by a party relying for its support on a fraction of the masses. Once in power, the party had established a merciless dictatorship in its own interests. "Of all the blows that history has delivered to revolutionary romanticism", wrote Aron, "this is the most serious".[27]

It was an illusion, he believed, to think that the proletarian or factory worker, as such, would ever come to hold power. The bourgeois, as lawyer or tradesman, could offer the state the knowledge and skill he had acquired in business; his was the kind of competence which governments required. A former worker could rise to the highest positions, but, in the very process of becoming a leader or politician, he cut himself off from his former fellows. In other words, when the proletariat took power, the latter was exercised either by men who had risen from the ranks of the working class, or by professional revolutionaries, writers, lawyers and agitators, who had generally originated from the bourgeoisie. Within the Bolshevik Party, both types of leader had existed, with the intellectuals predominating in the higher ranks of the party hierarchy.[28]

The Bolshevik Revolution and those of Mussolini and Hitler all provided a concrete but "tragically prosaic" indication of what the revolutions of the twentieth century involved: the seizure of power by an active minority, organized as a revolutionary party and mobilizing a fraction of the masses. The Revolution was not the collective awakening of a people, but a violent episode in the struggle between classes, parties and ideologies. The victorious party suppressed democratic processes because, if it did not, either it would not be assured of its majority (as was the initial case with the Bolsheviks) or it would relapse into the very paralysis that it aimed to overcome. Logically, it was not impossible to imagine a revolution of the type Marx described – a vast uprising of the exploited masses against a weak clique of exploiters. Historically, however, such an eventuality was out of the question in the twentieth century (except in the case of national insurrections against military occupants), for two reasons: the increasing differentiation of modern societies, and the link between the party of revolution and Soviet Russia.

For the events of the Russian Revolution – liquidation of the bourgeoisie and the Kulaks, collectivization of land, prolonged dictatorship of a single party, official ideology and political police – were enough to prevent social groups, and even progressive forces, from coming together. But, Aron concluded, in order to breathe life back into revolutionary romanticism, it was no longer enough to attack contemporary capitalism; it was also necessary to criticize the USSR. Today, it was Trotskyism which had all the strength and weakness of such messianism – "the strength of hope eternal, and the weakness of hope unrealized, and so often disappointed".[29]

Aron next considered "the myth of the classless society". Up until 1914, at a time when it was "miraculously improving the condition of men", capitalism was reviled without any attempt being made to define the regime, named socialism, which would succeed it:

It is easy to hate what we know and to enthuse over what we do not know. But such propaganda depended on a prior assumption that was based on sentiment rather than made explicit: the conviction that post-capitalism would realize the values in whose name capitalism was condemned. In this way every horse was backed: man's freedom was kept intact, the complicity of destiny was ensured, the Revolution was invested with the dignity of universal truth and, at the same time, embarrassing questions were avoided. It was known that the Marxist Revolution would mark the end of pre-history, but no one knew what sort of social relations would result from it.

Anyone who, today, resorts to such ideological jugglery is no longer naive, but *de mauvaise foi*. For no one, except those who are resolved to be so, is unaware that post-capitalism can be considerably worse than capitalism itself. . . Why should the substitution of one elite for another and of collective ownership for private ownership imply the fulfilment of that dream of the millenium which rocks to sleep the sufferings of humanity?[30]

As to the withering away of the state, Russia's experience had, to say the least, shaken that theory, for in no capitalist state had the coercive apparatus ever attained the degree of ubiquity to be found in Soviet Russia. First, was the theory correct? Was it true that the state was nothing more than an instrument in the service of the exploiting class? Was it true that, even at an ideal level, it was possible to move logically from the suppression of private property to the withering away of the state? If all that was meant was that the controllers of the means of production always exercised an influence on the state, and often a decisive influence, that was obviously true. Political and social power were interconnected in a thousand ways, both visible and invisible. But this did not imply either that the state was *nothing but* the instrument of a class, or that the fundamental relation between the governing elite and the masses was identical with that of the exploiters and the exploited and would disappear with the coming of collective ownership.

375

The elite of a modern capitalist society was divisible into distinct groups: the controllers of the economy, politicians, administrators and the leaders of the masses. The relative strengths of each group varied according to the country and the circumstances. In other words, it was a misunderstanding of the historical function of the state to contrast a ruling class on the one hand with, on the other, a set of public powers subject to the exclusive interests of that class – a mistake, moreover, which Marx, in his historical studies, never made. The reality, in all periods of history, was "a plurality of elite groups".[31]

In the USSR, by contrast, there was "a complete unification of the elite". The masters of the state were automatically masters of the economy; the distinction, characteristic of formal democracy, between elected politicians and administrators appointed according to the rules, did not exist; and the leaders of the masses and the political rulers were one and the same. The elite was *one* and was simply confronted by the mass of the nation. Thus it was essential to analyse the structure of the elite as well as the social class structure: these two structures were not independent of one another, but they were not a simple reflection of each other, either. Finally, in the USSR the "vertical battle" between employers and employed had disappeared with the elimination of the employers and the enslavement of the unions, but not the "horizontal battle" between occupational interest groups (workers and peasants, investment and consumer industries). This horizontal battle did not express itself visibly, but neither, for that matter, did the vertical battle between the worker masses and the ruling minority. "A 'classless society' of the Soviet type does not eliminate social conflicts, but represses them through despotism".[32]

However, it was not a question of choosing between either "capitalism" or "communism". Another possibility was the *travaillisme* of the Labour Party in Great Britain, which "aims at equality and respects liberties".[33] This was, in Aron's view,

the only method which offers a chance of attaining a post-capitalist society whose structure is not simplified to the point that despotism becomes inevitable and permanent... The safeguarding of a portion of private ownership, the preservation of sectors in which market-mechanisms operate, and respect for the moral traditions and humane relations of the past, are indications not of a kind of cowardice in the face of the future, but of wisdom. It is not the romanticism of Revolution, but steady patience, which improves the lot of man. To reconcile technical progress and the continuity of history – that is the outstanding task.[34]

* * *

Aron turned next to "the French schism". After an analysis of the three "decisive facts" of the years between 1944 and 1947 (the rapid disintegration of the "pseudo-unity" of the Resistance, the failure of the coalition governments, and the revision of the Constitution),[35] followed by an examination of the economic situation since the Liberation,[36] the conclusion seemed to him "obvious". A democratic regime was only viable on two conditions: a state must be sufficiently strong to impose its law on all occupational groupings, and sufficiently far-seeing and effective to ensure that its aims were achieved. Neither of these requirements had been met by the Fourth Republic. The Communist Party, which took its orders from abroad, would do all in its power to prevent the restoration of France, but the problem was a difficult one to resolve. To outlaw the Party presupposed the consent of a large majority of opinion and if such a step were taken without sufficient justification in the public's eyes, it might do more harm than good. "It is", Aron observed, "desirable, but not morally obligatory, to leave freedom to those who would refuse it to you, if they had the means. One does not owe the privileges of democracy to totalitarian parties". Because of the Soviet Union, Europe was engaged in a struggle to the death, in which the safety of the West was at stake.

Whether one liked it or not, he concluded, modern societies were vulnerable to agitators to the extent that pluralist regimes were paralysed and there existed revolutionary parties bent on fomenting chaos. Gaullism was an accident of French politics, but it posed two historically significant questions: how to restore the necessary authority to the state in an age in which society was dissolving into parties and trade unions? And how to defend itself against the permanent conspiracy of Soviet fifth columns? "I do not know", Aron wrote, "if the RPF will solve these problems; but I do know that these problems would have arisen without the RPF, just as they will continue to present themselves if it eventually fails or disappears. If the RPF did not exist, it would be necessary to invent it".[37]

* * *

In the light of the preceding analysis, Aron went on to recommend four kinds of reform – political, economic, social and intellectual. As far as political reform was concerned, the main question was: under what conditions was a pluralist regime, which would avoid both totalitarian unification and chaos, possible? The only way of ensuring that democracy was viable in France, Aron believed, was to create conditions analogous to those in the United States and Great Britain: the absence of a large revolutionary party, moderate trade unions, and a two-party system which gave the executive both the stability and the authority that derived from a lasting and relatively homogeneous majority. The "indispensable conditions" for the survival of democracy were threefold: the elimination of Communist Parties – at the very least, the exclusion of Communists from official positions and, at most, the outlawing of the Party; the restoration of the state over and above the intermediate bodies, in particular the unions; and the establishment of a cohesive majority, probably through the RPF. A revision of the Constitution – "one of the worst that France has had" – was also necessary, although Aron was again careful to point out that the conditions for the existence of pluralism were not just institutional, but also "political and human".[38]

Economically, France must do more than try to restore production to its pre-war level; it must make up for the time lost between the two world wars and overcome its backwardness in industry and agriculture. France must abandon the habits of the *rentier* and adopt a pioneering approach, for in the inter-war years the French people, both individually and collectively, had been inspired by the desire for an easy life rather than a concern for industrial strength and prosperity.[39] Today, the objectives must be, first, the struggle against inflation, then reconstruction and modernization, and finally the integration of France's economy into a larger grouping, like that of a Western federation.

But the main question underlying economic reform concerned the kind of regime – a planned or a free economy – best suited to attaining those objectives. At the time of the Liberation, Aron wrote, he had been in favour of a few years of limited planning, but that had failed, or, rather, it had been tried in conditions which made failure inevitable. Today, it seemed to him that economic liberalism, which was less unpopular and technically easier, would have more chance of success. He was "deeply convinced that the nations of Western Europe only have a future if they surmount their nationalism, first of all on an economic level". A federal Europe must not, however, be *dirigiste* or dictatorial, but rest on "internal freedom", the federation's authority being confined to determining frameworks and structures. The alternative was either a Hitlerite or Stalinist federation in which changes would be dictated, or a democratic federation in which, once monetary and fiscal conditions had been specified and external structures (exchange rates and commercial policy) established, market mechanisms would be allowed to operate freely.

Aron favoured, then, a "return to freedom", since this ought to create the most favourable climate for economic renovation. Herein lay "the heart of the problem". The aim was to increase productivity and one of the ways of injecting new life into the French economy was to open it up to competition once again. Not, Aron emphasized, that he was trying to re-establish "a dead liberalism". France was living under a mixed economy and would continue to do so. He was rejecting both extremes – that in which market mechanisms operated unhindered and that in which the state took planning to its limit. The task was to "make the mixed economy viable" and this, so far, had not been the case.[40]

The aim of social, as of political and economic, reform was to re-establish liberal and moderate institutions; but it was important, first of all, to establish the conditions in which such institutions could operate. These were: the conversion of trade-union militants to reformism and the elimination of communist agitators; reform of trade-union structure and an expansion of the economy, which would lead to a gradual but real, rather than fictitious, improvement in the condition of working people, while maintaining stability and not precipitating inflation. Any legislation, however, would be ineffective without a "psychological transformation" among workers and trade-union leaders. There were no easy answers. Communism still fed the hopes of millions of people and neither the RPF nor any other party had anything comparable to set against it. And yet, Aron declared:

Let us be perfectly clear. We do not have any doctrine or creed to set against the communist doctrine or creed, but we are not ashamed of it, because secular religions are always mystifications. They offer the masses an interpretation of the drama of history, and attribute humanity's misfortune to a single cause. But the truth is otherwise: there is no single cause and no one-dimensional evolution. There is no Revolution which, at a stroke, would inaugurate a new era of humanity. Communist religion has no rival; it is the latest of those religions which have piled up ruins and spread rivers of blood. It is the most redoubtable of them all and is perhaps destined to victory. But, to demand a comparable faith of anti-communists, to require of them an equally compact fabric of equally seductive lies, is to open the door to fascism. For they have the profound conviction that the fate of men is not improved by catastrophic means, equality is not promoted by state planning, and dignity and freedom are not ensured by abandoning all power to a sect that is both religious and military. We have no lullaby with which to send children to sleep. Will humanity, which no longer believes in God, live without idols?

Not having a creed, what shall we give the masses in order to reconcile them to their lot? There again, we are under no illusions. There are no dramatic gestures, there is no sensational new catchphrase, which, by linking capital and labour, will suddenly transform the climate. Our efforts, humble and patient, can be turned in three directions: the legal status of collective relations between employers and employed, work-committees, and the sharing of workers in profits.[41]

As to intellectual reform, Aron echoed what he had said three years earlier in his Introduction to *L'Âge des empires et l'avenir de la France*:[42] the French should be prepared to *"think* politics" and, abandoning their romantic and escapist dreams, come to recognize reality and the slow and thankless effort involved in trying to improve men's condition.[43] In particular, the French had neglected science. After the defeat of 1871, Ernest Renan had written that the great fault of the French was that they did not believe sufficiently in science. That diagnosis remained true today, though Aron was not, he pointed out, referring to the scientistic rationalism that was the more or less official philosophy of the University (Marxism and Durkheimianism), but to the neglect of science in the army, industry, agriculture and government.

France would not, Aron stated in conclusion, give way to an authoritarian regime, for that always degenerated into totalitarianism; but it would not rise again if it succumbed to the chaos of a powerless pluralism. Restoration of the state, stability of the executive, limitation of the power of occupational groups, improvement in administrative techniques and economic competence – none of these reforms was spectacular or sufficient in itself, but they would, if taken together, take France nearer the goal of a regime of moderate authority. The state would be strong, but not unlimited; parties and trade unions would be free, but not all-powerful; parliament would legislate and control, but not seek to govern; the economy would be guided, but not directed.

Utopia? I refuse that admission of powerlessness which leads to the alternative of communism or right-wing despotism. For in its present form, the Fourth Republic is not a solution. Capable of enduring, it is not capable of renovating.[44]

* * *

Le Grand Schisme, it is important to remember, was Aron's first book since the *Introduction to the Philosophy of History*, and in a *Note finale* he related the argument of *Le Grand Schisme* to themes which he had first discussed in his earlier and fundamental work. In *Le Grand Schisme*, he pointed out, he was arguing against "the two extreme forms of philosophy of history" of Marx and Spengler. According to Marx, the whole movement of history had a meaning: it was the unfolding of a rational necessity. The dialectic of contradiction and struggle led to the communism with which the meaning of mankind's previous history would be revealed. According to Spengler, history was the unfolding of an organic or biological necessity, by which cultures were born and died like plants. But these two philosophies, Aron stressed, were not the only ones alive in our time:

The expression, *plurality of systems of interpretation*, which I used ten years ago in the *Introduction to the Philosophy of History*, and which at the time was taken to be academic, today corresponds to a political reality. The conflicts between parties have developed into metaphysical conflicts. The whole of history has been called into question by the alternatives of our tragic age...An open philosophy, which humbly confesses the limits of our knowledge, avoids both rationalist pride and biological determinism, and ends neither in triumphant certainty nor a cry of despair.[45]

Europe's tragedy was not that the capitalists, in a search for new markets, had clashed in the violent conflict of the Great War, but that the combination of modern methods of production and political nationalism, which had been viable in the previous century, had proved untenable in the twentieth. Technology had imparted an inexpiable fury to a war which, in 1914, the diplomats had started as if by mistake. When, after the First World War, the division of Europe into twenty-five nations came to provide the framework for planned economies, the contradiction became a mortal absurdity. Germany, which suffered more than other countries, sought to overcome the absurdity to its advantage. Claiming to unify Europe, it was buried beneath the ruins of a continent. The crucial factors in this history were not, therefore, private ownership and the class struggle, but technological progress and national conflicts.[46]

Thus, the decisive fact of our time was not capitalism, socialism or class conflict, but "the adventure of science and technology". It was this which lay behind the social crisis in the countries of Europe and the threat of death that hung over them. What Spengler interpreted as the dissolution of collective life appeared, in the perspective of economic progress, as the inevitable troubles which accompanied the ripening of a new order. Certainly, such technical progress did not in itself imply moral or spiritual progress and nobody knew the conditions that were necessary for humanity's loftiest creations or for harmony to exist between man, his environment and his culture. It might be that a society became reconciled with itself as it overcame need. Perhaps prosperity would bring men to devote themselves to higher things. In any case, it would enable more people to share in those goods which, in the past, had been the privilege of a few. Only technical progress allowed one to glimpse, on the horizon of history, a civilization which would not be founded on slavery. Whatever else they might be, the enemies of technical progress were the supporters of slavery.[47]

381

"The only purpose of these reflections", Aron concluded, was

to release us from the spell of fear and despair. We are living through one of the most tragic, but also one of the most wondrous, periods of history. Humanity will perhaps blow itself up, while handling the toy which its genius has placed in its childlike hands. If it overcomes the schism and agrees to accept a common law, then, freed of its servitudes but not its anxieties, it will continue to interrogate the heavens and put questions to itself. History will never resolve the enigma of our destiny...

Let it suffice us to know that our efforts have a meaning. Let us stop dreaming and return to the daily task.[48]

* * *

Looking back on *Le Grand Schisme* and its successor, *Les Guerres en chaîne*, at the end of his life, Aron wondered why he had allowed himself to indulge in "such literature" – "an attempt at a kind of immediate philosophy of history-in-the-making which would serve as a framework and foundation for my daily or weekly commentaries and for the political positions I adopted".[49] Such works have, however, had convincing champions. To the future international relations specialist Pierre Hassner, for example, who came to France from Romania at the age of fifteen and discovered Aron's thought through *Le Grand Schisme*, Aron was the only writer in the West to speak of communism as Hassner had experienced it.[50] Unlike Aron, who preferred the more abstract, generalizing and "academic" works like the *Introduction to the Philosophy of History*, Hassner in fact considers the "hybrid", more "journalistic", books such as *Le Grand Schisme* and *Les Guerres en chaîne* to be superior. In Hassner's view, the more theoretical writings have a slightly strained (tendu) and static character which is not to be found in the historical works.[51] Similarly, to the Yugoslav Branko Lazitch, who had served on General Mihailovitch's staff during the war and become a political refugee in Geneva, Aron alone understood communism; *Le Grand Schisme*, he remarked after Aron's death, was "the first work in French which offered a global interpretation of the East-West confrontation".[52] Despite his own reservations, Aron believes that he probably received more letters and reviews in praise of *Le Grand Schisme* than for any other book, doubtless because in 1948 the work satisfied the curiosity of a public anxious to understand the consequences of the Second World War.[53]

Among the letters were those from two "princes of the mind" which he singled out for mention in his memoirs. The first was one of support from Alexander Koyré; the second was a critical letter from Lucien Febvre who, like so many French intellectuals of the time (and without, he

382

admitted, having yet read the book), naively objected to Aron's refusal to put "l'influence américaine" and "Stalinism" on a par.[54]

The reviewers were full of praise. "It is rare in France", wrote J.-J. Marchand in the RPF weekly, *Le Rassemblement*, "to find the science of political economy, a thorough knowledge of ideologies, and moral rectitude, all combined as they are here". The simplicity of its style made *Le Grand Schisme* easy to read, while the book was "a real manual for anyone who is seeking to understand the fundamental causes behind the events we are now experiencing".[55] Thierry Maulnier, Aron's colleague on *Le Figaro*, spoke of "the astonishingly rich contents of a work which considers almost every perspective on the present historical situation and reveals the main tendencies and *impasses*, the possibilities and contradictions, with a masterly lucidity".[56] Similar judgements were made by Roger Caillois,[57] Georges Bataille,[58] Gilbert Sigaux,[59] Jean de Fabrègues,[60] and Robert d'Harcourt and Michel de Saint-Pierre.[61]

The anonymous reviewer in the *Revue de métaphysique et de morale* was equally enthusiastic. "Among the new generation of French political philosophers and writers", he declared, "Raymond Aron is without doubt one of those whose mastery has been most precociously and completely confirmed. The importance of his theses, his studies of contemporary German sociology, his economic and political analyses, not to mention his vast philosophical culture, have helped to give him a leading role in the renovation of French thought in the years immediately before and after the Second World War". *Le Grand Schisme* did not claim, however, to be a scientific work, but – to put it in the language of the day – that of a militant *engagé* in action. Indeed, it was important to underline that whereas people usually tried to shroud partisan ends in the cloak of science, Aron "frankly recognizes that scientific analysis, however far it is taken, is powerless to justify political or social ends, because ultimately these always comprise philosophical values. And it is these values which inspire strictly political choices between parties claiming to put them into practice".[62]

Aron had already made such a choice "with *éclat*" on the national level during the Second World War, and the resolution with which he defended "man against the tyrants" and democratic values against Hitlerism was well known. Today a similar kind of choice was at issue – that between communism and anti-communism. Following the logic of his own thought, Aron had joined the party or *rassemblement* which seemed to him most likely to carry on the anti-communist fight effectively. Not that there was anything crude about his decision: it involved a number of reservations and sacrificed neither his freedom nor the right to speak the truth.

Finally, the reviewer was particularly struck by "the constructive and moderate character" of the reforms Aron proposed. Social reformers, especially revolutionaries, frequently adopted "the fervent tone of the prophet" ("un ton d'apôtre ou de devin"), but Aron was at the furthest pole from romanticism. At the same time, although he wrote that he had no doctrine or creed to set against communism and rejected the striking of spectacular attitudes, he clearly had a political and social faith, believing as he did in the values of freedom and justice which illuminated his action. Aron's strictly "partisan" views were, inevitably, debatable. The trenchant language which he occasionally used in order to defend them would provoke lively reactions in the opposite camp; but it was impossible to remain indifferent to such political considerations, in the broadest sense of the term, and the "scientific" works promised by Aron would be eagerly awaited.[63]

However, the most eloquent discussion of *Le Grand Schisme* was that by *Le Figaro littéraire*'s chief critic, André Rousseaux.[64] He began by justifying his decision to review, in what was after all a literary column, a book which "contains so much science and so many figures and statistics". *Le Grand Schisme* was, he confessed,

sufficiently rich in ideas and dazzling in style for such a question to have hardly crossed my mind. But then I shall never forget that it was literature in its purest form – poetry – which was the occasion of my first contact with Raymond Aron.

It was the winter of the Liberation, at a time when our hopes were battered and confused. A small book of poems reached me, bearing the posthumous message of Jean-Claude Diamant-Berger, who was killed in Normandy. I have never forgotten those poems. Through them the voice of a dead young man gave clear expression to the fervent hope we had then as now: that human existence should be noble and free, and that it was France's mission to uphold this ideal throughout the world. The Preface to this little book was by Raymond Aron, who had been Jean-Claude's friend in London. It did not just provide a commentary on the young poet's work, but bore witness to it. Jean-Claude Diamant-Berger was striving after a creative revolution; Raymond Aron was doing likewise.[65]

If today I recall those pages, it is because this masterly book, *Le Grand Schisme*, is inspired by the same energy...

Certainly, *Le Grand Schisme* abounds in analytical demonstrations which give us our fill of logical deductions, judicious observations and corrections to countless errors. A sovereign good sense never ceases to stimulate and, at the same time, comfort the mind. But the strength of the book lies in the fact that never for a moment does the free exercise of a mind in pursuit of truth become gratuitous. There is not one of its arguments that does not converge on the dominant truth on which the fate of the thought, the thinker and the reader all depend. For Raymond Aron shows the "great schism" – the division of the planet between Stalinist imperialism and American reaction – to be a crisis on which hangs the destiny of man's freedom on earth. Humanity is not at the crossroads in terms of a choice between America and Russia; it is faced, rather, with the alternative of death or survival, depending on whether Stalinism will enslave it or not. Thus resistance to Stalinism is a direct consequence of the Resistance itself, when the latter rallied every mind and heart that was determined, after 1940, to choose between freedom and death . . . In other words, the great schism does not so much mark a frontier between two rival empires as the boundary between what belongs to the human order and what is against it.

The importance of such a book at the present time is, therefore, clear. Although in many of its sections it gives the impression of being a very straightforward portrait of the political, economic and social physiognomy of our time, it far surpasses its descriptive aspect by the position it takes with regard to the salvation of humanism, in the broadest sense of the term. Even more, the demonstrations contained in its analysis provide material in support of this position of principle. This is why, instead of being overtaken by events, the work is served by them. Events move quickly in these times, and Raymond Aron's book, which was completed over six months ago, would have already slipped into the category of past history, if it had only been concerned to account for certain facts of the last few years. On the contrary, it is striking to see that the notable events that have taken place in France and the world since its author put down his pen only serve to confirm his views. Does this imply that his views are prophetic? Quite simply, Aron's analysis rests on one fundamental truth, which nothing can contradict. Even more simply, I would say that Raymond Aron is doing no more perhaps than calling things by their real name. White is not black, it is white. Only, it is more difficult to convince people of this when they are talking about freedom and progress . . . [66]

In *Le Monde*, the political scientist and journalist, Maurice Duverger, with whom Aron was often to cross swords on subsequent occasions, was, despite the praise he lavished on *Le Grand Schisme*, more equivocal.[67] "Intelligent almost to the point of being human" – this description of a character in one of Aldous Huxley's novels (the writer, Philip Quarles, in *Point Counter Point*) came irresistibly to mind when reading Aron's latest book:

All the crucial problems – political, social and economic – which torment the men of our time are posed here in terms that are stark and clear; the tangled web of causes and consequences is unravelled with a lucidity that is almost painful, such is its rigour. One would like a public opinion that is blinded by slogans which are contradictory in their terms, but identical in their stupidity, to start putting into practice on a regular basis this political summary of our time, for it would provide a real drying-out cure (cure de désintoxication).

Not that he was saying, Duverger stressed, that Aron had spoken the last word on every point he discussed. Aron himself, who at every step indicated the difficulties involved in social enquiry and the provisional and limited character of his conclusions, would claim no such thing. In Duverger's view, the essence of the book lay not so much in its conclusions, however important they might be, as in its method:

May the pseudo-Marxists of today, prisoners of a debilitating scholasticism, see from this example what can be offered by a true dialectic, a Marxism infinitely more authentic than theirs, in spite of everything that separates it from Marx! Thanks to it, Raymond Aron's subtle intelligence never loses touch with reality: it triumphantly resists the temptation to intellectuality.

What, then, prevented the book from being "entirely human"? In Duverger's opinion, it was a lack of passion. In his view, this was a strength, since social science laid claim to impassivity, detachment and distance from the event, and he considered *Le Grand Schisme* to be a work of science, "a sort of manual of contemporary political sociology". But it was precisely this which was strange: for Aron refused at the outset the very compliment – in Duverger's judgement, the highest of all – which Duverger paid the work. "This book is a partisan and not a scientific work", wrote Aron in his Preface. In other words, it seemed to Duverger that the author of the *Introduction to the Philosophy of History* was here giving way to the member of the National Council of the RPF: the latter did not wish to be judged by the same criteria as the former. It had to be said, then, that Aron the party member was not the equal of the scientist: "this excellent sociologist is a very poor partisan". Not only did he lack bad faith, but any faith at all. Since Koestler and Camus, the image of the Christian without faith had become familiar. It would probably be an exaggeration to say that Aron was a Gaullist without faith, but his faith was not one which could move mountains and his religion was somewhat lukewarm – or lucid, "which is roughly the same thing".

In joining the RPF, Duverger wrote, Aron was not merely moving with the likely direction of history: his motives were more complex and lofty than that. As every page of his book showed, he was "profoundly and sincerely liberal". As such, he sought to show that liberty was threatened throughout the world, and especially in France, where the anarchy of the Fourth Republic made the coming of a right- or left-wing fascism inevitable. He believed – probably rightly – that this anarchy could not be overcome within existing institutions. Consequently, of the two "movements" which presented themselves as the successors of the regime – Gaullism and communism – Aron chose the one which was least destructive of freedom, at the same time as he sought by his personal action to attenuate its authoritarian tendencies. Hence the last part of the book outlined a programme of moderate reforms which would allow Gaullism to renew the Republic without destroying it.

But this raised what for Duverger was the fundamental question. Was a democratic Gaullism possible, or was the tendency of the movement irresistibly dictatorial? Although Aron never posed the problem so directly, it seemed to Duverger to underlie every one of his arguments. Indeed, "the whole book is an attempt to show the possibility of a moderate Gaullism; but the demonstration lacks any warmth and its author seems to be trying to convince himself as much as his readers". For, in Duverger's view, an "abyss" separated the style of *Le Grand Schisme* from that of General de Gaulle, just as it separated Aron's Gaullism from the General's. In short, Duverger doubted if Aron himself – "this lucid and pitiless observer" – really believed in the moderate Gaullism he described in the book, although Duverger admitted that "the presence of liberals in a party that is by nature authoritarian...can sometimes serve to counterbalance the action of the extremists within the movement".[68]

Jean-Marie Domenach, in *Esprit*, shared a number of Duverger's reservations. *Le Grand Schisme* represented "an enormous expenditure of intelligence in return for a disappointing result". The book was "packed with ideas and interesting statistics", but contained a number of "simplistic notions (about the trade unions, for example) and disturbing omissions (not a word on the reform of the French Union)". At the heart of the argument, in "the best chapter in the book", Aron analysed France's economic regression with "a perfect mastery and clarity of exposition". Yet, added Domenach, thus revealing a naive and unsubstantiated faith in non-capitalist economies, it was "difficult to understand how so intelligent a sociologist cannot see that it is French capitalism itself which, even if it does undergo the political and social measures he proposes, constitutes the major obstacle to that technical development which is the road to salvation".[69]

"This lack of understanding", Domenach concluded (thereby ignoring some three-quarters of the book), "doubtless stems from a total absence of anything other than an economic perspective":

What is most lacking in this intelligent RPF theorist – who, in London, was one of the forerunners of today's anti-Gaullism – is a deeply-held conviction: the warmth and enthusiasm that are aroused by the vision of an ideal, the sense of coming revolution. Raymond Aron's progress, like his Gaullism, is cold.[70]

Finally, in an essay on "right-wing thought" published a number of years later, Simone de Beauvoir[71] took Aron to task as follows: "The bourgeois theorist", she wrote, "knowing that the future is slipping from his grasp, no longer even tries to be constructive: he defines himself in relation to communism, in opposition to it, in a purely negative way. Aron, for example, in his conclusion to *Le Grand Schisme*, does not ask:

'What do we believe in?', but: 'What can be opposed to communism?' His reply is: 'The affirmation of Christian and humanist values'. But it is clear to anyone who has read his books that these so-called values are the least of his concerns: the only thing that is important to him is the defeat of Communism".[72]

The very opposite of Simone de Beauvoir's charge is of course true, as is evident to anyone who has seriously read Part Four of *Le Grand Schisme*, where Aron makes many constructive proposals for political, economic, social and intellectual reform. In making such an accusation, she was also wilfully ignoring the affirmation of values contained in the final chapter – "Faith without Illusions" – of his next book, *Les Guerres en chaîne*, which appeared in 1951, four years before Simone de Beauvoir wrote the essay in question.

Notes

1. 1948a.
2. Ibid., p. 8.
3. Ibid., pp. 9–10.
4. Ibid., pp. 13–14.
5. Ibid., p. 15. Lord Altrincham, taking *Le Grand Schisme* as the starting-point for an article in the American journal, *Foreign Affairs*, drew attention to Aron's failure to mention the British Commonwealth at this point (Lord Altrincham, "The British Commonwealth and Western Union", *Foreign Affairs*, 27, 1949, pp. 601–17). This is one of the few references to *Le Grand Schisme* (which was never translated into English, or indeed any other language) in Anglo-American literature. Despite this reservation, Lord Altrincham believed that Aron –"a very distinguished representative of French political thought" – had discussed "with much insight the effect of the ideological division between the United States and the Soviet Union upon the world in general and France in particular" (ibid., p. 601).
6. 1948a, pp. 17–19.
7. Ibid., pp. 25–6.
8. Ibid., pp. 26–30.
9. Ibid., pp. 30–1.
10. Ibid., Chapter II.
11. Ibid., pp. 59–60.
12. Ibid., pp. 67–8.
13. Ibid., pp. 70–1.
14. Ibid., pp. 77–80.
15. Ibid., pp. 80–8. See also the series of articles Aron wrote on the German question in *Combat*, 26, 29, 31 January, 2, 7 February, 1947.
16. 1948a, pp. 89–90.
17. Ibid., pp. 91–2.

18. 1944o, 1944p. See Chapter 12, above.
19. 1948a, p. 97.
20. Ibid., pp. 108–9.
21. Ibid., p. 110.
22. Ibid., pp. 110–11.
23. Ibid., p. 112.
24. Aron was careful to examine the theory of relative pauperization, which Marxists frequently put forward: ibid., pp. 114–16.
25. Ibid., p. 114. Aron presented the evidence against the theory of proletarianization, ibid., pp. 116–19.
26. Ibid., pp. 119–25.
27. Ibid., pp. 125–6.
28. Ibid., p. 126.
29. Ibid., pp. 129–30.
30. Ibid., pp. 131–2.
31. Ibid., pp. 132–5.
32. Ibid., pp. 135–7.
33. Ibid., p. 156.
34. Ibid., p. 162.
35. Ibid., Chapter IX.
36. Ibid., Chapter X.
37. Ibid., pp. 234–6.
38. Ibid., Chapter XIII.
39. Ibid., pp. 237, 243.
40. Ibid., pp. 288–90.
41. Ibid., p. 302.
42. 1946b. See Chapter 12, above.
43. 1948a, p. 305.
44. Ibid., p. 323.
45. Ibid., pp. 327–8.
46. Ibid., pp. 331–2.
47. Ibid., pp. 339, 342.
48. Ibid., p. 343.
49. 1983a, p. 284.
50. *Volcano on Ice*, BBC Radio 3, 14 January 1985. Aron and Hassner were to become close friends and colleagues.
51. Hassner, 1985, p. 226.
52. Lazitch, 1985, p. 47. Aron and Lazitch met in 1950 and Aron agreed to write a preface to Lazitch's Geneva doctorate on Lenin and the Third International (1951b) – despite the initial reservations of the Swiss publisher, for whom Aron, the Cold War militant, was too controversial a figure.
53. 1983a, p. 90.
54. Ibid., pp. 288–90.
55. Marchand, 1948.
56. Maulnier, 1948. Before the war Thierry Maulnier (born 1909) had been one of the most brilliant young contributors to *L'Action française*. Reviewing his *La France,*

la guerre et la paix (1942) in *La France libre*, Aron had written that, unlike other conservatives such as Daniel Halévy, Maulnier was at least trying to define a way ahead for France ("Even if one does not accept the conclusions, one can salute the attempt"). In Aron's view, he was a genuine patriot who believed in fundamental liberties (1943s, p. 430). Later in the war Aron was to say of Maulnier that "one can loathe his ideas but one must acknowledge his talent and personality" (1944k; reprinted 1946b, p. 160).

57. Caillois, 1948.
58. Bataille, 1948.
59. Sigaux, 1948.
60. Fabrègues, 1948.
61. Harcourt and Saint-Pierre, 1948.
62. Anon., 1949.
63. Ibid.
64. Rousseaux, 1948.
65. The book of poems in question was published in London during the war (1945z) and Aron's Preface was reprinted in the review, *Renaissances* (1945z[1]). Jean-Claude Diamant-Berger was born in 1920 and moved in surrealist circles in Paris before the war. In June 1941 he went to the USA, where his parents already were, but in March 1942 joined the Free French in England as a parachutist. In June 1944 he was sent to France on a photographic mission and was killed during the battle of Caen in the following month. A collection of his poems was published after the war: Jean-Claude Diamant-Berger, *Poèmes d'Everlor* (Paris, 1951).
66. Rousseaux, 1948.
67. Duverger, 1948.
68. Ibid.
69. Domenach, 1949.
70. Ibid.
71. Simone de Beauvoir, "La Pensée de droite, aujourd'hui", *TM*, 10, 1955, pp. 1539–75.
72. Ibid., pp. 1543–4. In fact, the passage quoted by Simone de Beauvoir is not, as she states, from the conclusion of *Le Grand Schisme*, but from p. 169.

17

The Wars of the
Twentieth Century

———

Aron had announced at the end of *Le Grand Schisme* that he was hoping
to develop the discussion of "crises and wars", outlined there, in his next
book.[1] *Les Guerres en chaîne*[2] was written largely in 1950 – several of its
early chapters were published in journals during that year[3] – and
completed in April 1951. During its writing, however, Aron was struck
by personal tragedy. In July 1950 a daughter, Laurence, was born with
Down's Syndrome. Six months later, at the very end of December, his
second daughter, Emmanuelle, who had been born in England during
the war, died of leukaemia, after a three-week illness, at the age of six
and a half. "There is no apprenticeship to misfortune", he wrote in one
of the most moving passages of his *Memoirs*. "When it strikes us, we still
have everything to learn. I was a bad pupil, slow and rebellious".[4] For
three years he was "a virtual sleepwalker" and, in his opinion, wrote
nothing of value during that time. However, he "tried to come alive again"
and did so through the writing of *The Opium of the Intellectuals*, which
was for him "a kind of half-cure".[5] Aron hoped that the two blows he

suffered in 1950 were not apparent in his writing, but inevitably the marks were there: *Les Guerres en chaîne* itself makes one oblique reference to the death of his daughter[6] and Manès Sperber suggests that the book is characterized by "a new tone, a moving sensibility", which was absent from the earlier work.[7]

Originally to be called *Contradictions de la paix belliqueuse*[8] and then *Le Siècle des guerres*,[9] *Les Guerres en chaîne* (literally, *Wars in Chain Reaction*) was the first of Aron's books to be translated into English, under the title *The Century of Total War*.[10] Aron in fact took advantage of the translation, which appeared three years after the French original, to make a number of revisions to the text. As well as being slightly cut and re-arranged, the American edition leaves out three chapters[11] and includes a new one on the implications for the international situation of Stalin's death in 1953.[12]

As Aron pointed out in the Preface to *Les Guerres en chaîne*, which is regrettably omitted in the English translation, his specific starting-point in writing the book was an attempt to reply to a question put by a British reviewer of *Le Grand Schisme*: if peace was impossible and total war improbable in the foreseeable future, how was the international situation likely to evolve? In order to answer this question, it had seemed necessary to "go back to the beginning", to an analysis of the origins of the wars of the twentieth century.[13]

Aron attempted to do this in Part One of the book, "From Sarajevo to Hiroshima", starting with the First World War. There was no simple explanation of its origins to be offered, he argued, since the reasons behind the hostility among the nations of Europe were "manifold and complex". Wars were essentially unpredictable, but those of the twentieth century were especially so, because the very situations that brought about a modern war were destroyed in its wake: "It is the battle in and for itself, and not the origin of the conflict or the peace treaty, that constitutes the major fact and produces the most far-reaching consequences".[14]

In the case of the First World War, "between the aspiration and the fulfilment" there intervened what Aron called "the technological surprise" – the development (between the Franco-Prussian War of 1870–1 and the Balkan Wars of 1912–13) of such armaments as the mine, the torpedo, the submarine, the machine gun and rapid-firing artillery. Furthermore, in the age of democracy (with its compulsory military service) and of industry (with its potential for mass production and mass destruction), national wars tended to become total wars. What required explanation, however, was not how the 1914–18 war spread across Europe and became, as Pareto put it, "hyperbolic", but the fact that the nineteenth century was able to escape these twin consequences of the French and the Industrial Revolutions. The answer, Aron suggested, was that diplomacy had been able to localize the conflicts in nineteenth-century Europe, because none of them had posed a clear threat to the general balance of power. Examples of this were the Anglo-French victory over Russia in the Crimea and the German victory over France in 1871.

In 1914, it was the "technological surprise" which, in Aron's view, was "among the main causes of the geographical extension of the war and the growth of wartime passions".[15] For instance, America's historically significant decision to intervene, which assured the defeat of Germany, was provoked by the latter's declaration of unrestricted submarine warfare, and was due essentially to the technological amplification of the war. Certainly, ideology (of kinship and democracy) played a part in winning over American opinion to participate in the war, but "the fundamental consideration, nevertheless, was primarily materialistic. The Allies had sought American aid to help support the burden of the hyperbolic war. Economic participation became military partnership when the submarines tried to break the bond already existing between the European and American democracies, and so threatened to leave a navy regarded as hostile ruling the oceans and separating ancient Europe from the New World".[16]

There had been "incessant inquiry" into the origin of the First World War, but no one, Aron stated, had ever asked why it became hyperbolic:

Was it passion that produced technological excess, or technological excess that fomented passion? Not unreservedly or without qualification, and fully recognizing the interaction of the two phenomena, I would maintain that the motive force of the evolution, at that time, was technological. It was technology that imposed the organization of enthusiasm, condemned to failure the efforts at conciliation, drove out the old diplomatic wisdom, and contributed to the spread of the crusading spirit, finally producing a peace that created the situation from which the second world war started.[17]

For, Aron continued,

the principal causes of the Second World War resulted from prolongation of the first war and, above all, of the Russian Revolution and the Fascist reactions to it in Italy and Germany.

The war destroyed those traditional institutions that might have checked the tendency in Western societies toward social levelling and forms of collectivism. The monarchies that had crumbled in defeat would not have prevented the "democratization" of the regimes of Central Europe, but they would have reduced the risk of mass passions, secular religions, and totalitarian parties. Parliaments are soundly established insofar as they are the result of continuity and consent, and not violence.

Everything happens as if, at a certain point, violence becomes self-supporting. In war, as with fissionable materials, there is a critical mass. Since 1914, Europe has been shaken by wars in "chain reaction".[18]

The second war of the twentieth century, like the first, was lost by the aggressor; once more, however, now that the ordeal was over, the world remained unconverted to the values for which the West had fought. European democracy, freedom and civilization were the victims, even more than Germany, of a victory won in their name. "Leaving aside these fundamental analogies, the second war was nearly a replica of the first. Everything happened differently but the final outcome is much the same".[19] In Aron's view, the "decisive capitulation" in the 1930s was not the Munich agreement, but the failure of Britain and France to act after the German reoccupation of the Rhineland in March 1936. "From that date, war was not inevitable (what, indeed, is the meaning of inevitability, applied to a chain of historical events?), but it had become probable".[20]

It was easy, Aron wrote, to understand why the immediate causes of the Second World War should have been the subject of less controversy. The First World War had been the result of what had been termed "diplomatic failure". The Second World War had arisen from "Hitler's schemes of conquest":

It might have broken out a year earlier if the democracies had decided to fight for Czechoslovakia; it might have been delayed had the democracies not come to the aid of Poland. But it is impossible to see how Hitler could have stopped of his own accord, or how Great Britain and France could have saved themselves without stopping him, that is to say, without fighting. Thus, what really matter are the remote origins. What were the sources of Hitler's rise to power and Germany's imperial desires? Why did the conservative states give the Teuton Caesar time to accumulate enough arms, not for victory, but for his own burial beneath the ruins of a civilization?[21]

But the second war of the twentieth century had in its turn prepared the ground for a third war. It was in the Western allies' interest, Aron maintained, to weaken Germany, but not to destroy it.[22] Since their aim was to re-establish conservative (in the sense of non-revolutionary) regimes, they ought not to have wanted Germany to resist to the death. Yet they did nothing to detach from the regime those elements that opposed the Nazis, and nothing to allow the generals or the ordinary fighting man to envisage anything but unconditional surrender. The

Allies acted as if their aim was to unite the National Socialists and the rest of the German people; in other words, their actions were contrary to all reason. In order that the Second World War should be the "war to end wars", it was carried to its limit; and because it was carried to its limit, it gave rise to a successor.

The only thing that could be said in defence of the Western statesmen was that

their conduct of the war was characteristic of the democracies in our century: they submitted passively to the dynamism of hyperbolic war. They propagated the simplest and most convincing of myths: all the United Nations belonged on the side of the just, and the enemy was the incarnation of evil. Incapable of thinking about peace, which comes after war and is its real purpose, they went to the very limits of destruction, making no effort to detach the German people from Hitler's clique and taking no precautions against their ally, whose ambitions were hardly more of a mystery than those of Hitler. By the time the illusions of propaganda were dissipated and the governments in London and Washington had the support of public opinion in their will to resist, the benefits of victory had been lost: Eastern Europe had been Sovietized, Germany divided, and the Chinese Communists armed by courtesy of the Russian army. The Second World War had laid the foundations for the third...

Since, under a July sun, bourgeois Europe entered the century of war, men have lost control of their history and have been dragged along by the contradictory logics of technology and passion. Out of national war came a first imperial war. How far will we be dragged by the chain reactions of violence?[23]

To try to answer this question, Aron considered first "the Leninist myth of imperialism" – the Marxist view that "the industrial societies would be peaceful if they were not capitalist".[24] The ideas common to the Marxist theory of imperialism, as expressed in the writings of Rosa Luxemburg, Bukharin, Lenin and others, could be put in the form of three propositions. First, "capitalist economy cannot, because of its very structure, absorb its own production, and is therefore compelled to expand; the individual is not even aware of the mechanism that is carrying him away". Second, "the race among the European nations to win overseas territories for colonial exploitation is an inevitable consequence of competition". Third, "the European wars are the inevitable result of imperialism: their real stake is the division of the planet, even though they may be set off by some European dispute... Having reached the limits of the planet, the will to power that has driven the capitalists to the remotest corners of the world must now turn upon itself".[25]

This theory enjoyed "tremendous prestige even in non-Marxist circles". It was "intellectually satisfying" because it sought to account for a certain number of facts – for example, Britain and America's interest in the oil resources of the Near East, the link between the Boer War and the South African gold mines, and the support of the German coal and steel trusts for naval construction before 1914 and the financing of national socialism before 1933. But there were a number of objections to be made against the theory. First, there was "no relation between the purely economic need for expansion, such as should have obtained according to the theory, and the actual facts of colonial expansion". For example, "French capitalism was one of the least dynamic in Europe, yet the African empire that France acquired at the end of the nineteenth century was second in importance only to that of Great Britain". Again, "Russia, which at that time was only just beginning its capitalistic career and whose immense territory was still underdeveloped, was nevertheless diplomatically active in both Europe and Asia. The Russian interest in Manchuria and in the Slavic peoples of Europe was not dictated by economic considerations, nor was it the result of capitalist machinations".[26]

A second objection to the Leninist myth of imperialism was that "Neither the First nor the Second World War originated directly in a conflict over colonies". The twenty years prior to the First World War, for instance, were "probably among the most prosperous in the history of capitalism" and "the image of a Europe constrained by its economic contradictions to destroy itself" was, therefore, "a myth". Certainly, Aron agreed, "capitalism tends to incorporate undeveloped territories into its system" and "colonial conquest may be regarded as a function of economic expansion", but two questions remained. Were the African colonial empires founded in accordance with this pattern? And were the European wars a consequence of these quarrels for the division of the planet? "The facts, if invoked without bias", Aron replied, "answer these two questions negatively". For, apart from the Boer War,

none of the colonial undertakings that caused important diplomatic conflicts in Europe was motivated by the quest for capitalist profits; they all originated in political ambitions that the chancelleries camouflaged by invoking "realistic" motives. In other words, the actual relationship is most often the reverse of that accepted by the current theory of imperialism: the economic interests are only a pretext or a rationalization, whereas the profounder cause lies in the nations' will to power.[27]

The "central idea" of Lenin's theory was that, although the wars of the twentieth century were waged in Europe over European conflicts, it was the division of the planet which was at stake. However, to Aron the difficulty in trying to refute the theory was to see how it could either be proved or disproved. As far as the First World War was concerned,

396

despite the mythology, it was not the case that millions of men were sent to their deaths to open up industrial markets. The "essential cause" of the hostility between Britain and Germany was Germany's creation of a navy, since Britain's survival depended on its control of the sea – hence Aron's "main thesis", that military alignments are political in origin.[28] Turning to the Second World War, he of course accepted that the economic crisis of 1929 and the war of 1939 were connected, and was "far from denying the imperialistic potentialities of the economic policy adopted by the National Socialists"; he merely maintained that "the Third Reich was not driven to imperialism by residues of capitalism in its structure". If the economy had been collectivized, "the imperialistic temptation would not have been mitigated".[29] In other words, he stressed characteristically, the motives of the actors were primarily political.

However, at the very moment when economic progress was helping to cure some of the evils attributable to technology, war had brought about "the total mobilization of collectivities". The rule of the bourgeoisie might one day seem like a precarious transition from the military order of the aristocracies to the military order of the technocracies.[30] By effacing traditions, war "clears the way for the building of the totalitarian state. Wars always resemble the societies that wage them". Throughout the centuries, there had been "a reciprocal adjustment between tools and arms, between class relations and the structure of armies".[31] Thus "the supreme laws of the nation at war" could be summed up in two words, both of which were important in the industrial order: "organization" and "rationalization". Rules which, in time of peace, were applied only to certain enterprises were applied, in time of war, to society as a whole. In wartime, administrative centralization was "irresistible", and total mobilization came close to totalitarian order. But the process was not inevitable: although the First World War created a favourable opportunity for the seizure of power by the Bolsheviks in Russia and the National Socialists in Germany, the example of the Western democracies showed that mobilization perhaps implied a total, but not necessarily a totalitarian, state.[32]

Aron ended the first part of *The Century of Total War* with an outstanding passage in which he related his discussion of the two World Wars to the philosophy of history, and in particular the parts played in events by "necessity" and "accident":

If we want to think of the two wars as elements of one and the same whole, as episodes in a single struggle, we must not refer to "eternal Germany" but to the tragic interlocking of causes and effects and to the dynamism of violence which we have been trying to analyse. All the "monist" theories, those that hold Germany responsible as well as those that inculpate capitalism, are puerile. In the historical order they are comparable to the mythologies that served in place of natural science in the ages in which men were incapable of understanding the mechanism of natural forces. If we study the effect of the first war on the internal constitution of states, on the psychology of peoples, and on the disintegration of the world economy; if in our interpretation we take account of circumstances such as the seizure of power by the Bolsheviks or the personal rivalries of the dictators, and of phenomena that are determined and yet at the same time accidental, such as the exceptional acuteness of the world crisis of 1929, then we may succeed in following the history of the thirty years, a history of wars in chain reaction.

It is history in the full sense of the term, whose broad lines one may retrospectively trace, but without making the claim that the ultimate outcome could have been foreseen or was implicit in the principal forces of the time...

It is so obvious a story that one is astonished afterwards at not having seen beforehand what was coming. Yet it is all the more necessary to guard against any retrospective illusion of fatalism. During those thirty years there were moments when destiny was, so to speak, in suspense and quite different lines of evolution began to take form. It would have taken only a few more army corps to reverse the outcome of the Battle of the Marne...

After Hitler came to power, there were still opportunities to change the course of destiny. In March 1936, a military reply to the entry of the German troops into the Rhineland would at least have slowed down the pace of events, and might even have brought about the downfall of Hitlerism. It may be, though there can be no certainty on this point, that Anglo-French resistance in 1938 would have induced the anti-Hitler conspirators (who included some of the military commanders) to act. During the war, the British and Americans might have maintained or resumed contact with the German opposition, and tried to conquer Germany without destroying her, instead of pushing the war to the point at which the annihilation of the vanquished made a collision between the Allies inevitable. To spare the enemy when one is not sure of one's ally has always been the teaching of an honourable Machiavellian wisdom...

How mysterious is the evidence of history! In some epochs events forever betray the intentions of the actors. Peoples make war, but they never aspire so passionately to peace. Statesmen try first to appease conquerors and then to resist them, first to satisfy them and then to overawe them. They discover each time that these successive methods of diplomacy have been resorted to at the wrong time: resistance when compliance would have been better, and vice versa. However immense empires may be, they never satiate the appetite of the Caesars. Hitler refused hegemony over continental Europe, which would have satisfied the aspiration of the Hohenzollerns; the Kremlin is refusing an empire reaching from the Elbe to Indo-China, which would have satisfied Hitler's aspirations – at least for a time. From war to war the stake grows, until it now involves domination over the world.

That is why at times the philosopher meditates on the end result and invokes what Hegel calls "the Cunning of Reason". Is not the unity of mankind the aim, obscurely aspired to, that magnetizes not so much the desires of individuals as the dynamism of collective forces, attracting to itself, through blood and tears, the unfortunate peoples whose sufferings will receive the subsequent compensation of a precarious welfare? The lag between the causes and the results of events, between human passions and the effects of the acts they inspire, between conflicts of ideology and power and the real issue of wars, fascinates the observer, who is tempted at one moment to denounce the absurdity of history and at another to admit its broad rationality.

The only truth accessible to objective understanding is the recognition of these contradictions. If there is a Providence in this tragic chaos, it escapes us.[33] Mythologies consist of the substitution of a single factor for the plurality of causes, of lending unconditional value to a desired object, and of a failure to realize the distance between the dreams of men and the destiny of societies.

Men of learning have discovered the secret of fire but not that of history. Lenin, who dreamed of ending the class struggle, laid the foundation of the total state, of concentration camps, and of an omnipotent police. Millions of victims curse and will continue to curse the blindness of the revolutionary, but their curses do not permit us to anticipate with confidence the judgement of posterity.[34]

* * *

In Part Two, "Crossroads of History", Aron began by discussing the rise of the "peripheral states", the USA and the USSR, and then turned to an examination of the passage "from Marxism to Stalinism". The first problem he set himself was to try to explain the appeal – to Asian peasants as well as atomic scientists – of Marxism. Marxism was "a religion promising temporal salvation" and "a Christian heresy", "the modern form of millennialism" which "places the Kingdom of God on this earth, due to arrive after an apocalyptic revolution in which the old world will be engulfed". Its ideology combined three themes which, taken together, gave Marxism its "explosive force": the Christian theme ("All religions of salvation prophesy in one form or another the revenge of the humiliated"); the Promethean theme ("Man, having discovered the secret of fire, used it to extend more and more quickly his mastery over natural forces, as, on the distant horizon, he could see an earthly paradise"); and the rationalist theme ("Because they know the laws of their own history, men become capable of acting in complete lucidity", since "the final outcome – the creation of a humane society thanks to man's conscious action – is known in advance"). It was the synthesis of the revolt against inequality and injustice, together with a boundless faith in science and technology which, based on a pseudo-rationalist interpretation of history, gave Marxism its popular appeal.[35]

Intellectually, it was easy to explain the passage from Marxism through Leninism to Stalinism, for the "decisive stages" were clear: the creation of the revolutionary party, revolutionary civil war, the doctrine of

399

socialism in one country, and the assertion of the leading role of the Russian Bolshevik Party.[36] The aim of Soviet society today was unity; it allowed no rivalry, whether between temporal and spiritual power, between different social groups, or between society and the state. In forcing all its citizens and all its resources into the service of the state, it was like every other tyranny. Western societies, on the other hand, were characterized by their rejection of unity, for life in the West, "requiring creative struggle and effort", was made up of tensions that were "not so much overcome as controlled".[37]

Marxist ideology, however, when viewed as a continuation of the rationalist and humanist tradition of the West, still aroused sympathy. Despite Soviet reality, every element in the prestige enjoyed by Marxism worked to the profit of Stalinism. In order to tear away the veil of illusion, one needed direct experience of that reality. Paradoxically, therefore, there were probably more believers on this side of the Iron Curtain than on the other. "Communist faith dissolves as it spreads; it destroys itself through its victories". In every Sovietized country a minority supported the regime, but the religion probably found its believers mainly among the privileged or those who were too young to have known anything else.[38]

Aron turned next to an analysis of "the atomic age". Nowadays people were quick to label as anachronistic the kind of dispute which had traditionally existed over strategically important frontiers and regions. In fact, Aron contended, international diplomacy had not as yet been radically altered by the new weapon.[39] In 1946 and 1947, when American public opinion grasped the nature of Soviet ambitions and the military weakness of the democracies, the atomic bomb was of inestimable value in giving confidence to American diplomacy. But if it was asked whether the fate of Europe would have been different without the weapon, two questions arose. Even without the atomic bomb, would the United States have tolerated the expansion of the Soviet empire as far as the Atlantic? And would Stalin have been prepared to face the risk of world war?[40]

The answer to both questions, it seemed to Aron, was "no". In what one British reviewer has called "a remarkably convincing passage",[41] he argued that if anything, the Americans had lost rather than gained by their "famous atomic monopoly". It had been of no use in the Cold War and the United States had been led, by its atomic superiority, to adopt military and diplomatic attitudes whose dangers were now apparent. "Confident that the stock-pile of bombs would suffice to prevent the Soviet Union from employing regular armies in any part of the world, the United States reduced to a minimum its own aerial, naval, and – above all – land forces capable of immediate action. It thus allowed itself to be driven into a position where, in the event of any local aggression, it would have to choose between passivity or world war – a formidable choice for a nation aiming to avoid a world war".[42]

In a section entitled "Logic and Chance", Aron summarized the second part of *The Century of Total War*, as he had concluded the first, by relating his discussion to the philosophy of history:

The present world is situated, so to speak, at the meeting point of three processes of development. The first led to a planetary unity and a bi-polar diplomatic structure; the second to the diffusion in Asia and Europe of a secular religion of which one of the two giant powers claims to be the metropolis; and the third to the perfection of weapons of mass destruction, to a total war animated both by modern science and primitive fury, with the atom bomb and the guerrilla as the extreme manifestations of unlimited violence.

Each of these processes includes – to employ Cournot's expression – one part logic and one part chance...[43]

The meeting of these processes itself indicates a combination of logic and of chance. To some extent each begins in a common situation: the development of science, the application of science to industry, and the expansion of industrial civilization. It was industrial technique, even more than political democracy, that rendered unlimited and inexpiable a war which Europe, unaware, had undertaken as a war just like any other. It is industrial technique that weakens beliefs that have justified and upheld the age-long order of human societies; that uproots the urban masses and makes them dissatisfied with their humble lot; that makes poverty, long accepted as a decree of God or nature, a sort of scandal. It is this that precipitates the anti-white revolution in Asia and the insurrection of masses ever more numerous and wretched; and this that spurs the impatience of the peoples of Europe whose standard of living rises more slowly than their aspirations. This is what has made the political structure of the Continent an anachronism, has promoted the advent of continent-states, has favoured the diffusion of a secular religion – a substitute faith for souls deprived of the Gospel, and has made of Stalinism – the religion of the proletariat and the machine – a fetish for the worship of the semi-educated.

There is no justification, even after the event, for saying that things had to happen as they have in fact happened. The decisive events of this period – the 1914 explosion, the Russian Revolution, Hitler's rise to power, the coming of the second war, and the ineptitude of Anglo-American statesmanship can be explained reasonably. One can see the causes, however remote, which favoured them but one cannot ignore the interval between the cause and the effect; it is man, or rather it is men, who by their action or inaction, produced this history which they did not want, and we cannot even console ourselves with the thought that in the long run the consequences of their courage or cowardice, their blindness or foresight, will be effaced, for as far as the eye can see, there loom the consequences of Russia's industrialization in the Bolshevik and not in the Western manner.

To keep to the broadest phenomena, the present crisis is not the direct and inevitable result of industrial civilization, but of its collision with certain long-standing facts of

401

history. If the European communities have destroyed themselves, it is not because they have proved incapable of integrating their productive forces into a structure founded on private property. The eternal rivalry of nations has continued into the age of infernal machines; and nations, in their pursuit of power, have not found a way to agree either to a common law or to moderation and compromise. The techniques of modern war have made the survival of Europe incompatible with the continuance of conflicts that long antedate capitalism and that were due only in slight measure to competition between economic or social systems.

The revolt of Russia and of Asia is directed less against capitalism than against the civilization that came from the West. In Russia it began against a Westernized ruling class, in Asia against the dominance of Europeans. As a result of wars it has become an insurrection not of workers against the owners of the means of production, but of peoples of ancient civilization humiliated by the mysterious power of the creators of machines, and of wretched mobs with a vague sense of the incapacity of their traditional rulers to build a modern nation.

The recession of national states, the rise of the continent-states, the decline of Europe, the revolt against the West – all these were to a great extent foreseeable because they were implicit in industrial civilization and its material and moral repercussions. What was unforeseeable was the pace and manner of these changes. The two wars greatly hastened them and at the same time gave them a cataclysmic character. That Russia, the metropolis of a secular religion of universal dimensions, should stand at the borders of an exhausted Europe and an Asia in revolt, and should be checked in her ambition only by the far-off force of the United States, itself anxious about the future and accumulating a stock of atom bombs – such an encounter clearly was not predetermined by any historical necessity. The wars of the first half of the twentieth century have ripened a catastrophe that would be to the catastrophes of the past what the atom bomb is to Big Bertha.[44]

* * *

In Part Three, "Limited War", Aron argued that American diplomacy had at last realized that the enemies of yesterday – Germany and Japan – must be brought into the Western camp, if they were not to be "fatally" drawn into the Soviet orbit. However, American diplomacy had not drawn the full conclusions from that major fact, since Westerners were "too intelligent (or too stupid) to see simple things simply . . . How attractive it was to speculate on the neutrality of Germany and Japan, on armed neutrality and disarmed neutrality, on political neutrality and military neutrality!" But all those speculations "collapsed like a house of cards when the first shot was fired in Korea".[45] For the events of 1950 revealed one of the defects in American doctrine. Initially it was thought that there would be either a bellicose peace, without intervention by regular armies, or a total war, with air attacks on the main Russian cities. However, "a third possibility was discovered, which had not been foreseen – limited hot wars".[46]

402

The West, Aron believed, had the necessary resources to win a total war, should it come, and even more to re-establish the balance of armed forces in time of bellicose peace, while thus diminishing the risk of an explosion. The question was whether the democracies would have the courage to endure the sacrifices and efforts of semi-mobilization before the enemy moved. The world was living in a limited war. A semi-war required semi-mobilization, while "intercontinental equilibrium" necessitated additional duties: the West must resign itself either to losing valuable territories in the early weeks of fighting, or to keeping up a sufficient number of divisions in time of peace. Semi-mobilization would not guarantee that aggression would be repelled, but for defeatists the difficulty of resistance became a reason for passivity. Such an attitude was strictly absurd: an army of fifty divisions would not guarantee the absolute security of Europe (militarily speaking, was there such a thing?), but it would change the general strategic situation, reduce the probability of Soviet aggression, and help restore the confidence of the Europeans. For in the long run it was up to them to fill the void in Europe. If they did not make up their minds to do so, the day would come when the United States resigned itself to a strategy of intercontinental war, in response to European defeatism.[47]

The leaders of the Soviet Union considered the world-wide spread of communism to be the logical and inevitable outcome of the present crisis. The attitude of Western leaders was one of "live and let live", in their desperate hope for coexistence between the so-called socialist and the so-called capitalist countries. The Kremlin pursued an offensive strategy, the West a defensive one. Face to face with Stalin, as with Hitler, the democracies, instead of asking themselves, "What shall I do?", kept asking, "What will the Red Tsar of the Kremlin do?".[48] The Soviet Union's ultimate aim was plain to all except the wilfully blind: "That the historical concept of the Stalinists is catastrophic, that they look forward to a series of monstrous wars, civil and foreign, until the final triumph of what they call Communism, does not, it seems to me, admit of argument".[49] Such a doctrine implied preparation for the expected cataclysm, but not necessarily its cold-blooded provocation. It did not even necessarily imply a military struggle between the two regimes, although Aron thought this probable, for why else would the Kremlin keep so many divisions on a war-footing? In other words, "the Kremlin's goal is world conquest or universal diffusion of the Stalinist system".[50] Nevertheless, the Cold War was, he argued, probably a preparation rather than a substitute for total war.[51]

What of Europe? Could it live? Economically, Europe could only be "a fragment of the Atlantic universe".[52] Could it unite? The military, economic and moral arguments in favour of European unity were powerful and persuasive, but Aron doubted if the European states would "suddenly agree to surrender a fraction of their sovereignty in favour of a superstate".[53] In his view, the choice facing Europe was clear:

Of the two ideologies – European unity and Atlantic community – between which Western Europe hesitates, it is the latter that we must choose, if a choice must be made. Even united, Europe would be lost if the United States, because of discouragement, yielded to the temptation of isolationism. Europe, even divided, still has a chance of safety so long as the national states remain integrated in an Atlantic community, however imperfect.[54]

Did this mean, then, that the ideal of European unity should be abandoned altogether? "The anachronism of national states and the harm done by customs barriers are undeniable; but is Europe the supranational unit into which the national states ought to merge?" Aron's answer was that "Europe" denoted "a continent or a civilization, not an economic or political unit". The argument in favour of European unity was "still more doubtful" when one considered the position of Britain:

It has been repeated hundreds of times during the past few years, but these trite sayings are true: the government and people of the United Kingdom generally have the feeling of being Britons first and Europeans afterwards (assuming the word even means anything to them) . . . An Englishman is conscious of relationship in blood, culture and destiny with an Australian or a Canadian, and even with an American, much more than with an Italian, a German, or even a Frenchman.

. . . To ask Great Britain to make herself an integral part of an area, political or economic, called Europe, is to ask her to renounce her historic functions as an intermediary between the Continent and the rest of the world, the metropolis of a federation of nations, the centre of a subtle network of relations that are financial and commercial as well as moral. A symptom of this disparity is that no customs tariff would at the same time suit the countries of the Continent, which largely feed themselves, and the United Kingdom, which imports 60 per cent of its food.[55]

Thus the very idea of a great area, or even a "little Europe", was questionable. A united Europe would not have many advantages over the nation states; European free trade made only a limited contribution to the restoration of European economic life; and, political obstacles apart, the different countries were "too unlike in structure to be able to agree within a few years to a real fusion".[56]

What, therefore, Aron asked, was the basic element in the idea of Europe? "To my mind, it is a simple and almost obvious proposition, which Mr Churchill was quick to grasp and which propagandists and intellectuals have since obscured: namely, that Western Europe must build up its military strength, and that strength can only emerge from a reconciliation between France and Germany".[57] The only sphere in which the European idea was capable of being realized in the near future was that of the armed forces. Logically, political institutions should come first; in practice, they would emerge from the requirements of common defence.

The "brutality" of this conclusion might, Aron realized, come as a shock, but he could not see any realistic alternative. Not that, in his view, the military conception of European unity suffered from lack of imagination or excessive prudence. On the contrary,

My fear is that it may be too revolutionary. Patriotism is not made to order. It is easy to say, and it is true in the abstract, that national states are an anachronism, because they are incapable of unaided self-defence. But popular feeling does not change with the same speed as industrial progress. National passions are supposed to be on the way to extinction (although rivalries in sport are sufficient to revive them), but they are replaced by ideological passions. For example, those Frenchmen who are indifferent to the fate of France are either Communists, who love the country of their dreams and the empire in which their religion triumphs, or the purely self-centred. The European idea is empty; it has neither the transcendence of Messianic ideologies nor the immanence of concrete patriotism. It was created by intellectuals, and that fact accounts at once for its genuine appeal to the mind and its feeble echo in the heart.[58]

And yet, did Europe have "a historic vitality"? Depite its recent humiliation, Europe, west of the Iron Curtain, was still one of the rare and privileged places where the great majority of people escaped the danger of hunger and torture. From the point of view of living standards, personal rights and freedom from arbitrary interference, Europe remained almost exemplary compared with the Soviet bloc, where police violence struck at millions of innocent people, and compared with immense regions of Asia and Africa, where every year famine carried off millions of helpless victims.

While it was true that neither material prosperity nor formal liberty were the yardsticks by which to judge civilizations, the values which Europe realized less imperfectly than the greater part of mankind were the very ones of which the enemies of the West made empty boast. The Stalinists of France, the rationalists and the progressive Christians denounced economic inequality, the poverty of the masses and the abuse of power. A Soviet regime increased coal and steel production more rapidly than it improved living conditions. It eliminated landowners and capitalists, but it immediately replaced them with a hierarchy of functions and incomes, and subjected the people to the arbitrary authority of Party and police. If the struggle between the two Europes took the form of an examination in morality or in economic efficiency before an impartial tribunal, the verdict would not be in doubt. Unfortunately, that was not the character of historic conflicts. Victory might fall to the more virtuous, but that virtue had nothing to do with a sense of justice or respect for humanity. It was a matter of the stern qualities needed in difficult times – discipline and devotion on the part of the people, vision and resolution in their leaders. But did the Europeans still possess that kind of virtue?[59]

* * *

Aron ended *Les Guerres en chaîne* with a remarkable testament of "faith without illusions". He refused to accept the argument of the neutralists and those who rejected both Russia and America, that it did not matter who won the next war since the same fate awaited humanity:

We do not know a single supporter of the double refusal who would look to the East for freedom, in the event of an American occupation; but we know many who would look for it in the West, in the event of a Russian occupation. In the United States the economic system, the political institutions and the social order are loaded with injustices, as in all known societies. The principle of the equality of men of all races and all religions is proclaimed there, but not always followed. But in spite of everything, if we compare American capitalism and Russian communism in their actual concrete reality, we cannot, without aberration or bad faith, dismiss them both together and cover them with the same invectives. Whether we consider personal rights, the possibilities of opposition or creativity, or the effect of the methods of production and exchange on the welfare of the masses, the American system is the exact opposite of the Soviet system, and not another example of the same type.[60]

The defenders of neutralism claimed that there was a basic similarity between American and Russian civilization, because all mass societies had essentially the same characteristics. No one, Aron pointed out in reply, would deny that modern methods of production were accompanied by certain social and psychological consequences, such as a tendency to uniformity, manipulation of the masses and a permanent search for efficiency. But technology was not the sole factor. To regard it as such would be to fall into a crude Marxism, in which it was not the relations but the instruments of production that was the creative and determining force. The fact was that the builders of dams and blast-furnaces could treat people either as objects or as persons; they could believe in God or not, encourage the individual to think for himself or dictate what he was to read, restore an aristocracy of bureaucrats or reduce economic inequalities, and concentrate political power in a party-church or try to spread it among different groups. Adversaries who belonged to the same historical world always had something in common, but it did not follow that what was at issue in the rivalries between nations or parties was of no importance.[61]

Those who rejected both societies also had another argument: the condemnation of technology in itself. According to them, technology inevitably led to the horrors of concentration camps and totalitarianism. Man himself, they said, had lost his soul, now that he had handed it over to the cult of the machine. But, Aron retorted, only the ignorant could doubt the considerable rise in the living standard of whole populations in Western societies over the last century, as had been shown by Colin Clark and his French disciple, Jean Fourastié.[62] "In the strictly material order", he wrote, "the reasons for optimism seem to me to prevail in the long run over those for pessimism". Did "the romanticists of the anti-technology school" envy those societies in which famine was endemic and the expectation of life short? Nevertheless, Aron had no illusions about the limitations of technology: "Man is not, and probably never will be, the master and possessor of nature. Neither is he any longer her trembling slave or a resigned victim". At the same time, "serene optimism in the faith that social or spiritual progress will automatically follow scientific progress" was "dead", and there was "no need to dissect the corpse", for the raising of living standards was not enough "either to spread happiness or to satisfy people":[63]

Morally neutral, technology can be used for good or for evil, to give millions of men honourable conditions of existence or to exterminate millions of innocent people in a few minutes. The profit and loss account is not yet closed...Knowledge puts at the disposal of mankind a collection of instruments: it does not determine the use to be made of them.[64]

Recently an ex-Communist who was now an anti-Communist (Arthur Koestler, in fact) had written, "We are defending a half-truth against a total lie". Although this was true, said Aron, why feel the need to repeat it "with a mixture of guilty conscience and frankness"? On the contrary, he affirmed, for those in the West, "The right to choose one's God, the right to seek truth freely, and the right not to be at the mercy of the police, the bureaucrats and the psycho-technicians, are, or should be, ...values

407

as unconditional as the triumph of the Soviet Union for the Stalinists...
The survival of hope depends on the victory of the liberal societies".[65]

Are people disheartened because we have only half-truths to defend in this imperfect world?
I am not so sure. The real cause of scepticism is different. The lesson of the two wars has
been learned: the unleashing of violence settles nothing. Europe would be the victim of
a hyperbolic war, whatever its outcome. I have not sought to conceal this paradox of means
and ends. The object of the West is and must be to win the limited war in order not to have
to wage the total one. But the West will not succeed unless it is animated by an inflexible
resolution, unless it believes in itself and in its mission of liberty.

   Can the third world war be won without becoming total? No one knows. But we do know
that, in the limited war more even than in the total one, courage and faith count as much
as material resources. The will to win will not eliminate the perils that are to be our daily
lot for years, but it can give us a better chance of overcoming them.[66]

* * *

The philosopher and specialist on Comte, Henri Gouhier, wrote to Aron
that *Les Guerres en chaîne* seemed to him "the concrete illustration of the
Introduction to the Philosophy of History. The pages on necessity and chance
and the last paragraphs of the work form the connection". Furthermore,
"I learnt from Comte everything there was to know under the heading
'historical analysis'. I found the same again in your pages, with an
intelligence unprejudiced by the law of three estates".[67] The book
aroused another friend and correspondent, the "saintly" André Kaan,
to engage Aron in philosophical debate about historical determinism
("Small, apparently frail, sickly, awkward in gesture and speech, André,
a member of the Resistance, was captured by the Gestapo and deported
to a concentration camp").[68] Manès Sperber, on the other hand, was
frankly critical to his friend: "Between you and me, it's not so much a book
as a collection of articles..." (Aron later tended to agree) "...arranged
in an order which on this occasion is ill-assorted and even in contradiction
to your basic theses" (on this point Aron was not in agreement). "Hence
the repetitions which elsewhere are most uncharacteristic of you... You
are, my dear friend, almost as arrogant as myself, but this time you
have definitely underestimated yourself, bowing to the necessities of
journalism when you had things to say which journalists at best learn
but never teach". Nevertheless, Sperber concluded: "497 pages. 250,
notably in Part One and the second section of Part Two ('Impuissance
de l'Europe?'): among the best pages *in denen eine Epoche ihrer selbstbewusst
wird* (in which an age becomes conscious of itself). 247 pages: brilliant
journalism, the best today, but clearly repetitive and too insistent".[69]

To his colleague on *Le Figaro*, the veteran political scientist André Siegfried, Aron's mind in *Les Guerres en chaîne* was "like a precision telescope which can be focused with ease to look at things in close-up or at a distance, and in terms of a single day, a year or an epoch". Without being over-ambitious, Aron could have entitled his book *Explication de notre temps* (*An Explanation of Our Time*), for, as he himself wrote, its aim was "to understand and help others understand". Never once did Aron's "lucid mind" lose its way in the maze of twentieth-century wars. Siegfried particularly commended Aron's "penetrating analysis" of the Cold War and the chapters on the passage from Marxism to Stalinism which were "essential for an understanding of how far the notions of Marxism and the proletariat have been transformed in the process". In short, *Les Guerres en chaîne* was "un livre passionnant", whose author had been able, in spite of his lack of illusions, to "preserve his faith in the destiny of our civilization".[70]

"Philosopher, historian, economist and sociologist", wrote the historian, Jacques Chastenet, "Raymond Aron is one of the most lucid observers of the contemporary political scene". His new book could only confirm the reputation which he had earned through an *oeuvre* that was already important. Chastenet's one regret was that "the scope of its subject-matter, the author's natural subtlety, his intellectual scruples and the richness of his information have given the book a dense character which makes it somewhat difficult to read; but the lessons to be drawn from it repay the effort". *Les Guerres en chaîne* did not claim to offer magic solutions or even to throw an entirely new light on the dramatic events of the day. On a number of points, it seemed open to criticism. "But, with its solid documentation, wealth of insight and, above all, honesty of thought, it deserves to be read and pondered by all those who, in the general confusion, still have a taste for clarity of vision and believe that those who deliberately shut their eyes are guilty of the worst form of cowardice".[71]

In the opinion of François Bondy, the Editor of *Preuves*, *Les Guerres en chaîne*, even more than its "remarkable" predecessor, *Le Grand Schisme*, treated its subject-matter "in all its complexity, without literary effect". Aron's "appeal to lucidity and moral courage" justified "the severely objective character of an enquiry whose conclusion is hardly encouraging". This quest for truth, combined with moral choice, formed a unity, as Brunschvicg had shown in the case of mathematical thought. Indeed, wrote Bondy, Aron's style was often reminiscent of Brunschvicg's, aiming as it did at an "almost mathematical rigour"; however, Aron added "an empirical suppleness" which softened the possible harshness of his generalizations. The result was "a language which, by its integrity and, one might almost say, intellectual asceticism, renounces all evocative imagery and easy emotion. It is quite clear that Raymond Aron is reacting against the high-flown excesses of the literary style in political writing. In his rejection of mythologies and his affirmation of a 'faith without illusions', Raymond Aron associates liberty with the idea of complexity, just as he links totalitarianism with the urge to simplify". Bondy's one reservation was that Aron saw European unity only in a military, and not a political, light. That apart, the discussions of the relationship between the Russian Revolution and Marxist ideology, total war and the totalitarian state, and socialism and democracy, "carried conviction by their wealth of thought and knowledge".[72]

On the other hand, to Jean Desanti in the Marxist periodical, *La Nouvelle Critique*, Aron was "the leader of the warmongers", whose aim was to establish fascism in France. He was "a detestable example of intellectual dishonesty, mental licentiousness and conceptual impotence", who resorted to every kind of slander against the Communists. Aron believed, Desanti falsely claimed, that war should be declared on the Soviet Union and the country destroyed, but Aron ignored the fact that the USSR, as Stalin had put it "in magnificent terms", embodied the aspirations of the peoples towards peace. Since, Desanti simplistically alleged, Aron did not believe that objectivity was possible in history, his purpose was to "falsify the whole history of the last hundred years" and make people accept the war aims of the American imperialists as the final outcome of history. "In this way the sociological theories of the Diltheys and Max Webers of this world now lend considerable support to the designs of the aggressors". Faced with reality, however, Aron's behaviour was that of "a real paranoiac". Desanti particularly recommended psychiatrists to read the chapter on "Staline et l'ombre de Trotsky" ("Stalinism and the Shade of the Past"). He also asserted that whenever Aron tried to confront Marxist theory, as in "The Leninist Myth of Imperialism", he sank into "confusion and grandiloquent nonsense"[73] – a view not shared by the political scientist, François Goguel, to whom Aron had provided "a rigorous demonstration" of the inadequacy of Lenin's theory.[74]

Goguel's judgement on this point was echoed by Jean-Marie Domenach in *Esprit*, though the latter had other reservations about *Les Guerres en chaîne*. "Aron, so discriminating and subtle in his many analyses (some of them, like his critique of the Leninist thesis of imperialism as the source of the two world wars, seem altogether irrefutable) is suddenly guilty of over-simplification when he studies the causes of international tension; for he only presents one side of the question and shamelessly resorts to the use of propaganda (alleging, for example, the existence of of an East German army) – an attitude that cannot be ignored in one who never fails to have a dig· at 'irresponsible intellectuals'".[75] Thus Domenach complained that Aron made no attempt to justify his basic assumption that it was Stalinism which was primarily responsible for the Cold War – a surprising accusation in view of all the attention Aron had in fact given to this very question. Domenach went on to assert, equally erroneously, that Aron (like the other three "great RPF intellectuals", Malraux, Soustelle and Monnerot)[76] had an evolutionary view of history, tended to think in terms of global civilizations, and was "obsessed by the decadence of Western society"; as a result, ideologies, cultures and empires took on a dehumanized life of their own. Finally (ignoring Aron's conclusion, "Faith without Illusions") Domenach objected that Aron gave men no reason to live and hope, whereas to Domenach, "The task of intellectuals confronted by civilizations should be to strive for their renewal and humanization" (a sentiment with which Aron would not have disagreed), "not to pass on tips to warmongers" (an unworthy and wholly unjustified trivialization of Aron's thesis).

Lastly, Aron clashed with Maurice Duverger in what must surely be one of the latter's least convincing pieces to appear in *Le Monde*.[77] *Les Guerres en chaîne*, Duverger observed, confirmed the high opinion he had earlier expressed of *Le Grand Schisme*. However, he repeated his allegation that Aron was "a poor partisan", incapable of accepting the watchwords of any group to which he belonged, but "an excellent sociologist" – the chapters on the transformations of communism, the evolution of the Labour Party and the development of socialism, constituted "absolutely remarkable analyses". Duverger then proceeded to make the strange criticism that Aron's fundamental concern to stay close to the facts and express reality in all its complexity led him "constantly to refine his judgements in an extremely subtle way". The problem was, according to Duverger, that in doing so Aron demonstrated the defects of his qualities, thus aggravating tendencies which were already apparent in his earlier work. Aron's technique in *Les Guerres en chaîne* reminded Duverger of Monet's in "Les Nymphéas":

Claude Monet's desperate effort to render every shade of light, analyse its myriad iridescences and capture even the most subtle of its reflections, results in that golden haze in which the essential features of things become blurred, dissolve and fade away. Raymond Aron's constant concern to qualify every statement with a limiting clause, and then the latter with a return to the original statement, and so forth, in a kind of intellectual daisy-chain (par une série de lacets intellectuels), sometimes has analogous results.

411

Not, Duverger hastened to add, that he was implying any "real criticism": "This supple method is perhaps a better reflection of the facts than a rigid synthesis. . . After the grossly simplified assertions of the propagandists, a reaction is probably necessary".

Duverger's "real reproach" to Aron was that "the concern for objectivity, precision and nuance, evident in all the specific passages of the book as well as in the details of the analysis, does not reveal itself so clearly in the fundamental assumptions of the work". For it seemed to Duverger that the whole book rested on two basic assumptions, which were "nowhere made explicit, but underlie most of the arguments: the idea that the USSR is ultimately determined to unleash war in order to spread communism and that the danger of war is unilateral, i.e., attributable only to Russia, no risk being involved in current American policy".[78]

Aron replied vigorously to these charges, however, first in a letter to *Le Monde*[79] and then in two closely argued articles in *Liberté de l'esprit*,[80] in which he had little difficulty in showing that Duverger had seriously misrepresented his views. Goguel, too, in his comments on Aron's "polemic" with Duverger, clearly sided with Aron.[81]

In Britain, the French edition of *Les Guerres en chaîne* was reviewed in *The Economist*. Although Aron's book stood "among the most important political writings since the war", it was, the anonymous critic observed, "a hard nut to crack":

Not that it is long-winded or obscure; the book is a real thriller in its close-knit penetrating argument. The trouble lies rather in the analytical method and manner which, in spite of an apparent empiricism, remains essentially monist and Germanic. (Of French political writers M. Aron is perhaps the most deeply versed in German philosophy and sociology.) The author makes it clear that he is not a determinist or believer in any kind of historical metaphysic. Nor does he, like Professor Toynbee, invent a phraseology to express his own historical vision. His approach to the world is essentially activist and extraverted, and he contents himself with the current terms of politics, sociology, economics and industrial and military science. All this stuff he rams into the breech to fire a broadside at the average dejected citizen. In the frightful fifties M. Aron occupies something of the position held by Mr Aldous Huxley in the soppy thirties. Both writers (although Huxley far more widely) draw on modern social science to explain the situation; but whereas Huxley refused to concentrate on material resistance to mounting evil and preached personal detachment and spiritual integrity, M. Aron the militant is solely concerned with securing enough collective moral and material strength to oppose the Soviet power.

The result of this Tacitean objectivity towards organized evil is certainly a masterly analysis of Soviet operatives which must leave the chancelleries gaping in the wake. But for the ordinary individual whose business in life lies outside Sovietics, the book is cruelly short of air and humanity. M. Aron seems to identify an anti-Soviet programme

412

with the whole purpose of contemporary free society. Moreover, he is so concerned with naked power in geo-political and industrial terms that he has little time for the deep factors of human morale. "If we are late", he seems to say, "we cannot survive".

In a continent still sunk in political indifference and riddled with escapism it is perhaps right that at least one front rank intellectual should be frankly terroristic. But there are other roads to strength – in France, MM. Schuman and Monnet are following them – which are less hurried and less precisely charted. And is it realistic to pay so little heed as M. Aron does to the problem of Germany, which is psychologically far more serious (since a whole people is involved) than the nihilistic efforts of the few hundred thousand militant Communists of Western Europe? It is indeed not at all clear what is M. Aron's attitude to the human soul which it is the object of the whole exercise to save. The pessimism of his writing seems to derive from a belief in the possibility of its total destruction by evil agencies in history. But that is hardly a starting point for a historical analysis.[82]

Les Guerres en chaîne was also briefly but favourably noticed by the historian, David Thomson,[83] and he gave it a similar welcome when the translation, *The Century of Total War*, appeared in 1954.[84] D. W. Brogan called the latter a "remarkable tract for the times"[85] and Jules Menken in *The Spectator* was equally enthusiastic:

M. Aron's method is primarily analytical; his treatment is historical, sociological, economic or political as varying subordinate topics require; his view is wide and the knife of his thought cuts deep. This is a study in the great French intellectual tradition, cool, informed, scholarly, reasoned, reasonable; a work suffused by intelligence of the highest order and throwing light on the problems which intelligence can illumine; a book to be read, re-read, pondered by those who seek to understand the world of today or have responsibility for shaping opinion or framing policy.[86]

The *Times Literary Supplement*, too, welcomed Aron's "most brilliant and most timely book":

It is one reason for M. Aron's great prestige, inside France and outside it, that he is a realist in the modern "Anglo-Saxon" sense. For him words are words and formulas are formulas. Problems are both concrete and complex. Intellectual elegance in posing them and solving them is probably a trap. Long-distance wisdom is folly and the belief in one key to open all doors is greater folly still.

It is this attitude that makes M. Aron so refreshing to read and his counsel so persuasive. In his latest book the virtues that we associate with his work are very visible...

It should not be thought that M. Aron is in any sense a fatalist. He is not the prisoner of a doctrine. He allows a place for the accident, for personality, for human error...[87]

For Arnold Toynbee in *The Observer, The Century of Total War* was:

written with all the ability and acumen that would be expected by anyone who has read previous works by M. Aron and has had the pleasure of meeting him. It is also admirably objective, particularly in the numerous passages dealing with Germany. It would be difficult here to detect, from the internal evidence, that the writer was a Frenchman of Jewish extraction...

His book is not the less valuable for being deliberately inconclusive; for, in peering into the future, one can only see, and state, alternative possibilities. "The Cold War – Preparation or Substitute for Total War?" is the characteristic heading of one of his most interesting chapters.[88]

The one dissenter from opinions such as these was the Labour politician, R. H. S. Crossman, in the *New Statesman*. In his view, Aron had failed to "move with the times":

The brilliant columnist of *Figaro*, he is convinced of the decadence of the Fourth Republic and the consequent inevitability of accepting American suzerainty. *The Century of Total War* is a French book written in strict accordance with the theses of American Anti-Marxism. When it was first published in France and the USA, it was hailed as "a brilliant, incisive and thorough analysis". But history has run faster than its English publisher, and the modishness of its "faith without illusions" is already dated, along with a good many of the "facts" with which M. Aron supports it.

"Even the most gifted journalist", Crossman concluded, though he made no attempt to justify his strictures, "cannot be blamed for failing to foresee M. Mendès-France!".[89]

In the United States, the international relations specialist, Hans Morgenthau was also critical.[90] Aron's style was, he complained, "impressionistic". The book lacked a coherent structure. It had "no beginning or end, no centre or periphery, no top or bottom", even though there was "much to admire in detail". Still more questionably, Morgenthau went on to argue that Aron was "the intellectual *par excellence*" who "loves the work of the mind for its own sake". Aron's purpose was "not to prove a thesis, to develop a system, or to tell a coherent story". As a consequence, he had "no programme for action, no political philosophy, no history, but rather elements of one or another as the occasion arises". Thus the book contained perceptive and original discussions of Marxist theory and practice, the economies of Western Europe, and modern technology, yet it failed to illuminate the contemporary scene as a whole.

Furthermore, Aron did not always sustain his arguments, attacking a problem in the way a cat attacks a mouse: "He tosses it around, takes hold of it, lets it go, and catches it again; but, in contrast to the cat, he never consumes and digests more than part of it". Nevertheless, concluded Morgenthau (despite his earlier complaints about a lack of coherence),

two great themes hold the book together: the paramountcy, in our century, of politics over all other spheres of human endeavour, especially economics, and the organic inter-connectedness of the great wars of the century, the unsolved problems of one engendering the increasing fury of the next.

Upon these two themes, Aron brought to bear "his immense learning and great gifts as a thinker and writer".[91]

Notes

1. 1948a, p. 329, n.i.
2. 1951a.
3. 1950h, 1950i, 1950j, 1950k.
4. 1983a, p. 335.
5. R. A., interview with the author, 1977.
6. "Qui a assisté impuissant à la mort de son enfant ne sera jamais plus tenté de souscrire à l'orgueil prométhéen" ("Anyone who has helplessly witnessed the death of his child will never again be tempted by the pride of Prometheus"). 1951a, p. 490: tr. 1954a, p. 361.
7. Sperber, 1971, p. 547.
8. *Fig. Lit.*, 4 June 1949, p. 5.
9. 1950j.
10. Tr. 1954a. Apparently Aron himself would have preferred the title *A Half-Century of Total War*, since he came to think that the time of "total wars" was probably over ("Notre carnet", *Preuves* (58), December 1955, p. 103).
11. 1951a, Chs. X ("Contenir ou refouler"), XVII ("L'Europe est-elle capable de se défendre?") and – the most regrettable omission – the fine analysis of totalitarianism in the Conclusion, Ch. II ("Le Totalitarisme").
12. Tr. 1954a. Conclusion, Ch. II ("After Stalin"). First published 1953d.
13. 1951a, pp. 7–8.
14. Ibid., pp. 21–2: tr. 1954a, pp. 17–18 (R.C.).
15. Ibid., p. 27: tr. p. 22.
16. Ibid., p. 29: tr. p. 24.
17. Ibid., pp. 29–30: tr. pp. 24–5 (R.C.).
18. Ibid., p. 36: tr. p. 31 (R.C.).
19. Ibid., p. 37: tr. p. 32.
20. Ibid., p. 40: tr. p. 35.
21. Ibid., p. 42: tr. p. 36–7.
22. The 1954 translation is misleading at this point, since Aron's "Les Occidentaux avaient intérêt à affaiblir non à anéantir l'Allemagne" (ibid., p. 59) has been translated as "The Westerners were interested in weakening Germany, but not in

destroying her" (tr. p. 53), which is almost the opposite of what Aron was saying. One British reviewer described Aron's argument at this point as "a particularly damaging criticism of the policy of 'unconditional surrender' adopted by the Allies in the second world war" (Anon., 1954a).

23. 1951a, pp. 61-2: tr. 1954a, p. 55 (R.C.).
24. Ibid., p. 63: tr. p. 56.
25. Ibid., p. 64: tr. p. 57 (R.C.).
26. Ibid., p. 65: tr. p. 58 (R.C.).
27. Ibid., pp. 69-70: tr. p. 59. As evidence in support of his argument, Aron referred to E. Staley's *War and the Private Sector* (New York, 1935) and, in particular, the Russo-Japanese War and the establishment of French protectorates in Tunisia and Morocco.
28. Ibid., pp. 72-6: tr. pp. 62-6.
29. Ibid., pp. 82-3: tr. p. 72.
30. Ibid., p. 84: tr. p. 73.
31. Ibid., p. 100: tr. p. 85. Cf. 1942h. See above, Chapter 11.
32. 1951a, pp. 101-4: tr. pp. 87-9.
33. "S'il est une Providence, en ce chaos tragique, elle nous échappe". This sentence is omitted in the 1954 translation.
34. Ibid., pp. 109-12: tr. pp. 94-8 (R.C.).
35. Ibid., pp. 136-8: tr. pp. 116-18 (R.C.).
36. See ibid., pp. 139-51: tr. pp. 119-31.
37. Ibid., p. 153: tr. pp. 132-3. (R.C.).
38. Ibid., pp. 174-5: tr. pp. 144-5.
39. Ibid., p. 178: tr. p. 149.
40. Ibid., p. 181: tr. p. 151.
41. Anon., 1954a.
42. 1951a, pp. 191-2: tr. 1954a, pp. 153-4.
43. Ibid., p. 197: tr. p. 159. Antoine Cournot was a nineteenth-century philosopher of mathematics who specialized in political economy and probability theory.
44. Ibid., pp. 202-3: tr. pp. 164-5.
45. Ibid., p. 260: tr. p. 194. For Aron's reaction to the invasion of South Korea, as expressed in his *Figaro* editorials, see Chapter 18, below.
46. 1951a, p. 264: tr. 1954a, pp. 196-7.
47. Ibid., pp. 276-7: tr. pp. 207-8.
48. Ibid., p. 278: tr. 209.
49. Ibid., p. 279: tr. p. 210.
50. Ibid., p. 284: tr. p. 212.
51. Ibid., Chapter XIX: tr. pp. 226-38.
52. Ibid., p. 377.
53. Ibid., pp. 410-11: tr. pp. 311-12 (R.C.).
54. Ibid., p. 411: tr. p. 312.
55. Ibid., pp. 411-12: tr. pp. 313-14 (R.C.).
56. Ibid., p. 413: tr. p. 314.
57. Ibid.: tr. ibid. (R.C.).
58. Ibid., p. 415: tr. p. 316 (R.C.).

59. Ibid., pp. 416–17: tr. pp. 317–18.
60. Ibid., p. 486: tr. p. 357 (R.C.).
61. Ibid., pp. 486–7: tr. pp. 357–8.
62. Colin Clark, *The Conditions of Economic Progress* (New York, 1940); Jean Fourastié, *Machinisme et bien-être* (Paris, 1951). Some of the details of their evidence might be questionable, Aron believed, but not their general argument.
63. 1951a, p. 490: tr. 1954a, p. 361 (R.C.).
64. Ibid., pp. 491–3: tr. pp. 362–3 (R.C.).
65. Ibid., pp. 494–6: tr. pp. 365–7 (R.C.).
66. Ibid., p. 497: tr. pp. 367–8 (R.C.).
67. 1983a, p. 292.
68. Ibid., pp. 295–6.
69. Ibid., pp.291–2. In Aron's own view, the first two chapters, "The Technical Surprise" and "Dynamism of Total War" were "by far the best" (ibid., p. 296).
70. Siegfried, 1951. Compare Rousseaux, 1951.
71. Chastenet, 1951.
72. Bondy, 1951.
73. Desanti, 1951.
74. Goguel, 1951.
75. Domenach, 1951.
76. Jules Monnerot (born 1909) shared a number of Aron's concerns. He was the author of a critique of Durkheim, *Les Faits sociaux ne sont pas des choses* (Paris, 1946), *Sociologie du communisme* (Paris, 1949) and *La Guerre en question* (Paris, 1951).
77. Duverger, 1951.
78. Ibid.
79. 27 October 1951.
80. 1951i, 1952e.
81. Goguel, op. cit. In his memoirs, however, Aron stated (too generously) that Duverger's article, which had "irritated" him at the time, now seemed "largely justified" (1983a, p. 292).
82. Anon., 1951.
83. Thomson, 1952.
84. Thomson, 1955.
85. Brogan, 1954.
86. Menken, 1954. Compare *The Listener*: "M. Aron has written a searching analysis of the present world situation in the light of the vast changes that have taken place since the beginning of the twentieth century. The writer's scholarship is unquestionable, and his style clear and cogent in the best tradition of French political commentary. It may be objected that here and there he obtains his clear-cut effects by attaching insufficient weight to the more confusing aspects of the problem. But this is minor criticism of a book that is designed to provoke thought, and succeeds admirably in its purpose" (Anon., 1954a).
87. Anon., 1954c. *The Times* also welcomed Aron's "fascinating and important book" (Anon., 1954b).
88. Toynbee, 1954.
89. Crossman, 1954. Aron knew Crossman and in September 1950 had been present

at a "violent quarrel" between Koestler and Crossman at a dinner in the House of Commons, the other guests being John Strachey and Arthur J. Schlesinger Jr. "A political discussion between Strachey and Crossman on the one hand and Koestler on the other (all three at their most argumentative and aggressive) rapidly developed into an acrimonious argument, which in turn, fuelled by a great deal of drink, flared up into a furious slanging-match". Iain Hamilton, *Koestler: A Biography* (London, 1982), pp. 201–2.

90. Morgenthau, 1955.
91. Ibid.

18

The Future of Europe

In the Introduction to *L'Age des empires et l'avenir de la France*, completed in July 1945, Aron had argued that while some form of Western European federation, which would include France, Britain, Spain, Germany and Italy, should be the long-term aim, any hope of its realization in the circumstances then prevailing was "pure utopia": Britain, for example, was too committed to its empire and to its friendship with the United States, ever to be wholly linked to Europe.[1] Three years later, however, in 1948, Aron took part in the Hague Conference of the European Movement which, under Churchill's presidency, was to give rise to the European Assembly, the Council of Europe.[2]

In April of that year, in the context of the mounting tensions of the Cold War (the Communist *coup de Prague* had taken place a few weeks before) and shortly after the signing of the Brussels Pact,[3] Aron wrote in *Le Figaro* that: "Politically, Great Britain sees itself as an integral part of Western Europe". In order to provide a counterweight to the Soviet Union, nothing less than an alliance of West European nations was essential. Accordingly, for the first time, British opinion envisaged the unity of the old Continent "not with fear but with favour" ("Winston Churchill, with his customary clearsightedness, was the first to recognize and proclaim this reversal of opinion"). Militarily, Great Britain was aware that its very existence depended on the safety of Western Europe. In the economic sphere, austerity, the Marshall Plan, and the gradual return to the world conditions of the past, were seen by the British as grounds for optimism. Such a view did not, Aron believed, exclude either the coordination of particular European industries (such as aviation or steel), or greater cooperation between the partners of the Dunkirk Pact,[4] but it did forbid "a definitive commitment, a choice between a European role and a world role, between the old Continent and the Commonwealth".[5]

Some months later, Aron was expressing doubt that a European customs union of the kind proposed by the Belgian Foreign Minister, Paul Henri Spaak, would be enough; political union must come first. "Only an authority to which states have transferred part of their sovereignty will be capable of substituting the unity of a great economic area for the multiplicity of national economies, each enclosed within its own frontiers, regulations, and monetary and fiscal policy". Customs union, in the present age, no longer offered a path to political unity; the former presupposed the latter.[6]

But the obstacles to political unity were, of course, considerable:

That ancient nations, intensely conscious of their uniqueness and history and laden with the memory of their secular rivalries, should voluntarily renounce their unconditional sovereignty – such an event would deserve to be hailed as a masterpiece of lucidity, courage and wisdom.

And yet, the necessity is so obvious, the nations are so weary of their sterile conflicts and the external menace is so pressing, that there would be every ground for optimism if two immediate obstacles could be overcome: British hesitancy and French chaos.[7]

It was clear to Aron that Britain's leaders did not want to go any further than diplomatic and military cooperation between sovereign states. As soon as economic union or transfer of sovereignty was mentioned, the atmosphere changed. What, it was asked, would happen to the system of imperial preferences if Britain agreed to become an integral part of Western Europe? Any such decision, it was said, would be irrevocable. In other words, those who guided British policy believed that Britain would be able to manage on its own and that the present crisis did not require the kind of revolution implied by European union. "Willing to facilitate exchanges between the European states, they come back in the end, without always acknowledging it, to the national tradition: enlightened empiricism, refusal to make a final choice, adaptation to poverty, reduction of the standard of living, and a concentration on

420

exports. 'Hug the shore and we'll survive the storm'. *Qui vivra verra* – time will tell". As for the chaos in France, there was no doubt that the present combination of weak and ephemeral governments, industrial disorder, the increasing number of political groups, and interpersonal rivalry offered the best possible justification for Britain's hesitancy.[8]

When, six months later in January 1949, the Franco-British negotiations on a European Assembly were running into difficulties, Aron commented that while he understood and even "approved" British scepticism, there was a "decisive counter-argument" which needed stating: "A European Assembly would have an incomparable symbolic significance (une force de rayonnement incomparable)". It would put flesh on an idea which, despite all the propaganda, was still viewed as being far off in a utopian future. Aron doubted whether, militarily or economically, it would be particularly effective, but it *was* likely to have a unique influence on public opinion. Britain's refusal, he felt sure, was based not only on the administrative ineffectiveness of the European Assembly, but also on its "likely moral effectiveness".[9]

Herein, he reasoned, lay the heart of the debate. Neither the government nor the people of Britain envisaged, for the moment, embarking on an adventure whose ultimate end would be the setting up of a federal authority to which national governments would transfer part of their sovereignty. The road from a consultative assembly to a federal government was long but direct. Britain refused the former, because it did not want the latter. Concern for the Commonwealth and aversion to a decision whose consequences were unforeseeable were combined with the anxiety caused by the political and economic confusion in the Latin countries. As long as it was merely a question of organizing the defence of the West and coordinating, as best one could, a number of independently conceived economic plans, Britain's adhesion was sincere and total. But the moment the talk was of political unity, the answer was equally clear, but negative: "Semi-permanent organic alliance, yes. Federation, no". The best way to convince Britain, Aron believed, was for France to rediscover its moral unity and political stability and consider reconciliation with Germany, as Churchill had advocated in his Zurich speech in September 1946.[10]

Aron himself had long been an advocate of Franco-German reconciliation. He had, as Golo Mann recalls, lectured memorably on the subject at the University of Frankfurt as early as 1946.[11] He had frequently discussed the subject in his *Combat* column in 1946 and 1947,[12] as well as in *Le Grand Schisme*, and he returned to the theme in an eloquent and courageous article in the spring of 1949:

Obsessed as we are by our own disparate anxieties, we end up by forgetting the essential: the indispensable effort towards the reconciliation of the two peoples. I know that some of my readers will be surprised and shocked. And yet, if French and Germans are ever to put an end to a secular conflict which the transformation of the world has turned into an anachronism, could a moment ever be more propitious than this? Will Germany ever be weaker or more amenable (disponible) than she is today?

I am certainly not claiming that the Germans have once and for all renounced aggressive nationalism or that they have become good "democrats". But what Germany is tomorrow depends partly on what we do. The frank and resolute resumption of humane relations with the Germans is a not unworthy contribution that it is within our power to make to the restoration of the West.[13]

Such reconciliation was necessary for military reasons, too. At the same time, Western unification would be the strongest guarantee against any German adventurism, if Germany was gradually given back its freedom of action.[14]

As to German reunification, which was the subject of a long drawn-out Four-Power Conference in Paris in the early summer of that year, Aron was in favour, but on certain conditions, both political and economic. The former should include the suppression of the militarized "police" in Eastern Germany, the restoration of liberties there, the authorization of the Socialist Party and the Western press, and free elections under international control. Germany's economic structure should be decided by freely elected rulers and all the reforms carried out so far should be open to reconsideration.[15] But when, to Aron's evident exasperation, the talks eventually broke down, he agreed that a divided Germany and a sovietized Eastern Europe were likely to last for a long time: "Nonetheless, it is better not to resign oneself to it too quickly. A continent that is half free and half enslaved lives uneasily and the line of demarcation drawn up at Yalta ought to separate two allied armies, not two hostile worlds".[16]

* * *

Meanwhile, the great debate about neutralism and the formation of Nato had begun in France, among the most prominent critics of the Atlantic Pact being the Catholic philosopher Etienne Gilson and Hubert Beuve-Méry, its Editor, in the pages of *Le Monde*.[17] In reply, Aron had welcomed the idea of the Pact in an early article in *Le Figaro* in December 1948,[18] arguing that it was necessary to organize resistance to Stalin, as the free world had failed to do against Hitler,[19] the most effective barrier against Soviet expansion being a united and prosperous Europe.[20] He returned to the problem several times in *Le Figaro* in the weeks leading up to the formation of Nato in April 1949,[21] but his main response to Gilson came in an article published in *Liberté de l'esprit* at that time.[22] According to the periodical's Editor, Claude Mauriac, Aron's article may have helped persuade de Gaulle not to take a position against the Pact, as this extract from Mauriac's diary for 17 March 1949 shows:

I mentioned the article that Raymond Aron had sent me for the third number on the Atlantic Pact, and gave him the gist of it in a few words, because I was afraid that it might go against his policy and that of the RPF. It contained some very sharp criticisms of Etienne Gilson's two articles, in which he accused the Americans of wanting to buy French blood with their dollars. It censured the Atlantic Pact for not having given the French any guarantees on the time or place of American intervention in the event of a Russian invasion of Western Europe.

"But it's obvious that it's M. Gilson who's right", the General exclaimed. "...The error that...the Arons and the gentlemen on *Le Figaro* are committing lies in making us believe that the Atlantic Pact is all that's needed, and that the French can now sleep peacefully in their beds".[23]

Five days later Claude Mauriac wrote:

Following our conversation on 17 March, I sent Raymond Aron's article on the Atlantic Pact to the General today for his opinion.

After a summons from the General to come round at 7.00, I was certain that he would raise the strongest objections to the publication of the article just now in its present form. So I was astonished by the words with which the General greeted me:

"Well, it's not bad at all, that article you sent me".

The fact is that the General seems to have greatly modified his opinion of the Atlantic Pact in the last few days.

When he announced that he would explain to me the real crux of the matter, I told myself that he had no doubt forgotten that he had already disclosed his point of view to me at some length and that I was about to hear more or less the same speech. But it was nothing of the sort.

"It's certain – and Raymond Aron was right to stress the point – that the Pact, even without any definitive commitments, is of a kind to give Stalin food for thought. I don't say it ensures that he'll leave us alone, but at least he now knows that, if he occupies Western Europe, it'll mean war. And we might reasonably suppose that, if such a pact had existed in 1939, Hitler would not have embarked on his Polish venture. Obviously, it would have been better if Aron had emphasized the fact that a strong France would make the chances of war even smaller..." This does not alter the fact that such a Pact is better than no Pact at all, and that's where Raymond Aron did very well to point out the weakness of Gilson's arguments...

As I was leaving, de Gaulle said to me:

"Now you know how I view the matter. Naturally, you are free to publish the article or not, but I would not like Raymond Aron to think that I disapprove of the line he has taken".[24]

Aron welcomed the ratification of the Pact by the National Assembly at the end of July:

> Stalin's enterprise is of the same kind as Hitler's: it is no less ambitious in its ends and no less cynical in its means, but it employs a different technique.
>
> It is excellent to show Stalin that the recourse to arms at the expense of a country of Western Europe would constitute a *casus belli*. I tend to believe he knows it. Soviet expansion has come to a halt. In no country to the west of the Iron Curtain does the Communist Party still have a serious chance of seizing power either through elections or through a coup d'état. And it has been acknowledged, since 1945, that by crossing the line of demarcation, the Red Army would set the world on fire.

But other problems remained. Should Soviet expansion merely be contained or should it be driven back? Could Europe live in peace as long as, whether directly or through third parties, the Russian Empire stretched as far as Weimar? Could Germany remain cut in two? And how, and to whose advantage, would unity be restored? These were the issues at stake in the present phase of the Cold War.[25]

It was, Aron maintained, *morally* important that the signatories to the Atlantic Pact should give proof, to themselves and others, of their will to live and defend one another. But this testimony of their resolution did not depend exclusively on the United States. What was the good of several thousand tanks or several hundred aeroplanes if the men, the organization, the discipline and the tactical ideas, without which the best equipment was useless, were missing? The European nations had no time to lose, and only themselves to rely on, if they wanted to work out a strategic doctrine and create the essential conditions for rearmament in each country. It would be fatal if the legitimate call for American aid served as an excuse for inactivity.[26]

But the argument with *Le Monde* flared up again a few months later in February 1950, when he felt called upon once more to expose "the illusion of neutrality":

> Whether one likes it or not, in our age there is no choice between belligerency and neutrality: when one does not fight, as a free man, for oneself, one fights, as a slave, for a master.
>
> No one will deny that the Cold War imposes a painful ordeal on France. No one will deny that, if total war breaks out, the destiny of Europe will be tragic. But one does not diminish the ordeal or avoid the tragedy by dreaming of an impossible escape. Whatever people may say, the Europeans, to the west of the Iron Curtain, still retain enough resources to take on, with American help, the responsibility for their own defence. What they do not have is the courage to overcome outdated quarrels and together undertake the effort on which their future depends. The events of recent years do not

incline us to confidence. Democracies do not act in accordance with the rhythm of twentieth-century history. But a declaration of neutrality would only aggravate the consequences of this fatal passivity.

Let us call on the nations of Europe to unite and arm, instead of justifying defeatism with subtle reasoning. It is defeatism, no less than atomic bombs and Soviet divisions, which places Europe in mortal danger.[27]

The West should enter into a dialogue with Stalin only from a conscious position of strength.[28] The West's great weakness was that it did not believe in itself. No one should be surprised, therefore, that "the Machiavellians, the simple-minded, the 'fellow-travellers' and the false idealists – all those who lack the will to win, in other words to survive – should constantly seize upon the West's weak point and, by means of lies, subtle arguments and half-truths, provide justifications for defeatism".[29]

A few months later Aron became the unwitting subject of what came to be known as "the Gilson affair". During his stay in the United States in the autumn of 1950, he received a letter from Waldemar Gurian of the Catholic University of Notre Dame, saying that he was regretfully withdrawing Aron's invitation to lecture at the University. His reason was that "Etienne Gilson, who is currently at Notre Dame, has stated that you are a paid agent of the United States. There are witnesses who will confirm this accusation..." Aron states in his memoirs that he was "more surprised than upset" but "in the climate of the Cold War, all forms of polemic were becoming possible".[30]

On 27 January 1951 Gurian published an open letter to Gilson in the *Figaro littéraire*. Gurian criticized him for "spreading the dark gospel of defeatism" and for "solemnly accusing a well-known and much respected French writer and scholar of being in the pay of the Americans". As Gilson had, in the meantime, retired from the Collège de France in order to devote himself to the Institute for the Study of Mediaeval Philosophy which he directed at Toronto, he was accused of fleeing from France in order to find security on the other side of the Atlantic. As a consequence his colleagues at the Collège de France refused him the honorary membership which normally would have been automatically his.[31]

Gilson defended himself the following month and the controversy continued in the columns of the *Figaro littéraire* for several weeks. As for Aron, "I had and continued to have nothing to do with this quarrel among Catholics". Gurian's original letter had perhaps been inspired by a group of Catholic *bellicistes*, but Gurian was "certainly wrong to give to con-versations between friends a publicity that was out of all proportion to

425

their significance". Who could say, Aron asked in his memoirs, that Gilson had gone to Toronto, as was his right, because he was afraid of war and another Occupation? As to the alleged accusation against himself, Aron found it "hard to believe". Despite their disagreements, it did not accord with his knowledge of Gilson: in short, "Gurian had related somewhat unthinkingly (avec légereté) remarks that he had not himself heard and which Gilson always denied" [32] – although the death of Emmanuelle a few weeks before the "Gilson affair" broke out enabled Aron to put such matters into perspective.

* * *

In the meantime, in August 1949, the European Assembly, or Council of Europe, had opened in Strasbourg,[33] but without the Germans. Later that month, after West Germany's first elections since the war, Aron observed – with great sympathy and understanding – that it would be wrong to despair of "eternal Germany" and naive to think that a few years were enough to convert its people to formal democracy:

How could West Germany, overpopulated as it is, with a bourgeoisie largely pro-letarianized, its cities in ruins and millions of families destitute, suddenly become calm and peaceful, full of admiration for parliamentary games and respectful of the moral law, harbouring no resentments and nourishing no ambitions? To be frank, I am not in the least surprised that Germany should be nationalistic. My fear is that, at the rate things are going, it might become even more so in the future.[34]

The solution was for Germany to be accepted on terms of equality in a united Western Europe [35] and this, Aron repeated at the time of the allied conference in Paris the following November, was "inconceivable without a genuine reconciliation between French and Germans". It was "now or never" that French diplomacy must overcome the so-called "complexes" which inhibited it, and find the courage to adopt a positive attitude. The conditions for a Franco-German understanding had been more favourable two years before and in a year's time they would be worse. Germany would re-enter the concert of powers, but it depended in part on France's leaders whether or not that re-entry, instead of appearing as a defeat for France, "brings the promise of a reconciled West".[36]

By February 1950 Aron was arguing that "Consultative Assembly and administrative machinery remain powerless fictions, as long as the essential is missing: the European executive".[37] Shortly afterwards he

426

returned to the German question, arguing that although a Franco-German union was not a possibility at the present time, if France did not take the initiative in a reconciliation between the two countries, the whole of Western diplomacy would be paralysed. West Germany's leaders had given proof of their sincerity as democrats and, although one could never be *sure* of their feelings and those of the West German people, their future depended partly on France:

Reduce controls to a minimum; simplify international administrative machinery; restore to the Bonn government all the sovereignty compatible with the maintenance of a military occupation that is as discreet as possible; openly organize economic collaboration; increase contacts both between industrialists and between political parties as well as the youth of the two countries; freely grant to West Germany the rights it will probably obtain tomorrow; hasten the time when it will sit in the Committee of Ministers: such a policy will eliminate none of the dangers, immediate or long-term, inherent in the present situation. Germany's loyalty to the West cannot be vouchsafed for ever. The urge to recover the lost territories to the East or to recreate the unity of the Reich will continue to motivate a German government, whatever it might be. We shall at least, insofar as it lies within our power, have lessened the risk of a Germany being progressively undermined by communism or seeking, in despair, a way out in the direction of the Russian empire.[38]

In May 1950, three weeks after Aron wrote these words, the French Foreign Minister, Robert Schuman, launched his spectacular proposal for the pooling of the Franco-German coal and steel industries, other Western European countries being invited to take part in the future. Aron welcomed this French initiative, whose chief architect was Jean Monnet, on economic grounds; but he also, unlike many at the time, immediately saw its political significance.[39] Economically, the enterprise would only succeed, he believed, if it were supported by public opinion; for example, it would be "deplorable" if the Socialists, in Germany and France, were to be hesitant about joining. More importantly, in political terms the Schuman Plan represented a break with the German policy pursued by the Quai d'Orsay in recent years; instead of guarding against the perils of yesterday, Aron wrote, it was looking to the future.[40] Benelux was, he thought, likely to join, but British membership was "improbable". The many different motives – some specific to the Labour Party, others nationalistic – which lay behind Britain's reticent attitude to the OEEC [41] would act against the French proposal; and the way in which it had been presented, with no advance warning to the British Government, was unlikely to diminish the irritation, politely restrained, of France's allies in the Brussels Pact.

Nevertheless, a combination of Franco-German heavy industry could, it seemed to Aron, be the starting-point for an immediate transformation of European policy and for a long-term transformation of the European economy. The technical difficulties, and the twin dangers of state monopoly (étatisation) and private mergers were obvious; but the attempt to set up the conditions that were essential for economic integration in a limited sector was worth making. Even the diplomatic style, which was declamatory and in some respects displeasing to France's allies, could be justified if interpreted as a kind of commitment – a commitment to take seriously a slogan which was often heard but rarely applied: reconciliation between France and Germany, in order to lay the foundations for a united Europe.[42]

By the following month the Six had decided to go ahead with the coal and steel pool, notwithstanding Britain's abstention. "Part of British opinion", Aron wrote,

had given a favourable welcome to the Schuman Plan, but, in leading administrative and political circles, hesitation and reticence were at once apparent. Senior officials were somewhat taken aback by all the fuss that was being made over a plan that was as vague as it was grandiose. The tradition of independence and pragmatism arouses a kind of revolt against a leap into the unknown and against the required promise to abide by the decisions of an international Authority, in which no one knows how power and voting will be distributed. British coal and steel have no need of foreign assistance. At the present time they would have concessions to make rather than to seek...

British participation in the pool would have been desirable, but it was, in any case, improbable, at the outset at least. In itself, there is nothing surprising about this fact. Industrial agreements have regularly been concluded between the countries of the Continent; British producers have sometimes joined them after the event.[43]

But the main aim of the Schuman Plan, Aron repeated, was political rather than economic: reconciliation and dialogue between France and Germany. Concrete results must now follow: "In 1950, Europe cannot afford the luxury of disappointing its peoples and accepting the failure of such an undertaking".[44] "Personally", Aron added ten days later after the Labour Government's rejection of the Schuman Plan, he had "never believed that Britain would agree to sacrifice a fraction of its sovereignty on the altar of European unity", but it was not a reason at this stage to put off "an essential collaboration".[45]

One week later, on 26 June, Communist forces invaded South Korea. "The invasion", Aron declared the next day, "is the most serious event to have occurred since the end of the Second World War". The Soviet Union had been carrying on permanent aggression against the free world, but with limited means. Between 1946 and 1950, the conventions of the Cold War had seemed to forbid the direct use of armed forces. For the first time, that convention had been violated. Till now, the military frontiers drawn up at Tehran and Yalta, however absurd they might be, had been respected. A new step had been taken in the direction of unlimited war. Aron had, he said, no doubt that the worst possible solution would be passivity on the part of the United States. Unless there was a military reply by America, other attacks by Soviet satellites would follow, thus adding to the Soviet Empire. It was necessary to act now, he urged, in order not to repeat the diplomatic mistakes of the 1930s.[46]

Accordingly when, a few days later, the United States decided to intervene in Korea, Aron wrote that, "By not repeating the fatal mistakes made by France and Britain from 1935 to 1938, the United States have shown themselves worthy of the immense responsibilities they bear. They have restored hope to the Western world".[47] What, in his opinion, were the implications of the Korean War? The assumption had been that there would either be Cold War (without action by regular armies) or total war, whereas the situation was now an intermediate one of limited hot wars. As soon as possible, therefore, the United States, and indeed the Atlantic Pact, should considerably increase its forces. The lesson for France was the impossibility of neutrality: "Do people think that Soviet armies, in pursuit of American troops, would stop at the frontiers of France?...When one imagines the disasters which total war or an eventual occupation would bring...one wonders if the people of Europe have not simply lost the instinct for self-preservation".[48]

At the present time, whatever the strategy adopted – local withdrawals, local resistance or the decision to generalize partial conflicts – the "first imperative" was the rearmament of the USA and Europe.[49] It was not a question of either reassuring or alarming public opinion, but of convincing it of three propositions: the West as a whole was in grave danger, there was still time to save the situation with a determined effort, and nothing less would offer hope of salvation.[50]

In the event, in September the French Prime Minister, René Pleven, proposed the setting up of a European Defence Community (EDC),[51] which involved the creation of a European Army. The Pleven Plan, like the Schuman Plan, was the brainchild of Jean Monnet and represented a compromise between French hostility to German rearmament and American pressure for it. As Aron was to express it in a collaborative study of the EDC published in 1956,[52] this proposal marked "the first phase of the EDC story: an attempt to apply the Schuman Plan method to the settlement of the problem brought up the American demand for German rearmament". The Pleven Plan

substituted for the brutal term "German rearmament" the subtler formula of "German participation in the defence of Europe". The notion of a "Wehrmacht" was changed to one of "German divisions in the European army". The principle of equality was limited to the European Community, thus preventing the entry of Germany into the Atlantic Community.[53]

Pleven's EDC proposal was received with some scepticism in the West, especially in Washington, and negotiations among the Six were complex and difficult. Nevertheless, by the spring of 1951 the American leaders had come to favour the European army in preference to the German army for two reasons: French politicians had convinced them that the National Assembly would never ratify the formation of a German national army; and the link between West German rearmament and European unity pleased American opinion. General Eisenhower himself, Commander-in-Chief of Nato and soon to become US President, was an enthusiastic convert to Europeanism, believing that the Six would find an unprecedented prosperity within a federal union. Despite reservations in the State Department as well as the Pentagon, President Truman and the Secretary of State, Dean Acheson, decided to put their weight behind the "Europeans" in France and give their support to the EDC plan.

This position, which was well established by the middle of 1951, was formally agreed by the Foreign Ministers of the United States, Britain and France in Washington in September (though Britain refused to participate) – Aron, who was there for *Le Figaro*, wrote that the European Army was "a wager on the future that cannot be refused".[54] Ironically, however,

the crisis was approaching at the very moment when the French initiative began to find support in Washington, support that had been lacking at the beginning of the enterprise. The American leaders had "bought" the Pleven Plan so completely that they became its warmest propagandists. But now the idea had to be "sold" to the French Parliament.[55]

There was in fact strong opposition to German rearmament in the National Assembly. By the end of 1951, it was clear that although the Socialists were more willing to rally to the EDC than to accept the reconstitution of a German army, the Gaullists had decided that a German army was preferable to the loss of French military sovereignty.[56] Nevertheless, early in 1952, the Assembly voted to accept the principle of the

430

European Army,[57] just before the Lisbon Conference at which the nations of the Atlantic Alliance approved the formation of the EDC. When, however, the treaty was initialled at the end of May, Aron expressed the view that the signing of the agreement "could not be greeted with enthusiasm. A policy which sanctifies the division of Germany is perhaps necessary (I believe it is, in fact), but certainly does not accord with our preferences. What was not inevitable, on the other hand, is that such pains should have been taken, in different quarters, to stress that 'signing is not ratifying'" – a reference to views expressed in *Le Monde* and elsewhere. The agreement must, Aron reiterated, be presented as "an attempt at an authentic reconciliation" with Germany.[58]

Aron returned to the question of German rearmament the following autumn. In September the Six had set up a special assembly to devise a European constitution.[59] German rearmament, Aron wrote at the end of November, constituted "a moral commitment" on France's part towards all its allies, but an "honourable revision" of the treaty was perfectly possible. Its main features should include an elected European assembly, to which the Council of Ministers would be accountable. "Such an assembly would perhaps give the Europe of the Six a political, and in time a moral, reality".[60]

For my part, I am inclined to think that it is easy to exaggerate the advantages which would result, in the economic sphere at any rate in the short term, from the Federation of the Six. But I leave that argument aside. I grant the usefulness of cooperation between Germany, Belgium, the Netherlands, Italy and France. And I grant, if needs be, that such cooperation should, for reasons of geographical solidarity, take on a more close-knit, organic character than that which binds the other members of the Atlantic Pact. But I shall limit myself to one decisive point. What sort of unity is it desirable or possible to conceive among the Six?

Aron was, he implied, one of those who believed in a continental unity, convinced that a definitive reconciliation between France and Germany was only possible within the framework of federal institutions and that, once created, the Federation would receive, if not the adhesion, at any rate the frank collaboration, of Britain. To avoid chaos, he was also in favour of capping the specialized agencies of defence and coal and steel with a European political authority. But what would this entail?[61]

How would foreign policy be handled? It was a mistake to think in terms of a "European Government", comparable to national governments – that was at best a long-term objective. Aron was also opposed to the idea of a "federal government", because the conditions were not right. Collaboration between the Six must therefore be based on "agreements

431

between governments". Specialist agencies could be extended, but national sovereignties should not be disbanded while there was nothing to put in their place. At the present time, political power could only rest in a committee of ministers whose decisions must be unanimous, though a European assembly, chosen by the electors of the Six, could be added to this permanent ministerial committee. However, such modest but realistic proposals must be backed by the feelings and consent of the peoples of Europe: "to go too far would risk hastening the failure of the whole enterprise".[62] As to Britain's attitude, Aron wondered, after attending the Commonwealth Conference in London in December 1952 for *Le Figaro*, whether "attention to the Commonwealth and distraction from Europe" was "the height of wisdom".[63]

Meanwhile, although the EDC treaty had been signed in May 1952, Robert Schuman, the Foreign Minister, for reasons which in Aron's view had never been satisfactorily explained, only sent it to Parliament for ratification at the end of January 1953.[64] "These six months", Aron wrote in 1956, "were rather a loss than a gain, since the situation for the EDC deteriorated every month":

On the international level, little remained of the anxiety and urgency that had dominated all minds at the time of the Chinese intervention in the Korean war. Military operations had been stabilized on the Korean peninsula, and the risks of a generalization of the war were greatly reduced – in spite of the fact that the Armistice was not yet signed. The death of Stalin, the style adopted by his successors, and the conclusion of the Korean truce during the first half of 1953 – all these accentuated the impression of an easing world situation and made German rearmament even less acceptable.[65]

The period from January 1953 to August 1954 saw what Aron has described as "the greatest ideological and political debate France has known since the Dreyfus Affair; its most visible stake was German rearmament, but its ultimate significance concerned the very existence of the French national state".[66] During this time, opposition to the EDC grew within the governmental majority and in Parliament, as well as among public opinion.[67] In his *Figaro* articles in the early part of 1954, Aron had concentrated on events in Indo-China and their repercussions in France and elsewhere,[68] but he returned to "the eternal debate" on the EDC shortly before the project was defeated. Apart from the Gaullists, he wrote, who were uniformly hostile, and the MRP, who were uniformly in favour, Socialists, moderates and Radicals were divided:

I personally belonged to the group of moderate critics of the treaty. I was afraid that it would make German rearmament less acceptable to French public opinion, by linking it with an abandonment of sovereignty, that it would endanger the solidarity of the metropolis and the French Union, and that finally it would compromise the indispensable reconciliation with Germany.

On the other hand, once the treaty was ratified by the Four Powers, its non-ratification by the French Parliament seemed to me to present disadvantages that were so serious and obvious that I hoped for a compromise solution.[69]

Two weeks later, during the course of which Aron expressed his impatience with the Mendès-France Government's inability to reach a clear decision on the matter,[70] the National Assembly voted (by 319 votes to 264) to reject the EDC. "The end of the EDC must not be the end of Europe", ran the title of Aron's editorial on the "deplorable consequences" of the vote in the Assembly. The moment had come for Europeans to rethink their problems and maintain their objectives – Franco-German reconciliation, close co-operation between the Six, and a German contribution to the defence of Europe – while for the time being renouncing the idea of a federation, for which French opinion was not yet ready. Many of those who had not taken part in the battle of yesterday, or who were in the opposite camp because the terms of the treaty seemed dangerous, would join them tomorrow. The anti-EDC majority was an ephemeral one and its aim was purely negative. An imperfect treaty which had become the symbol of a necessary policy had been rejected. Communists and neutralists were triumphant and the intentions of the government obscure. "But the struggle for the reconciliation of Europe and the security of the free world continues".[71]

Faced with Soviet imperialism, the West must remain vigilant and united, although this was not easy for democracies, in contrast to "an empire built on military strength and a quasi-religious orthodoxy":

The Mendès-France team looks, for the moment, rather like a French version of "Bevanism". A certain amount of Bevanism, as an antidote to the military obsession of America's leaders, can serve a useful purpose. But, in the long run, the Atlantic Alliance would find it difficult to withstand the attitude readily adopted by our colleagues on *Le Monde* – an attitude of surrender or, at any rate, boundless indulgence towards the Soviet world, and recrimination or pitiless severity towards our American allies.

The enthusiasm with which the neutralists support you, Mr Prime Minister, does not prove that you agree with them; but it does prove that the meaning of your policy is ambiguous.

Economic expansion at home, liberal reforms in North Africa, and strengthening of Western solidarity – these are the three elements of a French policy worthy of the name. The first two are probably ensured, but not the third – the one which dominates all the others. The choice is not yet made, but there remains little time in which to make it.[72]

West Germany's entry into Nato, Aron believed, had now become inevitable.[73] He therefore welcomed as "a happy event for the West" and as "Eden's masterpiece" the London Agreement, early in October, whereby West Germany should be rearmed and its sovereignty restored, but with the guarantee that Britain would maintain a standing army and air force on the continent of Europe. The result, Aron remarked, would be "coalition" rather than "integration". The creation of a separate German army of twelve divisions did not constitute a danger and the decision safeguarded France's military sovereignty.[74] A week later the London Agreement was ratified by the National Assembly (350 votes to 113) and a fortnight afterwards the Paris Agreements, creating a new European organization, the Western European Union, and admitting West Germany and Italy into Nato, were signed ("That the London Agreements should, within a few weeks, have become the Treaties of Paris is", Aron observed, "a cause for unreserved congratulation").[75]

But the Paris Agreements still had to be ratified by the National Assembly. "Looking back on the manoeuvres of last summer", Aron wrote in December,

it must in all honesty be said that M. Mendès-France's responsibility in the rejection of the EDC is limited. He perhaps dealt it the *coup de grâce*; for my part, I think it was nearly dead already. The negotiations in September and October gave real proof of the new diplomacy. Unless, then, the mind is completely distorted by emotion, how is it possible to deny that M. Mendès-France took exactly the decisions which any sincere and lucid supporter of the Atlantic Alliance would have taken?[76]

The basic facts of the problem, Aron reasoned, had been these. In 1950 the French Government had proposed the EDC in order to stop an autonomous German army from coming into being and to prevent West Germany's entry into the Atlantic Alliance. If the aim was to avoid a serious crisis among the Allies, the rejection of the EDC inevitably implied assent to these two measures, condemned though they had been by the French Parliament. The day Mendès-France, in his talks with Eden in Paris, formally accepted West Germany's entry into Nato, he had taken the decisive step. It was understandable that the supporters of a federal Europe of the Six should judge the London Agreements to be inferior to the EDC and it was normal that they should continue their action in support of the supranational solution. But, after the failure of the EDC, the London Agreements were the only reasonable alternative.[77] The Paris Treaties marked a decisive phase in that political battle whose stake was Germany and which would decide the future of Europe. They must, therefore, be ratified.[78]

434

Nevertheless, the issue was to remain uncertain to the end. The debate in the National Assembly on the ratification of the Paris Agreements was held at the end of December 1954. At first, Article One of the agreement – the creation of Western European Union through the entry of West Germany and Italy into the Brussels Pact – was rejected (by 280 votes to 259), although the ending of occupied status in Germany and the Franco-German agreement on the Saar were accepted.[79] The Prime Minister, Mendès-France, however, decided to make the vote on the whole Bill a question of confidence. Three days later the Assembly voted (by 289 votes to 251) in favour of West Germany's entry into Nato, and three days after that, on 30 December 1954, the Paris Agreements were finally ratified when, by 287 votes to 260, the French Parliament gave its approval to German rearmament and the creation of Western European Union. This "indispensable" ratification was confirmed by the French Senate (184 votes to 110) the following March.[80]

The "greatest ideological and political debate France had known since the Dreyfus Affair" was at last over. It was soon to be replaced by another that was to prove infinitely more traumatic for the French nation – the debate over the Algerian War.

Notes

1. See Chapter 12, above.
2. 1983a, p.273. Here he met Daladier and listened to the passionate speeches of Churchill, Reynaud and Duncan Sandys – "incapable of rousing myself to take part in these rhetorical jousts".
3. The Treaty of Mutual Assistance between France, Britain, Belgium, the Netherlands and Luxembourg.
4. The Treaty of Alliance between France and Britain, signed in March 1947.
5. "La crise économique anglaise: II. La Grande-Bretagne et l'Europe", *Fig.*, 1 April 1948. Compare the discussion of European problems contained in *Le Grand Schisme*, which was also completed at this time (see Chapter 16, above).
6. "Du plan Marshall à l'Europe unie: III. Accords économiques ou union politique?", *Fig.*, 4 August 1948.
7. "Du plan Marshall à l'Europe unie: IV. Les obstacles", *Fig.*, 10 August 1948.
8. Ibid.
9. "L'échec des négociations franco-britanniques sur l'Assemblée européenne", *Fig.*, 26 January 1949.
10. Ibid.
11. Mann, 1985, p.148.
12. For example, France must, he wrote in February 1947, adopt a positive and constructive attitude towards "a Germany reconstituted in a peaceful Europe...

I think that the reconstruction of Germany will take place in spite of us if, through our fault, it takes place without us" ("Une autre Allemagne", *Combat*, 7 February 1947). Aron's articles on the Franco-German problem have been singled out for praise by the diplomat Jean-Marie Soutou (Soutou, 1985). More generally, see Löwenthal, 1985, and Rovan, 1985.

13. "Politique allemande: la tâche essentielle", *Fig.*, 30 March 1949.
14. "Politique allemande: l'éternelle menace", *Fig.*, 2-3 April 1949.
15. "Vers l'unité allemande?", *Fig.*, 19 May 1949.
16. "Futilité de la diplomatie", *Fig.*, 14 June 1949.
17. Aron has summarized their arguments in his memoirs (1983a, pp.256-60).
18. "Le pacte de l'Atlantique", *Fig.*, 21 December 1948.
19. "Est-il possible de mettre fin à la guerre froide? Staline et la révolution mondiale", *Fig.*, 29 January 1949.
20. "Fin de la guerre froide? Détente", *Fig.*, 8 February 1949.
21. "Le pacte atlantique: diplomatie et stratégie", *Fig.*, 21 February 1949; "Le pacte atlantique: Le cas de la Norvège", *Fig.*, 23 February 1949; "Le pacte de l'Atlantique et ses critiques", *Fig.*, 21 March 1949.
22. 1949e.
23. Claude Mauriac, *Un autre de Gaulle* (Paris, 1970), pp.340-1; tr. (by Moura Budberg and Gordon Latta) *The Other de Gaulle* (London, 1973), pp.312-13.
24. Ibid., pp.341-2: tr. pp.313-14. Aron in fact made it very clear in an article in *Le Figaro* the following August that he did not believe that, once the Atlantic Pact was signed, all the European nations need do was sit back and leave the defence of Europe to the Americans ("Le réarmament de l'Europe", *Fig.*, 5 August 1949).
25. "La ratification du pacte de l'Atlantique: Après le vote de l'Assemblée", *Fig.*, 28 July 1949.
26. "Le réarmement de l'Europe", 5 August 1949. Thus Aron did not subscribe to the view, at one time attributed to him by General de Gaulle, that the defence of Europe could be left to the Americans.
27. "L'illusion de la neutralité", *Fig.*, 17 February 1950.
28. "Conversation avec Staline?", *Fig.*, 23 February 1950.
29. "Contre le défaitisme", *Fig.*, 3 March 1950. See also the outstanding article, "Les communistes et la paix", *Fig.*, 18 March 1950.
30. 1983a, p.266.
31. Ibid.
32. Ibid., pp.267-8.
33. "Que peut-on attendre de l'Assemblée Européenne?", *Fig.*, 10 August 1949.
34. "Incorrigible Allemagne? I. Après les élections", *Fig.*, 22 August 1949.
35. "Incorrigible Allemagne? II. Que faire?", *Fig.*, 23 August 1949.
36. "La Conférence de Paris", *Fig.*, 9 November 1949.
37. "Fictions européennes", *Fig.*, 1 February 1950.
38. "L'Allemagne et Europe: V. Choix d'une politique", *Fig.*, 20 April 1950.
39. "L'initiative française", *Fig.*, 11 May 1950.
40. Compare 1956b, pp.1-2: tr. 1957c, pp.2-3: "This initiative marked the beginning of a new phase in French post-war diplomacy. France had tried between 1944 and 1947 to be mediator between East and West. From 1947 to 1950 French diplomacy

had faithfully but reluctantly adopted the Western view. And in 1950, for the first time, she endeavoured to make her own positive contribution to European and Western reconstruction. Instead of hindering the inevitable restoration of West Germany, the French Foreign Minister contrived a safeguard against German power by the offer of an honourable place for the Bonn Government within a United Europe".

41. The seventeen-member Organization for European Economic Cooperation set up in the wake of the Marshall Plan.
42. "L'initiative française", *Fig.*, 11 May 1950.
43. "Le pool industriel franco-allemand: II. L'Autorité internationale", *Fig.*, 7 June 1950.
44. Ibid.
45. "La demi-absence de la Grande-Bretagne", *Fig.*, 19 June 1950. "The full meaning of this event", as Aron was to put it in 1956, was that "France was stressing the importance of a supranational power and preferred to construct a new supranational Europe without Great Britain rather than a traditional international coalition with Great Britain. By insisting upon a supranational power, France took the lead for a federal type of organization, restricted to the six continental nations, Holland, Belgium, Luxembourg, West Germany, Italy and France" (1956b, p.2: tr. p.3).
46. "Epreuve de force", *Fig.*, 27 June 1950.
47. "Guerre chaude en Asie", *Fig.*, 4 July 1950.
48. "Guerre chaude en Asie: II. Leçon de la Corée", *Fig.*, 5 July 1950.
49. "En quête d'une stratégie", *Fig.*, 14 July 1950.
50. "Les conditions du salut", *Fig.*, 7 August 1950. Compare Aron's view in *Les Guerres en chaîne*, which he was writing at this time, that "Europe" would be most likely to develop through military, rather than economic or political, cooperation. See Chapter 17, above.
51. Known to the French as the Communauté Européenne de Défense (CED).
52. *La Querelle de la CED* (Paris, 1956). These "essays in sociological analysis" were published under the auspices of the Fondation Nationale des Sciences Politiques and edited by Aron and Daniel Lerner (see 1956b: tr. 1957c). The other contributors were Jacques Fauvet, Stanley Hoffmann, Alfred Grosser, Jacques Vernant, Jean Stoetzel and J.-J. Marchand. On its appearance Dorothy Pickles called the work "a fascinating study and a first-rate piece of research which will illuminate many facets of French thought for possibly years to come" (*IA*, 33, 1957, p.360).
53. 1956b, p.3: tr. p.4.
54. "L'armée européenne: un pari sur l'avenir qu'on ne peut pas refuser", *Fig.*, 17 September 1951.
55. 1956b, pp.5-6: tr. p.7
56. Ibid., p.6: tr. ibid.
57. "Après les débats de Bonn et de Paris: Le double dialogue", *Fig.*, 21 February 1952.
58. "Après la signature", *Fig.*, 30 May 1952.
59. "Fédération européenne: objectif ou mirage?", *Fig.*, 24 September 1952.
60. "Le réarmement de l'Allemagne: III. La possible révision", *Fig.*, 24 November 1952.
61. "La Fédération des Six", *Fig.*, 3 December 1952.
62. "Ce que peut être la Fédération des Six", *Fig.*, 4 December 1952.
63. "L'Angleterre s'interroge sur son avenir: VI. Le Commonwealth et l'Europe", *Fig.*, 23 December 1952.

64. "La querelle de l'armée européenne: Comment arriver à un accord indispensable", *Fig.*, 31 January 1953.

65. 1956b, p.7: tr. p.8.

66. Ibid., p.9: tr. p.10. Aron himself entered the debate early in 1954 in a polemic with Jacques Soustelle, who in a recent *Combat* article had expressed his opposition to German rearmament in any form ("Machiavel et Talleyrand", *Fig.*, 4 February 1954). Soustelle accused Aron of being "subservient to the will of America", a "deviation" which, irrelevantly in Aron's view, Soustelle traced back to the events of 1942 ("De l'indépendance française", *Fig.*, 8 February 1954).

67. For Aron's analysis of these developments, see 1956b: tr. 1957c.

68. See Chapter 19, below.

69. "L'éternel débat", *Fig.*, 17 August 1954.

70. "'Gouverner, c'est choisir'", *Fig.*, 26 August 1954.

71. "La fin de la CED ne doit pas être la fin de l'Europe", *Fig.*, 3 September 1954.

72. "Le choix n'est pas encore fait", *Fig.*, 6 September 1954.

73. "De Bruxelles à Londres", *Fig.*, 25 September 1954.

74. "L'accord de Londres", *Fig.*, 4 October 1954.

75. "Les accords de Paris", *Fig.*, 25 October 1954.

76. "Ni refus, ni annexion", *Fig.*, 2 December 1954.

77. Ibid.

78. "Subtilités inutiles", *Fig.*, 8 December 1954.

79. "Les surprises d'un débat", *Fig.*, 23 December 1954; "Quelques faits et quelques mots", *Fig.*, 27 December 1954.

80. "Avant la ratification: La France, l'Allemagne et la Sarre", *Fig.*, 11 March 1955; "La ratification indispensable", 22 March 1955. For Aron's final thoughts on the EDC, see his memoirs (1983a, pp.274-7).

19

France and the Empire

In considering France's post-war future in 1945, Aron had stated his belief that it should hold on to its colonies, especially (for economic reasons) in North and West Africa; at the same time, he had argued that liberal reforms (though he left these unspecified) were essential to the Empire's survival.[1] The following July, Aron published his first article on the problem of France's empire in *Combat*. Clearly, he wrote,

colonialism, in the sense given to the word towards the end of the previous century, from now on belongs to a bygone age. No task is more urgent or of greater significance for France than the progressive elaboration, in theory and in practice, of the system destined to take the place of colonialism.

However, Aron was opposed to "independence pure and simple", because in most cases this would deliver the newly emancipated territories to other forms of imperialism and was likely to prove "an illusory solution". At the same time, the concept of the French Union ("L'Union Française") – the new title and status that was to be given to the Empire under the new Constitution – though "rich in possibilities", still remained vague. Any "Federation", Aron pointed out, implied that its members should first become conscious of themselves as autonomous personalities.

It also seemed to him essential that France should invest in heavy industry in the overseas territories – an idea which met with much opposition. Thus the Labonne Plan for the economic development of Morocco was as important as the Monnet Plan for France, but both depended on "the consent and even the enthusiasm of the nation".[2]

Less than six months later, on 19 December 1946, Vietminh nationalists rose against the French in Hanoi. The Indo-China War, which was to last nearly eight years, had begun. "Maintenir" ("Hold fast"), urged the title of Aron's editorial in *Combat* three days afterwards: France must do all it could to renounce violence.[3] One month later, in an article on "The Tragedy of Indo-China", he wrote that:

For anyone who escapes the obsession with current events and party quarrels, one question dominates all, because it involves the historic destiny of France: the fate of our overseas territories. Will we, or will we not, succeed in replacing the colonial regime of yesterday with a new system of economic, political and moral relations, which will correspond both to the wishes of their inhabitants and to our determination to maintain our imperial mission? Will we, or will we not, succeed in making of the French Union, which is still only a name, a reality?

The events in Indo-China are tragic in themselves. But their seriousness is increased even more by the repercussions they inevitably have in the four corners of our Empire. Two dangers lie in store for us (although most observers persist in only seeing one). Abdication or lack of resolution on our part will encourage violence, but intransigence is likely to drive our protégés of yesterday to despair. Our history is full of examples, both from the recent and the remote past, of how we have ended up losing everything by dint of yielding nothing...[4]

There was no question, Aron continued, of that reconquest of Indo-China which Léon Blum, before being re-elected Prime Minister that December, had vigorously condemned. But Vietnam must not be seen as a uniform block. It was important to distinguish those politicians in Vietnam who were in favour of an agreement with France and those who saw a negotiated settlement simply as a strategem by which to gain time and gather their forces together for the decisive struggle. The question was how to strengthen the moderates and weaken the extremists. The moderates must not be blamed for the Hanoi insurrection on 19 December; within the Indo-Chinese Federation, Vietnam must not be reduced to a sense of powerlessness or despair; and there must be a dialogue not simply with France's protégés, but above all with those who enjoyed the confidence of the people. If these were not the intentions of the French authorities and they thought that the occupation of key military positions was enough to bring total pacification, it would be

440

even more important to confront French opinion with the realities and state openly what France's policy was.[5]

"Who with any heart", asked Aron two months later, after an Assembly debate on Indo-China, "does not feel a dull anguish and a kind of guilty conscience at the thought that the troops of a liberated France are fighting in a distant land?" The military position had improved, but Aron was impatient at the lack of political movement and progress.[6] Only a few days later, however, rebellion broke out in Madagascar as well and, in another far-sighted article in *Combat*, Aron called for "the courage to innovate":

It is difficult to delude oneself about the character and significance of the movement which is carrying the victims of colonialism towards freedom. It can never be said enough: this system is dead. The loss of power and prestige of the European nations; the spread of ideas borrowed from the colonizers themselves; the awakening or reawakening of political consciousness in the native populations; the propaganda, at home and abroad, of the great empires of the twentieth century, the Soviet Union and the United States, whose conflicting ideologies are both opposed to the preservation of the status quo: all these "realistic" reasons are enough, without even resorting to moral arguments, to condemn the absurd pretension to prolong the established order, or the so-called established order.[7]

On the other hand, it was no less clear, Aron maintained, that world diplomacy abhorred a vacuum and that even if France's colonies gained a theoretical independence, they would represent a vacuum which others would soon fill. Thus he hoped that their evolution towards an authentic independence could take place within the framework of the French Union.

Force was no solution, for how long would such a solution last? And what would be the value "for France, its authority in the world, its vocation and its very power" of an Empire held only by violence? Whether one liked it or not, for the nation's conscience as well as its temporal destiny, there was "no hope in a return to the past". Yet there *was* hope in "boldness and generosity":

In Indo-China, as in Madagascar and North Africa, the moderates will win insofar as we give them proof of our sincerity and demonstrate that the French Union is not simply a phrase designed to cloak the reality of yesterday, but a future that accords with our duties and their aspirations.

France must help with industrialization as well as the accession of indigenous elites to responsible posts. There again one must look and plan ahead, instead of merely adapting to the pressure of circumstances – "a matter of intelligence and faith". But in order to do this, France could only count on itself.[8]

Even as Aron wrote those words, however, brutal repression in Madagascar was under way. "This paper", he declared in *Combat* in mid-April, "has never been accused of colonialism":

We have never underestimated the gravity of the crisis that is spreading to the whole Empire and the only hope we see is in generosity and boldness. But the likelihood of peacefully achieving deep-seated reforms depends on the image of ourselves which we offer to the indigenous peoples, and also on the clarity of our plans and the strength of our will. That the different government parties each support one of the indigenous parties, including those against which our troops are at this very moment being ordered to fire, increases the risks of an explosion – that is, of a disaster for all.

In the months ahead French politics will be dominated, not by a shortage of bread or meat, but by events in the French Union. Whether we like it or not, such events contain within them the seeds of a political crisis in which the fall of a Ministry will seem no more than a tiny episode.[9]

The aim of the French Union, Aron stated a month later in May 1947, after General de Gaulle had made a speech on the subject at Bordeaux, was "to allow every country to administer itself, without breaking the ties which attach them to France". But he had to admit that "this goal is as simple and obvious as the means to attain it are complex and difficult".[10]

Shortly afterwards Aron left *Combat* for the more conservative *Le Figaro*. The war in Indo-China dragged on, but over six years were to pass before he again discussed the problem in his newspaper articles. Commenting at the end of his life, Aron did not regret this public reticence; he was convinced that any editorials which he might have written on French policy in Indo-China would have changed "absolutely nothing", since those who had any influence knew perfectly well, from private conversations, exactly what he thought.[11] Furthermore, he had strongly criticized France's Indo-China policy in *Les Guerres en chaîne*, which was published in 1951:

We have brought into being (or we did not know how to avoid) the very thing we should have feared above all else: an endless war against an Indo-Chinese resistance which, though led by the Communists, is supported by a majority of nationalists. From the outset we had a choice of two methods: either to grant Ho Chi Minh's main demands – Indo-China's independence, the union of the three countries, together with a more or less vague link with the French Union – or, if we thought it impossible to negotiate with Ho Chi Minh, to bring about a national government to which we would have granted, in all essentials, what we would have refused to an agent of Stalin. But instead of making a resolute choice of policy and sticking to it, we hesitated. We recognized Ho Chi Minh as the chief of national resistance in 1946; we negotiated with him and solemnly invited him to France. But, at the same time as we gave him additional prestige by these very actions, we appeared to be playing a double game. We should have sought an independent and friendly Indo-China...It may be that such a goal was unattainable from the start; perhaps an independent Indo-China would have become communist. But from France's point of view, such an eventuality would have cost us less dear than war.

...France, which lacks the means to defend its own territory, is squandering its resources in an adventure that is perhaps justifiable in terms of global anti-communist diplomacy, but not in terms of the self-interest of the country.[12]

The occasion which led Aron to break his newspaper silence on Indo-China was the trip he made to the Far East at the end of 1953. While in Saigon he wrote one despatch for *Le Figaro* on "The Meaning of a War"[13] and he published two further articles on "The Indo-China Tragedy" on his return to France.[14] Since 1947 it had become the aim of French policy in Indo-China to give support to the ex-Emperor, Bao Dai, against the Vietminh under Ho Chi Minh. Having abdicated in 1945, Bao Dai had resumed his title in 1948, when France agreed to recognize the independence of Vietnam. He had subsequently formed a provisional central government in Saigon and in March 1949 had signed an agreement with President Auriol by which Vietnam became an Associated State of the French Union.

One could, Aron wrote, argue about the likelihood of this policy succeeding, but one fact was beyond dispute – the necessity of recognizing the genuine nationalism of the Bao Dai Government. In order to be taken seriously in Indo-China, this nationalism had to be affirmed against France, and it was important, Aron stressed, that this should be understood. In other words, the Bao Dai Government wanted Vietnam to leave the French Union and this much, Aron implied, must be accepted. The real issue, on the other hand, concerned the consequences for South-East Asia of a Sovietization of Indo-China: it was this which, in Aron's view, gave meaning to the joint efforts of France and Vietnam. American intervention would, he believed (though he was to modify this view a few weeks later), involve China and lead to a second Korea. Unless Vietnamese nationalism was satisfied, "victory – that is, an honourable end to the war – is out of the question".[15]

The "tragedy" of Indo-China was that the French used the argument that the French Union must remain intact in order to justify a struggle which in fact was aggravating the growing crisis in North Africa. "The navy dreams of preserving bases (what ships are they to shelter?) and the politicians want to respect the terms of the Constitution. But the disproportion between the sacrifices made and the issue at stake gives cause for anxiety".[16] The worst solution, Aron argued in a particularly incisive article, was the refusal to make a choice, and the choice, it seemed to him, lay between three possibilities. The first was direct negotiation with the Vietminh. This would result in the withdrawal of French troops and the Sovietization of Indo-China, but at least it would lead to the end of the war. The second possibility was to continue with the present policy. This would lead either to victory over the Vietminh, or an improved position from which to negotiate – or French defeat. Thirdly, France could appeal to the United States to intervene directly. The war could not, in Aron's view, be justified in terms of France's interest. But if it was granted that defeat in Indo-China was not in the interest of the free world (and would, for instance, lead to the Sovietization of Thailand and Burma), then the third solution appeared to be necessary – unless, of course, it was argued that Indo-China was only of secondary importance. In spite of all the drawbacks, it was this third solution that Aron favoured.[17]

He returned to the problem at the beginning of 1954:

Let us speak clearly. The alternative is as follows: either the Western nations – America and Britain, as well as France – believe it essential to halt the Communist advance towards South-East Asia, in which case they must all play their part in the task; or they do not consider the safeguarding of Indo-China to be indispensable in a general strategic context, in which case France, having regard to her interest alone, must decide in favour of negotiation.

In other words, France should tell its allies that "they should choose between participating in the struggle or accepting the loss of a position which they themselves regard as vital".[18]

As to the question of negotiations over Indo-China, Aron was equally opposed to those who categorically refused them at any price and those who were prepared to accept any conditions. France would have to negotiate one day ("Un jour ou l'autre il faudra traiter"). Meanwhile, the government must make its conditions known concerning the security of French forces, the participation of the Vietnamese Government, and the method by which the people of Vietnam would choose their leaders. In other words, France must not prepare a disguised surrender.[19]

By the time Aron wrote about Indo-China again, at the end of April,

444

the peace conference had opened at Geneva and American help was now being given, but the military situation was desperate. In mid-March the Vietminh forces encircling the huge French garrison at Dien Bien Phu had begun their attack on the stronghold and its fall was only a question of time. Aron, clearly exasperated at what he called "the tragic events in Indo-China" and "the catastrophe of Dien Bien Phu",[20] referred bitterly to "the blind obstinacy" as a result of which, for the past seven years, the French government "has not found the means to demonstrate our disinterestedness by solemnly granting, in a few simple words, full and complete independence to Vietnam". He was also critical of "the mixture of jingoistic nationalism and weakness which paralyses our diplomacy". Direct Anglo-American intervention, he argued, would neither have aimed at nor resulted in the spreading of the war, but the re-establishment of the local balance of power, the condition of an honourable peace. But Britain had refused such a step and this would serve to reinforce American in-activity. The United States must now act by using its influence to get the Russians and the Chinese to agree to a compromise, and the USA must guarantee that compromise by maintaining its presence south of the demarcation line. If it did not do this or if, instead of intervening in a limited way to improve the local situation with a view to negotiation, the United States continued in its present attitude of inaction, France would soon be compelled simply to withdraw from Indo-China. If, Aron warned, Western solidarity crumbled in Indo-China, it would not easily survive elsewhere.[21]

Just four days later, on 7 May, despite fierce resistance, the stronghold surrendered.[22] After "the atrocious and heroic folly of Dien Bien Phu", as Aron called it, the French government's sole objective, he emphasized, must be the safety of the expeditionary force. "For many years the prevention of Communist victory in Indo-China has been the sole justification for the war. Now that this justification is no longer considered to be valid by all the Western powers, we have the right – no, we have the duty – to draw the logical conclusion".[23]

Aron was clearly irritated at the attitude being shown by the British – both by the Eden Government and by the Labour opposition, which had put down a parliamentary motion critical of what it called "French colonial-ism". Nevertheless, he admitted that France had much with which to reproach itself, in particular the failures of military and political foresight in Vietnam. The task now was to "make clear to the expeditionary corps that it has the support of the nation, establish specific and limited objectives both in the military and in the political sphere, and stop the contagious disease of defeatism from spreading":

Is the world to say tomorrow that while there are still Frenchmen ready to die a heroic death, the French state is incapable of facing the ordeal? Are we not ashamed to make a local defeat even worse through tears and recriminations, instead of responding, as a major nation, by a will to act?[24]

By now, however, the Laniel Government was in its last days, and on 17 June Pierre Mendès-France became the new Prime Minister, publicly setting himself the now famous deadline of 20 July by which to negotiate a cease-fire or resign. Aron's reaction came in an editorial a few days later entitled "The Thirty Days".[25] Mendès-France had, Aron began, "two indisputable claims to a presumption in his favour". The first was that he had resigned from the Provisional Government in the spring of 1945 in protest against an economic and financial policy of which he disapproved. Such an example of courage, Aron observed, had become so rare in the last ten years that the resignation had in retrospect taken on a symbolic significance and conferred on its author a well-deserved prestige. Secondly, Mendès-France had also been right – "unfortunately" – about Indo-China. He had declared that the situation would get worse every year and he had repeatedly said that the only solution was direct negotiation with Ho Chi Minh. Aron agreed that this was probably so, although even now no one could tell what the Vietminh response would have been to a French initiative at different times. Mendès-France had not, in Aron's view, been in favour of Vietnam leaving the French Union altogether, but seemed to believe in a French Union of equal and independent nations; and, Aron added, events in North Africa showed at least that the path followed till now was leading to an increasingly serious crisis.[26]

However, that presumption in Mendès-France's favour – "and we say this with equal frankness" – was, Aron continued, "tinged with anxiety". Some of the Prime Minister's supporters seemed to be hoping for a reversal of foreign policy and a breaking off of alliances that would have radical consequences for the country; and they had gone so far in their criticisms that they had ended up by "irritating those who do not succumb to *la folie parisienne*". But Mendès-France's "Donnez-moi trente jours et je vous apporte la paix" ("Give me thirty days and I shall bring you peace") was also worrying, in Aron's view, because "one should not play double or quits with the Government of France or with the outcome of international negotiations". As a result, Molotov and Chou En Lai were now the arbiters of French politics, free to cause or prevent a governmental crisis. If they granted a cease-fire within the stated time, Mendès-France would inevitably become suspect, because he would look like the favourite of those whom he himself called France's enemies. And if, on 20 July, the Cabinet was forced to resign, should public opinion conclude that a policy of war was going to succeed one of peace?

Our fear is that M. Mendès-France has ill-advisedly risked his prestige – which was one of the last remaining assets in a discredited system – in a wager that he should not have made. Indeed, let us say quite specifically here and now: if the cease-fire is not concluded in thirty days' time, M. Mendès-France will perhaps feel duty-bound to resign (though I am not sure about that), but France will in no way be forced to change her policy. This will continue to be to seek a negotiated peace, the terms of the compromise being determined less by the provisional occupant of the Hotel Matignon than by events on the spot together with the general diplomatic situation.

In the atmosphere created by the enthusiasm of his friends, M. Mendès-France is likely to take these remarks the wrong way. Let me repeat, therefore, my admiration for the character and intellectual honesty of the Prime Minister. I do not, however, believe that patent-medicine advertising of this kind (les promesses de style publicitaire) can symbolize the will for national recovery.[27]

The press was becoming increasingly "Mendèsiste"[28] and, as Aron had foreseen, his editorial was the subject of considerable criticism. Ten days later, therefore, he added a "Postscript" to what he had said earlier: "I have already given voice to the high hopes and also to a number of anxieties aroused by the new government. Having said that, I do not consider myself to be any more 'anti-government' today than 'pro-government' yesterday".[29]

The truth of this was shown shortly afterwards when Aron defended the government's decision to evacuate the southern part of the Tongking Delta; such an act was, he argued, justifiable both on military grounds and in terms of the current negotiations at Geneva. The American press had been critical of France. But, Aron asked, "Why should France strive on her own to contain Communist expansion in South-East Asia, if neither the United States nor Britain nor the independent countries of Asia consider Vietnam to be vital? Why urge on France an intransigence which the Americans themselves rejected when it was Korea that was the issue and GIs were fighting there?" The decisions which led to the Indo-China War, Aron argued, were taken in 1945 and 1946 by the French and not at the instigation of the American leaders; indeed, at that time the latter, "obsessed as they were by anti-colonialism, if anything showed sympathy for Ho Chi Minh". Since 1950, however, the Indo-China War had appeared to Washington to be part of the struggle against Communism. But, for a variety of reasons, French governments had never desired, nor American governments accepted,

447

the internationalization of the war. Despite, therefore, the economic aid it had given France, the United States, which had taken no part in the fighting and had no wish to do so now, had neither the moral authority nor the diplomatic justification to prohibit France from trying to reach a settlement. The search for an agreement implied negotiations with China – "in the British manner and contrary to American liking". It could have been otherwise, but there was no point now in dwelling on the past. The Prime Minister had received a clear mandate from the Assembly and public opinion, and Aron was "confident that he will not subscribe to any agreement that is contrary to the fundamental interests of France or the Atlantic Alliance".[30]

Ten days later Aron addressed some ironical remarks to Mendès-France's supporters:

When M. Mendès-France makes an approach to Washington, he is defending the independence and dignity of France. The same approach made by M. Bidault would have been clear proof of French subjection. Why be indignant that the prospect of power should be the beginning of wisdom? If a change of government was necessary in order to rally a fraction of the opposition – our colleagues on *Le Monde*, in particular – to the Atlantic policy, then the price does not appear to us to have been too high.

Let M. Mendès-France obtain, between now and the end of the parliamentary session, an honourable armistice and the ratification of a European defence treaty, and he will have deserved well, not so much of his supporters as of those who, through the accident of parliamentary battle, appear to be his opponents. Let us say that he will have done a service to the country.

It is often difficult, in French politics, to remain faithful both to men and to ideas. For my part, if a choice has to be made, I prefer to be faithful to ideas.[31]

Three days afterwards, on 20 July, the cease-fire was signed at Geneva. Mendès-France had beaten his deadline. It was, Aron wrote, "a bet well won":[32]

M. Mendès-France has won his bet in conditions which do not lend themselves to criticism. Not that the terms of the cease-fire are good: they are not and they could not be. But they reflect the local situation, without making it worse. One could not, in all honesty, ask for more.

In Aron's view, the demarcation line gave the Vietnamese state a chance to survive in the south. The neutralization of Laos and Cambodia did not guarantee the independence of these small countries, but neither did it make their imminent absorption into the Soviet universe inevitable. After the Anglo-American shirking of the issue in April, and considering

Britain's resolve to negotiate with few cards and America's determination not to negotiate at all, the agreement was better than could be expected. Nevertheless, Aron concluded,

If M. Mendès-France is to be congratulated, it would be indecent, after so many sacrifices and so many painful surrenders, to rejoice too loudly. The event will be interpreted, throughout the whole of Asia, as a defeat for the West, and for the United States just as much as France, since people hold the USA responsible for what it does not do as well as for what it does. But this setback is not irremediable and its consequences can be limited, if the West learns from the past in order not to make the same mistakes again.[33]

Aron subsequently added that the thirty-day deadline, which to him had seemed open to criticism at the time, had been justified not so much by the successful outcome as by the military argument put forward by Mendès-France in his speech to the National Assembly. But the Prime Minister had also stated that negotiations were already seriously under way when he took office and he had thus implicitly acknowledged the exaggerated character of some of the attacks made in his Assembly speech on 9 June, before he came to power. As to the future of South-East Asia, open aggression seemed to Aron to be unlikely in the next few years (China wanted to re-enter the international orbit and to concentrate on economic development), although guerrilla activity was probable in Laos, Cambodia, Thailand and South Vietnam. In the long term, however, China could help national Communist Parties to power, though it should, in Aron's view, be admitted to the United Nations. The task of the West was to help those countries which felt threatened and wanted to defend themselves, but at the same time the West must avoid giving India or Indonesia pretexts for denouncing its actions as mere colonialism or warmongering. "From now on in Asia it is up to the Asians to contain the expansion of communism".[34]

Meanwhile, French attention had been forced to shift from Indo-China to Tunisia. In July 1954 the terrorism of the main nationalist party, the Néo-Destour (whose leader, Habib Bourguiba, was interned in France), had grown alarmingly and, on the day the above article appeared in *Le Figaro*, Mendès-France made a dramatic flight to Tunis. As a result he affirmed the Tunisian right to internal sovereignty (although foreign policy and the armed forces would remain in French hands) and proposed the formation of a Tunisian government which would prepare democratic institutions for an independent state (within days such a government was set up under the moderate nationalist leader, Tahar ben Ammar).

Aron was under no illusion that such proposals went far enough. "Personally", he wrote, "I do not believe that France has adopted the policy which, in an age of nationalism, offers the best chance of maintaining the Franco-Tunisian community":

When a party has been recognized by a large section of opinion as representing national feeling, there is no point in looking for other people to act as intermediaries, on the ground that they are moderates. In order to compel recognition, these moderates will inevitably be driven to make demands that are pitched almost as high as those of the extremists, without disarming the latter. Besides, those to whom all outlets are blocked themselves become extremist, while those to whom the responsibilities of power and the practice of cooperation reveal the virtue of progressive methods can become moderate.[35]

France, Aron believed, had made this mistake with the non-Communists in Vietnam. He was also opposed to such slogans as "First restore order" and "No negotiation with those responsible for terrorism". Furthermore, it was important that "elites trained in our universities, who are deeply imbued with a love of our culture" should not be driven to despair. But what of the rest of North Africa? His conclusion was generous, realistic and unequivocal:

The repercussions in Algeria, where the situation is quite different, and in Morocco, where the evolution of events has not reached the same point, are not easy to foresee...but, between the risks of a liberal policy and those of other policies, there can be no hesitation. The risks of the liberal policy are probably less great and they are certainly more noble.[36]

Less than three months later, on 1 November 1954, the Algerian War had begun. Within a year, in October 1955, a few weeks after his election to the Sorbonne and in – of all places – the conservative *Figaro*, Aron was to begin his courageous and powerfully argued campaign in favour of the independence of France's North African colonies, including Algeria.[37]

Notes

1. 1946b, p.350. See Chapter 12, above.
2. "L'industrialisation de l'Empire", *Combat*, 24 July 1946. Cf. "A propos de l'Union française", *Combat*, 15 September 1946.

3. "Maintenir", *Combat*, 22 December 1946. Aron discussed this article, which Sartre apparently described as "embarrassed" and which Aron reread "without too much shame or remorse", in his memoirs (1983a, pp.211-12).

4. "La tragédie d'Indochine", *Combat*, 29 January 1947.

5. Ibid. Compare 1983a, pp.212-13: this article, "too moderate for my taste today, nevertheless reiterated the rejection of military reconquest and the necessity for talks not only with our protégés but, above all, with those who enjoyed the confidence of the people as a whole".

6. "En pleine confusion", *Combat*, 20 March 1947.

7. "Le courage d'innover", *Combat*, 3 April 1947.

8. Ibid.

9. "Crise permanente", *Combat*, 18 April 1947.

10. "L'Union Française", *Combat*, 16 May 1947.

11. 1981a, pp.147-9: tr.1983b, pp.126-8.

12. 1951a, p.228. This passage is omitted from the English translation (tr.1954a).

13. "Signification d'une guerre", *Fig.*, 16 November 1953.

14. "La tragédie d'Indochine", *Fig.*, 3 December 1953; "La tragédie d'Indochine: Le refus du choix est la pire solution", *Fig.*, 4 December 1953.

15. "Signification d'une guerre", *Fig.*, 16 November 1953.

16. "La tragédie d'Indochine", *Fig.*, 3 December 1953.

17. "La tragédie d'Indochine: Le refus du choix est la pire solution", *Fig.*, 4 December 1953.

18. "Le dilemme indochinois", *Fig.*, 1 January 1954.

19. "Le désarroi français", *Fig.*, 22 January 1954.

20. "Raison garder", *Fig.*, 26 April 1954.

21. "Savoir ce qu'on veut", *Fig.*, 3 May 1954.

22. "Le sang-froid et l'action", *Fig.*, 11 May 1954.

23. "Le salut du corps expéditionnaire", *Fig.*, 17 May 1954.

24. "Fascination du désastre", *Fig.*, 21 May 1954. See also "Agir et négocier", *Fig.*, 29 May 1954.

25. "Les trente jours", *Fig.*, 22 June 1954.

26. Ibid.

27. Ibid.

28. Alexander Werth, *France 1940-1955* (London, 1957), pp.680-1.

29. "Rigidité américaine, souplesse britannique", *Fig.*, 1 July 1954.

30. "Nécessités", *Fig.*, 6 July 1954. The next day the *Figaro* spoke of the "lucidity" of this article.

31. "Paradoxes", *Fig.*, 17 July 1954.

32. "Un pari bien gagné", *Fig.*, 22 July 1954.

33. Ibid.

34. "En Asie du Sud-Est après le cessez-le-feu", *Fig.*, 31 July 1954. Compare the discussion of Mendès-France in Aron's memoirs (1983a, pp.277-8) and Aron's tribute to him on his death in 1982: "Valiant, competent, a man of character, capable of authority", he was a statesman whose virtues destined him to govern well but left him little chance of heading a government ("Le solitaire", *L'Express* (1633), 29 October 1983).

35. "Risques et réalités", *Fig.*, 6 August 1954.
36. Ibid.
37. For Aron's writings on the Algerian War, see Volume 2, Chapter 3.

20

The Opium of the Intellectuals

In 1950 Aron became a member of the Executive Committee of the Congress for Cultural Freedom (Congrès pour la Liberté de la Culture). Founded at a moment of great international tension (its first conference, in Berlin, opened on 26 June, the day of the Communist invasion of South Korea), it aimed to bring together intellectuals, artists and scientists to defend freedom of thought and expression against the threat of totalitarianism. Its Honorary Presidents were Benedetto Croce, John Dewey, Karl Jaspers, Salvador de Madariaga, Jacques Maritain and Bertrand Russell. The Executive President was Denis de Rougemont and the Secretary-General Nicolas Nabokov. Besides Aron, the members of the Executive Committee included Georges Altman, T. R. Fyvel, Arthur Koestler,[1] David Rousset, Ignazio Silone and (from September 1955, although he had been associated with the work of the Congress from the beginning) Manès Sperber. Despite such names as these, Aron has been described as the organization's "most eminent recruit", even if his "Atlanticism" aroused suspicion in the minds of some of his colleagues.[2]

Aron took a major part in the international conferences held by the

Congress – for example, those at Berlin in 1950,[3] Hamburg (1953),[4] Milan (1955),[5] Oxford (1956),[6] Rheinfelden (1959)[7] and the tenth anniversary meeting at Berlin in 1960.[8] In addition, from March 1951 the organization began publishing a French monthly, entitled *Preuves*, under the editorship of François Bondy. Its aim was to

defend and embody the liberty that is most seriously threatened in our century: the freedom of critical and creative thought that resists propaganda and partisan slogans.

We shall defend this freedom by bringing proof (preuves) of totalitarian oppression, wherever the latter acts – whether openly or in secret – to the detriment of culture.

We shall embody this freedom by inviting intellectuals of different tendencies to speak in their own name, and thus freely and responsibly. Their evidence will, equally, provide proof (preuves) of that critical spirit which is our best weapon against the immense deception that results where thought is controlled.[9]

Aron published his first article in *Preuves* in October 1951[10] and soon became its leading contributor.[11] Altogether he wrote some fifty articles for the journal – an average of three or four a year – between 1951 and 1966, when Bondy ceased to be its Editor. Furthermore, Aron often presided or spoke at an annual series of Tuesday lectures organized by the review and entitled "Les Mardis de *Preuves*".[12] He also had a long-standing association with *Preuves*' English-language counterpart, *Encounter*, in which he was to publish over thirty articles – often translations of those which first appeared in *Preuves* – from August 1954.[13]

Years later, of course, it transpired that the Congress had been largely funded by the American Government through the Central Intelligence Agency. Aron and his colleagues thought that it was financed by various American foundations, but should they have found out, or at least guessed, the truth? The answer Aron gives in his *Memoirs* is that he and his friends lacked curiosity and should have been alerted by many clues; but it was reasonable to believe that the Congress was funded by such foundations and, in any case, when he spoke at meetings or wrote in *Preuves*, he said exactly what he thought. He was not paid by the Congress and it gave him the opportunity to speak up for ideas which, at the time, had need of champions.

Secondly, even if they had known about it, would they have accepted the financial support of the CIA? Aron doubted it, although ultimately such a refusal would have seemed to him unreasonable. Neither *Preuves*, in which he expressed himself with the same freedom as in any other periodical, nor *Encounter* – "the best monthly magazine in English" – would have flourished if they had appeared as instruments of the American Secret Service; but the Congress could only accomplish its task (and did

454

so) through subterfuge (le camouflage) or, if one preferred, lying by omission. Nevertheless, Aron did not regret taking part in its activities, because they had a considerable influence on European intellectuals, even if the lie continued to weigh on his memories of the Congress.[14]

* * *

The period from the beginning of 1951 till the middle of 1954 was a particularly difficult one for Aron. Still numbed by the death of his daughter and by the birth of his handicapped child, he desperately sought consolation in work. But, he wrote in his memoirs, "The more I plunged into this illusory refuge, the more I destroyed myself. Conscious of so doing, I suffered even more, beyond the misfortune itself, from the wounds that time did not heal".[15] Nevertheless, it was through the writing of *The Opium of the Intellectuals*, between July 1954 and January 1955, that he began to come alive again – a process that was to be continued, however imperfectly, through his appointment to the Sorbonne in the summer of 1955. It so happens that his colleague on *Le Figaro*, Roger Massip, has left this description of a visit he paid to Aron at this time:

Raymond Aron was spending his holidays a thousand metres up in a small village in the Savoie...I found him, at the far end of the house, in a darkened room, writing *The Opium of the Intellectuals* by the light of a table-lamp. Beyond the closed shutters there stood a landscape of sunlit mountains.

I have often thought back to the image I had of Raymond Aron that day – the prisoner of his thought processes, refusing to be distracted for a single moment from the page that he was covering with his illegible writing (illegible, that is, to all except his wife).

Intellectual qualities, when carried to such extremes, are often desiccating, but with Raymond Aron this is by no means the case. A fine sensibility, a deep feeling for friendship and a sense of courtesy that never fails him even in the heat of the sharpest exchanges – all these go to make up an engaging personality, to which one other quality must be added: courage.[16]

L'Opium des intellectuels[17] in fact began its life as an introduction to *Polémiques*[18], a collection of articles published early in 1955, but the introduction soon grew into a much larger book in its own right. The essays in *Polémiques* were written between 1949 and 1954 and were aimed not so much at the Communists as at fellow-travellers such as Sartre and Merleau-Ponty.[19] Aron made no secret of the "passion" that inspired these polemics. Although the essays were not all aimed at specific texts or particular writers, they were, he acknowledged, "clearly inspired

455

by the desire to refute ideas, criticize attitudes or suggest certain interpretations of the present-day world. I confess, quite unequivocally, that
a polemical intent runs right through the collection".[20]

Why was it, he asked, that the French, who were apparently ranged
in opposing camps, so rarely consented to listen and reply to one another?
Aron suggested three possible reasons. First, that they did not take their
debates wholly seriously, because they realized that they involved an
element of theatricality. Secondly, the fact that everyone declared their
faith in the same values created confusion and ambiguity, for the Soviets,
too, claimed that they were achieving true democracy. Thirdly, too often
the arguments seemed to take place in a world of unreality: the non-
communist intellectuals derived too much pleasure from denouncing the
"American occupation" to feel a real desire for "liberation". "They have
no wish to think seriously about the world or to change it; they merely
wish to denounce it". However, because Aron was, in his own words,
"naturally inclined towards optimism", he still hoped to incite certain
people in the two camps to think:

If, having read my book, the faithful adherent of *Les Temps modernes* has a clearer
understanding of why I do not adopt the same positions as M. Jean-Paul Sartre, the
result will not be negligible. The true purpose of a polemic is not to convert but to help
each person understand *the other*.[21]

This point was underlined by Thierry Maulnier, himself no mean
polemicist, in his review of Aron's "very important collection of essays".
He confessed that at first he had wondered if the title fitted the book:

The author's approach in the discussion is calm, there is no abuse, the irony is courteous;
no attempt is made to discredit the opponent in a personal way...And then one ends
up by realizing that it is the author who is right...

To engage in a polemic is to engage in a fight...and in order to fight it is essential
to understand. The most effective weapon against error or fraud is not abuse but analysis.

Of course, when he sees Jean-Paul Sartre, in the full flush of his progressivist zeal,
portraying his opponents as "a bunch of tender, whey-faced intellectuals parroting polite
phrases about culture and freedom", Raymond Aron does not, by way of reply, miss
a dig at "the tough guys of *Les Temps modernes*", reminding us that people like Koestler
and Malraux have grappled with the dangers of the century further afield than the
pedestrian crossings of Saint-Germain-des-Prés. But only enough to let Jean-Paul Sartre
know that, if necessary, one is just as capable as he is of adopting such a tone, and
that it resolves nothing...[22]

In *The Opium of the Intellectuals*, as the Italian liberal, Enzo Bettiza,
pointed out nearly a quarter of a century later,[23] Aron was "the first

systematic demystifier of the new drug and the new religion which, in spite of all its promises of the total redemption of man on this earth, was to contribute more than any other to his enslavement and humiliation". It was impossible to overestimate "the enormous intellectual merit of the work and the enormous moral courage that its author must have possessed in order to conceive and publish it in the Paris of twenty years ago". For Aron was, of course, writing before the conspiracy of silence over Stalinism was broken at the Twentieth Congress of the Soviet Communist Party in February 1956 and before the Polish and Hungarian uprisings in October of that year opened the eyes of some Communist and fellow-travelling intellectuals to the nature of Soviet imperialism.

None of this had happened, however, when in 1955 Aron, the lucid neo-liberal, armed only with his doctrine, was the first to go into battle. He was isolated and under fire in a city occupied by the ideologies of the Marxist-existentialist-Christian Left. The Soviet myth still kept its prestige intact; de-Stalinization seemed out of the question; and the few Trotskyites or followers of Djilas who dared to loosen their tongues were immediately confined to the ghetto and branded with infamy...The High Priests of French militant culture...were Sartre and Merleau-Ponty. The new (monthly) Holy Scriptures were *les Temps modernes* and *Esprit*. And whilst the two principal existentialist parties – one atheist, the other Christian – found reconciliation in Marxism and the myth of the revolutionary proletariat, one voice could be heard, solitary and yet limpid, mocking and anticonformist...Aron's.[24]

The philosopher, Jeanne Hersch, has recorded an episode from that time which serves as an admirable illustration of Bettiza's point:

During the 1950s, both a little before and after Stalin's death, in other words, in the Soviet Union's most Stalinist period, pro-communist intimidation was at its height in the Latin Quarter. It was at this time that the Catholic Centre for French Intellectuals (Centre Catholique des Intellectuels Français) organized a debate with Raymond Aron. For me the occasion remained unforgettable because I witnessed what one can only call the naked confrontation between a smug and self-satisfied collective conscience, fortified by a virtuous anti-capitalist guilty conscience, and the sober, solitary reflection of a single man whose clear voice referred to facts, figures and historical situations as it spoke the truth about the USSR. He was criticized, there as everywhere, for his coldness and insensitivity towards social injustice and the sufferings of the exploited. You could hear those tender hearts vibrating. But he did not attempt to defend himself. He made no concession and his voice remained unaltered. He was the embodiment of a style, both moral and intellectual, which nothing – not even he himself – could alter. I thought he was the prince of truth.[25]

As we have seen, *The Opium of the Intellectuals* took its title from a phrase Aron had used in the course of a polemic with Sartre some years earlier.[26] His purpose in writing the book was to "explain the attitude of the intellectuals, merciless towards the failings of the democracies but ready to tolerate the worst crimes as long as they are committed in the name of the proper doctrines". In doing this he "soon came across the sacred words, Left, Revolution, Proletariat" – the three "political myths" he analysed in Part One. This led him to "reflect on the cult of History" in Part Two ("The Idolatry of History"), and then to examine in Part Three ("The Alienation of the Intellectuals") "a social category to which sociologists have not yet devoted the attention it deserves: the intelligentsia". The book dealt, therefore,

both with the present state of so-called left-wing ideologies and with the situation of the intelligentsia in France and in the world at large. It attempts to give an answer to some of the questions which others besides myself must have asked themselves. Why has Marxism come back into fashion in a country whose economic evolution has belied the Marxist predictions? Why are the ideologies of the proletariat and the Communist Party all the more successful where the working class is least numerous? What circumstances control the ways of speech, thought and action of the intellectuals in different countries?[27]

People asked where on the Right Aron himself was to be placed, but he rejected such simplistic labels:

Personally, as a Keynesian with a certain nostalgia for economic liberalism, as a supporter of agreement with Tunisian and Moroccan nationalism, as one who is convinced that the strength of the Atlantic Alliance is the best guarantee of peace, I shall be classed as either left-wing or right-wing according to whether economic policy, the North African problem, or relations between East and West are taken as the criterion.

The confusion of French ideological quarrels will never be clarified until these ambiguous concepts are rejected. One has only to face reality, and set oneself specific aims, to realize the absurdity of these politico-ideological compounds which are the playthings of big-hearted but light-headed revolutionaries and ambitious journalists.[28]

Regretfully, therefore, he now had no alternative but to make a decisive break with the "spiritual family" to which he belonged:

Beyond all short-term quarrels, beyond all the constantly changing coalitions, one may perhaps discern family ties of thought and feeling. Everyone, whatever he may say, is conscious of his elective affinities...But, having finished writing this book which is devoted to the family of which I am myself a member, I feel inclined to break all ties with it, not for the sake of wallowing in solitude but in order to choose my companions among those who know how to fight without hatred and rancour and who refuse to regard the quarrels of the Forum as the key to human destiny.[29]

* * *

Aron began, then, in Part One by analysing the three "political myths" of the Left, the Revolution and the Proletariat.

"The Left" was a myth, he argued, because ever since the Revolution of 1789 the different groups which in France thought of themselves as left-wing had never been deeply united. The so-called "unity of the Left" had been "less a reflection than a distortion of the reality of French politics" and was no more than "a retrospective myth":

Because it was incapable of attaining its objectives without twenty-five years of chaos and bloodshed, the party of progress conceived, after the event, a new and over-simplified dichotomy – between good and evil, the future and the past. Because it failed to integrate the working class with the rest of the nation, the bourgeois intelligentsia dreamed of a Left which would include the representatives both of the Third and of the Fourth Estates. This Left was not entirely mythical. Sometimes it presented a united front to the electorate. But just as the revolutionaries of 1789 became united only retrospectively, when the Restoration had thrown Girondins, Jacobins and Bonapartists together into opposition, so the Radicals and the Socialists were genuinely agreed only in their hatred of a vague, impersonal enemy – "reaction" – and in out-of-date battles against clericalism.[30]

At the same time, a "dissociation of values" had occurred. In continental Europe, the decisive ideological event of the century had been the double schism, splitting the Right as well as the Left, produced by fascism and communism; in the rest of the world, the decisive event had been the dissociation between the political and social values of the Left. "The appearance of ideological chaos arises from the clash and the confusion between a strictly European schism and the dissociation of European values in societies outside the Western sphere of civilization".[31] The appeal of totalitarian parties grew strong whenever a crisis revealed a disparity between the capabilities of representative regimes and the problems of governing mass industrial societies. The temptation to sacrifice political liberties for the sake of vigorous action had not disappeared with Hitler and Mussolini. By its identification of the Party with the State, its curbing of independent bodies, its transformation of a minority doctrine into a national orthodoxy, the violence of its methods and the unlimited power of the police, did not the Hitlerite regime have more in common with Bolshevik Russia than with the daydreams of the counter-revolutionaries? Did not Right and Left, or Fascist pseudo-Right and Communist pseudo-Left, meet in totalitarianism?[32] And did not the progress of the Left bring with it a worse oppression than the one it rose against?[33]

This came about through "a dialectic of revolutionary and counter-revolutionary regimes", in which

an optimistic interpretation of history with the liberation of humanity as the ultimate goal is replaced by a pessimistic version according to which totalitarianism, the enslavement of mankind body and soul, is the inevitable result of a movement which begins with the abolition of ancient wrongs and ends with the destruction of every human liberty. The example of Soviet Russia encourages this pessimism, already envisaged by some of the more lucid minds of the nineteenth century. Tocqueville, for example, foretold with devastating clarity what the irresistible impetus of democracy would lead to if representative institutions were swept away by the impatience of the masses, if the sense of liberty, aristocratic in origin, fell into decay. Historians like Burckhardt and Renan dreaded a return to the tyrannies of the dark ages far more than they hoped for the reconciliation of mankind.[34]

But, Aron maintained, there was no need to accept either of these extreme views, for the inevitable transformations of economic techniques and structures and the expansion of the state did not necessarily involve either liberation or enslavement. In a given regime, it was a matter of reaching a reasonable compromise between demands which, if carried to extremes, were incompatible. Under capitalism, for example, there had to be limits to equality of incomes, because this was inseparable from the very principle of competition; while, in a completely planned economy, the planners would understandably increase wage differentials in order to encourage individual effort, and their estimate of the value of their own services was unlikely to be less than that of their capitalist predecessors. The rewarding of the most active and the most talented was not only just but also necessary in the interests of efficiency. "Whatever the regime – aristocratic, bourgeois or socialist – neither freedom of thought nor human fellowship is ever completely guaranteed. The true Left is that which continues to invoke, not liberty or equality, but fraternity, in other words, love".[35]

Unlike in Britain, there was a gap between idea and reality in French political thought. It was by no means impossible, Aron believed, to define an anti-capitalist or a Keynesian Left in France, but on condition that one did not become trapped in the Right-Left straitjacket or that of Marxist dogma, and that one recognized the diversity of current disagreements, social groupings, problems and solutions. "Historical awareness should make this diversity clear: ideology, even when it is dressed in the tawdry finery of the philosophy of history, obscures it".[36]

It seemed to Aron, in conclusion, that the Left was

animated by three ideas, which are not necessarily contradictory, but usually divergent: *liberty*, against arbitrary power and for the rights of the individual; *organization*, for the purpose of substituting a rational order in place of tradition or the anarchy of private enterprise; and *equality*, against the privileges of birth or of wealth.

The *organizing* Left tends to become *authoritarian*, because free governments act slowly and are held in check by the opposition of private interests or prejudices; *national*, if not nationalist, because the state alone is capable of fulfilling its programme; and sometimes *imperialist*, because the planners tend to require more space and bigger resources. The *liberal* Left turns against socialism, because it cannot but be aware of the hypertrophy of the state and the return to arbitrary rule, this time bureaucratic and anonymous, and against the nationalist Left which repudiates the ideal of inter- nationalism. As for the *egalitarian* Left, it seems to be condemned to a perpetual opposition against the rich and against the powerful, who are sometimes the same people and sometimes in rivalry. Which, one may ask, is the true Left. . .?[37]

One of the editors of *Esprit* – "those Leftists par excellence" – had unwittingly answered this question when he described the true man of the Left as being opposed to all orthodoxies and moved by all human suffering.[38] Was the Communist, therefore, Aron asked, for whom the Soviet Union was always right, a man of the Left? What of those who demanded liberty for all the peoples of Asia and Africa, but not for the Poles or the East Germans? "The language of the historical Left may have triumphed in our day", he reflected bitterly, but "the spirit of the eternal Left is surely dying, when pity itself is a 'one-way' virtue".[39]

The second "political myth" which Aron examined was that of the Revolution. If the idea of continuous Progress was implicit in the myth of the Left, the myth of the Revolution was both complementary and opposed to the idea of Progress; for the myth of the Revolution "fosters the expectation of a break with the normal trend of human affairs". Sociologically, revolution meant "the sudden and violent supplanting of one regime by another" and was characterized by certain "essential traits": "the exercise of power by a minority which ruthlessly suppresses its adversaries, creates a new state, and dreams of transfiguring the nation".[40] Revolutionary power was

by definition a tyrannical power. It operates in defiance of the law, it expresses the will of a minority group, it is not, and cannot be, concerned with the interests of this or that section of the people. The duration of the tyrannical phase varies according to the circumstances, but it is never possible to dispense with it – or, more exactly, when it is avoided, there has been reform but no revolution. The seizure and exercise of power by violence presuppose conflicts which negotiation and compromise have failed to resolve – in other words, the failure of democratic procedures. Revolution and democracy are contradictory notions.[41]

461

The man of reason, therefore, "especially the man of the Left",

> must surely prefer therapeutic methods to the surgeon's knife, must prefer reform to revolution, as he must prefer peace to war and democracy to despotism.[42]

Experience had shown, too, in the case of Britain and the United States, that political stability and social change were not necessarily incompatible. In both countries, the system of government had given evidence of "the supreme virtue, which is a mixture of steadfastness and flexibility" and had preserved tradition by renewing it.[43] On the other hand, history had not provided any examples of a revolution that accorded with Marxist predictions. It was clear from the experience of the Russian and the Chinese Revolutions that the idea of a procession of the social classes, passing the torch on from one to the other, was "no more than an illustration in a children's picture book". The reason why the revolution of the Marxist type had never occurred was that "its very conception was mythical": neither the development of the forces of production nor the coming of age of the working class paved the way for the overthrow of capitalism by the workers conscious of their mission. So-called proletarian revolutions, like all past revolutions, simply entailed the violent replacement of one elite by another. There was nothing about them to justify their being hailed as "the end of pre-history".[44]

A reform at least changed something, whereas a revolution appeared capable of changing everything, simply because it was impossible to say exactly what it would change:

> To the intellectual who turns to politics for the sake of diversion, or for a cause to believe in or a theme for speculation, reform is boring and revolution exciting. The one is prosaic, the other poetic, one is the concern of mere functionaries, the other that of the people risen up against their exploiters. Revolution provides a welcome break with the everyday course of events and encourages the belief that all things are possible...
>
> In love with ideas and indifferent to institutions, uncompromising critic of private life and unamenable, in politics, to reason and moderation, the Frenchman is quintessentially the revolutionary in theory and the conservative in practice.[45]

But the myth of the Revolution had also benefited – dubiously, Aron contended – from the prestige of other ideas such as aesthetic modernism, moral non-conformism, and revolt.[46] The liveliest polemics, however, were not those between rebels or nihilists, but between intellectuals who, while agreeing on the ultimate aim, differed over the sacred word: Revolution.

This was illustrated most famously by the exchange of letters and articles betwen Sartre and Camus in *Les Temps modernes* in 1952.[47] Aron would not, he observed ironically, "presume to adjudicate the fight point by point or to analyse its rights and wrongs, but merely to try to grasp the significance of the revolutionary myth as represented by two distinguished writers during the seventh year of the Cold War". The metaphysical positions of the two protagonists were similar, as were their attitudes to current problems:

When they come to express their approval or disapproval – the latter more frequent than the former – they reveal like values. Both are humanitarian: they want to alleviate human suffering, to free the oppressed; they are against colonialism, Fascism, capitalism. Whether over Spain, Algeria or Vietnam, Camus has never been guilty of departing from progressive ideology. When Spain was admitted to Unesco, he wrote an admirable letter of protest; when Soviet Russia and Czechoslovakia joined, he remained silent. He too belongs, to all intents and purposes, to the conformist Left (la gauche bien-pensante).[48]

Why then, the split? The origin seemed to have been "the question which, in the West, is continually setting brothers, comrades and friends at one another's throats: the question of what attitude to adopt towards the Soviet Union and Communism".[49] The difference between them was that in the last resort Camus would choose the West and Sartre the East (providing, of course, that he could go on living in the West). Camus was not merely a critic of certain aspects of Soviet reality; he regarded the Communist regime as a total tyranny, inspired and justified by a philosophy. He accused the revolutionaries of denying all basic moral values which transcend the class struggle and of sacrificing living men to an allegedly absolute good, a historical end whose very idea was contradictory and incompatible with existentialism. Camus' analysis of Marxism in *L'Homme révolté* "offered nothing one could not have found elsewhere, but it was on several points not easily contestable". At the same time, both it and, even more, Camus' letter to *Les Temps modernes* were "vulnerable":

In the book, the main lines of his argument lost themselves in a succession of loosely connected essays, while the style of the writing and the moralizing tone militated against philosophical exactitude. The letter sought to confine the existentialists within too narrow a metaphysical straitjacket (Sartre was given a nice opportunity of pointing out that Marxism is not exclusively confined to a prophetism and a methodology, but also comprises a philosophy).[50]

Nevertheless, Camus put some crucial questions which Sartre and

Jeanson found it difficult to answer: did they, or did they not, regard the Soviet regime as having accomplished the revolutionary "project"?

The concept of Revolution, Aron concluded, would not fall into disuse any more than the concept of the Left. It too expressed a nostalgia, which would last as long as societies remained imperfect and men eager to reform them. All known regimes could be criticized in terms of an *abstract* ideal of equality or liberty, but only the Revolution or a revolutionary regime seemed capable of attaining the goal of perfection, the former because it gave promise of adventure and the latter because it accepted the permanent use of violence. The myth of the Revolution served as "a refuge for utopian intellectuals" and became "the mysterious, unpredictable intercessor between the real and the ideal":

No one, as Herodotus says, is insane enough to prefer war to peace.[51] The observation should also be applicable to civil wars. And yet, although the romance of war was buried in the mud of Flanders, the romance of civil war has managed to survive the dungeons of the Lubianka. There are times when one wonders whether the myth of the revolution is not indistinguishable from the Fascist cult of violence. At the end of Sartre's play, *Le Diable et le Bon Dieu*, Goetz cries: "The reign of man has come at last. And a good beginning, too! Come on, Nasty, let's do some killing...We've got this war to fight and I'll fight it".

Must the reign of men be the reign of war?[52]

The last of the three "political myths" to be considered was that of the Proletariat. "In Marxist eschatology", Aron wrote,

the proletariat is cast in the role of collective saviour. The expressions used by the young Marx leave one in no doubt as to the Judaeo-Christian origins of the myth of the class elected through suffering for the redemption of humanity. The mission of the proletariat, the end of prehistory thanks to the Revolution, the reign of liberty – it is easy to recognize the millenarian mould of his thinking: the Messiah, the break with the past, the Kingdom of God.[53]

The proletarian, according to Marx and his followers, was "alienated" by the private ownership of the means of production. But, Aron responded, many of the workers' grievances had nothing to do with the pattern of ownership. Inadequate pay, excessive working hours, discontent with factory organization, the feeling of being trapped in their condition without hope of promotion, the consciousness of being the victims of a basic injustice, either because the system did not allow workers a fair share of the national wealth or because it refused them any part in the management of the economy – the same grievances persisted when the means of production belonged to the state. The one exception, Aron admitted, was the threat of unemployment – "one of the evils of any regime based not so much on private property as the market". There was "no point in denying this drawback; its effects must be reduced as far as possible".[54]

This led Aron to make an important distinction between two forms of working-class emancipation – "real" and "ideal":

The first, which is never finally completed, consists of a multiplicity of partial and *ad hoc* measures: the remuneration of the workers rises as productivity rises; social legislation protects families and the old; trade unions freely discuss conditions of work with the employers; and the extension of education increases the chances of promotion. This form of emancipation can be called *real* emancipation: it is characterized by concrete improvements in the condition of the proletariat; it allows certain grievances to persist, such as unemployment and discontent within the organization; and it cannot entirely eliminate opposition on the part of a minority, big or small, to the principles of the regime itself.[55]

This was to be contrasted with the "ideal" emancipation to be found in Communist regimes:

A revolution on the Soviet model gives absolute power to the minority which claims to represent the proletariat and transforms many workers or sons of workers into engineers or commissars. Does this mean that the proletariat itself, that is to say the millions who work with their hands in factories, is "emancipated"?

The standard of living has not suddenly leapt up in the People's Democracies of Eastern Europe; rather has it diminished, since the new ruling classes probably do not consume any less of the national wealth than the old. Where there existed free trade unions, there are now only bodies which are subject to the state and whose function is to incite to effort, not to fight for the workers' rights. The risk of unemployment has disappeared, but so have the free choice of job or of place of work and the free election of union leaders and governments. The proletariat is no longer alienated, because it is theoretically the ultimate owner of the means of production and even of the state. But it has not been freed from the risk of deportation, or from the tyranny of the labour permit, or from the authority of the managers.[56]

In countries, therefore, where the economy continued to expand and the standard of living had risen, why should the real liberties of the proletariat, however partial, be sacrificed to a total "liberation" which was curiously indistinguishable from the omnipotence of the state? Perhaps, in the latter case, workers who had not experienced trade unionism or Western socialism were given an impression of progress;

but in the eyes of the East German or Czech workers, who had known real liberties, "ideal" emancipation was nothing but a mystification.[57]

To "progressive Christians", on the other hand, ideal emancipation was seductive in so far as it expressed itself in terms borrowed from Christian tradition, while to Sartrean existentialists, obsessed by human solitude, it appeared to offer a mystical community. To both it contained "the poetry of the unknown, of the future, of the absolute".[58] At the same time, the "real" emancipation of the worker in Great Britain or Sweden was, to the intellectuals of *Esprit* and *Les Temps modernes*, "prosaic" and "as boring as an English Sunday", whereas the "ideal" emancipation of the Soviet worker was "as exciting as a leap into the future or a cataclysm".[59] And yet, Aron maintained, "if suffering confers a vocation", it was not the proletariat but "the victims of racial, ideological and religious persecution who should be the chosen of today".[60]

Left, Revolution, Proletariat – these fashionable concepts, Aron wrote in conclusion to Part One of *The Opium of the Intellectuals*, were "the latter-day counterparts of the great myths which once inspired political optimism: Progress, Reason, the People". Yet such notions ceased to be rational and became mythical as a consequence of an intellectual error:

To re-establish the continuity of the Left across the centuries or to disguise the divisions inside the Left in any given epoch, it is necessary to forget the dialectic of regimes, the shifting of values from one party to another, the adoption by the Right of liberal values against planning and centralization, the necessity of establishing a common-sense compromise between contradictory aims.

The historical experience of the twentieth century reveals the frequency and the causes of revolutions in the industrial age. The error is to attribute to the Revolution a logic which it does not possess, to see it as the logical end of a movement which is based on reason, and to expect it to produce benefits which are incompatible with its very essence. It is not unprecedented for a society to return to the path of peace, after a revolutionary explosion, with a positive balance sheet. But revolutionary means remain on balance contrary to the ends envisaged. Internecine violence is the negation, perhaps sometimes inevitable, of the mutual sympathy which should unite the members of a community. By uprooting tradition and mutual respect, it risks destroying the foundation of civil peace.[61]

The source of such errors lay in "a kind of visionary optimism combined with a pessimistic view of reality", for it was "nothing but raving optimism to designate the proletariat for a task which is beyond it, and excessive pessimism to put the other classes beyond the pale".[62] The proletariat, subjected to the rude discipline of the factory, did not change its nature in changing its master, any more than it changed the nature of societies, because it did not change the essence of *homo politicus*:

466

Neither public order nor the power of the state constitutes the sole objective of politics. Man is also a moral animal and a society is human only in so far as it allows every one of its members to participate. But the basic imperatives survive all changes of regime: no miracle can give political man an exclusive preoccupation with the public good or the wisdom to be content with the place which chance or merit have given him. The dissatisfaction which prevents societies from becoming crystallized in an arbitrary structure, the appetite for honours which inspires both the great builders and the petty intriguers, will continue to convulse the body politic even after the Left has transformed it, the Revolution has done its work and the Proletariat won its victory. For this supposed victory raises as many problems as it resolves. If the privileges of the nobility are destroyed all that is left is the authority of the state or of those who draw their pay from it. The disappearance of the privileges conferred by birth allows free reign to those acquired through money. The destruction of local communities reinforces the prerogatives of the central power. Two hundred functionaries take the place of the "two hundred families". When the Revolution has stamped out respect for tradition and spread hatred of the privileged, the masses are ready to bow down before the leader with the sword until the day comes when passions are spent, order is restored, and the counsels of reason have regained the ascendancy.

These three myths – the Left, the Revolution and the Proletariat – are refuted not so much by their failure as by the successes they have achieved. The Left, in opposing the Ancien Régime, stood for freedom of thought, for the application of science and reason to the organization of society, for the rejection of hereditary rights: clearly, it has won its battle. Today there is no longer any question of advancing always in the same direction, but of balancing planning with initiative, fair shares for all with incentives to effort, the power of the bureaucracy with the rights of the individual, economic centralization with the safeguard of intellectual liberties.[63]

* * *

In Part Two of *The Opium of the Intellectuals*, Aron turned to an examination of "The Idolatry of History", beginning with an analysis of "Churchmen and the Faithful" – non-Stalinist revolutionaries and especially, in Parisian intellectual circles, existentialists like Sartre and Merleau-Ponty who had "given a kind of philosophical respectability to a revolutionary idealism which the tragic life of Trotsky together with the realism of Stalin would seem to have condemned". Merleau-Ponty's *Humanisme et terreur* seemed to Aron "the most systematic statement" of a way of thought in which, whether Christian or rationalist, rebels in search of a revolution returned to Marx's youthful writings "just as the Protestants whose spiritual hunger the Church failed to satisfy were wont to re-read the Gospels".[64] It was at times "quite startling in its naive dogmatism", expressing as it did "the conviction of so many intellectuals throughout the world: that Marxism must be identified with *the* philosophy of history, must be definitively true".[65] But, Aron asked,

467

Why should the supreme test, of Marxism as of History, have to take place in the middle of the twentieth century and why should it necessarily be identified with the Soviet experiment? If the proletariat fails to set itself up as a universal class and fails to take upon itself the destiny of mankind, why not admit, instead of despairing of the future, that the philosophers were wrong to designate the industrial workers for such a unique mission? Why should not the "humanization" of society be the common aim and task, never fully achieved, of a humanity incapable of eliminating the gap between the real and the ideal, but also incapable of resigning itself to it? Why should the seizure of power by a totalitarian party be the indispensable prelude to this never-ending task?

To judge societies by their ideology and not by the lot which they mete out to their members is to fall into an error which Marx himself, to his eternal credit, was the first to denounce. "It is a signal merit of Marxism and conducive to the progress of Western civilization to have taught us to confront ideas with the social functions they are supposed to inspire, to confront our outlook with that of others, our morals with our politics". This could not be better said. But why should the revolutionaries be preserved from this confrontation?[66]

Two errors, "apparently contradictory but in fact connected", lay at the origin of the idolatry of History: "churchmen and the faithful" allowed themselves to fall into the trap of absolutism, and then to indulge in a limitless relativism. However, Aron maintained, employing the self-same arguments he had first developed in the *Introduction to the Philosophy of History*, the twin errors of absolutism and relativism were both refuted by a logic of the retrospective knowledge and understanding of human facts. The historian, the sociologist and the jurist could bring out the *multiple* meanings of actions, institutions and laws, but they could not discover *the* meaning of the whole; history was not absurd, but no living being could grasp its *one* ultimate meaning.[67] The "plurality of meanings" did not, however, imply the failure of understanding but the richness of reality and the *renewal* of historical interpretation. It offered a protection against the worst form of relativism – that which was combined with dogmatism:

Specific meanings are first of all ignored; efforts are made to reduce philosophical works to the meaning they assume in the consciousness of the non-philosopher; "experienced" meanings are interpreted on the basis of what is known as a dominant fact, such as the class struggle; and, finally, a single meaning, decreed by the historian, is given to the world of man, reduced to a single dimension. The multiplicity of historical entities, real and ideal, should preclude the fanaticism which refuses to recognize the diversity of roles played by individuals in a complex society, the interlacing of the systems within which human activity revolves. Historical reconstruction must inevitably retain an unfinished character, because it never succeeds in unravelling all relationships or exhausting all possible meanings.[68]

468

At the same time, and for similar reasons, Aron rejected the view that human history was a "unity" and society a "totality"; the elements of a society were interdependent and they influenced one another reciprocally, but they did not constitute a totality.[69] For example, Marxists who imagined that the "economic factor" was the unifying force were confusing a causal primacy with a primacy of values or interest. The most that one could say was that the adventure of mankind through time had *one* meaning to the extent that all men were collectively seeking to achieve salvation; but "logic confirms what successive doctrines suggest: philosophies of history are secularized theologies".[70]

"Churchmen" and "the faithful", who subscribed to dubious notions like "the end of history", were guilty of fanaticism because they

reject, with indifference or contempt, the rules of wisdom that statesmen have elaborated in order to harness for the good of the collectivity the egoism and the passions of individuals. Constitutional government, the balance of power, legal guarantees, the whole edifice of political civilization slowly built up over the course of the ages and always incomplete, is calmly pushed aside...

Statesmen who do not claim to know history's last word sometimes hesitate before embarking on an enterprise, however attractive, the cost of which would be too high. "Churchmen" and "faithful" ignore such scruples. The sublime end excuses the revolting means. Profoundly moralistic in regard to the present, the revolutionary is cynical in action. He protests against police brutality, the inhuman rhythm of industrial production, the severity of bourgeois courts, the execution of prisoners whose guilt has not been proved beyond doubt. Nothing, short of a total "humanization", can appease his hunger for justice. But as soon as he decides to give his allegiance to a party which is as implacably hostile as he is himself to the established disorder, we find him forgiving, in the name of the Revolution, everything he has hitherto relentlessly denounced. The revolutionary myth bridges the gap between moral intransigence and terrorism.

There is nothing more commonplace than this double game of inflexibility and tolerance, of which, in our day, the idolatry of history is the manifestation if not the intellectual origin. On the pretext of discovering the meaning of history, the unavoidable constraints of thought and action are totally disregarded.

The plurality of meanings which we ascribe to an act reveals not our incapacity but the limits of our knowledge and the complexity of reality. Only when we recognize that the world is essentially equivocal have we any chance of reaching the truth. Our understanding is not incomplete because we lack omniscience, but because the plurality of meanings is implicit in the object of our understanding.[71]

Political choice was essentially historical because it was inseparable from particular circumstances; sometimes reasonable, it was never finally proved and never of the same nature as scientific truths or moral imperatives. The impossibility of proof was due to the intractable laws of social existence and the plurality of values. Incentives were needed

469

in order to increase productivity; an edifice of authority must be built up in order to persuade quarrelsome individuals to cooperate; these ineluctable necessities symbolized the gap between the history we live and the end of history we conceive. Not that work or obedience as such were contrary to man's predestined lot, but they became so if born of constraint. And violence had never ceased to play a part in any known society. In this sense, politics had always been based on the notion of the lesser evil, and they would continue to be so as long as men remained fundamentally unchanged.[72]

What passed for optimism was most often the result of an intellectual error. It was both permissible and reasonable to prefer planning to the free market, but anyone who expected planning to usher in the reign of plenty misjudged the efficiency of bureaucrats and the extent of available resources. It was not absurd to prefer the authority of a single party to the slow deliberations of the parliamentary system, but anyone who counted on the dictatorship of the proletariat to bring about freedom misjudged human nature and ignored the inevitable results of the concentration of power in a few hands. It was possible to transform writers into engineers of the soul and to recruit artists into the service of propaganda; but anyone who wondered why philosophers imprisoned in dialectical materialism, or novelists enslaved by socialist realism, were lacking in genius, misjudged the very essence of the creative process. The idolators of history caused more and more havoc, not because they were inspired by good or bad sentiments, but because their ideas were wrong.[73]

Human reality in process of development, Aron concluded, had a structure:

every action has a place in a complex of actions; individuals are bound up with regimes; ideas organize themselves into doctrines. One cannot ascribe to the conduct or the thoughts of others a meaning arbitrarily deduced from one's own interpretation of events. The last word is never said and one must not judge one's adversaries as if one's own cause were identified with the ultimate truth.

A true understanding of the past recalls us to the duty of tolerance; a false philosophy of history breeds only fanaticism.[74]

Because historical explanation was no more than probabilistic in character, it was an illusion to think that it was possible to predict the evolution of economic regimes or prove that capitalism destroyed itself and that socialism would necessarily follow it, even though one knew neither when nor how.[75] Historical "destiny", in retrospect, was "simply

470

the unalterable crystallization of our actions"; as far as the future was concerned, historical "destiny" was "always undecided". Not that this implied that man's freedom was absolute; it was "limited by the heritage of the past, by human passions and by collective servitudes". But such limitation on our freedom did not "compel us to submit in advance to a detestable system", for there was "no such thing as a global determinism".[76] Revolutionaries were inclined to exaggerate both the margin of their freedom and the power of destiny. Fanatical in hope or despair, they continued to theorize about an inevitable future, one that they were incapable of describing but which they claimed to be able to foretell. There was, however, "no law, either human or inhuman", which could "direct the chaos of events to a definite end, be it radiant or horrific".[77]

History is made by men who act, in circumstances which are not of their own choosing, according to their appetites or their ideals, and their imperfect knowledge, sometimes succumbing to their environment, sometimes conquering it, bowed down under the weight of immemorial customs, or uplifted by a spiritual force. At first glance, it seems both a chaos of events and a tyrannical whole; each fragment is significant and the whole devoid of meaning.[78]

But historical awareness, unlike the idolatry of history, showed us the limits of our knowledge and taught us respect for *the other*, even when we were engaged in fighting him. The idolatry of history, on the other hand, convinced that it was acting with a view to achieving the only worthwhile future, "sees, and wants to see *the other* merely as an enemy to be eliminated, and a contemptible enemy at that, since he is incapable of wanting the good or of recognizing it".[79]

* * *

In Part Three, "The Alienation of the Intellectuals", Aron made a start on what he saw as a long overdue sociology of the intelligentsia. The term itself was not easy to define and could be made to refer either to "the category of individuals who have acquired, in universities or technical schools, the qualifications needed for the exercise of techno-bureaucratic functions" (as in the USSR), or to "those whose 'principal occupation is to write, to teach, to preach, to appear on the stage or to practise art or letters'" (the meaning usually employed in the West).[80] The term "intelligentsia" had first been used in Russia in the nineteenth century, where

471

those who had been through a university and acquired a culture which was for the most part of Western origin constituted a small group external to the traditional class structure. They were recruited from the younger sons of aristocratic families and the sons of the bourgeoisie or even the better-off peasantry. Detached from the old society, they felt themselves united by the knowledge they shared and by the attitude they adopted towards the established order. All this, together with the new scientific spirit and liberal ideas, inclined them towards revolution.

In societies where modern culture developed spontaneously and progressively from the traditional soil, the break with the past was less abrupt. University graduates were not so clearly distinguishable from other social categories; they did not unconditionally reject the age-old structure of communal life. They were nonetheless accused, and they are still accused, of fomenting revolutions – an accusation which the left-wing intellectual would accept as a tribute, pointing out that without the revolutionaries' determination to transcend the present, the ancient abuses would still survive.

In a sense, the accusation is ill-founded. It is not true that intellectuals as such are hostile to all societies. The writers and scholars of old China "defended and illustrated" the doctrine, more moral than religious, which put them in the front rank of their society and consecrated the hierarchy. Kings and princes, crowned heroes and wealthy merchants, have always found poets (not necessarily bad ones) to sing their praises. Neither in Athens nor in Paris, neither in the fifth century before Christ nor in the nineteenth century of our era, did the writer or the philosopher incline spontaneously towards the party of the people, of liberty or of progress. Admirers of Sparta were to be met with in no small quantity within the walls of Athens, just as, in our day, admirers of the Third Reich or the Soviet Union could be met with in the cafés of the Left Bank.

All doctrines, all parties – traditionalism, liberalism, democracy, nationalism, fascism, communism – have had and continue to have their oracles and their thinkers. In each camp, the intellectuals are those who transform opinions or interests into theories; by definition, they are not content merely to live, they want to *think* their existence.

There remains, nevertheless, a basis of truth in the hackneyed notion, which has been taken up in a more subtle form by certain sociologists (Schumpeter, for example), of the intellectuals as revolutionaries by profession.[81]

The "occupational disease" of intellectuals was their tendency to criticize the established order and to judge their country and its institutions by comparing present realities with theoretical ideas rather than with other realities – the France of today with their own idea of what France ought to be rather than with the France of yesterday. No human institution, Aron pointed out, could stand up to such a test without suffering some damage.[82] The basis of their criticism was a moralism which earned them the glory of being "righters of wrong" ("les redresseurs de torts") and of always adopting a negative attitude, but also the less flattering reputation of professional word-spinners who ignored the rude constraints of action:

472

It is a long time since criticism could be regarded as a proof of courage, at least in our free Western societies. The public prefers to find in its newspapers arguments which justify its resentments or its claims rather than motives for admitting that, in the given circumstances, the action of the government could not have been very different from what it was. In criticizing, one evades responsibility for the unpleasant consequences entailed by a measure which may be desirable on the whole. The oppositionist, however violent his polemics, seldom suffers for his so-called heresies. To sign petitions on behalf of the Rosenbergs or against the rearming of Western Germany, to denounce the bourgeoisie as a mob of gangsters or regularly to take up a position in favour of the side against which France is preparing to defend herself – none of this damages the career even of a servant of the state.[83] How often have the privileged taken to their bosoms the writers who execrated them! The Babbits of America were to a great extent responsible for the success of Sinclair Lewis. The bourgeoisie and the sons of the bourgeoisie, denounced by the writers of yesterday as philistines, by those of today as capitalists, have been the salvation of the rebels and the revolutionaries. Success is to those who transfigure the past or the future: it is doubtful whether, in our day, it is possible with impunity to defend the moderate opinion that the present is in many respects neither better nor worse than any other period.[84]

France itself was often thought of as "the intellectuals' paradise" and yet, paradoxically, French intellectuals had the reputation of being revolutionaries.[85] Why did so many intellectuals loathe – or say they did – a society which provided them with an honourable standard of living, placed no limitations on their activity, and proclaimed that the works of the mind represented the highest values? The answer, Aron believed, lay in the fact that most politically minded intellectuals were embittered because they felt they had been cheated of what was theirs by right: whether docile or rebellious, they had the feeling that, under a Fourth Republic that was "rich in negative virtues" and "conservative in a changing world", they were crying in the wilderness.[86] They dreamed of a Europe which, in appearance at any rate, had regained its freedom of action, and herein lay the source of their anti-Americanism. Some of Sartre's writings, for example, at the time of the Korean War or the Rosenberg case, recalled "those of the Nazis against the Jews. The United States is represented as the embodiment of everything most detested, and then all the resentment and hatred and gall which accumulates in people's hearts in a time of troubles is heaped on this symbolic figure".[87] The fact was, Aron argued further, that the European Left had a grudge against the United States mainly because the latter had become successful through means which conflicted with the favoured ideology: "Prosperity, power, the tendency towards uniformity of economic conditions – these results have been achieved by private initiative, by competition rather than state intervention, in other words by capitalism, which every well brought-up intellectual has been taught to despise".[88]

If the Paris of the Left Bank was the writers' paradise, then the United States could be considered the writers' hell. And yet, if France exalted its intellectuals, only to be rejected by them, America, who made no concessions to its intellectuals, was adored by them. The French, Aron believed, were reacting to the humiliation of their country and the Americans to the grandeur of theirs.[89] Of the Western countries it was probably Britain which treated its intellectuals in the most reasonable manner. By not taking their intellectuals so seriously, the British managed to avoid both the militant anti-intellectualism to which American pragmatism sometimes led and the uncritical admiration shown to intellectuals in France.[90]

Turning from this examination of "The Intellectuals and their Homeland" to "The Intellectuals and their Ideologies", Aron suggested four "basic factors" of the current world situation. The first of these was that, in the West, the quarrel between capitalism and socialism was in the process of losing its emotional potential. The so-called socialist societies, like the capitalist West, had to ensure the development of productive forces and this entailed the necessities inherent in any modern economic system: hierarchies of authority, incentives, production bonuses and all the demands of economic arithmetic.

Another basic factor was the challenge to representative institutions brought about by the failure of parliamentary regimes in most European countries between the wars and the rise of a totalitarian state, the Soviet Union, to the forefront of world power. Thirdly, a "pre-established harmony" existed between the denunciation of nineteenth-century capitalism by a Western intellectual (Karl Marx) and the passions felt by intellectuals in Asia and Africa today:

That the be-all and the end-all of the West is the search for profits; that the religious missions and Christian beliefs are the smoke-screen or the alibi for cynical interest; that finally, the victim of its own materialism, the West must destroy itself by imperialist wars – such an interpretation is partial, misleading and unjust. It nevertheless convinces peoples in revolt against foreign masters.[91]

Lastly, "the great schism" between the Soviet camp and the West was differently interpreted in London and Bombay, Washington and Tokyo. In Britain, the debate was primarily a technical one rather than an ideological debate about conflicting values:

...elsewhere, people argue about the various choices with which they themselves are faced; the British argue about the choices facing others. The editors of the *New Statesman and Nation* are carried away with enthusiasm at the idea of collaboration between socialists and communists – in France, of course, not in Britain.

If the rest of the world were as sensible as Great Britain, the great debate would collapse from sheer boredom. Luckily, American senators, French intellectuals and Soviet commissars will provide inexhaustible opportunities for dispute.[92]

There were also, Aron suggested, striking parallels between the situation of Japanese intellectuals in Japanese society and their counterparts in France (the majority of Japanese writers and artists were not far short of being communist and, as in France, disapproved of the alliance with the United States).[93] However, the position was different in those Asian countries which had been formerly ruled by Britain. Indian or Burmese intellectuals, for example, while also for the most part "progressives", were not communists. Although they inclined more to anti-imperialism than to anti-communism in what they said, deep-down they were more uneasy about the intentions of Mao Tse-tung than those of President Eisenhower. Here the determining factors seemed to Aron to be threefold: national variations in Western influence, the attitude towards religion and the past, and the relative strength of liberal or socialist convictions.[94]

Parallels had frequently been drawn between socialism and religion, and between the spread of Christianity throughout the ancient world and that of Marxism in our time. The expression "secular religion", which Aron himself had coined in *La France libre* during the war,[95] had become a commonplace:

The Marxist prophetism, as we have seen, conforms to the typical pattern of the Judaeo-Christian prophetism. Every prophetism condemns what is and sketches an outline of what should or will be; it chooses an individual or a group to cleave a path across the no-man's land which separates the unworthy present from the radiant future. The classless society which will bring social progress without political revolution is comparable to the dreams of the millennium. The misery of the proletariat proves its vocation and the Communist Party becomes the Church which is opposed by the bourgeois/pagans who stop their ears against the good tidings and by the socialists/Jews who failed to recognize the Revolution which they themselves had been heralding for years.[96]

But in Aron's view the Christian could never be a genuine Communist, as the French worker-priests had recently advocated,[97] any more than the Communist could believe in God or in Christ. There was a fundamental incompatibility between the two beliefs, which was ignored by "progressive" Christians: communism was an atheistic secular religion and, in complete contrast to Christianity, taught that man fulfilled his destiny uniquely in the temporal sphere, here on earth.[98]

Thirty years earlier, Julien Benda had immortalized the expression "the betrayal of the intellectuals" with the title of his book *La Trahison des clercs*. Benda's argument had been that the intellectuals in the early years of the century had betrayed their mission – which was to serve timeless values such as truth and justice – by giving an articulate and pseudo-rational form to the interests of states and the hatred between peoples. Where, Aron asked, were the traitors now?

I can only give my own personal answer to the question. The intellectual who sets some store by the just and reasonable organization of society will not be content to stand on the side-lines, to put his signature at the bottom of every manifesto against every injustice. Although he will endeavour to appeal to the consciences of *all* parties, he will take his stand in favour of the one which appears to offer humanity the best chance – a historical choice which involves the risk of error which is inseparable from the historical condition. He will not refuse to become involved, and when he participates in action he will accept its consequences, however harsh. But he must try never to forget the arguments of the adversary, or the uncertainty of the future, or the faults of his own side, or the underlying fraternity of ordinary men everywhere.[99]

* * *

Aron's conclusion was couched in the form of a question: had "the end of the ideological age" been reached? Of course, he stressed, he was "not so naive as to expect peace to blossom forth in the immediate future", because once the revolutionaries who had seized power had become disillusioned or been liquidated, the bureaucrats would continue to reign. Nevertheless, the peoples of the West were perhaps entering an age of greater scepticism and political tolerance. Neither the optimist who conjured up a vision of fraternity thanks to material plenty, nor the pessimist who visualized a consummate tyranny extended over human minds with the help of the new instruments of mass communication and torture, was quite refuted by the experience of the twentieth century. Their dialogue, which began at the time of the first factories, was still being pursued; but it did not, Aron maintained, take the form of an ideological debate, because the opposing themes were "no longer connected with a particular class or party".

476

The last great ideology was born of the combination of three elements: the vision of a future consistent with human aspirations, the link between this future and a particular social class, and trust in human values above and beyond the victory of the working class, thanks to planning and collective ownership. Confidence in the virtues of a socio-economic technique has begun to wane and one looks in vain for this class which is supposed to bring about the radical renewal of institutions and ideas.[100]

The theory of the class struggle, which was of course still current, had been falsified by a spurious analogy, according to which the proletariat would finish the work begun by the bourgeoisie in their struggle against the aristocracy at the time of the French Revolution. But, Aron contended, the rivalry between bourgeoisie and proletariat was essentially different from that between artistocracy and bourgeoisie. A case might be made that the working class and the bourgeoisie differed in life-style and values – the sense of solidarity versus the desire for possessions, participation in the community as opposed to individualism and egoism, or the generosity of the impoverished as against the avarice of the wealthy. But, whatever the bourgeois intellectuals who set themselves up as the ideologists of the proletariat might say,

the proletariat has never had a conception of the world opposed to that of the bourgeoisie; there has been an ideology of what the proletariat should be or should do, an ideology whose historical ascendancy was most powerful when the number of industrial workers was smallest. The so-called proletarian party, in the countries where it has seized power, has had peasants rather than factory workers as its troops, and intellectuals, exasperated by the traditional hierarchy or by national humiliation, as its leaders. . .

It was in the hope of accomplishing fully the ambitions of the bourgeoisie – the conquest of Nature, social equality or equality of opportunity – that the ideologists handed on the torch to the proletariat. The contrast between technological progress and the misery of the workers was a crying scandal. How could one help but impute to private ownership and the anarchy of the market the survival of ancestral poverty which was in fact due to the exigencies of accumulation (capitalist or socialist), insufficient productivity and increases in population. Soft-hearted intellectuals, revolted by injustice, seized on the idea that capitalism, being in itself evil, would be destroyed by its contradictions and that its victims would eventually overthrow the privileged. Marx achieved an ingenious synthesis between the Hegelian metaphysic of history, the Jacobin interpretation of the Revolution, and the pessimistic theory of the market economy developed by British authors. To maintain the continuity between the French Revolution and the Russian Revolution, it was only necessary to call Marxist ideology proletarian. But one has merely to open one's eyes to be rid of the illusion.

The market economy and total planning are rival models – which no existing economy actually reproduces – not successive stages in evolution. There is no necessary link between the phases of industrial development and the predominance of one model or the other. Backward economies approximate more to the model of the planners than

477

do advanced economies. Mixed systems are not monsters incapable of surviving, or transitional forms on the way to the pure type; they are the normal thing. In a planned system one will find most of the categories of the market economy, more or less modified. As the standard of living rises and the Soviet consumer has more freedom of choice, the benefits and the problems of Western prosperity will appear on the other side of the Iron Curtain.[101]

No intelligentsia, it seemed to Aron, suffered as much as the French from what he called "the loss of universality": hankering after a truth applicable to humanity as a whole, French intellectuals watched and waited upon events. For some time after Yugoslavia's excommunication by Moscow, Saint-Germain-des-Prés was Titoist; then Tito, without abandoning communism, concluded military alliances analogous to those with which the progressives reproached the Western states, and his prestige immediately sank to zero. Now, at the end of 1954, Mao Tse-tung's China had succeeded Tito's Yugoslavia in their esteem; but, Aron asked, what possible model could Mao's regime offer France?

Yet, to those French intellectuals with a yearning for universalism, Aron had this to say:

Many of the tasks which should compel the attention and the energies of France in the middle of the twentieth century would have a significance far transcending our frontiers. To organize a genuine community between Frenchmen and Moslems in North Africa, to unite the nations of Western Europe so that they are less dependent on American power, to cure the technological backwardness of our economy – such tasks as these might well arouse a clear-sighted and practical enthusiasm. None would revolutionize the condition of men on this earth, none would make France the soldier of the ideal, none would rescue us from the tiny foreland of Asia with which our fate is linked; none would have the glamour of metaphysical ideas, none the apparent universality of socialist or nationalist ideologies. By placing our country in its exact position in the planetary system, by acting in accordance with the teachings of social science, our intellectuals could achieve the only political universality which is accessible in our time. They might give to mechanical civilization a form attuned to the traditions and the maturity of the nation, and organize with a view to prosperity and peace the zone of the planet over which our power and our thought can still extend their influence.

To these immediate and attainable prospects, the French intellectuals seem indifferent. One has the feeling that they aspire to recapture, in a philosophy of immanence, the equivalent of the lost eternity, and that they murmur to one another: "What's the point of it all, if it isn't universal?"[102]

The essential difference between the West and the Soviet universe was not, as was sometimes argued, that the West represented a "Christian" civilization, but that it admitted itself to be divided, whereas the Soviet

478

universe "politicized" the whole of existence. The least important, though most frequently cited, aspect of plurality was the party system. This had its disadvantages: it maintained an atmosphere of discord in the body-politic, blurred the sense of communal necessity and compromised internal peace and friendship. Nevertheless, it was tolerated, in spite of everything, as a means of giving expression to irreplaceable values and as a symbol of them; it was a means of limiting arbitrary power and ensuring a legal expression of discontent, and a symbol of the lay impartiality of the state and the autonomy of the human mind.[103]

Aron ended with a rejection of fanaticism, coupled with a plea for tolerance, but this did not mean that a faith based on reason should be replaced by scepticism. The refusal to idealize one class, one form of action and one ideological system did not, Aron made clear, imply that one no longer desired a more just society and a less cruel lot for humanity:

> ...the man who no longer expects miraculous changes either from a revolution or an economic plan is not obliged to resign himself to the unjustifiable. It is because he likes individual human beings, participates in living communities and respects the truth, that he refuses to surrender his soul to an abstract ideal of humanity, a tyrannical party and an absurd scholasticism.[104]

And yet, perhaps only a strong cure of scepticism could rid intellectuals of their fanaticism. If so, there was a place for tolerant scepticism as well as reasonable faith:

> It is not as though we are surrounded by indifference.[105] Men have not yet reached the point where they have no further occasion or motive for killing one another. If tolerance is born of doubt, let us teach everyone to doubt all models and utopias, to challenge all the prophets of salvation and the heralds of catastrophe.
> Let us pray for the advent of the sceptics, if they alone can abolish fanaticism.[106]

* * *

Not surprisingly, *The Opium of the Intellectuals* "created a furore"[107] and was peppered with hostile notices in both the Marxist and the fellow-travelling press.[108] Annie Besse, for example, in the Communist *Nouvelle Critique*, had the misfortune to open her review with the words: "M. Raymond Aron has done the most vulgar thing possible; he has gone back on his youth. As a young man, he was full of generous ideas. He has become a writer on the *Figaro*. He cannot get over it. And he drugs his shame with opium".[109] Shortly afterwards she left the Party and, as Annie Kriegel, became one of the foremost historians of French communism. A forthright anti-communist, she is now a columnist on *Le Figaro* and a fervent Aronian, affirming after Aron's death that *The Opium of the Intellectuals* "remains a classic".[110] Another interesting case was Jean-Jacques Sorel in *France-Observateur*: "It is", he argued speciously, "as if the drugs squad came to the conclusion, at the end of a 300-page investigation, that there are no grounds for further enquiry because the opium taken by *les intellectuels de gauche* turns out, too, to be nothing but a phoney wonder-drug (la poudre de perlimpinpin)". If Aron maintained that the Left was a myth, then he and his book proved that the Right was a reality.[111] In the years that followed, Sorel, as Jean-Jacques Salomon, eventually turned away from Sartre and towards Aron – partly through the influence of Georges Canguilhem – and Aron and Canguilhem became his thesis supervisors and examiners after 1968.[112]

Perhaps the most venomous attack, however, came from Aron's old adversary, Maurice Duverger, in *Le Monde*.[113] The very title of his piece, "Opium des intellectuels ou trahison des clercs?", with its deliberate echoing of the title of Benda's book and its implication that Aron was some kind of "traitor", set the tone and summarized the main theme of the review. Aron's "dialectical power" was, Duverger stated, "impressive but unconvincing". This "admirable intellectual machine" was functioning perfectly but "without engaging with reality". Aron had failed to touch the heart of Marxism. He had merely demolished – "quite rightly", as Duverger admitted – "a kind of Marxist integrism", but one did not dispose of Christianity simply by refuting the *Syllabus* or denouncing the Inquisition. The proletariat was not just a myth and the class struggle remained a reality. The form of economic oppression had perhaps changed since *The Communist Manifesto*, but it existed nonetheless: freedom was as much threatened by money as by the state. The essence of Marxism lay not in any Hegelian metaphysic but "in the fact that at the present time Marxism offers the only general theory of social injustice".

It was this which explained its attraction for intellectuals. Aron's analysis was "most ingenious"; the motives he distinguished were, Duverger granted, "not false", but "of secondary importance". The intellectual, and especially the French intellectual, he continued, presenting an unwitting parody of the very position Aron had been attacking,

does not believe that his job is merely to understand, but also to judge and to act in accordance with his judgement. He believes he is always more or less invested, if not with a mission, then with responsibilities. Having noted the existence of social injustice, he sees it as his duty to fight that injustice. His natural tendency leads him to side with the weak against the strong, with the victims against the executioners, and with the oppressed against the oppressors.

Therein lay "the fundamental explanation" for the attraction of the Left: the latter, asserted Duverger, ignoring Aron's own critique of the "myth of the Left", was the party of the weak and the oppressed. However, the "drama" facing contemporary intellectuals, was, Duverger acknowledged, that the oppression was not all one-way: the political police, totalitarian systems and deportation camps all existed, but so did social injustice, capitalist domination and colonialism. And the situation was such, he stated with a questionable logic, that "to take a position for certain victims is to take a position against others".

What was the intellectual to do in the face of such contradictions? Were there "good" victims to be pitied and "bad" victims to be ignored or abused? That was the position of the orthodox Communists and it was also, said Duverger, grotesquely seeking to tar Aron with the same brush, "in the last analysis" Aron's position, too. The attempts of the Communists to justify the Soviet camps were comparable to Aron's attempts to justify capitalism – even if the latter's arguments were more subtle. Both were betraying the role of the intellectual.

In fact, Duverger's own view of the task of the intellectual – "to determine, in each particular case, the attitude which will be most effective in reducing injustice and hastening the end of oppression" – was not one with which Aron would have been likely to disagree. But he then went on to present a travesty of Aron's intellectual activity as well as an argument for doing nothing in the face of injustice: "Simply to denounce the Soviet deportation camps, day in and day out, to the 'Amis de la Liberté' and in the pages of *Preuves*, in no way helps to bring the freedom of the deportees any nearer". Such denunciations could even, Duverger argued dubiously, "aggravate the tension between the two blocs, which tends to prolong the existence of the camps and the sufferings of the deportees". At the same time, Duverger claimed for himself the right "ceaselessly to denounce social injustice and capitalist domination in France", since this could "to some extent help bring about their end".

Such an approach was, Duverger admitted, difficult to put into practice and implied "many hesitations, nuances and even contradictions and about-turns"; it was quite easy, he added sarcastically, for "brilliant dialecticians to demonstrate their logical fragility". But Aron should also have attacked those intellectuals who, while loudly proclaiming their sympathy for the oppressed in remote and inaccessible places, closed their eyes to the victims on their own doorstep. For *les clercs* were not blind to their own motives and, when they betrayed, they did so consciously.

When seen in this light, the "deep pathos" of Aron's book stood revealed; for its real significance lay in the fact that it was "a confession in disguise". According to Duverger, what Aron most loathed about left-wing intellectuals was that he himself was no longer one of them. "The left-wing intellectual of the 1930s, the brilliant para-Marxist of the pre-war years" (the description made Aron sound much more of a left-winger before the war than he had ever been) was "too lucid not to see the exact role he is playing today": his task was to provide the bourgeoisie with the kind of arguments which would give it a clear conscience and undermine its opponents. Aron knew that "the courageous positions" which, Duverger grudgingly admitted, "he sometimes adopts on particular points of detail", were not enough to compensate for this basic attitude; on the contrary, they were "part of the system, since they more or less give the illusion of objectivity". In fact, Aron was trying to convince himself rather than his readers: there had to be sinners in order that he himself might be innocent.

If Aron did not succeed in his readers' eyes, this was because, Duverger claimed, he had failed in his own. Was it not revealing that Aron had in recent years been fascinated by the theme of betrayal? In his discussions of Marxist dialectic Aron had often analysed the opposition between manifest and latent meaning. Such a distinction was equally applicable to his own dialectic: "it is its latent meaning which, in the last analysis", Duverger concluded sardonically, "gives to *The Opium of the Intellectuals* its exceptional interest".[114]

But the work was not short of defenders, among them Pierre-Henri Simon in *Carrefour*.[115] To Maurice Schumann, it was an "epoch-making book" – notwithstanding Aron's reluctance to commit himself to the General.[116] The historian and writer, Claude Delmas, in a major two-part essay in *Critique*,[117] rightly underlined the continuity that ran through Aron's work from the *Introduction to the Philosophy of History* to *The Opium of the Intellectuals*. The former constituted a philosophical and methodological introduction to all of his subsequent studies, and in particular to *Les Guerres en chaîne* and *The Opium of the Intellectuals*, Aron's most important books since his thesis. Indeed, the works could be said to form a trilogy.

But the reviewer who spoke out most eloquently in favour of *The Opium of the Intellectuals* was the philosopher, Gabriel Marcel.[118] The book's quality was, he wrote, "indisputable", its first merit being its "rigour" and "unflinching capacity for judgement":

Its author is, as we have known for a long time, one of the few indestructibly courageous spirits of our time. But why is it that, in an age and in a country in which so many men have fought with heroic valour against every kind of physical and moral ordeal, adversity and even torture, such spiritual courage should be so clearly exceptional, and indeed its very value called into question?

Marcel would not, he stated, be surprised if there formed around the book the kind of conspiracy of silence which automatically enveloped any work whose aim was not to flatter or provoke but to seek after truth. Aron's "austere and pure" book discouraged the snobberies of intellectual fashion and no faction could claim his essentially critical conclusions for its own. What had to be strongly underlined was that

if these categories still have any meaning (and it is by no means clear that they do), then the author remains a man of the Left, who is deeply attached to the unchanging values inherent in any democracy worthy of the name. Not that this will be enough to prevent him, in certain circles, from being called a Fascist. No matter. All those who, in France or abroad, read this book without losing their *sang-froid*, will see in it irrefutable evidence of the continued existence of that Reason which, at certain dark moments of our history, we might have thought had been destroyed.

In the United States the French original of *The Opium of the Intellectuals* was reviewed in *Social Research* by Albert Salomon, in whose judgement Aron's "sweeping generalizations" about American, German and British intellectuals were "sometimes brilliant, always impressionistic, and never completely true". He agreed with Aron that Marxist-Leninist doctrines had become a secular religion, but thought it "misleading" to say that Marxism was a Christian heresy, since "Marxism presupposes the complete rejection of all previous religions". The philosophy of history which Aron opposed to the Hegelian-Marxist system, a philosophy which stressed man's capacity for choice and decision in the context of a complex web of historical conditions that determined our lives, was "close to that of Dilthey and Isaiah Berlin"; and Salomon concluded with the hope that Aron, who had now returned to the University, would "continue his valuable Proustian work *à la recherche de Montaigne perdu*, revitalizing the discipline of scepticism and the moral integrity of its uncertainties".[119]

The publication in Paris of *L'Opium des intellectuels* quickly attracted attention in Britain, the *Times Literary Supplement* devoting a front-page article (its author was in fact Denis Brogan) to Aron's "brilliant" and "most stimulating and most valuable book".[120] *The Economist*, on the other hand, thought that the work was "unlikely to add much to his reputation". Though parts of it were "suggestive" and "challenging", the book was "labouring the obvious" in its analysis of the appeal of Soviet ideology to French intellectuals and was marred by "an unusual opacity of style".[121]

When, however, Terence Kilmartin's readable and accurate English translation appeared two years later (the work has also been translated into German, Italian, Spanish, Polish, Japanese, Portuguese and Russian), the book was widely noticed in the literary and political journals. It was the subject of a fine appraisal from Irving Kristol in *The Observer*:

M. Raymond Aron is probably the most brilliant political analyst of our day. He is also one of the most paradoxical. He tantalizingly evades all efforts to fix him on the Right or the Left of the political spectrum: as a columnist for the right-wing daily, *Le Figaro*, he opposed the Suez affair and has been the only prominent non-Communist bold enough to urge the immediate recognition of Algerian independence. He is both a liberal and a pessimist – an unsentimental spokesman for reform and progress whose vision of the human condition does not inspire him to consider politics as particularly relevant to the problem of human happiness.

He is "typically French" in the perfect lucidity and painstaking logic with which he handles ideas; but he is also "typically English" in his passionate and stubborn verification of large ideas by the small, plain facts. He is a political philosopher who would certainly agree with G. K. Chesterton that "unless a man has a philosophy...he will stagger on to a miserable death with no comfort but a series of catchwords"; but the greater part of his energy goes into the sceptical and destructive examination of how philosophers are used to conceal prejudice and bad faith. The oddest thing about these and other paradoxes is that, in reading M. Aron, one is not aware of them as paradoxes at all. They add up to a consistent point of view.

The riddle dissolves if one puts M. Aron in his place – which is in the line of descent from Montaigne and the *politiques* of the sixteenth and seventeenth centuries. These men lived, as we do today, in the midst of ideological wars; and they learned that, important as it is to have a consistent view of the world, it is not the most important thing *in* the world. They gave people more weight than ideas, proposed a kind of negative humanism – negative, in that it simply aimed to protect men from themselves. Their main enemies, like M. Aron's, were less people who were in intellectual error than those who insisted that everyone else was: the dogmatists, in short. The *politique* has his personal opinions about what is the best political order, but also realizes that in practice the scales are, in the most favourable conditions, usually tipped in favour of the second-best.

This tradition goes deep in France, but in the post-war period it has been overwhelmed by a tide of Teutonic romanticism. M. Aron stands like a lonely survivor of classical

French political thinking in the midst of all the neo-Marxists and Young Hegelians who, for some peculiar reason calling themselves "existentialists", now dominate French intellectual life. *The Opium of the Intellectuals* is directed against them and their fashionable opinions. It is a polemic, but so cool, patient, and cogent that one can only regret that those who stand most to gain by it are the least likely to read it. . . [122]

Another enthusiastic reviewer was Philip Toynbee in *Encounter*, who saw Aron as "an independent liberal markedly to the left of centre". The difficulty in reviewing *The Opium of the Intellectuals* was that

it is a book written for Frenchmen, about France, which sometimes seems to have amazingly little relevance to political realities and attitudes in England. In fact, for us the main value of the book may well lie in its demonstration of the deep political differences between the two countries – just as the main temptation of an English reviewer will be to thank God that we are not as Frenchmen are. It is a temptation which must be fiercely resisted. M. Aron's brilliant and absorbing book is an analytical castigation of the French Left – it is typical of his radical position that he does not think the French Right is *worth* attacking, except *en passant*. We should remind ourselves as we read it that a quite different but scarcely less devastating attack could be launched, from the same position of informed good-sense, against the *British* Left. [123]

Toynbee found himself in agreement with Aron's critiques of the myths of the Revolution and of the Proletariat, but not with the myth of the Left. Aron had been "greatly, and rightly, concerned with the fellow-traveller" and had demonstrated "as clearly as I have ever seen it demonstrated, that the advent of Communism has been, for the Left, a cruel fall from the comparative innocence which they enjoyed at the time of the Dreyfus case". Nevertheless, it still seemed to Toynbee that

there is a general attitude to life and society which can usefully be described as left-wing, and another which can usefully be described as right-wing. Far from destroying this distinction, as he has tried to do throughout this book, M. Aron has simply revealed himself as a very pure, very convinced but very disillusioned Man of the Left. [124]

To the anonymous reviewer in *The Listener*,

Monsieur Raymond Aron is a very clever man indeed: and his *Opium des intellectuels* was rightly hailed on its appearance in 1955 as one of the most valuable and stimulating contributions made by "the higher journalism" to the political discussions of our day. The fact that M. Aron passes in his own country as a representative of the Anglo-Saxon tradition of thought should in no way diminish the interest of his book for the English reader. Indeed, if anything it should increase it. For his thought is as good an example of the difference between things as they are and things as others see them as *zuppa inglese* or *le jardin anglais*. [125]

His book contained "three different messages": "a scorching and vivid indictment of the post-war political activities and opinions of what passes for the left-wing intelligentsia in certain European countries, notably France"; "a destructive analysis of the traditional classification of all political opinions into the two categories of left and right"; and "a subtle and devious attack upon a conception of politics that would seem to be characteristic of, if not essential to, all left-wing theory".

On the first score Aron had secured "total victory":

He deals in a devastating way with the various appeals that have been made to History and other abstractions in justification of fellow-travelling politics: he unravels the monstrous Hegelian terminology in which the simplest political points have come to be muffled. His treatment of writers like M. Merleau-Ponty is not only very effective, it is also very funny.

Nevertheless, it was the other two messages which were "most likely to arouse interest and provoke discussion", the book's "great merit" being that it should encourage the reader to "distinguish within his own political ideas what is genuine belief and what is hot air".[126]

The historian, Geoffrey Barraclough, was more non-committal. Aron's new book was "opportune" because it made one think again about the old categories of Left and Right, even if it did not contribute any new lines of thought. However, it had "singularly little relevance" to the conservative England of 1957. Aron had failed to provide the kind of analysis of why both Right and Left were "so utterly at sea" which "we had every right to expect from a man of M. Aron's calibre". He offered "some telling examples" of how the old antithesis between Left and Right had lost touch with reality; and he was at his "most trenchant" when discussing public and private ownership and planned and free economies. However, Barraclough ended with the unwarranted accusation that Aron appeared to welcome the development of a technocratic pragmatism in which political values and aspirations played no part.[127]

The Opium of the Intellectuals was also the subject of a characteristically waspish review by A. J. P. Taylor in the *New Statesman*. Aron was, Taylor wrote,

both clever and wise, a rare combination. He scores debating points with the zest of an undergraduate, yet never loses sight of his cautious, sensible conclusion. He admires English ways – perhaps to excess; and in return we reward him by finding him as nearly sympathetic as a French writer can be. But he cannot altogether escape his national character. He assumes that all problems are already known to the reader, and comments allusively on them, much as a preacher might assume a knowledge of the scriptures. The title of his book is a case in point. Marx said that religion was the opium of the people. Marxism itself has become a religion, but it is the opium of the intellectuals. This is as smart a piece of dialectics as anything constructed by Marx himself. But the book does little to develop it. One might have expected a detailed examination of books by Marxist intellectuals, showing where their reasoning broke down and how Marxism puts them in blinkers. M. Aron remains abstract. He quotes one or two French fellow-travellers, though only to denounce them. He makes no attempt to analyse Marxism as a system of thought. M. Aron is a sociologist by profession, and this book confirms my suspicion that sociology is history with the history left out.[128]

Taylor went on to make the extraordinary accusation that Aron "does not mind political criminals", but could not bear muddled thinking. Aron, Taylor alleged, "believes only in scepticism. He wants to see the end of ideologies and looks forward to a world in which nobody believes anything, a world of universal tolerance, where every solution is regarded with equal indifference". But this too, Taylor concluded, was a Utopia. To hope that everyone would one day be as sensible as M. Aron was "the last and greatest of the intellectual myths".[129]

A few years later, in his indulgent study of *Communism and the French Intellectuals*, David Caute put forward the specious argument that Aron's lack of sympathy with left-wing ideas disqualified him from entering the debate at all:

. . . it is essential in appraising the actions of communist intellectuals, not only to avoid regarding them as psychological misfits, strangers to reason, but also to accept, for the purposes of discussion, left-wing premises, or at least those shared not only by communists but, broadly, by Trotskyists, idealists, the advocates of a Third Force. Otherwise the essential problem of ends and means is lost sight of in a welter of technical and indecisive arguments. Thus M. Aron has attempted to explain (or ridicule) the behaviour of Marxist intellectuals while denying all their premises, while discarding as myths the basic ideas of the Left, of the Revolution and of the Proletariat. M. Aron believes in a guided capitalism, in technical adjustments, in reform. The logic of his complete demolition of Marxism as a doctrine relevant to the mid-twentieth century, and his refusal to regard his opponents as complete fools, leads inexorably to the "opium" theory. He refuses to set one "reason" against another. Consequently he tells us more about Marxism than about Marxists.[130]

In the United States, *The Opium of the Intellectuals* was the subject of hostile reviews by Harold Rosenberg in *Dissent*[131] and George Lichtheim in *Commentary*,[132] but the main interest it aroused there was in connection with what came to be known as "the end of ideology thesis". The idea that advanced industrial society would be marked by a decline in ideology of course existed well before Aron. The theme has

487

in fact been traced back to writers of such varied political persuasions as Engels, Weber and Mannheim, as well as – after the Second World War – Camus, T. H. Marshall, Isaiah Berlin, H. Stuart Hughes, and members of the Frankfurt School.[133] Indeed, it was the latter who published the conclusion to *The Opium of the Intellectuals*, "Fin de l'âge idéologique?" ("End of the Ideological Age?") – with a question mark – in one of their volumes.[134]

But it was the appearance of the English translation of *The Opium of the Intellectuals* which was to provide an important stimulus to the "end of ideology" debate, especially in the United States. Thus Edward Shils, who had earlier taken up the theme in his *Encounter* report of the Milan Conference of the Congress for Cultural Freedom in September 1955,[135] made *The Opium of the Intellectuals* the starting-point for his argument in favour of a "civil politics" as opposed to an "ideological politics".[136] At the same time, in an article written in English for the *Partisan Review* and published in 1958, Aron sought to extend the end of ideology thesis from the sphere of ideas to "the field of world politics".[137]

By 1960, when Daniel Bell's *The End of Ideology* and S. M. Lipset's *Political Man* were published, the idea had gained wide currency. Throughout the 1960s, however, the thesis was to be the subject of constant charge and counter-charge – both Aron and Bell, for example, were the targets of attack by the Harvard philosopher, H. D. Aiken.[138] As will be recounted in the second volume of this work, Aron himself joined in the debate with a long essay, "Fin des idéologies, renaissance des idées" ("The End of Ideology and the Renaissance of Ideas"), written in 1964.[139] When, a few years later, a collection of writings representing both sides of the debate was published in America,[140] he returned to the fray with some ironically titled "Remarques sur le nouvel âge idéologique" ("Remarks on the New Ideological Age").[141] Eventually, towards the end of his life, in an essay written in honour of Edward Shils, he was to characterize his position on "the end of ideology" issue as follows:

The authentic liberal doubts everything and patiently searches for truth. But he will never doubt his firmest moral and intellectual convictions. I was not wrong in opposing this attitude to that of true believers, the faithful of secular religions. I was wrong to call one ideological and the other not. We would do better to look to Pascal and speak of "the proper use of ideologies".[142]

Notes

1. For Aron's assessment of Koestler – "one of the last and greatest of those *intellectuels engagés* who, born in the early years of the century (and so too young to take part in the First World War), were tossed about in the turbulent 1920s and '30s, alternately enchanted and disenchanted by secular religions in search of the absolute" – see "Koestler: un des plus grands", *L'Express* (1653), 18 March 1983: tr. 1983c.

2. H. R. Lottman, *La Rive gauche: Du Front populaire à la guerre froide* (Paris, 1981), p. 358. For a while Aron was also a member of the Comité Promoteur of the Société Européenne de la Culture, which had been established in Venice in 1950 under the auspices of the Biennale. It had attracted the signatures of a large number of French intellectuals, among them Sartre and François Mauriac, and published a journal, *Comprendre*. However, Aron resigned in 1952, on the grounds that the organization's directors were guilty of bad faith: they had published, without prior consultation, a political manifesto which implied a fellow-travelling neutralism vis-à-vis the Soviet Union. Aron argued that this was unacceptable for an association which claimed to stand for cultural freedom (1952l, 1952o).

3. 1950l.

4. 1954h: tr. 1955a.

5. Aron wrote a preliminary paper for the Milan conference and with Michael Polanyi, Sidney Hook and Nicolas Nabokov "conceived the conference and guided it". Edward Shils, "Letter from Milan: The End of Ideology?", *Encounter*, November 1955, pp. 52–8. See also tr. 1956b.

6. 1957h.

7. 1960b: tr. 1963a.

8. 1960c: tr. 1960b. Through the Congress he met such people as its Estonian founder, Michaël Josselson, George F. Kennan, Robert Oppenheimer ("The Father of the Bomb") and, above all, Michael Polanyi (1983a, pp. 238–41). Another participant was Arthur Schlesinger Jr. (see Schlesinger, 1985).

9. *Preuves*, November 1951.

10. 1951l.

11. Other contributors to *Preuves* during its first year included Rémy Roure, Georges Altman, François Bondy, James Burnham, Benedetto Croce, T. R. Fyvel, Jean Guéhenno, Sidney Hook, Karl Jaspers, Melvin Lasky, Herbert Lüthy, Salvador de Madariaga, Gabriel Marcel, Denis de Rougemont, Maximilien Rubel and Ignazio Silone.

12. See, e.g., 1959r.

13. Tr. 1954c. As well as *Preuves* and *Encounter*, the Congress for Cultural Freedom published journals in Spanish (*Cuadernos*), German (*Forum*) and Italian (*Tempo Presente*).

14. 1983a, pp. 237–8.

15. Ibid., p. 335.

16. Massip, 1963.

17. 1955b: tr. 1957b. A paperback version, containing a new preface, was published in 1968 (1968c), and the original edition was reprinted after Aron's death (1983b).

18. 1955a.

19. 1955b, p. 9: tr. p. xi. See, for example, Aron's double critique of Sartre's "Les Communistes et la paix" (1952d, 1954a) and his attack on Merleau-Ponty's justification of Stalinism in *Humanisme et terreur* (1949h), as well as his epilogue to the French edition of *The God that Failed* (1950f). Aron also became involved at this time in a polemic with Isaac Deutscher over the latter's book, *Russia After Stalin* (see 1953i; Deutscher, 1954; 1954j).
20. 1955a, pp. 14, 7.
21. Ibid., pp. 8–9.
22. Maulnier, 1955. Not surprisingly, Jean-Marie Domenach, in *Esprit*, took a different view. Although Aron was "the bourgeoisie's most intelligent ideologist", Domenach was "disappointed" by *Polémiques*, with the exception of the "remarkable" essay, "Histoire et politique" (1949a). Aron, wrote Domenach, aimed too low, distorting but cheapening the arguments of those he was discussing. But he filled his role to perfection, which was "to use, in defence of privilege, the most remarkable intellectual instrument that has ever been formed for human liberation", while venting his guilty conscience on "the *intellectuel de gauche* he might have been" (Domenach, 1955a).
23. Bettiza, 1979. Enzo Bettiza is a writer, journalist (he is an Editor of the Milan newspaper, *Il Giornale*) and Liberal member of the Italian Senate.
24. Ibid., pp. 267–8. Bettiza went on to argue that *L'Opium des intellectuels* had the same impact as Julien Benda's *La Trahison des clercs* a generation earlier. See also Bettiza, 1985.
25. Hersch, 1985, p. 170. Aron's opponent happened to be Georges Suffert, later Editor of the news magazine *Le Point*, who recalled the occasion after Aron's death: "I quickly got on with things – all the more so because a careful reading of *The Opium* had shaken me: what if Aron was right? He must have sensed my discomfiture because, throughout the evening, he remained courteous and amused. Irritated by his arguments, his knowledge of the facts and his rigour, I tried to deliver some cheap blow below the belt. He did not even reply, but simply pinched the microphone. Not a sound. The platform burst out laughing and Aron brilliantly concluded the evening. We left together. I felt ashamed and a little humiliated. Suddenly he turned to me, held out his hand and said with a smile, 'At least you've learnt one thing this evening: never let go of the microphone at a public meeting. *A bientôt*'" (Suffert, 1985, p. 88). The two subsequently became political friends.
26. 1949g, p. 141. See Chapter 15, above.
27. 1955b, pp. 9–10: tr. p. ix.
28. Ibid., pp. 10–11: tr. p. x.
29. Ibid., p. 11: tr. pp. x–xi.
30. Ibid., pp. 21–2: tr. p. 10.
31. Ibid., p. 23: tr. p. 11.
32. Ibid., p. 26: tr. p. 14.
33. Ibid., p. 28: tr. p. 17.
34. Ibid., pp. 32–3: tr. p. 21.
35. Ibid., p. 36: tr. p. 24. In the 1968 paperback edition, Aron replaced the last phrase, "c'est-à-dire l'amour", with a question: "Existe-t-elle?" ("Is there such a thing [as fraternity]?") (1968c, p. 52).
36. 1955b, p. 43: tr. p. 32.

37. Ibid., pp. 43–4: tr. ibid.

38. J.-M. Domenach, "Confrontation", *Esprit*, 20 (196), November 1952.

39. 1955b, p. 45: tr. p. 34.

40. Ibid., pp. 46, 47, 49: tr. pp. 35, 36, 37 (R.C.).

41. Ibid., pp. 50–1: tr. p. 39.

42. Ibid., p. 51: tr. p. 40.

43. Ibid., p. 52: tr. p. 41.

44. Ibid., p. 53: tr. p. 42.

45. Ibid., p. 54: tr. p. 43.

46. Ibid., pp. 54–62: tr. pp. 43–50.

47. The quarrel had begun when Sartre's colleague, Francis Jeanson, wrote a harsh review of Camus' *L'Homme révolté*, *TM*, 7 (79), May 1952. Camus had objected in a letter to "Monsieur le Directeur" and Sartre and Jeanson had replied in the same number (August 1952).

48. 1955b, pp. 62–3: tr. p. 51. The last sentence is omitted in the English translation. Aron came to regret his "disagreeable remarks" about Camus, and the two men in fact ended on good terms (1981a, pp. 178–9: tr. 1983a, p. 153).

49. 1955b, p. 63: tr. pp. 51–2.

50. Ibid., pp. 65–6: tr. p. 54.

51. "Nul homme n'est assez dénué de raison pour préférer la guerre à la paix". These were the words which Aron later had inscribed on his Academician's sword when he entered the Académie des Sciences Morales et Politiques in 1965. See Volume 2, Chapter 1.

52. 1955b, pp. 76–7: tr. p. 65.

53. Ibid., p. 78: tr. p. 66 (R.C.).

54. Ibid., p. 86: tr. p. 74.

55. Ibid., p. 87: tr. p. 75 (R.C.).

56. Ibid., p. 88: tr. pp. 75–6.

57. Ibid., p. 90: tr. p. 78.

58. Ibid., p. 97: tr. p. 85.

59. Ibid., p. 102: tr. p. 90.

60. Ibid., p. 103: tr. p. 91.

61. Ibid., pp. 107–8: tr. p. 96.

62. Ibid., pp. 108, 109: tr. pp. 96, 97.

63. Ibid., pp. 110–11: tr. pp. 98–9.

64. Ibid., p. 125: tr. p. 115.

65. Ibid., p. 126: tr. p. 116. Despite Aron's various "polemics" with Merleau-Ponty ("un homme adorable"), the two men never fell out. In Aron's view, Merleau-Ponty accepted dissent more easily than Sartre. Aron remained on intermittently friendly terms with Merleau-Ponty. The latter wrote him some "very affectionate" letters, for example, at the time of the Algerian question (1981a, p. 179: tr. p. 153). For a recent discussion of Merleau-Ponty's political attitudes, see Simone Goyard-Fabre, "Merleau-Ponty et la politique", *RMM*, 80, 1980, pp. 240–62; and for his final thoughts on the man, see Aron's memoirs, 1983a, pp. 312–16.

66. 1955b, p. 130: tr. p. 120 (R.C.). The 1957 English translation is misleading here because it leaves out the reference to ideology in the first sentence of the second paragraph, as well as a crucial negative.

67. Ibid., pp. 145, 146: tr. pp. 135, 136.
68. Ibid., p. 152: tr. p. 142.
69. Compare Merleau-Ponty, *Humanisme et terreur*, pp. 165–6: "A philosophy of History presupposes that human history is not a simple sum of juxtaposed facts – individual decisions and adventures, ideas, interests, institutions – but that it is, instantaneously and sequentially, a totality moving towards a privileged state which will give meaning to the whole". Aron agreed that society was certainly not a "simple sum of juxtaposed facts", but neither was it an "instantaneous and sequential totality".
70. 1955b, p. 159: tr. p. 149.
71. Ibid., pp. 166–7: tr. pp. 156–7.
72. Ibid., pp. 168–9: tr. p. 158.
73. Ibid., p. 169: tr. pp. 158–9.
74. Ibid., pp. 169–70: tr. p. 159.
75. Ibid., p. 182: tr. p. 171.
76. Ibid., p. 193: tr. p. 182 (R.C.).
77. Ibid., pp. 200–1: tr. p. 190.
78. Ibid., p. 203: tr. p. 192 (R.C.).
79. Ibid., p. 205: tr. p. 194.
80. Ibid., pp. 217–18: tr. pp. 207–8. Aron's second sense of "intelligentsia" followed Crane Brinton's definition in *The Temper of Western Europe* (Harvard, 1954): tr. *Visite aux Européens* (Paris, 1955), p. 14.
81. 1955b, pp. 218–19: tr. pp. 208–9.
82. Ibid., p. 220: tr. p. 210.
83. David Caute, drawing on a number of examples of the alleged dismissal of French Communists from state positions during the Cold War, believes that this claim of Aron's "requires some modification". But Caute relies on the accounts given in *L'Humanité* and *La Nouvelle Critique*, both Party organs, and adds: "Nevertheless, the communists have often exaggerated their case, and it is perhaps not a case which comes well from those who, if given power, would be unlikely to show a liberal attitude toward their academic opponents. . . In certain areas of France, it has been a positive advantage, when applying for a teaching position, or even for a job as a *fonctionnaire*, to be a Party member. Communist scholars are everywhere to be found in the universities; in 1962, Roger Garaudy was appointed by the state to a chair at Clermond Ferrand despite protests from the faculty". David Caute, *Communism and the French Intellectuals, 1914–1960* (London, 1964), pp. 354–5.
84. 1955b, p. 222: tr. p. 212.
85. "English writers of the avant-garde, whose names are probably unknown in the House of Commons, are overcome with rapture when they come to Paris and settle down in Saint-Germain-des-Prés. They at once develop a passionate interest in politics, a subject the dispiriting sobriety of which at home discourages their attention. And indeed the discussions they will hear in Paris are elaborated with a subtlety that cannot but enthral those who live by the mind. The latest article by Jean-Paul Sartre is a political event, or at least it is greeted as such by a circle of people which, though narrow, is convinced of its own importance". Ibid., p. 229: tr. p. 219 (R.C.).
86. Ibid., pp. 230–1: tr. p. 220.

87. Ibid., pp. 234–5: tr. pp. 224–5. In support of this claim, Aron provided a lengthy quotation from Sartre's article, "Les Animaux malades de la rage", *Libération*, 22 June 1953.
88. 1955b, p. 237: tr. p. 227.
89. David Caute has argued that "Aron's paradox. . .appears singularly inappropriate when applied to the large fraternity of communist intellectuals and their occasional allies, unless one were to confuse 'France' with any single political system or government" (Caute, op. cit., p. 213).
90. 1955b, pp. 238–45: tr. pp. 228–35. Although, Aron wrote, the left-wing intellectual in Britain experienced "a kind of solidarity with all the revolutionaries of the world", he had "not yet broken with his country. He shows himself to be no less attached to British parliamentary institutions than the conservatives he detests. He reserves for foreigners the benefits of the Popular Front, from which he himself is protected by the weakness of the British Communist Party. He would readily admit that the strength of Communism in each country is in inverse ratio to the merits of the regime.

   "Thus he would pay tribute to the excellence of the British parliamentary system, would recognize the legitimacy of Communism in France, Italy or China, and would declare himself to be a good patriot as well as a good internationalist. The Frenchman dreams of international reconciliation by the conversion of all non-Frenchmen to France. The Englishman is tempted to believe that no-one outside his happy island is altogether worthy to play cricket or the parliamentary game. It is an odd mixture of arrogance and modesty, which perhaps will have its reward: the peoples of India, of Africa and elsewhere, educated and emancipated by the British, will continue to play cricket and the parliamentary game" (ibid., pp. 244–5: tr. pp. 234–5).
91. Ibid., pp. 248–9: tr. p. 238.
92. Ibid., p. 250: tr. p. 240.
93. See pp. 258–64: tr. pp. 248–54.
94. See pp. 265–73: tr. pp. 254–64.
95. 1944o, 1944p. See Chapter 12, above.
96. 1955b, p. 276: tr. p. 267.
97. *Les Prêtres-ouvriers* (Paris, 1954).
98. 1955b, p. 283: tr. p. 274.
99. Ibid., p. 311: tr. pp. 302–3.
100. Ibid., pp. 319–20: tr. p. 309.
101. Ibid., pp. 320–2: tr. pp. 310–12 (R.C.).
102. Ibid., pp. 327–8: tr. pp. 317–18 (R.C.).
103. Ibid., p. 332: tr. p. 322.
104. Ibid., p. 334: tr. pp. 323–4.
105. "Nous ne sommes pas menacés par l'indifférence". The English translation – "Indifference will not harm us" – is misleading at this point and certainly does not represent Aron's view.
106. Ibid.: tr. p. 324 (R.C.).
107. 1968b, p. 25: tr. 1969f, p. 13. See also the discussion of the book's reception – and in particular the review by Father Dubarle (Dubarle, 1955) – in Aron's memoirs (1983a, pp. 322–31).
108. E.g., Pouillon, 1956; Domenach, 1955b; Nadeau, 1955.

109. Besse, 1955.
110. Kriegel, 1985, p. 60.
111. Sorel, 1955.
112. Salomon, 1985.
113. Duverger, 1955.
114. Ibid.
115. Simon, 1955.
116. Schumann, 1955.
117. Delmas, 1955a, 1955b.
118. Marcel, 1955.
119. Salomon, 1956.
120. Anon., 1955b. It may be deduced from a reference in Aron's memoirs (1983a, p. 336) that Brogan was the author of the review. See also Volume 2, Chapter 1, n.4.
121. Anon., 1955a.
122. Kristol, 1957.
123. Toynbee, 1957, p. 81.
124. Ibid., pp. 82–3.
125. Anon., 1957b.
126. Ibid.
127. Barraclough, 1957.
128. Taylor, 1957.
129. Ibid.
130. Caute, op. cit., pp. 364–5. Caute himself has been criticized, on the other hand, for his failure to assemble "in any one section all the *anti*-Communist arguments put forward by French intellectuals. He refers to them incidentally, but in such a way that an intelligent anti-Communist like Raymond Aron hardly seems to get fair treatment". J. G. Weightman, "The Mandarin Left", *Commentary*, 39 (3), March 1965, pp. 96–8.
131. Rosenberg, 1958.
132. Lichtheim, 1958. "Discursive and rambling", he wrote, "*The Opium of the Intellectuals* is best regarded as a bulky specimen in the great French tradition of essay-writing".
133. S. M. Lipset, "The End of Ideology and the Ideology of the Intellectuals", in J. Ben-David and T. N. Clark (eds), *Culture and its Creators: Essays in Honour of Edward Shils* (Chicago, 1977).
134. 1955o.
135. Edward Shils, "Letter from Milan: The End of Ideology?", *Encounter*, November 1955, pp. 52–8. See n.5, above.
136. Shils, 1958.
137. Tr. 1958d.
138. Aiken, 1964.
139. In 1966a: tr. 1967c. See Volume 2, Chapter 10.
140. Chaim I. Waxman (ed.), *The End of Ideology Debate* (New York, 1968). See tr. 1968g.
141. 1971e, reprinted 1973h.
142. Tr. 1977d. For a brief but illuminating essay on *The Opium of the Intellectuals*, written after Aron's death, see Furet, 1985.

Chronological Table, 1905–1955

———

Personal	National	International
		1904
		Anglo-French entente
1905		
14 March. Born, Paris		
	1906	
	Dreyfus rehabilitated	
1913	*1913*	
Pupil, Lycée Hoche, Versailles	Poincaré President	
	1914	*1914*
	Battle of the Marne	First World War
	1916	
	Battle of Verdun	
	Battle of the Somme	
	1917	*1917*
	Clemenceau Government	Russian Revolution
	1918	
	Nov. Armistice	
	1919	*1919*
	Electoral victory of Bloc National	Treaty of Versailles

Personal	National	International
	1920 Socialist Party Conference at Tours	
1922 Pupil, Lycée Condorcet, Paris	1922 Poincaré Government	
		1923 French occupation of Ruhr
1924 Student, Ecole Normale Supérieure, Paris	1924 Electoral victory of Cartel des Gauches Herriot Government	
	1925 Fall of Herriot Briand's Foreign Ministry	1925 July. Evacuation of Ruhr Oct. Locarno Pact.
	1926 Poincaré Government of National Unity	
1928 Agrégé de philosophie Military service	1928 Poincaré electoral victory	
	1929 Retirement of Poincaré	1929 Sept. European Federal Union proposed by Briand Oct. Wall Street crash
1930 Lektor, University of Cologne		1930 June. French evacuation of Rhineland Sept. Spectacular Nazi gains in Reichstag elections
1931 Lektor, French Institute, Berlin (1931-3)		
	1932 Electoral victory of Cartel des Gauches Herriot Government	1932 March. German presidential election April. Hindenberg re-elected Chancellor July. Further Nazi successes in Reichstag elections
1933 Sept. Marries Suzanne Gauchon Philosophy teacher, Lycée du Havre (1933-4)	1933 Stavisky affair	1933 Jan. Hitler becomes Chancellor Feb. Reichstag fire March. Nazi-Nationalist majority in Reichstag
1934 Birth of eldest daughter, Dominique Secretary, Centre de Documentation Sociale, Paris (1934-9)	1934 Feb. Street riots Fall of Daladier Dec. Laval Government	

Personal	*National*	*International*
1935		**1935**
Lecturer (part-time), Ecole Normale d'Instituteurs, Saint-Cloud (1935–9)		Jan. Saar votes for reunification with Germany
		Sept. Italian invasion of Abyssinia
		Dec. Hoare-Laval Pact
	1936	**1936**
	Jan. Fall of Laval Government	March. German reoccupation of Rhineland
	May. Electoral victory of Popular Front: Blum Government	April. Franco-Soviet Pact ratified
	Occupation of factories Matignon agreements	July. Spanish Civil War begins
	Oct. Devaluation of franc	
1937	**1937**	
Lecturer (temporary part-time), University of Bordeaux (1937–8)	March. Blum's "pause" June. Fall of Blum Government	
1938	**1938**	**1938**
March. Defence of doctoral theses	April. Daladier Government	March. German annexation of Austria
		Sept. Munich
		Dec. Franco-German Declaration of Friendship
1939	**1939**	**1939**
Aug. Appointed Lecturer, University of Toulouse. War service (1939–40)	Sept. War declared Daladier dissolves Communist Party	March. German occupation of Czechoslovakia
		April. Anglo-French guarantee to Poland
		Aug. Franco-Russian Non-Aggression Pact
		Sept. Germany invades Poland.
		Britain and France declare war on Germany.
		Russia invades Poland
1940	**1940**	**1940**
June. Joins Free French in England	May. French front broken near Sedan	May. Germany invades Holland and Belgium
Editor, *La France libre*, London (1940–4)	Reynaud Government	Germany invades France
	June. Pétain obtains Armistice	June. Italy enters war
	July. Government moves to Vichy	De Gaulle in London
	Pétain Head of State	July. British attack French fleet at Mers-el-Kébir
	Laval Chief Minister	Sept. Free French expedition to Dakar
	Oct. Anti-Jewish laws	
	Hitler-Pétain meeting at Montoire	
	Dec. Laval dismissal	

Personal	*National*	*International*
	1941	1941
	Feb. Darlan Chief Minister	June. British and Free French attack on Syria
		Germany invades Russia
		Dec. United States enters war
		Free French landing on Saint-Pierre-et-Miquelon
	1942	1942
	Feb. Trial at Riom of Blum and Daladier	Nov. Allied invasion of French North Africa
	April. Laval returns as Chief Minister	Dec. Darlan assassinated in Algiers
	Nov. Germans enter Unoccupied Zone	Giraud Head of Government in North Africa
	French fleet scuttled at Toulon	
1943	1943	1943
July. Wife and daughter reach London	Nov. Laval's collaborationist Government	June. Committee of National Liberation formed in Algiers
		De Gaulle eliminates Giraud
		Nov. Tehran Conference
1944	1944	1944
June. Birth of second daughter, Emmanuelle, in London	Jan. Darnand Minister of Interior	Jan. Brazzaville Conference
Sept. Returns to Paris	June. Allied landings in Normandy	
	Aug. Liberation of Paris	
	Sept. Provisional Government of National Unanimity under de Gaulle	
1945	1945	1945
Editorial Board, *Les Temps modernes*	April. Mendès-France resigns from Government	Feb. Yalta Conference
Lecturer, Institut d'Etudes Politiques and Ecole Normale d'Administration	Trials of Pétain (July) and Laval (Oct.)	March. Vietnam proclaims independence
March. Joins weekly, *Point de vue*	Oct. Referendum ends Third Republic	April. Truman succeeds Roosevelt
Nov. *Directeur de cabinet* in Malraux's Ministry of Information (till Jan. 1946)	Election of Constituent Assembly	May. Germany surrenders
	Nov. De Gaulle Head of Government	Insurrection and repression in Algeria
		July. Potsdam Conference
		Aug. Atomic bombs on Japan
		Japan surrenders
		Sept. Vietminh proclaims Vietnamese independence
		Dec. Franco-Soviet Pact
1946	1946	1946
April. Joins *Combat*	Jan. Resignation of de Gaulle	March. Churchill's Fulton speech
	Feb. Gouin Government	
	May. Referendum "no" to first Constitution	

Personal	*National*	*International*
	June. Election of second Constituent Assembly De Gaulle's Bayeux speech. Bidault Government Sept. De Gaulle's Epinal speech Oct. Referendum "yes" to second Constitution Nov. National Assembly elections Dec. Blum Government	Sept. Churchill's Zurich speech Oct. Creation of French Union Nov. French shelling of Haiphong Dec. Indo-China War begins
1947 Awarded Legion of Honour June. Joins *Figaro* Member of National Council, RPF	1947 Jan. Auriol President Ramadier Government March. De Gaulle's Bruneval speech April. De Gaulle's Strasbourg speech Formation of RPF May. Communist-supported strikes Ramadier dismisses Communist Ministers De Gaulle's Bordeaux speech Autumn. Further strikes Oct. RPF victory in local elections Nov. Schuman Government	1947 March. Dunkirk Pact Revolt in Madagascar June. Marshall Plan Aug. Algerian Statute adopted
1948 Editor of Calmann-Lévy series, *Liberté de l'Esprit*	1948 July. Marie Government Sept. Schuman Government Queuille Government Oct. Wave of strikes	1948 Feb. Communist *coup* in Prague March. Brussels Pact May. Hague Conference June. Berlin blockade July. Yugoslavia breaks with Moscow Creation of OEEC
	1949 July. National Assembly ratifies Atlantic Pact Oct. Bidault Government	1949 Jan. Council of Europe set up April. Atlantic Pact: NATO formed May. Four-Power Conference on Germany Aug. European Assembly opens in Strasbourg First West German elections Adenauer Chancellor Oct. Communist victory in China

Personal	*National*	*International*
1950	**1950**	**1950**
Executive Committee, Congress for Cultural Freedom	July. Queuille Government	May. Schuman Coal and Steel Plan
July. Birth of third daughter, Laurence	Pleven Government	June. Communist invasion of South Korea
Nov. First visit to USA	Autumn. "Gilson Affair"	Sept. Pleven EDC Plan
Dec. Death of Emmanuelle Aron		
1951	**1951**	**1951**
Sept. Attends San Francisco and Washington Conferences	March. Queuille Government	May. American H-bomb exploded
	June. General Election: RPF set-back	Sept. Japanese Peace Treaty, San Francisco
	Aug. Pleven Government	Washington Conference on EDC
	1952	**1952**
	Jan. Faure Government	Feb. Lisbon Conference approves EDC
	Feb. National Assembly accepts principle of EDC	May. EDC treaty signed
	March. Pinay Government	Sept. Creation of European Constituent Assembly
1953	**1953**	**1953**
Visiting Professor, Tübingen	Jan. Mayer Government	Jan. Eisenhower President
Oct. Visits Far East	April. RPF losses in local elections	March. Death of Stalin
	May. De Gaulle disbands RPF	July. East Berlin riots
	June. Laniel Government	Korean Armistice signed
		Aug. Sultan of Morocco deposed
		Sept. Khruschev attains power
	1954	**1954**
	Jan. Coty President	Jan. Berlin Conference
	June. Mendès-France Government	April. Geneva Peace Conference on Indo-China
	Aug. National Assembly rejects EDC	May. Fall of Dien Bien Phu
	Oct. Ratifies London	July. Indo-China cease-fire signed at Geneva
	Dec. Ratifies Paris Agreement	Mendès-France Tunisian Agreement
		Oct. London Agreement on German rearmament
		Paris Agreement on Western European Union
		West Germany enters NATO
		Nov. Algerian War begins
1955	**1955**	**1955**
Professor of Sociology, Sorbonne	Feb. Faure Government	Jan. Soustelle Governor of Algeria
	March. Senate ratifies Paris Agreement	May. Warsaw Pact signed
		July. Terrorism in Morocco
		Aug. Philippeville massacres in Algeria

500

Bibliography, 1905–1955

This bibliography of Aron's writings and interviews published in French and English up to and including 1955 is as complete as possible; a similar bibliography for the years 1956–85 is to be found in Volume 2. For reasons of space, I have not included works in other languages or the four to five thousand editorials which comprise Aron's regular journalism for *Point de vue* (1945), *Combat* (1946–7), *Le Figaro* (1947–77), *Réalités* (1967–9), *Le Progrès de Lyon* (1977) and *L'Express* (1977–83). I have, however, listed Aron's occasional journalism in these and other newspapers and periodicals.

Other, very incomplete, bibliographies are to be found in 1959b (reprinted in 1961a); Aron's *Festschrift* (Casanova, 1971); Fessard, 1980 (reprinted in 1981a); and 1985q. Perrine Simon of the Institut Raymond Aron is currently compiling a bibliography of all Aron's writings in every language. This is based on my own earlier bibliography (Colquhoun, 1982), which Aron described on the last page of his *Mémoires* as the only "scientific bibliography" of his works in existence (1983a, p. 759). I am grateful to Perrine Simon for the help I have received from her, and to Paul Janssens of the University Faculty of Saint Aloysius, Brussels, for sending me a copy of his work-in-progress on the same subject.

A. Aron's Publications in French, 1905–1955

1928   "A propos de *La Trahison des clercs*", *LP*, avril, pp. 176–8.
1929   "L'influence d'Alain", *La Psychologie et la vie: Revue de psychologie appliquée*, 3 (1), janvier, pp. 10–11.
1930   "Lettre d'Allemagne", *LP*, décembre, p. 570.

1931a   "De Man, *Au delà du Marxisme*", *LP*, janvier, pp. 43–7 (review). Reprinted 1975f.

1931b   "Simples Propositions du pacifisme", *LP*, février, pp. 81–3.

1931c   "Lettre d'Allemagne. Cologne, le 26 février 1931", *LP*, mars, pp. 138–40.

1931d   "Révision des traités: Lettre d'Allemagne", *LP*, mai, pp. 221–3.

1931e   "Lettre d'Allemagne: *List der Venunft* (Ruse de la Raison)", *LP*, juin, pp. 258–9.

1931f   "Lettre d'Allemagne: De l'Anschluss à Hoover. Cologne, 7 juillet", *LP*, juillet, pp. 306–9.

1931g   "'Autre impasse' ou 'devenir présent'", *Europe*, février, pp. 281–6.

1932a   "La Pensée de M. Léon Brunschvicg: à propos de son dernier ouvrage" (*De la Connaissance de soi*), *Revue de synthèse*, 4, octobre, pp. 193–207.

1932b   "Sur le Problème des réparations", *LP*, janvier, pp. 38–40. Reprinted in *Commentaire*, 8 (28–9), 1985, pp. 284–6.

1932c   "Lettre d'Allemagne. Berlin, 29 janvier 1932", *LP*, février, pp. 88–91.

1932d   "Lettre d'Allemagne. Berlin, le 5 mars 1932", *LP*, mars, pp. 151–3.

1932e   "Combien l'Allemagne a-t-elle payé?", *LP*, mai, pp. 250–5.

1932f   "Réflexions de Politique réaliste. Lettre d'Allemagne. Berlin, le 26 avril 1932", *LP*, mai, pp. 265–8.

1932g   "Combien l'Allemagne a-t-elle payé? Remarques et rectifications", *LP*, juin, p. 313.

1932h   "Lettre d'Allemagne. Berlin, le 1er juin 1932", *LP*, juin, pp. 314–17.

1932i   "Elections allemandes: perspectives", *LP*, août, pp. 414–15.

1932j   "Désarmement ou union franco-allemande?" *LP*, août, pp. 422–5.

1932k   "Hess, G., *Alain (Emile Chartier), in der Reihe der franzoesischen Moralisten*", *LP*, octobre, pp. 537–8 (review).

1932l   "D'une Lettre d'Allemagne. Berlin, le 11 novembre", *LP*, novembre, p. 592.

1932m   "Nouvelles Perspectives allemandes", *Europe*, février, pp. 295–305.

1932n   "Allemagne, juin 1932", *Europe*, mai-août, pp. 489–98.

1932o   "Après les Elections", *Europe*, décembre, pp. 625–30.

1932p   "Fried, F., *La Fin du capitalisme*", *Europe*, décembre, pp. 647–8 (review).

1933a   "Réflexions sur le 'pacifisme intégral' (A propos de la brochure, *La Paix sans aucune réserve*, thèse de Félicien Challaye. Documents des *Libres Propos* (1) 1932)", *LP*, janvier, pp. 96–9.

1933b   "Malraux, A., *La Condition humaine*", *LP*, décembre, pp. 653–7 (review). Reprinted in *Commentaire*, 8 (28–9), 1985, pp. 287–90.

1933c   "La révolution nationale en Allemagne", *Europe*, septembre, pp. 125–38.

1933d   "Comte, A., *Lettres inédites à C. de Blignières*; Delvolve, J., *Réflexions sur la pensée comtienne*", *ZS*, 2, pp. 281–3 (reviews).

1933e   "Lettre ouverte d'un jeune Français à l'Allemagne", *Esprit*, 1, pp. 735–43.

1934a   "De l'Objection de conscience", *RMM*, 41, pp. 133–45. Reprinted in 1972a, and in *Commentaire*, 8 (28–9), 1985, pp. 291–7.

1934b   "Note sur l'objet et les divisions de la sociologie et ses rapports avec la philosophie", *AS*, Série A, fascicule 1, pp. 101–16. (Review article on: *Handwörterbuch der Soziologie*, Hrsg. von Vierkandt; *Soziologie von Heute*, Hrsg. von Thurnwald; Mannheim, K., *Die Gegenwartsaufgaben der Soziologie; Ihre Lehrgestalt*; Schütz, A., *Der sinnhafte Aufbau der sozialen Welt*; Sombart, W., *Nationalökonomie und Soziologie*; Steding, C., *Politik und Wissenschaft bei Max Weber*; Bienfait, W.,

Max Webers Lehre vom geschichtlichen Erkennen; Seidler, E., *Die sozialwissenschaftliche Erkenntniss.*)

1934c "Note: Individus et groupes. Société et communauté," *AS*, Série A, fascicule 1, pp. 150–60. (Review article on: Freyer, H., *Soziologie als Wirklichkeit-wissenschaft; Handwörterbuch der Soziologie* (Vierkandt); Hartmann, N., *Das Problem des geistigen Seins*; Jerusalem, F., *Grundzüge der Soziologie*; Seidler, E., *Die sozial-wissenschaftliche Erkenntnis*; Spann, O., *Geschichtsphilosophie*; Tönnies, F., *Ein-führung in die Soziologie*; Von Wiese, L., *System der allgemeinen Soziologie als Lehre von den sozialen Prozessen und den sozialen Gebilden der Menschen*; Leemans, F., *F. Tönnies et la sociologie contemporaine en Allemagne.*)

1934d "Philosophie de l'histoire et sociologie", *AS*, Série A, fascicule 1, pp. 191–200. (Review article on: Heussi, *Die Krisis des Historismus*; Kaufmann, F., *Geschichts-philosophie der Gegenwart*; Weber, A., 'Kultursoziologie' in Vierkandt, A. (ed), *Handwörterbuch der Soziologie*; Mannheim, K., 'Wissenssoziologie' ibid.; Hartmann, N., *Das Problem des geistigen Seins.*)

1934e "Sociologie systématique et sociologie de la culture", *AS*, Série A, fascicule 1, pp. 230–43. (Review article on: Landshut, *Kritik der Soziologie*; Neurath, *Empirische Soziologie*; Rumpf, "Deutsche Volkssoziologie" in *Rahmen einer Sozialen Lebenslehre*; Rumpf, *Soziale Lebenslehre*; Freyer, H., *Soziologie als Wirklichkeitswissenschaft*; Freyer, H., *Einleitung in die Soziologie*; Tönnies, F., *Einfuhrung in die Soziologie*; Jcrusalem, F., *Grundzüge der Soziologie*; Von Wiese, L., *System der allgemeinen Soziologie*; Sombart, 'Grundformen des menschlichen Zusammenlebens' in Wierkandt, A. (ed.), *Handwörterbuch der Soziologie.*)

1934f "Gouhier, H., *La Jeunesse d'Auguste Comte et la formation du positivisme*: 1. *Sous le signe de la liberté* ", *ZS*, 3, pp. 274–5 (review).

1934–5a "Grünwald, E., *Das Problem der Soziologie des Wissens*; Schmidt, F., *Die Theorie der Geisteswissenschaften vom Altertum bis zur Gegenwart*; Landshut, H., *Kritik der Soziologie*; Freyer, H., *Soziologie als Wirklichkeits wissenschaft*", *RP*, 4, pp. 442–6 (reviews).

1934–5b "Cornu, A., *La Jeunesse de Karl Marx. De l'hégélianisme au matérialisme historique (1818–1845); Moses Hess et la gauche hégélienne*", *RP*, 4, pp. 509–11 (rcviews).

1935 *La Sociologie allemande contemporaine* (Paris: Alcan). Tr. 1957a.

1935–6 "Gomperz, H., *Über Sinn und Sinngebilde. Verstehen und Erklären*; Pfister, H., *Die Entwicklung zum Idealtypus*", *RP*, 5, pp. 460–5 (reviews).

1936a "Une Révolution antiprolétarienne: idéologie et réalité du national-socialisme", in Halévy, E. et al., *Inventaires. La Crise sociale et les idéologies nationales* (Paris: Alcan). Reprinted in *Commentaire*, 8 (28–9), 1985, pp. 299–310.

1936b "Descamps, P., *La Sociologie expérimentale*", *AS*, Série A, fascicule 2, pp. 90–2 (review).

1936c "Note sur l'histoire des idées et l'idéologie", *AS*, Série A, fascicule 2, pp. 129–38. (Review article on: Borkenau, F., *Der Uebergang vom feudalen zum buergerlichen Weltbild*; Kafka, G., *Geschichtsphilosophie der Philosophie-Geschichte*; Böhm, F., *Ontologie der Geschichte*; Rothacker, E., *Geschichtsphilosophie*; De Man, *L'Idée socialiste*; Grünwald, E., *Das Problem der Soziologie des Wissens.*)

1936d "Etcheverry, A., *L'Idéalisme français contemporain*", *ZS*, 5, p. 109 (review).

1936e   "Gurvitch, G., *L'Expérience juridique et la philosophie pluraliste du droit*", ZS, 5, pp. 118–19 (review).

1936f   "Fauré-Frémiet, P., *Pensée et récréation*", ZS, 5, pp. 130–1 (review).

1936g   "Arquillière, H. X., *L'Augustinisme politique. Essai sur la formation des idées au Moyen Age*", ZS, 5, pp. 132–3 (review).

1936h   "*La Foule*. Exposés faits par MM. Bohn, Hardy, Alphandéry, Lefebvre, Dupréel. Centre International de Synthèse, 4ᵉ Semaine Internationale (Alcan, 1934)", ZS, 5, p. 151 (review).

1936i   "*Science et loi*. Par MM. Rey, Gonseth, Mineur, Berthoud, Cuénot, Wallon, Halbwachs, Simiand, Chapot. Centre International de Synthèse, 5ᵉ Semaine Internationale (Alcan, 1935)", ZS, 5, pp. 151–2 (review).

1936j   "Desgrippes, G., *Etudes sur Pascal. De l'Automatisme à la foi*", ZS, 5, p. 272 (review).

1936k   "Berr, H., *L'Histoire traditionnelle de la synthèse historique*", ZS, 5, pp. 274–5 (review).

1936l   "Lote, R., *Histoire de la 'culture allemande'*", ZS, 5, p. 292 (review).

1936m   "Hauser, H., *La Paix économique*", ZS, 5, pp. 318–19 (review).

1936n   "Landsberg, P. L., *Essai sur l'experience de la mort*", ZS, 5, pp. 420–1 (review).

1936o   "Bourthoumieux, C., *Essai sur le fondement philosophique des doctrines économiques. Rousseau contre Quesnay*. Raynaud, B., *La Loi naturelle en économie politique. 1. L'Idée de la loi naturelle en économie politique*", ZS, 5, p. 430 (review).

1936p   "Ancel, J., *Géopolitique*", ZS, 5, p. 468 (review).

1936q   "Le Branchu, Y., *Les Origines du capitalisme en Angleterre*", ZS, 5, p. 480 (review).

1936r   Contribution to "Discussion": Elie Halévy, "L'Ere des tyrannies", Séance du 28 novembre 1936, BSFP, 36, pp. 226–8.

1937a   "Les Rapports de la politique et de l'économie dans la doctrine marxiste", in Aron, R. et al., *Inventaires II: L'Economique et le politique* (Paris: Alcan). Reprinted (with minor alterations) in 1972a.

1937b   "La Sociologie", in Aron, R. et al., *Les Sciences sociales en France: enseignement et recherche* (Paris: Hartmann).

1937c   "Réflexions sur les problèmes économiques français", RMM, 44, pp. 793–822. Reprinted in *Commentaire*, 8 (28–9), 1985, pp. 311–26.

1937d   "L'Idéologie", RP, 6, pp. 65–84. Reprinted 1978m.

1937e   "Gouhier, H., *La Jeunesse d'Auguste Comte et la formation du positivisme. T. II: Saint-Simon jusqu'à la restauration*", ZS, 6, p. 188 (review).

1937f   "Alain, *Histoire de mes pensées*; Guéhenno, J., *Jeunesse de la France*; Simon, P.- H., *Les Catholiques, la politique et l'argent*; Fernandez, R., *L'Homme, est-il humain?*; Maulnier, T., *Mythes socialistes*; George, W., *L'Humanisme et l'idée de patrie*; Suarès, A., *Valeurs*", ZS, 6, pp. 223–5 (reviews).

1937g   "*Recherches philosophiques*, 5, 1935–6; Fondane, B., *La Conscience malheureuse*; Hersch, J., *L'Illusion philosophique*; Bachelard, G., *La Dialectique de la durée*", ZS, 6, pp. 417–19 (reviews).

1937h   "De la Harpe, J., *De l'Ordre et du hasard. Le Réalisme critique d'Antoine Augustin Cournot*", ZS, 6, pp. 419–20 (review).

1937i   "Cuvillier, A., *Introduction à la sociologie*", ZS, 6, p. 424 (review).

1937j   "Dolléans, E., *Histoire du mouvement ouvrier. Tome 1: 1830–1871*", ZS, 6, pp. 452–3 (review).

1937k   "Viallate, A., *L'Activité économique en France de la fin du XVIIIe siècle à nos jours*", *ZS*, 6, pp. 487–8 (review).

1937l   "La Sociologie de Pareto", *ZS*, 6, pp. 489–521. Reprinted 1978l.

1937m   "Troisième Centenaire du *Discours de la Méthode*", *ZS*, 6, 648–53 (review of articles and books on Descartes).

1937n   "*Annales sociologiques*, 1936–7", *ZS*, 6, pp. 664–5 (review).

1937o   "Hauser, H., *Recherches et documents sur l'histoire des prix en France de 1500 à 1800*", *ZS*, 6, pp. 731–2 (review).

1937p   "Lettre de M. Raymond Aron" (à propos de Jean Wahl, "Subjectivité et transcendance", séance du 4 décembre 1937), *BSFP*, 37, pp. 205–7.

1937–9   "Monnaie et crédit" (à propos d'un livre récent: Charles Rist, *Histoire des doctrines relatives au crédit et à la monnaie, depuis Law jusqu'à nos jours), Thalès*, 4, pp. 235–53.

1938a   *Essai sur la théorie de l'histoire dans l'Allemagne contemporaine: la philosophie critique de l'histoire* (Paris: Vrin).

1938b   *Introduction à la philosophie de l'histoire: Essai sur les limites de l'objectivité historique* (Paris: Gallimard). Tr. 1961a.

1938c   "Note sur la sociologie de la culture", *AS*, Série A, fascicule 3, pp. 76–83. (Review article on: Weber, A., *Kulturgeschichte als Kultursoziologie*; Mannheim, K., *Mensch und Gesellschaft im Zeitalter des Umbaus*; Tönnies, F., *Geist der Neuzeit*.)

1938d   "Pirou, G., *Economie politique et facultés de droit*", *ZS*, 7, p. 320 (review).

1938e   "Lévy-Bruhl, L., *L'Expérience mystique et les symboles chez les primitifs*; Richard, G., *La Conscience morale et l'expérience morale*; Richard, G., *La Loi morale*; Caillois, R., *Le Mythe et l'homme*; Joussain, A., *Psychologie des masses*; Halbwachs, M., *Morphologie sociale*; Lhomme, J., *Le Problème des classes*; Centre International de Synthèse. Sixième semaine de synthèse: *La notion de progrès devant la science actuelle* (Alcan, 1938); Sartiaux, F., *La Civilisation*; Seignobos, C., *Essai d'une histoire comparée des peuples d'Europe*", *ZS*, 7, pp. 412–18 (reviews).

1938f   "Sociologie et sciences sociales en Allemagne", in *Les Convergences des sciences sociales et l'esprit international*, pp. 33–8. Travaux de la Conférence Internationale des Sciences Sociales, Paris, juillet 1937. Centre d'Etudes de Politique Etrangère. Travaux des groupes d'études. Publication n° 9 (Paris: Hartmann).

1939a   "Le Concept de classe", in Aron, R. et al., *Inventaires III. Classes moyennes* (Paris: Alcan).

1939b   "*L'Ere des tyrannies* d'Elie Halévy", *RMM*, 46, pp. 283–307. Reprinted in *Commentaire*, 8 (28–9), 1985, pp. 328–40.

1939c   "Remarques sur l'objectivité des sciences sociales", *Theoria* (Gothenburg), 5, pp. 161–94.

1939d   "Lévy, H., *Henri Wölfflin. Sa Théorie, ses prédécesseurs*", *ZS*, 8, pp. 293–4 (review).

1939e   With Jean Cavaillès, "Introduction", Albert Lautman, *Nouvelles Recherches sur la structure dialectique des mathématiques* (Paris: Hermann).

1940a   "La Capitulation", *FL*, 1 (1), novembre, pp. 19–26. Reprinted in 1945r.

1940b   "Le Machiavélisme, doctrine des tyrannies modernes", *FL*, 1 (2), novembre, pp. 45–54. Reprinted in 1944a, 1946a.

1940c   "La France était-elle à la veille d'une révolution?", *FL*, 1 (2), décembre, pp. 128–37.

1940d "Chronique de France", *FL*, 1 (2), décembre, pp. 184–96. Reprinted in 1945r, Ch. II.

1941a "Kaufmann, F., *Methodenlehre der Socialwissenschaften*", *AS*, Série A, fascicule 4, pp. 25–9 (review).

1941b *The Social Sciences: Their Relations in Theory and in Teaching* (London 1936); Dugdale, J. E. (ed.), *Further Papers on the Social Sciences: Their Relations in Theory and in Teaching* (London, 1937)", *AS*, Série A, fascicule 4, pp. 30–2 (review).

1941c "Elias, N., *Uber den Prozess der Zivilisation. Vol. I: Wandlungen des Verhaltens in den weltlichen Oberschichten des Abendlandes*", *AS*, Série A, fascicule 4, pp. 54–6 (review).

1941d "*La Notion de progrès devant la science actuelle* (VIᵉ Semaine internationale de Synthèse, 1938); Sartriaux, F., *La Civilisation*", *AS*, Série A, fascicule 4, pp. 56–8 (review).

1941e "Mandelbaum, M., *The Problem of Historical Knowledge: An Answer to Relativism*", *AS*, Série A, fascicule 4, pp. 59–61 (review).

1941f "Korsch, K., *Karl Marx* (London, 1938)", *AS*, Série A, fascicule 4, pp. 93–6 (review).

1941g "Rabaud, E., *Phénomène social et sociétés animales*", *AS*, Série A, fascicule 4, pp. 115–17 (review).

1941h "Gurvitch, G., *Essai de sociologie*", *AS*, Série A, fascicule 4, pp. 117–19 (review).

1941i "Philosophie du pacifisme", *FL*, 1 (3), janvier, pp. 267–74. Reprinted in 1944a, 1946a.

1941j "Chronique de France: Le nouveau régime: les hommes et les idées", *FL*, 1 (3), janvier, pp. 288–99. Reprinted in 1945r.

1941k "Chronique de Francc: Organisation de la misère", *FL*, 1 (4), février, pp. 356–65. Reprinted in 1945r.

1941l "Chronique de France: Le Gouvernement des notables", *FL*, 1 (5), mars, pp. 449–60. Reprinted in 1945r.

1941m "Le Romantisme de la violence", *FL*, 1 (6), avril, pp. 550–9. Reprinted in 1944a, 1946a.

1941n "Chronique de France: Le Problème du ravitaillement", *FL*, 1 (6), avril, pp. 568–76. Reprinted in 1945r.

1941o "Réflexions sur la philosophie bergsonienne", *FL*, 2 (7), mai, pp. 42–54. Reprinted in *Commentaire*, 8 (28–9), 1985, pp. 351–8.

1941p "Chronique de France: Propagandes et opinion", *FL*, 2 (7), mai, pp. 65–71. Reprinted in 1945r.

1941q "Naissance des tyrannies", *FL*, 2 (8), juin, pp. 131–41. Reprinted in 1944a, 1946a.

1941r "Chronique de France: Culture et société", *FL*, 2 (8), juin, pp. 155–66. Reprinted in 1945r.

1941s "Mythe révolutionnaire et impérialisme germanique", *FL*, 2 (9), juillet, pp. 219–27. Reprinted in 1944a, 1946a.

1941t "Chronique de France: Collaboration et exploitation: un an après l'armistice", *FL*, 2 (9), juillet, pp. 243–52. Reprinted in 1945r.

1941u "Louis Lévy, *The Truth about France*", *FL*, 2 (9), juillet, p. 273 (review).

1941v   "Prestige et illusions du citoyen contre les pouvoirs", *FL*, 2 (11), septembre, pp. 416–25. Reprinted in 1944a, 1946a.

1941w   "Chronique de France: Du Gouvernement des notables au régime policier", *FL*, 2 (11), septembre, pp. 426–34. Reprinted in 1945r.

1941x   "A propos de la Morale cartésienne", *FL*, 2 (12), octobre, pp. 492–501.

1941y   "Chronique de France: Etatisme et corporation: la nouvelle organisation de l'industrie française", *FL*, 2 (12), octobre, pp. 521–7. Reprinted in 1945r.

1941z[1]   "Bureaucratie et fanatisme", *FL*, 3 (13), novembre, pp. 49–59. Reprinted in 1944a, 1946a and in *"La France libre". Numéro anthologique: novembre 1940–septembre 1945* (Paris, n.d.).

1941z[2]   "Chronique de France: Défense de l'esprit français", *FL*, 3 (13), novembre, pp. 60–70.

1941z[3]   "Chronique de France: Finances de défaite", *FL*, 3 (14), décembre, pp. 162–9. Reprinted in 1945r.

1942a   "Chronique de France: Autorité de l'état et confiance du peuple", *FL*, 3 (15), janvier, pp. 241–9.

1942b   "Tyrannie et mépris des hommes", *FL*, 3 (16), février, pp. 291–300. Reprinted in 1944a, 1946a.

1942c   "Chronique de France: L'Organisation de la jeunesse française", *FL*, 3 (16), février, pp. 330–9.

1942d   "De la Liberté politique: Montesquieu et Jean-Jacques Rousseau", *FL*, 3 (17), mars, pp. 374–83. Reprinted in 1944a, 1946a.

1942e   "Chronique de France: Crise agricole et bureaucratie", *FL*, 3 (17), mars, pp. 416–22.

1942f   "Défi à Hitler: la France et le procès de Riom", *FL*, 3 (18), avril, pp. 435–43. Reprinted in 1945r.

1942g   "Chronique de France: Prix et salaires en France", *FL*, 3 (18), avril, pp. 498–503.

1942h   "La Stratégie totalitaire et l'avenir des démocraties", *FL*, 4 (19), mai, pp. 29–37. Reprinted in 1944a, 1946a.

1942i   "Chronique de France: Mise au pas?", *FL*, 4 (19), mai, pp. 58–65. Reprinted in 1945r.

1942j   "Henri Bergson, *Essais et témoignages inédits recueillis par Albert Béguin et Pierre Thévenaz*", *FL*, 4 (19), mai, p. 81 (review).

1942k   "Démocratie et enthousiasme", *FL*, 4 (20), juin, pp. 89–96. Reprinted in 1944a, 1946a.

1942l   "Défaite d'hier, leçons actuelles: Le problème militaire au procès de Riom", *FL*, 4 (21), juillet, pp. 209–24. Reprinted in 1945r.

1942m   "Chronique de France: La Comédie politique", *FL*, 4 (22), août, pp. 303–10. Reprinted in 1945r.

1942n   "Bataille des propagandes", *FL*, 4 (23), septembre, pp. 372–9. Reprinted in 1944a, 1946a.

1942o   "Aux Sources de la pensée française" (A propos de Léon Brunschvicg, *Descartes et Pascal, lecteurs de Montaigne*), *FL*, 4 (24), octobre, pp. 441–8 (review).

1942p   "Chronique de France: Nouvelle technique d'exploitation", *FL*, 4 (24), octobre, pp. 465–72. Reprinted in 1945r.

1942q   "La Menace des Césars", *FL*, 5 (25), novembre, pp. 24–31. Reprinted in 1944a, 1946a.

1942r   "Chronique de France: Au Service de l'ennemi", *FL*, 5 (25), novembre, pp. 70–8. Reprinted in 1944a, 1946a. Tr. 1945a.

1942s   "Au Service de l'ennemi – II", *FL*, 5 (26), décembre, pp. 138–45. Reprinted in 1944a, 1946a.

1942t   "Chronique de France: Problèmes du ravitaillement", *FL*, 5 (26), décembre, pp. 152–7. Reprinted in 1945r.

1943a   "De la Violence à la loi", *FL*, 5 (27), janvier, pp. 195–207. Reprinted in 1944a, 1946a.

1943b   "Chronique de France: La Désagrégation du régime de Vichy", *FL*, 5 (27), janvier, pp. 215–22. Reprinted in 1945r.

1943c   "Au Service de l'ennemi – III", *FL*, 5 (28), février, pp. 268–74. Reprinted in 1944a, 1946a.

1943d   "Chronique de France: Collaboration ou abstention?", *FL*, 5 (28), février, pp 303–9. Reprinted in 1945r.

1943e   "Destin des nationalités", *FL*, 5 (29), mars, pp. 339–47. Reprinted in 1944a, 1946a.

1943f   "Chronique de France: Empire de Charlemagne et testament de Richelieu", *FL*, 5 (29), mars, pp. 377–84. Reprinted in 1945r.

1943g   "Du Pessimisme historique", *FL*, 5 (30), avril, pp. 439–46. Reprinted in 1944a, 1946a.

1943h   "Pensée française en exil: I. Le message de Bernanos", *FL*, 6 (31), mai, pp. 22–8.

1943i   "Chronique de France: Le Chaos économique", *FL*, 6 (31), mai, pp. 69–76. Reprinted in 1945r.

1943j   "Vive la République!", *FL*, 6 (32), juin, pp. 81–4.

1943k   "Les Racines de l'impérialisme allemand", *FL*, 6 (32), juin, pp. 110–17. Reprinted in 1944a, 1946a.

1943l   "Chronique de France: Epreuve aggravée", *FL*, 6 (32), juin, pp. 151–7. Reprinted in 1945r.

1943m   "Pensée française en exil: II. Jacques Maritain et la querelle du Machiavélisme", *FL*, 6 (33), juillet, pp. 209–15.

1943n   "Chronique de France: L'Afrique française dans la guerre", *FL*, 6 (33), juillet, pp. 232–6.

1943o   "L'Ombre des Bonapartes", *FL*, 6 (34), août, pp. 280–8. Reprinted in 1946b, and in *Commentaire*, 8 (28–9), 1985, pp. 359–68.

1943p   "Chronique de France: Appauvrissement de la nation", *FL*, 6 (34), août, pp. 310–15. Reprinted in 1945r.

1943q   "Homme d'Etat ou démagogue?", *FL*, 6 (35), septembre, pp. 347–55.

1943r   "A propos de l'Assemblée consultative", *FL*, 6 (36), octobre, pp. 401–4.

1943s   "Remarques sur quelques préjugés politiques", *FL*, 6 (36), octobre, pp. 430–7. (A propos de: Daniel Halévy, *Trois Epreuves, 1814–1871–1940*; Henri Massis, *Les Idées restent*; Thierry Maulnier, *La France, la guerre et la paix*.)

1943t   "Chronique de France: La Fin des équivoques", *FL*, 6 (36), octobre, pp. 463–9. Reprinted in 1945r.

1943u   "Du Renouvellement des élites (I)", *FL*, 7 (37), novembre, pp. 30–8. Reprinted in 1946b.

1943v   "Chronique de France: Note sur l'avenir du franc", *FL*, 7 (37), novembre, pp. 66–72.

1943w   "Du Renouvellement des élites (II)", *FL*, 7 (38), décembre, pp. 111–19. Reprinted in 1946b.

1943x   "René Balbaud, *L'Entente à l'épreuve*", *FL*, 7 (38), décembre, pp. 157–8 (review).

1944a   *L'Homme contre les tyrans* (New York: Editions de la Maison Française).

1944b   "Vers une Assemblée constituante", *FL*, 7 (39), janvier, pp. 161–4.

1944c   "Pour l'Alliance de l'occident", *FL*, 7 (39), janvier, pp. 178–86. Reprinted in 1946b.

1944d   "Chronique de France: Dernières illusions", *FL*, 7 (39), janvier, pp. 230–5. Reprinted in 1945r.

1944e   "Remarques sur l'instabilité politique de la France", *FL*, 7 (40), février, pp. 262–9. Reprinted in 1946b. Tr. 1945b.

1944f   "Donald Monroe", *FL*, 7 (41), mars (obituary).

1944g   "Le Renforcement du pouvoir – I: De l'instabilité ministérielle", *FL*, 7 (41), mars, pp. 342–9. Reprinted in 1946b.

1944h   "Chronique de France: Les Gangsters au pouvoir", *FL*, 7 (41), mars, pp. 374–9. Reprinted in 1945r.

1944i   "Le Renforcement du pouvoir – II: De l'efficacité gouvernementale", *FL*, 7 (42), avril, pp. 447–54. Reprinted in 1946b.

1944j   "Chronique de France: Vers la deuxième bataille de France", *FL*, 7 (42), avril, pp. 458–62. Reprinted in 1945r.

1944k   "Garanties de la liberté", *FL*, 8 (43), mai, pp. 32–9. Reprinted in 1946b.

1944l   "La Philosophie de Léon Brunschvicg", *FL*, 8 (44), juin, pp. 105–12. Reprinted 1945s. (Commemorative lecture on death of Brunschvicg, delivered on 28 April 1944 at French Institute, London.)

1944m   "En France libérée: Monnaie et ravitaillement", *FL*, 8 (45), juillet, pp. 176–81.

1944n   "Jean Schlumberger, *Nouveaux Jalons*", *FL*, 8 (44), juin, pp. 152–3 (review).

1944o   "L'Avenir des religions séculières – I", *FL*, 8 (45), juillet, pp. 210–17. Reprinted in 1946b, and in *Commentaire*, 8 (28–9), 1985, pp. 369–76.

1944p   "L'Avenir des religions séculières – II", *FL*, 8 (46), août, pp. 269–77. Reprinted in 1946b, and in *Commentaire*, 8 (28–9), 1985, pp. 376–83.

1944q   "En France libérée: Situation de l'industrie", *FL*, 8 (46), août, pp. 297–301.

1944r   "Redevenir une grande puissance", *FL*, 8 (47), septembre, pp. 322–30. Reprinted in 1946b.

1944s   "En France libérée: Esquisse de la situation politique", *FL*, 8 (47), septembre, pp. 371–6.

1944t   "Organisation des partis", *FL*, 8 (48), octobre, pp. 402–7. Reprinted in 1946b.

1944u   "En France libérée: Le Gouvernement provisoire de la République", *FL*, 8 (48), octobre, pp. 444–8.

1944v   "Nouvelle Entente", *FL*, 9 (49), novembre, pp. 1–4.

1944w   "En France libérée: Malaise et espérance (Paris, fin octobre 1944)", *FL*, 9 (49), novembre, pp. 52–8.

1944x   "Le Nerf de la paix", *FL*, 9 (50), décembre, pp. 77–9.

1944y   "Signification des problèmes français", *FL*, 9 (50), décembre, pp. 80–7. Reprinted in 1946b.

1944z[1]   "Chronique de la France libérée: Au Seuil de l'hiver (Paris, fin novembre 1944)", *FL*, 9 (50), décembre, pp. 129–34.

1944z[2]   With Stanislas Szymonzyk, *L'Année cruciale: juin 1940–juin 1941*. Par le critique militaire de la revue, *La France libre* (London: Hamish Hamilton).

1944z[3]   "Préface", *Offrande à la France* (London: Société des Editions de la France Libre).

1944z[4]   "Léon Brunschvicg", *France*, 18 février.

1944z[5]   "Les Conditions de la grandeur française", *Combat*, 25 octobre.

1945a   "Diplomatie élastique", *FL*, 9 (51), janvier, pp. 151–4.

1945b   "Chronique de la France libérée: La Scène politique", *FL*, 9 (51), janvier, pp. 201–5.

1945c   "Pierre-Henri Simon, *La France à la recherche d'une conscience*; André Hauriou, *Le Socialisme humaniste*", *FL*, 9 (51), janvier, pp. 218–24 (review).

1945d   "Politique sur le continent", *FL*, 9 (52), février, pp. 242–9. Reprinted in 1946b.

1945e   "Victoire idéologique?", *FL*, 9 (53), mars, pp. 333–40. Reprinted in 1946b.

1945f   "Chronique de la France libérée: Vers la Sortie du tunnel", *FL*, 9 (53), mars, pp. 365–70.

1945g   "Jacquier-Bruère, *Refaire la France – l'effort d'une génération*", *FL*, 9 (53), mars, pp. 382–4 (review).

1945h   "Esquisse des problèmes de la réforme de l'enseignement – I", *FL*, 9 (54), avril, pp. 413–17. Reprinted in 1946b.

1945i   "Chronique de la France libérée: Gouvernement, Assemblée, nation", *FL*, 9 (54), avril, pp. 443–9.

1945j   "Simone de Beauvoir, *Pyrrhus et Cinéas*", *FL*, 9 (54), avril, pp. 468–70 (review).

1945k   "L'Age des empires", *FL*, 10 (55), mai, pp. 13–20. Reprinted in 1946b.

1945l   "Chronique de France: L'Expérience Pleven", *FL*, 10 (55), mai, pp. 60–70.

1945m   "Esquisse des problèmes de la réforme de l'enseignement – II", *FL*, 10 (56), juin, pp. 92–6. Reprinted in 1946b.

1945n   "Dominique Parodi, *Le Problème politique et la démocratie*", *FL*, 10 (56), juin, pp. 160–1 (review).

1945o   "Révolution et rénovation – I", *FL*, 10 (58), août, pp. 267–76. Reprinted in 1946b.

1945p   "Révolution et rénovation – II", *FL*, 10 (59), septembre, pp. 352–6. Reprinted in 1946b.

1945q   "Jean-Jacques Bernard, *Le Camp de la mort lente*", *FL*, 10 (59), septembre, pp. 403–4 (review).

1945r   *De l'Armistice à l'insurrection nationale* (Paris: Gallimard).

1945s   "La Philosophie de Léon Brunschvicg", *RMM*, 50, pp. 127–40. Reprint of 1944l.

1945t   With Stanislas Szymonzyk, *1940–41: La Grande Bretagne contre la menace hitlérienne*. Texte tirée de *L'Année cruciale*, livre du critique militaire de la revue *La France libre* (Paris: Sans nom d'éditeur).

1945u   "A propos de la Constitution de la IVᵉ République", in Aron, R. and Clairens, F., *Les Français devant la Constitution* (Paris: Editions Défense de la France), pp. 81–133.

1945v   "Les Désillusions de la liberté", *TM*, 1, pp. 76–105.

1945w   "Après l'Evénement, avant l'Histoire", *TM*, 1, pp. 143–62.

1945x   "La Chance du socialisme", *TM*, 1, pp. 227–47.

1945y   "Jean Cavaillès", *Le Monde*, 12 juillet (obituary).

1945z   "Préface", Jean-Claude Diamant-Berger, *Poèmes* (London: Kelihir, Hudson and Kearns). Reprinted in 1945z[1].

1945z[1]   "Jean-Claude Diamant-Berger", *Renaissances* (17), décembre, pp. 50–1. Reprint of 1945z.

1946a   *L'Homme contre les tyrans* (Paris: Gallimard). New edn of 1944a.

1946b   *L'Age des empires et l'avenir de la France* (Paris: Editions Défense de la France).

1946c   "Remarques sur la politique étrangère de la France", in 1946b. Tr. 1945c.

1946d   "Etats démocratiques et Etats totalitaires", *BSFP*, 40, pp. 41–92 (paper to the Société Française de Philosophie, 17 June 1939, with discussion by MM. Basch, Berthod, Boegner, Maritain, Mantoux, Maublanc, Parodi, Rist, Vermeil). Reprinted (abridged) 1983f.

1946e   "Une Constitution provisoire", *TM*, 1, pp. 1627–41.

1946f   "Les Limites de la théorie économique classique", *Critique*, 1, pp. 510–19 (review of Jacques Rueff, *L'Ordre social*; Jean Lescure, *Etude sociale comparée des régimes de liberté et des régimes autoritaires*).

1946g   "Préface", Etienne Mantoux, *La Paix calomniée ou Les Conséquences économiques de M. Keynes* (Paris: Gallimard).

1947a   "Méditations sur la défaite", *Critique*, 2, pp. 439–47 (review of Marc Bloch, *L'Etrange Défaite*).

1947b   "Préface", General John R. Deane, *L'Etrange Alliance* (Paris: Stock).

1947c   "France-Angleterre dans la reconstruction européenne", *Cahiers du Monde Nouveau*, 3 (7), septembre, pp. 117–23. Reprinted 1947d.

1947d   "Conclusion: France-Angleterre dans la reconstruction européenne", in A.-H. Adrian et al. *Angleterre 1947* (Paris: Editions du Monde Nouveau). Reprint of 1947c.

1947e   Contribution to "Discussion" of "Communication" by Jacques Rueff, "Sur les Fondements de l'ordre dans les sociétés humaines". Séance du 25 mai 1946, *BSFP*, 41, pp. 67–101.

1947f   "Qui gouverne la France?", *Réalités* (23), décembre, pp. 37–48.

1947g   "Réponse aux 'Questions du communisme'", *Confluences*, 8 (18), pp. 17–24.

1948a   *Le Grand Schisme* (Paris: Gallimard).

1948b   *Introduction à la philosophie de l'histoire: Essai sur les limites de l'objectivité historique* (Paris: Gallimard). New edn of 1938b. Tr. 1961a.

1948c   "Avant-propos", Elie Halévy, *Histoire du socialisme européen* (Paris: Gallimard).

1948d   "Remarques sur les rapports entre existentialisme et marxisme", in *L'Homme, le Monde, l'Histoire* (Paris: Arthaud). Lecture at the Collège Philosophique, 6 February 1947. Reprinted as "Marxisme et existentialisme" in 1970b. Tr. 1969b.

1948e   "L'Editorialiste", in Fondation Nationale des Sciences Politiques, *Problèmes et techniques de la presse* (Paris: Editions Domat-Montchrestien), pp. 65–83 (lecture at the Institut d'Etudes Politiques). Reprinted in *Commentaire*, 8 (28–9), 1985, pp. 387–96.

511

1948f   *Les Conséquences sociales de la guerre* (Paris: Collège Libre des Sciences Sociales et Economiques, roneo). (Six lectures: "La Structure de la politique mondiale et le destin de l'Europe"; "Du Gaullisme au RPF"; "Problèmes économiques de trois années"; "Théorie et pratique de la IVᵉ République"; "En quête d'un régime politique"; "Conclusion".)

1948g   "Discours à des étudiants allemands sur l'avenir de l'Europe", *TR* (1), janvier, pp. 63–86 (lecture to a student audience in Munich).

1948h   "Paix impossible, guerre improbable", *TR* (3), mars, pp. 411–33. Extract from 1948a, pp. 13–30.

1948i   Contribution to "Discussion" of "Communication" by Jean Hyppolite, "La Structure du *Capital* et de quelques présuppositions philosophiques dans l'oeuvre de Marx". Séance du 10 avril 1948, *BSFP*, 42, pp. 169–203.

1948j   "Du Gaullisme au RPF", *Cahiers du Monde Nouveau*, 4 (3), mars, pp. 5–19. Reprinted in 1948k.

1948k   "Du Gaullisme au RPF", in *Bilan français depuis la Libération* (Paris: Editions du Monde Nouveau), pp. 5–19. Reprint of 1948j.

1948l   "Lettre de Raymond Aron", *TM*, 4, p. 957.

1948m   "L'ONU vivra-t-elle?", *Réalités* (32), septembre, pp. 8–9.

1948n   "En causant avec James Burnham", *Fig. Lit.*, 10 janvier.

1948o   "Témoignage". Unpublished evidence, collected by Madame Granet, 26 octobre 1948. Archives, Bibliothèque du Comité d'Histoire de la Deuxième Guerre Mondiale, Paris.

1948p   "De la Stabilité à la confiance", *France Illustration*, 7 août, p. 127.

1948q   "Le Mode de scrutin déterminera-t-il l'avenir de la Quatrième République?", *France Illustration*, 18 décembre, p. 576.

1949a   "Note sur les rapports de l'Histoire et de la Politique", *RMM*, 44. Reprinted in 1955a. Tr. 1978i.

1949b   "Introduction à l'étude des partis politiques" (Paris: Fondation Nationale des Sciences Politiques), pp. 9–28. (Association Française de Science Politique. Journées d'études des 26 et 27 novembre 1949. Les Partis politiques. Le Vocabulaire politique. Le Role des croyances économiques dans la vie politique.)

1949c   "Témoignage", *In Memoriam Paul Desjardins (1859–1940)*. Bulletin de l'Union pour la Vérité, Cahiers de Pontigny (Paris: Les Editions de Minuit), pp. 75–8.

1949d   "Le Monde déchiré" (pp. 331–6) and "Conclusion" (pp. 421–2), *Trente ans de l'histoire: 1918–1948: de Clemenceau à De Gaulle* (Paris: Edition Sant'Andrea).

1949e   "Le Pacte atlantique", *LE* (3), avril, pp. 52–4. Reprinted in *Commentaire*, 8 (28–9), 1985, pp. 397–402.

1949f   "Réponse à Jean-Paul Sartre" (1), *LE* (5), juin, pp. 101–3.

1949g   "Réponse à Jean-Paul Sartre" (2), *LE* (6), été, pp. 137–41.

1949h   "Messianisme ou sagesse?", *LE* (7), décembre, pp. 159–62. Reprinted in 1955a.

1949i   "Les Chances d'un règlement européen", *PE*, 14 (3), juin, pp. 249–62 (lecture at Centre d'Etudes de Politique Etrangère, 29 March 1949).

1949j   "Les Deux Voix de la tyrannie: Introduction à *Timoléon, Réflexions sur la tyrannie*, de Amédée Ponceau", *L'Age Nouveau* (42), octobre, pp. 43–4. Extract from 1950e.

1949k   "Perspectives de la guerre froide", *Réalités* (37), février, pp. 12–14.

1949l   "Transformations du monde de 1900 à 1950: Déplacement du centre de gravité international", *Réalités* (47), décembre, pp. 70–2, 108–12.

1949m   "Mystique de l'emprunt", *France Illustration*, 12 février, pp. 147–8.

1950a   *La Sociologie allemande contemporaine* (Paris: Presses Universitaires de France). New edn of 1935. Tr. 1957a.

1950b   *La Philosophie critique de l'histoire: essai sur une théorie allemande de l'histoire* (Paris: Vrin). New edn of 1938a.

1950c   "Philosophie de l'histoire", in *L'Activité philosophique contemporaine en France et aux Etats-Unis. Tome Second. La Philosophie française* (Paris: Presses Universitaires de France), pp. 320–40. Tr. 1950b.

1950d   "Démocraties au XXᵉ siècle", *Encyclopédie politique de la France et du monde* (2ᵉ édition). *La France et l'Union française, Tome premier* (Paris: Editions de l'Encyclopédie Coloniale et Maritime), pp. 159–74.

1950e   "Introduction", Amédée Ponceau, *Timoléon: Réflexions sur la tyrannie* (Paris: Editions du Myrte).

1950f   "Fidélité des apostats". Postface, *Le Dieu des ténèbres* (Paris: Calmann-Lévy). Reprinted 1950g, and in 1955a.

1950g   "Fidélité des apostats", *TR* (30), juin, pp. 52–65. Reprint of 1950f.

1950h   "La Surprise technique", *TR* (34), octobre, pp. 54–75 (extract from 1951a, Ch. I).

1950i   "Dynamisme de la guerre totale", *TR* (35), novembre, pp. 21–43 (extract from 1951a, Ch. II).

1950j   "Le Mythe léniniste de l'impérialisme (1)", *LE* (10), mai, pp. 65–8, 96 (extract from 1951a, Ch. III, pp. 63–72). Tr. 1951f.

1950k   "Le Mythe léniniste de l'impérialisme (2)", *LE* (11–12), juin-juillet, pp. 136–41 (extract from 1951a, Ch. III, pp. 72–84). Tr. 1951f.

1950l   "Impostures de la neutralité", *LE* (13), septembre, pp. 151–6. Reprinted in 1955a. Text of speech written for the first Congress for Cultural Freedom, Berlin, June 1950.

1950m   "Du Messianisme à la tyrannie", *LE* (16), décembre, pp. 247–8. Reprinted 1951b.

1950n   *L'Economie française au carrefour* (Paris: Publicis).

1950o   "La Paix, c'est peut-être la guerre froide", *Réalités* (52), mai, pp. 32–3.

1950p   "Les Trusts: légendes et réalités", *Réalités* (55), août, pp. 61–5.

1950q   "La Science politique en France", in *La Science politique contemporaine. Contribution à la recherche, la méthode et l'enseignement* (Paris: Unesco), pp. 52–68. Tr. 1950c.

1951a   *Les Guerres en chaîne* (Paris: Gallimard). Tr. 1954a.

1951b   "Préface", Branko Lazitch, *Lénine et la IIIᵉ Internationale* (Neuchâtel: Editions de la Baconnière). First published 1950m.

1951c   "De la Trahison", Preface to André Thérive, *Essais sur les trahisons* (Paris: Calmann-Lévy). Reprinted 1951d, and in 1955a. Tr. (in part) 1954e.

1951d   "De la Trahison", *TR* (47), novembre, pp. 48–69. Reprint of 1951c. Tr. (in part) 1954e.

1951e   "Carrefour de l'Histoire", *LE* (19), mars, pp. 69–73. Reprinted 1951a, pp. 108–12, 197–203.

1951f   "La Guerre et l'Etat total", *LE* (20), avril, pp. 101–4. Reprinted 1951a, Ch. IV, pp. 98–107.

1951g   "Foi sans illusions", *LE* (22), juin, pp. 161–5. Reprinted 1951a, Conclusion, III, pp. 486–97.

1951h   "Du Préjugé favorable à l'égard de l'Union Soviétique", *LE* (24), octobre, pp. 225–30 (text of written contribution to the 1951 Congress of the Société du Mont-Pélérin).

1951i   "Réflexions sur la guerre possible" (1), *LE* (26), décembre, pp. 289–93 ("A propos d'une polémique avec *Le Monde*") (see Duverger, 1951).

1951j   "De la Paix sans victoire: note sur les relations de la stratégie et de la politique", *RFSP*, 1, pp. 241–55. Reprinted in 1972a.

1951k   "De la Vérification en histoire", *Revue internationale de philosophie* (Brussels), 5, pp. 367–80.

1951l   "Conditions d'une détente", *Preuves* (8), octobre, pp. 3–5 (on George Kennan, "America and the Russian Future", *Foreign Affairs*, April 1951).

1951m   "Préface", Harold D. Lasswell and Daniel Lerner (eds), *Les "Sciences de la politique" aux Etats-Unis: The Policy Sciences in the United States*, pp. xi–xvi. Cahiers de la Fondation Nationale des Sciences Politiques, 19 (Paris: Armand Colin).

1951n   "Les Contradictions de la démocratie", *La Nef*, avril-mai, pp. 68–87 (extract from 1951a).

1951o   "Le Dilemme américain", *Réalités* (62), mars, pp. 34–5. Tr. 1951g.

1951p   "Comment l'Etat doit choisir ses grands commis", *Réalités* (64), mai, pp. 40–1.

1951q   "Incertitude au Kremlin", *Réalités* (70), novembre, p. 16.

1951r   "L'Allemagne et l'Europe", *Mouvement Européen. Rapport I* (Hamburg).

1952a   "Remarques sur la pensée politique d'Alain", *RMM*, 57, pp. 187–99. Reprinted in *Commentaire*, 8 (28–9), 1985, pp. 403–11.

1952b   "Alain et la politique", *NRF*, septembre. Reprinted in 1972a.

1952c   "Préface", George F. Kennan, *La Diplomatie américaine* (Paris: Calmann-Lévy).

1952d   "Jean-Paul Sartre et le prolétariat ou la grande peur du mal-pensant", *Fig. Lit.*, 27 septembre. Reprinted in 1955a.

1952e   "Réflexions sur la guerre possible" (2), *LE* (27), janvier, pp. 15–18.

1952f   "En quête d'une stratégie: I. Le partage du monde", *LE* (29), mars, pp. 65–70.

1952g   "En quête d'une stratégie: II. Les fausses alternatives", *LE* (30), avril, pp. 111–16.

1952h   "Séduction du totalitarisme et justification de la liberté", *LE* (31–2), mai-juin, pp. 129–36. Reprinted in 1955a. Tr. 1953b. (Lecture to the Congrès des Amis de la Liberté, Paris, 18 May 1952.)

1952i   "Science et politique chez Max Weber et aujourd'hui" (1), *LE* (34), octobre, pp. 235–40 (expanded version of lecture at University of Tübingen).

1952j   "Science et politique chez Max Weber et aujourd'hui" (2), *LE* (35), novembre, pp. 264–70.

1952k   "Le Dialogue des Quatre sur l'Allemagne", *PE*, 17 (3), juin-juillet, pp. 135–42 (lecture at Centre d'Etudes de Politique Etrangère, 10 April 1952).

1952l   "A propos de la 'Société Européenne de Culture'", *Preuves* (13), mars, pp. 31–6. Reprinted 1952o.

1952m   "Les Deux Tentations de l'européen", *Preuves* (16), juin, pp. 9–10. Tr. 1952m and 1952n.

1952n   "Discours aux étudiants allemands", *Preuves* (18–19), août, pp. 3–9 (lecture at Frankfurt University, 30 June 1952). Reprinted in part in *Commentaire*, 8 (28–9), 1985, pp. 412–15.

1952o   "La Liberté de la culture", *Comprendre* (5/6), juillet, pp. 214–20 (reprint of 1952l, together with reply by Umberto Campagnolo).

1952p   "L'Unité économique de l'Europe", *La Revue libre*, octobre, pp. 3–22.

1952q   "L'Inflation", *Réalités* (72), janvier, pp. 63–6, 103. Tr. 1952h.

1952r   "Comment financer les dépenses d'équipement", *Réalités* (74), mars, pp. 80–1, 114, 117. Tr. 1952i.

1953a   "Postface", James Burnham, *Contenir ou libérer* (Paris: Calmann-Lévy).

1953b   "En quête d'une philosophie de la politique étrangère", *RFSP*, 3, pp. 69–91. Reprinted in 1972a. Tr. 1960g.

1953c   "Superstition de l'Histoire", *LE* (38), février, pp. 33–6. Reprinted in 1955a.

1953d   "Après Staline", *LE* (41), juin-juillet, pp. 129–34. Tr. 1954a, pp. 329–40.

1953e   "La Politique américaine des visas", *Preuves* (23), janvier, pp. 68–70. Tr. 1952b.

1953f   "James Burnham et la politique de libération", *Preuves* (27), mai, pp. 3–17. Reprint of 1953a.

1953g   "Risques et chances d'une économie dominante", *Preuves* (29), juillet, pp. 5–17.

1953h   "Réponse de M. Raymond Aron", *Preuves* (29), juillet, pp. 94–5 (reply to letter from Jan Ulatowski, "A propos de 'James Burnham et la politique de libération'" (1953f)).

1953i   "La Russie après Staline", *Preuves* (32), octobre, pp. 5–13 (review of Isaac Deutscher, *Russia after Stalin*).

1953j   "La Vérité sur les procès derrière le rideau de fer", *Réalités* (87), avril, pp. 98–103.

1953k   "Les Contradictions internes de la société soviétique", *Réalités* (89), juin, pp. 84–7, 111.

1954a   "Jean-Paul Sartre, le prolétariat et les communistes", *La Revue de Paris*, juin, pp. 88–99. Reprinted in 1955a.

1954b   "De quoi disputent les nations?", *La Nouvelle NRF* (22), octobre, pp. 612–37. Reprinted in 1955a. Tr. 1955e.

1954c   "De l'Analyse des constellations diplomatiques", *RFSP*, 4, pp. 237–51 ("Extrait d'une *Introduction à une sociologie des relations internationales*"). Reprinted in 1972a.

1954d   "Note sur la Stratification du pouvoir", *RFSP*, 4, pp. 469–83.

1954e   "L'Essence du totalitarisme", *Critique* (80), janvier, pp. 51–70 (review article: Hannah Arendt, *The Origins of Totalitarianism*; Léon Poliakov, *Bréviaire de la haine*; Crane Brinton, *The Anatomy of Revolution*; A. Weissberg, *L'Accusé*; F. Beck and W. Godin, *Russian Purge and the Extraction of Confession*). Reprinted in part in *Commentaire*, 8 (28–9), 1985, pp. 416–25.

1954f   "L'Avenir du Japon", *Preuves* (36), février, pp. 33–43.

1954g   "La Révolte asiatique connaît-elle ses limites?", *Preuves* (37), mars, pp. 44–54.

1954h   "Les Concepts de vérité de classe et de vérité nationale dans le domaine des sciences sociales", *Preuves* (37), mars. Supplément: "Science et Liberté", Rapports et débats du Congrès pour la Liberté de la Culture, Hambourg, 23–26 juillet 1953, pp. 14–21. Tr. 1955a.

1954i   "L'Asie entre Marx et Malthus: Le mirage de la méthode soviétique d'industrialisation", *Preuves* (39), mai, pp. 21–32. Tr. 1954c.

1954j   "Un Croisé de l'anti-anticommunisme", *Preuves* (39), mai, pp. 66–70 (reply to Deutscher, 1954).

1954k   "La Rencontre de l'Asie et de l'Occident: La revanche militaire de l'Asie", *Preuves* (41), juillet, pp. 8–19.

1954l   "La Coopération nécessaire: en quête d'une méthode", *Monde Nouveau Paru*, 10 (80–81), juin-sept., pp. 29–38.

1954m   "Problèmes actuels de la diplomatie en Extrême-Orient", *PE*, 19 (1), février-mars, pp. 29–44 (lecture at the Centre d'Etudes de Politique Etrangère, 18 December 1953).

1954n   "Les Conditions de la paix en Indochine", *Réalités* (98), mars, pp. 72–6. Tr. 1954f.

1954o   "Ce que signifie le développement des échanges avec l'Est", *Réalités* (99), avril, pp. 74–9. Tr. 1954g.

1954p   "Qui gouverne l'URSS?", *Réalités* (100), mai, pp. 111–13. Tr. 1954h.

1955a   *Polémiques* (Paris: Gallimard). Contains 1952d, 1954a, 1949h, 1950f, 1951c, 1952h, 1953c, 1949a, 1950l, 1954b.

1955b   *L'Opium des intellectuels* (Paris: Calmann-Lévy). Tr. 1957b.

1955c   "Dialogue entre Raymond Aron et l'auteur", in Crane Brinton, *Visite aux Européens* (Paris: Calmann-Lévy), pp. 119–209.

1955d   "Réflexions sur la politique et la science politique française", *RFSP*, 5, pp. 5–20. Reprinted in 1972a.

1955e   "Electeurs, partis et élus", *RFSP*, 5, pp. 245–66. Reprinted in 1972a.

1955f   "Les Intellectuels français et l'utopie", *Preuves* (50), avril, pp. 5–14.

1955g   "Visage du Communisme en France et en Italie", *Preuves* (54), août, pp. 38–41 (text of Preface to Italian edn of *Polémiques*).

1955h   "A l'Age atomique peut-on limiter la guerre?", *Preuves* (58), décembre, pp. 30–9. Reprinted in 1972a. Tr. 1956c.

1955i   "Ouvriers, prolétaires et intellectuels", *Diogène* (10), pp. 38–56. Tr. 1955d.

1955j   "La Haine, ses origines religieuses et sociales", *Evidences* (53), décembre, pp. 43–6.

1955k   "L'Ethnologue entre les primitifs et la civilisation", *Fig.Lit.*, 24 décembre (review of Claude Lévi-Strauss, *Tristes Tropiques*).

1955l   "La Situation dans le Sud-Est asiatique: de Bangkok à Bandoeng", *PE*, 20 (3), juin-juillet, pp. 283–98 (lecture at the Centre d'Etudes de Politique Etrangère, 29 April 1955).

1955m   "Idéologie communiste et religion", *La Revue de Paris*, mai, pp.70–7 (extract from 1955b, pp. 293–303).

1955n   "L'Opium des intellectuels ou le mythe du prolétariat", *Nouvelle NRF*, 3 (mai), pp. 788–813.

1955o   "Fin de l'Age idéologique?", in *Frankfurter Beitrage zur Soziologie. Band 1: Soziologica* (Frankfurt), pp. 219–33 (reprint of 1955b, Conclusion).

1955p   "L'Asie entre l'URSS et les Etats-Unis", *Les Annales: Revue mensuelle des lettres françaises*, mars, pp. 24–38.

B. English Translations and Writings in English, 1905–1955

1945a   "Serving the Enemy". Tr. of 1942r, in J. G. Weightman (ed. and translator), *French Writing on English Soil* (London: Sylvan Press).

1945b   "Reflections on the Political Instability of France". Tr. of 1944e, in J. G. Weightman (ed. and translator), *French Writing on English Soil* (London: Sylvan Press).

1945c   "Reflexions on the Foreign Policy of France". Tr. of 1946c by Daphne and Marjorie Kirkpatrick, in *IA*, 21, pp. 437–47.

1947   "Frustration in France", *The Times*, 26 July (letter to the Editor).

1949a   "The Crisis of the Fourth Republic", *Partisan Review*, 16, pp. 400–6.

1949b   *France and Europe*. The Human Affairs Pamphlets (Hinsdale, Illinois: Henry Regnery Company).

1950a   "The Philosophy of History". Tr. of 1961b, in *Chambers's Encyclopedia*. Reprinted in tr. 1978a.

1950b   "The Philosophy of History". Tr. of 1950c, in Martin Farber (ed.), *Philosophic Thought in France and the United States: Essays Representing Major Trends in Contemporary French and American Philosophy*. University of Buffalo Publications in Philosophy (New York: Buffalo).

1950c   "Political Science in France". Tr. of 1950q, in *Contemporary Political Science: A Survey of Methods, Research and Teaching* (Paris: Unesco), pp. 48–64.

1950d   "Social Structure and the Ruling Class (1)", *BJS*, 1, pp. 1–16 (text of three lectures delivered at the London School of Economics).

1950e   "Social Structure and the Ruling Class (2)", *BJS*, 1, pp. 126–43 (text of three lectures delivered at the London School of Economics).

1950f   "The Atomic Bomb and Europe", *BAS*, 6, pp. 110–14, 125–6.

1950g   "An Appreciation of the Cold War", *The Listener*, May 4 (BBC Home Service talk).

1950h   "Politics and the French Intellectuals", *Partisan Review*, 17, pp. 595–606.

1951a   "Does Europe Welcome American Leadership?", *The Saturday Review of Literature*, 13 January. Reprinted in tr. 1951b.

1951b   "Transatlantic Relations: Does Europe Welcome American Leadership?", in Lewis Galantière (ed.), *America and the Mind of Europe* (London: Hamish Hamilton). Reprint of tr. 1951a.

1951c   "American Policy: Europe and Asia", *BAS*, 7, pp. 81–8 (tr. of extracts from series of articles written for *Le Figaro* between 8 and 22 December 1950. Also published in *The Manchester Guardian*).

1951d   "France, Still the Third Republic", *Foreign Affairs*, 30, pp. 145–51.

1951e   "Britain after the Election", *The Listener*, 22 November (BBC Third Programme talk).

1951f   "The Leninist Myth of Imperialism". Tr. of 1950j, 1950k, by Norbert Guterman, in *Partisan Review*, 18, pp. 646–62.

1951g   "The American Dilemma". Tr. of 1951o, in *Realities*, 15 March, pp. 6–7.

1951h   "Can Germany be United?", *European Review* (5), March, pp. 2–3. Tr. of

"L'unification de l'Allemagne est-elle possible?", *Fig.*, 3–4 mars 1951.

1952a   "French Public Opinion and the Atlantic Treaty", *IA*, 28, pp. 1–8.

1952b   "American Visa Policy". Tr. of 1953e, in *BAS*, 8, pp. 234–5.

1952c   "Ought Europeans to Criticise the United States?", *The Listener*, 3 April (eighth of nine talks on "The Impact of American Power in Europe", BBC European Service).

1952d   "M. Pinay's Experiment", *The Listener*, 17 April (BBC Third Programme talk).

1952e   "The Two Temptations of a European". Tr. of 1952m, in *European Review* (21), July, pp. 16–18.

1952f   "Allies – Not Satellites!". Tr. of 1952m, in *American Mercury*, September, pp. 10–14 (also tr. 1952e).

1952g   "The Prospects for Peace with the Soviets: Can We Negotiate a Settlement Now? Armchair Strategy vs. Political Reality", *Commentary*, 13, pp. 515–20.

1952h   "Inflation". Tr. of 1952q, in *Realities*, February, pp. 39–42.

1952i   "Inflation and Capital Equipment". Tr. of 1952r, in *Realities*, April, pp. 48–9, 73.

1953a   "The Diffusion of Ideologies", *Confluence*, 2 (1), March, pp. 3–12.

1953b   "Totalitarianism and Freedom". Tr. of 1952h, in *Confluence*, 2 (2), June, pp. 3–20.

1953c   "Has the Commonwealth Become a Luxury?", *European Review* (27), January, pp. 14–15. Tr. of "Le Commonwealth est-il devenue un luxe?", *Fig.*, 19 décembre 1952.

1953d   "Is France Too Much of a Welfare State?", *The Listener*, 8 October (BBC Third Programme talk).

1954a   *The Century of Total War*. Tr. of 1951a by E. W. Dickes and O. S. Griffiths (London: Derek Verschoyle/Garden City, New York: Doubleday). Reprinted tr. 1981a.

1954b   "Limits to the Powers of the United Nations", *AAAPSS* (296), pp. 20–6.

1954c   "Asia – between Malthus and Marx". Tr. of 1954i, in *Encounter*, August, pp. 44–9.

1954d   "French Thoughts on the Berlin Conference", *The Listener*, 11 March (BBC Third Programme talk).

1954e   "On Treason". Tr. (in part) of 1951c, 1951d, in *Confluence*, 3 (3), September, pp. 280–94.

1954f   "Indo-China: A Way Out of the Wood". Tr. of 1954n, in *Réalités* (English edn), March, pp. 8–12.

1954g   "The Impact of East-West Trade". Tr. of 1954o, in *Réalités* (English edn), April, pp. 8–13.

1954h   "Can Russia's Rulers Keep the Lid On?". Tr. of 1954p, in *Réalités* (English edn), July, pp. 8–15.

1955a   "The Concepts of 'Class Truth' and 'National Truth' in the Social Sciences". Tr. of 1954h, in *Science and Freedom* (London: Secker and Warburg), pp. 156–70 (proceedings of a conference of the Congress for Cultural Freedom, Hamburg, July 1953).

1955b   "Europe and Air Power", *AAAPSS* (299), pp. 95–101.

1955c   "Realism and Common Sense in Security Policy", *BAS*, 11, pp. 110–12.

1955d   "Workers, Proletarians and Intellectuals", Tr. of 1955i, in *Diogenes* (10), pp. 31–46.

1955e   "Nations and Ideologies". Tr. of 1954b, in *Encounter*, January, pp. 24–33.

1955f   "France: Stability and Instability", *Yale French Studies* (15), Winter, pp. 17–23.

1955g   "Permanence and Flexibility in Soviet Foreign Policy", *Problems of Communism*, 4 (3), May-June, pp. 8–13.

C. Writings on Aron Mentioned in Volume 1

Abel, T., 1958, *"German Sociology"*, *AAAPSS* (316), p. 177. Review of tr. 1957a.

Acton, H. B., 1939, "Philosophical Surveys: Philosophy in France", *Philosophy*, 14, pp. 341–4. Review of *Essai sur la théorie de l'histoire dans l'Allemagne contemporaine* (1938a) and *Introduction à la philosophie de l'histoire* (1938b).

Aiken, H. D., 1964, "The Revolt Against Ideology", *Commentary*, 37 (4), April, pp. 29–39.

Anon., 1936, *"La Sociologie allemande contemporaine"*, *RMM*, 43 (2), avril, Supplément, pp. 14–16. Review of 1935.

Anon. 1938a, *"Introduction à la philosophie de l'histoire"*, *RMM*, 45 (3), juillet, Supplément, pp. 12–13. Review of 1938b.

Anon., 1938b, "Thèses de doctorat". Compte rendu sommaire des deux thèses de R. Aron présentées devant la Faculté des Lettres de Paris en vue du doctorat ès lettres, mars 1938, *RMM*, 45 (3), juillet, Supplément, pp. 28–30.

Anon., 1939, *"Essai sur la théorie de l'histoire dans l'Allemagne contemporaine"*, *RMM*, 46, pp. 175–6. Review of 1938a.

Anon., 1944, "Tracts for the Times", *TLS*, 19 August, p. 402. Review of 1944a.

Anon., 1947, *"L'Homme contre les tyrans"*, *RMM*, 52, pp. 95–6. Review of 1946a.

Anon., 1949, *"Le Grand Schisme"*, *RMM*, 54, pp. 217–19. Review of 1948a.

Anon., 1951, "From Sarajevo to Hiroshima", *The Economist*, 17 November. Review of *Les Guerres en chaîne* (1951a).

Anon., 1954a, *"The Century of Total War"*, *The Listener*, 23 September, p. 491. Review of tr. 1954a.

Anon., 1954b, "Legacy of War: The Predicament of Europe", *The Times*, 1 September. Review of *The Century of Total War* (tr. 1954a).

Anon., 1954c, "Dragons' Teeth", *TLS*, 15 October, p. 651. Review of *The Century of Total War* (tr. 1954a).

Anon., 1955a, "Political Interpreter", *The Economist*, 13 August. Review of *L'Opium des intellectuels* (1955b).

Anon., 1955b, "The Role of the Intellectuals", *TLS*, 16 September. Review of *L'Opium des intellectuels* (1955b).

Anon., 1957a, "Man in his Social Setting", *TLS*, 12 April. Review of *German Sociology* (tr. 1957a).

519

Anon., 1957b, "*The Opium of the Intellectuals*", *The Listener*, 14 November, p. 803. Review of tr. 1957b.

Arnaud, P., 1966, "*La Sociologie allemande contemporaine*", *L'Année sociologique*, 3ᵉ série, 17, pp. 215–16. Review of 1966b.

Arnaud, P., 1968, "*Introduction à la philosophie de l'histoire*", *L'Année sociologique*, 3ᵉ série, 19, pp. 175–6. Review of new edn of 1938b.

Barraclough, G., 1957, "Dead Riflemen", *The Spectator*, 9 August, p. 194. Review of *The Opium of the Intellectuals* (tr. 1957b).

Barraclough, G., 1961, "*Introduction to the Philosophy of History*", *The Listener*, 2 March, p. 401. Review of tr. 1961a.

Bataille, G., 1948, "Du sens d'une neutralité morale dans la guerre russo-américaine", *Critique*, 4, pp. 832–8. Review of *Le Grand Schisme* (1948a).

Baverez, N., 1985, "Raymond Aron et le Père Gaston Fessard: Le drame de l'existence historique au XXᵉ siècle", *Commentaire*, 8 (28–9), pp. 193–9.

Becker, H., 1939, "*Essai sur la théorie de l'histoire dans l'Allemagne contemporaine*", *ASR*, 4, pp. 911–13. Review of 1938a.

Becker, H., 1959, "*German Sociology*", *AJS*, 64, p. 536. Review of tr. 1957a.

Berger, G., 1985, "Les Français et la raison économique: Raymond Aron commentateur économique dans les années 1957–1959", *Commentaire*, 8 (28–9), pp. 274–7.

Bertaux, P., 1985, "Amitiés normaliennes", *Commentaire*, 8 (28–9), pp. 13–15.

Besse, A., 1955, "Monsieur Aron bouleverse la science", *NC* (67), juillet-août, pp. 92–109. Review of *L'Opium des intellectuels* (1955b).

Bettiza, E., 1979, "*L'Opium des intellectuels*, un quart de siècle après", *Commentaire*, 2 (6), pp. 266–70.

Bettiza, E., 1985, "L'Auteur de *L'Opium des intellectuels*", *Commentaire*, 8 (28–9), pp. 135–6.

Birnbaum, N., 1958, "*German Sociology*", *BJS*, 9, pp. 83–4. Review of tr. 1957a.

Bloom, A., 1985, "Le dernier des libéraux", *Commentaire*, 8 (28–9), pp. 174–81.

Bondy, F., 1951, "Guerres en chaîne, hommes enchaînés", *Preuves* (7), septembre, pp. 24–6. Review of *Les Guerres en chaîne* (1951a).

Bourricaud, F., 1985, "Entre 1947 et 1950", *Commentaire*, 8 (28–9), pp. 32–4.

Brogan, D. W., 1954, "The Power of the Political Myth", *Encounter*, December, pp. 77–9. Review of *The Century of Total War* (tr. 1954a).

Bundy, M., 1985, "Aron et l'équilibre de la terreur", *Commentaire*, 8 (28–9), pp. 127–9.

Caillois, Roger, 1948, "D'où vient le prestige du marxisme", *Fig. Lit.*, 23 octobre. Review of *Le Grand Schisme* (1948a).

Callois, Roland, 1946, "La Pensée politique de Raymond Aron", *Critique*, 1, pp. 430–7. Review of *L'Homme contre les tyrans* (1946a) and *L'Age des empires et l'avenir de la France* (1946b).

Casanova, J.-C., 1971, (ed.), *Science et conscience de la société*. Mélanges en l'honneur de Raymond Aron. Two volumes (Paris: Calmann-Lévy).

Casanova, J.-C., 1985, "Raymond Aron et la politique française: Trois Républiques et leurs institutions", *Commentaire*, 8 (28–9), pp. 252–68.

Catlin, G., 1961, "*Introduction to the Philosophy of History*", *Political Studies*, 9, p. 317. Review of tr. 1961a.

Chambliss, R., 1958, *"German Sociology"*, *Social Forces*, 36, p. 280. Review of tr. 1957a.

Chastenet, J., 1951, *"Les Guerres en chaîne"*, *RTASMP*, 2ᵉ semestre, pp. 187–9. Review of 1951a.

Cohen, J., 1951, *"La Philosophie critique de l'histoire"*, *Philosophical Quarterly*, 1, pp. 376–7. Review of 1950b.

Colquhoun, R. F., 1982, *Raymond Aron: An Intellectual Biography, 1905–1955* (Thesis submitted for the degree of Doctor of Philosophy at the London School of Economics and Political Science). Available at the British Library of Political and Economic Science, London; the University of London Library; and the Institut Raymond Aron, Paris.

Conant, M. B., 1978, "Preface" to tr. 1978a.

Cordier, D., 1985, "René Avord à Londres", *Commentaire*, 8 (28–9), pp. 22–7.

Crossman, R. H. S., 1954, "Retreat from Anti-Marxism", *The New Statesman*, 30 October, pp. 542–4. Review of *The Century of Total War* (tr. 1954a).

Dahrendorf, R., 1980, "The Achievement of Raymond Aron", *Encounter*, May, pp. 29–35.

Delmas, C., 1951, "Devant l'Histoire avec Raymond Aron", *LE* (17), janvier, pp. 20–2. Review of new edition of *Introduction à la philosophie de l'histoire* (1948b).

Delmas, C., 1955a, "Un Effort de compréhension de l'histoire: Raymond Aron (I)", *Critique* (102), novembre, pp. 992–9.

Delmas, C., 1955b, "Un Effort de compréhension de l'histoire: Raymond Aron (II)", *Critique* (103), décembre, pp. 1077–91.

Desanti, J. T., 1951, "Raymond Aron et Cie, avocats de la guerre", *NC* (31), décembre, pp. 3–13. Review of *Les Guerres en chaîne* (1951a).

Deutscher, I., 1954, *"L'URSS après Staline*: Réponse aux critiques", *Esprit*, mars, pp. 350–67. Discussion of 1953i. For Aron's reply, see 1954j.

Domenach, J.-M., 1949, *"Le Grand Schisme"*, *Esprit*, février, p. 329. Review of 1948a.

Domenach, J.-M., 1951, "La Guerre limitée", *Esprit*, décembre, pp. 904–8. Review of *Les Guerres en chaîne* (1951a).

Domenach, J.-M., 1955a, *"Polémiques"*, *Esprit*, avril, pp. 733–4. Review of 1955a.

Domenach, J.-M., 1955b, "Les Intellectuels et le communisme", *Esprit*, juillet, pp. 1200–14. Review of *L'Opium des intellectuels* (1955b).

Draus, F., 1983, "La Dialectique de la liberté dans la pensée de Raymond Aron", *Revue européenne des sciences sociales* (Geneva), 21, pp. 143–84.

Draus, F., 1984, "Sur la Perspective théorique de l'engagement politique de Raymond Aron", *Revue européenne des sciences sociales* (Geneva), 22, pp. 15–40.

Draus, F., 1985, "Un Etudiant venu de l'Est: l'éducation à la liberté", *Commentaire*, 8 (28–9), pp. 143–6.

Dubarle, D., 1955, "Les Chrétiens et l'opium des intellectuels", *La Vie intellectuelle*, août-septembre, pp. 22–35. Review of *L'Opium des intellectuels* (1955b).

Duverger, M., 1948, *"Le Grand Schisme* ou croisade sans croix", *Le Monde*, 8 octobre. Review of 1948a.

Duverger, M., 1951, "Les guerres sans chaîne", *Le Monde*, 21–22 octobre. Review of *Les Guerres en chaîne* (1951a).

521

Duverger, M., 1955, "Opium des intellectuels ou trahison des clercs?", *Le Monde*, 27 août. Review of *L'Opium des intellectuels* (1955b).

Fabrègues, J. de, 1948, "*Le Grand Schisme*", *La Nef* (49), décembre, pp. 120–2. Review of 1948a.

Falck, C., 1961, "Lucid Disillusion", *The Spectator*, 17 March, pp. 372–3. Review of *Introduction to the Philosophy of History* (tr. 1961a).

Febvre, L., 1948, "Deux Livres de Raymond Aron", *Annales*, n.s. 3 (2), avril-juin, pp. 244–5. Review of *De l'Armistice à l'insurrection nationale* (1945r) and *L'Homme contre les tyrans* (1946a).

Fessard, G., 1938, "*Essai sur la théorie de l'histoire dans l'Allemagne contemporaine* and *Introduction à la philosophie de l'histoire*", *Etudes*, 5 novembre, pp. 410–12. Review of 1938a and 1938b.

Fessard, G., 1971, "Raymond Aron, philosophe de l'histoire et de la politique", in Casanova, 1971, vol. 1, pp. 51–88.

Fessard, G., 1980, *La Philosophie historique de Raymond Aron* (Paris: Julliard).

Freund, J., 1972, "*Etudes politiques*", *L'Année sociologique*, 3ᵉ série, 23, pp. 217–20. Review of 1972a.

Friess, H. L., 1940, "*Essai sur la théorie de l'histoire dans l'Allemagne contemporaine*", *Social Research*, 7, pp. 105–7. Review of 1938a.

Froment-Meurice, H., 1985, "Division et convergence", *Commentaire*, 8 (28–9), pp. 42–5.

Furet, F., 1985, "La Rencontre d'une idée et d'une vie", *Commentaire* 8 (28–9), pp. 52–4.

Gellner, E., 1961, "Time Machines", *Time and Tide* (42), 3 February, pp. 176–7. Review of *Introduction to the Philosophy of History* (tr. 1961a).

Gellner, E., 1966, "On Democracy in France", *Government and Opposition*, 1, pp. 255–64. Review of *Essai sur les libertés* (1965b). Reprinted in Ernest Gellner, *Contemporary Thought and Politics* (London: Routledge and Kegan Paul, 1974).

George, F., 1985, "Un trop bref dialogue", *Commentaire*, 8 (28–9), pp. 111–13.

Goguel, F., 1951, "L'Enchaînement belliqueux du XXᵉ siècle vu par Raymond Aron", *RFSP*, 1, pp. 548–57. Review of *Les Guerres en chaîne* (1951a).

Gorer, G., 1957, "A New Library of Sociology", *The Observer*, 10 February. Review of *German Sociology* (tr. 1957a).

Gouhier, H., 1939, "Connaissance historique et philosophique de l'histoire", *La Vie intellectuelle*, 63, 25 avril, pp. 260–6. Review of *Essai sur la théorie de l'histoire dans l'Allemagne contemporaine* (1938a) and *Introduction à la philosophie de l'histoire* (1938b).

Groethuysen, B., 1939, "Une Philosophie critique de l'histoire", *NRF*, 53, octobre, pp. 623–9. Review of *Essai sur la théorie de l'histoire dans l'Allemagne contemporaine* (1938a) and *Introduction à la philosophie de l'histoire* (1938b).

Halbwachs, M., 1937, "Les Courants de la pensée sociologique en Allemagne", *Annales d'histoire économique et sociale*, 9, pp. 622–3. Review of *La Sociologie allemande contemporaine* (1935).

Halévy, E., 1985, "Lettre d'Elie Halévy à Raymond Aron", *Commentaire*, 8 (28–9), p. 298.

Hall, J. A., 1981, *Diagnoses of Our Time: Six Views on Our Social Condition* (London: Heinemann).

Harcourt, R. d', and Saint-Pierre, M. de, 1948, "*Le Grand Schisme*", *Cahiers du Monde Nouveau*, 4 (7), pp. 97–8. Review of 1948a.

Hartman, J., 1948, "Les Cours de faculté: à l'Ecole d'Administration, Raymond Aron 'réfute' le marxisme (1)", *NC* (1), décembre, pp. 107–14.

Hartman, J., 1949, "Les Cours de faculté: à l'Ecole d'Administration, Raymond Aron 'réfute' le marxisme (2)", *NC* (2), janvier, pp. 85–94.

Hassner, P., 1985, "L'Histoire du XXe siècle", *Commentaire*, 8 (28–9), pp. 226–33.

Hauser, H., 1939, "*Essai sur la théorie de l'histoire dans l'Allemagne contemporaine* and *Introduction à la philosophie de l'histoire*", *Revue d'économie politique*, 53, pp. 867–8. Review of 1938a and 1938b.

Hepp, J., 1985, "Souvenirs des années 20", *Commentaire*, 8 (28–9), pp. 9–11.

Hersch, J., 1980, "Dialogue sur la philosophie de l'histoire: Le Père Gaston Fessard et Raymond Aron", *Commentaire*, 3 (11), pp. 384–91. Reprinted in Fessard, 1980 ("Préface").

Hersch, J., 1985, "Style moral contre 'belle âme'", *Commentaire*, 8 (28–9), pp. 169–73.

House, F. N., 1939, "*Introduction à la philosophie de l'histoire*", *AJS*, 44, pp. 287–8. Review of 1938a.

Hughes, H. S., 1966, *The Obstructed Path: French Social Thought in the Years of Desperation 1930–1960* (New York: Harper and Row).

Ionescu, G., 1975, "Raymond Aron: A Modern Classicist", in Anthony de Crespigny and Kenneth Minogue (eds), *Contemporary Political Philosophers* (New York: Dodd, Mead/London: Methuen, 1976).

Janelle, E., 1939, "*La Sociologie allemande contemporaine*", *L'Année politique française et étrangère*, 14, pp. 81–3. Review of 1935.

Koyré, A., 1944–5, "*L'Homme contre les tyrans*", *Renaissance* (New York), 2–3, p. 488. Review of 1944a.

Kriegel, A., 1985, "L'art de vivre de la haute Université", *Commentaire*, 8 (28–9), pp. 58–61.

Kristol, I., 1957, "Western Malady", *The Observer*, 4 August. Review of *The Opium of the Intellectuals* (tr. 1957b).

Labedz, L., 1977, "Raymond Aron's 'Vindication'", *Encounter*, September, pp. 63–6.

Lazitch, B., 1985, "Aron et le communisme", *Commentaire*, 8 (28–9), pp. 47–9.

Lichtheim, G., 1958, "French Neo-Liberalism", *Commentary*, 25 (2), February, pp. 176–8. Review of *The Opium of The Intellectuals* (tr. 1957b) and *German Sociology* (tr. 1957a).

Löwenthal, R., 1985, "L'Europe partagée", *Commentaire*, 8 (28–9), pp. 242–7.

McGill, V. J., 1936, "*La Sociologie allemande contemporaine*", *The Journal of Philosophy*, 33, pp. 275–6. Review of 1935.

MacIntyre, A., 1961, "Beyond Max Weber?", *The New Statesman*, 3 February, pp. 181–4. Review of *Introduction to the Philosophy of History* (tr. 1961a).

Malraux, A., 1985, "Lettre d'André Malraux à Raymond Aron", *Commentaire*, 8 (28–9), p. 290.

Manent, P., 1985, "Raymond Aron éducateur", *Commentaire*, 8 (28–9), pp. 155–68.

Mann, G., 1984, "The Committed Guardian: Remembering Raymond Aron", *Encounter*, January, pp. 74–8.

Mann, G., 1985, "Aron vu d'Allemagne", *Commentaire*, 8 (28–9), pp. 148–50.

Marcel, G., 1955, "Vraie et fausse rigueur", *Fig.*, 9 juin. Review of *L'Opium des intellectuels* (1955b).

Marchand, J.-J., 1948, "*Le Grand Schisme*", *Le Rassemblement*, 28 août. Review of 1948a.

Marjolin, R., 1985, "Les années 30", *Commentaire*, 8 (28–9), pp. 19–22.

Marrou, H.-I., 1939 (Henri Davenson), "Tristesse de l'historien", *Esprit* (79), avril, pp. 11–47. Review of *Introduction à la philosophie de l'histoire* (1938b).

Marrou, H.-I., 1954, *De la Connaissance historique* (Paris: Seuil).

Marrou, H.-I., 1971, "Introduction à la philosophie de l'histoire: le point de vue d'un historien", in Casanova, 1971, vol. 1, pp. 37–47.

Marrou, H.-I., 1975, *De la Connaissance historique* (Paris: Seuil). New edn of Marrou, 1954.

Massip, R., 1963, "Raymond Aron, rigoureux enchanteur", *Fig. Lit.*, 28 novembre.

Maulnier, T., 1948, "La Paix belliqueuse", *Fig.*, 4 septembre. Review of *Le Grand Schisme* (1948a).

Maulnier, T., 1955, "Les Sottises de l'intelligence", *Fig.*, 22 février. Review of *Polémiques* (1955a).

Menken, J., 1954, "Cold War and Total War", *The Spectator*, 10 September, pp. 320–2. Review of *The Century of Total War* (tr. 1954a).

Mesure, S., 1984, *Raymond Aron et la raison historique* (Paris: Vrin).

Millet, R., 1946, "Renouvellement des élites", *Le Monde*, 19 juin. Review of *L'Age des empires et l'avenir de la France* (1946b).

Moïsi, D., 1985, "Souvenirs des années 70", *Commentaire*, 8 (28–9), pp. 107–8.

Morgenthau, H. J., 1955, "Foreign Policy: The Conservative School", *World Politics*, 7 (2), January, pp. 284–92. Review of *The Century of Total War* (tr. 1954a).

Nadeau, M., 1955, "MM. Aron, Merleau-Ponty et les intellectuels", *Les Lettres nouvelles*, 3, pp. 892–903. Review of *L'Opium des intellectuels* (1955b).

Palle, A., 1985, "Il y a cinquante ans...", *Commentaire* 8 (28–9), pp. 15–18.

Pierce, R., 1963, "Liberalism and Democracy in the Thought of Raymond Aron", *The Journal of Politics*, 25, pp. 14–35.

Pierce, R., 1966, *Contemporary French Political Thought* (London: Oxford University Press).

Piquemal, A., 1978, *Raymond Aron et l'ordre international* (Paris: Editions Albatros).

Pirou, G., 1936, "*La Sociologie allemande contemporaine*", *Revue d'économie politique*, 50, p. 1452. Review of 1935.

Pouillon, J., 1956, "Confessions d'un mangeur d'opium", *TM* (122), pp. 1314–21. Review of *L'Opium des intellectuels* (1955b).

Prévost, P., 1946, "*L'Age des empires et l'avenir de la France*", *La Nef* (21), août, pp. 153–4. Review of 1946b.

Priouret, R., 1959, "*Immuable et changeante*", *Fig.*, 30 mai. Review of 1959a.

Raynaud, P., 1985, "Raymond Aron et Max Weber: Epistémologie des sciences sociales et rationalisme critique", *Commentaire*, 8 (28–9), pp. 213–21.

Rosenberg, H., 1958, "Twilight of the Intellectuals", *Dissent*, 5, pp. 221–8. Review of *The Opium of the Intellectuals* (tr. 1957b).

Rousseaux, A., 1948, "*Le Grand Schisme*", *Fig. Lit.*, 20 novembre. Review of 1948a.

Rousseaux, A., 1951, "*Les Guerres en chaîne*", *Fig. Lit.*, 28 juillet. Review of 1951a.

Rovan, J., 1985, "Raymond Aron et l'Allemagne", *Commentaire*, 8 (28–9), pp. 248–51.

Ruff, M., 1985, "Souvenirs très anciens", *Commentaire*, 8 (28–9), pp. 12–13.

Salomon, A., 1956, "*L'Opium des intellectuels*", *Social Research*, 23, pp. 489–93. Review of 1955b.

Salomon, J.-J., 1985, "Un Parcours aronien", *Commentaire*, 8 (28–9), pp. 66–70.

Schlesinger, A., 1985, "L'Intelligence et l'action", *Commentaire*, 8 (28–9), pp. 134–5.

Schumann, M., 1955, "Raymond Aron aux prises avec le démiurge", *Fig. Lit.*, 23 juillet. Review of *L'Opium des intellectuels* (1955b).

Schwartz, M., 1936, "*La Sociologie allemande contemporaine*", *ZS*, 5, pp. 425–6. Review of 1935.

Semmel, B., 1961, "*Introduction to the Philosophy of History* and *Dimensions de la conscience historique*", *AAAPSS* (338), pp. 184–5. Review of tr. 1961a and 1961a.

Shils, E., 1958, "Ideology and Civility: On the Politics of the Intellectual", *Sewanee Review*, 66, pp. 450–80. Review of *The Opium of the Intellectuals* (tr. 1957b).

Siegfried, A., 1951, "*Les Guerres en chaîne*", *Fig.*, 21 août. Review of 1951a.

Sigaux, G., 1948, "Le sens du Grand Schisme", *TR* (11), novembre, pp. 1910–12. Review of 1948a.

Simon, P.-H., 1955, "Intelligence et révolution", *Carrefour*, 22 juin. Review of *L'Opium des intellectuels* (1955b).

Sirinelli, J.-F., 1982, "Quand Aron était à gauche de Sartre...", *Le Monde dimanche*, 17 janvier.

Sirinelli, J.-F., 1984, "Raymond Aron avant Raymond Aron (1923–1933)", *Vingtième Siècle: revue d'histoire* (2), avril, pp. 15–30.

Sorel, J.-J., 1955, "'L'Opium des intellectuels'", *France Observateur*, 23 juin. Review of 1955b.

Soutou, J.-M., 1985, "Aron devant l'histoire-se-faisant", *Commentaire*, 8 (28–9), pp. 38–41.

Sperber, M., 1971, "Raymond Aron", in Casanova, 1971, vol. 2, pp. 545–9.

Stark, W., 1965, "*German Sociology*", *Social Forces*, 44, pp. 140–1. Review of tr. 1964a.

Stewart, W. McC., 1948, "*De l'Armistice à l'insurrection nationale*", *IA*, 24, p. 436. Review of 1945r.

Strong, T. B., 1972, "History and Choices: The Foundations of the Political Thought of Raymond Aron", *History and Theory*, 11, pp. 179–92.

Suffert, G., 1985, "L'Homme des amitiés tenaces", *Commentaire*, 8 (28–9), pp. 87–9.

Taylor, A. J. P., 1957, "A Sceptic at Large", *New Statesman*, 31 August, pp. 252–3. Review of *The Opium of the Intellectuals* (tr. 1957b).

Tazerout, 1936, "*La Sociologie allemande contemporaine*", *Revue internationale de sociologie*, 44, pp. 321–3. Review of 1935.

Thomson, D., 1952, "*Les Guerres en chaîne*", *IA*, July, pp. 362–3. Review of 1951a.

Thomson, D., 1955, "*The Century of Total War*", *IA*, January, p. 76. Review of tr. 1954a.

Toynbee, A., 1954, "The Prospect Before Us", *The Observer*, 19 September. Review of *The Century of Total War* (tr. 1954a).

Toynbee, A., 1961, "Problems of History", *The Observer*, 19 February. Review of *Introduction to the Philosophy of History* (tr. 1961a).

Toynbee, P., 1957, "The 'True Left'", *Encounter*, September, pp. 81–4. Review of *The Opium of the Intellectuals* (tr. 1957b).

Uri, P., 1985, "Souvenirs décousus", *Commentaire*, 8 (28–9), pp. 116–19.

Vignaux, P., 1936, "*La Sociologie allemande contemporaine*", *Politique*, 10, pp. 184–6. Review of 1935.

Werner, E., 1973, "Raymond Aron et le problème de la guerre", *RMM*, 78, pp. 218–34.

Wilson, C., 1957, "De Profundis", *The Spectator*, 29 March, pp. 418–19. Review of *German Sociology* (tr. 1957a).

Winch, P., 1959, "*German Sociology*", *Philosophy*, 34, pp. 84–5. Review of tr. 1957a.

Wolton, D., 1985, "Je ne suis pas la conscience universelle...'", *Commentaire*, 8 (28–9), pp. 109–11.

Index